T0366226

Tacit Knowledge in Organizational Learning

Peter Busch
Macquarie University, Australia

IGI PUBLISHING

Hershey • New York

Acquisition Editor:	Kristin Klinger
Senior Managing Editor:	Jennifer Neidig
Managing Editor:	Sara Reed
Development Editor:	Kristin Roth
Copy Editor:	Jennifer Young
Typesetter:	Amanda Appicello
Cover Design:	Lisa Tosheff
Printed at:	Yurchak Printing Inc.

Published in the United States of America by
    IGI Publishing (an imprint of IGI Global)
    701 E. Chocolate Avenue
    Hershey PA 17033
    Tel: 717-533-8845
    Fax: 717-533-8661
    E-mail: cust@igi-pub.com
    Web site: http://www.igi-pub.com

and in the United Kingdom by
    IGI Publishing (an imprint of IGI Global)
    3 Henrietta Street
    Covent Garden
    London WC2E 8LU
    Tel: 44 20 7240 0856
    Fax: 44 20 7379 0609
    Web site: http://www.eurospanonline.com

Library of Congress Cataloging-in-Publication Data

Busch, Peter, 1967-
  Tacit knowledge in organizational learning / Peter Busch.
    p. cm.
  Summary: "This book offers academians and practitioners an illustration of the importance of tacit knowledge to an organization, presenting a means to measure and track tacit knowledge in individuals and recommendations on firm attributes and their ideal utilization of the tacit knowledge resource"--Provided by publisher.
  Includes bibliographical references and index.
  ISBN-13: 978-1-59904-506-1 (hardcover)
  ISBN-13: 978-1-59904-503-0 (ebook)
  1. Knowledge management. 2. Tacit knowledge. 3. Social networks. 4. Organizational learning. I. Title.
  HD30.2.B872 2008
  658.4'038--dc22
               2007032058

British Cataloguing in Publication Data
A Cataloguing in Publication record for this book is available from the British Library.

All work contributed to this book is new, previously-unpublished material. The views expressed in this book are those of the authors, but not necessarily of the publisher.

Tacit Knowledge in Organizational Learning

Table of Contents

Section I

Section V

Appendices

Foreword

Knowledge management now is seen as one of the major challenges in developing strategies for competitive advantage. Businesses continually must collect and assess knowledge to decide on the kinds of products and services and processes to deliver them to remain competitive. Many businesses have approached knowledge management by collecting explicit knowledge and storing it for easy retrieval. However, it now is widely recognized that such stored knowledge must be interpreted using people's expertise and knowledge of context to result in innovative outcomes. It increasingly is recognized that it is essential to find ways to utilize this tacit knowledge to improve competitiveness and innovation in enterprises. Tacit knowledge is thus now seen as the critical knowledge needed to develop new ideas that lead to innovative products and services. However, very little is known on how to utilize such tacit knowledge.

This book provides many answers on ways to find and utilize tacit knowledge. It presents the results of a serious and long term study on tacit knowledge by the author from all its dimensions. It begins by introducing tacit knowledge with wide references to earlier work it then continues with a more systematic and measured way to identify knowledge flows using tools such a social networks and the tested methodologies applying these tools. It considers aspects of organizational culture and its influence on tacit knowledge flows and diffusion through the organization, making distinctions between small and large companies. It does not focus simply on improving socialization or team structures, but also introduces ways to integrate it into organizational processes.

Furthermore, it is not simply a qualitative discussion, but also looks at ways to identify and even measure the flow of tacit knowledge as well as ways to improve its utilization. The description of the application of social networking methods in analysing the flow of tacit knowledge is unique in this field. This application of social networks is based on numerous studies and the techniques and their application success clearly is outlined.

The book concludes with a description with valuable recommendations for ways that organizations can utilize their knowledge to improve their organizational performance. It is a book to be recommended to all readers interested in developing greater agility in their enterprises through the ability to use their expertise to respond quickly to opportunities and improve their competitive position.

Igor Hawryszkiewycz, University of Technology, Sydney, Australia
(http://www-staff.it.uts.edu.au/~igorh/)

Preface

Organizational memory is a frame of reference in which managers interpret what they will do. Organizational memory is developed through sharing memories of what has worked and what has not worked in the past. Then, business "recipes" are developed to help to interpret future actions. The problem is that new situations might demand totally new "frameworks," since old recipes may become obsolete. Being aware of this is another "soft" aspect that needs to be considered during the creation and transfer of organizational knowledge (Guzman & Wilson, 2005 p. 70).

A substantial amount of literature in the last few decades has been devoted to the discipline of knowledge and its management. Doubtless various definitions for data, information, and knowledge exist. In short, there is evidence to suggest that a sliding scale exists between what we commonly ascribe as data, information, and knowledge. "*Data* consists of raw facts … *Information* is a collection of facts organised in such a way that they have additional value beyond the value of the facts themselves … *Knowledge* is the body of rules, guidelines, and procedures used to select, organise and manipulate data to make it suitable for a specific task …" (Stair & Reynolds, 1998, p. 5 [italics added]). This is all very well, but presupposes that what is dealt with are the codified stocks of knowledge that exist in our daily lives and more relevantly the workplace or organisational domain.

Organisations to date generally have been successful at creating and maintaining their codified knowledge stocks, but the tacit component is a phenomenon that is only just now starting to receive serious attention. This is not to say that tacit knowledge has not existed for millennia; of course it has. But the serious management or attempt at explicating it and storing it into databases is far more recent. Given that a large proportion of the information made use of is in the form of non-verbal communication, with words in themselves comprising only some 20 percent of our communication (Raghuram, 1996), we begin to understand the issue of tacit knowledge, and in turn the importance of its management. To a large degree what has prompted this is the global economy, or globalisation as it is more popularly known. Western economies are far less reliant today on income from secondary industry; they simply cannot compete on a manufacturing basis with the labour costs of developing or less developed nations. Primary industry in the west is far less labour intensive than it was 100 years ago. Certainly the tertiary employment sector still needs to be based in the west, but this sector is not quite as knowledge intensive as say the quaternary or quinary sectors. In order to gain competitive advantage in the global economy, developed nations need to turn to maximising their information and knowledge assets. To use an analogy, they need to become the head whilst the less developed nations become the body (Wood, 2003).

The Challenges

In order to achieve greater competitiveness, organizations will need to pay greater attention to managing their soft knowledge such as tacit knowledge, judgement, and intuitive abilities. These parameters could be said to fall under the purview of a recent discipline referred to today as Knowledge management (KM). Broadbent (1998) provides one interpretation of KM, where she considers Knowledge management to be about managing two key assets of the organisation. The first of these relates to maximising the knowledge assets organisations have available to them. The second application relates to making use of the skills employees themselves bring to bear on the company. Indeed at a lower level in the company, the firm may want to improve the performance of its teams, thereby maximising usage of organisational intellectual capital (Curtain, 1998; Jorgensen, 2004; Malik, 2004).

Tacit knowledge management is also important because of the overall economic benefit it brings. Whereas codified knowledge is usually available either freely or through direct payment for patents or intellectual property settlements, tacit knowledge tends to be withheld from direct transfer. The latter knowledge plays a direct role in enabling an organisation to attain a competitive advantage as the knowledge is itself difficult to acquire (Johannessen, Olsen & Olaisen, 1997; Lei, 1997). The ultimate value of any new knowledge, including of course tacit knowledge, is that codification leads to a greater return on investment, increased workplace efficiency, and overall lower organisational costs (Arora, 1996; Nonaka, 1991). For all of these reasons, tacit knowledge often tends to be a resource that employees tend to keep to themselves, for loss of it can represent a loss of power.

One particularly important element of knowledge management is in establishing intra-organisational knowledge flows (Liebowitz, 2005). Both Bloodgood and Salisbury (2001) and Syed-Ikhsan and Rowland (2004) mention the organisational advantages to successful knowledge transfer in firms. One good example of organisational knowledge transfer is knowledge mapping, where the firm seeks to determine bottlenecks or alternatively, particularly rich depots of knowledge. The advantage of conducting such an exercise is that new staff is more easily acclimatised to the culture of the organisation, but more importantly all staff is more easily able to understand what intellectual capital exists in various parts of the company. Management also benefits as it gains a picture of the health of the organisation through studying the interactions of staff and areas where they may be avoiding one another and so not passing on their knowledge. Alternatively particular groupings or cliques of personnel may represent areas where a great deal of tacit knowledge may be being transferred.

There are many techniques to better understanding knowledge flows varying from storytelling (Snowden, 2005, 2002) or narrative knowing and telling (Küpers, 2005). Whatever the case, there is no doubting the role of teams in the modern organisation and their function in tacit knowledge management is critical (Jorgensen, 2004). Groups of people working on a given project tend to collaborate closely together and share their knowledge.

Probably even more than defining the discipline of KM, defining the term "tacit knowledge" can be a vexatious exercise indeed. The need to define is perhaps even more important in research that actually tries to be empirical. Using grounded theory is one way of doing so. Following an examination of 64 recently published documents (Busch, Richards, & Dampney, 2001), we developed a tacit knowledge hermeneutic unit or database in lay terms, examining terms that were most often used to describe tacit knowledge. What is apparent from our grounded theory exercise is that tacit knowledge is typically knowledge (80 instances in the literature), *individualistic* (50 instances), it is heavily *organisationally based* (46 instances), it is directly related at least to *skill* (35) and it is *context specific* (24). Furthermore it tends to be *practically* (9) rather than theoretically *oriented* in nature, also it is acquired in conditions of *low environmental support* (7) (Sternberg, Wagner, Williams, & Horvath 1995), tying in with its economic importance. One other very important issue, often not realised with tacit knowledge is the need for *understanding* (9) on the part of the *receiver*, again making tacit knowledge highly contextual. Our grounded theory analysis of the literature allowed us to establish a definition of tacit knowledge which forms the basis for the phenomenon in this book, namely that of *articulable implicit managerial IT workplace knowledge.*

One Solution

Through this empirical study, it was intended to define the term tacit knowledge in the context of this study and next was to measure the tacit knowledge in ICT personnel, in a given number of organisations. The study sought to examine the relationships among personnel to see whether there were likely to be factors that would enhance or decrease the likely tacit knowledge flows between them. As a means of increasing rigour associated with this research it was felt (Busch & Richards, 2000) beneficial to adopt a triangulated approach (Jick, 1979) which would incorporate (a) a psychological testing instrument; (b) Social Network Analysis as a tool to track the soft knowledge dissipation cycle, and (c) Formal Concept Analysis as a means to balance results with those achieved by way the (a) psychological method, and the dissipation (through personnel) of tacit knowledge viewed by way of (b) Social Network Analysis (SNA). Formal Concept Analysis is a mathematical lattice based means of interpreting or visualising data. Social Network Analysis is also graphical and maps the relationships between individuals.

In testing for tacit knowledge itself, approaches are limited. Arguably the greatest amount of *empirical* tacit knowledge based research has arisen out of the Yale-based psychology group under the directorship of Professor Robert Sternberg. The Sternberg technique has evolved over time and one approach is to incorporate a means of assessment normally using a questionnaire, whereby measurement typically used consists of a set of work-related situations, with anywhere between 5 to 20 response items (Wagner & Sternberg, 1991a; 1991b). Similar to Sternberg's group, we were also interested in determining whether workplace proficient personnel were developing or using tacit knowledge in different ways from novices. To evaluate data, psychological testing usually uses statistics for interpretation. A Wilcoxon nonparametric statistical test (Siegel, 1956) was performed, which permits a one-tailed test of statistical significance on data to determine whether in fact *statistically*, experts and novices were answering the scenario questions in different ways. At the same time, the intention of this research was also to identify other individuals who attained results similar to that of experts but were not necessarily recognised by their peers as such. What made this work quite different from previous such work was the adoption of Formal Concept Analysis which occurred for a number of key reasons. First, there was a desire to model the tacit knowledge inventory results (elicited by way of a questionnaire) in a visual environment, which would permit finer interpretive granularity. Secondly, it was expected that the sample sizes would be too small to permit effective quantitative interpretation of the datasets along traditional psychology lines.

Remember that the second and perhaps a very major goal was to examine knowledge flows amongst individuals. There are many parameters that can affect knowledge flows in organisations, but at the level of the individual there are limited logistically means with regard to how measure of flows can take place. Social Network Analysis permits a viable means of measuring such flows. Pivotal in Social Network Analysis (SNA) has been the work of Granovetter (1973). It is the ties between individuals that constitute a fundamental principle in Social Network Analysis. Eventually, through using such tools, we are able to build up a knowledge map. These knowledge maps may represent staff at the level of the whole organisation, or at the level of the individual. This research tends to focus more at the organisational level as a whole.

Given that the research is conducted in organisations, it is useful to use some categorisation of company type. Just as Sternberg is one of the better known experts in the area of empirical tacit knowledge research, so too is Mintzberg (1991a-e) well known for his research into organisations. To ground the work, the research was conducted in three organisations, which will be referred to as X, Y, and Z. Using Mintzberg's typology, we could declare Organisation X to be a very large nationally based diversified company; however, the IT branch within that firm, which is the section under study, operates as a combination of a machine bureaucracy and a professional bureaucracy. Although the IT branch acts as a support structure for the diversified organisation, professionals within the wider company nevertheless conduct a lot of knowledge work, which is far from standard on a day to day basis. Organisation Y, a small specialised firm, is either an operating adhocracy or a professional bureaucracy. Such a classification disparity depends on the type of work being undertaken by the firm. As an IS/ICT management consultancy, some of their work would be routine, other knowledge work would be unique. The IT group in organisation Z is in fact similar to the IT group in organisation X, except on a much smaller scale, such that it too comprises a machine or professional bureaucracy.

To gather data, a tacit knowledge inventory questionnaire was programmed, which incorporated a biographical, social network analysis and tacit knowledge inventory component. This was the research instrument that permitted the gathering of data. When statistical testing was applied to the results, the results did not reveal significant differences between experts and others. The use of Formal Concept Analysis did however allow the identification of individuals whose answers were consistently like those of experts. It was found experts did tend to answer the IT tacit knowledge inventory items differently from those of novices. At the same time, a whole group of expert-novices were identified who were not officially identified by their peers as being experts but whose results did place them in an expert category.

Perhaps one of the more obvious findings uncovered here is that there are a number of parameters that are going to affect tacit knowledge utilisation and transfer. Starting externally, the classification type of the organisation is going to have some affect. Certain organisations are by their very mission going to be tacit knowledge rich and others far more heavily reliant on a codified knowledge base. Within the organisation itself, the number of employees and number of departments of work teams is going to affect how reliant the company is on codifying their knowledge and trying where possible to codify their tacit knowledge. At the level of the employees themselves, there also are a number of parameters that will affect how well the tacit knowledge is going to flow. Ethnic differences, how well a common language such as English is utilised by the employees, their gender, and their age group—for example along generational lines—will all have a bearing on how well tacit knowledge is made use of and then transferred.

It was found in Organisation X specifically that the soft knowledge of ICT contractors is not being transferred in the Organisation as well as it could have been. In addition to this, certain key personnel were akin to gatekeepers in their ability to either transfer or withhold tacit knowledge. It also was established that there were quite a number of groupings or cliques in this firm, where some of these cliques were comprised of very tacit knowledge rich individuals, where other cliques were quite knowledge poor with regard to limited access to experts. In Organisation Y, the small cottage industry size of the firm meant that higher densities of communication were taking place between the far lower numbers of personnel. Electronic communication which can act as a tacit knowledge barrier was also minimal here, for much face-to-face interaction was taking place instead. The CIO seemed to play a more prominent role in knowledge transferral in Organisation Z. In many ways however the parameters affecting Organisation Z were similar to those of X, except on a smaller scale. Their staff complements were similar in composition and skill levels proportionately speaking. It would be easy to say that Organisation Y provided the best opportunity for tacit knowledge utilisation and transferral; however, by itself this would be simplistic. What is certain is that organisations and their employees need to be more aware of their current knowledge assets and focused on their future opportunities.

Both organisations and individuals are challenged to deal with continuing demands for flexibility. While companies are adapting their managing and organisational structures, demands on employees include continuous self-directed learning, adjusting to new work organisation, and changing job profiles. Employees' ability to deal with those changes largely determines their future employability (Loogma, Ümarik, & Vilu, 2004 p. 323).

Contributions to Knowledge

This book presents a number of original contributions to research in the tacit knowledge area. First, the research incorporated a triangulated approach to analysing tacit knowledge diffusion within an IT domain. This approach was comprised of firstly a phenomenological interpretation of tacit knowledge, secondly the inclusion of tacit knowledge testing, and thirdly the adoption of techniques to test for its transfer, none of which in combination have been previously offered. Prior research typically has *discussed* tacit knowledge, or when actually taken a step further, merely performed tests at the level of the individual. This research, however, actually has examined aspects of *diffusion* of soft knowledge in IT organisational settings.

Secondly, a very substantial literature review was conducted with a view to incorporating this within a grounded theory analysis of tacit knowledge. The results of this research can be seen in part B of chapter 2. The conduct of grounded theory enabled further research to commence with regard to articulating the phenomenon of tacit knowledge as clearly as possible.

The third original contribution to research in the tacit knowledge area relates to the creation of an IT specific tacit knowledge inventory. This questionnaire with its IT workplace scenarios represents a research and industry tool that has practical applications in the knowledge management domain. It is anticipated that the inventory will be adopted by some organisations (certain requests have already been made). Similarly, the Social Network Analysis specific component of the questionnaire already has been requested by other organisations.

Fourth, whereas it was noted that the overwhelming majority of tacit knowledge research *is* descriptive, that small component that actually is *empirical* typically resides within the domain of psychology. The point being the research presented here is unique insofar as it makes novel use of Formal Concept Analysis as a means of interpreting tacit knowledge related workplace scenarios. Indeed the identification of expert non-experts was only possible through the use of this technique.

And fifth, perhaps the most significant contribution has been that the research has taken place in the "real world" with the involvement of three IT, but nevertheless quite different organisations. All too commonly a great deal of both academic scholarship and research is conducted for the sake of logistical simplicity on captive undergraduate student populations, the results of which then are extrapolated onto the outside world. This empirical study purposely sought to avoid this so that any generalisations that did arise could be better placed with regard to the organisational environments in which they were discovered.

Organisation of the Book

The book is organised into five sections and 15 chapters, followed by appendices. A brief description of each of the chapters follows:

Section 1: Background

Chapter I: Identifies the existing areas of concern with regard to the domain of tacit knowledge. Difficulties inherent in undertaking tacit knowledge research are explored as well as why researchers and scholars would wish to do so.

Chapter II: Provides a background to this area of research through an examination of knowledge management. Having discussed knowledge management in general, the focus turns to knowledge management with regard to tacit knowledge.

Chapter III: Focuses on tacit knowledge specifically. In coming to an agreement on what constitutes tacit knowledge for this book, ground theory is utilised to arrive at a suitable definition to this form of knowledge.

Section 2: Methodological Foundations

Chapter IV: Describes the issues that currently exist with regard to testing for tacit knowledge. The chapter explains that testing typically takes place at the level of an individual. Although a great deal of literature discussing tacit knowledge exists, testing almost wholly takes place in psychological disciplines; little empirical tacit knowledge research tends to take place outside this discipline.

Chapter V: Discusses the concept of organisations, using Mintzberg's typology. The organisations under study in this book are then introduced, being named X, Y and Z.

Chapter VI: Introduces the concept of knowledge flows as a means of learning and knowledge transfer.

Chapter VII: Establishes arguably the major means of illustrating knowledge flows is through relationships between individuals. The technique introduced here is Social Network Analysis.

Section 3: Methodology

Chapter VIII: Outlines the methodology used as a technique to eliciting tacit knowledge. The chapter then explores the data analysis necessary for interpretation of results.

Section 4: Results

Chapter IX: Provides the reader with initial results, introducing in detail the test instrument that was used in the research process. Results of a statistical test (Wilcoxon) also are presented.

Chapter X: Presents results through a different technique, namely that of Formal Concept Analysis (FCA). Using this form of investigation we can visually interpret data that would otherwise be lost in numerical obscurity

Chapter XI: Examines the results from the first of our three organisations, in this case Organisation X.

Chapter XII: Continues the result presentation and discussion with Organisation Y.

Chapter XIII: Concludes the presentation of results with Organisation Z.

Section 5: Discussion, Conclusion, and Recommendations

Chapter XIV: Provides a summary of the work covered in the book.

Chapter XV: This concluding chapter makes brief recommendations for organisations.

Appendices

Appendix A: Prior definitions of tacit knowledge

Appendix B: Tacit knowledge maps created through a qualitative analysis of tacit knowledge definitions

Appendix C: The structure charts for Organisation X

Appendix D: Social Network Analysis sociograms on overhead transparencies, should the reader which to see an overlay of the diagrams from one to the next

Appendix E: Extra Social Network Analysis supporting data

Appendix F: The questionnaire used in the research

Appendix G: Glossary of common terms used in this book

Clarifications for the Reader

There are a few points that need to be clarified for the benefit of the reader.

Firstly, one will note that the authors make use of *both* the Harvard and endnote referencing styles. The Harvard system is nevertheless the customary approach utilised. When however the number of citations becomes excessive or a particular point is emphasised, end-noting is utilised as an aid to maintaining flow.

Secondly, the reader will note that key words are often italicised.

Thirdly, not *all* quotes cited throughout the text and citations listed in the bibliography include page numbers, the reasons being that these documents were available electronically in HTML format, in which page numbers do not appear.

References

Bloodgood, J., & Salisbury, D. (2001). Understanding the influence of organisational change strategies on information technology and knowledge management strategies. *Decision Support System,* 31, 55-69.

Broadbent, M. (1998). The phenomenon of knowledge management: What does it mean to the information profession? *Information Outlook, 2*(5), 23.

Busch, P., & Richards, D. (2000). Triangulated measurement of articulable tacit knowledge with an emphasis on formal concept analysis. In T. Chan & C. Ng (eds.), *Proceedings of the 11th Australasian Conference on Information Systems,* December 6-8, Brisbane Australia.

Busch, P., Richards, D., & Dampney, C. (2001). Visual mapping of articulable tacit knowledge. In P. Eades & T. Pattison (Eds.), *Australian Symposium on Information Visualisation* (InVIS'2001), December 10-11, Melbourne, pp. 37-47.

Curtain, R. (1998). The workplace of the future: Insights from futures scenarios and today's high performance workplaces. *Australian Bulletin of Labour, 24*(4), 279-294.

Granovetter, M. (1973). The strength of weak ties. *American Journal of Sociology, 78*(6), 1360-1380.

Guzman, G., & Wilson, J. (2005). The "soft" dimension of organizational knowledge transfer. *Journal of Knowledge Management, 9*(2), 59-74.

Jick, T. (1979). Mixing qualitative and quantitative methods: Triangulation in action. *Administrative Science Quarterly, 24,* 602-611.

Johannessen, J., Olaisen, J., & Olsen, B. (2001). Mismanagement of tacit knowledge: The importance of tacit knowledge, the danger of information technology and what to do about it. *International Journal of Information Management, 21,* 3-20.

Jorgensen, B. (2004). Individual and organisational learning: A model for reform for public organisations. *Foresight, 6*(2), 91-103.

Küpers, W. (2005). Phenomenology of embodied implicit and narrative knowing. *Journal of Knowledge Management, 9*(6), 114-133.

Lei, D. (1997). Competence building, technology fusion and competitive advantage: The key roles of organisational learning and strategic alliances. *International Journal of Technology Management, 14*(2/3/4), 208-237.

Liebowitz, J. (2005). Linking social network analysis with the analytic hierarchy process for knowledge mapping in organizations. *Journal of Knowledge Management, 9*(1), 76-86.

Loogma, K., Ümarik, M., & Vilu, R. (2004). Identification-flexibility dilemma of IT specialists. *Career Development International, 9*(3), 323-348.

Malik, K. (2004). Coordination of technological flows in firms. *Journal of Knowledge Management, 8*(2), 64-72.

Mintzberg, H. (1991a). The professional organisation. In *The Strategy Process: Concepts, Contexts, Cases,* 2nd Ed. Englewood Cliffs, NJ: Prentice Hall, pp. 704-717.

Mintzberg, H. (1991b). The entrepreneurial organisation. In *The Strategy Process: Concepts, Contexts, Cases,* 2nd Ed. Englewood Cliffs, NJ: Prentice Hall, 604-613.

Mintzberg, H. (1991c). The machine organisation. In *The Strategy Process: Concepts, Contexts, Cases,* 2nd Ed. Englewood Cliffs, NJ: Prentice Hall, pp. 630-646.

Mintzberg, H. (1991d). The diversified organisation. In *The Strategy Process: Concepts, Contexts, Cases,* 2nd Ed. Englewood Cliffs, NJ: Prentice Hall, pp. 666-677.

Mintzberg, H. (1991e). The innovative organisation. In *The Strategy Process: Concepts, Contexts, Cases,* 2nd Ed. Englewood Cliffs, NJ: Prentice Hall, pp. 731-746.

Nonaka, I. (1991). The knowledge creating company. *Harvard Business Review, 69*(6), 96-104.

Raghuram, S. (1996). Knowledge creation in the telework context. *International Journal of Technology Management, 11*(7/8), 859-870.

Siegel, S. (1956). *Nonparametric statistics: For the behavioural sciences.* New York: McGraw-Hill.

Snowden, D. (2002). Narrative patterns: Uses of story in the third age of knowledge management. *Journal of Information and Knowledge Management. 00,* 1-5.

Snowden, D. (2005). From atomism to networks in social systems. *The Learning Organization, 12*(6), 552-562.

Stair, R., & Reynolds, G. (1998). *Principles of information systems: A managerial approach.* Cambridge, MA: Course Technology/Nelson ITP.

Sternberg, R., Wagner, R., Williams, W., & Horvath, J. (1995). Testing common sense. *American Psychologist, 50*(11), 912-927.

Syed-Ikhsan, S., & Rowland, F. (2004). Knowledge management in a public organization: A study on the relationship between organizational elements and the performance of knowledge transfer. *Journal of Knowledge Management, 8*(2), 95-111.

Wagner, R., & Sternberg, R. (1991a). *TKIM: The common sense manager: Tacit knowledge inventory for managers: Test booklet.* San Antonio: The Psychological Corporation Harcourt Brace Jovanovich.

Wagner, R., & Sternberg, R. (1991b). *TKIM: The common sense manager: Tacit knowledge inventory for managers: User manual.* San Antonio: The Psychological Corporation Harcourt Brace Jovanovich.

Wood, J. (2003). Australia: An under performing knowledge nation? *Journal of Intellectual Capital, 4*(2), 144-164.

Acknowledgment

There probably are more people I need to thank in writing this book than I can remember. But of those I can, thanks must first of all go to my mentor, the late Associate Professor C.N.G. "Kit" Dampney, who guided me through my "research apprenticeship." I also must thank my wife, Associate Professor Debbie Richards, who has lovingly supported me in this lengthy undertaking, and my good colleague Dr. Lee Flax. I also would like to extend thanks to Dr. Mark Werner and Dr. James Giesecke from the University of Adelaide days for all the sound advice they have provided over the years. And last but certainly not least of all, I thank my parents Peter and Renate Busch for having given me the guidance and encouragement to value higher education and lifelong learning, to which end I hope this book helps others in those two endeavours.

Section I

This first section of the book comprising chapters I, II, and III introduces the reader to the domain of knowledge. Where there is knowledge, there is a need for management of this resource. We understand that data collected in an informative way comprises information, and when this latter form of abstraction becomes meaningful it is said to become knowledge. What is somewhat less well known is that knowledge itself is often for better or worse divided into two categories, explicit or codified and tacit. The former subset the reader will already be well acquainted with, for this category comprises essentially all print and electronic material with a history dating back to humankind's first recorded writing. The latter subset is equally as old, but far less well known or documented. Whilst documentation with regard to tacit knowledge may seem somewhat of a paradox, it is actually possible to articulate some tacit knowledge, but not all of it. The question then remains, why should we choose to do so? Reasons for undertaking tacit knowledge research tend to be varied, but typically focus on organisational self-improvement. More specific examples include a focus on enhancing work team performance, attaining some sort of competitive advantage over rival firms and generally recognising the economic benefits that good utilisation of an organisation's tacit knowledge assets brings.

Just as the discipline of Knowledge Management is difficult to define, so too do researchers and practitioners face the same hurdles with regard to defining tacit knowledge. There is certainly a quite correct notion that truly tacit knowledge is precisely that, it is tacit, it cannot be articulated. There is however another school of thought that acknowledges the presence of other forms of unwritten knowledge that is articulable. Such knowledge is commonly referred to as "trade secrets," "street smarts," "tricks of the trade" and so on. It is this latter category of tacit knowledge that forms the subject material under study here.

Conducting a literature review is the usual means of gaining a thorough understanding of relevant subject material. An arguably better approach is to conduct grounded theory where a clearer understanding of the literature emerges through a deeper immersion in the *subject matter. The use of grounded theory on 64 documents sought to establish what other authors had defined as tacit knowledge. This process led to a definition being formulated that is used throughout this book. The definition established here was that of articulable implicit managerial IT workplace knowledge. Articulable insofar as it represents that subset that can be spoken or written and transferred. Implicit because it is knowledge that often tends not to be articulated. Managerial because after much research we have established that for all intents and purposes we are dealing with a form of management knowledge. Finally, this research is limited to the IT workplace focusing on IT professionals, for that is the background of the author.*

Chapter I

Introduction

At the dawn of a new century, the principal assets of many (perhaps most) corporations are now held in the intangible form of intellectual capital. The primary market value of Microsoft, for example, lies not in its buildings, equipment, or receivables, but instead in the smarts of its people, software development capacity, patents, copyrights, and trademarks (Housel & Bell, 2001 p. xi).

Introduction

There is evidence to suggest that a sliding scale exists between data, information, and knowledge. "***Data*** consists of raw facts … ***Information*** is a collection of facts organised in such a way that they have additional value beyond the value of the facts themselves … ***Knowledge*** is the body of rules, guidelines, and procedures used to select, organise and manipulate data to make it suitable for a specific task…" (Stair & Reynolds, 1998, p. 5 [italics added]). ***Codified*** **knowledge** for Microsoft is the software that has been developed, the patents, copyrights, and trademarks that have also arisen out of the software development process. The "smarts" that Housel and Bell (2001) refer to represents a far more important concept, namely that of the *tacit* knowledge that the employees have within their heads and that which is typically not written down.

Organisations to date have generally been successful at creating and maintaining their codified knowledge stocks, but the tacit component is a phenomenon that is only just now starting to receive serious attention. It has for example been shown (Baumard, 1999), that whilst codified knowledge has always permitted managerial decisions to be *planned*, it was the tacit knowledge component that was often called upon in emergency situations to provide decisions in a fast changing situation. Nevertheless it should be acknowledged that the structures of organisations themselves (Mintzberg 1991a-e, 1983) also affect tacit **knowledge transfer** (Lam, 2000).

Equally important is the "**stickiness**" factor that features prominently in discussions of knowledge (Audretsch, 1998; Bush & Tiwana, 2005; Dosi, 1988; Ghemawat, 1991; Hoskisson & Hitt, 1994; Lei, 1997; Polanyi, 1967; Ramaprasad & Rai, 1996; von Hippel, 1994; Wright 1994). Stickiness refers to the way in which knowledge adheres to particular individuals or contexts. Codified knowledge tends to be far less sticky than tacit knowledge, to which end tacit knowledge almost always requires human contact for transfer. The factors in turn that affect **knowledge transfer** relate directly to the ability of the receiver to receive knowledge, the years and more importantly the type of experience, that the giver of knowledge may have, and the nature of the knowledge itself. The latter point in particular relates to the competitive nature of the knowledge in question, with many organisations seeking to retain whatever advantage in the form of knowledge they may hold over their opposition.

Given that a large proportion of the information we make use of is in the form of non-verbal communication, with words in themselves comprising only some 20 percent of our communication (Raghuram, 1996), one can begin to understand the issue of tacit knowledge, and in turn the importance of tacit **knowledge management**. From an organisational point of view, it should be realised that some 50 to 90 percent of organisational knowledge is actually tacit, and that such knowledge is one of the 10 factors affecting the successful implementation of knowledge management (Horak, 2001). On the one hand, it is recognised that *information management,* which falls under the purview of knowledge management, is considered important by organisational researchers. On the other hand, *Information Systems* (IS) as a discipline has treated information management as the management of information technology (Anand, Manz & Glick, 1998; Southon, 1997). Many of these concepts are summarised in the following quote:

"... to achieve effective information management, organizations will need to pay greater attention to managing soft knowledge such as tacit knowledge, judgement and intuitive abilities. The development of advanced information and communication technologies has increased the need for adopting an organization–level approach to information management. Consequently, efforts to implement technically oriented management information systems can contribute to effective information processing only when accompanied by an appropriate set of organizational strategies .... [Furthermore], there is also increasing pressure for increased externalization of soft knowledge that may be required for constructing and structuring problems in the face of incomplete information (Daft & Weick, 1984; Huber, 1991, in Anand et al., 1998 pp. 797, 806).

Tacit Knowledge: An Initial Definition

Simplistically put, tacit knowledge is essentially the opposite of codified knowledge. Codified knowledge exists in print or electronic form, is available either freely, free of charge but through restricted access or at cost. What is often referred to as codified knowledge is not necessarily knowledge, but information. In other words, it does not become knowledge until the receiver understands what it is they are receiving. Technically speaking tacit knowledge on the other hand *is* knowledge, not data or information, insofar as the term tends to be used to describe knowledge that is far more heavily based on **personal understanding** or experience.

Data are a [sic] formalised representation of information, making it possible to process or communicate that information. Information is not the same as data. ... The concept of information is close to the concepts of knowledge and competence, but it also involves the concepts of interpreting and making ideas explicit. To produce information, we have to interpret what we experience and make explicit what we know ... Information comes in bits and pieces; knowledge and competence do not. Information is explicitly expressed in the paper, or electronically lit pixels on a screen. In contrast, knowledge and competence are personal and intrinsically related to each individual's practice (Dahlbom & Mathiassen, 1999, pp. 26-27).

Strictly speaking, tacit knowledge cannot be codified; rather what passes for tacit knowledge is actually the implicit knowledge that we as individuals make use of to greater or lesser degrees of success. What is meant by implicit knowledge is that component that is not necessarily written anywhere, but we *tacitly* understand that using such knowledge is likely to lead to greater personal success. Stated another way, tacit knowledge is "knowledge that usually is not openly expressed or taught ... by our use of tacit in the present context we do not wish to imply that this knowledge is inaccessible to conscious awareness, unspeakable, or unteachable, but merely that it is not taught directly to most of us" (Wagner & Sternberg, 1985, pp. 436, 439). Or as Baumard (1999) differentiates, "on the one hand it is implicit knowledge, that is something we might know, but we do not wish to express. On the other hand, it is tacit knowledge that is something that we know but cannot express" (p. 2). For the purposes of this book, the term chosen to describe this implicit set of knowledge is that of articulable Tacit Knowledge (aTK). The use of aTK refers to the "**articulable implicit managerial IT knowledge**" made use of to varying degrees of success by IS organisational personnel, where IT refers to Information Technology professionals and IS the broader computing discipline.

Primary Reasons for Undertaking Tacit Knowledge-Based Research

... people management is already a critical issue for Australian business. For example, when asked to identify the single most important factor impacting their business 42 percent of Australian CEOs responded with "acquisition and retention of talent" (Best Employers Australia, 2003, in Jorgensen, 2004, p. 98).

Reasons for undertaking tacit knowledge related research are many and varied, but almost overwhelmingly relate to the organisation with a particular emphasis on improved **workplace** performance.

Knowledge Management in the Workplace with a Tacit Knowledge Perspective

From a **workplace** point of view, the study of tacit knowledge is usually but not necessarily concerned with the area that has come to be known as **Knowledge Management**, a discipline examined in further detail in the following chapter. The capturing of tacit knowledge has been noted as being fundamental to such management. It was noted that "through 2001, more than 50 percent of the effort to implement knowledge management will be spent on cultural change and motivating knowledge sharing (0.8 probability)," which Casonato and Harris (1999) had envisaged as including the more effective utilisation of tacit knowledge.

In addition Broadbent (1998) considers Knowledge Management to be about managing two key assets of the organisation. The first of these relates to maximising the knowledge assets organisations have available to them. The second application relates to making use of the skills employees themselves bring to bear on the company. Because of these factors, effective management policies are needed to harvest the tacit knowledge of employees. Generally speaking,

knowledge management practices aim to draw out the tacit knowledge people have, what they carry around with them, what they observe and learn from experience, rather than what is usually explicitly stated. In firms that appreciate the importance of knowledge management, the organizational responsibilities of staff are not focused on the narrow confines of traditional job descriptions (Broadbent, 1998).

Knowledge capture in itself is all very well; however Tuomi (1999/2000) in relation to the Information Technology environment has summed up one aspect of this process quite succinctly:

If the design principles and methodology cannot address the tacit component, it cannot tell us where and how much we should invest in the explication of knowledge. In general, it can be argued that there has been too little emphasis on the sense - making aspects of information systems. This is becoming an increasingly important issue as information systems are increasingly used for collective meaning processing (p. 111).

Indeed, the increasing sophistication of **Information** and Communications Technology (ICT) has been a major factor in a number of organisational changes, for example the migration from technology management to human-based knowledge management. Another is the move from an information based view to a knowledge based view of organisational assets. A further example concerns the move from a hierarchical organisational view to a work activity view, for example the use of people on short term teams, based not upon their hierarchy in the organisation but the skills they bring to the team. One final example is that information systems are now not just information processing machines, rather they are now being geared towards providing a means of **knowledge transfer**, as in the example of Lotus Notes systems (Anand et al., 1998; Raghuram, 1996; Suchman, 1995; Sveiby, 1997).

Improvement of Work-Team Performance

At a lower level in the company, the firm may want to improve the performance of its teams, thereby maximising usage of organisational **intellectual capital** (Curtain, 1998; Jorgensen, 2004; Malik, 2004). Another commonly cited reason relates to capturing the **expertise** of professionals, the most notable examples occurring within the *sensu latu* medical domains (Chambers, 1998; Cimino, 1999; Goldman, 1990; Meerabeau, 1992; Patel, Arocha, & Kaufman, 1999; Scott, 1990; Southon, Sauer, & Dampney, 1997). The capturing of professional expertise usually means articulating tacit knowledge in the form of generalisable principles so that these principles may then be transferred to others (Scott, 1992), so that novices will preferably be in a position to gain from a more **experience**d, yet perhaps not always present mentor. The expertise of a guru may permit knowledge to be formulated and entered into an expert system or at the very least a Lotus Notes system as for example at Roche (Broadbent 1998). Granted such knowledge has been explicated, but it was often tacit to begin with. Taking into account that a generation of OECD "baby boomers," that is, those born in the immediate post-war period are nearing retirement, then the need to somehow "capture" the know how in the minds of knowledge workers of this generation becomes all the more pressing (Walczak, 2005; Wood, 2003).

Other practical reasons for examining tacit knowledge are "improv[ing] the quality of a person's or a team's performance, help[ing] to communicate knowledge to another person, keep[ing] one's actions under critical control by linking aspects of performance with more or less desirable outcomes, [and] construt[ing] artefacts that can assist decision making or reasoning" (Eraut, 2000, p. 134). All of the latter arguments for researching tacit knowledge point to intra-organisational self improvement (Curtain, 1998), with an emphasis on the individual. Yet it is interesting to note that the tacit knowledge literature, especially within the domain of knowledge management tends to focus at the macro-organisational level (Athanassiou & Nigh, 2000; Cantwell & Santangelo, 2000; Donaldson, 2001; Marcotte & Niosi, 2000; Thorburn, 2000; Walczak, 2005). A substantially smaller proportion of literature is concerned with the actual *testing* of such knowledge focusing on the level of the individual (Colonia-Willner, 1999; Herbig, Büssing, & Ewert, 2001; Larkin, 1980; Reber, 1993; Sternberg, 1999). Notably however, those focused on tacit knowledge at the individual level tend to be psychologists. Certainly from a psychological perspective, one of the leading reasons for undertaking tacit knowledge research is the improvement to intra-organisational welfare that tacit knowledge testing brings (Ramaprasad & Rai, 1996). For example, it has now become very popular for professional organisations to implement practical knowledge tests (i.e., practice wisdom or clinical judgement [Scott, 1990, 1992; Sternberg, Wagner, Williams, & Horvath, 1995]), which ask potential employees questions in relation to soft knowledge situations (Coates, 2001). These tests are largely along the lines of tacitly enquiring as to whether employees are likely to fit into the *culture* of the organisation. They do not actually test for a candidate's knowledge of codified information per se, bearing in mind the tests for tacit knowledge at least in the Yale example, are not considered to be intelligence tests in disguise (Sternberg et al., 1995).

The Economic Benefits of "Capturing" Tacit Knowledge

Another major factor encouraging the study of tacit knowledge relates to the overall economic benefit it brings. The very issue of the economics of tacit knowledge is debateable and researchers tend to differ in their interpretations of tacit knowledge along philosophical lines, from the holism of system sciences to the methodological individualism adopted by economists. On the one hand, it is argued that *some* tacit knowledge can never actually be articulated (Langlois, 2001; Leonard & Sensiper, 1998). Others argue that *all* tacit knowledge by definition is unable to be articulated. Strictly speaking, the latter interpretation is correct. Nevertheless it is interesting to note that economists arguing in reductionist terms consider that "only cost considerations prevent residual forms of tacit knowledge [from being] codified" (Ancori, Bureth, & Cohendet, 2000, p. 281). A more extreme economic interpretation is "that tacit knowledge is just knowledge not codified (but potentially codifiable)" (Cowan, David, & Foray, 2000).

The ultimate value of any new knowledge, including of course tacit knowledge, is that codification leads to a greater return on investment, increased workplace efficiency and overall lower organisational costs (Arora, 1996; Nonaka, 1991). Such benefits are all but defeated in an organisation that employs a high proportion of contract staff who upon termination walk out of the door carrying their soft knowledge with them (Wood, 2003). In such a situation retaining longer tenured staff would indeed prove beneficial (Berry, Berry, & Foster, 1998). Either way the economics of knowledge and particularly tacit knowledge mean that its transference tends to be limited by distance and means of transfer (Audretsch, 1998; Jones, Hesterly, & Borgatti, 1997).

Attaining Competitive Advantage

Whereas **codified knowledge** is usually available either freely or through direct payment for patents or intellectual property settlements, tacit knowledge tends to be withheld from direct transfer. The latter knowledge plays a direct role in enabling an organisation to attain a **competitive advantage** as the knowledge is itself difficult to acquire (Johannessen, Olsen, & Olaisen, 1997; Lei, 1997). Or as Sternberg (*et al.*, 1995) would say, "is acquired [in the face of] low environmental support," meaning we do not receive much help as individuals in acquiring this knowledge. If the knowledge is difficult to acquire it is also difficult to transfer. This last point explains why a considerable proportion of tacit knowledge research is focused on attempting to make tacit knowledge explicit, a process that Nonaka, Takeuchi, and Umemoto (1995) refer to as externalisation. Broadly speaking tacit knowledge is gained either through (a) personal **experience** over time (and perhaps place),[a] or (b) by serving in an "apprenticeship" with someone who is senior and able to pass on the knowledge to the "trainee" (Goldman, 1990). The significant point to note is that tacit knowledge cannot by its very nature be passed in written format, as at this stage the knowledge is no longer tacit, but explicit. Some of the consequences of codification from an organisational point of view have been summarised by Tuomi (1999/2000):

When tacit knowledge is articulated and data are created out of it, a lot of flexibility in interpretation is lost. This may lead to organizational rigidity. It may look attractive, for example to create organization wide information systems where the data repositories of data are used in all organizational processes. Underlying this view is sometimes an exceedingly empiristic and objectivistic belief that when we get the semantics "right" the organization will be able to function as a perfect machine. In some cases, one could argue that, indeed, the organization has become a perfect machine that is fixed in its operation by the information systems it has implemented. Therefore a major challenge for the designer of organization memory and knowledge management systems is to understand, not only the relationships between tacit and explicit stocks of organizational knowledge but also the costs of changing their relationships when the world changes (pp. 111-112).

It is precisely the competitive nature of tacit knowledge Colonia-Willner (1999) notes, which leads organisations to adopt competitive strategies from an *inter*-organisational or rather *extra*-organisational point of view, meaning that firms are likely to contain the tacit knowledge they hold to the best of their abilities. From an *intra*-organisational perspective, research (Pierce & Delbecq, 1977) had shown that those workplaces high in intra-organisational communication were more likely to innovate with all of the respective benefits this would bring. The primary such benefit however was that of enabling experts to pass their knowledge on to non-experts. The flow-on effect from such a practice was noted to be "minimising [the] cost of work, build[ing] adaptability to changing competitive market conditions, [which] as a result may produce a fast return on investments, and a gain in market share" (Colonia-Willner, 1999, p. 609). With such points in mind one can easily be of the impression research into tacit knowledge is a must, nevertheless it is not without its difficulties.

Difficulties Inherent in Tacit Knowledge Research

One of the major hurdles to tacit knowledge related research stems from its soft nature which by definition does not lend itself easily to articulation and therefore to measurement. Sternberg (1999; *et al.*, 1995; Wagner & Sternberg, 1985) and his research team shows us that tacit knowledge is able to be tested for,[b] where a majority of researchers seem typically to be content with discussing its existence. Sternberg's technique is to take workplace related scenarios with answer options, and to test a respondent's approaches to dealing with these workplace situations for which no clear answer necessarily exists.

On the other hand, Reber (1993; 1989), and Lewis (1977) have provided an alternative means of testing for tacit knowledge, drawing upon the research of others (Dulany, Carlson, & Dewey, 1984; Perruchet & Pacteau, 1990). Admittedly, such research is along the lines of expecting control groups to undertake various grammatical and memorisation tasks as a means of later expecting the groups to explicate their tacitly learned knowledge. Within the

IS domain, researchers are constrained by the fact that they do not necessarily have captive control groups on whom they are able to employ grammatically based testing regimes, to which end the Sternberg-based approaches are more feasible, especially as in the case of this study we seek also to map diffusion of such knowledge within the organisational domain.

Eraut (2000) provides an interesting insight into some tacit knowledge elicitation problems:

1. Our series of encounters with another person are unlikely to provide a typical sample of his or her behaviour: the reasons and circumstances for the meetings will largely determine the nature of those encounters, and our own presence is also likely to affect what happens;

2. We are most likely to remember events within those encounters that demand our attention, that is, those that are most "memorable" rather than those which are most common;

3. Preconceptions, created by earlier encounters, affect both parties' behaviour on later occasions, so the sample is not constructed from genuinely independent events;

4. People develop personal constructs (Kelly, 1955), or ways of construing their environment, as a result of their life experiences; and these affect their understanding of, and hence behaviour towards, those whom they meet (pp. 121-122).

Nonetheless, few alternative approaches remain for attempting to explicate and in some way measure this pervasive but all too often underestimated intelligence source, other than that proposed by Sternberg's Yale University research group. In order to combat the predispositions of individuals to answering tacit knowledge tests in a certain way, expert vs. novice comparisons of results achieved, should at least partially enable the above difficulties to be negated. What this means is comparing the results of peer selected "experts" to those of everyone else for any one particular type of tacit knowledge experiment.

Means of Undertaking Tacit Knowledge Research

Whereas many researchers in the knowledge management domain attempt to focus on the tacit component (Athanassiou & Nigh, 2000; Donaldson, 2001; Horak, 2001; Osterloh & Frey, 2000; Thorburn, 2000), few means actually exist to measure this type of knowledge, among which Sternberg's (1999) Yale University based approach could be said to be the most practical because of its more applied nature. Other known approaches to tacit knowledge measurement involve mental scanning (Reed, Hock, & Lockhead, 1983), or grammatical memorisation tasks (Reber, 1993). The latter two approaches tend to involve lengthy testing sessions with captive subjects. The Yale-based approach alternatively tends to be more workplace oriented and involves situational workplace inventories, for which employees are asked to make decisions as to how they would handle soft knowledge situations. These same respondents can be expected to provide an answer for how they would deal with workplace situations ethically (in other words what *should* you *ideally* do when confronted with a situation?) and realistically (that is to say what *would* you *actually* do in practice?).

In order to determine if there is any likelihood of knowledge being transferred in the organisational environment, other tools will need to be utilised. It is the addition of Social Network Analysis (SNA) that provides us with a particularly good means of viewing the social relationships between individuals (Koehly & Shivy, 1998; Paxton, Schutz, Wertheim, & Muir, 1999; Sbarcea, 1999; Scott, 1991; Wasserman & Faust, 1994), which in turn permits assumptions to be made on the likelihood of knowledge transferral. Alternatively, Scott (1992; 1990), had used Participant Observation to provide a check on what participants had stipulated in their questionnaires in relation to tacit knowledge situations. She had noted for example that what was stated in her tacit knowledge questionnaire was not in agreement with what she had later observed. The adoption of Participant Observation, or Complete Observer/Complete Participant for that matter (Leedy, 1997), is considered impractical from an Information Systems workplace point of view. The nature of IS work differs from the physical roles carried out by nurses (Scott, 1992, 1990), insofar as the IS role tends to be more computer-monitor centric.

In addition to providing descriptive statistics as a means of viewing questionnaire results, use will also be made of Formal Concept Analysis (FCA). Such an approach permits results that respondents provide to be viewed in a graphical lattice as a means of visualising patterns, rather than only examining at numerical results. The use of FCA is considered useful particularly if questionnaire sample sizes are small, as the quantitative **data** may not be substantial enough to permit valid statistical conclusions to be drawn.

Due to the nature of the research being undertaken, participants will not be anonymous as clear individual identification is required, in order to determine with whom people interact (i.e., using Social Network Analysis). Furthermore individual identification is required to permit conclusions to be drawn about the types of qualifications, ethnicity, age, gender, and a range of other factors and the bearing this has on the individuals interacting with others in the **workplace**.

Goals of the Book

It is known from prior research (Sternberg et al., 1995), that tacit knowledge "tends to increase with **experience** on the job;" as such can we expect to see senior IT staff with higher tacit knowledge scores? It has been noted, that it is not necessarily age that is an indicator of tacit knowledge usage (Sternberg et al., 1995), but the experience that one has gained at the workplace that determines effectiveness of tacit knowledge usage. To that end, another aim is to determine which factors differentiate individuals who have accumulated more tacit knowledge from those with significantly less tacit knowledge. Results from the research may thus lead to more complete conclusions relating to how tacit knowledge can be articulated and how tacit knowledge may be transferred to those with less. Ultimately the study of intra-organisational tacit knowledge leads towards more complete organisational memory systems whereby the information is either captured if it can be codified, or retained in the form of skilled or permanent staff if the knowledge is truly tacit (Anand et al., 1998). The alternative is organisational rigidity with a lack of flexibility in data interpretation (Tuomi, 1999/2000).

The three major goals of the book are as follows. *To test for articulable Tacit Knowledge^c (aTK) in individuals*. Any research that goes beyond merely writing about tacit knowledge needs to perform some sort of testing to assess who has more of this resource, and what differentiates these individuals. Sternberg's (2000) work, and to a lesser extent Reber's (1993, 1989), together with Lewis (Reber & Lewis, 1977), have to date been the most enlightening in this regard. The research contained in this book will focus on the IT sector as its research domain. Formal Concept Analysis will be utilised as a means of interpreting tacit knowledge results by way of providing a finer level of granularity than statistical interpretation permits. A logical extension to the testing of tacit knowledge is the mapping of likely tacit knowledge flows.[d]

The second goal of the book is: *To map the likelihood of intra-organisational diffusion of aTK among IS personnel*. The term *likelihood* is used here, because *absolute* knowledge transfer is difficult to prove other than through the ability of reading another's mind. In order to gain an insight into knowledge flows, we need to be able to map the social relationships that take place between employees. The application of Social Network Analysis permits us to illustrate such relationship patterns.

The *supra-goal* that rests upon these first two goals is to observe any patterns between personnel types based for example, on years of experience, ethnic background, occupation type, and whether this affects the likelihood of tacit knowledge diffusion.

The third goal is thus: *To determine if there are differences between population groups (age, gender, ethnicity, educational background, employment tenure) and the levels of tacit knowledge present within the groups, and whether this knowledge is likely to be passed from and among these different groups.*

Summary

Reasons for undertaking tacit knowledge research tend to be varied, but typically focus on organisational self-improvement, where the most common example of such self-improvement philosophies is that of knowledge management. What is meant by tacit knowledge for the purposes of this research is **articulable implicit managerial IT knowledge**. The ability to test for such knowledge is however limited to only few approaches, among which Sternberg's (Wagner & Sternberg, 1991a, b) is generally considered the most widely acceptable. Sternberg's technique is to make use of an organisational situational inventory with answer options for which respondents are asked to select pragmatic and ethical values for each given answer option. Instead of just utilising statistics to interpret data, a finer degree of analytical granularity will be achieved with the use of Formal Concept Analysis to interpret the data.

Rather than focus only on ascertaining the characteristics of tacit knowledge, what is sought here is to map the *likelihood* of knowledge flows between intra-organisational personnel. To that end, Social Network Analysis will permit a visualisation of the *likelihood* of tacit knowledge flowing from one employee to the next. There is no *absolute* way of determining whether knowledge is being transferred intra-individually, other than through the reading of minds, which is not possible. It is expected that there will be differences between population groups and their tacit knowledge utilisation. It also is expected that transferral of tacit knowledge will be determined by the population group type.

References

Anand, V., Manz, C., & Glick, W. (1998). An organizational memory approach to information management. *The Academy of Management Review, 23*(4), 769-809.

Ancori, B., Bureth, A., & Cohendet, P. (2000). The economics of knowledge: The debate about codification and tacit knowledge. *Industrial & Corporate Change, 9*(2), 255-287.

Arora, A. (1996). Contracting for tacit knowledge: The provision of technical services in technology licensing contracts. *Journal of Development Economics, 50*(2), 233-256.

Athanassiou, N, & Nigh, D. (2000). Internationalization, tacit knowledge and the top management teams of MNCs. *Journal of International Business Studies, 31*(3), 471-487.

Audretsch, D. (1998). Agglomeration and the location of innovative activity. *Oxford Review of Economic Activity, 14*(2), 18.

Baumard, P. (1999). *Tacit knowledge in organisations* (originally published as Baumard, P., (1996), *Organisations déconcertées: La gestion stratégique de la connaissance.* London: Sage Publications.

Berry, F., Berry, W., & Foster, S. (1998). The determinants of success in implementing an expert system in State Government. *Public Administration Review, 58*(4), 293.

Best Employers Australia (2003). *Best employers to work for in Australia 2003.* Retrieved July, 2006 from http://was7.hewitt.com/bestemployers/anz/

Broadbent, M. (1998). The phenomenon of knowledge management: What does it mean to the information profession? *Information Outlook, 2*(5), 23.

Bush A., & Tiwana, A. (2005). Designing sticky knowledge networks. *Communications of the ACM, 48*(5), 67-71.

Cantwell, J., & Santangelo, G. (2000). Capitalism, profits, and innovation in the new techno-economic paradigm. *Journal of Evolutionary Economics, 10*(1-2), 131-157.

Casonato, R., & Harris, K. (1999). Can an enterprise really capture "tacit knowledge:" We answer two top questions on knowledge management from the Electronic Workplace 1999 Conference. *Gartner Group Research Note Select Q&A,* March 16.

Chambers, D. (1998). Tacit knowledge. *Journal of the American College of Dentists, 65*(3), 44-47.

Cimino, J. (1999). Development of expertise in medical practice. In R. Sternberg & J. Horvath (Eds.) *Tacit knowledge in professional practice: Researcher and practitioner perspectives.* Mahwah, NJ: Lawrence Erlbaum and Associates, pp. 101-120.

Coates, P. (2001). Headhunters and collectors. *The Weekend Australian,* Saturday, July, 7, 1st edition.

Colonia-Willner, R.(1999). Investing in practical intelligence: Ageing and efficiency among executives. *International Journal of Behavioral Development, 23*(3), 591-614.

Cowan, R., David, P., & Foray, D. (2000). The explicit economics of knowledge codification and tacitness. *Industrial & Corporate Change, 9*(2), 211-253.

Curtain, R. (1998). The workplace of the future: Insights from futures scenarios and today's high performance workplaces. *Australian Bulletin of Labour, 24*(4), 279-294.

Daft, R., & Weick, K. (1984). Toward a model of organizations as interpretation systems. *Academy of Management Review, 28*, 57-91.

Dahlbom, B., & Lars Mathiassen, L. (1999). *Computers in context: The philosophy and practice of systems design.* Oxford, UK: Blackwell.

Donaldson, L. (2001). Reflections on knowledge and knowledge – Intensive firms. *Human Relations, 54*(7), 955-963.

Dosi, G. (1988). Sources, procedures, and microeconomic effects of innovation. *Journal of Economic Literature, 26*, 1120-1170.

Dulany, D., Carlson, R., & Dewey, G. (1984). A case of syntactical learning an judgement: How conscious and how abstract? *Journal of Experimental Psychology: General, 113*, 541-555.

Eraut, M. (2000). Non-formal learning and tacit knowledge in professional work. *British Journal of Educational Psychology, 70*(1), 113-136.

Ghemawat, P. (1991). *Commitment: The dynamic of strategy.* New York: Free Press.

Goldman, G. (1990). The tacit dimension of clinical judgement. *The Yale Journal of Biology and Medicine, 63*(1), 47-61.

Herbig, B., Büssing, A., & Ewert, T. (2001). The role of tacit knowledge in the work context of nursing. *Journal of Advanced Nursing, 34*(5), 687-695.

Horak, B. (2001). Dealing with human factors and managing change in knowledge management: A phased approach. *Topics in Health Information Management, 21*(3), 8.

Hoskisson, R., & Hitt, M. (1994). *Downscoping: Taming the diversified firm.* New York: Oxford University Press.

Housel, T., & Bell, A. (2001). *Measuring and managing knowledge.* New York: International Edition McGraw-Hill Irwin.

Huber, G. (1991). Organizational learning: The contributing processes and the literatures. *Organization Science, 2*, 88-115.

Johannessen, J., Olaisen, J., & Olsen, B. (2001). Mismanagement of tacit knowledge: The importance of tacit knowledge, the danger of information technology and what to do about it. *International Journal of Information Management, 21*, 3-20.

Jones, C., Hesterly, W., & Borgatti, S. (1997). A general theory of network governance: Exchange conditions and social mechanisms. *Academy of Management Review, 22*(4), 911.

Jorgensen, B. (2004). Individual and organisational learning: A model for reform for public organizations. *Foresight, 6*(2), 91-103.

Kelly, G. (1955). *The psychology of personal constructs, Vol 1: A theory of personality.* New York: W. W. Norton & Co.

Koehly, L., & Shivy, V. (1998). Social network analysis: A new methodology for counseling research. *Journal of Counseling Psychology, 45*(1), 3-17.

Lam, A. (2000). Tacit knowledge, organizational learning, and societal institutions: An integrated framework. *Organization Studies, 21*(3), 487-513.

Langlois, R. (2001). Knowledge, consumption, and endogenous growth. *Journal of Evolutionary Economics, 11*(1), 77-93.

Larkin, J. (1980). Skilled problem solving in physics: A hierarchical planning model. *Journal of Structural Learning, 6*(4), 271-297.

Leedy, P. (1997). *Practical research: Planning and design, 6th. Ed.* New York: Merrill.

Lei, D. (1997). Competence building, technology fusion, and competitive advantage: The key roles of organisational learning and strategic alliances. *International Journal of Technology Management, 14*(2/3/4), 208-237.

Leonard, D., & Sensiper, S. (1998). The role of tacit knowledge in group innovation, *California Management Review Berkeley, 40*(3).

Malik, K. (2004). Coordination of technological flows in firms. *Journal of Knowledge Management, 8*(2), 64-72.

Marcotte, C., & Niosi, J. (2000). Technology transfer to China: The issues of knowledge and learning. *Journal of Technology Transfer, 25*(1), 43-57.

Meerabeau, L. (1992). Tacit nursing knowledge: An untapped resource or a methodological headache? *Journal of Advanced Nursing, 17*(1), 108-112.

Mintzberg, H. (1991a). The professional organisation. In *The Strategy Process: Concepts, Contexts, Cases,* 2nd Ed. Englewood Cliffs, NJ: Prentice Hall, pp. 704-717.

Mintzberg, H. (1991b). The entrepreneurial organisation. In *The Strategy Process: Concepts, Contexts, Cases,* 2nd Ed. Englewood Cliffs, NJ: Prentice Hall, 604-613.

Mintzberg, H. (1991c). The machine organisation. In *The Strategy Process: Concepts, Contexts, Cases,* 2nd Ed. Englewood Cliffs, NJ: Prentice Hall, pp. 630-646.

Mintzberg, H. (1991d). The diversified organisation. In *The Strategy Process: Concepts, Contexts, Cases,* 2nd Ed. Englewood Cliffs, NJ: Prentice Hall, pp. 666-677.

Mintzberg, H. (1991e). The innovative organisation. In *The Strategy Process: Concepts, Contexts, Cases,* 2nd Ed. Englewood Cliffs, NJ: Prentice Hall, pp. 731-746.

Mintzberg, H. (1983). *Structures in fives: Designing effective organisations.* Englewood Cliffs, NJ: Prentice Hall Inc.

Nonaka, I. (1991). The knowledge creating company. *Harvard Business Review, 69*(6), 96-104.

Osterloh, M., & Frey, B. (2000). Motivation, knowledge transfer, and organizational forms. *Organization Science, 11*(5), 538-550.

Patel, V., Arocha, J., & Kaufman, D. (1999). Expertise and tacit knowledge in medicine. In R. Sternberg, J. Horvath (Eds.), *Tacit knowledge in professional practice: Researcher and practitioner perspectives.* Mahwah, NJ: Lawrence Erlbaum and Associates.

Paxton, S., Schutz, H., Wertheim, E., & Muir, S. (1999). Friendship clique and peer influences on body image concerns, dietary restraint, extreme weight – loss behaviours, and binge eating in adolescent girls. *Journal of Abnormal Psychology, 108*(2), 255-266.

Perruchet, P., & Pacteau, C. (1990). Synthetic grammar learning: Implicit rule abstraction or explicit fragmentary knowledge? *Journal of Experimental Psychology: General, 119,* 264-275.

Pierce, J., & Delbecq, A. (1977). Organization structure, individual attitudes and innovation. *Academy of Management Review, 2*(1), 26-37.

Polanyi, M. (1967). *The tacit dimension.* London: Routledge & Kegan Paul.

Raghuram, S. (1996). Knowledge creation in the telework context. *International Journal of Technology Management, 11*(7/8), 859-870.

Ramaprasad, A., & Rai, A. (1996). Envisioning management of information. *Omega: International Journal of Management Science, 24*(2), 179-193.

Reber, A. (1989). Implicit learning and tacit knowledge. *Journal of Experimental Psychology: General, 118*(3), 219-235.

Reber, A. (1993). *Implicit learning and tacit knowledge: An essay on the cognitive unconscious.* Oxford Psychology Series No. 19. New York, Oxford: Oxford University Press, Clarendon Press.

Reber, A., & Lewis, S. (1977). Implicit learning: An analysis of the form and structure of a body of tacit knowledge. *Cognition, 5*(4), 333-361.

Reed, S., Hock, H., & Lockhead, G. (1983). Tacit knowledge and the effect of pattern recognition on mental scanning. *Memory & Cognition, 11*(2), 137-143.

Sbarcea, K. (1999). Mapping the pathways to knowledge. *Image & Data Manager,* September/October, 32-33.

Scott, D. (1990). Practice wisdom: The neglected source of practice research. *Social Work, 35*(6), 564-568.

Scott, D. (1992). Reaching vulnerable populations: A framework for primary service expansion. *American Journal of Orthopsychiatry, 62*(3), 333-341.

Scott, J. (1991). *Social network analysis: A handbook.* London: Sage Publications.

Southon, F., Sauer, C., & Dampney, C. (1997). Information technology in complex health services: Organisational impediments to successful technology transfer and diffusion. *Journal of the American Medical Informatics Association, 4*(2), March/April, 112-124.

Southon, G. (1997). The roles and functions of information systems: Challenges for organisations and management. Discussion Paper for *WG13 Workshop on Organisational Issues Asia Pacific Association of Medical Informatics Conference (APAMI 1997),* Darling Harbour August.

Stair, R., & Reynolds, G. (1998). *Principles of information systems: A managerial approach.* Cambridge, MA: Course Technology/Nelson ITP.

Sternberg, R. (1999). Epilogue – What do we know about tacit knowledge?: Making the tacit become explicit. In R. Sternberg & J. Horvath (Eds.) *Tacit knowledge in professional practice: Researcher and practitioner perspectives.* Mahwah, NJ: Lawrence Erlbaum and Associates, 231-236.

Sternberg, R. (2000). Wisdom as a form of giftedness. *Gifted Child Quarterly, 44*(4), 252-260.

Sternberg, R., Wagner, R., Williams, W., & Horvath, J. (1995). Testing common sense. *American Psychologist, 50*(11), 912-927.

Suchman, L. (1995). Transforming work: Collaboration, learning and design. *CACM,* 9, 33-44.

Sveiby, K. (1997). *The new organisational wealth: Managing & measuring knowledge-based assets.* San Francisco: Berrett – Koehler.

Thorburn, L. (2000). Knowledge management, research spinoffs, and commercialisation of R&D in Australia. *Asia Pacific Journal of Management, 17*(2), 257-275.

Tuomi, I. (1999/2000). Data is more than knowledge: Implications of the reversed knowledge hierarchy for knowledge management and organizational memory. *Journal of Management Information Systems, 16*(3), 103-177.

von Hippel, E. (1994). Sticky information and the locus of problem solving. *Management Science, 40,* 429-439.

Wagner, R., & Sternberg, R. (1985). Practical intelligence in real – world pursuits: The role of tacit knowledge. *Journal of Personality and Social Psychology, 49*(2), August, 436-458.

Wagner, R., & Sternberg, R. (1991a). *TKIM: The common sense manager: Tacit knowledge inventory for managers: Test booklet.* San Antonio: The Psychological Corporation Harcourt Brace Jovanovich.

Wagner, R., & Sternberg, R. (1991b). *TKIM: The common sense manager: Tacit knowledge inventory for managers: User manual.* San Antonio: The Psychological Corporation Harcourt Brace Jovanovich.

Walczak, S. (2005). Organizational knowledge management structure. *The Learning Organization, 12*(4), 330-339.

Wasserman, S., & Faust, K. (1994). *Social network analysis: Methods and applications.* Cambridge, UK: Cambridge University Press.

Wood, J. (2003). Australia: An under performing knowledge nation? *Journal of Intellectual Capital, 4*(2), 144-164.

Wright, R. (1994). The effects of tacitness and tangibility on the diffusion of knowledge based resources. *Academy of Management Proceedings,* 52-56.

Endnotes

a   Personal communication with Dr. John Antonakis, PACE centre, Yale University, October 2001.

b   Again only insofar as we understand the tacit knowledge we are testing for is a form of 'street smarts', or articulable tacit knowledge, not the true in-articulable subset.

c   This will be explained in detail in the following chapters. For the benefit of the reader, the brief definition here is that of a form of tacit knowledge, which can be verbalised or passed on from one individual to another.

d   Which was considered a rather novel approach by Sternberg's group at Yale as of October 2001.

Chapter II

Knowledge Management

The true standard of success for knowledge management is the number of people who access and implement ideas from the knowledge networks. Those bring state of the art ideas and/or best practices into one place and time, thereby collapsing the organisation into areas of critical mass that imply standardization for ideas that work, and everyone can make comments to improve those standards. Even the newest novice to the organisation can look at the materials and make recommendations based on personal insight, creativity, and experience (Harrington, 2005, p. 113).

Introduction

Delving into tacit knowledge flows requires at least a cursory understanding of its parent discipline, namely Knowledge Management (KM). In turn, discussion of KM is not possible without briefly discussing knowledge and more specifically organisational knowledge. Knowledge Management is a discipline that is quite recent, having been exposed largely in the 1990s. Perhaps the most frustrating aspect of KM is that no one true definition, rather like with tacit knowledge, exists. If one were pressed to define KM, it would be the process whereby an organisation has in place plans or actions to maximise its knowledge assets both codified and soft to its best advantage. At this stage, let us examine the issues regarding this discipline and later examine how they relate to tacit knowledge management specifically Concepts of knowledge relating specifically to tacit knowledge are discussed in much greater detail in the following chapter.

What is Knowledge?

By definition, one cannot discuss Knowledge Management without giving at least the briefest of attention to the concept of knowledge itself.[a] Knowledge as an idea is covered in more detail in the following chapter, where the focus is on tacit knowledge specifically. Although postmodernists would argue there is no universal foundation for knowledge, rather just the consensus of the community (Kakabadse, Kakabadse, & Kouzmin, 2003), let us for the time being use a more commonly held view of the "**knowledge hierarchy**." Data are generally ascribed as raw facts, un-interpreted in this form. When organised in some way, they become information; finally, knowledge is that information that has human meaning attached to it (Bhatt, 2001 in Rowley, 2003). An alternative view is that knowledge has been ascertained from information through tests of proof (Lee & Bai, 2003). Ultimately, one could consider **wisdom** to encompass judicious use (by humans of course) of knowledge (Sternberg, 2000). Perhaps more importantly for this chapter, there needs to be an understanding that knowledge may be categorised as existing at the individual or organisational level (Merx-Chermin & Nijhof, 2005; Nonaka, 1991; Sveiby, 1997). The former more so encompasses tacit knowledge that is not necessarily written down but may be depending upon the circumstances, as will become clear in the following chapter. **Organisational knowledge**, on the other hand, could also be tacit, but also includes explicit knowledge, and in many ways forms the backbone of KM.

What is Organisational Knowledge?

How is organisational knowledge best summarised? Some would argue it comprises knowledge about the company, its operations, customers and supply chain (Siemieniuch & Sinclair, 2004). Unsurprisingly, authors are generally of the opinion **organisational knowledge** is both tacit and explicit (Guzman & Wilson, 2005). Obviously, it is built up from that which resides in its employee's minds and in their interactions in the workplace (Hustad, 2004). As a result of those parameters, it is partly automatic; meaning employees are to some extent aware of it, yet at the same time apply the knowledge without full consideration to its presence. It is collective insofar as it comprises the knowledge of a number of personnel, not just that of the CEO. At the same time, it is emergent, as it arises over time, rather than comprising a "snapshot" of a company's knowledge. It, like tacit knowledge, is also contextual; it is typically tied to one particular organisation, although this is not to say, like tacit knowledge that it *absolutely* cannot be transferred to another firm (Guzman & Wilson, 2005).

An important component of organisational knowledge obviously is the input of personnel. More significantly, it must be remembered that individuals are not islands or silos of knowledge, but their connectivity to other staff constitute a very large component of organisational know-how, that is to say "the whole is greater than the sum of its parts." Whilst once it may have been efficient in a Taylorist model to have employees specialising in only one area of the production process, the workplace of today has changed significantly insofar as individuals seek more of a sense of belonging and fulfilment, with current work practices relying more heavily on cooperation and effective decision making, and an acknowledgement of "**Human Capital**" (Jorgensen, 2004). Whereas Human Capital relates to personnel broadly, **Social**

Capital (SC) relates to the intricate relationships between personnel.[b] These relationships include all such ingredients as trust, reciprocity and norms all working toward the achievement of workplace goals. In a nutshell, "social capital is valuable to an organisation because it improves efficiency of action and facilitates the development of new forms of association and innovation" (Jorgensen, 2004, p. 97). With an increase in workplace knowledge available to us, more educated staff and employees demanding more input into the workplace, it is little wonder companies need to consider some form of knowledge management.

What is Knowledge Management?

One could trace the origins of knowledge management as far back as the development of the cuneiform language at around 3,000 BC. Scholars do seem to agree that both the ancient East and the West were interested in emphasising and understanding knowledge.[c] It was not however until 1959 that Drucker coined the term "knowledge worker" and later the term "**knowledge society**" to reflect in the case of the West at least, the rising importance of knowledge as a form of capital. With the 1990s and 2000s, Kakabadse et al. (2003) note that knowledge management had evolved to a group focus, from the individual knowledge focus of the previous two decades. But what is Knowledge Management? Beginning with a simple dictionary definition, *knowledge* is defined as "the body of truths or facts accumulated by humankind in the course of time" (Macquarie Dictionary, 1997, p. 1186), where *management* is defined as "the act or manner of managing; handling, direction, or control" (Macquarie Dictionary, 1997, p. 1307). Therefore, KM is managing or controlling facts gathered by a company over a period of time. Doubtless such an approach to KM is simplistic, as we have seen in attempting to define organisational knowledge. Just as it is tricky to define knowledge, others claim there is no universal definition for knowledge management (Goh, 2005). What is agreed is that organisations seek to value-add to their knowledge assets by exploiting (Ng & Lee, 2003) or managing what they have (Goh, 2005). Others take a slightly more technology oriented approach to definition, suggesting "the role of KM is to facilitate communication between members of the organisation through tools such as email, intranets, groupware, and discussion boards" (Rowley, 2003, p. 435). Some see KM as a process of codifying individual knowledge and placing this in **databases** or data warehouses (e.g., Hansen, 1995), others (e.g., Davenport & Prusak, 1998) see KM as trying to enable better access by employees to knowledge; or trying to change the knowledge environment by valuing knowledge as an asset (Rowley, 2003). Either way, it can be concluded that KM is as its name suggests, an approach used by forward thinking organisations to best manage their articulated and tacit knowledge assets to competitive advantage.

The reason for a certain amount of imprecision with regard to definitions of KM relates to the youthful age of the discipline (Al-Ghassani et al., 2004). Like Information Systems (IS), KM has arisen, or at the very least been influenced by, a number of other disciplines. Examples of such disciplines include "*philosophy*, in defining knowledge; *cognitive science* (in understanding knowledge workers); *social science* (understanding motivation, people, interactions, culture, environment); *management science* (optimizing operations and integrating them within the enterprise); *information science* (building knowledge-related capabilities); *knowledge engineering* (eliciting and codifying knowledge); *artificial intelligence* (automating routing and knowledge-intensive work) and *economics* (determining priorities)" (Kakabadse et al., 2003, p. 79; *italics added*). With such expansive input from other fields, it is little wonder KM is still evolving, although what does seem to be apparent is that it is divided into either *process-oriented* or *outcome-oriented* camps. The former sees KM as controlling the formation, exploitation, and distribution of knowledge, whilst the latter approach focuses on benefits to the company from having KM in place (Al-Ghassani et al., 2004). Whether or not KM is viewed as process or outcome oriented, like many disciplines or theories KM tends to develop in stages.

Knowledge Management Evolution/Classification

There is little doubt that KM improvement in firms occurs over time. One good example of KM developmental maturity is presented by Gottschalk and Khandelwal (2003). They note that in stage 1, *tools*, in other words a fairly standard range of hardware and software platforms, are made available for end users. Generally speaking, knowledge workers at this point in time will use word-processors, spreadsheets, and other tools usually available in the office environment today.

By stage 2, the organisation starts to *map* information about their staff along the lines of "who knows what." The company starts to build an internal directory listing the staff members and their areas of knowledge, either hard or soft. The knowledge at this stage resides in the individual. Should one need to learn from another, face to face contact takes place or emails are sent. That is to say there is a certain amount of personalisation (Hansen, 1999) applied by the firm and individuals. The use of tools is not diminished at this stage; rather employees make use of these tools to find colleagues who can help them with their queries in the firm.

Stage 3 sees a move to *storing* data. The knowledge is taken from the individual and stored so that perhaps some data mining techniques may be put to use so that other individuals (and perhaps some stakeholders outside the firm) can have access to the expertise that reside within. Lotus notes could be one tool made use of at this stage, but there could be others.

Stage 4 introduces the concept of information systems *processing* knowledge for the benefit of workers. Perhaps some neural networks, **expert systems**, or other AI techniques come into the fore. Through an examination of the stored data, coincidences may be brought to light between one piece of knowledge and another. At this stage the organisation has clearly moved beyond one individual talking to the next. Tacit knowledge can be incorporated into the system as well. This tacit knowledge is articulable however; it is as we shall see a form of "street smarts." The higher (Gottschalk & Khandelwal, 2003) or lower (Dampney & Busch, 2000) tacit knowledge, depending on ones orientation, that is to say the in-articulable component, is much harder to codify and this takes place only over an extended period of time.

Why Conduct Knowledge Management?

Many studies of firms have clearly indicated there has been a benefit from the practice of knowledge management. These include Buckman Laboratories, Texas Instruments, Dow

Chemical, Chevron, Ford Motor Company (Chua, 2003), Ericsson (Hustad, 2004), British Petroleum, Ernst and Young, Hewlett Packard, Microsoft, Siemens, Skandia (Kankanalli, 2003), BICC Cables, Corning, ICI and Pilkington (Malik, 2004), Océ (Merx-Chermin & Nijhof, 2005), John Deere, and the U.S. Army[d] (Desouza & Evaristo, 2004). More specifically, why is KM so popular and being adopted by increasing number of organisations? Tiwana (2000) had identified a number of reasons apart from knowledge aiding in decision making, including the move toward a knowledge intensive work environment, where capital (that is to say finance), had been pre-eminent until recently.

Another reason concerns the **Knowledge Society** of today, which is a product of globalisation. Learning and more specifically lifelong learning is a key ingredient of a **Knowledge Society** (Merx-Chermin & Nijhof, 2005). **Globalisation** by definition means that competitors exist globally. The only way to differentiate product is to work innovatively and produce innovatively, to think globally and act locally—in other words, "glocally" (Hustad, 2004). The instability of modern markets, particularly in western societies, necessitates innovative thinking relying less on materially manufactured goods with a stable structure, rather more on knowledge-rich end products. Those innovative companies in turn become the leaders and are more likely to survive. Innovation at the same time forces a certain degree of cross collaboration, which in turn utilises complex knowledge. More importantly, the tacit component is all too easily lost from the organisation if knowledge management principles are not established to minimise this drainage.

Globalisation brings with it some less obvious problems, chief among these being the influence of culture.[e] A considerable portion of Tacit Knowledge literature emphasises the differences between western (usually meaning Anglo-American) and eastern (often meaning Japanese) experiences. Similarly, KM literature also acknowledges cultural differences with regard to the impact they have on Knowledge Management. The Japanese employee, it has been widely noted (Burrows, Drummond, & Martinsons, 2005, Nonaka, 1991; Nonaka, Ray, & Umemoto, 1998; Nonaka, Takeuchi, & Umemoto, 1996), is encouraged to share in knowledge creation with middle management (Burrows et al., 2005). Much like the Japanese, the Chinese also prefer to learn through observation and benchmarking of competitors and acquiring knowledge through informal networks; however, they are less likely to share explicit knowledge. Unlike Japanese companies however, Chinese companies are less likely to have learning take place from bottom-up, as managers rarely acquire knowledge from subordinates given issues of "hierarchy" and "loss of face" (Burrows et al., 2005). In summary, "in eastern cultures, where the group is stressed above the individual, members of organisations are more likely than in western cultures to rely on informal discussions and networks. Such cultural preferences have important consequences for the most important KM strategy" (Rowley, 2003, p. 436).

Finally, motivation is another issue for engaging in KM. For example, it has been noted (Amar, 2004) that Generation Y (1977-1994) is not motivated in the same way as X (1964-1976) or the Baby Boomers (1945-1963) before them.[f] Whereas Boomers and Xers expected to graduate from education and work their way up the company ladder one step at a time, generation Y expects to change jobs every couple of years, are far less interested in the corporate ladder, and require motivation to stay in the same position and/or company. What will happen with the Millennium generation (1995-present) remains to be seen. At the same time, our Western societies have changed substantially. With hugely increased participation of minorities and more particularly women in the workforce over the last few decades, the character of the workplace has changed almost out of sight (Amar, 2004). Where once it was typical for a (male) worker to devote his energies to his workplace first and personal life second, the feminisation of the (western) workforce has seen a new worker that is often (1) part time and as a consequence may (2) job share with others, and (3) is as committed to life outside the company as within. If we combine these factors with a less tradition-ally euro-centred multicultural environment, we have a renewed necessity to capitalise on knowledge that is in the heads of employees, who (a) may either not be as present on a day to day basis as workers in the past, and (b) may have trouble communicating as effectively or perhaps may communicate in another way as compared with workers of the past.

Organisational Learning

Let us return to the concept of Social Capital. **Organisational Learning** (OL) is another term of recent invention, dating from the early 1990s that is actually very closely linked (if not the same) as Social Capital (Jorgensen, 2004). The transfer of OL within a company represents another branch of the conventional KM tree (Guzman & Wilson, 2005). Just as definitions have been difficult to arrive at with KM, so too has a similar situation been the case with OL (Lee & Bai, 2003; Sunassee & Haumant, 2004). Concepts arising over the last decade related to, or examples of OL, include learning organisations, knowing organisations (from Choo), knowledge creating companies (from Nonaka) and innovative organisations (Merx-Chermin & Nijhof, 2005). What generally is accepted as comprising OL are concepts like knowledge being stored in procedures and rules gradually becoming accumulated amongst the staff over time (Lee & Bai, 2003). An organisation learns at a number of levels however; at the level of the individual, the team, the company itself and inter-organisationally, and for each of these there are noted by Sun and Scott (2005) to be strengths and weaknesses. Within the firm, Sunnasee and Haumant (2004) note that learning takes place at the single loop level, the double loop, deutero double loop, and triple loop levels. An example of a single loop learning process is improving workplace efficiency. A double loop example would be questioning how or why an inefficiency occurred in the first place and to a lesser extent the undertaking of innovative thinking. Deutero means learning how to learn, but as an example of this level in organisational learning, what is meant is some form of critical self-reflection (of processes) (Merx-Chermin & Nijhof, 2005). Finally an example of triple loop learning would be an organisation continually challenging or questioning its very purpose and directions (Sunnasee & Haumant, 2004).

To further "muddy the waters," scholars differentiate between OL and the **Learning Organisation** (LO) the latter term a more recently derived concept.[g] While the former focuses on processes such as single loop through to triple loop learning or the activity of knowing, the LO championed by Senge (1990), uses the findings of the former as a prescription with regard to how firms can continuously learn. Nonaka and Takeuchi (as noted by Merx-Chermin and Nijhof, 2005) illustrate some differences between the two concepts (OL vs. LO). Firstly, knowledge creation is seen as central to OL, but apparently missing from theories in LO. Second of all, OL is considered (by Nonaka and Takeuchi) to be another concept for learning at the level of the individual, and from an examination of concepts covered so far, this would largely seem to be true. Third, OL appears to be rather retrospective, examining the ways firms have undertaken tasks in the past, more so than focusing on the understanding of the knowledge creation process itself. Finally, the double loop learning process in OL is again perceived to be too disconnected from the ongoing knowledge creation process, with double loop's focus on past actions. Another way of differentiating the two would be that OL is about understanding the *processes* by which organisations learn, whereas LO is focused more on *how* organisations learn. Perhaps the following quote by Sunassee and Haumant (2004) best sum up the seemingly minute differences between the two concepts:

Organisational Learning is the way in which individuals in an organisation learn, from the approach they take to addressing a task-related challenge, to their understanding of how they should learn, while a Learning Organisation is one in which processes are imbedded in the organisational culture that allow and encourage learning at the individual, group and organisational level and be transferred between these levels (p. 266).

One can begin to understand why definitions of OL and LO are still in the formative stage. The author is of the opinion, for the purposes of this book at least, that the differences between OL and LO are less important than understanding or appreciating how the knowledge is transferred within the company, and for that reason the next section explores organisational knowledge transfer.

Organisational Knowledge Transfer

A particularly important element of knowledge management is in establishing intra-organisational knowledge flows (Liebowitz, 2005). Bloodgood and Salisbury (2001), as well as Syed-Ikhsan and Rowland (2004), mention the organisational advantages to successful knowledge transfer in firms. Success in this case is subjective, as there is a time factor with regard to the relevance of knowledge being transferred (Davenport & Prusak, 1997), as well as the importance of the individual receiving it. Obviously there is little sense in transferring irrelevant knowledge to the relevant person and vice versa.

One good example of organisational knowledge transfer is knowledge mapping, where the firm seeks to determine bottlenecks or alternatively, particularly rich depots of knowledge. The advantage of conducting such an exercise is that new staff are more easily acclimatised to the culture of the organisation, but more importantly all staff are more easily able to understand what intellectual capital exists in various parts of the company. The understanding of knowledge flows also helps a company ascertain the likelihood of knowledge loss should a particular staff member skilled in a specialised area leave the firm. All of this sounds very simple, but it should be realised that organisational knowledge transfer is actually quite complex for reasons of individual interpretation which in turn are shaped by contextual rules and resources relative to each staff member or even section of the company (Guzman & Wilson, 2005). In other words, it is difficult enough for staff to transfer knowledge amongst themselves if they are of similar mindset, educational background, section of the firm, and so on. The complexity of knowledge transfer becomes exponentially greater when the dissimilarity along several axes increases. Indeed, understanding knowledge flows at the intra-organisational level is difficult enough; at the inter-organisational and multi-national level it becomes multifarious indeed. However the knowledge flows under study in this book are concerned only with those at the intra-organisational level.

It has been noted (Albino, Garavelli, & Gorgoglione, 2004), that two approaches to knowledge transfer are considered feasible. Firstly, either treating knowledge as an object which can be observed, stored, and so on, or along the lines of Sveiby (1997), by treating it as a process, in which case we see a flow of changes in people who learn. Focusing at the level of the individual, Guzman and Wilson (2005) argue that transfer takes place along Nonakian lines with socialisation, externalisation, combination and internalisation. The first involves the transfer of knowledge (in this case tacit knowledge) between people. The second deals with articulating ones tacit knowledge. The third involves combining both explicit and tacit knowledge and finally internalisation is the process of taking codified knowledge and making sense of it by us as individuals.

ICT in Knowledge Management

Opinions are divided on the role of **ICT** in KM.[h] Certain authors (Jorgensen, 2004; Ng & Li, 2003) argue that technology cannot necessarily make an organisation more knowledgeable. For those firms interested in increasing the levels of socialisation amongst their employees, Hansen, Nohria, and Tierney (1999) note that ICT can have a divisive effect, if exchanging tacit knowledge is what is called for. For the presence of ICT often means that employees may resort to an email rather than a face-to-face meeting for example. Goh (2005) notes, as early as the 1980s the focus had been on IT as a saviour for knowledge creation. One such example is **expert systems** on stand-alone platforms, which were seen as a benefit to a company. At the risk of oversimplifying, the **Artificial Intelligence** (AI) approach sought (and indeed still does) attempt to "capture" knowledge from experts and place such expertise in "knowledge bases." Through a sequence of "backward" and "forward chained" "rule sets" **expert systems** programmers can take the unwritten expertise of experts in a knowledge "domain" and codify these rules as best as possible. The idea being that a novice can come along at some later stage, query the "knowledge base" and at least subconsciously "pretend" to be an expert themself. Typical expert system domains include medicine and the physical sciences. Given a set of symptoms what is the condition the human or animal is suffering from? Or in the case of the latter example, what exactly is the object in question being examined? The expert system approach conversely was not necessarily the best way forward for "part of the problem was that developers have focused too much, perhaps overly so, on developing 'thinking machines' using, for instance, **artificial intelligence** (AI) techniques, rather than designing these 'machines' to augment 'human thinking'" (Goh, 2005).

There is also some agreement among a number of authors (Daft & Lengel, 1986; Goh, 2005; Hustad, 2004; Roth, 2003; Syed-Ikhsan & Rowland, 2004; Tsui, 2005), that ICT can have a positive impact on KM. Nevertheless there seems to be some general consensus that machines really process information, for codified or tacit knowledge must be handled by humans (Albino et al., 2004). Examples of computer use include control of global logistics such as Just in Time (JIT) inventory control (Hustad, 2004). Nonetheless, "knowledge as the object of knowledge management is not necessarily the same as knowledge as stored in a knowledge-based system" (Ng & Li, 2003, p. 170). In summary technology can be beneficial from a knowledge management point of view. Technology decreases distance, increases speed of transfer and provides a means of conformity (Albino et al., 2004), but one should remember "ICT fits in better with a knowledge management strategy aimed at codification, i.e. storing descriptive amounts of tacit knowledge for the purpose of reusability" (Ng & Li, 2003, p. 169). Finally, there is a need to understand that the Internet has offered the organisation a new salvation to knowledge management, in the form of groupware conferencing systems or Group Decision Support Systems (GDSSs) or the intranet (Goh, 2005, p. 8). At this stage there is a need to examine knowledge management with a focus on tacit knowledge more specifically.

Knowledge Management with Regard to Tacit Knowledge

Tacit knowledge has a specific role to play in knowledge management: it is a factor in knowledge transfers that explains or predicts the stickiness of the transfer (Mooradian, 2005, p. 110).

Some would argue tacit knowledge sits at the very heart of knowledge management. KM research tends to treat tacit knowledge as the target of KM practice. Capturing tacit knowledge is seen as the challenge to organizations that want to spread knowledge throughout the organization or spur greater innovation. It is treated as a reserve deposited deep within the ground that needs to be detected and then pumped out. Explicit knowledge, by contrast, is treated as a kind of surface pool that is easier to detect and capture, but which represents only a fraction of the organizational knowledge. Theorists differ on the nature of tacit knowledge. Nonaka and Takeuchi describe it as subjective and mental, as opposed to being objective and external. Hence, to continue the reserve metaphor, they treat the deep buried reserve as having different chemical properties or being in a different physical state. Merely "pumping it out" will not suffice to make it useful. It needs to be processed and converted into a new form (Mooradian, 2005, p. 107).

Briefly, for tacit knowledge is examined in more detail in the following chapter, how is it possible to define such knowledge? Harrington (2005), defines it as knowledge

.... formed around intangible factors embedded in individual's experiences. It is personal, context-specific knowledge that resides in an individual. It is knowledge that an individual gains from experience or skills that he or she develops. It often takes the form of beliefs, values, principles, and morals. It guides the individual's actions. I like to call this soft knowledge. It is embedded in the individual's ideas, insights, values, and judgement. It is only accessible through the direct corroboration and communication with the individual that has the knowledge (p.113).

It is known that organisations have made relatively longstanding use of the codified knowledge assets. Organisations have after all migrated from an era of paper filing to the electronic world of flat file **databases**, to hierarchical and networked examples, through to relational databases and now the era of the object-relational and fully object oriented database is with us. All of this is not to say that database have had their day and are on their way out. Certainly given many firms investments in relational database technology, the data storage structures utilising keys and records stored in flat matrices, requiring a structured query language to access the data are likely to be with us for quite some number of years yet. With regard to object databases, whether truly object oriented, or just pretending to be (i.e., object-relational), such databases are very much a recent technology and have not been taken up by the mainstream at this point in time. The reasons for this are many, but include the fact that the technology is new and not fully mature, and that in some ways the move to full objectivity means records become hard coded through links to other records returning us to a paradigm that existed with hierarchical and networked databases. Such linking of records typically requires the expertise of programmers.

One should at this stage not think of tacit knowledge as contrasting with its codified cousin, rather as complimenting it. Databases will still have their use and are not likely to disappear altogether. Nevertheless what is new to a lot of firms, many would argue most, is the recognition of the role tacit knowledge plays in the knowledge management process. The "street smarts" of employees, once not consciously considered by employers are now much in demand. Managers have come to realise that with the departure of the employee from the firm goes the soft or tacit knowledge. So what are the approaches used by organisations to minimise TK disappearing "out of the door?"

Knowledge Bases

One means of making the most of a firms tacit knowledge rests with Lotus Notes **databases**, **knowledge repositories** (Bush & Tiwana, 2005), or similar such technology, where employees are encouraged to enter their workplace tricks of the trade. Should a staff member, experienced or otherwise, have a knack for solving a particular problem, they are able to enter this information into a knowledge base. And "even knowledge that cannot be codified or stored in a knowledge repository can be shared through hyperlinks, pointers, multimedia ….." (Bush & Tiwana, 2005, p.70). In the case of some organisations, personnel are *more than* strongly encouraged to enter their know-how, for one of the biggest problems facing firms is changing from a knowledge hording to knowledge sharing culture (Harrington, 2005). One such prime example is that of Buckman Laboratories (Chua, 2003), with its head office in Memphis, Tennessee, but with offices around the world:

Buckman Labs has organised its employees and their work around its knowledge network – K'Netix. …. Not long after K'Netix went online, Buckman made his expectations clear: 'Those of you who have something intelligent to say now have a forum in which to say it. Those of you who will not or cannot contribute also become obvious. If you are not willing to contribute or participate, then you should understand that the many opportunities offered to you in the past will no longer be available (Robbins, Bergman, Stagg, & Coulter 2003, pp.298-299).

Admittedly Buckman spends some $7,500 per employee each year (as of 2003) to enable such knowledge networking (Kankanalli, Tanudidjaja, Sutanto, & Tan, 2003). Another approach to tacit knowledge management has been storytelling.

Storytelling

Stories provide context and stimulation (Snowden, 2002) that is often missing from more traditional forms of information and **knowledge repositories** such as manuals and databases. They allow the past, current and future cultures surrounding the story to be both explained and created. Wiig (2003) provides a practical example in the following quote:

Much of what we know is in the form of isolated knowledge elements. We often link these isolated elements with other knowledge elements. We integrate and synthesise to create a weave--a mental model, a story-like construct for a particular context ... That is why it is so hard for a mechanical engineering graduate who knows all the theoretical principles to design a working machine before she has formed a "story" in her mind of how all the details fit together (pp. 15-16).

Storytelling (Snowden, 2005, 2002) or narrative knowing and telling (Küpers, 2005) is an approach that is gaining currency with regard to managing or at the very least appreciating the knowledge available to firms (Gordon & Ganesan, 2005; Roth 2003). The use of stories in knowledge management has been explored by others, such as Schultze and Boland (1997) who have suggested a discussion database as an effective way of communicating organisational memory. Mitroff, Nelson and Mason (1974) suggest that data only becomes information when "tied to an appropriate story that has personal meaning to the individual who needs the information, the organisation in which he is located, and the type of problem that he faces." They call such a system a Management Myth-Information System. Storytelling permits individuals to elucidate thoughts, make use of metaphors and transfer body language all at the same time. The combination of such "techniques" is of course much richer than a message sent through e-mail. In short, stories permit a lot of embodied "emotional knowledge" and "meta knowledge" to be transferred (Küpers, 2005).

Teams and Communities (of Practice)

There is no doubting the role of teams in the modern organisation and their function in tacit knowledge management is critical (Jorgensen, 2004). Groups of people working on a given project tend to collaborate closely together and share their knowledge. The makeup of the team will also have an impact of the likelihood of knowledge transfer. Some argue that diverse teams can negatively influence the transfer of knowledge, insofar as "people tend to feel part of a social group (functional) to which they assign superior or at least more positive, characteristics, skills and knowledge, with a tendency to assign negative characteristics to other groups" (Camelo-Ordaz, Hernández-Lara, & Valle-Cabrera, 2005 p. 698). And whilst this negativity may be true at the inter-team level (Bush & Tiwana, 2005), within the team itself, others (Malik, 2004) are of the opinion, heterogeneity along the lines of intellectual and occupational background can actually increase knowledge creation and transfer in novel ways.[i] What is clear with regard to tacit knowledge management is that if the knowledge is not already available within the group then it must be brought in from outside the team; similarly, if a worker leaves a team then he or she take their tacit knowledge with them, a process akin to socialisation (Nonaka, 1991) or horizontal knowledge transfer (Walczak, 2005).

It would not be unreasonable to consider communities as teams on a larger scale. The Community of Practice (CoP) model (Lave & Wenger, 1991) based on an apprenticeship system is widely distributed. Hustad (2004) notes the CoP model has a number of variants, namely *communities of knowing* (from Boland & Tenkasi, 1995), *communities of practitioners* (from Blackler, 1995) and *microcommunities of knowledge* (from Krogh von, Ichijo, & Nonaka 2000). The idea behind such communities is that they aim to provide personalised knowledge exchange. The tractor manufacturer John Deere is an example of one organisation that "recognises" hundreds of CoPs within the firm for enabling knowledge exchange. The company refers to its CoP system as *MindShare*, whereby videoconference, email and discussion groups are integrated (Desouza & Evaristo, 2004).

Sticky Knowledge Networks

Finally, but certainly not the only remaining means of undertaking tacit knowledge management, is that of establishing knowledge networks. Once again knowledge and particularly tacit knowledge, is sticky by nature (Bush & Tiwana, 2005; Dosi 1988; Ghemawat, 1991; Hoskisson & Hitt, 1994; Polanyi, 1967; Ramaprasad & Rai, 1996; von Hippel, 1994 in Raghuram, 1996; Wright, 1994 in Lei 1997). That is to say, the more valuable the knowledge becomes, the less likely we are to want to lose it or otherwise transfer it. There are a multitude of studies that indicate sharing of knowledge; again particularly tacit knowledge makes either the team or individual less valuable to the organisation (Desouza & Evaristo, 2004).

In addition the more that is invested in building up a team, workgroup or knowledge network, the less likely we are to want to abandon this precious resource (Bush & Tiwana, 2005). But it is the nature of the team or networks Snowden (2005) remarks, which is also of relevance to the "stickiness" of knowledge. He argues that informal self-formed networks carry more inherent trust than any formal network established by the senior hierarchy in a firm. That is to say, employees who form their own workgroups are more likely to be successful at sharing their experiences, and more significantly, employees who are on the receiving end of important knowledge are better likely to gain from the experiences of their more enlightened peers.

Summary

What has been ascertained with regard to knowledge management, organizational learning and tacit knowledge? Basically "a majority of KM programmes are still predominantly centred on building databases or computerised repositories for documenting and disseminating best practices. For organisations to benefit fully from their KM efforts, the real payoff lies in the ability to harness knowledge for innovation" (Goh, 2005, p. 9). Clearly, knowledge is not just codified, but also tacit. Of course, the tacit component with its ethereal nature is also the hardest knowledge phenomenon to research. Many studies remain relatively unsuccessful because they either tend to be largely descriptive in nature, or they fail because they do not adequately address what *they* mean by tacit knowledge in a knowledge management context. With this last point in mind, the following chapter focuses on defining tacit knowledge for this book.

References

Albino, V., Garavelli, A., & Gorgoglione, M. (2004). Organization and technology in knowledge transfer. *Benchmarking: An International Journal, 11*(6), 584-600.

Amar, A.D. (2004). Motivating knowledge workers to innovate: A model integrating motivation dynamics and antecedents. *European Journal of Innovation Management, 7*(2), 89-101.

Blackler, F. (1995). Knowledge, knowledge work and organizations: An overview and Interpretation. *Organization Studies,* (16), 1021-1046.

Bloodgood, J., & Salisbury, D. (2001). Understanding the influence of organisational change strategies on information technology and knowledge management strategies. *Decision Support System,* 31, 55-69.

Boland, R., & Tenkasi, R. (1995). Perspective making and perspective taking in communities of knowing. *Organization Science,* (6), 350-372.

Burrows, G., Drummond, D., & Martinsons, M. (2005). Knowledge Management in China. *Communications of the ACM, 48*(4), 73-76.

Bush A., & Tiwana, A. (2005). Designing sticky knowledge networks. *Communications of the ACM, 48*(5), 67-71.

Camelo-Ordaz, C., Hernández-Lara, A., & Valle-Cabrera, R. (2005). The relationship between top management teams and innovative capacity in companies. *Journal of Management Development, 24*(8), 683-705.

Chua, A. (2003). Knowledge sharing: A game people play. *Aslib Proceedings, 55*(3), 117-129.

Daft, R., & Lengel, R. (1986). Organizational information requirements, media richness, and structural design. *Management Science, 32*(5), 554-71.

Davenport, T., & Prusak, L. (1998). *Working knowledge: How organisations manage what they know.* Boston: Harvard Business School Press.

Desouza, K.C., & Evaristo, J.R. (2004). Managing knowledge in distributed projects. *Communications of the ACM, 47*(4), 87-91.

Dosi, G. (1988). Sources, procedures, and microeconomic effects of innovation. *Journal of Economic Literature, 26,* 1120-1170.

Duedahl, M., Andersen, J., & Sein, M.K. (2005). When models cross the border: Adapting IT competencies of business managers. *SIGMIS-CPR '05,* April 14–16 Atlanta, Georgia, 40-48.

Ghemawat, P. (1991). *Commitment: The dynamic of strategy.* New York: Free Press.

Goh, A.L.S. (2005). Harnessing knowledge for innovation: An integrated management framework. *Journal of Knowledge Management, 9*(4), 6-18.

Gottschalk, P., & Khandelwal, V. (2003). Determinants of knowledge management technology projects in Australian law firms. *Journal of Knowledge Management, 7*(4), 92-105.

Guzman, G., & Wilson, J. (2005). The "soft" dimension of organizational knowledge transfer. *Journal of Knowledge Management, 9*(2), 59-74.

Hansen, M. (1999). The search-transfer problem: The role of weak ties in sharing knowledge across organizational subunits. *Administrative Science Quarterly, 44*(1), 82-111.

Hansen, M., Nohria, N., & Tierney, T. (1999). What's the strategy for managing knowledge? *Harvard Business Review, 77*(2), 106-116.

Harrington, H.J. (2005). The five pillars of organizational excellence. *Handbook of Business Strategy,* 107-114.

Hoskisson, R., & Hitt, M. (1994). *Downscoping: Taming the diversified firm.* New York: Oxford University Press.

Hunt, D.P. (2003). The concept of knowledge and how to measure it. *Journal of Intellectual Capital, 4*(1), 100-113.

Hustad, E. (2004). Knowledge networking in global organizations: The transfer of knowledge. *SIGMIS '04,* April 22–24, Tucson, Arizona, 55-64.

Jorgensen, B. (2004). Individual and organisational learning: A model for reform for public organizations. *Foresight, 6*(2), 91-103.

Kakabadse, N., Kakabadse, & Kouzmin, A. (2001). From tacit knowledge to knowledge management: Leveraging invisible assets. *Knowledge and Process Management, 8*(3), 137-154.

Kankanhalli, A., Tanudidjaja, F., Sutanto, J., & Tan, B. (2003). The role of IT in successful knowledge management initiatives. *Communications of the ACM, 46*(9), 69-73.

Küpers, W. (2005). Phenomenology of embodied implicit and narrative knowing. *Journal of Knowledge Management, 9*(6), 114-133.

Lave, J., & Wenger E. (1991). *Situated learning: Legitimate peripheral participation.* Cambridge, UK: Cambridge University Press.

Lee, G, & Bai, R. (2003). Organizational mechanisms for successful IS/IT strategic planning in the digital era. *Management Decision, 41*(1), 32-42.

Lei, D. (1997). Competence building, technology fusion, and competitive advantage: The key roles of organisational learning and strategic alliances. *International Journal of Technology Management, 14*(2/3/4), 208-237.

Liebowitz, J. (2005). Linking social network analysis with the analytic hierarchy process for knowledge mapping in organizations. *Journal of Knowledge Management, 9*(1), 76-86.

Macquarie Dictionary (1997). Published by the Macquarie Library, 3rd. ed. Macquarie University, Australia: Macquarie Library.

Malik, K. (2004). Coordination of technological flows in firms. *Journal of Knowledge Management, 8*(2), 64-72.

Merx-Chermin, M., & Nijhof, W. (2005). Factors influencing knowledge creation and innovation in an organization. *Journal of European Industrial Training, 29*(2), 135-147.

Mitroff, I., Nelson, J., & Mason, R. (1974). *On management myth-information systems.* U.S. Department of Health, Education, and Welfare's National Institute of Education Publication.

Mooradian, N. (2005). Tacit knowledge: Philosophic roots and role in KM. *Journal of Knowledge Management, 9*(6), 104-113.

Ng, J.M., & Li, K.X. (2003). Implications of ICT for knowledge management in globalization. *Information Management & Computer Security, 11*(4), 167-174.

Nonaka, I. (1991). The knowledge creating company. *Harvard Business Review, 69*(6), 96-104.

Nonaka, I., Ray, T., & Umemoto, K. (1998). Japanese organizational knowledge creation in Anglo – American Environments. *Prometheus, 16*(4), 421-439.

Nonaka, I., Takeuchi, H., & Umemoto, K. (1996). A theory of organisational knowledge creation. *International Journal of Technology Management, 11*(7/8), 833-845.

Polanyi, M. (1967). *The tacit dimension.* London: Routledge & Kegan Paul.

Raghuram, S. (1996). Knowledge creation in the telework context. *International Journal of Technology Management, 11*(7/8), 859-870.

Ramaprasad, A., & Rai, A. (1996). Envisioning management of information. *Omega: International Journal of Management Science, 24*(2), 179-193.

Robbins, S., Bergman, R., Stagg, I., & Coulter, M. (2003). *Management,* 3rd. ed. French's Forest, NSW Australia: Prentice Hall/Pearson Education.

Roth, J. (2003). Enabling knowledge creation: Learning from an R&D organization. *Journal of Knowledge Management, 7*(1), 32-48.

Rowley, J. (2003). Knowledge management – The new librarianship? From custodians of history to gatekeepers to the future. *Library Management, 24*(8/9), 433-440.

Schultze, U., & Boland, R. (1997). Hard and soft information genres: An analysis of two notes databases. *Proceedings of the 30th Hawaii International Conference on System Sciences. Digital Documents Track.* Los Alamitos, CA: IEEE Computer Society Press.

Senge, P. (1990). *The fifth discipline: The art and practice of the learning organization.* New York: Doubleday.

Siemieniuch, C.E., & Sinclair, M.A. (2004). A framework for organisational readiness for knowledge management. *International Journal of Operations & Production Management, 24*(1), 79-98.

Snowden, D. (2002). Narrative patterns: Uses of story in the third age of knowledge management. *Journal of Information and Knowledge Management, 00*, 1-5.

Snowden, D. (2005). From atomism to networks in social systems. *The Learning Organization, 12*(6), 552-562.

Sternberg, R. (2000). Wisdom as a form of giftedness. *Gifted Child Quarterly, 44*(4), 252-260.

Sun, P., & Scott, J. (2005). An investigation of barriers to knowledge transfer. *Journal of Knowledge Management, 9*(2), 75-90.

Sunassee, N., & Haumant, V. (2004). Organisational Learning versus the Learning Organisation. *Proceedings of SAICSIT, 264* – 268.

Sveiby, K. (1997). *The new organisational wealth: Managing & measuring knowledge-based assets.* San Francisco: Berrett – Koehler.

Syed-Ikhsan, S., & Rowland, F. (2004). Knowledge management in a public organization: A study on the relationship between organizational elements and the performance of knowledge transfer. *Journal of Knowledge Management, 8*(2), 95-111.

Tiwana, A. (2000). *The knowledge management toolkit.* Upper Saddle River, NJ: Prentice-Hall Inc.

Tsui, E. (2005). The role of IT in KM: Where are we now and where are we heading? *Journal of Knowledge Management, 9*(1), 3-6.

von Hippel, E. (1994). Sticky information and the locus of problem solving. *Management Science, 40*, 429-439.

von Krogh, G., Ichijo, K., & Nonaka, I. (2000). *Enabling knowledge creation: How to unlock the mystery of tacit knowledge and release the power of innovation.* New York: Oxford University Press, Inc.

Walczak, S. (2005). Organizational knowledge management structure. *The Learning Organization, 12*(4), 330-339.

Wassenaar, D.A., & Katsma, C. P. (2004). IT- based innovation in a digital economy - A social learning perspective. In M. Janssen, H. Sol, & R.W. Wagenaar (Eds.), *ICEC'04 Sixth International Conference on Electronic Commerce*166-176.

Wiig, K. (2003). A knowledge model for situation-handling. *Journal of Knowledge Management, 7*(5), 6-24.

Wright, R. (1994). The effects of tacitness and tangibility on the diffusion of knowledge based resources. *Academy of Management Proceedings, 52-56.*

Endnotes

[a]   Defining knowledge has long been a difficult exercise. There does seem to be some general consensus that data represent the most basic building blocks of knowledge, and wisdom the most accomplished outcome of knowledge. For those of us interested in tacit knowledge, knowledge

then (and usually only then) becomes subdivided into articulated or codified knowledge as opposed to tacit knowledge.

[b]   Social Capital is more valuable than ever before. With the rise of the knowledge worker and the need for western firms to obtain a competitive advantage with regard to knowledge work (given that much manufacturing now takes place offshore), social capital provides the oil that lubricates the knowledge work wheel.

[c]   Kakabadse et al., (2003) wittily portray KM as an ancient discipline. However the generally held view by most KM researchers and practitioners seems to be that it is an area of study arising over the last two decades.

[d]   The U.S. Army is noted for taking a centralised approach to KM. The Army Publishing Agency produces thousands of publications annually for members of the Armed Forces. Benefits include faster access to lessons and protocols to be learnt (Desouza & Evaristo, 2004).

[e]   As we shall see with regard to tacit knowledge, cultural examples when associated with KM, also tend to be split along eastern and western lines. Although some (e.g., Snowden) are not convinced by Nonaka's cyclic approach to knowledge, Nonaka nevertheless remains popular with regard to descriptions of Japanese approaches to KM and TK specifically. When discussing eastern vs. western perspectives, the Japanese vs. Anglo-American approaches tend to be norm. Burrows, Drummond, and Martinsons (2005) provide refreshing evidence for Chinese approaches toward KM. In both Japanese and Chinese firms, implicit knowledge is prized, more so than in western firms. It seems to be the case in Chinese organisations specifically, that knowledge only flows upward, unlike the Japanese example.

[f]   The author has chosen to use these dates, as sources seem to vary with regard to start and end dates for these generations.

[g]   Either way, both OL and LO refer to a sub-branch of KM that values connectedness between team members and a willingness of employees to learn from their own and each others' experiences.

[h]   The role of ICT in KM, and particularly with regard to knowledge diffusion is complex. Opinions are divided as to whether ICT aids or inhibits the transferral of knowledge, particularly tacit knowledge. There is of course general consensus that the increased amount of knowledge needing to be processed nowadays requires and is aided by ICT. At the same time it is felt in certain quarters that (truly) tacit knowledge cannot by definition be transferred electronically.

[i]   Hansen (1999) comments that knowledge transfer is likely to be heavily affected by amongst other things; the strength of ties amongst teams. For example strong ties within a group itself, may actually constrain a team to satisfying its information demands from within. Weaker ties will conversely encourage a team to search for information (and of course knowledge) from other work groups in a company. How exactly 'weaker' and 'stronger' is defined is not made clear.

Chapter III

Tacit Knowledge Defined

We have no idea how we do a lot of the things that we know how to do. Among those are the very fast feats of perception, recognition, attention, information retrieval, and motor control. We know how to see and smell, how to recognise a friend's face, how to concentrate on a mark on the wall ... These definitely are tacit competencies. If there are rules involved, we have no idea what they might be (Dahlbom & Mathiassen, 1999, p. 33).

Introduction

As Dahlbom and Mathiassen (1999) state, even though we may not be able to articulate a lot of our "know how" as opposed to "know what" or "know that" (Garud, 1997), it is felt there is a proportion that can be. Within an organisational context, people make use of knowledge that is not necessarily codified or even articulated, this knowledge is said to be tacit, yet comprises not only a viable source of information to be articulated but provides an organisation with a competitive edge. The separation between **articulable** and **inarticulable tacit knowledge** has its foundations in the work of others. "… It is important to distinguish between tacit knowledge, which is embodied in skills and can therefore be copied, and tacit knowledge which cannot be demonstrated and so is very difficult to transfer (e.g., the recognition of a musical note)" (Senker, 1995a, p. 102). Although recognition is given to **inarticulable tacit knowledge**, or *true* tacit knowledge, the bulk of this monograph is concerned with the articulable component.

This chapter accomplishes two tasks. Part A provides the reader with a general background to knowledge with a view to where tacit knowledge fits into this spectrum. A broad review of the literature then is presented with tacit knowledge explored from different perspectives. Exemplars will include the effect of culture on the importance of tacit knowledge to the competitive process, as well as the significance of the receiver understanding what it is they are being given in the form of knowledge. In addition, the role of metaphors and analogies in the tacit knowledge transfer process is explored. Part B explores *definitions* of tacit knowledge through a qualitative grounded theory approach. As a result of this process a *working definition* for the remainder of this book is established.

Part A: The Knowledge Background

Aside from postmodernist viewpoints with regard to definitions of knowledge (Kakabadse, Kakabadse, & Kouzmin, 2003), one can postulate that data is said to comprise pieces of unrelated code or facts (Busch & Dampney, 2000; Rowley, 2003), which become meaningful within a human mind when formed into information and thereto into knowledge (Hustad, 2004) for "there is evidence to suggest that a sliding scale exists between data, information and knowledge. Data consists of raw facts … Information is a collection of facts organised in such a way that they have [by virtue of what is implied in a human mind], additional value beyond the value of the facts themselves ….Knowledge is the body of rules, guidelines, and procedures used to select, organise and manipulate data to make it suitable for a specific task ….." (Stair & Reynolds, 1998, 5 [italics added]). *The Macquarie Dictionary* defines value as "that property of a thing because of which it is esteemed, desirable, or useful, or the degree of this property possessed; worth, merit, or importance" (1997, p. 2337). Note the implied context that value is relative to human judgement, interpretation and assessment. Dahlbom and Mathiassen (1999) differ,[a] insofar as they see data being a representation of information, implying that information is a component of data. The key issue here is that data is a representation of a particular purpose viz: communication and in reality communication within an implied or explicit context. Thus, information is more than data--as there may be several possible contexts (aspects, perspectives) of the reality represented in the data. Data is thus a projection of information for a particular purpose, even if other purposes may also be supported. Information on the other hand requires interpretation and processing, leading inevitably to the requirement to articulate the means and skills, that is knowledge, supporting an interpretation. To summarise, and as Figure 1 illustrates, data is the minimum we are able to communicate, information elaborates but knowledge truly represents what we know both articulately and tacitly.

Knowledge is a manifestation of skills and means expressed by humans, making use of both data and information. Sveiby (1997) states that "knowledge cannot be described in words because it is mainly tacit … it is also dynamic and static," furthermore, "information and knowledge should be seen as distinctly different. Information is entropic (chaotic); knowledge is nonentropic. The receiver of the information – not the sender – gives it meaning. Information as such is meaningless" (pp. 38, 49). Although it should be realised that data is the most basic representation of information and that organised information requires a component of knowledge, taking this reasoning one step further, one may envisage a knowledge hierarchy as illustrated in Figure 2. What begins as TK (Stage 1) (components of which may never be articulated), ultimately becomes separated from that which is able to be articulated (Stage 2), and eventually is so (Stage 3). In due course knowledge becomes categorised (Stage

Figure 1. An interpretation of data, information, and knowledge

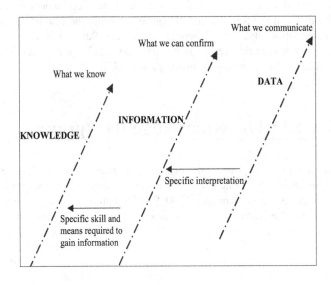

Figure 2. The knowledge hierarchy

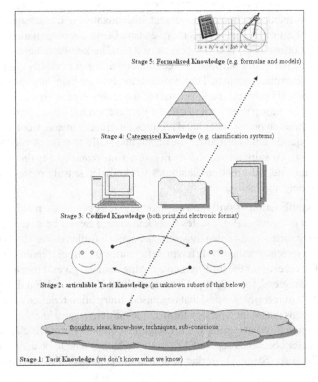

4) and thereafter codified into rule sets (stage 5). The definitive examples of **codification** include mathematical, chemical or other scientific formulae. Finally, but not absolutely, the formulae are based on the axioms of the mathematics, which cannot be both complete and consistent (based on the work of Gödel), and on the decision that the interpretation of the axioms is valid in the domain in which they are being applied. **Codification** rests ultimately on continuing agreement to decisions previously made--no absolute or complete articulation is therefore ever possible. This book is largely concerned with the transference process from stage 2 to stage 3. Stage 1 merely serves as a foundation to knowledge extraction, and stages 4 and 5 are already well researched in most disciplines.

It also is important to realise that a proportion of tacit knowledge can never actually be articulated (Leonard & Sensiper, 1998), for "much of it is not introspectable or verbally articulable (relevant examples of the latter would include our tacit knowledge of grammatical or logical rules, or even of most social conventions)" (Pylyshyn, 1981, p. 603).

Social conventions such as etiquette sets or what constitutes proof, become codified over time as a practical matter (Busch & Dampney, 2000), because the parties involved accept, agree or submit to the conventions, rules, laws (or the means of arriving at them) as the case may be. From an organisational point of view, tacit knowledge is typically placed under the heading of intangible assets (Howells, 1995a).

An Introduction to Tacit Knowledge

Given the volume of literature concerned with tacit knowledge, there is little alternative but to treat the tacit knowledge literature as discrete topics of enquiry. At the same time, the breadth of definitions with regard to tacit knowledge necessitates some means of deriving a sound definition for the purposes of *this* book. Definitions for tacit knowledge are dealt with in depth in the second part of this chapter; nevertheless, a brief introduction to defining such knowledge is necessary in the first section. With these points in mind, an examination of the tacit knowledge literature takes place under a number of headings beginning with the tacit versus articulate knowledge debate. Finally, this chapter concludes with a suitable working of tacit knowledge based upon grounded theory analysis.

Tacit Knowledge vs. Articulate Knowledge

It has become usual to consider articulable and tacit knowledge as separate types. However it is acknowledged by a number of researchers (e.g., Küpers, 2005) that "some have been critical to a purely taxonomic perspective, because it treats knowledge as a set of discrete elements ... total separation is impossible, since tacit knowledge is a necessary component of all knowledge" (Tsoukas, 1996, in Hustad, 2004, p.58). Nevertheless, the approach adopted in this book treats tacit knowledge as separate from its explicit cousin for simplicity's sake. We may define explicit knowledge as "what is usually described as knowledge, as set out in written words or maps, or mathematical formulae," and tacit knowledge, "such as we have of something we are in the act of doing" (Polanyi, 1958).

Tacit knowledge is that component of knowledge that is widely embodied in individuals (Küpers, 2005), but not able to be readily expressed. It is expertise, skill or 'know how', as opposed to codified knowledge. Alternatively, "tacit knowledge is the personal knowledge resident within the mind, behavior and perceptions of individuals. Tacit knowledge includes skills, experiences, insight, intuition and judgment. It is typically shared through discussion, stories, analogies and person-to-person interaction; therefore, it is difficult to capture or represent in explicit form. Because individuals continually add personal knowledge, which changes behavior and perceptions, tacit knowledge is by definition uncapped" (Casonato & Harris, 1999).

Articulate Knowledge is acquired through formal education, writing, books, rule-sets, legal code, and so on to provide but a few examples. Conversely, tacit knowledge either is acquired through an "intimate" relationship between a "master" and an "apprentice," or through learned experience over time. It usually is transferred orally, by way of example or by sight. "Apprenticeship" refers to both the knowledge transfer process (typically by an expert or senior person) and the concurrent acquisition of knowledge (typically by a novice or junior person) within a given domain.

The Tacit Knowledge Conversion Process

It has been shown "… that *new* tacit knowledge is generated as former tacit knowledge becomes codified" (Senker, 1995a, p. 104). In fact the transition to codified knowledge is not so sudden. What begins as an initial process of socialisation as pointed out by Nonaka (1991) and Nonaka, Takeuchi, and Umemoto (1996), characteristic of experts showing novices "the ropes," becomes a gradual **codification** process. A graphical interpretation of this principle is provided in Figure 3.

Before the "blue" codification phase takes place, tacit knowledge becomes formalised in "unspoken rules" that exist within the organisational sphere. We may refer to these as "etiquette sets." Over time even etiquette becomes codified. We find codified examples of such

Figure 3. The tacit knowledge codification cycle (Busch & Dampney, 2000)

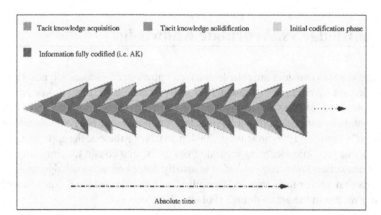

rule sets in almost every society which dictate how behaviour should be conducted in all manner of situations (often social), from dining behaviour to what may be deemed acceptable relationships between the genders. One step further along, the partial codification phase characterises an environment where notes are available but not in any "official capacity." Examples would include "research in progress," "draft documents," material which is "not to be quoted" and so on. Such material is far from being tacit, nonetheless fully codified it is not. Finally complete codification includes all manner of printed and electronic material.

It is appropriate at this juncture to consider several other points. The process just outlined is thought by Busch and Dampney (2000) to be cyclical, but not necessarily symmetrical. In other words, although tacit knowledge becomes chronologically codified, the transference from one individual to another does not take place equally. Senior people typically tend to teach junior people tacit knowledge and experts tend to teach novices. A novice, however, may be senior and the expert junior, especially in the sciences and technology where young people may be more up to date technologically.

Another important aspect is that codified knowledge combined with tacit knowledge is said to produce competitive advantage as Sternberg, Wagner, Williams, and Horvath (1995) point out.

Tacit knowledge is acquired without direct help from others ... Tacit knowledge is acquired under conditions of minimal environmental support ... there are three characteristic features of tacit knowledge: (a) procedural structure, (b) high usefulness, and (c) low environmental support for acquisition ... Knowledge acquired in the face of low environmental support often confers a comparative advantage and thus tends to be practically useful in a competitive environment. When knowledge must be acquired in the face of low environmental support, the probability that some individuals will fail to acquire it increases. When some individuals fail to acquire knowledge, others who succeed in acquiring the knowledge may gain a competitive advantage over those who fail to acquire it ... (p. 917).

It is also known that the loss of tacit knowledge can lead to a loss of self-esteem, "... Tacit knowledge emerges and develops through closeness to the work processes ... for the people in question, loss of recognition of this type of tacit knowledge could lead to reduced motivation, [and] propensity and ability to get involved in the organisational processes" (Johannessen, Olsen, & Olaisen, 1997, p. 103). Such loss of self-esteem for the individual almost certainly is likely to lead to employees being less in a position to competitively market themselves. Those individuals with more marketable skills (both articulable and tacit knowledge), are more likely to find employment at a salary that satisfies them.[b]

Another important factor is that work practices can also be affected by the absence of TK. For instance it has been noted that telecommuting can have a detrimental effect on junior employees, as they are unable to pick up many of the workplace cues they require for on the job success.[c] It may thus be argued **telework** is satisfactory for is the expeditious transfer, manipulation and creation of articulable knowledge but not tacit knowledge. This last point is important, for a premium is placed on tacit knowledge being acquired by the novice to the extent that "some organisations mandate that newcomers should not telework" (Raghuram, 1996, p. 863). With these points in mind, let us now turn our attention to what has been written about tacit knowledge in the literature, beginning from a historical perspective.

Tacit Knowledge Historically

In turning our attention to historical issues it should not be inferred that tacit knowledge has an inception date that is necessarily tied to any one particular period or socio-cultural location. Naturally tacit knowledge is as old as humankind; however the way in which it was dealt with historically is interesting. One of the most commonly cited historical examples of tacit knowledge in action was that of Collins' work dealing with the building of lasers. Scientists, whose lasers actually worked, were shown to have incorporated tacit knowledge into their methodology (Collins, 1974; Henderson, 1995; Meerabeau, 1992). There are also other historical examples of tacit knowledge usage. For example, Ivins (1953 in Henderson, 1995) noted that ancient Greek citizens often faced technological advancement hurdles. First due to a Platonic mind/body schism,[d] and secondly the fact that slaves worked directly with technological know–how in performing their many acts of labour. Such slave labour, which was not considered worthy of any energy saving innovation on the part of the citizens, meant that the Greeks themselves were not attaining the tacit knowledge.

Another example concerned artists historically (and still today). One particular reference is given with regard to engravers depicting Newcomen engines (an early form of steam engine). "… Artists either failed to understand the principles of the valve gear, and drew it indistinctly or inaccurately, or else they copied their predecessors' work" (Rolt in Henderson, 1995, p. 205). Historically, Chinese copies of western technical drawings seemed to represent a similar problem, namely a failure to incorporate perspective, and therefore an understanding of how the technology worked (Edgerton, 1980 in Henderson, 1995). Hindle (1981 in Henderson, 1995) had gone further, declaring that as the apprentice system of learning was lost (meaning the ability to transfer tacit knowledge), and a consequent rise in explicit or (articulate) drawings became necessary, to the extent that we have CAD/CAM (Computer Aided Design/Computer Aided Manufacturing) equipment today.

Explicit knowledge whilst nevertheless valuable is obtainable in print or electronic format. Alternatively such knowledge is available through intellectual property innovations in the form of patents, which over time become available to all. Many examples of innovation begin in military or armament circles. A famous case in point from the 1860s-1870s is provided in the form of the Rollin-White patent for metallic cartridges. This patent enabled Smith & Wesson™ to gain a substantial lead on Colt™ in the firearms market. When the patent had expired, Colt™ was able to be more successful in developing handguns, which were able to utilise metallic cartridges, and eventually gained a lead over its rival with its now famous Colt .45 revolver (Wilson, 1985). Nevertheless Colt firearms had faced barriers to success as far as tacit knowledge was concerned when attempting to manufacture firearms overseas.[e] The point being that apart from having machinery and codified blueprints, unless technical help relevant to that area of expertise is available, success does not necessarily automatically follow. Once again Colt™ was to face similar problems shortly after the Second World War. Having laid off many skilled staff the company was unable to "resume commercial manufacturing until c.1947-1948, partly because of a lack of drawings for re-tooling, and the departure of so many top hands who were capable of setting up machines from memory" (Wilson, 1985, pp. 272, 275). Yet another martial example is provided by the fact that "during the First World War, the French, needing an additional supply of their 75-mm field guns, sent their blueprints to the US. However, the Americans could only produce guns of the required quality after a team of [French] workmen went to show them how" (Landes, 1999 in Roberts, 2001). Having examined some historical examples of the role of tacit knowledge in society, what part does culture play?

Tacit Knowledge and Culture

Saint-Onge (1996) includes intuition, perspectives, beliefs, and values people form as a result of their experiences in his definition of tacit knowledge. When Saint-Onge's description of tacit knowledge at the individual level is congregated into an organizational level, it can approach the definition of culture (Hatch, 1993; Schein, 1985 in Brockmann & Anthony, 1998).

It was revealed how knowledge management was affected by cultural viewpoints in the previous chapter. Culturally knowledge management (and by default tacit knowledge management) is often split along western (typically Anglo-American) and eastern (usually Japanese) lines (Prahalad & Hamel, 1990 in Lei, Hitt, & Bettis, 1996). Some understanding was gained with regard to how Japanese attitudes through Nonaka's work (Guzman & Wilson, 2005; Nonaka, 1991; Nonaka et al., 1996), contrasted with the Chinese approach to managing organisational knowledge (Burrows, Drummond, & Martinsons, 2005).

Within a western environment, the importance attached to articulated knowledge has always been paramount and far superseded that attached to what has traditionally been seen as "fuzzy," "soft," dare one say "unreliable" tacit knowledge. Computers were designed as numerical processing instruments, and as such dealt with articulated knowledge. Computers can deal with unarticulated knowledge by mimicking expertise. Expertise in this case refers to the patterns of fact employed to diagnose conditions even though the facts do not reduce to a sound set of principles. This, coupled with the fact that western managers see the organisation as a centre for "scientific management," with computers as machines for information processing (Takeuchi, 1998), means that a western perspective has always tended to play down the role of tacit knowledge within organisational knowledge creation.

The Japanese approach towards knowledge management differs from a western one, from anything as taken for granted as *nemawashi* (discussion behind the scenes to finalise a deal), to agreement on contracts, which is typically tacit in the Japanese case, to more formally contracted in the U.S. example (Yamadori, 1984). The differences in the cultures have also meant that Japanese car designers for example, but not their U.S. counterparts, were able to detect reasons why a vehicle had not been selling well because of the shape of its grille and headlights (Leonard & Sensiper, 1998). Another cultural example of tacit knowledge differences is given by way of Japanese work practices. The Japanese approach is to conduct a morning discussion session where staff "air" their viewpoints and transfer their tacit knowledge (a process the Japanese refer to as *cho rei*). Such an approach has often appeared to visiting U.S. staff as a waste of time (Nonaka & Takeuchi in Durrance, 1998).

Japanese firms also appear to differ with respect to knowledge sharing at an intra-organisational level. The Japanese approach is often to involve many people. The western approach tends to reflect a "need-to-know" basis, meaning that knowledge (both codified and more particularly tacit) is not so readily transmitted (Hamel, 1991 in West & Meyer, 1997). Certainly the Australian approach tends to follow the U.S. example. Meetings are conducted on a basis of only involving directly concerned personnel and information is typically transferred on a "need to know basis." From an articulate/codified knowledge point of view, this makes sense and indeed is practical given the "information overload" of most professional personnel today. What we do not have sitting on our desks in front of us, we can easily acquire, either through libraries or the internet. The disadvantage culturally within western spheres is that **articulable tacit knowledge** is not being transferred because of the codified knowledge management "mindset." At this stage, we are beginning to see the role the organisation plays in regard to soft knowledge. The following section thus explores the relationship between the workplace and tacit knowledge further.

The Role of Tacit Knowledge in Organisations

Tacit knowledge "… emerges and develops through closeness to the work processes" (Johannessen et al., 1997, p. 103) and so may be lost because tacit knowledge held by an individual is taken to the new workplace. If work processes change, the competence developed by a person in the form of tacit knowledge may be made superfluous and new knowledge needs to be developed in relation to the work processes. Most tacit knowledge measurement or articulation is conducted at the level of the individual, largely because measurement is conducted by psychologists. Group tacit knowledge is nevertheless a reality insofar as collective tacit knowledge takes place when individuals interact (Leonard & Sensiper, 1998). The ideal goal of any workplace is to tap into the collective tacit knowledge that individuals possess and to store this in a database format (not necessarily relational). Indeed this practice has been adopted in a number of organizations, one of which has been the Hewlett Packard (HP) Corporate Education Division where all manner of tips, "tricks of the trade," and other "tacit forms" of knowledge were "captured" by being placed within a Lotus Notes™ database and thereby made available to some 2,000 HP trainers (Davenport, De Long, & Beers, 1998). A similar process has taken place between Xerox™ France and Xerox™ Palo Alto, California (Durrance, 1998).

Such information elicitation and storage is usually found under the banner of knowledge management today. Its purpose is to inform not just other members of staff, but particularly newcomers. The importance of tacit knowledge transfer to new staff is particularly important. One such example is provided by Raghuram (1996), whereby she notes some organisations actually forbid **teleworking** by junior staff, due to their inability to acquire tacit knowledge from more experienced staff as physical contact has been removed. From an organisational point of view even if we admit that not all tacit knowledge is suitable for inclusion within the knowledge management (KM) paradigm,[f] we still need to consider that "the traditional work environment is embedded with cues, nuances, gossip and other unspoken, unwritten sources of vital information" (Raghuram, 1996, p. 861). What is missing is not articulated knowledge, rather tacit knowledge and indeed not just tacit knowledge, but more specifically **articulable tacit knowledge**. True tacit knowledge can only be acquired by the individual through sense experience; it cannot actually be acquired from *another* individual. Another way of defining such demarcation is contingency versus rule-governed behaviour within a framework of *Verstehen* (understanding):

When a person learns a behaviour from direct experience, without any rules of verbal guidance from others, the behaviour is said to be contingency shaped behaviour. The child who learns not to touch bees after having been stung while playing in the clover has learned contingency shaped behaviour. When a person learns a behaviour by following rules which are explicitly or implicitly encoded in verbal statements, the behaviour is said to be rule-governed (Baldwin & Baldwin, 1978, p. 336 italics added).

Such a view reinforces the concept of tacit knowledge as implicit rather than explicit, more as Baldwin and Baldwin (1978) note, a matter of ***Verstehen*** rather than ***Erklären*** (explanation or articulation/externalisation).

Organisational tacit knowledge can also be subdivided into intra-firm, intra-organisational tacit knowledge or inter-firm inter-institutional tacit knowledge. The former concerns personnel moving *within* the firm and taking knowledge with them. The latter refers to staff collaborating with each other on projects. Howells (1995a) defines this as horizontal transfer. Vertical transfer refers to staff in differing industries collaborating. An example at the macro inter-institutional level is where university staff may perhaps align their tacit expertise with that of public or private institutional research staff (Howells, 1995a). Arguably the more commonplace example is likely to be the first example, where personnel *within* the firm provide their knowledge to other less experienced staff. Nevertheless the spectre of staff leaving and taking their tacit knowledge with them is well documented (Howells, 1995a; Walczak, 2005), and certainly advantageous to the hiring firm (Senker, 1995a). Contrarily, a less beneficial aspect to companies can be the competitive nature of tacit knowledge as we shall see.

Tacit Knowledge and Competitive Advantage

By far and away a major factor concerning tacit knowledge in general is its competitive potential. It is that subset of tacit knowledge, for example, "open culture, employee empowerment and executive commitment" (Powell, 1995), more so than the subset of **articulable tacit knowledge**, and certainly more than articulated/codified knowledge that permits an "edge" either at the personal or organisational level. Sternberg and his associates (Sternberg et al., 1995; Torff & Sternberg, 1998) have noted extensively how tacit knowledge is acquired within what they term conditions of "low environmental support" and this provides the owner of the knowledge with an advantage over those who do not have such knowledge. Indeed colloquially this process can be termed sorting the "sheep from the goats" or the "men from the boys."[g] It is the competitive capability of tacit knowledge that is of greatest importance to organisations, for it is such context specific knowledge and its associated skills that make it difficult for competitors to rival other firms (Ree & DeFillippi, 1990 in Lei, 1997). Codified knowledge on the other hand is available to all, unless it is locked into patents, which even then are potentially illegally reproduced in any case.[h]

The competitive attribute of tacit knowledge which the blue collar sector labels "trade secrets," can lead in turn to "industrial espionage" in both white and blue collar domains. Capturing codified knowledge can easily enough be accomplished either through reading literature or practically through "reverse engineering" where an object is disassembled to gain an understanding of how and with what materials it was constructed. Extreme examples of reverse engineering include the capture and testing of enemy equipment during wartime. Taking this one step further with the inclusion of tacit knowledge, it could well be argued that what the Allies had sought to achieve at the conclusion of the Second World War with the "capture" of German scientists, was not just codified "rocket science," but the tacit component stored within the minds of these detainees. One should not really be surprised at this example however, for capturing the tacit knowledge of scientists (and engineers) is still very much *de rigeur* today (Senker, 1995a; Zucker & Darby, 1998; Zucker, Darby, & Armstrong, 2001; Zucker and Darby, 1998).

Within the IS domain[i] a great deal of importance is placed on the tacit component of competitive advantage. Unfortunately as is all too often the case, intellectual property theft is also commonplace even within the IS sector. Typical examples include the illegal reproduction of Microsoft™ software (or even the pirating of music by Metallica™ which usually requires Information Systems for duplication to be successfully undertaken). What IS firms seek to do is recruit personnel who will provide their organisations with a competitive edge over others. To the point that today third party firms specialise in selecting personnel for client organisations, depending on their relevant codified and tacit knowledge. Actually, it is the tacit component that a senior/experienced IS person brings to the firm that commands the highest levels of respect and consequent high salaries or vice versa. The senior person is less likely to be working with codified knowledge, and if so, then highly summarised knowledge. Rather they are likely to have greater ability to tacitly process the information they have in front of them (Busch & Dampney, 2000). What *actualises* the tacit competitive component of the knowledge is the often-unique interrelationship of personnel, "routines and technologies" (Lei, Hitt, & Bettis, 1996). Perhaps the ultimate example here is once again provided by the military, where the unique interrelationship of the above factors leads to one army overcoming another (Horvath, Forsythe, Bullis, Sweeney, Williams, McNally, Wattendorf, & Sternberg, 1999; Ulmer, 1999). To summarise, the competitive nature of tacit knowledge is a question of essentially two things, first "regional specificity" (Foss, 1996 in Lawson & Lorenz, 1999), or the ability of such knowledge to be housed within certain conditions, for example firms, organisations or collections of personnel. The second factor relates to "imperfect imitation," the *in*ability to *easily* copy the valuable tacit component (Maskell & Malmberg, 1999), which relates to Sternberg et al's (1995) acquisition in conditions of low environmental support. In short "determining when to make articulable knowledge explicit (i.e., exploiting an opportunity) and when to leave inarticulable knowledge in its 'native' form (respecting both the inherent strengths and limits of tacit knowledge) is central to managing an appropriate balance between tacit and explicit knowledge" (Zack, 1999).

The Economics of Tacit Knowledge: The Significance of Geography

Given the competitive benefits of tacit knowledge, it is hardly surprising that it or at least *unarticulated* knowledge has been the source of economic study for quite some time, starting with Friedrich von Hayek (1948 in Desrochers, 2001). Economists such as von Hayek have argued that a distinction exists between information and knowledge where "the former may be marketed and traded, the latter may not" (Fransman, 1994). If one considers tacit knowledge to be knowledge and not information, then this would indicate that it is non-tradeable. In addition something that is to be consumed by the individual who created it is considered to be a *product*, but if it is to be consumed by another it attains the status of a *commodity*. Where does this then place tacit knowledge? Is personal tacit knowledge a product, and our learning it from another person, a commodity?

From the point of view of innovation, tacit knowledge has historically been intertwined with the development of certain specialised industrial regions where the know-how (rather than know-what) has enabled clustering of industries to take place (Audretsch & Feldman, 1995). The concentration of the industrial German Ruhr and British Midlands provide such examples (Desrochers, 2001). It has been noted that clustering was prevalent at the immature stage of industrial development, whereas upon industrial maturity, dispersion of economic activity (and therefore tacit knowledge) may take place. Knowledge spillovers, leading to the concentration of certain industrial sectors, have traditionally taken place where the role and importance of tacit knowledge has been the greatest. Once again, this ties back to tacit knowledge being knowledge and not information, therefore it becomes difficult to package and commodify (Audretsch & Feldman, 1995).

... New economic knowledge is said to spill over when the unit of observation which utilises the new economic knowledge is distinct from the one that produced it. These knowledge spillovers do not, however, transmit costlessly with respect to geographic distance. Rather, location, and proximity matter. That is, while the costs of transmitting information may be invariant to distance, presumably the cost of transmitting knowledge and especially tacit knowledge rises along with distance (Audretsch & Feldman, 1995, p. 6).

Such geographical concentration would also help to explain why certain companies maintain their R&D branches in the home country, whereas much of the less "original" work is permitted to be outsourced, or perhaps still in-sourced (if a multi-national), but offshore (Cantwell & Santangelo, 2000; Malik, 2004).[j] Unlike codified information, which is available in the form of printed or electronic documentation or perhaps as patents, tacit knowledge cannot necessarily be said to comprise a public good. If it is not widely available because of its competitive advantage and the economic benefits it bestows on the holder, what then are its practical applications?

Examples of Tacit Knowledge in Action

Having examined tacit knowledge historically, culturally and now economically, let us turn our attention to some practical examples, beginning with the domain of health. In the pharmaceutical industry originally, knowledge creation was often not dependent on scientific theory (in other words articulate knowledge), but rather gauging how patients reacted to new medicines (Liebenau, 1984; Swann, 1988 in Howells, 1995a). It was only later that systematised codified rules were developed to explain phenomena. Similarly in diabetes research, tacit knowledge first described how insulin effected pancreatic extracts (Swann, 1988 in Howells, 1995a), "... it was often only subsequently that scientific discoveries and advances were able to explain and systematise the initial observations and practice that arose out of them in medicine" (Howells, 1995a, p. 11). In the area of medical practice specifically, Goldman (1990) has identified how clinical judgement is by no means a solely codified knowledge process, even though the dominant view would tend to indicate otherwise. Tacit knowledge is made use of, for "… it is the knowledge which goes beyond the physical findings, lab data, and clinical rules when the intensivist fine tunes the controls of a mechanical ventilator. It is all that knowledge which integrates and permits the choice and use of the appropriate explicit rules and methods" (p. 53). Similarly the radiologist is able to interpret x-rays based on codified rule sets; nevertheless a degree of tacit knowledge is used in making judgements (Goldman, 1990). Paediatric examples are also known, where clinicians are able to diagnose quickly, important cases from less important ones. In other words, these are examples relying on more than codified rule sets (Goldman, 1990). Specifically within the field of dentistry, Chambers (1998) argues that his discipline makes even more than (medically) usual usage of tacit knowledge.

In the aeronautical arena, Dreyfus, Dreyfus, and Athanasiou (1986) had noted how accomplished helicopter pilots would fly aircraft in a different manner from that of novice pilots. Apparently skilled pilots utilised holistic flying, whereas novices adopted conscious problem solving. This was to such a point that in the United States Air Force it was once discovered that flight instructors did not actually fly the way they were teaching trainee pilots.[k]

In the engineering domain, practical knowledge rather than purely codified knowledge was responsible for the development of scientific instrumentation (von Hippel, 1976 in Howells, 1995a). Viewed another way, it is often the lack of tacit knowledge that prevents progress in technical domains, as in the case of manufacturing:

Application knowledge which was a core capability in developing competence in FMS [Flexible Manufacturing Systems] was highly tacit in nature and centred around the ability to specify and describe the order of events and the flow of information, tools and workpieces that could only be gained via interaction with advanced customers and hence the ability to gain tacit application knowledge meant that they effectively remained blocked in gaining entry to the new technology (Howells, 1995a p. 11).

A similar example is noted with regard to the export of technology to developing nations where the tacit knowledge is missing. Although blueprints for technology may be complete, if the tacit knowledge is missing, receivers of the knowledge are unable to follow even highly detailed plans (Arora, 1996; Malik, 2004; Pavitt, 1987; Woherem, 1991), which is also considered to be the case even in advanced nations (Arora, 1996). Given the number of examples with regard to the role of the sender, what of the role of the receiver in the tacit knowledge transferral process?

The Importance of the Receiver

Knowledge remains tacit because the emitter and/or the receiver have no knowledge about how to exchange knowledge (Ancori, Bureth, & Cohendet 2000, p. 273).

What we must realise, is that tacit knowledge is precisely that: knowledge. It is only knowledge if the receiver is in a position to understand to what we are referring. "… There will always be significant knowledge that cannot be communicated due to lacking receiver competence … It is "tacit" to those who don't understand" (Eliasson in Lamberton, 1997 p. 75). Sveiby (1997) also agrees with this point of view. For example in a master-apprentice situation, the apprentice is never likely to attain tacit knowledge if the frame of mind is not willing to accept the subtle skills passed on by the master. Nonaka (1991) provides us with a classic example where a significant amount of effort was required by an Osaka whitegoods manufacturer to duplicate the bread making skills of a master baker/pastry cook. The idea being that such skills could be incorporated into a bread making machine the company had been working on. It was only the ability of the relevant software engineer to notice how the dough was being twisted by the baker that led to the machine ultimately being perfected. One could equally argue that those who do not wish to understand, or those "who do not wish to see," are unlikely to acquire tacit knowledge.

In relation to contingency-based knowledge, the receiver can only acquire the tacit component if they themselves have experienced similar contingency-based experiences (Baldwin and Baldwin, 1978). For instance, the act of underwater swimming being likened to a weightless gliding sensation would make little sense to someone who has never experienced either flight or swimming. Nonetheless, it is acknowledged that at least partial codification of even this knowledge type is able to take place,[1] and this certainly is true of the information systems domain. The complexity of knowledge that is dealt with in the IS arena requires a greater level of knowledge than that of the purely articulated component.

Although computing is not as practically oriented as medicine or dentistry with the need for hands on skills where computing tends to be more keyboard focused, the skills required by IT professionals demand that much more than just processing of articulated information take place. Some possible examples include the interpretation of body language in interviews that suggest that the client may not fully be explaining what the problem with the old system might be. Or learning to deal with the data communications manager who states that she is open to opinion, but eye contact seems to reveal that her mind is closed. Another example would be the system administrator confronting a group of staff about "unethical" Internet access, and then determining from facial expressions who the guilty parties might be (without necessarily even having checked access logs). Such experiences allow us to formulate rule sets for dealing with situations, from determining who an ideal future manager in the organisation might be; through to deciding which employee would make a good "front" person for an organisation. Experiences such as these lead us to form rule sets with regard to handling such situations. Indeed Sternberg et al. (1995) have provided similar examples in relation to staff coping with their boss depending on the current circumstances. One easily could argue based on evidence such as this that certain occupations within the IS domain are likely to require personnel with higher tacit knowledge aptitude; for instance systems analysts, data administrators, knowledge engineers and of course managers. That is to say "front office" personnel who are more likely to have to liaise with people, rather than work with machines. The latter group alternatively are often characterised as "back office" personnel.

To summarise, it must be realised that all of our explicit knowledge nevertheless is based on our tacit understanding of the underlying principles. Examining the IS domain for example, it could be argued all of our knowledge resides at an underlying tacit level. There would be little point explaining to a stone age hunter-gatherer what recursion within software code entails, without the hunter-gatherer having first seen how a computer is structured of hardware and software, and that the latter (with the addition of electricity [in itself requiring an understanding of tacit knowledge]) runs the former. Indeed, examining disciplines as complex as computing, based as they are on a multitude of other disciplines (mathematics, electronics, logic, heuristics, linguistics, ergonomics), it is necessary to draw upon tacit knowledge to interpret not just computing specific concepts such as data communications bus typologies, but all of the tacit knowledge inherent in the underlying fields.

But what is it about tacit knowledge that enables us to convey to others what we are trying to say? Certainly words or writing tend to be the main instrument of knowledge transferral (Nonaka et al., 1996). What if words in themselves are not ordinarily adequate to transfer the knowledge? A principle means by which such problems are overcome is through the use of metaphors and analogies.

Metaphor and Analogy

Nonaka et al. (1996) consider the articulate/tacit knowledge process to be broken into four phases. *Socialisation* (tacit to tacit), *internalisation* (explicit to tacit), *combination* (explicit to explicit) and *externalisation* (tacit to explicit). With regard to the last of these four phases, the most obvious form of externalisation is that of the act of writing (Nonaka et al., 1996). Nonetheless, what enables the externalisation of tacit knowledge to a large degree is the role played by both **metaphors** and **analogies**. *Metaphor* may be defined as "a figure of speech in which a term or phrase is applied to something to which it is not literally applicable, in order to suggest a resemblance" (*Macquarie Dictionary,* 1997, p. 1353). An *analogy* is "a partial similarity in particular circumstances on which a comparison may be based ... A form of reasoning in which similarities are inferred from a similarity of two or more things in certain particulars" (*Macquarie Dictionary,* 1997, p. 72). What is more, "contradictions between two thoughts in a metaphor are then harmonised by analogy, which reduces the unknown by highlighting the 'commonness' of two different things. Metaphor and analogy are often confused. Association of two things through metaphor is driven mostly by intuition and holistic images and does not aim to find differences between them. On the other hand, association through analogy is carried out by rational thinking and focuses on structural/ functional similarities between two things and hence their differences. Thus, analogy helps us to understand the unknown through the known and bridges the gap between an image and a logical model" (Nonaka et al., 1996, p. 839).

The role of metaphor and analogy is reinforced by the fact that language (syntax and se-mantics) often is not powerful enough to capture knowledge that we may wish to transmit (Guzman & Wilson, 2005). An emphasis needs to be placed at this stage on the fact that we refer not to data or information, rather knowledge. In other words that combination of data and information with attached human processed meaning. Put another way, knowledge is said to incorporate a "tacit" component, whereas information is purely articulate in nature and words.

Within the IS domain much product innovation takes place, and metaphors abound. For example the term "Web" is used to describe a software interface to the Internet, which links computers globally. Literally, of course, the Web is quite unlike a spider's web, for it is not biological, nor typically symmetrical, nor emanating from necessarily any one centre, nor "sticky," even though knowledge may be described as sticky (Bush & Tiwana, 2005; Dosi, 1988; Ghemawat, 1991; Hoskisson & Hitt, 1994; Polanyi, 1967; Ramaprasad & Rai,1996; von Hippel, 1994 in Raghuram, 1996; Wright, 1994). Other metaphorical examples include *firing up* an application or document, but at no stage is flame involved. Another analogy is that of *rebooting* a machine, even though we do not actually kick the machine. Yet another example relates to *spreadsheeting*, although we do not actually spread a sheet out, rather we manipulate figures and text in matrices. Yet another example is that of *debugging*, whereby the removal of insects or arachnids from programs does not take place, even if this may once have occurred. The basic point here as Lei et al. (1996) had noted, is that it is difficult for outsiders to decode metaphors. Unless one has had experience with computers, the novice is unlikely to understand the concept of debugging, let alone actually perform the task. Nor is the novice likely to understand *pipelining*, whereby data is passed by way of commands to another process. We obviously do not literally attempt to thread the data needle with "chunks" of data we can see and feel. As an aside, it is interesting to note that these last points re-emphasise the role of the receiver in the tacit knowledge process.

Tacit Knowledge and the IS Domain

Are individual differences in tacit knowledge domain-general? Are measures of tacit knowledge highly domain-specific tests of knowledge, analogous to a test for mechanics that requires identifying a crescent wrench, or do they represent some more general construct? The evidence to date is more compatible with the view that measures of tacit knowledge assess a relatively general construct (Sternberg et al., 1995, p. 919).

Management is a tacit skill (Castanias & Helfat, 1991; Coff, 1997; Goldman, 1990; Sternberg, 1999; Wagner & Sternberg, 1987), even if traditionally such skills may not be *formally* recognised by *western* management (Agor, 1986 in Giunipero, Dawley, & Anthony, 1999; Nonaka, 1991; Nonaka et al., 1996; Takeuchi, 1998). Following Sternberg's lead, one can imply that testing for the ability of a software engineer to identify the missing lines of code in a program, along the lines of Soloway et al. (1982, in Wagner & Sternberg, 1985), is more a domain-specific test of codified knowledge, rather than a general test for tacit knowledge per se. When testing for tacit knowledge within the IS domain, what is in fact being tested is management potential. Those of our employees who are best able to exploit their own and others tacit knowledge, are more likely to make the most proficient managers, this concept ties in with Sternberg's (Sternberg, Wagner, & Okagaki, 1993; Wagner & Sternberg, 1985), three types of tacit knowledge, management of "oneself, others, and one's career." The former refers to maximising ones own productivity, or to rephrase this informally, "it is easy to work hard, but difficult to work smart." The second relates to the ability to successfully manage others, typically to one's own (or perhaps the organisation's) advantage. The third relates to the ability to organise the directions one takes so as to maximise one's career

Given that tacit knowledge is a management skill, and all humans are essentially managers (if only at the "oneself" level, meaning of their own personal lives), are there likely to be certain occupations within the computing domain making greater use of tacit knowledge? If as previous research confirms, senior more experienced personnel are likely to have higher levels of tacit knowledge (Sternberg et al., 1995; Wagner & Sternberg, 1985), while junior personnel make greater use of codified rule sets (Wagner & Sternberg, 1985), it also is highly likely that senior computing people are just as likely to have greater proficiency of tacit knowledge than junior personnel. Senior need not necessarily mean older, merely more experienced (Busch & Dampney, 2000).

A Tacit Knowledge Model

"A picture is worth a thousand words" is a saying that is familiar to all of us, and for that reason the best means of conceptualising the ideas covered in the literature so far is through diagrammatical means. An examination of the model in Figure 4 reveals that tacit knowledge can be perceived to be spiral in form. The reader should note that the model is a generalisation of an *individual's* information acquisition over a career within either one or several organisations. At the start of one's career, tacit knowledge is typically minimal. The graduate is encumbered with a great deal of articulable knowledge sustained from a tertiary education and must come to terms with learning "the ropes" within a new organisation. A great deal of knowledge encountered by first the student and then the new employee is of a codified nature. As an employee within a workplace, one begins to make greater usage of ones tacit knowledge.

Figure 4. Schematic model illustrating the adoption of TK by an individual over a career (Busch & Dampney, 2000)

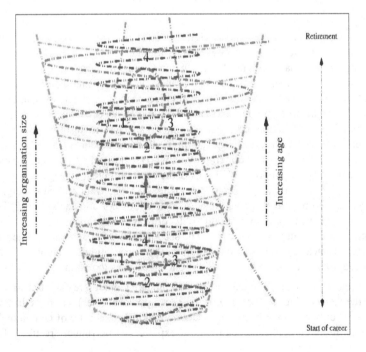

Several spirals comprise the model. The first inner blue spiral could be said to represent the articulable knowledge learning "adoption" of the individual over a career lifetime, which is significant when first employed, gradually becoming less important as one becomes more senior within the organisation. There exists significant evidence (Sternberg et al., 1995; Wagner & Sternberg, 1985) that senior/more experienced people tend to score "higher" on a tacit knowledge scale, while making less use of more formalised rule sets, algorithms, or procedures (Wagner & Sternberg, 1985).

The red spiral represents tacit knowledge, while minimal when the apprentice enters the workforce, is likely to increase significantly over the years. In fact, the pattern is not likely to be a simplistic outward branching spiral, but rather a waveform like spiral that will continually oscillate with an individual's career.

The green "cone" represents the external interface with which an individual interacts with "knowledge" or "people." The access to knowledge stems from either articulable knowledge or tacit knowledge represented by expertise, which over time becomes codified and is passed on in an "apprenticeship" situation. In due course, it is inevitable that one will come into contact with increasingly more people and forms of knowledge. As such, Busch and Dampney (2000) expect the cone will increase rather than decrease in size. Only retirement is likely to bring about a significant change in the knowledge acquisition cycle, with an expected decline in the articulable and tacit knowledge procurement.

The inner "volume" of the cone represents the individual for whom articulable and tacit knowledge is "stored' over time, and able to be transferred to other individuals. The external surface of the cone represents the individuals *Weltanschauung*.[m] The brown dashed lines in Figure 4 illustrate the relationship between tacit knowledge and the size of an organisation. It has been noted (Caves & Uekusa, 1976; Hedlund, 1994; Imai, 1980), that Japanese firms for example are generally smaller than western ones and that this is likely to influence tacit knowledge adoption. This in turn would indicate that the smaller the firm, the more likely the firm is to make use of this "soft" knowledge. Extreme such examples comprise the craft or cottage industries whereby people working from home in the past and again today would transfer much of their knowledge in a tacit way. So to restate, the larger the firm, the less tacit knowledge utilised proportionately and the more articulable knowledge is utilised (for all manner of cultural and legal reasons), particularly within western societies. The smaller the organisation (and typically the less complicated the organisation), the greater the expectation the firm will make use of tacit knowledge.

The purple "rings" represent Nonaka (1991) and Nonaka et al.'s (1996) four stages of explicit and tacit knowledge transfer. Busch and Dampney (2000) take Nonaka's approach further, explaining there is likely to be a difference in the extent to which any of the above four stages occurs throughout an individual's career. They are (1) **Socialisation** (tacit to tacit transfer); (2) **Externalisation** (tacit to articulate transfer); (3) **Combination** (articulate to articulate transfer); and (4) **Internalisation** (articulate to tacit transfer). For instance, it is anticipated that at a junior level there is likely to be a fairly even amount of each of the four stages being utilised. However, the more senior/experienced/older one becomes the greater amount of internalisation is made use of as the individual matures drawing upon ever-greater use of soft knowledge resources.

The model illustrated represents one view of tacit knowledge from the standpoint of the individual that has arisen through an interpretation of the literature. Another approach to defining tacit knowledge is through the use of grounded theory examining texts whereby authors have sought to define the phenomenon of tacit knowledge. Ultimately as the reader will see, such an exercise will to a definition of tacit knowledge suitable for the empirical work presented herein.

Part B: Qualitative Analysis of Tacit Knowledge

Definitions: A Consensus by Association

On the one hand, it is argued that *some* tacit knowledge can never actually be articulated (Leonard & Sensiper, 1998). On the other hand, economists arguing in reductionist terms consider that: "only cost considerations prevent residual forms of tacit knowledge [from being] codified" (Ancori et al., 2000, p. 281). It often is accepted "that tacit knowledge (as distinct from intangible investment more generally) is non-codified, disembodied know how that is acquired in the informal take-up of learned behaviour and procedures" (Howells, 1995a, p. 2). Tacit knowledge also has its traces in Gärdenfors' Conceptual Spaces (Gärdenfors, 2000). Research by Aisbett and Gibbons (2001) identifies the "subconceptual layer" of Gärdenfors as being representable, for example, by neural nets. This suggests that if one equates the brain's subconscious with tacit knowledge, then an explanation of tacit knowledge processing as subconscious pattern matching in the human mind is possible. Such pattern matching is not explicitly codified of course, until an effort is made to make such knowledge conscious, articulate it and then codify it.

A literature review established that much mention is made of tacit knowledge both within the organisational domain and external to it (Johannessen et al., 1997; Lei, 1997; Nonaka et al., 1996; Raghuram, 1996; Ramaprasad et al., 1996; Scott, 1992, 1990; Senker, 1995a). One could start with as general a definition of tacit knowledge as constituting "the hallmark of a profession" (Atkinson, Reid, & Sheldrake, 1977; Meerabeau, 1992; Jamous & Peloille, 1970). Polanyi (1967; 1958) who may be credited as the "father" of tacit knowledge, with the terms conception in the 1950s, defined tacit knowledge as "such as we have of something we are in the act of doing," indicating it was knowledge either nonverbalised or nonverbalisable. Tacit knowledge is thus that vast store of experiences, technical know-how, skill sets, wisdom that permits us to function from a basic survival level, to interacting in our complex knowledge-rich western societies. It is "knowledge that resides in the minds of the people in an organization but has not been put in structured, document-based form" (Davenport et al., 1998). Tacit knowledge also has been likened to intuition (Casonato & Harris, 1999; Giunipero et al., 1999; Hedlund, 1994; Howells, 1995a; MacKenzie, 1996; Takeuchi, 1998), but in reality intuition is more likely "used to access tacit knowledge" (Brockmann & Anthony, 1998). The author believes much tacit knowledge is articulable, whereas intuition is less so, lying more within the subconscious spectrum. There is naturally much more to it than this.

Tacit and particularly **articulable tacit knowledge** transfer typically takes place between individuals in the form of a "master-apprentice" relationship, for example the transfer of such knowledge between scientists in Japanese universities and research institutions (Zucker et al., 1998). In many instances one is unaware of one's own tacit knowledge, and what individuals often feel to be correct ways of performing actions may not actually be what they perform in practice. MacKay (1974) as an example had alluded to the differences between articulable and inarticulable tacit knowing:

3. The "tacit" aspect of knowledge, as Polanyi himself has pointed out, is what we have in common with lower animals, presumably all of their "knowing" is tacit.

4. Therefore, we must distinguish between what we can say we know, and what a suitably equipped observer could say we know; between what we cannot put into words, and what cannot be put into words.

5. It is scientifically inappropriate to regard knowledge we can express in words as paradigmatic, and tacit knowledge as a peculiar special case. What we need from the outset is a methodology that can cope with tacit knowledge, taking verbalisable knowledge as a special case (p. 94).

Certainly such instances tie in with Polanyi's concepts of tacit knowledge being related to "knowing more than we can tell," or "knowledge that cannot be articulated;" however, it is realised now that only a subset, even if a large subset, of tacit knowledge is truly not articulable (Figure 4; Busch & Dampney, 2000). And that this subset is normally representing physical skill-sets which simply do not lend themselves to **codification**, but can only be transferred through the "indwelling" of the individual learning the new skill for themselves. Let us deal for the moment with tacit knowledge as a complete entity. Polanyi (1958) also refers to *subsidiary* and *focal* awareness. More specifically, Polanyi (1967) had actually contemplated a triad of 1) subsidiary particulars, 2) a focal target, and 3) the knower who links the particulars to the focal target. By *focal* awareness he refers to our use of meaning systems to interpret what we see, hear or read, whereas our *subsidiary* awareness arouses within us past experiences which guide our ability to further understand what it is we are experiencing. In short, "tacit knowledge is manifestly present ..., not only when it exceeds the powers of articulation, but even when it exactly coincides with them, as it does when we have acquired it a moment before by listening to or reading a text" (p. 92). The latter concept would also relate to Polanyi's concept of "indwelling," or assimilating outside influences within (Polanyi, 1967), so typical of the tacit knowledge acquisition process. Another way of looking at this is to say "it exists between the lines" (Bundy, 1975; Greeno, 1987). Many of these definitions are noted in appendix A, should the reader wish to examine them further.

How else can tacit knowledge be defined? The *Oxford English Dictionary* (1989) views it as: "not openly expressed or stated, but implied, understood, inferred" (Vol XVII, p. 527). From a theoretical point of view, this has certainly come to appear mainstream. Although we may consider this to be the "normal" definition of tacit knowledge, little mention is made in the above quote of the practical skills often located within tacit knowledge. For example, we might choose to state that tacit knowledge is *"learning by doing"* (Arrow, 1962 in Howells, 1995a; Chambers, 1998; Itami, 1987; Lamberton, 1997; Lei, 1997; Nonaka et al., 1996), or *"learning by using"* (Badaracco, 1991; Dierickx & Cool, 1989; Dosi, 1988; Itami, 1987; Lei, 1997; Lei et al., 1996; Polanyi, 1967; Reed & deFillippi, 1990; Rosenberg, 1982; Sahal, 1981; Teece, Rumelt, Dosi, & Winter, 1992). It is precisely the skill component, which the latter two terms embody, which also ties the term tacit knowledge back to the workplace

(Howells, 1995a). One may argue that tacit knowledge is not necessarily workplace specific, and that all of us to some degree or another make use of it. Nonetheless, as it is "knowledge gained through apprenticeship" (Woherem, 1991), it unequivocally has workplace connotations. As added evidence for the "workplace" nature of tacit knowledge, Raghuram (1996) uses such terms as "traditions," "values," and "organisational culture." Hedlund (1994) uses "corporate culture." Baldwin and Baldwin (1978) mention "shop lore." While Arora (1996) exercises "rules of thumb", "tricks of the trade" and the fact that transfer of it "requires face to face contact". The writer chooses to disagree with the latter component, for voice intonation could be said to comprise a tacit component of knowledge, as it is possible to derive from phone conversations more than just the focal content of a message, at the same time it is also possible to deduce the tacit subsidiary particulars of the conversation. Nevertheless as will be explained later, information technology which typifies indirect contact, does impact negatively on tacit knowledge transfer.

"Learning to learn" (Guzman and Wilson, 2005; Grieves and Mathews, 1997; Howells, 1995a), otherwise known as "deutero learning" (Guzman and Wilson, 2005; Robinson, Clemson and Keating, 1997; Argyris and Schön, 1978), also expresses a way in which tacit knowledge is linked to the ability of the individual not only to actually learn the "focal" component of that which it is they need to know, but also incorporates the "subsidiary" learning process itself. Another example is "tip of the tongue" (Jüttner, 1980; Brown and McNeill, 1966) knowledge which corresponds with the subsidiary awareness, for it is not exactly what we are focused on, but represents a movement from the subsidiary particular to the focal component of knowledge. Perhaps this movement from subsidiary to focal knowledge is what metaphors and analogies more successfully permit us to do?

Another all too common definition is "something which cannot be easily codified or learnt" or "not directly codifiable via artefacts" (Howells, 1995a). Codification by artefact is taken to mean, made into articulate form, where the artefact in question might represent printed media in either paper or electronic format. Such definitions also tie in with a personal concept of tacit knowledge which is exemplified by Nonaka's (1991) and Takeuchi's (1998) definitions of it being "deeply rooted in an individual's action and experience, as well as in the ideals, values or emotions he or she embraces", or "customs" (Baldwin and Baldwin, 1978) that could be said to represent human etiquette at a societal (or organisational) rather than an individual level.

With regard to temporal aspects, tacit knowledge is "not a static stock of knowledge" (Howells, 1995a), in as far as knowledge is unchanging, particularly within a competitive organisational context. All the same Wagner and Sternberg (1985) mention that it is "not automatically acquired with years of experience", in other words, it is really what we have learnt from our experience that separates us from people who are less capable of making use of their tacit resources of knowledge, hence sorting "the sheep from the goats". And while this is certainly true, Olsson and Gullberg (1988) are probably still quite correct when they state that tacit knowledge is characteristically "formed under long tradition and experience", which given its nature tends to "var[y] from one situation to another" (Sveiby, 1997). It is the context dependency of tacitness that comes to the fore when dealing with such knowledge, and it is this parameter more so than tacit knowledge's "soft" character that indicates articulated knowledge is not simply a "time-stamped" snapshot of tacit knowledge.

A Working Definition of Tacit Knowledge

Tacit knowledge, depending on one's interpretation, may vary from developing physical skills such as "learning to ride a bicycle", through to acquiring "tricks of the trade" in a workplace situation. The tacit knowledge deliberated for the empirical research in *this* book refers to

... those components of technology that are not codified into blueprints, manual patents and the like. In other words, tacit knowledge [that] is intangible knowledge, such as rules of thumb, heuristics, and other "tricks of the trade" (Arora, 1996, p. 234).

For the *practical* purposes of *this* IS research, tacit knowledge in the IT arena could be said to comprise the *articulable implicit IT managerial knowledge* that IT practitioners draw upon when conducting the "management of themselves, others, and their careers" (Wagner & Sternberg, 1991a; 1991b). This approach to the IT managerial nature of **articulable tacit knowledge** follows closely along the lines of Bassellier, Horner-Reich, and Benbasat (2001). When such tacit knowledge is shared from mutual experience and culture it gains a dimension within an organisation. It thus requires an added dimension to the theory to take into account the nature of learning that is particularly applicable to *knowledge evolution*. It is also possible to examine more formal approaches to defining tacit knowledge.

Approaches to Definition

Definition, *n*. 1. The act of defining or making definite or clear. 2. The formal statement of the meaning or signification of a word, phrase, etc. (*Macquarie Dictionary,* 1997, p. 567).

Tacit knowledge is heavily individualistic and based on self–experience, which leads ultimately to a greater understanding for situations which individuals confront in the future. The latter aspect of tacit knowledge ties in directly with Polanyi's epistemology, whilst the useful nature of TK for improving ones future understanding of situations ties in with Sternberg's epistemology where such knowledge is considered to be a management asset (Wagner & Sternberg, 1991a; 1991b). Interpretation will be examined first of all.

Interpretation: Qualitative Content Analysis of Tacit Knowledge in the Research Literature

Given the overwhelmingly textual nature of tacit knowledge definitions, the adoption of grounded theory[n][o] provides an opportunity to explore descriptions to TK in depth. Very briefly, grounded theory is an approach within the interpretive framework that seeks deep immersion in an area of research *before* attempting the establishment of research questions. Indeed the questions themselves, as in the case of the work presented here, may only come about at the *conclusion* of the grounded theory process. Further material explaining grounded theory is provided in the endnotes to this chapter. An added advantage to using grounded theory (particularly with software such as Atlas.ti™ [p]), is that one can output pictures such as graphs from textual input. Such "network maps" as the graphs are termed, are able to best represent the initially submerged underpinnings in the tacit knowledge literature. To that end an analysis of the literature has been conducted along qualitative research lines using Atlas. ti, which permitted the "coding" of text from primary text documents. The grounded theory process using the Atlas.ti software proceeds along the following lines. After the creation of an established *hermeneutic unit* or related set of primary text documents, which represents the information to be coded or marked-up, one can then code up the text, whereby the codes or nodes correspond to anchor points. The term code and node are used concomitantly here, for they stand for essentially the same thing. Having established codes we are then able to "map" these into network diagrams (Appendix B), which require the concurrent establishment of relationships or links between the codes (or nodes). The underlying basis of these network maps is not dissimilar to graph theory. A subjective component is implicit within the creation of nodes as well as the creation of relationships between the nodes.

An examination process of 64[q] documents took place in which many authors defined tacit knowledge (discussed in detail in Busch, Richards, & Dampney, 2001). These documents were placed in what was referred to as a tacit knowledge hermeneutic unit to use a grounded theory term. Utilising grounded theory, the following terms appeared the most widely cited, in descending order of groundedness.[r] The terms given are subjectively coded "themes" that have been derived from the literature, rather than direct terms, as they exist per se. Only those codes that have a groundedness of greater than 2 instances in the literature are provided here, beginning with *Knowledge* (80 instances/groundedness in the 64 papers examined):

Knowledge (80); Individuals (50); Organisational domain (46); Skill (35); Non-Codification (28); Non-verbal (27); Experience (26); Context specific (24); Intuition (20); Learned (16); Know how (15); Not formal (13); Action (12); Expertise (11); Culture (10); Contingency based (9); Environment (9); Externalisation (9); Knowing (9); Not easily communicated (9); Practical (9); Sub-consciousness (9); Understanding (9); Cognitive (8), Internalisation (8); Mental models (8); Not directly taught (8); Not easily transmitted (8); Process (8); Abilities (7); Apprenticeship (7); Low environmental support (7); Management (7); Practice (7); Society (7); Two dimensional (7); Behaviour (6); Beliefs (6); Conscious (6); Direct contact (6); Face to face transfer (6); Goal attainment (6); Inferences (6); Learning by doing (6); Maxims (6); Non-awareness (6); Pattern recognition (6); Perceptions (6); Procedural in nature (6); Routine (6); Subjectivity (6); Tasks (6); Technology (6); Values (6); Common sense (5); Decision making (5); Embodied (5); Implicit (5); Implied (5); Information (5); Judgement (5); No idea (5); Not easily codifiable (5); Sharing (5); Taken for granted (5); Unconscious (5); Everyday situations (4); Interaction (4); Job knowledge (4); Know more than we can tell (4); Not easily formalised (4); Not formal instruction (4); Others (4); Physical control (4); Riding a bicycle (4); Rule (4); Schema (4); Time (4); Touch sensitivity (4); Wisdom (4); Abstraction (3); Access constraints (3); Awareness (3); Communal (3); Competitive advantage (3); Embedded (3); Emotions (3); Experientially established cognitive structures (3); Focal awareness (3); Groups (3); Holism (3); Ideals (3); Importance of language (3); Information retrieval (3); Insight (3); Learning by using (3); Meaning (3); Mind (3); Motor skills (3); Observation (3); Oneself (3); Particular uses/particular situations (3); Performance (3); Practical intelligence (3); Procedures (3); Resistance to revelation (3); Rules of thumb (3); Selective comparison (3); Semantics (3); Sense perception (3); Transmission (3).

The above list is not complete, and a significant number of codes remain that contain a groundedness of one and two instances in the literature,[s] which were considered too trivial for inclusion. What is apparent from our grounded theory exercise is that tacit knowledge is typically; *individualistic* (50) {beliefs (6); oneself (3)}, it is heavily *organisationally based* (46), it is directly related at least to *skill* (35) and it is *context specific* (24). Furthermore it tends to be *practically* (9) rather than theoretically *oriented* in nature {practice (7); learning by doing (6); learning by using (3); practical intelligence (3)}; and given the nature of human competition, it is acquired in conditions of *low environmental support* (7) (Sternberg et al., 1995), which leads to it's being used for *competitive advantage* (3). One other very important issue, often not realised with tacit knowledge is the need for *understanding* (9) {internalisation (8); others (4); awareness (3); meaning (3); oneself (3)} on the part of the *receiver*.

As had previously been alluded to, "knowledge cannot be described in words because it is mainly tacit … it is also dynamic and static" (Sveiby, 1997, p. 38). The dynamic nature of tacit knowledge also ties in with its contextual character (Snowden, 2005). It is often rooted to a particular time and place, but not necessarily limited to this. Furthermore, "information and knowledge should be seen as distinctly different. Information is entropic (chaotic); knowledge is non-entropic. The receiver of the information—not the sender—gives it meaning. Information as such is meaningless" (Sveiby, 1997 p. 49). In other words, tacit knowledge is not knowledge if it is not understood by the receiver. This may help explain why tacit knowledge is so culturally loaded (10) {environment (9); society (7); beliefs (6); values (6); ideals (3); importance of language (3)}, and why others of for example NESB (Non-English Speaking Background), may not understand immediately what is taking place, even if they do happen to understand the syntax and semantics of English. Over time the tacit knowledge component, in addition to the already acquired syntax and semantics, aids in improved communication amongst people.

The content analysis[t] provided a balance or "reality check" in addition to formalising what could be said to comprise tacit knowledge. The definitions provide a view of what many other authors have considered comprises tacit knowledge. The importance in particular of the individualistic nature of tacit knowledge serves, if nothing more, to establish the contextual nature of this knowledge and its reliance upon an individual's *Weltanschauung*. The disadvantage of attempting any such form of content analysis is that authors' definitions often tend to vary wildly and as such finding any one "true" definition can be difficult, if not impossible. Truth, like the contextual nature of tacit knowledge can be a subjective assessment.

Formalisms

In his authoritative work on Information Systems, Weber (1997) had provided set theory based formalisms to better explain the underpinnings of this field. He did this by trying to establish phenomena that had not been accounted for through other theories. In part this was to legitimise the discipline of Information Systems for "… it is only via substantive contributions to theory that the IS discipline can rightly claim to be its own and that we will lay the foundations for legitimacy and disciplinary progress" (p. 32). Where some aspects of Information Systems had not previously been uncovered by existing theories, Weber (1997) had proposed an ontology for IS drawing upon the works of Bunge (1979). It is in a similar vein that one can *postulate* the following definitions and constructions of tacit knowledge at a superficial level along the subsequent lines.

It may be stated that there exist both *articulable* and ***inarticulable* tacit knowledge** properties. Consider the *articulable* properties that have been selected to exemplify tacit knowledge:

$\{a, \ldots, n\} \subseteq aTK$

where $\{a \ldots n\}$ is the set of the following **articulable tacit knowledge** constructs taken through grounded theory from the literature. They are hereby presented as identified constituents, which demonstrate the extent of tacit knowledge about any system, beginning with the *articulable* subset:

{Abstract high level plans, Abstraction, Access constraints, All purpose algorithms, Analogies, Aphorisms, Artistic vision, Assumptions, Behaviour, Beliefs, Business knowledge, Common sense, Competitive advantage, Complex multiconditional rules, Concepts, Constructs, Content, Contradiction, Convincing people, Crafts, Culture, Customer's attitudes, Customs, Data, Decision making, Descriptors, Discussion, Everyday situations, Examples can be articulated, Expectations, Externalisation, Face to face transfer, Goal attainment, Grammatical rules, Gut feel, Habits, Heuristics, Hunches, Ideals, Imitation, Impressions, Information, Information placed in meaningful context - eg. Message, Innovation, Interaction, Job knowledge, Judgement, Justified true belief, Know how, Knowledge base that enables us to face the everyday world, Knowledge of designs, Logical rules, Maxims, Meaning, Methods, Negotiation, Observation, Perceptions, Performance, Perspectives, Political correctness, Practical know how, Practice, Prescriptive knowledge, Principles, Private knowledge, Procedural in nature, Procedures, Process, Proverbs, Reproduction, Riding a bicycle, Ritual, Routine, Rule, Rules of thumb, Schema, Script/Scripted, Semantics, Shop lore, Stories, Subjectivity, Swimming, Task management, Tasks, Team coordination, Technique, Technology, Theories, Tradition, Trial and error, Tricks, Understanding, Understanding of categories, Values, Way things are done, Wisdom} $\subseteq aTK$

The subset above provides tacit knowledge examples that are considered articulable. Again these terms have been taken in a qualitative fashion from those researchers who have sought to define tacit knowledge to date.

Copyright © 2008, IGI Global. Copying or distributing in print or electronic forms without written permission of IGI Global is prohibited.

We also are able to identify the following as specifically constituting examples of tacit knowledge that *cannot*, or rather *do not*, lend themselves to being articulated, which we shall refer to as *inarticulable* **tacit knowledge** ITK:

$$\{a' \dots n'\} \subseteq iTK$$

where $\{a' \dots n'\}$ include the following *inarticulable* tacit constructs:

{Abilities, Accidental, Accomplishment, Action, Action oriented know how, Action slips, Ad hoc, Adaptation, After the fact, Analysis, Application, Attention, Automatic, Automatic knowledge, Awareness, Background knowledge, Between the lines, Body language, Charisma, Concentration, Coordination, create and enjoy challenges, Diagnostic closure, Emotions, Executive commitment, Exists, Experience, Expertise, Focal awareness, Force/tension required, Gaining promotion, Gaining respect, Getting one's feet wet, Hands on teaching, Have a feeling, Here and now, Hidden, High level goals, Holistic in nature, How to seek out, Idiosyncratic, Immutable, Implicit, Implied, Indeterminacy, Inferences, Inferred from actions/statements, Informating, Ingrained, Insight, Inspiration, Instinctive reaction, Intangibility, Intimacy, Intuition, Involuntary, Know more than we can tell, Know why, Knowing, Knowledge possessed by itself, Learning by doing, Learning the ropes, Lip service, Management, Managing relationships, Managing subordinates, Manual dexterity, Meaning requires tacit component, Mediation, Mental models, Metacognitive understanding, Motivation, Motor skills, Networking, No idea, Noiseless, Non awareness, Non focus on parts, Orientation, Out of the corner of the eye, Paradigms, Pattern recognition, Personality, Physical control, Place, Possessed, Power, Practical intelligence, Practice wisdom, Preciousness, Presuppositions, Principles, Product of process, Proximal knowledge, Psychomotor skills, Recognition, Recognition of musical note, Reflection in action, Reflection upon reflection, Relativity, Residual category, Rooted, Second hand, Second nature, See as' rather than see, Selective comparison, Semiconscious, Sense perception, Short term, Skill, Smell, Socialisation, Society, Spatial awareness, Spontaneity, Sub-consciousness, Thinking in practice, Tool, Touch sensitivity, Unanalysed, Unconscious, Vision, Vivid, Way things ought to be, Weltanschauung, Wholeness} $\subseteq$ iTK

Summary

Tacit knowledge has the following characteristics. It is the source of knowledge in that it is the basis for knowledge gathering, generation and diffusion. It eventually becomes codified in practice as individuals, organisations and finally all of us learn by its successful application. It becomes codified in theory by its reduction to simple underlying principles. We use these principles as a basis for drawing an analogy. Tacit knowledge is used as the starting point for gathering experience, forming patterns which in turn leads to the act of knowing, at first with oneself, then within an organisational context whether social, professional or business. By comparison, it is argued that tacit knowledge is within the unconscious mind first of the individual and then by a mix of articulated explanation and other transfer, it is developed within the mind of the organisation.

In conclusion, one may feel tempted to ask whether tacit knowledge is not simply another test for intelligence, yet evidence (Brockmann & Anthony, 1998; Wagner & Sternberg, 1985), would seem to suggest that it is not. Rather it is more a general level of "ability", which tends to separate the successful from the less successful. What is defined as tacit knowledge for the remainder of this book is *articulable implicit managerial IT workplace knowledge*, where managerial is understood to be along Sternberg's lines, namely management of oneself, others, and ones career. The focus of the book now moves onto the research issues relating to testing for tacit knowledge and more importantly, the issues that affect its diffusion in the organisational domain.

Sources Used in Grounded Theory

Arora, A. (1995). Licensing tacit knowledge: Intellectual property rights and the market for know-how. *Economics of Innovation and New Technology, 4*(1), 41-59.

Arora, A. (1996). Contracting for tacit knowledge: The provision of technical services in technology licensing contracts. *Journal of Development Economics, 50*(2), 233-256.

Baldwin, J., & Baldwin, J. (1978). Behaviorism on Verstehen and Erklären. *American Sociology Review, 43*(3), 335-347.

Brockmann, E., & Anthony, W. (1998). The influence of tacit knowledge and collective mind on strategic planning. *Journal of Managerial Issues, 10*(2), 204(19).

Casonato, R., & Harris, K. (1999). Can an enterprise really capture "tacit knowledge:" We answer two top questions on knowledge management from the Electronic Workplace 1999 Conference. *Gartner Group Research Note Select Q&A*, March 16.

Chambers, D. (1998). Tacit knowledge. *Journal of the American College of Dentists, 65*(3), 44-47.

Chaseling, C. (1994). Beyond finances-audits that explore. *Directions in Government, 8*(8), 16-18.

Coff, R. (1997). Human assets and management dilemmas: Coping with hazards on the road to resource-based theory. *The Academy of Management Review*, April.

Dahlbom, B., & Lars Mathiassen, L. (1999). *Computers in context: The philosophy and practice of systems design*. Oxford, UK: Blackwell.

Davenport, T., De Long, D., & Beers, M. (1998). Successful knowledge management projects. *Sloan Management Review, 39*(2), 43-57.

Devinney, T. (1997). *Knowledge, tacit understanding and strategy*. Working paper 97-022, October AGSM, UNSW, Sydney, Australia.

Durrance, B. (1998). Some explicit thoughts on tacit learning (Cover Story). *Training & Development, 52*(12), 24(6).

Fleck, J. (1997). Contingent knowledge and technology development. *Technology Analysis & Strategic Management, 9*(4), 383(15).

Fodor, J. (1968). The appeal to tacit knowledge in psychological explanation. *The Journal of Philosophy, 65*(20), 627-640.

Giunipero, L., Dawley, D., & Anthony, W. (1999). The impact of tacit knowledge on purchasing decisions. *Journal of Supply Chain Management, 35*(1), 42-49.

Goldman, G. (1990). The tacit dimension of clinical judgement. *The Yale Journal of Biology and Medicine, 63*(1), 47-61.

Greeno, J. (1987). Instructional representations based on research about understanding. In A. Schoenfeld (Ed.), *Cognitive science and mathematics education.* Hillsdale, NJ: Lawrence Erlbaum Associates, 61-88.

Hedlund, G. (1994). A model of knowledge management and the N-form corporation. *Strategic Management Journal, 15*(Special Summer issue), 73-90.

Henderson, K. (1995). The visual culture of engineers. In S. Star (Ed.), *The cultures of computing.,*Oxford: Blackwell publishers/The sociological review, 196-218.

Hicks, D. (1995). Published papers, tacit competencies, and corporate management of the public/private character of knowledge. *Industrial and Corporate Change, 4*(2), 401-424.

Howells, J. (1995a). *Tacit knowledge and technology transfer.* Working paper No. 16, ESRC Centre for Business Research and Judge Institute of Management studies, University of Cambridge U.K. September.

Howells, J. (1995b). A socio-cognitive approach to innovation. *Research Policy, 24*(6), 883-894.

Johannessen, J., Olsen, B., & Olaisen, J. (1997). Organising for innovation. *Long Range Planning, 30*(1), 96-109.

Joly, P., & Mangematin, V. (1996). Profile of public laboratories, industrial partnerships, and organisation of R & D: The dynamics of industrial relationships in a large research organisation. *Research Policy, 25*(6), 901-922.

Lamberton, D. (1996). A telecommunications infrastructure is not an information infrastructure. *Prometheus, 14*(1), 31-38.

Larkin, J. (1980). Skilled problem solving in physics: A hierarchical planning model. *Journal of Structural Learning, 6*(4), 271-297.

Lawson, C., & Lorenz, E. (1999). Collective learning, tacit knowledge and regional innovative capacity. *Regional Studies,* June, Cambridge.

Lei, D. (1997). Competence building, technology fusion, and competitive advantage: The key roles of organisational learning and strategic alliances. *International Journal of Technology Management, 14*(2/3/4), 208-237.

Lei, D., Hitt, M., & Bettis, R. (1996). Dynamic core competences through meta – learning and strategic context. *Journal of Management, 22*(4), 549-569.

Leonard, D., & Sensiper, S. (1998). The role of tacit knowledge in group innovation, *California Management Review Berkeley, 40*(3).

MacKenzie, D. (1995). Tacit knowledge, weapons design, and the invention of nuclear weapons. *American Journal of Sociology, 101*(1), 44-99.

Macquarie Dictionary (1997). Published by the Macquarie Library, 3rd. ed. Macquarie University, Australia: Macquarie Library.

McAulay, L., Russell, G., & Sims, J. (1997). Tacit knowledge for competitive advantage. *Management Accounting,* December, London.

Meerabeau, L. (1992). Tacit nursing knowledge: An untapped resource or a methodological headache? *Journal of Advanced Nursing, 17*(1), 108-112.

Nelson, D. (Ed.) (1998). *Dictionary of Mathematics* 2nd Ed. London: Penguin Books.

Nightingale, P. (1998). A cognitive model of innovation. *Research Policy, 27*(7), 689-709.

Nonaka, I. (1991). The knowledge creating company. *Harvard Business Review, 69*(6), 96-104.

Nonaka, I., Ray, T., & Umemoto, K. (1998). Japanese organizational knowledge creation in Anglo – American Environments. *Prometheus, 16*(4), 421-439.

Olsson, H., & Gullberg, M. (1988). Nursing education and importance of professional status in the nurse role. Expectations and knowledge of the nurse role. *International Journal of Nursing Studies, 25*(4), 287-293.

Oxford English Dictionary (1989). 2nd Ed. Oxford: Oxford University Press.

Polanyi, M. (1967). *The tacit dimension.* London: Routledge & Kegan Paul.

Powell, T. (1995). Total quality management as competitive advantage: A review and empirical study. *Strategic Management Journal, 16*(1), 15-37.

Pylyshyn, Z. (1981). The imagery debate: Analogue media versus tacit knowledge. In A. Collins & E. Smith (Eds.), *Readings in cognitive science: A perspective from Psychology and Artificial Intelligence,*Chapter 6.5, San Mateo, CA: Morgan Kaufman, 600-614.

Raghuram, S. (1996). Knowledge creation in the telework context. *International Journal of Technology Management, 11*(7/8), 859-870.

Sako, M. (1999). From individual skills to organisational capability in Japan. *Oxford Review of Economic Policy, 15*(1), 114-126.

Schmidt, F., & Hunter, J. (1993). Tacit knowledge, practical intelligence, general mental ability, and job knowledge. *Current Directions in Psychological Science: A Journal of the American Psychological Society, 2*(1), 8-9.

Scott, D. (1990). Practice wisdom: The neglected source of practice research. *Social Work, 35*(6), 564-568.

Senker, J. (1995a). Networks and tacit knowledge in innovation. *Economies et Societes, 29*(9), 99-118.

Senker, J. (1995b). Tacit knowledge and models of innovation. *Industrial and Corporate Change, 4*(2), 425-447.

Sternberg, R. (1995). Theory and management of tacit knowledge as a part of practical intelligence. *Zeitschrift für Psychologie, 203*(4), 319-334.

Sternberg, R. (1998a). Applying the triarchic theory of human intelligence in the classroom.

In R. Sternberg & W. Williams (Eds.), *Intelligence, Instruction and Assessment: Theory into Practice.* Mahwah, NJ: Lawrence Erlbaum Associates, 1-15.

Sternberg, R. (1998b). A balance theory of wisdom. *Review of General Psychology, 2*(4), 347-365.

Sternberg, R., Forsythe, G., Hedlund, J., Horvath, J., Wagner, R., Williams, W., Snook, S., & Grigorenko, E. (2000). *Practical intelligence in everyday life.* Cambridge: Cambridge University Press.

Sternberg, R., & Wagner, R. (1989). The fate of the trait: A reply of the Cantor and Kihlstrom" *Advances in Social Cognition Vol 2: Social Intelligence and Cognitive Assessments of Personality* (Wyer, R., Srull, T., eds.) Lawrence Erlbaum Associates Hillsdale New Jersey U.S.A. pp. 175-185.

Sveiby, K. (1997). *The new organisational wealth: Managing & measuring knowledge – based assets.* San Francisco: Berrett – Koehler.

Takeuchi, H. (1998). Beyond knowledge management: Lessons from Japan. *Monash Mt. Eliza Business Review, 1*(1), 21-29.

Torff, B. (1999). Tacit knowledge in teaching: Folk Pedagogy. In R. Sternberg & J. Horvath (Eds.), *Tacit knowledge in professional practice: Researcher and practitioner perspectives.* Mahwah, NJ: Lawrence Erlbaum and Associates, 195-213.

Turner, S. (1989). Tacit knowledge and the problem of computer modelling cognitive processes in science. In S. Fuller, M. de Mey, T. Shinn, & S. Woolgar (Eds.), *The cognitive turn: Sociological and psychological perspectives on science.* Dordrecht, The Netherlands: Kluwer Academic Publishers, 83-94.

Wagner, R., & Sternberg, R. (1985). Practical intelligence in real – world pursuits: The role of tacit knowledge. *Journal of Personality and Social Psychology, 49*(2), August, 436-458.

Wagner, R., & Sternberg, R. (1987). Tacit knowledge in managerial success. *Journal of Business and Psychology, 1*(4), 301-312.

Wagner, R., & Sternberg, R. (1990). Street smarts. In K. Clark & M. Clark (Eds.), *Measures of Leadership.* West Orange, NJ: Leadership Library of America, 493-504.

West, G., & Meyer, G. (1997). Communicated knowledge as a learning foundation. *International Journal of Organizational Analysis,* January.

Woherem, E. (1991). Expert systems as a medium for knowledge transfer to less developed countries. *Science and Public Policy, 18*(5), 301-309.

Zack, M. (1999). Managing codified knowledge. *Sloan Management Review,* Summer, Cambridge.

References

Aisbett, J., & Gibbon, G. (2001). A general formulation of conceptual spaces as a meso-level representation. *Artificial Intelligence, 133,* 189-232.

Anand, V., Manz, C., & Glick, W. (1998). An organizational memory approach to information management. *The Academy of Management Review, 23*(4), 769-809.

Ancori, B., Bureth, A., & Cohendet, P. (2000). The economics of knowledge: The debate about codification and tacit knowledge. *Industrial & Corporate Change, 9*(2), 255-287.

Argyris, C., & Schön, D.A. (1978). *Organizational learning: A theory of action perspective.* Reading, MA: Addison-Wesley.

Arora, A. (1996). Contracting for tacit knowledge: The provision of technical services in technology licensing contracts. *Journal of Development Economics, 50*(2), 233-256.

Arrow, K. (1962). Economic welfare and the allocation of resources for invention. In R. Nelson (Ed.), *The rate and direction of inventive activity.* Princeton, NJ: Princeton University Press.

Atkinson P., Reid, M., & Sheldrake, P. (1977). Medical mystique. *Sociology of Work and Occupations, 4*(3), 243-280.

Audretsch, D., & Feldman, M. (1995). *Innovative Clusters and the Industry Life Cycle.* Discussion paper No. 1161, April. London: Centre for Economic Policy Research.

Badaracco, J. (1991). *The knowledge link.* Boston: Harvard Business School Press.

Baldwin, J., & Baldwin, J. (1978). Behaviorism on Verstehen and Erklären. *American Sociology Review, 43*(3), 335-347.

Bassellier, G., Horner-Reich, B., & Benbasat, I. (2001). Information technology competence of business managers: A definition and research model. *Journal of Management Information Systems, 17*(4), 159-182.

Blackburn, S. (1996). *The Oxford Dictionary of Philosophy.* Oxford: Oxford University Press.

Brockmann, E., & Anthony, W. (1998). The influence of tacit knowledge and collective mind on strategic planning. *Journal of Managerial Issues, 10*(2), 204(19).

Brown, R., & McNeill, D. (1966). The tip-of-the tongue phenomenon. *Journal of Verbal Learning and Verbal Behavior, 5*, 325-337.

Bundy, A. (1975). *Analysing mathematical proofs, or reading between the lines.* Research Report 2, May. Department of Artificial Intelligence, University of Edinburgh, U.K.

Bunge, M. (1979). *Treatise on Basic Philosophy: Vol. 4 Ontology II: A World of Systems.* Boston: Reidel.

Burrows, G., Drummond, D., & Martinsons, M. (2005). Knowledge Management in China. *Communications of the ACM, 48*(4), 73-76.

Busch, P., & Dampney, C. (2000). Tacit knowledge acquisition and processing within the computing domain: An exploratory study. *2000 Information Resources Management Association International Conference,* Anchorage, AK, 1014-1015.

Busch, P., Richards, D., & Dampney, C. (2001). Visual mapping of articulable tacit knowledge. In P. Eades & T. Pattison (Eds.), *Australian Symposium on Information Visualisation (InVIS'2001),* December 10-11, Melbourne, pp. 37-47.

Busch, P., Richards, D., & Dampney, C. (2002). Tacit knowledge characteristics: A research methodology. In A. Wenn, M. McGrath, & F. Burstein (Eds.), *Proceedings of the*

Thirteenth Australasian Conference on Information Systems, Vol 1. December 4-6, 87-101.

Bush A., & Tiwana, A. (2005). Designing sticky knowledge networks. *Communications of the ACM, 48*(5), 67-71.

Cantwell, J., & Santangelo, G. (2000). Capitalism, profits, and innovation in the new techno-economic paradigm. *Journal of Evolutionary Economics, 10*(1-2), 131-157.

Casonato, R., & Harris, K. (1999). Can an enterprise really capture "tacit knowledge:" We answer two top questions on knowledge management from the Electronic Workplace 1999 Conference. *Gartner Group Research Note Select Q&A,* March 16.

Castanias, R., & Helfat, C. (1991). Managerial resources and rents. *Journal of Management, 17*(1), 155-171.

Caves, R., & Uekusa, M. (1976). *Industrial organization in Japan.* Washington, DC: Brookings Institution.

Chambers, D. (1998). Tacit knowledge. Journal of the American College of Dentists, 65(3), 44-47.

Coff, R. (1997). Human assets and management dilemmas: Coping with hazards on the road to resource-based theory. *The Academy of Management Review,* April.

Collins, H. (1974). The TEA set: Tacit knowledge and scientific networks. *Science Studies, 4*(2), 165-186.

Cutcliffe, J. (2000). Methodological issues in grounded theory. *Journal of Advanced Nursing, 31*(6), 1476-1484.

Dahlbom, B., & Lars Mathiassen, L. (1999). *Computers in context: The philosophy and practice of systems design.* Oxford, UK: Blackwell.

Davenport, T., De Long, D., & Beers, M. (1998). Successful knowledge management projects. *Sloan Management Review, 39*(2), 43-57.

Desrochers, P. (2001). Geographical proximity and the transmission of tacit knowledge. *The Review of Austrian Economics, 14*(1), 25-46.

Dierickx, I., & Cool, K. (1989). Asset stock accumulation and sustainability of competitive advantage. *Management Science, 33,* 1504-1511.

Dosi, G. (1988). Sources, procedures, and microeconomic effects of innovation. *Journal of Economic Literature, 26,* 1120-1170.

Dreyfus, H., Dreyfus, S., & Athanasiou, T. (1986). *Mind over machine: The power of human intuition and expertise in the era of the computer.* New York: The Free Press, Macmillan.

Durrance, B. (1998). **Some explicit thoughts on tacit learning** (Cover Story). *Training & Development, 52*(12), 24(6).

Fransman, M. (1994). Information, knowledge, vision and theories of the firm. *Industrial and Corporate Change, 3*(3), 713 57.

Gärdenfors, P. (2000). *Conceptual spaces: The geometry of thought.* Massachusetts: MIT Press.

Garud, R. (1997). On the distinction between know – how, know – why, and know – what. *Advances in Strategic Management, 14,* 81-101.

Ghemawat, P. (1991). *Commitment: The dynamic of strategy.* New York: Free Press.

Giunipero, L., Dawley, D., & Anthony, W. (1999). The impact of tacit knowledge on purchasing decisions. *Journal of Supply Chain Management, 35*(1), 42-49.

Glaser, B. (1992). *Basics of grounded theory analysis: Emergence vs. forcing.* Mill Valley, CA: Sociology Press.

Goldman, G. (1990). The tacit dimension of clinical judgement. *The Yale Journal of Biology and Medicine, 63*(1), 47-61.

Greeno, J. (1987). Instructional representations based on research about understanding. In A. Schoenfeld (Ed.), *Cognitive science and mathematics education.* Hillsdale, NJ: Lawrence Erlbaum Associates, 61-88.

Grieves, J., & Mathews, B. (1997). Healthcare and the learning service. *The Learning Organization, 4*(3), 88-98.

Gummesson, E. (2003). All research is interpretive. *Journal of Business & Industrial Marketing, 18*(6/7), 482-492.

Guzman, G., & Wilson, J. (2005). The "soft" dimension of organizational knowledge transfer. *Journal of Knowledge Management, 9*(2), 59-74.

Greeno, J. (1987). Instructional representations based on research about understanding. In A. Schoenfeld (Ed.), *Cognitive science and mathematics education.* Hillsdale, NJ: Lawrence Erlbaum Associates, 61-88.

Henderson, K. (1995). The visual culture of engineers. In S. Star (Ed.), *The cultures of computing.,*Oxford: Blackwell publishers/The sociological review, 196-218.

Horvath, J., Forsythe, G., Bullis, R., Sweeney, P., Williams, W., McNally, J., Wattendorf, J., & Sternberg, R. (1999). Experience, knowledge and military leadership. In R. Sternberg & J. Horvath (Eds.), *Tacit knowledge in professional practice: Researcher and practitioner perspectives.* Mahwah, NJ: Lawrence Erlbaum and Associates, 39-57.

Hoskisson, R., & Hitt, M. (1994). Downscoping: Taming the diversified firm. NewYork: Oxford University Press.

Howells, J. (1995a). *Tacit knowledge and technology transfer.* Working paper No. 16, ESRC Centre for Business Research and Judge Institute of Management studies, University of Cambridge U.K. September.

Hustad, E. (2004). Knowledge networking in global organizations: The transfer of knowledge. SIGMIS'04, April 22–24, Tucson, Arizona, 55-64.

Imai, K. (1980). *Japan's industrial organization and its vertical structure.* Tokyo: Institute of Business Research, Hitotsubashi University.

Itami, H. (1987). *Managing invisible assets.* Cambridge, MA: Harvard University Press.

Jamous H., & Peloille, B. (1970). The French university-hospital system. In J. Jackson (Ed.), *Professions and professionalization.* Cambridge: Cambridge University Press.

Johannessen, J., Olsen, B., & Olaisen, J. (1997). Organising for innovation. *Long Range Planning, 30*(1), 96-109.

Jüttner, C. (1980). Nichtbewuβtes Wissen, Mustererkennung und der Entwurf eines Ge-dächtnismodells. *Psychologische Beiträge, 22*(1), 70-87.

Kakabadse, N., Kakabadse, A., & Kouzmin, A. (2003). Reviewing the knowledge management literature: Towards a taxonomy. *Journal of Knowledge Management, 7*(4), 75-91.

Küpers, W. (2005). Phenomenology of embodied implicit and narrative knowing. *Journal of Knowledge Management, 9*(6), 114-133.

Lamberton, D. (1997). The knowledge-based economy: A Sisyphus model. *Prometheus, 15*(1), 73-81.

Lawson, C., & Lorenz, E. (1999). Collective learning, tacit knowledge and regional innova-tive capacity. *Regional Studies,* June, Cambridge.

Lei, D. (1997). Competence building, technology fusion, and competitive advantage: The key roles of organisational learning and strategic alliances. International Journal of Technology Management, 14(2/3/4), 208-237.

Lei, D., Hitt, M., & Bettis, R. (1996). Dynamic core competences through meta – learning and strategic context. *Journal of Management, 22*(4), 549-569.

Leonard, D., & Sensiper, S. (1998). The role of tacit knowledge in group innovation, Cali-fornia Management Review Berkeley, 40(3).

MacKay, D. (1974). The mechanics of "Tacit Knowing." *IEEE Transactions on Systems, Man and Cybernetics, 4*(1), 94-95.

MacKenzie, D. (1996). Moving toward disinvention. *Bulletin of the Atomic Scientists,* (Editorial), *52*(5), 4.

Macquarie Dictionary (1997). Published by the Macquarie Library, 3rd. ed. Macquarie University, Australia: Macquarie Library.

Malik, K. (2004). Coordination of technological flows in firms. *Journal of Knowledge Management, 8*(2), 64-72.

Maskell, P, & Malmberg, A. (1999). Localised learning and industrial competitiveness. *Cambridge Journal of Economics, 23,* 167-185.

McAulay, L., Russell, G., & Sims, J. (1997). Tacit knowledge for competitive advantage. *Management Accounting,* December, London.

Meerabeau, L. (1992). Tacit nursing knowledge: An untapped resource or a methodological headache? *Journal of Advanced Nursing, 17*(1), 108-112.

Muhr, T. (1997). *ATLAS.ti: The Knowledge Workbench: Short User's Manual.* Berlin: Sci-entific Software Development.

Nonaka, I. (1991). The knowledge creating company. *Harvard Business Review, 69*(6), 96-104.

Nonaka, I., Takeuchi, H., & Umemoto, K. (1996). A theory of organisational knowledge creation. *International Journal of Technology Management, 11*(7/8), 833-845.

Olsson, H., & Gullberg, M. (1988). Nursing education and importance of professional status in the nurse role. Expectations and knowledge of the nurse role. *International Journal of Nursing Studies, 25*(4), 287-293.

Oxford English Dictionary (1989). 2nd Ed. Oxford: Oxford University Press.

Partington, D. (2000). Building grounded theories of management action. *British Journal of Management, 11*(2), 91-102.

Pavitt, K. (1987). The objectives of technology policy. *Science and Public Policy, 14*(4), 182-188.

Polanyi, M. (1958). *Personal knowledge: Towards a post-critical philosophy.* London: Routledge & Kegan Paul.

Polanyi, M. (1967). *The tacit dimension.* London: Routledge & Kegan Paul.

Polanyi, M. (1968). Logic and psychology. *American Psychologist, 23*(1), 27-43.

Powell, T. (1995). Total quality management as competitive advantage: A review and empirical study. *Strategic Management Journal, 16*(1), 15-37.

Pylyshyn, Z. (1981). The imagery debate: Analogue media versus tacit knowledge. In A. Collins & E. Smith (Eds.), *Readings in cognitive science: A perspective from Psychology and Artificial Intelligence,*Chapter 6.5, San Mateo, CA: Morgan Kaufman, 600-614.

Raghuram, S. (1996). Knowledge creation in the telework context. *International Journal of Technology Management, 11*(7/8), 859-870.

Ramaprasad, A., & Rai, A. (1996). Envisioning management of information. *Omega: International Journal of Management Science, 24*(2), 179-193.

Reed, R., & deFillippi, R. (1990). Causal ambiguity, barriers to imitation and sustainable competitive advantage. *Academy of Management Review, 15,* 88-102.

Roberts, J. (2001). The drive to codify: Implications for the knowledge-based economy. *Prometheus, 19*(2), 99-116.

Robinson, T., Clemson, B., & Keating, C. (1997). Developing of high performance organizational learning units. *The Learning Organization, 4*(5), 228-234.

Rosenberg, N. (1982). *Inside the black box: Technology and economics,* Cambridge: Cambridge University Press. (particularly Chapter 11: "The international transfer of technology: Implications for the industrialized countries," 245-279).

Rowley, J. (2003). Knowledge management – The new librarianship? From custodians of history to gatekeepers to the future. *Library Management, 24*(8/9), 433-440.

Sahal, D. (1981). *Patterns of technological innovation.* Reading, MA: Addison-Wesley.

Scott, D. (1990). Practice wisdom: The neglected source of practice research. *Social Work, 35*(6), 564-568.

Scott, D. (1992). Reaching vulnerable populations: A framework for primary service expansion. *American Journal of Orthopsychiatry, 62*(3), 333-341.

Senker, J. (1995a). Networks and tacit knowledge in innovation. *Economies et Societes, 29*(9), 99-118.

Snowden, D. (2005). From atomism to networks in social systems. *The Learning Organization, 12*(6), 552-562.

Stair, R., & Reynolds, G. (1998). *Principles of information systems: A managerial approach.* Cambridge, MA: Course Technology/Nelson ITP.

Sternberg, R. (1995). Theory and management of tacit knowledge as a part of practical intelligence. *Zeitschrift für Psychologie, 203*(4), 319-334.

Sternberg, R. (1999). Epilogue – What do we know about tacit knowledge?: Making the tacit become explicit. In R. Sternberg & J. Horvath (Eds.) *Tacit knowledge in professional practice: Researcher and practitioner perspectives.* Mahwah, NJ: Lawrence Erlbaum and Associates, 231-236.

Sternberg, R., Wagner, R., & Okagaki, L. (1993). Practical intelligence: The nature and role of tacit knowledge in work and at school. In J. Puckett (Ed.), *Mechanisms of everyday cognition.* Hillsdale, NJ: Lawrence Erlbaum Associates, 205-227.

Sternberg, R., Wagner, R., Williams, W., & Horvath, J. (1995). Testing common sense. *American Psychologist, 50*(11), 912-927.

Sveiby, K. (1997). *The new organisational wealth: Managing & measuring knowledge-based assets.* San Francisco: Berrett – Koehler.

Takeuchi, H. (1998). Beyond knowledge management: Lessons from Japan. *Monash Mt. Eliza Business Review, 1*(1), 21-29.

Teece, D., Rumelt, R., Dosi, G., & Winter, S. (1992). *Understanding corporate coherence: Theory and evidence,* Working paper, University of California at Berkeley.

Torff, B., & Sternberg, R. (1998). Changing mind, changing world: Practical intelligence and tacit knowledge in adult learning. In M Smith & T. Pourchot (Eds.), *Adult learning and development: Perspectives from educational psychology.* Mahwah, NJ: Lawrence Erlbaum Associates, 109-126.

Tsoukas, H. (1996). The firm as a distributed knowledge system: A constructionist approach. *Strategic Management Journal, 17,* 11-25.

Ulmer, W. (1999). Military learnings: A practitioners perspective. In R. Sternberg & J. Horvath (Eds.), *Tacit knowledge in professional practice: Researcher and practitioner perspectives.* Mahwah, NJ: Lawrence Erlbaum and Associates, 59-71.

Wagner, R., & Sternberg, R. (1985). Practical intelligence in real – world pursuits: The role of tacit knowledge. *Journal of Personality and Social Psychology, 49*(2), August, 436-458.

Wagner, R., & Sternberg, R. (1987). Tacit knowledge in managerial success. *Journal of Business and Psychology, 1*(4), 301-312.

Wagner, R., & Sternberg, R. (1991a). *TKIM: The common sense manager: Tacit knowledge inventory for managers: Test booklet.* San Antonio: The Psychological Corporation Harcourt Brace Jovanovich.

Wagner, R., & Sternberg, R. (1991b). *TKIM: The common sense manager: Tacit knowledge inventory for managers: User manual.* San Antonio: The Psychological Corporation Harcourt Brace Jovanovich.

Walczak, S. (2005). Organizational knowledge management structure. *The Learning Organization, 12*(4), 330-339.

Weber, R. (1997). *Ontological foundations of information systems.* Coopers & Lybrand Accounting Research Methodology Monograph No. 4, Melbourne, Victoria, Australia.

Wilson, R. (1985). *Colt: An American legend,* Sesquicentennial edition. New York: Abbeville Publishing.

Woherem, E. (1991). Expert systems as a medium for knowledge transfer to less developed countries. *Science and Public Policy, 18*(5), 301-309.

Wright, R. (1994). The effects of tacitness and tangibility on the diffusion of knowledge based resources. *Academy of Management Proceedings,* 52-56.

Yamadori, Y. (1984). Office automation in Japan. *Science and Technology in Japan, 3*(10), 24-26.

Zack, M. (1999). Managing codified knowledge. *Sloan Management Review,* Summer, Cambridge.

Zucker, L., & Darby, M. (1998). Capturing technological opportunity via Japan's star scientists: Evidence from Japanese firms' biotech patents and products. *NBER Working Paper Series, Working paper 6360.* National Bureau of Economic Research, Cambridge Massachusetts, January.

Zucker, L., Darby, M., & Armstrong, J. (1998). Geographically localised knowledge: Spillovers or markets? *Economic Inquiry, 36*(1), 65(22).

Endnotes

[a] Data are a formalised representation of information, making it possible to process or communicate that information. Information is not the same as data. ... The concept of information is close to the concepts of knowledge and competence, but it also involves the concepts of interpreting and making ideas explicit. To produce information, we have to interpret what we experience and make explicit what we know ... Information comes in bits and pieces; knowledge and competence do not. Information is explicitly expressed in the paper, or electronically lit pixels on a screen. In contrast, knowledge and competence are personal and intrinsically related to each individual's practice (Dahlbom & Mathiassen, 1999, pp. 26-27).

[b] Personal communication with Dr. James Giesecke, Research Economist and Senior Research Fellow, CoPS centre, Monash University, Australia, September 2002.

[c] In the traditional workplace, organisational members can interact with each other frequently, thereby converting existing tacit knowledge to new tacit knowledge. Very often, these meetings with colleagues follow an impromptu mode where people "bump" into each other, be it near the elevator, the coffee percolator, the water cooler or the photocopying machine. Meetings also might take the less impromptu form of going out for lunch or for an after hours' drink. Invariably these informal meetings follow a pattern where people share news about their work related problems and how they went about solving these problems... Telework cuts out a lot of nonverbal communication. Because of the limited physical cues, telework has the potential for weakening the links between experience – based learning and acquisition of tacit knowledge (Raghuram, 1996, p. 862).

[d] "For many people understanding the place of mind in nature is the greatest philosophical problem. Mind is often thought to be the last domain that stubbornly resists scientific understanding ... The mind-body problem in the modern era was given its definitive shape by Descartes, although the dualism that he espoused is far more widespread and far older, occurring in some form wherever there is a religious or philosophical tradition whereby the soul may have an existence

apart from the body. While most modern philosophies of mind would reject the imaginings that leads us to think that this makes sense, there is no consensus over the best way to integrate our understanding of people as bearers of physical properties on the one hand and as subjects of mental lives on the other" (Blackburn, 1996, p.245).

[e]   In the 1850s the British government succeeded in introducing American gun-making machinery by employing a large number of American mechanics and managers. At the same time, Samuel Colt, who had been [extremely] successful in the United States, failed to produce firearms with American machinery and British workers. Rosenberg (1970) insisted that "where the transfer of technology involved places geographically distinct from one another, the reliance upon the migration of trained personnel (at least temporarily) was very strong" (Takii, 2000, p. 4).

[f]   … some expert knowledge is extremely complex or abstract and is difficult to understand without benefit of demonstration or explanation. This class of knowledge is often not suitable for KM since the normal communication channel is one-way through a workstation. On the other hand, knowledge that is very simple may not benefit from a KM approach since it may not stimulate collaboration or innovation. Similarly, tacit knowledge that changes frequently, and hence requires a too frequent update and renewal may require more effort than value. Tacit knowledge suitable for KM should be able to be captured and transferred to others. This means the provider can explain it and the user can understand the knowledge via text, diagrams, pictures or frameworks. The characteristics would exclude any skill or art that requires hands-on training. Other aspects of tacit knowledge that may not be easily transferable/useable include cultural differences (Casonato & Harris, 1999).

[g]   It is knowledge that is unspoken, underemphasized, or poorly conveyed relative to its importance for practical success … When knowledge must be acquired in the face of low environmental support, the probability that some individuals will fail to acquire it increases. When some individuals fail to acquire knowledge, others who succeed in acquiring the knowledge may gain a competitive advantage over those who fail to acquire it … one may speculate that knowledge acquired under conditions of low environmental support is often particularly useful. This knowledge is more likely to differentiate individuals than is highly supported knowledge (Sternberg et al., 1995, pp. 917-918).

[h]   Depending of course on the complexity of the knowledge involved.

[i]   Tacit knowledge as a source of competitive advantage is well documented in a number of disciplines, such as the financial domain for example (McAulay, Russell, & Sims, 1997).

[j]   Recent research on the economic payoff from new technology has emphasised the importance of tacit knowledge or know – how (Arora, 1996, p. 233) … With knowledge increasingly becoming a source of competitive advantage (Grant, 1996), differences in organizational abilities to tap soft knowledge from external sources can conceivably become significant determinants of organizational outcomes (Anand, Manz, & Glick, 1998, p. 806).

[k]   Instructor pilots teach beginning pilots how to scan their instruments. The instructor pilots teach the rule for instrument scanning that they themselves were taught and, as far as they know, still use. At one point, however, Air Force psychologists studied the eye movements of the instructors during simulated flight and found, to everyone's surprise that that instructor pilots were not following the rule they were teaching. In fact, as far as the psychologists could determine, they were not following any rule at all … The instructors, after years of experience, had learned to scan the instruments in flexible and situationally appropriate ways (Dreyfus, Dreyfus, & Athanasiou, 1986, pp. 152).

[l]   … if the second person listens to the message and utilises the encoded information, the second person's behaviour will be rule governed rather than contingency-shaped, and it will not be associated with the kinds of tacit knowledge—feelings, emotional responses and attached meanings—found in the first person's behaviour … Even though rules never capture all of the

wisdom, feelings and sensitivity to individual cases that are found in tacit knowledge, people learn to be rule creators: the rewards of passing on information and helping others to learn rapidly condition people into becoming rule creators (Baldwin & Baldwin, 1978, p. 336).

[m]   World view, philosophy on life, world outlook.

[n]   A grounded theory is a theory that is induced from the data rather than preceeding them (Cutcliffe, 2000; Partington, 2000). "Grounded theory strives to be realistic and valid. To start a theory generating a research project by first designing clear-cut categories and criteria in a complex and dynamic domain ... might kill or mutilate reality. As long as the search is directed to an area of interest, patterns will emerge with the gentle assistance of the researcher, not through forcing" (Gummesson, 2003, p. 489; Glaser, 1992).

[o]   "Grounded Theory (GT) is a research method most often associated with the social sciences, for example as psychology. Developed by the sociologists Barney Glaser (b. 1930) and Anselm Strauss (1916-1996). Their collaboration in research on dying hospital patients led them to write the book *Awareness of Dying*. In this research they developed the *constant comparative method* later known as Grounded Theory ... Grounded theory was developed as a systematic methodology, and its name underscores the generation of theory from data. When the principles of grounded theory are followed, a researcher using this approach will formulate a theory, either substantive (setting specific) or formal, about the phenomena they are studying that can be evaluated ... Since their original publication in 1967, Glaser and Strauss disagreed on "how to do" GT ... According to Kelle (2005), "the controversy between Glaser and Strauss boils down to the question whether the researcher uses a well defined 'coding paradigm' and always looks systematically for 'causal conditions,' 'phenomena/context, intervening conditions, action strategies' and 'consequences' in the data, or whether theoretical codes are employed as they emerge in the same way as substantive codes emerge, but drawing on a huge fund of 'coding families.'" ("Grounded Theory" URL: http://en.wikipedia.org/wiki/Grounded_theory accessed 14th June 2007).

[p]   ATLAS/ti™ is a powerful workbench for the qualitative analysis of large bodies of textual, graphical and audio data. It offers a variety of tools for accomplishing the tasks associated with any systematic approach to "soft" data, for example, material which cannot be analysed by formal, statistical approaches in meaningful ways. In the course of such a *qualitative analysis* ATLAS/ti™ helps to uncover the complex phenomena hidden in the data in an exploratory way (Muhr, 1997 p. 1).

[q]   See the reference list for grounded theory provided at the end of the chapter.

[r]   Groundedness in grounded theory refers to the number of times a term appears in the literature. Where literature in this instance refers to the 64 marked up articles.

[s]   The code total came to 1,310, with many codes having a groundedness of 1 or 2 in the literature and so on.

[t]   Content analysis refers to the process in grounded theory where we establish the groundedness of terms in the literature.

Section II

The second section of the book covering Chapters IV, V, VI, and VII introduces the reader to the logistical hurdles of conducting research in the tacit knowledge area. A great deal of literature in the knowledge management domain generally and in the tacit knowledge area specifically tends to be descriptive. The little research that is empirical is either conducted at the whole of organisational level by way of case studies, or at the level of individuals. If conducted at the level of the individual, the majority of tacit knowledge research tends to be undertaken by psychologists. The work presented here is somewhat unique in that it fits within the knowledge management domain, is focused at the level of the individual, is psychological in its approach, but is being conducted by researchers in the ICT field. The technique adopted to test for tacit knowledge follows in the line of that of Prof. Robert Sternberg, formerly at Yale and now at Tufts University. Workplace scenarios provide the means by which a form of soft knowledge can be tested in individuals. The way in which different individuals deal with soft knowledge situations is compared and contrasted. Although the results from the research instrument are interpreted using statistics, the main approach is somewhat more novel through the incorporation of an approach referred to as Formal Concept Analysis, which has a lattice theory underpinning.

As the research is empirical and what is being tested are knowledge flows amongst organisational personnel, it is necessary to ground the work within ICT companies. It would make little sense to discuss companies, without first providing some background to the concept of organisations. Mintzberg is perhaps one of the better-known identities in the organisation science field. His typology has become well known and is adopted here. They comprise the entrepreneurial firm, the machine organisation, the diversified company, the professional bureaucracy, and the innovative firm. Three organisations were used as case studies in this book, which will be referred to as Organisation X, Organisation Y, and Organisation Z. Within Mintzberg's framework, the first would be a combination of a machine bureaucracy and a *professional bureaucracy, the second would either an operating adhocracy or a professional bureaucracy and the third is very like the Organisation X except on a smaller scale.*

Last, but certainly not least, the important aspect to the work being presented relates to the likely flow of knowledge. What is taking place is not only testing for tacit knowledge, but also examining the flows of knowledge that are likely to occur within an ICT organisation. It is the flow or possible blockage of knowledge that can present a significant knowledge management issue for an organisation. Parameters affecting knowledge flows are covered in this section. One very viable means of assessing flows amongst individuals is that of Social Network Analysis. Such a technique which can be incorporated into the same research instrument as that testing for tacit knowledge, allows us to gauge the level of interaction amongst employees in a firm. Social Network Analysis is graph based like Formal Concept Analysis, but here the similarity ends. The former approach uses nodes to represent people and edges to represent relationship types. The latter uses a lattice structure to illustrate connections between objects.

Chapter IV

Testing for Tacit Knowledge

... organizational knowledge is abstract and possesses "soft" features, which are related to subtle, implicit, embedded and invisible knowledge, presumptions, values, and ways of thinking which permeate behaviour, decisions, and actions. As such, organizational templates are ill-defined, do not have clear boundaries, and they are context-dependent. Outcomes and performance of organizational knowledge are also difficult to specify, understand and measure (Guzman & Wilson, 2005, p.61).

Introduction

It is acknowledged that there exists a need for organisationally-based tacit knowledge research.[a, b] Perhaps the major hurdle to undertaking any form of tacit knowledge testing however, is attempting to gain data that for all intents and purposes is not strictly speaking codified, even if aspects of it may be articulable (Dampney, Busch, & Richards, 2002). Given the often ethereal nature of tacit knowledge, testing must be based upon sound definitions. The definition arrived at for this study was that of "articulable implicit IT managerial knowledge," which fits within Fleck's (1997) designation of "informal knowledge." What follows in this chapter is a discussion on the current research issues relating to *testing* for tacit knowledge.

Research Underpinnings

Whilst Fleck (1997) describes tacit knowledge at the whole organisational level as being a form of meta (knowledge about knowledge) or cultural knowledge, the purpose of the book is to examine tacit knowledge in individuals and more particularly the likely diffusion of such knowledge through the (IT) organisation. To that end, an individualistic approach is adopted, as well as a **case study** style, for "in general, case studies are the preferred strategy when "how" or "why" questions are being posed, when the investigator has little control over events, and when the focus is on a contemporary phenomenon within some real life context" (Yin, 1994, p. 1). Furthermore, given the exploratory nature of the work being reported here, the **case study** lends itself well to investigating a current phenomenon within a real life context using a variety of sources of information (Wassenaar & Katsma, 2004). Nonetheless difficulties in performing tacit knowledge testing from a case study point of view have been noted in Baumard's (1999) seminal work on tacit knowledge in organisations:

The case study method disturbs organizations by its investigative nature, its high cost in terms of hours of interviews, and the difficulty of promising quantifiable results. Spending time within a company encourages it to expose itself to the researcher's scrutiny, which company directors are not generally favourable to; and executives themselves are reticent about responding to an investigation which is interested in the manner in which they acquire and manage their knowledge during difficult periods (p. 4).

These hurdles aside, the case study is the most suitable approach for studying the phenomenon of tacit knowledge given the research takes place within a real life context and the investigator has little control over organisational events.

Again, the topic covered here is *exploratory* in nature. One interpretation of **exploratory** research is that it is not regarded as a complete study on its own, rather acting as a prelude to further research (Yin, 1994). Gregor (2002) had identified five different theory types depending on the type of research problem that needed to be solved. These were type 1: *for Analysing and Describing*; 2. *for Understanding*; 3. *for Predicting*; 4. *for Explaining and Predicting*; 5. *for Design and Action*. This **exploratory** research makes use of the first two types of theory, namely analysing/describing and understanding. The first theory is utilised as part of the explication process leading to the definitions of tacit knowledge covered in the previous chapter.[c] The second theory on the other hand explains how and why something takes place. The second theory thus covers the use of case studies and surveys/questionnaires as a means of eliciting the empirical component to the research.

The Ontological and Epistemological Perspectives

Given the information systems nature of the research in this **empirical** study, it is considered advisable to explain the ontological and epistemological perspectives adopted. The ***ontological*** perspective adopted is that the theories utilised, possess a separate existence from that of subjective human understanding. This is along the lines as noted by Gregor (2002) of that of Habermas (1984) and Popper (1986).

Habermas (1984) recognises three different worlds – the objective world of actual and possible states of affairs, the subjective world of personal experiences and beliefs, and the social world of normatively regulated social relations. These three worlds are related to Popper's worlds 1, 2, and 3 (Popper, 1986). World 1 is the objective world of material things, World 2 is the subjective world of mental states, and World 3 is an objectively existing but abstract world of man-made entities – language, mathematics, knowledge, science, art, ethics and institutions (Gregor, 2002, p.15).

Ontologically the view is also taken of tacit knowledge at the *individual* level, being a form of *embodied*[i] knowledge, which is able to be made explicit, that is to say to some extent *embrained*[k] (Lam, 2000). The author's view of tacit knowledge is that it is directly tied to human subconscious thought and that what is being measured comprises an articulable component. Scharmer (2001) and Lam (2000) had noted the epistemological distinctions between explicit and tacit knowledge, where the latter knowledge belonged to Popper's World 2, and explicit knowledge to Popper's World 3. As *implicit IT managerial knowledge* is what is being *empirically* tested for, the theory, methods and tools that are used to conduct the measurement exist outside of human subconscious thought. To that end the ***epistemology*** adopted is *largely* positivistic,[f][g] insofar as the tools and methodologies utilised, place the researcher at a distance from the subjects being studied. To be precise the researcher makes use of tools to extract the data from a questionnaire and then interprets the data as objectively as is possible.

Along the lines of Stenmark (2000/2001), an interpretivist approach (Neuman, 1997) had initially been adopted by the researcher in conducting qualitative analysis, except that this research made use of *Atlas.ti*™ as a means of gaining an improved understanding of the "phenomenon" of tacit knowledge. The initial interpretivist approach allowed the researcher to independently determine the shape of tacit knowledge through the groundedness and network density of codes[h] that had arisen through an extensive literature review (Dampney et al., 2002).

To reiterate, the outcomes of the interpretive analysis conducted by way of grounded theory on the 64 documents, enabled the author to conclude a number of key points. The first of these was the importance of *organisational domains*. The second major point to arise through grounded theory examining the tacit knowledge literature was the *contextual nature of tacit knowledge*. The third point related to the highly *individualistic nature of such knowledge*. These key points enabled the researcher to conclude a number of further points. First of all that the research should ideally be conducted within an *external workplace* (the IT industry), rather than an academic domain, which in the case of the latter almost always implies testing on undergraduate populations. The second point is that the use of *case studies* in this research is appropriate given the practical nature of the research. Third that *intra-organisational testing* was appropriate given the contextual nature of the knowledge. That is to say it is appropriate that testing takes place amongst a group of personnel within each organisation and that these participants choose colleagues they consider to be rich in experience and therefore tacit knowledge. Fourth, given the individualistic nature of tacit knowledge uncovered through the qualitative analysis, the use of an *individual question-naire* was felt to be appropriate.

The dispositional perspective adopted herein is *reductionist* (Lansbury & Spillane, 1991). It is believed that personality types likely will affect the results to be found in tacit knowledge testing. In other words, language other than English (Walsham, 2001), seniority on the job (Wagner & Sternberg, 1991a), gender (Horgan & Simeon, 1990; Koehly & Shivy, 1998), age (as opposed to seniority), to name but a few, are all felt to affect tacit knowledge measures. In short it is expected that personal attributes will affect the way people answer tacit knowledge questionnaires. At the same time the researcher acknowledges that he is limited by the principles of *bounded rationality* (Augier, Shariq, & Vendelø, 2001; Roberts, 2001), through which an improved but nevertheless limited view of tacit knowledge flows will be obtained.

What are the actual techniques that are going to be utilised to, firstly test for tacit knowledge, and secondly map the diffusion *or* non-diffusion in the workplaces under study? Bearing in mind that the ideal outcome of this monograph is to produce replicable results along positivist lines, how then will the mechanisms utilised allow others to follow in the author's footsteps? It is the aim of this chapter to introduce the reader to the methodological underpinnings of the tools and techniques that produce the results ultimately displayed in the following chapters. At the same time a brief discussion is provided of alternatives to techniques adopted here. What then are the approaches to conducting tacit knowledge related research?

A Triangulated Approach to Tacit Knowledge Research

The majority of *empirical* tacit knowledge research takes place in psychology where the emphasis is on testing at the individual level, along the lines of "who possesses more tacit knowledge than others." As a means of increasing rigour associated with this research it was felt[i] beneficial to adopt a **triangulated** approach (Jick, 1979) which would incorporate (a) a **Sternberg** based psychological testing instrument; (b) Social Network Analysis as a tool to track the soft knowledge dissipation cycle, and (c) **Formal Concept Analysis** as a means to balance results with those achieved by way of (a) Sternberg's method, and the dissipation (through personnel) of *aTK* viewed by way of (b) Social Network Analysis (SNA) (Figure 1).

Participant observation in a triangulated methodology dealing with nursing interaction had been used by Scott (1992, 1990) to provide balance to the methodology proposed by Sternberg et al.: "the questionnaire identified liberal attitudinal norms … In contrast, the observational methods identified behavioural norms that were conservative … The qualitative methods thus acted as a check on the quantitative method and provided valuable data on proposed role modification at the program development and practice levels" (Scott, 1990, p. 567). Direct observation (Leedy, 1997) rather than **participant observation** would have been more appropriate in the studies presented here, given the tendency of ICT work to be undertaken at a computer monitor where body language and otherwise obvious workplace

Figure 1. Macro-methodology utilising triangulation to test for articulable tacit knowledge at the individual level

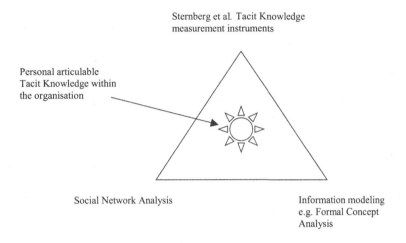

activities are minimised. A more appropriate technique is the application of Social Network Analysis (Koehly & Shivy, 1998; Paxton, Schutz, Wertheim, & Muir et al., 1999; Wasserman & Faust, 1994) which will be used to ascertain how articulable Tacit Knowledge (aTK) is conveyed from one individual to another. The Social Network Analysis questions will be incorporated within the Tacit Knowledge inventory/questionnaire so that it is possible to ascertain with whom personnel in organisations are experiencing positive and negative working relationships. One would expect for instance, that a negative working relationship within IS is likely to diminish the transfer of aTK, a positive relationship on the other hand enhancing transference.

A further means of providing balance in relation to tacit knowledge testing is that of modelling and comparing the results of Sternberg et al. using a set-theoretic approach known as Formal Concept Analysis (FCA) (Ganter & Wille, 1999; Wille, 1997). With these points in mind, a number of these approaches are presented in finer detail, beginning with the means for tacit knowledge testing.

Tacit Knowledge Testing

A large amount of literature exists *discussing* tacit knowledge at the macro organisational level, especially within the knowledge management domain (Athanassiou & Nigh, 2000; Cantwell & Santangelo, 2000; Donaldson, 2001; Jorgensen, 2004; Marcotte & Niosi, 2000; Thorburn, 2000). The significantly smaller proportion of literature concerned with the *testing* of such knowledge focuses at the level of the individual (Colonia-Willner, 1999; Herbig, Büssing,

& Ewert, 2001; Larkin, 1980; Reber, 1993; Sternberg, 1999). Those researchers focused at the level of the individual tend to be psychologists. From a psychological perspective, one of the leading reasons for undertaking tacit knowledge research is the improvement to intra-organisational welfare that tacit knowledge testing brings (Ramaprasad & Rai, 1996). For example, it has now become very popular for professional organisations (including those in the IT domain) to implement practical knowledge (meaning largely tacit knowledge) tests that ask potential employees questions in relation to soft knowledge situations (Coates, 2001). These tests are largely along the lines of tacitly enquiring as to whether employees are likely to *fit* into the *culture* of the organisation. They do not actually test for a candidate's knowledge of codified information per se. Once again the tests for tacit knowledge (at least in Sternberg's case), are not considered to be intelligence tests in disguise.

Approaches to Tacit Knowledge Testing

Let us examine some of the approaches that have been adopted as a means of *empirically* testing for tacit knowledge, concluding with the approach taken here. The tactics generally tend to codify the tacit knowledge problem solving process, or determine how subjects undertake the completion of tasks for which not all instructions are necessarily obvious to the uninitiated. The first approach is that which Larkin adopted as far back as the late 1970s.

Larkin (1980)

Larkin's (1980) "information processing approach" focused on one research participant in particular, whom the reader comes to know as "FR". The subject domain in which this research takes place is that of physics. In essence, Larkin (1980) seeks to study the tacit knowledge-based approach FR uses to solve certain undergraduate level physics problems, the details of which are captured by a non-automated program. The processing model achieved does not necessarily include the temporal data that indicates at which point in time a certain step in solving the problem is achieved, nevertheless the main steps are "captured".

The approach Larkin adopted to codify FR's tacit steps for physics problem solving were as follows. Firstly asking FR to "think aloud" as much as possible during which time Larkin transcribed notes which were later edited. The second step involved producing a process model incorporating the major steps taken by FR. The "program" used by Larkin (1980) had come to be labelled HIPLAN (for HIerarchical PLANner, along similar lines conducted by Ernst & Newell, 1969 in Larkin, 1980). In addition, the HIPLAN program could call upon a sub-routine of procedures. The HIPLAN program is at this stage automated, the precise details for which Larkin does not provide. Running the program performs a "trace," which duplicates as closely as possible how the human subject attempted the problem solving exercise. A comparison is then made with the human subject's original protocols. The testing then takes place once again with a different set of data variables. In summary, Larkin (1980) identifies four main stages in the explication of the tacit knowledge: *Assembly* of information from the problem; *planning* of the problem solution; *solving* the problem, and finally *checking* of the solution.

Scott (1992, 1990)

Scott (1992, 1990) whose approach has been mentioned briefly previously used a triangulated combination of (1) interviewer-administered survey-questionnaire, (2) participant observation and (3) day-to-day observation of the work conducted by nurses. Her studies reflected her social work background and she was interested in the working environment of nurses in maternity wards and their interaction with new mothers. The work conducted was ethno-methodological in its approach with Scott (1992, 1990) immersing herself in the hospital environment.

Reed, Hock, and Lockhead (1993)

Drawing upon the work of Pylyshyn (1981) and others (Kosslyn & Pomerantz, 1977 in Reed et al., 1993; Mitchell & Richman, 1980), Reed et al. (1993) conducted research on the effect of tacit knowledge on visual scanning. Similar to Larkin (1980),[j] undergraduates were the research participants for measuring usage of tacit knowledge. Two experiments were conducted which aimed to test the subject's ability to determine the length of images they were shown. In the first experiment, subjects were split into two groups. "Subjects in both the perception and image groups participated in two tasks. For the perception condition, six of the subjects did the scanning task first and the other six did the length estimation task … The task was designed to study how well people can estimate the lengths of lines … For the image condition, the other 12 subjects followed the same procedure as the perception group, except that the patterns were presented for only 0.5 sec and the subjects were instructed to base their judgements on a visual image of the pattern" (Reed et al., 1993 p. 139).

The second experiment followed along the same lines of the first, except that subjects themselves estimated the time required for scanning the patterns without actually being required to scan the patterns. The results of the experiments seemed to indicate that "scanning a maze should take longer than scanning a spiral and scanning a spiral should take longer than scanning a line … it appears from the data … that tacit knowledge is inadequate to account for all mental scanning data" (Reed et al., 1993, pp. 142-143).

Reber (1993); Reber (1989); Reber and Lewis (1977)

Reber (1989, 1993; Reber & Lewis, 1977) bases his work on tacit knowledge in relation to implicit learning. As early as 1977 Reber and Lewis were conducting psychological experiments involving undergraduates being asked to solve anagram puzzles based on the syntax of an artificial grammar. Over time participants would become slowly more competent in articulating the rule system in use. To summarise, the experimentation was individualistic in nature insofar as testing was conducted at the level of the individual. The empirical tacit knowledge research was aimed at the *explication* of tacit knowledge, that is to say articulating grammatical rules for the solving of anagram puzzles. Similar research challenged chess players to explicate their moves (DeGroot, 1965 in Reber, 1993). Two major approaches were adopted, first grammar learning, and secondly probability learning. The former approach involves "an acquisition phase, during which subjects acquire knowledge of the rules of the grammar, and a testing phase, during which some assessment is made of what they have learned" (1993, p. 220). The latter approach incorporates the subject observing a sequence of rapidly presented events and then a testing phase at which stage the subjects make predictions based on the probability of a certain event taking place. The conclusions from the research seemed to be that "the operations of implicit learning are shown to take place independently of consciousness; their [the subject's] mental products have been demonstrated to be held tacitly; their functional controlling properties have been shown to operate largely outside of awareness" (1993, p. 233).

Noh, Lee, Kim, Lee, & Kim (2000)

Noh et al. (2000) take more of an Artificial Intelligence (AI) approach with regard to working with tacit knowledge. The researchers employ cognitive maps (CM) to explicate tacit knowledge along archetypal AI lines (Stenmark, 2001). The use of **Case Based Reasoning** (CBR) is subsequently used to re-apply the articulated tacit knowledge to other cases. The approach used by Noh et al. (2000) is to firstly draw mental maps of an individual's usage of tacit knowledge. The mental map is composed of nodes with a sequence of relationships between those nodes. For each given relationship a set of causality values can be calculated. One condition is likely to lead to another based on a given heuristic. Following such an approach the CBR software is then able to apply the mental map to a given problem domain. The CBR software thus heuristically determines the commonality between cases represented in its case base and the new case it has been presented with. The tool was applied to a credit analysis problem domain as a means of determining whether a given firm was in a healthy financial position. Noh et al., found that their tool and system performed adequately.

Herbig et al. (2001)

Herbig et al. (2001) explore the tacit knowledge dimension within the nursing domain. Similar to the **Sternberg** approach, which will be explored next, they adopt a workplace-oriented approach to examining usage made of tacit knowledge, in this case by nursing practitioners. A study involving 16 experienced nurses was conducted with the research questions comprising: "do nurses who successfully deal with a critical nursing situation differ in their tacit knowledge from nurses who less successfully deal with the same situation?; and what kind of difference between these two groups can be found and how do they relate to experience-guided working?" (p. 2). In essence the work is based on the **Delphi method** (Linstone & Turoff, 1975 in Herbig et al., 2001), though to some extent the approach follows the simulation technique first proposed by Frederiksen (1966).

As with a Sternberg-based approach to tacit knowledge testing, critical workplace situations are articulated by experts in the subject domain, whereupon significant incidents are prioritised into actor "scripts". The explication process was along the line first promulgated by Kelly's repertory grid technique (Kelly, 1955) whereby the individual is considered to subjectively construe his or her own world and has the ability to provide feedback more detailed than would ordinarily be the case with interviews and questionnaires. Novices are then "trained" on the basis of these scripts to act as patients with certain ailments. The nurses are then presented with a brief patient record, whereupon the actors (both nurses and patients) "act out" the patient nurse scenario relating to the illness the patient apparently has. The actions taking place in the scenario are video recorded in combination with a half structured interview. Results are thus able to be determined in relation to the extent to which nurses are drawing upon their tacit knowledge to deal with medical situations. The results seemed to indicate "the unsuccessful nurses in contrast to the successful nurses seem to have a sequential organisation of their tacit knowledge and seem to use a sequential-analytical procedure in dealing with the situation. This sequential organisation is compared to the concept of experience-guided working which includes a holistic perception of the situation" (p. 694).

Sternberg et al.

Arguably the greatest amount of *empirical* tacit knowledge based research has arisen out of the formerly Yale, now Tufts-based psychology group under the directorship of Professor Robert Sternberg. Whilst Sternberg may have his critics (Jensen, 1993; Ree & Earles, 1993; Schmidt & Hunter, 1993), he is very well known and accepted for his tacit knowledge related research within the psychology community.[k]

In order to understand the Sternberg approach to tacit knowledge research, it is necessary to bear in mind the open acknowledgement made by the group at Yale in relation to what *they* consider to be tacit knowledge, "practical know-how that rarely is expressed openly or taught directly" (Oxford English Dictionary, 1933 in Wagner & Sternberg, 1991a). What the Sternberg group concedes they are testing for is "management knowledge", either management of oneself, others, or one's career, in either a local or global context, whether such knowledge is of an idealistic orientation ("ideally how good is a solution"), or of a more practical persuasion ("just how workable is a solution", or what would you *actually* do in this situation).

Sternberg's (Sternberg, 1995, 1999; Sternberg, Wagner, & Okagaki, 1993; Sternberg, Wagner, Williams, & Horvath, 1995; Torff & Sternberg, 1998; Wagner & Sternberg, 1985, 1987, 1990), approach tends to be applied, yet has involved to quite some degree, testing on undergraduate student populations. The current research direction has diversified; moving amongst other things towards conducting research within the US military domain (Horvath, Forsythe, Bullis, Sweeney, Williams, McNally, Wattendorf, & Sternberg, 1999).[l] Sternberg's research is broadly based upon two major approaches. The former is that of the **"critical incident technique"** (Flanagan, 1954; McClelland, 1976 in Wagner & Sternberg, 1985), and the latter is that of the **"simulation approach"** (Fredericksen, 1966; Thornton & Byham, 1982; Wagner & Sternberg, 1985). The former approach involves interviewing personnel within the subject domain and eliciting information in relation to workplace tasks that were performed particularly well and those tasks performed poorly. Statistics are then used by the Yale team to identify issues that have been identified as being important. The latter approach (which is considered to have face validity), involves the observation of individuals undertaking tasks. "In and out basket tests" (Frederickson, 1966; Wagner & Sternberg, 1985), fall into this sort of category where employees are given a range of tasks to perform that appear in their "in-baskets." The delegation of onward responsibility for certain tasks based on what is in their in-basket, is an example of employees making use of their workplace tacit knowledge.

The Sternberg technique has evolved over time to incorporate a workplace-oriented means of assessment normally using a questionnaire (Wagner & Sternberg, 1991a; 1991b). "The measurement instruments typically used consist of a set of work-related situations, each with between 5 and 20 response items. Each situation poses a problem for the participant to solve, and the participant indicates how he or she would solve the problem by rating the various response items" (Sternberg et al., 1995, p. 918). The respondent is at the same time asked to identify for each of the answer items, how they would answer *ethically* (remembering *ethically* relates to how one should *ideally* deal with a situation), as well as *realistically* (what one would *actually* do in *practice*). In Figure 2 we see one example (no. 8) from the actual test booklet for managers (Wagner & Sternberg, 1991a, p. 9). Respondents are asked to rate *each* of the responses (1-10 shown) of a Likert Scale from 1 (extremely bad) through 4 (neither good nor bad) to 7 (extremely good).

An alternative approach developed by Williams and Sternberg (mentioned in Sternberg et al., 1995), had been for respondents to rate a given set of workplace actions in relation to how they themselves carried out particular tasks. Alternatively, one approach posited was asking participants to write "plans of action" for how they would handle certain situations.

Wagner (1997 in Sternberg et al., 1995) has also been actively involved in developing tacit knowledge measurement indices. One approach developed by Wagner involved the "up front" identification of "practically" intelligent academic psychologists through a nomination process, to whom a tacit knowledge test was administered. The scores of this "proficient" group were averaged and used as a basis for what an expert sample would comprise.

Another approach by the same research group (Wagner, Rashotte, & Sternberg, 1992 in Sternberg et al., 1995) involved collating "rules of thumb" gathered both through a literature review and interviewing process. Based on such rules of thumb, test-banks of workplace scenarios along the lines given above were formulated. The response items (along the lines of 1-10 in the box above) were manipulated so that some followed the logical rules of thumb

Figure 2. Illustrating a sample scenario from the tacit knowledge inventory for managers (Wagner & Sternberg, 1991a, p. 9)

8. You are looking for a new project to tackle in the coming year. You have considered a number of possible projects and desire to pick the project that would be best for you.

1. The project is the one my immediate superior most desires to be completed.
2. Doing the project would require my developing skills that may enhance my future career success.
3. The project should attract the attention of the local media.
4. Doing the project should prove to be fun.
5. The risk of making a mistake is virtually nonexistent.
6. The project will require my interacting with senior executives whom I would like to get to know better.
7. The project is valued by my superior even though it is not valued by me.
8. The project will enable me to demonstrate my talents that others may not be aware of.
9. The project is in an area with which I have a lot of experience.
10. The project is the one I most want to do.

for dealing with the relevant scenario, whilst others represented an incorrect rule of thumb for that scenario. Respondents were then assessed on the basis of the extent to which they chose the correct application of the rule of thumb for that given workplace scenario.

Yet one other approach (Williams & Sternberg, 1995 in Sternberg et al., 1995) involved interviews and the observation of personnel to construct both a general and a level specific tacit knowledge measure. In addition to testing this measurement approach within four high technology companies, information was sought within the organisations as to who was considered overachieving *as well as underachieving* within their levels. Being able to then ascertain who the successful (and unsuccessful) personnel were, allowed the Yale group to determine what tacit knowledge existed (and was effectively utilised) by the "experts" at each level (lower, middle and upper management). Such knowledge in turn permitted the researchers to identify the type of knowledge the experts had, that their poorer performing colleagues did not.

The Wilcoxon Matched Pairs Signed Rank Test

The approach taken by the Yale group has been to process their data using statistics along characteristic psychology lines. Such an approach tends to require large sample populations, which partly explains why much testing takes place on undergraduate students or other captive sample groups, such as the military. Furthermore the Sternberg approach along with the majority of questionnaire data gathering techniques tends to use anonymous data. Because it was not expected that sample populations would be a) random, b) large, or c) captive in the IT domain, alternative means of data presentation to statistical approaches were sought. The alternative approach taken was that of **Formal Concept Analysis** with its lattice based means of representing data. Nevertheless some statistical processing of the data did take place. The Wilcoxon nonparametric[m] statistical test[n] (Siegel, 1956) permits a one tailed [o] test of statistical significance on data to determine whether in fact *statistically*, experts and novices were answering the scenario questions in different ways. At the same time the intention of this research was also to identify other individuals who attained results similar to that of experts but were not necessarily recognised by their peers as such. This group we label "*expert non-experts*" (expert novices), as such the term acronym ENE will be utilised from time to time. The *results* for this test are presented in chapter 9. Two key points should be considered. First the statistical tests utilise summarised numerical data in the form of means or medians, thus a great deal of information is lost. A graphical approach to identifying potential tacit knowledge savvy personnel provides us with greater data sensitivity.

The adoption of Formal Concept Analysis has occurred for a number of key reasons. First there was a desire to model the tacit knowledge inventory results (elicited by way of a questionnaire) in a visual environment, which would permit finer interpretive granularity. Secondly it was expected that the sample sizes would be too small to permit effective quantitative interpretation of the datasets along traditional Sternberg/psychology lines. As will be revealed later, the author's intuitions regarding the suitability of statistical testing were confirmed. Thirdly the graphical Formal Concept Analysis (lattice theory) approach, permitted the uncovering of a group of individuals who behaved similarly to their peer-identified experts henceforth being labelled as "expert non-experts". What then is this alternative approach to the processing of questionnaire data?

Formal Concept Analysis

A further means of providing balance in relation to tacit knowledge testing is that of modelling and comparing the results of Sternberg's approach by using a set-theoretic technique known as Formal Concept Analysis (FCA) (Ganter & Wille, 1999; Wille, 1997). Formal Concept Analysis, as its name suggests is based on the philosophical notion of concepts. Each "concept" is comprised of an *intension* and *extension*. The former term represents the attributes/properties or features of the object. The latter term relates to the set of objects, which "meet" or fulfil the attributes in the intension component (Fischer, 1993). Each concept thus forms a pair of mutually fitting sets (A,B), where A in this instance represents the set of objects, whilst B represents the set of attributes, corresponding to the former's set of objects. The terms in German, given the Darmstadt origins of FCA research, are those of: (G)egenstande for the objects, (M)erkmale for the attributes, and the relationship between them: (I)deale. The combination of (G,M,I) is referred to as a formal context. A binary K(ontext) (in German) may be formally expressed thus:

$$K := (G, M, I)$$

A multivalued context may be expressed as a quadtuple:

$$K := (G, M, W, I) \text{ and } I \subseteq G \times M \times W$$

where the relationship I is a subset of the combined components of Objects (G), Attributes (M) and merkmalsWerte (W) (Attribute-values). In short, "the aim of FCA is to find (formal) concepts and construct the hierarchy between them. To achieve this aim, the many valued context must be transformed into a single valued one by so-called conceptual scaling" (Ganter & Wille, 1989 in Bartel & Brüggemann, 1998 p. 24). The act of converting a many valued context into a single valued one is in fact converting multi-valued data into binary format. Either a value exists at the intersection of a particular object and attribute, or it does not.

Table 1. Representing the application of FCA concepts to the questionnaire data

K = Formal table with its corresponding data	G = The participant
M = The responses	W = The value of the response
I = Relationship between the responses, their values and the participants	

The result of the binary "conversion" process produces a cross-table. The cross-table in turn is used to create a lattice which graphically represents the binary data.

Along the lines of Kollewe (1989) and Spangenberg and Wolff (1988), the FCA approach is able to process questionnaire data. Using the Sternberg approach it is possible to interpret the responses to the Sternberg-style scenario as a formal context, a cross table of which may be constructed thus (Table 1).

Kollewe's (1989) use of questionnaire data treated the units of questioning as the objects (G), the questions as the attributes (M) and the answers to the questions as the attribute-values (W). In a pilot study (Richards & Busch, 2000), it was decided to represent the data differently as it seemed more intuitive. The author regarded the participant as the object (G) that has a number of features (M) such as age and position in addition to a set of responses and their values. This approach made data entry and validation easier as there was a one-to-one correspondence between the survey returned and the participant.

First it is necessary to construct the cross-table. Given the responses to the questionnaire are electronic; they can easily be manipulated into database or spreadsheet format. One takes the responses to the questionnaire and begins to implement them in a cross-table using the associated FCA Anaconda™ᴾ software. An example of a cross-table for a concept lattice appears in Figure 3.

Note that only one combination of any row of data is permissible. A careful examination of the figure will reveal that no two rows contain the same combination of points. From a practical point of view the data represented left most in the diagram consists of a set of embedded Structured Query Language (SQL) statements that in turn access the data from a relational database (MSAccess™). The column data given at the top right of the figure represents the titles for the concepts to later appear in the concept lattice (figure included further down). In this instance the cross-table represents data concerning the occupation of a respondent now, three years ago and six years ago. The lattice for the cross-table in Figure 3 is illustrated in Figure 4. Note that the FCA lattice is yet another practical implementation of Hasse diagrams (Bartel & Brüggemann, 1998).

Figure 3. Illustrating a crosstable in Anaconda™, the fundamental construct for constructing a concept lattice

Figure 4. Illustrating a concept lattice in Anaconda™, produced by way of the cross-table featured in Figure 3

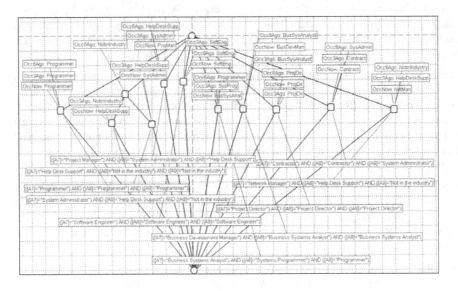

For those familiar or interested in the formalisms, the standard construction of the formal concepts takes place through the notion of a Galois connection. Formal concepts are found by determining the set of attributes shared by a set of objects or conversely the set of objects, which share a set of attributes. More formally, the derivation operators (see Table 1 for explanation of symbols) are as follows:

$$X \subseteq G : \quad X \mapsto X' := \{m \in M \mid gIm \text{ for all } g \in X \} \qquad \text{(Formula 1)}$$

$$Y \subseteq M: \quad Y \mapsto Y' := \{g \in G \mid gIm \text{ for all } m \in Y\} \qquad \text{(Formula 2)}$$

are used to construct all formal concepts of a formal context, by finding the pairs (X'',X') and (Y',Y''). It is possible to obtain all extents X' by determining all row-intents $\{g\}'$ with $g \in G$ and then finding all their intersections. Alternatively Y' can be obtained by determining all column-extents $\{m\}'$ with $m \in M$ and then finding all their intersections. This is specified as:

$$X' = \bigcap_{g \in X} \{g\}' \qquad \text{(Formula 3)}$$

$$Y' = \bigcap_{m \in Y} \{m\}' \qquad\qquad\qquad\qquad \text{(Formula 4)}$$

Having found the set of formal concepts it is possible to order these using the subsumption relation $\geq$ on the set of all concepts formed such that $(X_1,Y_1) \leq (X_2,Y_2)$ iff $X_1 \subseteq X_2$. By finding the predecessors and successors of each concept one can produce a visualisation of the concepts as a complete lattice given in Figure 4. The general idea when constructing the lattice is that objects (Gegenstande) are shown below the concept circles, whilst the attributes are illustrated above the actual concept circles. In this instance, the reader may note from the figure that the embedded SQL query fragments are shown as comprising the objects, whilst the title of the concepts to which these SQL queries refer comprise the attributes. In practice, what this means is that the personnel (or rather their database key identifiers), who meet the arguments of the SQL query will be shown as the objects in the final concept lattice. Concomitantly, the attributes relating to these personnel will be shown above the concept circles where the relevant personnel have been identified.

For a family (Xi,Yi) of formal concepts of K the greatest subconcept, the join, and the smallest superconcept, the meet, are according to the theory of FCA given by:

$$\bigvee_{i \in I} (X_i, B_i) := ((\bigcup_{i \in I} A_i)'', \bigcap_{i \in I} B_i) \qquad\qquad \text{(Formula 5)}$$

$$\bigwedge_{i \in I} (X_i, B_i) := (\bigcap_{i \in I} A_i, (\bigcup_{i \in I} B_i)'') \qquad\qquad \text{(Formula 6)}$$

Having examined the formalisms of FCA and how this relates to the use of it for processing questionnaire data specifically, an example of the approach is now illustrated.

Applying Formal Concept Analysis to Questionnaire Data: A Working Example

The main data collection instrument adopted was an online survey questionnaire. The questionnaire will be discussed in greater detail in the following chapter. This section provides a working example of the use made of FCA in the conduct of the research, with particular regard to the tacit knowledge component of the questionnaire. The approach adopted here is unique. Apart from a slightly similar method by Kollewe (1989), no evidence has been found for the use of FCA in processing survey questionnaire data. The questionnaire utilised in this study may be seen in appendix G. The reader may also care to note that Figures 5 and 9 come from this questionnaire. The following represents an example of processing the questionnaire data.

Many of the data items in the survey are of one-dimensional ordinal type. For example, for the tacit knowledge component of the questionnaire specifically, it is asked only that respondents select a value from extremely bad through to extremely good. An example of a

Figure 5. Illustrating a Likert scale (of ordinal type) used in the tacit knowledge testing process

Likert scale may be seen in the following diagram (Figure 5). Although the respondent filling out the questionnaire is not presented with numerical values, in actual fact "Extremely Bad" equates to 1, and "Extremely Good" takes on the value of 7. "Neither Good nor Bad" thus takes the value of 4. The remaining Likert scale points take on their relevant numerical values. Converting the textual data to numerical data permits this to be stored within a database format.

Upon converting the Likert scale into a cross-table (Figure 6), it is possible to see how the data presented in the rows represents the Likert value provided in the diagram above. For example note how ([A24]="1") corresponds to a Structured Query Language statement whereby A24 represents the column in the database table, and 1 equates to the value "Extremely Bad." Similarly ([A24]="2") represents the embedded SQL statement for a "Very Bad" value. The pattern is repeated up until the value ([A24]="7") for "Extremely Good." The SQL statement is thus able to look for the value within column A24 of the database table to find either "1", "2", "3", "4", "5", "6" or "7." Should one of these values be present (and there may be only one), the SQL query will return the value so that this value may then be used in the concept lattice.

Turning our attention to the concept lattice (Figure 7), it is possible to see how the values end up being represented. On the advice of a technical expert in the area of Formal Con-

Figure 6. Illustrating the crosstable for the likert scale data

(7/7) (7/7)	Extremely Bad	Very Bad	Bad	Neither Good nor Bad	Good	Very Good	Extremely Good
([A24]="1")	X						
([A24]="2")		X					
([A24]="3")			X				
([A24]="4")				X			
([A24]="5")					X		
([A24]="6")						X	
([A24]="7")							X

Figure 7. Illustrating the concept lattice from the concept table featured in the earlier figure

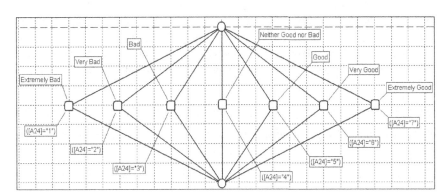

cept Analysis,[q] it was determined that the most appropriate means of representing the tacit knowledge Likert scale data was along the lines presented in Figure 7. It was felt that this approach provided the best way by which the Likert scale questionnaire data would be able to be visualised, as an alternative to viewing the data statistically.

Through using the complementary FCA Toscana™ [r] software, which takes the Anaconda™ data, one is able to eventually construct the complete concept lattice as illustrated in Figure 8. Note how the concept lattice now contains the actual data as it exists in the database. In this instance one can visualise the keys (in the relational database sense) of individuals who have chosen particular values for an actual tacit knowledge answer option.

Figure 8. Illustrating the concept lattice in Toscana™ with data included from the database table. Note how the diagram shows results for the values Extremely Bad (2 respondents), Very Bad (2 respondents) and Good (1 respondent)

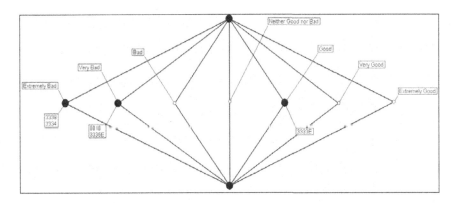

Turning our attention to a biographical question from the same questionnaire, the reader will be able to see how the subsumption relation is brought into play, taking the biographical question, *"please select the highest formal qualification (or equivalent) you have obtained"* as an example (Figure 9).

Examining the cross-table for this biographical question (Figure 10), one can see that subsumption takes place. Notice how the subsumption is to some degree subjective insofar as the researcher must make the decision to determine which qualification subsumes the other.

Figure 9. Illustrating a biographical question, in this instance highest formal qualification obtained

12. Please select the HIGHEST formal qualification (or equivalent) you have obtained

Highest qualification?   Qualification?

`<PLEASE SELECT>`

<PLEASE SELECT>
High School Leaving
High School Certificate
Trade Diploma
Associate Diploma
Bachelor Degree
Honours Bachelor Degree
Graduate Certificate
Graduate Diploma
Graduate Bachelor
Masters (Coursework)

13. Do you have any TECHNICAL (COMP...   ...lifications?

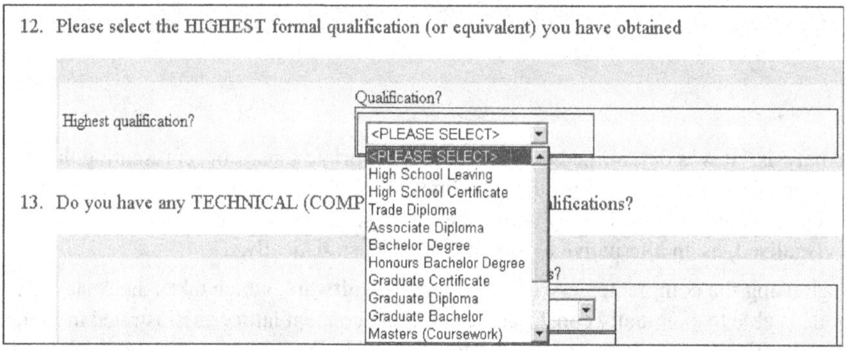

Figure 10. Illustrating a cross-table for the highest qualification obtained question

([A18]="Graduate Diploma") (7/12) (12/12)	High School Leaving	High School Certificate	Trade Diploma	Associate Diploma	Bachelor Degree	Honours Bachelor Degree	Graduate Certificate	Graduate Diploma	Graduate Bachelor	Masters	Doctorate	Higher Doctorate
([A18]="High School Leaving")	X											
([A18]="High School Certificate")		X										
([A18]="Trade Diploma")	X		X									
([A18]="Associate Diploma")	X			X								
([A18]="Bachelor Degree")		X			X							
([A18]="Honours Bachelor Degree")		X			X	X						
([A18]="Graduate Certificate")		X			X		X					
([A18]="Graduate Diploma")		X			X			X				
([A18]="Graduate Bachelor")		X			X				X			
([A18]="Masters")		X			X	X				X		
([A18]="Doctorate")		X			X	X				X	X	
([A18]="Higher Doctorate")		X			X	X				X	X	X

For example, in Germany,[s] academic paths tend to be firmly set. High schools are already subdivided into three categories based to some degree on how one performs in primary or elementary school. The high school chosen can have a direct bearing on whether one enters university, undertakes a trade, or perhaps obtains some other job. Within the university system itself, studies can be structured towards whether one eventually progresses into the doctoral stream. There is, in other words far less opportunity for "mind-changing" in later life. Due to the egalitarian nature of Australian society (Spillane 1983), such educational streaming would be considered elitist and exclusionist. The point being, that in constructing concept lattices where a subsumption principle may be said to apply (as in the case of educational qualifications), careful consideration needs to be given as to how the concept lattice will actually be assembled. For example, note how in Figure 10 below, that when one is in receipt of a higher school certificate, one would not normally be said to be holding high school leaving qualifications (the box for *high school certificate* is checked, but not the *high school leaving* box).

If one has pursued the option of obtaining a trade qualification, then we could reasonably expect the recipient to have completed high school leaving, rather than the high school

Figure 11. Illustrating a concept lattice for highest formal qualification obtained where a subsumption relation applies

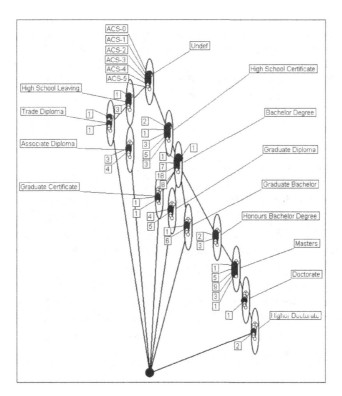

certificate. Having obtained a bachelor's degree, one would normally be in receipt of a high school certificate, and so on. A subsumption relation can be seen with the build up of crosses in any given row. A subjective judgement is necessary in constructing just such a cross-table. The ramifications of cross-table construction become clear when examining the corresponding concept lattice (Figure 11). Note how higher doctorate is at the bottom, and there are several branches to the tree-like structure represented in the figure. This multi-ordinal scale affects how the Gegenstande or objects will be placed. It will not be possible to move higher doctorate above that of doctorate. The subsumption relation works on the principle that one with a higher doctorate will have a doctorate. One with a doctorate will have a master's degree and so on, hence the subsumption relation.

Summary

In summarising the methodological underpinnings covered in this chapter, the reader needs to consider the suitability of means for conducting tacit knowledge testing. The Sternberg approach is considered to be the most practical if undertaking empirical organisational study. Underlying much psychological assessment is the need for descriptive and analytical statistics. Allowing for smaller sample sizes, given that this study was going to be conducted in a non-anonymous format partially negated the benefits of using a purely statistical approach to data analysis, nevertheless a Wilcoxon test was undertaken. An alternative means of displaying data is via Formal Concept Analysis, which allows the visualisation of questionnaire data whilst at the same time still providing legitimacy to data interpretation. Finally, FCA proved useful for interpreting the biographical and tacit knowledge inventory results components of the questionnaire. The other cornerstone of the work being reported here is that of examining likely soft knowledge flows amongst ICT personnel, and for that a different technique is required, namely Social Network Analysis.

References

Athanassiou, N, & Nigh, D. (2000). Internationalization, tacit knowledge and the top management teams of MNCs. *Journal of International Business Studies, 31*(3), 471-487.

Augier, M., Shariq, S., & Vendelø, M. (2001). Understanding context: Its emergence, transformation and role in tacit knowledge sharing. *Journal of Knowledge Management, 5*(2), 125-137.

Bartel, H-G., & Brüggemann, R. (1998). Applications of formal concept analysis to structure-activity relationships. *Fresenius Journal of Analytic Chemistry, 361*(1), 23-28.

Baumard, P. (1999). *Tacit knowledge in organisations* (originally published as Baumard, P., (1996), *Organisations déconcertées: La gestion stratégique de la connaissance*. London: Sage Publications.

Busch, P., & Richards, D. (2000). Triangulated measurement of articulable tacit knowledge with an emphasis on formal concept analysis. In T. Chan & C. Ng (eds.), *Proceedings of the 11th Australasian Conference on Information Systems,* December 6-8, Brisbane Australia.

Cantwell, J., & Santangelo, G. (2000). Capitalism, profits, and innovation in the new techno-economic paradigm. *Journal of Evolutionary Economics, 10*(1-2), 131-157.

Cavusgil, S.T., Calantone, R.J., & Zhao, Y. (2003). Tacit knowledge transfer and firm innovation capacity. *Journal of Business and Industrial Marketing, 18*(1), 6-21.

Coates, P. (2001). Headhunters and collectors. *The Weekend Australian,* Saturday, July, 7, 1st edition.

Colonia-Willner, R.(1999). Investing in practical intelligence: Ageing and efficiency among executives. *International Journal of Behavioral Development, 23*(3), 591-614.

Dampney, C., Busch, P., & Richards, D. (2002). The meaning of tacit knowledge. *Australian Journal of Information Systems,* December, 3-13.

Donaldson, L. (2001). Reflections on knowledge and knowledge – Intensive firms. *Human Relations, 54*(7), 955-963.

Fischer, W. (1993). Formal concept analysis as a research tool in mathematics education. *Hiroshima Journal of Mathematics Education, 1*, 1-35.

Fleck, J. (1997). Contingent knowledge and technology development. *Technology Analysis & Strategic Management, 9*(4), 383(15).

Fredericksen, N. (1966). Validation of a simulation technique. *Organizational Behaviour and Human Performance, 1*, 87-109.

Ganter, R., & Wille, R. (1999). *Formal concept analysis: Mathematical foundations.* Berlin: Springer-Verlag.

Gregor, S. (2002). Design theory in information systems. *Australian Journal of Information Systems,* Special Issue, 14-22.

Habermas, J. (1984). *Theory of communicative action Vol 1: Reasoning and the rationalization of society.* London: Heinemann.

Herbig, B., Büssing, A., & Ewert, T. (2001). The role of tacit knowledge in the work context of nursing. *Journal of Advanced Nursing, 34*(5), 687-695.

Horgan, D., & Simeon, R. (1990). Gender, mentoring, and tacit knowledge. *Journal of Social Behaviour and Personality, 5*(4, Special Issue), 453-471.

Horvath, J., Forsythe, G., Bullis, R., Sweeney, P., Williams, W., McNally, J., Wattendorf, J., & Sternberg, R. (1999). Experience, knowledge and military leadership. In R. Sternberg & J. Horvath (Eds.), *Tacit knowledge in professional practice: Researcher and practitioner perspectives.* Mahwah, NJ: Lawrence Erlbaum and Associates, 39-57.

Jensen, A. (1993). Test validity: G versus "Tacit Knowledge." *Current directions in psychological science: A Journal of the American Psychological Society, 2*(1), 9-10.

Jick, T. (1979). Mixing qualitative and quantitative methods: Triangulation in action. *Administrative Science Quarterly, 24*, 602-611.

Jorgensen, B. (2004). Individual and organisational learning: A model for reform for public organisations. *Foresight, 6*(2), 91-103.

Kelly, G. (1955). *The psychology of personal constructs, Vol 1: A theory of personality.* New York: W. W. Norton & Co.

Koehly, L., & Shivy, V. (1998). Social network analysis: A new methodology for counseling research. *Journal of Counseling Psychology, 45*(1), 3-17.

Kollewe, W. (1989). Evaluation of a survey with methods of formal concept analysis. In *Conceptual and Numerical Analysis of Data: Proceedings of the 13th Conference of the Gesellschaft für Klassifikation e. V. University of Augsburg, April 10-12, 1989.* Berlin: Springer-Verlag, 123-134.

Lam, A. (2000). Tacit knowledge, organizational learning, and societal institutions: An integrated framework. *Organization Studies, 21*(3), 487-513.

Lansbury, R., & Spillane, R. (1991). *Organisational behaviour: The Australian context, 2nd.* Ed. Melbourne, Australia: Longman Cheshire.

Larkin, J. (1980). Skilled problem solving in physics: A hierarchical planning model. *Journal of Structural Learning, 6*(4), 271-297.

Leedy, P. (1997). *Practical research: Planning and design, 6th. Ed.* New York: Merrill.

Marcotte, C., & Niosi, J. (2000). Technology transfer to China: The issues of knowledge and learning. *Journal of Technology Transfer, 25*(1), 43-57.

Mooradian, N. (2005). Tacit knowledge: Philosophic roots and role in KM. *Journal of Knowledge Management, 9*(6), 104-113.

Nelson, D. (Ed.) (1998). *Dictionary of Mathematics* 2nd Ed. London: Penguin Books.

Neuman, W. (1997). *Social research methods: Qualitative and quantitative approaches,* 3rd ed. Boston: Allyn and Bacon.

Noh, J., Lee, K., Kim, J., Lee, J., & Kim, S. (2000). A case-based reasoning approach to cognitive map-driven tacit knowledge management. *Expert Systems with Applications, 19,* 249-259.

Paxton, S., Schutz, H., Wertheim, E., & Muir, S. (1999). Friendship clique and peer influences on body image concerns, dietary restraint, extreme weight-loss behaviours, and binge eating in adolescent girls. *Journal of Abnormal Psychology, 108*(2), 255-266.

Popper, K. (1986). *Unended quest: An intellectual autobiography.* Glasgow: Fontana.

Pylyshyn, Z. (1981). The imagery debate: Analogue media versus tacit knowledge. In A. Collins & E. Smith (Eds.), *Readings in cognitive science: A perspective from Psychology and Artificial Intelligence,*Chapter 6.5, San Mateo, CA: Morgan Kaufman, 600-614.

Ramaprasad, A., & Rai, A. (1996). Envisioning management of information. *Omega: International Journal of Management Science, 24*(2), 179-193.

Reber, A. (1989). Implicit learning and tacit knowledge. *Journal of Experimental Psychology: General, 118*(3), 219-235.

Reber, A. (1993). *Implicit learning and tacit knowledge: An essay on the cognitive unconscious.* Oxford Psychology Series No. 19. New York, Oxford: Oxford University Press, Clarendon Press.

Reber, A., & Lewis, S. (1977). Implicit learning: An analysis of the form and structure of a body of tacit knowledge. *Cognition, 5*(4), 333-361.

Ree, M., & Earles, J. (1993). G is to psychology what carbon is to chemistry: A reply to Sternberg and Wagner, McClelland, and Calfree. *Current Directions in Psychological Science: A journal of the American Psychological Society, 2*(1), 11-12.

Reed, S., Hock, H., & Lockhead, G. (1983). Tacit knowledge and the effect of pattern recognition on mental scanning. *Memory & Cognition, 11*(2), 137-143.

Richards, D., & Busch, P. (2000). Measuring, formalising and modelling tacit knowledge. In F. Naghdy (Ed.), *International Congress on Intelligent Systems and Applications (ISA'2000)*, December 12-15. Academic Press, 58-64.

Roberts, J. (2001). The drive to codify: Implications for the knowledge-based economy. *Prometheus, 19*(2), 99-116.

Scharmer, C. (2001). Self-transcending knowledge: Sensing and organizing around emerging opportunities. *Journal of Knowledge Management, 5*(2), 137-151.

Schmidt, F., & Hunter, J. (1993). Tacit knowledge, practical intelligence, general mental ability, and job knowledge. *Current Directions in Psychological Science: A Journal of the American Psychological Society, 2*(1), 8-9.

Scott, D. (1990). Practice wisdom: The neglected source of practice research. *Social Work, 35*(6), 564-568.

Scott, D. (1992). Reaching vulnerable populations: A framework for primary service expansion. *American Journal of Orthopsychiatry, 62*(3), 333-341.

Siegel, S. (1956). *Nonparametric statistics: For the behavioural sciences.* New York: McGraw-Hill.

Smith, E. (2000). Applying knowledge – Enabling methods in the classroom and in the workplace. *Journal of Workplace Learning: Employee Counselling Today, 12*(6), 236-244.

Spangenberg, N., & Wolff, K. (1988). Conceptual grid evaluation. In N. Spangenberg & E. Wolff (Eds.), *Classification and related methods of data analysis.* Amsterdam: North Holland, 577-580.

Spillane, R. (1983). *Stress at work: A review of Australian research.* Department of Psychology, University of Stockholm, Report Number 35.

Stenmark, D. (2000/2001). Leveraging tacit organizational knowledge. *Journal of Management Information Systems, 17*(3), 9-24.

Sternberg, R. (1995). Theory and management of tacit knowledge as a part of practical intelligence. *Zeitschrift für Psychologie, 203*(4), 319-334.

Sternberg, R. (1999). Epilogue – What do we know about tacit knowledge?: Making the tacit become explicit. In R. Sternberg & J. Horvath (Eds.) *Tacit knowledge in professional practice: Researcher and practitioner perspectives.* Mahwah, NJ: Lawrence Erlbaum and Associates, 231-236.

Sternberg, R., Wagner, R., & Okagaki, L. (1993). Practical intelligence: The nature and role of tacit knowledge in work and at school. In J. Puckett (Ed.), *Mechanisms of everyday cognition.* Hillsdale, NJ: Lawrence Erlbaum Associates, 205-227.

Sternberg, R., Wagner, R., Williams, W., & Horvath, J. (1995). Testing common sense. *American Psychologist, 50*(11), 912-927.

Subramaniam, M., & Venkatraman, N. (2001). Determinants of transnational new product development capability: Testing the influence of transferring and deploying tacit overseas knowledge. *Strategic Management Journal, 22,* 359-378.

Thorburn, L. (2000). Knowledge management, research spinoffs, and commercialisation of R&D in Australia. *Asia Pacific Journal of Management, 17*(2), 257-275.

Thornton, G., & Byham, W. (1982). *Assessment centers and managerial performance.* New York: Academic Press.

Torff, B., & Sternberg, R. (1998). Changing mind, changing world: Practical intelligence and tacit knowledge in adult learning. In M Smith & T. Pourchot (Eds.), *Adult learning and development: Perspectives from educational psychology.* Mahwah, NJ: Lawrence Erlbaum Associates, 109-126.

Wagner, R., & Sternberg, R. (1985). Practical intelligence in real – world pursuits: The role of tacit knowledge. *Journal of Personality and Social Psychology, 49*(2), August, 436-458.

Wagner, R., & Sternberg, R. (1987). Tacit knowledge in managerial success. *Journal of Business and Psychology, 1*(4), 301-312.

Wagner, R., & Sternberg, R. (1990). Street smarts. In K. Clark & M. Clark (Eds.), *Measures of Leadership.* West Orange, NJ: Leadership Library of America, 493-504.

Wagner, R., & Sternberg, R. (1991a). *TKIM: The common sense manager: Tacit knowledge inventory for managers: Test booklet.* San Antonio: The Psychological Corporation Harcourt Brace Jovanovich.

Wagner, R., & Sternberg, R. (1991b). *TKIM: The common sense manager: Tacit knowledge inventory for managers: User manual.* San Antonio: The Psychological Corporation Harcourt Brace Jovanovich.

Walsham, G. (2001). Knowledge management: The benefits and limitations of computer systems. *European Management Journal, 19*(6), 599-608.

Wassenaar, D.A., & Katsma, C. P. (2004). IT- based innovation in a digital economy - A social learning perspective. In M. Janssen, H. Sol, & R.W. Wagenaar (Eds.), *ICEC'04 Sixth International Conference on Electronic Commerce* 166-176.

Wasserman, S., & Faust, K. (1994). *Social network analysis: Methods and applications.* Cambridge, UK: Cambridge University Press.

Wille, R. (1997). Conceptual graphs and formal concept analysis. In D. Lukose, H. Delugach, M. Keelr, L. Searle, & J. Sowa (Eds.), *Conceptual Structures: Fulfilling Peirce's Dream, Proceedings of the Fifth International Conference on Conceptual Structures (ICCS'97).* August 3 - 8, University of Washington, Seattle. Lecture Notes in Artificial Intelligence, Number 1257. Berlin: Springer Verlag, 290-303.

Yin, R. (1994). *Case study research: Design and methods.* Applied Social Science Research Methods series, Vol. 5. Beverly Hills, CA: Sage.

Endnotes

a   "Owing to the difficulty in interpreting and transferring it [tacit knowledge], previous studies are mostly descriptive in nature. Detailed research on it is lacking" (Cavusgil, Calantone, & Zhao, 2003, p. 7).

b   "… lacking are empirical studies validating the growing belief that tacit knowledge may have a significant impact on firm capabilities" (Subramaniami & Venkatraman, 2001, p. 360).

c   Personal communication with Professor Shirley Gregor A.N.U., October 2002.

d   "*Embodied* knowledge (individual-tacit) is action oriented; it is the practical, individual type of knowledge on which Polanyi (1962, 1966) focused. In contrast with embrained knowledge (see below) which depends on abstract theoretical reasoning ("knowing"), embodied knowledge builds upon "bodily" or practical experience ("doing"). It has a strong automatic and voluntaristic component; its generation and application does not need to be fitted into or processed through a conscious decision-making schema (Spender, 1996b; 67), Embodied knowledge is also context specific; it is particular knowledge' which becomes relevant in practice only "in the light of the problem at hand" (Barley, 1996). "Its generation cannot be separated from application" (Lam, 2000, p. 492, italics added).

e   "*Embrained* knowledge (individual-explicit) is dependent on the individual's conceptual skills and cognitive abilities. It is formal, abstract of theoretical knowledge. Scientific knowledge, which focuses on the rational 'understanding' and 'knowing' of universal principles or laws of nature, belongs to this category. Embrained knowledge enjoys a privileged social status within Western culture. The high occupational status of science compared with engineering reflects this. Moreover, the historical attempt by engineers in Britain and the United States to emphasize the conceptual components of their activity represents a conscious attempt to seek status enhancement in society" (Layton, 1974, 1976 in Lam, 2000, p. 492, italics added).

f   Personal communication with Associate Professor Frada Burstein, Monash University, December 2001.

g   "Polanyi developed the concept of tacit knowledge as part of a problematic directed at a philosophic conception of science and scientific theorizing prominent in his time and still influential today (Polanyi, 1958, 1966, 1969). The theory under attack, logical positivism, held that scientific knowledge was a purely objective matter, being constituted by logically specifiable rules of inference and verification. Scientific hypotheses could be understood as generalizations with specifiable empirical consequences that could be tested using objective methods and devices. Logic, mathematics, objective truth conditions, and a precise vocabulary were the materials of which science was made according to the positivist conception. Polanyi, by contrast, argued that science had a subjective side; that it was not a purely objective affair. His theory of tacit knowledge was the centerpiece of that argument. It was the element in scientific thinking and in thinking in general, that undermined the claim to pure objectivity" (Mooradian, 2005, p. 105).

h   ATLAS.ti™ had permitted interpretivistic analysis of tacit knowledge. The use of grounded theory permitted the focus of the research to narrow on tacit knowledge usage by individuals at an intra-organisational level. In other words the creation of network maps had shown in the literature that tacit knowledge was contextual, individualistic, and oftentimes organisationally based.

i   Discussed in further detail in Busch and Richards, 2000.

j   And the majority of *empirical* tacit knowledge research.

k   Personal communication with Assoc. Prof. Brett Myors, Organisational Psychologist, formerly Macquarie University, now at the Department of Psychology, Griffith University, Queensland; Semester 1, 2000.

l   Personal communication with Dr. Anna Ciancolo, PACE centre, Yale University, October 2001.

m   "Nonparametric methods: Inference procedures in which no assumptions are made about any population parameter. The term is often taken to be synonymous with distribution free methods, and is widely used this way ... The distinction is more one of logic than one of practical importance, so the term 'nonparametric' is commonly used somewhat loosely when 'distribution-free' would be logically more appropriate" (Nelson, 1998, p. 298).

n   "The Wilcoxon test is a most useful test for the behavioural scientist. With behavioural data, it is not uncommon that the researcher can (a) tell which member of a pair is 'greater than' which, i.e., tell the sign of the difference between any pair, and (b) rank the differences in order of absolute size. That is, he can make the judgement of 'greater than' between any pair's two performances, and also can make that judgement between any two difference scores arising from any two pairs" (Siegel, 1956, p. 75-76).

o   A one-tailed test is used to predict an effect in a particular direction, whereas the two-tailed test is not and is used when the direction of results is unsure beforehand. In this case a test is being conducted for clear differences between how experts differ from the rest of the sample population in terms of how they have answered the tacit knowledge inventory.

p   Anaconda™ is the software environment, which is first used to establish the crosstables. It does this through means of embedded SQL query statements to a database (established separately). Once the crosstables have been constructed, the partner software (Toscana™) is able to take over from there. Anaconda™ at this stage is only available in the German language.

q   Communication with Mr. Bastian Wormuth, visiting research fellow, Technische Hochschule, Darmstadt, February 2002.

r   Toscana™ takes the crosstables created in Anaconda™ as the structure for drawing the finished lattice. In order to present *results* however, Toscana™ has to access database tables via the embedded SQL queries in Anaconda™. Having accessed the data, the data is presented in the Toscana™ interface as a series of black dots at the appropriate place.

s   Personal communication with Mr. Bastian Wormuth, FCA software specialist, Technische Hochschule, Darmstadt, Germany.

Chapter V

Organisations

Research (e.g., Pierce & Delbecq, 1977) has shown that corporations that are high in in-tra-organisation communication are more likely to innovate. If this is true, when we help to make tacit strategies explicit, we are conceivably empowering organisations to store its practical intelligence, upgrade it, sell its products, and, above all, find ways to transfer it in house, improving business processes by bringing non-expert capabilities closer to the performance of experts. This, in turn can minimise cost of work, build adaptability to chang-ing competitive market conditions, and as a result may produce a fast return on investments, and a gain in market share (Colonia-Willner, 1999, p. 609).

Introduction

There is little sense in undertaking research on tacit knowledge and its intra-organisational diffusion without some discussion on organisations themselves. Rather than undertake a longitudinal study in one firm, the research covered in this book examines three IT firms (or IT branches of firms) at one point in time (late 2001-early 2002). There is evidence to suggest (Lam, 2000) that the nature of the organisation will influence tacit knowledge transfer, both with regard to organisational mission and whether the company is private or public sector in nature (Syed-Ikhsan & Rowland, 2004). Lam's (2000) work utilised **Mintzberg**'s (1983, 1991a, b, c, d, e) typology and it is for this reason in addition to the latter's prominence in the discipline of organisational theory that this chapter will introduce **Mintzberg**'s typology. The three firms under study will then be introduced in some detail, with an emphasis on the biographical composition of the staff participating in the research being presented here. The chapter will conclude with a placement of the three organisations within the Mintzberg framework.

The Influence of Organisational Type on Tacit Knowledge Utilisation

Evidence indicates that high performance workplaces in the US and Australia are far more likely to benefit through the nurturing of intellectual capital, chief among which is the effective utilisation of tacit knowledge (Curtain, 1998). But how do organisations differ in their usage or transference of tacit knowledge? Can scholars expect to see a difference of tacit knowledge utilisation depending on different organisational types along **Mintzberg**'s (1991a, b, c, d, e) lines? Lam (2000) for example argues "the knowledge of the firm is socially embedded; it is rooted in firms' coordination mechanisms and organizational routines which, in turn, are heavily influenced by societal institutions" (p. 488). One should remember that tacit knowledge in particular is socially rooted, as qualitative research had initially shown (Dampney, Busch, & Richards 2002). Recent evidence (Cavusgil, Calantone, & Zhao, 2003) seems to suggest that firm *size* does not have any effect on the strength of relationships between individuals and the extent to which tacit knowledge is likely to be transferred, however the *type* of organisation at the macro level as noted by Lam (2000) does. With these points in mind, let us examine the organisation types beginning with that of the entrepreneurial firm.

The Entrepreneurial Firm

Mintzberg had classified organisations into principally five types, being those of entrepreneurial, machine, diversified, professional and finally innovative. Lam (2000) also mentions the J-form (J for Japanese) organisation. The *entrepreneurial firm* (Mintzberg, 1991b) as its name suggests tends to have a small staff compliment. The labour in such a firm is divided amongst those staff in a somewhat flexible fashion. Given the minimal staff, the management structure is typically flat and in turn small in number. The CEO (chief executive officer) tends to be the driving force of this firm, and may have been the originator or inventor of the product produced by the company. A good example of such a firm would be AIMTEK (http://www.aimtek.com.au/) chaired by Dr. Don Fry, an innovator with a long history of groundbreaking technology. Mintzberg notes that the structure of entrepreneurial firms are characterised by the simpler nature of the products they produce, permitting strong leadership at the top. In contrast firms producing more complex goods or services must necessarily rely on a larger number of staff who bring with them a wider range of skills necessary for the production of such products. Dr. Fry's firm certainly has strong leadership at the top, but the products they produce are far from simple, one case in point being their recent development in collaboration with the University of Queensland and NASA on the "scramjet" (http://www.aimtek.com.au/aerospace.html). The entrepreneurial firm can be expected to make large scale use of tacit knowledge as a means of transferring soft knowledge from one staff member to the next, given the smaller number of staff and the closeness with which the staff operate. Dr. Fry has without doubt been instrumental in transferring much of his tacit knowledge to the more than 1,000 apprentices over the years under him, with whom he has often had a mentoring relationship.

The Machine Organisation

The *machine organisation* (Mintzberg, 1991c) is exemplified by routine work, typically simple in nature, which means in turn that workflow processes can become highly standardised. Communication in such organisations tends to be formalised, with a well-formed middle management structure to enable such communication flows. A good example of such firms would be subcontractors in the automotive industry such as Monroe shock absorbers (http://www.monroe.com.au/). Machine organisations rely heavily on encoded, that is to say explicit collective forms of knowledge (Lam, 2000). The role of tacit knowledge is minimised as knowledge is formalised quickly, for "the machine bureaucracy seeks to minimise and control tacit knowledge. It operates on an 'impoverished' knowledge base" (Lam, 2000, p. 498).

The Diversified Company

The *diversified company* (Mintzberg, 1991d) represents a modern structure caused by subdivisions within the firm having a central administrative headquarters. Such a structure has often come about because organisations have grown over time, with the end result being that certain divisions ultimately begin to specialise in certain fields. It is possible that tacit knowledge transference may take place within the individual divisions; however the central headquarters structure of such an organisation would likely diminish the importance placed on tacit knowledge, in favour of structured articulated knowledge, at least in the case of western organisations (Nonaka, Takeuchi, & Umemoto, 1996). A good example of a diversified company would be General Motors Holden (the Australian branch of the US parent company) (http://www.holden.com.au/www-holden/). Notable in such an organisation are a number of sub-divisions, for example manufacturing, new car and second hand car dealerships, a special vehicle division (http://www.hsv.com.au/vz_intro.html), a financial and insurance arm as well as the corporate headquarter component.

The Professional Bureaucracy

The *professional bureaucracy* (Mintzberg, 1991a) carries out complex work by way of its normally tertiary educated staff. The output of the firm is heavily based on knowledge work although the products and services do tend to be relatively standardised. Lam (2000) notes that professional bureaucracies derive much of their capability from *embrained* knowledge (Blackler, 1995), that is to say individual conceptual skills or cognitive abilities. "The professional bureaucracy contains and circumscribes tacit knowledge within the boundary of individual specialization. Tacit knowledge plays only a limited role in a professional bureaucracy: its transfer is inhibited by functional segmentation" (Lam, 2000, p. 498). Because professionals often work independently, they are often reluctant to share their tacit knowledge, one more extreme such example of this problem being noted in law firms[a] (Terrett, 1998), but also documented in other firms (Desouza & Evaristo, 2004). Consequently "the lack of a shared perspective and the formal demarcation of job boundaries inhibit the transfer of non-routine tacit knowledge in the day-to-day work. Moreover the power and status of 'authorised experts' inhibits interaction and the sharing of knowledge with 'non-experts'" (Lam, 2000, p. 495). Furthermore it has been noted (Syed-Ikhsan & Rowland, 2004) that the larger the firm the more likely employees are to regard knowledge as power and withhold it for personal advantage, particularly in public sector organisations. The Minter Ellison law firm (http://www.minterellison.com/public/connect/internet/) would be a good example of a professional bureaucracy with hundreds of professional staff drawing upon stores of tacit knowledge, which in the case of senior partners will have been garnered over many years.

The Innovative Firm

The *innovative firm* (Mintzberg, 1991e) or *operating adhocracy* (Mintzberg, 1983) is often characterised by high technology firms, or companies making one-off specialised products. Teams of people tend to form around particular projects. Given the nature of the product and the intense group work, one need hardly be surprised if a great deal of tacit knowledge is made use of in the company. "The knowledge base of an operating adhocracy is diverse, varied and 'organic.' A large part of the knowledge in use is organic, i.e. tacit knowledge generated through interaction, trial-and-error and experimentation … The frequent re-structuring and shifting of individuals between project teams means that tacit knowledge may not be fully and adequately articulated before an individual moves on" (Lam, 2000 p. 7). In some ways the innovative firm is the opposite to that of the professional bureaucracy. The innovative firm is less stable, makes use of high degrees of collaborative tacit knowledge (where say a legal firm makes use of individualised tacit knowledge), and the tacit knowledge is even less likely to be fully articulated where it may eventually be in bureaucratic firm. It is arguable that AIMTEK mentioned as an entrepreneurial firm, may in fact be an innovative firm, however the structure of AIMTEK as an engineering company indicates stability less likely to be seen in innovative firms. Perhaps a better example of an innovative firm would be a cutting edge software company such as Google (www.google.com), where teams of (typically) young, highly technologically savvy individuals work in and out of different teams on enhancements to the Google products.

The J-Form Organisation

Finally the *J-Form organisation* (Lam, 2000) combines the structure of a bureaucracy with the flexibility of an adhocracy. As noted by Nonaka, many Japanese firms do comprise efficient bureaucratic structures, yet nevertheless permit individual teams a great deal of creative leeway in designing products. The strong corporate culture is important for providing a sense of company togetherness. "The J-form organization has a superior capacity for mobilizing and accumulating tacit knowledge. It allows a team to operate in tandem with a formal hierarchy and stable social organization" (Lam, 2000, p. 499). Perhaps a good example would be the Toyota Company in Japan (http://www.toyota.co.jp/en/) (Rósza, 2003), where Toyota represents a good example of a typical large Japanese firm with a strong management structure but incorporating the Japanese mindset for bottom up innovation and strong teamwork principles.

Having examined organisational types via a very popular typology, it is time to introduce the Organisations under examination in this study, which will be labelled X, Y, and Z for reasons of anonymity.

Large Organisation (X)

Organisation X was founded in 1925, being at that time based in NSW and the ACT. It is now nationally based, operating in every state and territory. Under the Organisation X umbrella, IT service provision takes place for 3.8 million customers within Australia and further 700,000 customers in New Zealand. Today the company has several core businesses, emerging businesses and a recognition given to growth business. The core businesses are those of insurance for motor vehicles, home and contents, compulsory third party for motor related personal injury, workers compensation and asset management. The emerging business component includes the recognition given to the rising prominence of SMEs (Small and Medium sized Enterprises) and their consequent insurance needs, along with emerging business issues such as health insurance and providing retirement solutions. Finally, the growth business component of Organisation X represents a view towards international expansion of the general insurance business of the company. In all, some 10,000 staff in Australia and New Zealand conduct the core business of the organisation.

The IT group in Organisation X exists, as one would expect to support the general business requirements of the firm. In all more than 1,400 personnel are employed in the IT section. The breadth of expertise covered by the IT branch is evidenced through the comprehensive set of workgroup sections.[b] As it turns out the personnel who were actually sent letters were from only a number of these sections, the structure charts for *some* of which[c], are shown here (Figures 5.0a, b, c, d, e, f, g, h, and i in appendix c). The addresses were in fact quite limited, being a group in one location in Melbourne, Victoria, and the main group in one building of George St. in Sydney. A further five letters of the 164 total being sent to a section of Organisation X in Villawood of Sydney. In the case of the Melbourne address the staff were all located on the same floor. In the case of the George St. Sydney address, the staff were located across seven different floors. These last parameters will of course play a role in the upcoming social network analysis. Obviously the type of relationship between individuals is likely to vary enormously dependent upon the physical addresses of staff concerned. For example one would expect physically disparate personnel to make greater use of email and so on. Of the one hundred and eight personnel who did actually participate in the study all were from the Melbourne and George St. Sydney address.

Examining the sample population in depth (Table 1) there were noted to be 32 out of 108 personnel who were rated by their peers at being more than usually proficient in what they did, attaining the label of "expert." In relation to gender, although males made up the overall

Table 1. Demographic details for Organisation X

Response rate			Business Development Manager	1
No. questionnaires mailed	165		Business Systems Analyst	3
Response rate	1 0 8 (65%)		Clerical Support	1
			Computer Engineer	1
Experts vs. Normal			Computer Systems Engineer	1
Experts	32		Contractor	9
Normal	76		Data Administrator	1
Gender			Data Architect	1
Females	40		Database Administrator: Junior	1
Males	68			
Age			Information Modeller	1
20 – 24 years	6		IT Salesperson/Consultant	1
25 – 29 years	9		Network Manager	1
30 – 34 years	6		Programmer	2
35 – 39 years	28		Project Director	1
40 – 44 years	26		Project Manager	19
45 – 49 years	19		Software Engineer	24
50 – 54 years	9		Systems Administrator	5
55 – 59 years	3		**Years of IT Experience**	
60 - 64 years	1		0 – 4 years	15
Undef.	1		5 – 9 years	13
Qualifications			10 – 14 years	23
High School Leaving	4		15 – 19 years	22
Trade Diploma	2		20 – 24 years	19
High School Certificate	14		25 – 29 years	12
Associate Diploma	7		30 – 34 years	2
Bachelor Degree	35		35 – 39 years	1
Honours Bachelor Degree	5		**Position**	
Graduate Certificate	2		Permanent	81
Graduate Diploma	9		Contract	27
Graduate Bachelor	7		**Years with the organization**	
Masters	19		0 – 6 months	9
Doctorate	1		7 – 12 months	20
Higher Doctorate (probably Doctorate)	2		1 – 2 years	34
			3 – 4 years	16
Undef.	1		5 – 6 years	7
Job Titles			7 – 8 years	3
Account manager	1		9 – 10 years	2
Analyst	4		11+ years	17
Analyst: Business	6		**Subordinates responsible for**	
Analyst: Technical	11		None	68
Application programmer	13		1 – 4	15

Table 1. continued

5 – 9	14
10 – 14	2
15 – 19	2
20 – 24	2
25 – 29	1
40 – 44	1
50+	1
Undef.	2
ACS Level	
ACS-0	4
ACS-1	3
ACS-2	25
ACS-3	59
ACS-4	15
ACS-5	1
Undef.	1

sample majority (68), a considerable female cohort also existed (40). Examining the age ranges, the reader can perhaps sense practitioners who are not typically recent graduates, rather having had some workplace experience. One can see for example that the age span tends to form a fairly standard bell curve with the peak age range being 35 to 49 years.

There is evidence (Jorgensen, 2004) to suggest that life-long learning is also important in the modern western organisation for reasons varying from personnel self development through to keeping up with the ever increasing need for a range of skills.[d] And whilst some have found no direct evidence between higher levels of education or training and knowledge transfer in a firm (Syed-Ikhsan & Rowland, 2004), others (Smith, 2001) are of the opinion that at least adequate levels of training arc likely to help employees translate their knowledge into a company's explicit and tacit know how.[e]

With regard to the occupations listed by the respondents, what is noticeable is that a large proportion (roughly 65 percent) identifies themselves as {Technical Analysts, Application Programmers, and Software Engineers} or {Project Managers}. In relation to highest formal qualification obtained by the respondents we see that a substantial minority (about 20 percent) have no more than high school qualifications. Nevertheless roughly 80 percent of the sample are tertiary educated, some even to the level of a doctorate. Perhaps even more importantly, around 10 to 24 years of IT experience claimed by the respondents in Organisation X. Although a number of people are junior with regard experience, there are actually few that have more than 30 years of IT experience, which matches closely with the age ranges mentioned.

What is interesting in the case of Organisation X are the 25 percent of staff on contract employment. Also fascinating are the numbers of staff who have been with the organisation for a relatively short space of time. Whilst this is not atypical for the IT industry, this last trait in combination with high numbers of contract-based staff would present problems from a soft knowledge diffusion point of view. In this case roughly 75 percent of the staff have been with the organisation for less than four years. Note also the number of senior staff (in the order of 15 percent), with more than eleven years service in the organisation. In terms of responsibility levels, one can see that in the order of 65 percent of the staff have no subordinates. Balancing this with the fact that a large proportion of the staff occur in the ACS 2 to 4 level[f], one begins to establish a staff profile of independently working knowledge professionals. It is thus apparent that the organisation whilst having some hierarchy is nevertheless not over hierarchical, which is considered to be helpful from a knowledge creation viewpoint (Jorgensen, 2004).[g]

Scrutinizing the staff breakdown a little more closely through an examination of Figure 1, the reader should remember the lattice structure is read from outside to inside, from top to bottom. Starting with the outer top ellipse, we note there is a lattice structure inside. Reading the lattice from left to right the nodes represent age bands. Moving down to the next level the ellipses from left to right represent males and females in that order. By combining the ellipse (either male on the left, or female on the right) with the internal lattice nodes, a map is created of which ages are well represented for the relevant gender.

In Figure 1, it is possible to see that the age by gender balance is not markedly dissimilar. In other words, there are not many junior female staff with senior male staff, a trend that has historically been associated with female clerical staff leaving employment upon marriage. The age ranges illustrated show almost even breakdowns for each gender for each age range; although admittedly one female did not answer this question (it was not made compulsory).

Of the female staff (Figure 2), one can see that whilst no female ACS-5 exists, a high proportion of the females are ACS level 3s, in other words these females are IT specialists, but not necessarily senior managers. Where the male sample appears to differ is the greater number of ACS level 4s, representing greater numbers of the male sample in middle management,

*Figure 1. Illustrating gender * age*

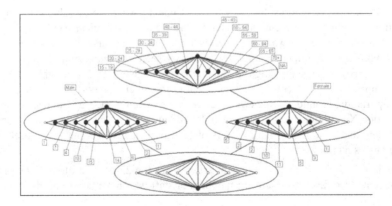

*Figure 2. Illustrating gender * ACS breakdown, numbers of people (males left; females right)*

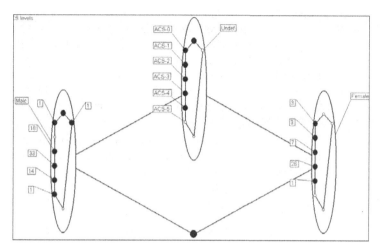

*Figure 3. Illustrating highest qualification * ACS level (everyone)*

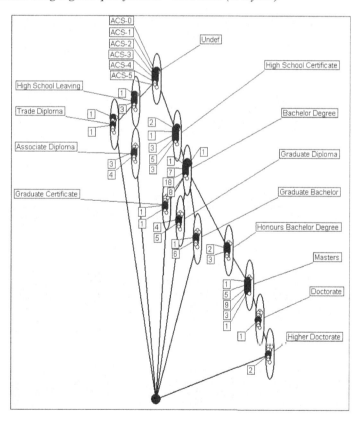

with responsibility for a number of work teams. A quick glance at figure 5.3 reveals no direct correlation[h] between ACS levels and higher formal qualification.

Although one could argue that the CIO holds a masters degree, there are still substantial numbers of ACS level 3s and 4s who have only a bachelor's degree or indeed only a high school certificate. And our doctors are all only level 3s, which may reflect the extra years spent in the educational system at the expense of "on the job" learning. Examining the expert sample specifically (Figure 4), it is interesting to note the lack of doctorates, the presence of high school or trade diploma qualifications, and the relatively low ACS levels. That is to say only six experts are level 4 (roughly 5 percent) of the sample population. Note the number of experts at levels 1 and 2.

Examining the computing specific qualifications (Figure 5), what is most noticeable are the number of IBM qualified personnel (33 staff in all), and the number of staff with Microsoft (28) and Novell qualifications (14). Note also the lack of popularity of Sybase (2 staff),

*Figure 4. Illustrating highest qualification * ACS level (experts specifically)*

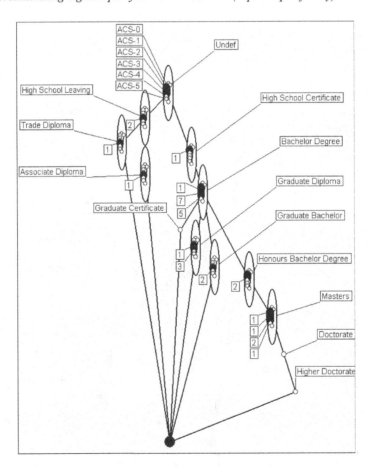

Figure 5. Illustrating computing specific qualifications (everyone)

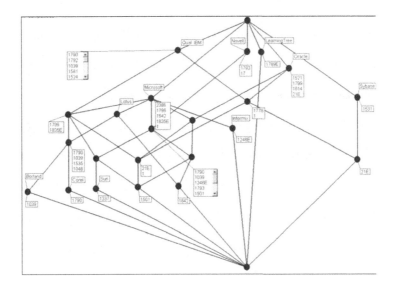

Learning Tree (1), Sun (1), Corel (1) and Borland (1) qualifications. And the relative lack of popularity of Oracle qualifications (10 staff), considering the popularity of Oracle for forming the basis of many organisational applications. Widely popular SAP[i] as a HR[j] package provides us with just one such example of a system with an Oracle backend.

Perhaps the above figures represent the specialisation factor of the software. For example, Novell is Local Area Networking (LAN) specific, being likely to appeal to Network Managers. Whilst Oracle is relational database specific, being likely to appeal to Database Administrators.

Even more marked are the very low numbers of experts specifically with computing technical qualifications (five experts) (Figure 6). Perhaps this reflects either one of two things. First the experts have *so* many technical computing qualifications; they have decided not to list them. Alternatively they really are not trained formally with technical qualifications; rather they are experts because they have learned much of their proficiency on the job.

Remember, experts have not been chosen on the basis of how they answered the tacit knowledge inventory (questionnaire) or because they happen to have computing specific qualifications, or because they have Ph.D.s. Experts have been identified as such by their peers on the basis of being workplace savvy. Of the qualifications they do actually have, these are Learning Tree (1 expert), Informix (2), Oracle (1), Sybase (1), Microsoft (2), Novell (1) and finally IBM (3 experts). This does mean there are 11 individuals, because as the lattice is read the reader will note there are some individuals (e.g. 21E) who have qualifications from all of Sybase, Oracle, Informix and IBM.

Moving onto the influence of multiculturalism (Figure 7), an examination of the languages other than English utilised by respondents in Organisation X is also interesting. For example,

Figure 6. Illustrating computing specific qualifications (experts only)

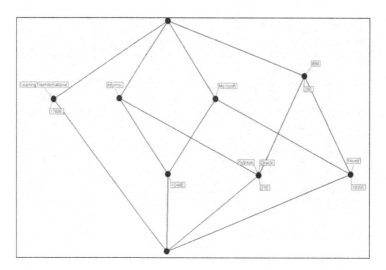

note (1) the number of Chinese speakers, whether Mandarin, Hokkien, Hakka, or Cantonese. Observe also (2) the numbers of experts who speak these languages, but Cantonese primarily. The number of such experts could also imply one of two things. Firstly, those Chinese speakers are in some way proportionately more expert than non-Chinese speakers. If this is the case, then it would suggest that people from these backgrounds have had to try even harder than native English speakers in gaining expertise, given the language difficulties people from such backgrounds ordinarily have to face. Or secondly, those Chinese speakers are perhaps choosing other Chinese speakers as experts. There is also evidence of a certain

Figure 7. Illustrating language other than English

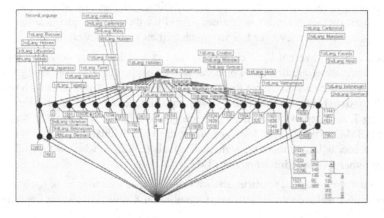

amount of cliquing taking place among Cantonese speakers. This last point in particular has serious ramifications for likely tacit knowledge transfer.

Simplifying language along the following lines (Table 2), a slightly different representation of language groups (Figure 8) is revealed. Nevertheless the point still remains that East

Table 2.Illustrating simplified language groups (LOE)

Original Lang.	Simplified Language
Assyrian	MiddleEast
Belorussian	EastEurope
Bosnian	EastEurope
Bulgarian	EastEurope
Cantonese	EastAsia
Chinese	EastAsia
Croatian	EastEurope
French	WestEurope
German	WestEurope
Greek	SouthEurope
Hakka	EastAsia
Hebrew	EastEurope
Hindi	SouthAsia
Hokkien	EastAsia
Hungarian	EastEurope

Indonesian	SouthEastAsia
Japanese	EastAsia
Kanada	SouthAsia
Korean	EastAsia
Lithuanian	EastEurope
Malay	SouthEastAsia
Mandarin	EastAsia
Mauritian Creole	Mauritian
Persian	MiddleEast
Russian	EastEurope
Serbian	EastEurope
Spanish	SouthEurope
Tagalog	EastAsia
Tamil	SouthAsia
Ukrainian	EastEurope
Vietnamese	EastAsia
Yiddish	EastEurope

Figure 8. Illustrating language groups (LOE) of Organisation X

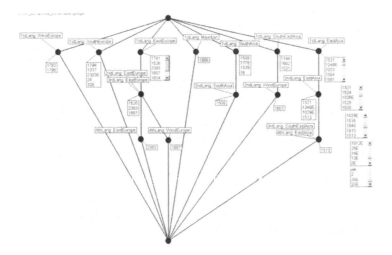

Figure 9. Illustrating job now (experts only)

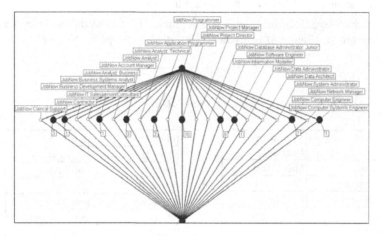

Asian languages (meaning largely the Chinese languages) predominate as second languages spoken amongst respondents in Organisation X. Once again note the numbers of experts in this group.

Whilst on the subject of experts, pay particular attention to the jobs the experts currently hold. Examining Figure 9 below, the occupations have generally been laid out from soft on the left to hard on the right in terms of the computing spectrum. Occupations presently held by the experts include contractor (3 experts), IT sales person/consultant (1) {business analyst (1), analyst (3), software engineer (9), information modeller (1), also project manager (10), network manager (1) computer systems engineer (1) and application programmer (2). There seems to be a grouping of experts in the business analysis domain with an emphasis on determining the organisation's information systems needs. Alternatively there is another grouping of experts who are managers, either of projects or networks. Finally there are some other experts, much smaller in numbers who have more specific technical jobs such as the computer systems engineers or application programmers.

What were the experts doing three years ago? First, a brief examination of Figure 10 reveals that the roles appear more diverse than the roles they currently hold. Re-grouping the occupations according to job similarity and we find experts {were not in the industry (2 experts)}, contacting (2), {information management consultants (1), business systems planners (1), business systems analysts (1), analysts (2), implementation officers (1)}. A number were managing tasks: {project managers (1), data architects (2) and network administrators (1)}. Finally, note also the numbers employed as application programmers (1), programmers (1) database administrators (1), software engineers (5), systems programmers (1), computer systems engineers (1), and computer scientists (1), in other words technical roles. Two points arise from these observations. Firstly, as mentioned the experts three years ago were more diverse in their occupations than they currently are. Secondly, they appear to have been better represented in technical roles than they presently are.

Figure 10. Illustrating occupation 3 years ago (experts)

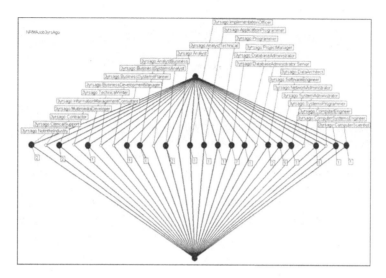

Organisation X Summary

In conclusion what type of profile can be established for respondents in Organisation X? The experts can be defined to some degree by their proportionately larger presence in "softer" computing roles, which become clear when comparing the results from the concept lattice with the numbers of people for each of the computing roles shown in the initial table (Table 1). Organisation X is quite multicultural, for 53 of the 108 staff actually speak at least one language other than English. Although only 18 experts out of a total sample population of 108 do speak a foreign language, it is interesting to note the proportion that speaks one of the Chinese languages. The differences between experts and novices in the way of technical computing qualifications are also interesting. Why is it that experts have so few in comparison? In terms of the gender makeup of our sample, the populations are actually relatively evenly spread. Granted there are more male than female respondents, the proportions in the age and ACS categories are quite even. This tends to imply that gender roles are not necessarily clearly delineated which would be expected for knowledge professionals. Admittedly, there are slightly larger numbers of males proportionately in the senior ACS levels. The sample population is composed predominantly of IT professionals (with a few clerical staff) clustered around a middle management level. A large proportion (38 out of 108 participants) is responsible for supervising at least one individual, indicating there are a number of project teams or technical groups working together. The staff is around 35 to 50 years of age. They typically have 10 to 15 years IT experience. They have not necessarily been with the present organisation for a long time, most less than four years. They tend to be tertiary educated, a small proportion even hold doctorates. They mostly are permanently employed by the organisation. The experts also seem to have slightly lower academic qualifications than the average respondents. Having established a feel for Organisation X, the next company presents a very different type of firm, both in terms of mission and size.

Small Organisation (Y)

Preparing the organization is the first step in developing a "knowledge culture" and often involves changing the culture of the organization, changing the way employees work and interact. Organizational culture shifts are difficult to accomplish (Roth, 2004). Smaller organizations, 200 or fewer employees, and newer entrepreneurial organizations will have an advantage in making the prescribed culture shift over larger and older organizations that have a long history of corporate culture and a more rigid managerial structure (Becerra-Fernandez, Gonzalez, & Sabherwal, 2004 in Walczak, 2005, p. 331).

Organisation Y is in many ways quite different from that of Organisation X. It is an independent Australian management consultancy, which was founded in 1983. With very much of a management focus on corporate information and the usage of IT in these processes, Organisation Y's workforce also differs with a leaning toward what would be labelled "front office" as opposed to "back office" IT staff (Figure 11). Indeed, the company actively recruits staff along the lines of Information Specialists, Information Managers, Information Architects, Project Managers, Strategic Planners and Business Analysts. These recruitment areas of interest are reflected in a staff profile where almost all staff has had some prior management experience. Figure 11 also reveals where the experts are located (in green), which will be discussed in further detail Chapter 12.

The organisation sees itself as able to inform business as to the strengths and weaknesses of IT. In other words the company's expertise is grounded not so much in fixing specific technical problems at the machine level, or indeed in implementing new systems, rather

Figure 11. Structure chart of Organisation Y

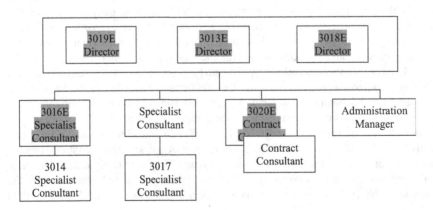

advising businesses what types of systems or strategies would best suit their needs. Unlike the IT group under study in Organisation X, Organisation Y is very externally focused. Its source of revenue comes from various State and Commonwealth agencies as well as private companies throughout Australia. Its particular strength is familiarity with the NSW Government's information management and technology direction.

Staff in the organisation number 15, of whom eight IT staff were invited by the CIO to participate in the research. Seven personnel eventually ended up doing so. These staff were the core IT professionals of the organisation. The remaining staff members are administrative. An examination of Table 3 reveals that only one of the seven staff is female and that the ages represented vary from 30 to 34 up to as old as 55 to 59 years of age.

Notice how the range of jobs is limited; all seem to be either {Business Analysts or Information Management Consultants}. Observe also that no-one has anything less than a bachelor's degree with two also having a master's degree. Considering the size of the group, one may also note that the range of IT experience tends to be weighted towards more senior personnel, with five of the seven respondents having more than 10 years of IT experience. The staffing also seems to be relatively stable with only one of the staff members being on contract. With regard to the years served with the organisation, one may note the presence of some relatively junior staff having been with the firm less than four years. Nevertheless, this is evenly balanced with four of the staff members having served anywhere from five to more than 11 years. One can see that of the seven consultants, five have no subordinates, with two having between five to nine subordinates. This would tend to imply the structure of the firm is quite flat with a group of professionals conducting their knowledge work and one or two superiors who handle the overall executive decisions of this organisation. Indeed, discussions with the CIO, or rather CKO (chief knowledge officer in this instance), confirms this is actually the case. Finally the ACS levels reveal an even spread of staff experience ranges, with perhaps some concentration at the level 3 and 4 range.

Let us examine the staff profile of Organisation Y in a little further detail. There is one female who is between 35 to 39 years of age. The remaining males are generally toward to the senior end of the spectrum, for five of them are in their 50s. The remaining male is young like the female staff member, in this case 30 to 34 years of age. The experts have all been identified as being males and their ACS levels range from level 2 up to level 5. The only two novices are one male and the female both at ACS level 3. There appears to be a perfect positive correlation between the age of the males and the incidence of them being declared experts. All of the males aged in their 50s (5 of them) have been considered by their peers to be "proficient at what they do".

Investigating the formal qualifications of the staff in Figure 12 below, the reader may note the one female holds a masters degree. Only one other male holds this level of qualification. This male is an "expert." At the other end of the spectrum the other novice (male) holds a bachelors degree. The remaining males (all experts) hold at least a bachelors degree, if not a graduate diploma or an honours bachelor's degree.

Turning our attention to the very important construct of years of IT experience and whether or not the employee is permanently employed (Figure 13), there is one expert with 10 to 14 years of IT experience who is on contract. Although this solitary staff member may only be considered a singular individual, being an expert on contract may mean that important knowledge will be lost if the contract expires within the short term.

Table 3. Demographic details for Organisation Y

Response rate	
No. questionnaires mailed	8
Response rate	7 (87.5%)
Gender	
Female	1
Male	6
Age	
30 – 34 years	1
35 – 39 years	1
50 – 54 years	4
55 – 59 years	1
Highest Qualification	
Bachelor Degree	2
Graduate Diploma	1
Honours Bachelors Degree	2
Masters	2
Current job title	
Analyst: Business	1
Business Systems Analyst	2
Information Management Consultant	4
Years of IT Experience	
0 – 4 years	1
5 - 9 years	1
10 – 14 years	3
30 – 34 years	2
Position	
Permanent	6
Contract	1
Years with the organization	
1 – 2 years	2
3 – 4 years	1
5 – 6 years	2
11+	2
No. of Subordinates	
None	5
5 – 9	2
ACS levels	
ACS-2	1
ACS-3	3
ACS-4	2
ACS-5	1

*Figure 12. Illustrating highest qualification * ACS level*

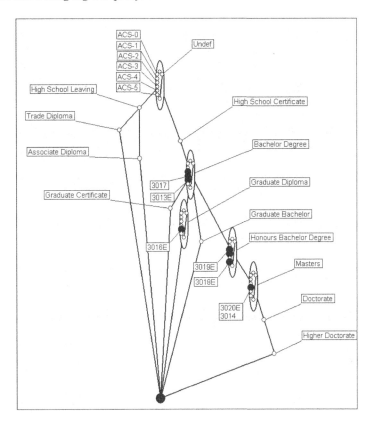

Examining both the current and prior occupations of our respondents (Figure 14), the major observable difference between the experts and novices seems to be that in the case of the latter, they were not in the IT industry three years ago (both the male and female, female = 3014) or even six years ago (just the male).

Examining a slightly more complex concept lattice (Figure 15), observe experts 3020, 3013, 3018, and 3016 seem to be closer to one other. Expert 3019, whilst nevertheless noted by peers to be an expert, appears to share certain attributes with the two novices, for example his job title (Business Systems Analyst). Interestingly his ACS level (2) is also fairly low for this organisation.

As a final point of note, the one female is also the multicultural individual. She speaks Cantonese and Malay as languages other than English.

*Figure 13. Permanent vs. contract employee * years of IT experience*

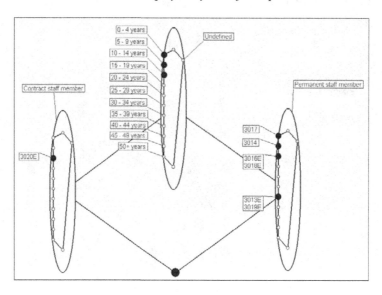

Figure 14. Illustrating occupation now, three years ago and six years ago

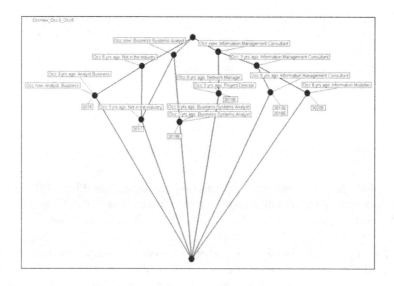

*Figure 15. Illustrating age * current job title * years of IT experience * current ACS level*

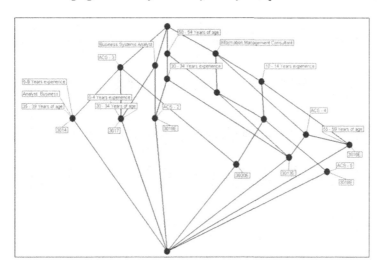

Organisation Y Summary

An examination of this firm provides us with a staff profile that is senior in terms of age; basically mono-cultural and made up of very experienced staff for the size of the organisation. This last point should not surprise us given the mission of the company is to sell management expertise. All of the staff is tertiary educated. The structure of the firm appears very flat. The proportion of individuals identified as experts would indicate quite a close working relationship with one another. This organisation would indeed appear to be a professional bureaucracy along Mintzberg lines. The next company presents a profile similar to Organisation X, although on a smaller scale.

Medium Organisation (Z)

The IT group in Organisation Z (Figure 16) were essentially similar to that of **Organisation X**, insofar as they were a support group for the wider organisation. This company deals in home and office furnishings and was first founded in 1981 at St. Leonards in N.S.W. By 1984 the organisation had branched into Victoria and in 1986 into the A.C.T. By 1998 the firm had 36 stores both in Australia and New Zealand and began to acquire other companies. The company had grown to 62 stores throughout Australia and New Zealand by the year 2000, employing 1,700 people.

Figure 16. Structure chart for Organisation Z

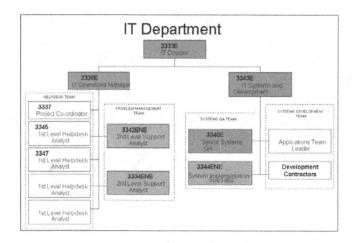

The IT support section is heavily involved in sustaining the logistics section whose job it is in turn to make sure the shops are reliably supplied with goods through various sourcing, tracking and distribution systems. This infrastructure supports not only the needs of the store in determining whether the warehouse has the product in stock, but also the customer who expects to be able to have something delivered within a few days at most. The IT group consists of 16 personnel of whom 13 elected to participate in the study. Of these 13, one chose not to provide biographical information. One can see from Figure 16 that the experts (green) and expert non-experts (ENE) (blue) are dispersed around the group, although the experts seem to be concentrated somewhat more in the senior ranks. Turning our attention to examining their biographical details in some depth, Table 4 reveals that the population is overwhelmingly male, with one female.

The ages tend to be evenly spread from 20 up to 59 years of age. Current job roles tend to vary from contracting through to help desk support and programming. Other job titles are those of project director or project manager. The Organisation Z sample appears to be tertiary educated with the overwhelming majority holding at least a bachelors degree with a couple possessing a master's degree. With respect to the samples' general years of IT experience, this is seen to vary from 0-4 years (5 people) and up to 20-24 years for a couple of them. Generally they are permanent employees with only three noting they are on contract employment. In terms of how long the sample group has been with the company, this tends to vary from one who has been with the organisation for less than a year, through to someone has been with the organisation up to 10 years. In fact this last individual is the CIO. The ACS levels of the personnel vary, but they do tend to be at least level 2, and two have indicated they are at CIO level. The CIO himself is obviously one of these. Our expert sample is all male, from ACS level 2 up to level 5. The experts themselves are specifically ACS level 2, 3 and 5. The one female happens to be a level 2. In addition the experts seem to either be young (25 –34) or senior (55-59) in age.

Table 4. Demographic details for Organisation Z

Response rate		
No. questionnaires mailed		16
Response rate	13 (81%)	
Gender		
Female		1
Male		10
Undef		2
Age		
20 – 24 years		3
25 – 29 years		2
30 – 34 years		3
35 – 39 years		2
50 – 54 years		2
55 – 59 years		1
Highest Qualification		
High School Certificate		2
Bachelor Degree		6
Graduate Certificate		1
Graduate Diploma		1
Masters		2
Current job title		
Business Development Manager		1
Business Systems Analyst		1
Contractor		1
Help Desk Support		3
Network Manager		1
Programmer		1
Project Director		1
Project Manager		1

Software Engineer	1
System Administrator	1
Undef	1
Years of IT Experience	
0 – 4 years	5
5 - 9 years	3
10 – 14 years	2
20 – 24 years	2
Position	
Permanent	9
Contract	3
Years with the organization	
7 – 12 months	1
1 – 2 years	3
3 – 4 years	1
5 – 6 years	3
7 – 8 years	2
9 – 10 years	1
No. of Subordinates	
None	6
1 – 4	3
5 – 9	2
15 – 19	1
ACS levels	
ACS-2	4
ACS-3	5
ACS-4	1
ACS-5	2

Examining Figure 17, one can see that an expert lies in the 55-59 years of age bracket (3340E), but is an ACS-3. Another expert is 50 to 54 years of age, but is actually an ACS level 5; this individual is actually the CIO. Interestingly, the other ACS level 5 is a male aged 30-34 years of age. One gets the impression this individual is either very good or perhaps egotistical. Notice the youngest age bracket 20-24 years of age, seems to have no experts.

Qualification-wise, most of the experts (4) have a bachelor's degree whilst one has a master degree. The novices seem for the most part to have bachelor's degrees (2), graduate certificates (1), graduate diplomas (1) and one has a master's degree. What largely differentiates the novice group is that two of them have nothing higher than a high school certificate. In

*Figure 17. Age * ACS level*

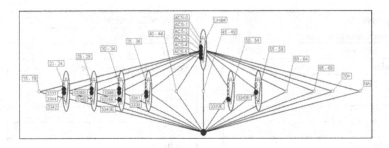

short, whilst the experts are on the whole relatively well educated formally, the novice's formal qualifications tend to be variable.

The computing specific qualifications (Figure 18) obtained by the sample population in Organisation Z are those of Oracle (2 individuals), Sun Microsystems (1), Lotus Notes (2), and Microsoft (6). Of the experts, one has an Oracle qualification; the other has a qualification from Microsoft. As an aside it is interesting to note that once again along the lines of Organisation X, the expert sample are not necessarily well qualified with regard to computing specific qualifications. This may just be because the experts had too many computing qualifications (as opposed to formal qualifications) and couldn't be bothered listing them.

Figure 18. Computing specific qualifications

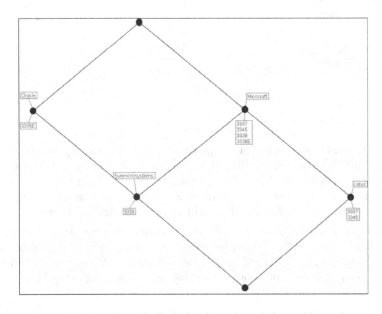

Alternatively, this phenomenon could be due to the fact that our experts *are* experts because of their practical know-how rather than because they have gained other workplace specific qualifications.

In terms of employment type, one of the experts happens to be a contract employee. The other experts are all permanent staff members. At the same time, the expert who is a contract employee has been with Organisation Z for between seven and eight years. The remaining experts who are on permanent staff have between five and 10 years with the organisation. The novice sample on both permanent and contract employment tend to have less than five years of experience with the firm in which they are employed. With regard to their IT experience however, the picture is a little more complex, in that although there may be other people who have longer periods of IT experience, this does not necessarily make them experts. Indeed, with regard to the contract staff, the expert has five to nine years of IT experience, but there are another couple of staff members with 10 to 14 years of IT experience who are not considered to be experts. In a somewhat similar fashion with regard to the permanent staff, only one staff member with zero to four years of IT experience is considered an expert, another four in the same category are not. Nevertheless one expert does have five to nine years of IT experience, whilst another two experts on permanent staff do have 20-24 years of IT experience.

In terms of the relationship between superiors and subordinates, there does appear to be a strong correlation between a higher number of subordinates and being identified as an expert. The number of people subordinate to experts varies anywhere from five to 19. There is however one expert who is a contract member of staff with no subordinates. Alternatively, we have a contract novice who is responsible for five to nine personnel. Generally speaking, the novices seem to have no subordinates except some have anywhere from one to four staff members under them.

The occupations held by experts (Figure 19) also reveal some interesting patterns. In terms of the occupations held at present by this group of personnel, they tend to be {Project

Figure 19. Illustrating occupation six years ago, three years ago and now

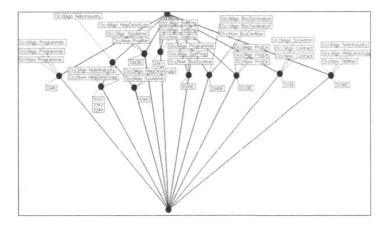

Manager, Project Director}, {Business Systems Analyst, Business Development Manager} and {Network Manager}. The novices on the other hand seem to currently be concentrated in roles such as {Programmer, Software Engineer and Systems Administration} or {Help Desk Support}. Occupations have been grouped according to similarity. There is almost a perfect positive correlation between experts being concentrated in managerial or otherwise "front office" positions, with novices heavily concentrated in "back office" or more technical roles. Perhaps this is indicative of the smaller size of Organisation Z? In the previous organisation, experts were grouped in managerial roles, as this company was a management consultancy. In Organisation X experts were located in "softer" computing roles, but not necessarily always in a management capacity.

Three years ago, as one would expect, their roles were somewhat different (Figure 19). The experts were {Systems Administrator, Systems Programmer}, {Business Systems Analyst}, {Project Director} and {Help Desk Support}. The novices were {Not in the industry}, {Programmer, Software Engineer}, {Help Desk Support}. What this seems to indicate is that the experts had previously "done some time" in the technical areas, but were nevertheless in the IT industry, whereas some of the novices at this stage were not necessarily involved in a computing related job.

Six years ago, the picture changes slightly once again (Figure 19). As one would expect a slightly higher number were not in the industry. Beginning with the experts, their jobs were {Help Desk Support}, {Programmer}, {Business Systems Analyst}, {Project Director}, {Not in the industry}. In other words, the backgrounds become more diversified. Examining the

Figure 20. Illustrating language groups (LOE) for Organisation Z

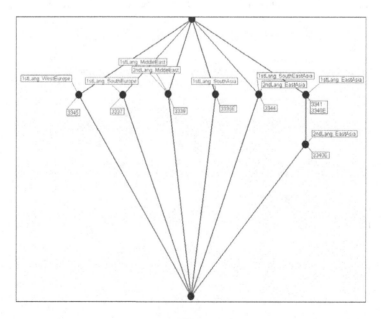

novice sample we find their positions were {Programmer}, {Not in the industry}, {Software Engineer}, {Systems Administrator}.

Languages other than English spoken by the IT staff in Organisation Z reveals quite some degree of multiculturalism, taking language other than English spoken as an indication of this characteristic. Remembering that one participant did not include biographical details, we still find seven out of 13 respondents spoke a language other than English. In all, eight languages other than English were represented. They were in order of popularity {Cantonese, Mandarin}, followed by at least one instance each of {Greek, French, Hindi, Persian, Assyrian and Indonesian}. Of the experts, one spoke Hindi, the other spoke Cantonese as well as Mandarin. The remaining experts (3) spoke no language other than English. Simplifying the language groups we can see the language breakdown in the following concept lattice (Figure 20), with a noticeable orientation again toward the east-Asian language grouping.

Organisation Z Summary

To summarise, we find Organisation Z is quite different from Y. It is substantially more multicultural with effectively 50 percent of its IT staff being non-Anglo-Celtic Australian. Next, the expert sample quite noticeably differs from the novices in terms of job profiles. That is to say, the experts seem to be in more managerial and/or "front office" type positions. Conversely, novices appear to be in more technical roles. Furthermore, there appears to be a strong positive correlation between being considered to be an expert and having a number of subordinates. There seems only to be a weak positive correlation between IT experience in this Organisation and being considered to be an expert. There is a strong positive correlation in this company with expertise and length of tenure in the organisation. Experts have generally been present for more than 5 years; the opposite is true of novices. Again, the experts are not particularly well qualified from a technical computing qualification point of view; however they are consistently better formally educated *on the whole* than the novices as a group. The experts appear to be either "young guns" or they are "grey haired".

Organisations and Mintzberg

Reflecting on the categories of organisations as defined by Mintzberg (1991a-e), of the three firms (X, Y, and Z) examined in this study (Table 5), **Organisation Y** (a small specialised firm) could be said to comprise either an *operating adhocracy* or a *professional bureaucracy*. Such a classification disparity depends on the type of work being undertaken by the firm. As an information systems management consultancy company, some of their work would be routine, other knowledge work would be unique. **Organisation X** is in reality a very large nationally based *diversified company*, however the IT branch within that firm, which is the section under study, operates as a combination of a *machine bureaucracy* and a *professional bureaucracy*. That is to say, although the IT branch acts as a support structure for the *diversified organisation*, professionals within the wider company nevertheless conduct a lot of knowledge work, which is far from standard on a day to day basis. The IT group in

Table 5. Mintzberg organisational types with our Organisations under study (TK = Tacit Knowledge) (Busch 2006)

	Entrepreneurial	Diversified	Machine	Professional	Innovative	J-Form
Staff Nos.	Few	Many	Many	Few	Few	Many
Leadership	Flat	Hierarchical	Hierarchical	Flat	Flat	Hierarchical
Work Type	Semi-routine	Semi-routine	Routine	Complex	Complex	Semi-routine
Products	Tang./Intang.	Tangible	Tangible	Intangible	Tang./Intang.	Tang./Intang.
TK usage	High	Medium	Low	Inhibited	High	Medium

········ = Organisation X   ⌣ = Organisation Y   ⌐ = Organisation Z

Organisation Z is in fact similar to the IT group in organisation X, except on a much smaller scale. At the same time, we also are able to classify these firms by size. These firms were also chosen because they represented examples of what may be called small (Y), medium (Z), and large (X). The first two firms in this case being SMEs,[k] the definition for which is that they employ up to 250 personnel.[l m]

Summary

The Organisations under study have been introduced. Organisation X was an insurance firm with a large IT component. Organisation Y was a much smaller ICT management consultancy. Organisation Z was essentially a smaller version of X. The staff complement varied in each of the firms, perhaps most noticeably with regard to ethnic makeup, from highly multicultural firms (X, Z) to very mono-culturally Anglo-Celtic Australian (Y). To provide some framework to organisational context, Mintzberg's categories have been applied to Companies X, Y, and Z. Remembering the reasons for the application of such a framework, are firstly that it is easier to comprehend the company type dealt with and also because there is some evidence that organisation type is likely to have an effect on soft knowledge flows. Using Mintzberg's classification, Organisations X, Y, and Z are noted to be either machine or professional in nature. Having examined organisations, the attention is now directed toward the topic of knowledge flows in firms.

References

Becerra-Fernandez, I., Gonzalez, A., & Sabherwal, R. (2004). *Knowledge management challenges, solutions, and technologies.* Upper Saddle River, NJ: Pearson Prentice Hall.

Betcherman, G., & Chaykowski, R. (1998). *The Changing Workplace and Public Policy.* Retrieved July 14, 2006 from: http://www.sdc.gc.ca/en/cs/sp/sdc/pkrf/publications/bulletins/1997-000006/page10.shtml

Blackler, F. (1995). Knowledge, knowledge work and organizations: An overview and Interpretation. *Organization Studies, (16),* 1021-1046.

Busch, P. (2006). Organisation design and tacit knowledge transferal: An examination of three IT firms. *Journal of Knowledge Management Practice, 7*(2).

Cavusgil, S.T., Calantone, R.J., & Zhao, Y. (2003). Tacit knowledge transfer and firm innovation capacity. *Journal of Business and Industrial Marketing, 18*(1), 6-21.

Colonia-Willner, R.(1999). Investing in practical intelligence: Ageing and efficiency among executives. *International Journal of Behavioral Development, 23*(3), 591-614.

Curtain, R. (1998). The workplace of the future: Insights from futures scenarios and today's high performance workplaces. *Australian Bulletin of Labour, 24*(4), 279-294.

Dampney, C., Busch, P., & Richards, D. (2002). The meaning of tacit knowledge. *Australian Journal of Information Systems,* December, 3-13.

Desouza, K.C., & Evaristo, J.R. (2004). Managing knowledge in distributed projects. *Communications of the ACM, 47*(4), 87-91.

Glenn, G. (1995). *Serving Australia: The Australian defence force in the twenty first century.* Retrieved October 18, 2002 from: http://defweb.cbr.defence.gov.au/documents/DATA/DEFPUBS/PORTDOCS/SERVAUST/SERVPRE.PDF

Hall, C. (1995). *APEC and SME POLICY: Suggestions for an Action Agenda.* Retrieved July 14, 2006 from: http://www.apec.org.au/docs/iss1.htm

Johnston, D. (1998). Lifelong learning for all. *OECD Observer,* No. 214, October/November. Retrieved July 14, 2006 from: http://www1.oecd.org/publications/observer/214/editorial_eng.htm

Jorgensen, B. (2004). Individual and organisational learning: A model for reform for public organisations. *Foresight, 6*(2), 91-103.

Lam, A. (2000). Tacit knowledge, organizational learning, and societal institutions: An integrated framework. *Organization Studies, 21*(3), 487-513.

Mintzberg, H. (1991a). The professional organisation. In *The Strategy Process: Concepts, Contexts, Cases,* 2nd Ed. Englewood Cliffs, NJ: Prentice Hall, pp. 704-717.

Mintzberg, H. (1991b). The entrepreneurial organisation. In *The Strategy Process: Concepts, Contexts, Cases,* 2nd Ed. Englewood Cliffs, NJ: Prentice Hall, 604-613.

Mintzberg, H. (1991c). The machine organisation. In *The Strategy Process: Concepts, Contexts, Cases,* 2nd Ed. Englewood Cliffs, NJ: Prentice Hall, pp. 630-646.

Mintzberg, H. (1991d). The diversified organisation. In *The Strategy Process: Concepts, Contexts, Cases,* 2nd Ed. Englewood Cliffs, NJ: Prentice Hall, pp. 666-677.

Mintzberg, H. (1991e). The innovative organisation. In *The Strategy Process: Concepts, Contexts, Cases,* 2nd Ed. Englewood Cliffs, NJ: Prentice Hall, pp. 731-746.

Mintzberg, H. (1983). *Structures in fives: Designing effective organisations.* Englewood Cliffs, NJ: Prentice Hall Inc.

Nelson, D. (Ed.) (1998). *Dictionary of Mathematics* 2nd Ed. London: Penguin Books.

Nonaka, I., Takeuchi, H., & Umemoto, K. (1996). A theory of organisational knowledge creation. *International Journal of Technology Management, 11*(7/8), 833-845.

Pierce, J., & Delbecq, A. (1977). Organization structure, individual attitudes and innovation. *Academy of Management Review, 2*(1), 26-37.

Rósza, A. (2003). Just-in-time system in terms of real options. *Proceedings of Conference on Institutional and Policy Diversity-Its role in Economic Development,* Debrecen, Hungary, November 3-5, 1-11.

Roth, G. (2004). Lessons from the desert: Integrating managerial expertise and learning for organizational transformation. *The Learning Organization, 11*(3), 194-208.

Smith, E. (2001). The role of tacit and explicit knowledge in the workplace. *Journal of Knowledge Management, 5*(4), 311-321.

Syed-Ikhsan, S., & Rowland, F. (2004). Knowledge management in a public organization: A study on the relationship between organizational elements and the performance of knowledge transfer. *Journal of Knowledge Management, 8*(2), 95-111.

Terrett, A. (1998). Knowledge management and the law firm. *Journal of Knowledge Management, 2*(1), 67-76.

UK Cabinet Office (2001). *In demand-adult skills in the 21st century, Part 2.* Retrieved July 14, 2006 from: http://www.strategy.gov.uk/downloads/su/wfd_2/report/downloads/su-adult-skills.pdf

Van der Heijden, B. (2002). Prerequisites to guarantee life-long employability. *Personnel Review, 31*(1), 44-61.

von Krogh, G., Ichijo, K., & Nonaka, I. (2000). *Enabling knowledge creation: How to unlock the mystery of tacit knowledge and release the power of innovation.* New York: Oxford University Press, Inc.

Walczak, S. (2005). Organizational knowledge management structure. *The Learning Organization, 12*(4), 330-339.

Wyn, J. (2001). Education and training in the new economy: Future, funding, policy, and industry outcomes. *The First National Conference for the Education for Work Coalition.* University of Melbourne, Australia: Centre for Public Policy.

Zimmer, I., & McKern, B. (2000). *A review into military postgraduate education.* Retrieved from July 14, 2006 from: http://www.defence.gov.au/dpe/dpe_site/publications/zimmer.pdf

Endnotes

[a]   Terrett (1998) notes that lawyers, partly due to their competitive nature are often reluctant to work with another or in teams. The implicit feeling being that knowledge is power, particularly

the tacit component. We should understand however that the feeling of knowledge as power is not limited to law firms, but often to companies in general (Desouza & Evaristo, 2004).

[b]   Account Management; Account Services; Business Intelligence Systems; Business Requirements Engineering Team; Business Solutions; Business Solutions Management; CFO (Chief Financial Officer) Information Services; Claims Systems; CTP (Compulsory Third Party)/Workers Compensation Team; Customer Data Management; Customer Support Services; Deliver 2001 Host IS; Deliver 2001 Workbench IS; Development Environments & Tools; Documentation Design & Development; Financial Services; H Development; H Services; Infrastructure Projects; IS Commercial Management; IS Front End Development; IS H Core System; IS IT Victoria; IS Lotus Notes Team; IS Management Services; IS Operations; IS Program Office; IS SAP Basis; IS SAP Development; Manager Administration Support; Member Services IT&T; Middleware; National Product Platform User Group; National Test Centre; Online Receipting; Operations; Print Logistics; Print Logistics Team; Printing & BMT; Product Analysis; Product Services & Claims; Production Enablement; Production Support; Project Assurance; SAP Contract Development Team; SAP Systems; SE - CRM & Integration System; SE (Software Engineering) SD&I Claims; SE Application Architecture; SE Environment Support; SE Insurance Systems; SE Member Services & Receipting Systems; SE Professional Development; SE Quality & Productivity; S IT Group Facilities; S IT Business Systems; S IT Group Communication & Desktop Sys; S IT Technical Services; Software Development Esprit IT; Software Engineering; Software Engineering Victoria; Sol Development IBM/GSA; Contractors; Solutions Development Staff; South Australia Business Solutions; Strategy Planning & Architecture; Victoria Workers Compensation; Western Australia Business Solutions; Windows & Unix Solutions.

[c]   Only some organisational structure charts were provided for the researcher by Organisation X. Further charts were noted as being unavailable.

[d]   "The rationale for life-long-learning comes from the needs and aspirations of the individual, the technological developments that demand a continuous renewal and updating of skills and the evolving job descriptions associated with the rapidly diversifying market conditions of the modern economy" (Glenn, 1995; Johnston, 1998, in Jorgensen, 2004, p. 94).

"Study and work increasingly overlap and careers are less secure (Wyn, 2001) ... Zimmer and McKern (2000) argue that the reliance on individual effort to achieve postgraduate qualifications (part-time), in the absence of broader organisational support, places significant stress on individuals ... there is a trend in the West for life-long learning to become an essential for both employability and career progression" (Betcherman & Chaykowski, 1998; UK Cabinet Office, 2001; Van der Heijden, 2002, in Jorgensen, 2004, p. 95).

[e]   "Zackarias et al. (2001, p. 7) and Smith (2001, p. 421) claim that adequate training may enable employees to translate their knowledge into the organisations tacit and explicit knowledge, whereas those who lack training will have to struggle to keep up. However, the Spearman test shows that there is no significant relationship between training and knowledge transfer performance but shows a positive significant relationship with knowledge assets" (Syed-Ikhsan & Rowland, 2004, pp. 108-109).

[f]   ACS stands for the Australian Computer Society. There are basically five levels of relevance here, beginning with **Level 1** (recent graduate):

Level 1: "Little practical experience in IT work, may be supervising ancillary staff"

Level 2: "Experienced and capable of performing a wide range of IT work"

Level 3. "Experienced in specialised IT areas, well developed liaison skills"

Level 4: "Managing a number of teams and the allocation of resources"

Level 5: "Typically report to CEO, manage major function, extensive IT coordination"

Copyright © 2008, IGI Global. Copying or distributing in print or electronic forms without written permission of IGI Global is prohibited.

Finally **Level 0**: "Clerical computing work, not graduate level" was added by the author to permit a few secretarial staff to participate in the study.

[g]   "... the literature suggests that traditional forms of hierarchy and control can interfere with the development of the strong relationships required to enable knowledge creation" (van Krogh, Ichijo, & Nonaka, 2000, in Jorgensen, 2004, p. 95).

[h]   "... correlation between two or more quantities denotes an interdependence between them ... Data pairs that show a close relationship are said to be highly correlated. High correlation need not imply causal relationship" (Nelson, 1998, p. 88). Correlation in this empirical study is used in the social science sense of the term whereby an implication is drawn there is some relation between two or more variables. Typically the term would be used in relation to either a weak, strong or perfect positive or alternatively negative correlation.

[i]   Systeme, Anwendungen, Produkte/Systems, Applications, Products: Popular German software for most facets of organisational usage.

[j]   Human Resources.

[k]   Small and Medium sized Enterprises. This is a term that has become popular in recent times, particularly with the introduction of electronic commerce.

[l]   The term SME varies somewhat from country to country, however it is noted that "over 95 percent of SMEs employ less than 100 people, and most employ less than 50 people" (Hall, 1995).

[m]   We must remember that whilst Organisation Z employed 1,700 people nationally, the IT sector was much smaller (with 16 personnel). Organisation X on the other hand had more than 1,400 people employed in the IT section alone, and was clearly not an SME for this reason.

Chapter VI

Knowledge Flows

Tacit knowledge is automatic, resembles intuition, and is oral (Stewart, 1997 in Smith, 2000) ... Tacit knowledge cannot be shared electronically ... Electronic networks and the steadily increasing pace of business drastically reduce the time people can spend discussing and challenging each other's knowledge and overall expertise .... Managers and team leaders must begin to make better use of key knowledge-building activities to guide, control, and inspire their workforces by encouraging more face-to-face transfer of tacit knowledge (Smith, 2000).

Introduction

Recalling from previous discussions, this book is not concerned solely with discussing knowledge management or testing for tacit knowledge. The former topic is well handled through a great deal of literature dating from the 1990s to the present day. The latter subject as we saw in the previous chapter tends to take place at the level of the individual and although a variety of techniques exist, the one by Sternberg's group is arguably the most practical. It is the flow of (tacit) knowledge in an organisation that should also be considered for the richness it provides both at the level of the staff member and holistically at the company-wide level. As one would expect, the measurement of knowledge flows brings with it another set of complexities including but not limited to, the culture of the firm, the cultural background of the individual employee, the degree to which ICT is in place within the company, the size of work groups and the formality or structure of the groups themselves. A study of intra-organisational flows needs to understand the parameters that will have an impact on the likelihood of soft knowledge being transferred from one individual to the next.

Tacit Knowledge Management

It only was in the 1990s that knowledge management arose as a discipline in business and academic circles (Roberts, 2001), where the discipline may be defined as "the process of creating, capturing, and using knowledge to enhance organisational performance" (Bassie, 1997, p. 25). Another definition that has been proposed acknowledges the importance of the role of the individual; for example, "knowledge management is about encouraging individuals to communicate their knowledge by creating environments and systems for capturing, organising, and sharing knowledge throughout the company" (Martinez, 1998, p. 89). All too often however, knowledge management has been about the codification of knowledge (Clark, Carter, & Szmigin, 2000).

As discussed in Chapter II, knowledge management in the context of western firms (including of course Australian ones) has to date meant the overemphasis on codified knowledge (Durrance, 1998; Platts & Yeung, 2000). Whilst such an approach is broadly acceptable, it nevertheless misses out on the role that tacit knowledge plays (Broadbent, 1998). Until we realise that some ninety percent of any organisational knowledge is embedded and created in the minds of staff (Bonner, 2000; Lee, 2000; Smith, 2001; Wah, 1999), the western organisation will never fully utilise the most valuable resource it possesses. Nevertheless, in western society, it has been shown that the use made by management in arriving at decisions is often a combination of almost *equal* amounts of tacit and explicit knowledge (Giunipero, Dawley, & Anthony, 1999). Evidence would seem to suggest that the two types of knowledge are indeed complementary, rather than alternatives (Lawson & Lorenz, 1999).

One major impediment to conducting empirical tacit knowledge investigations has been the lack of appropriate tools (Bloodgood & Salisbury, 2001). There have, however, been other factors that have affected studies of tacit knowledge and its role in the organisation, let us examine these beginning with the role of culture.

The Effect of Culture on Tacit Knowledge Flows

Knowledge management is heavily influenced by the role of **culture** (Syed-Ikhsan & Rowland, 2004) as is Tacit Knowledge more specifically. Culture in this instance need not necessarily refer to the macro/country level, rather the role of culture is important even down at the ethnic[a] [b] level. For example, in Finland much tacit knowledge is transferred in the sauna (Koskinen, 2000), understandably this has led to present-day difficulties as women begin to participate in business (Rosendo n.d.), to the extent that business in Finland is now moving towards western style boardrooms. The complexity for modern western organisations in particular is to integrate the tacit knowledge backgrounds of its (often) highly multicultural staff, for "cross-cultural working involves the interaction of people whose tacit knowledge has been developed in different ways, and who have learnt different approaches to sense-reading and sense-giving. A necessary first condition for trying to facilitate effective cross-cultural working is to take these cultural differences seriously" (Walsham, 2001, p. 606). Another such example was provided by Walsham (2001) whereby British and Japanese engineers were forced to work together. The British approach had been sequential and hierarchical with a view toward self-containment of their knowledge. Distrustful at first of each other's approaches to design tasks, the formalised British soon came to appreciate the Japanese approach to multi-functional teams permitting a far greater degree of tacit flow between team members.

With regard to the findings being reported in this book, Organisation X in particular is highly multicultural, with over 50 IT staff members (out of 108 participating), speaking over 35 languages other than English. Organisation Y is quite the opposite, with only one staff member speaking Cantonese and Malaysian, the remainder of the staff (seven) being essentially Anglo-Celtic Australian. Organisation Z had seven IT staff members (out of 13 participating) who spoke nine languages other than English. To what extent can we expect the varying levels of multiculturalism displayed in all three organisations to affect the tacit knowledge flow process?

Current Approaches to Tacit Knowledge Diffusion

One is almost led to believe organisations currently have no means for sharing tacit knowledge, given the logistical hurdles of its transfer. Let us very briefly examine some of the traditional means by which these hurdles have been overcome. At face value the approaches adopted vary from the esoteric to the more practical. The Japanese believe in the value of "*ba*", whereby feelings, emotions, experiences, mental models in a face-to-face environment are shared. Metaphors represent a dominant means by which this knowledge can be transferred. One must understand however that *ba* comprises not just the content but also rather the context and the place where such knowledge is transferred (Nonaka, Takeuchi, & Umemoto, 1996; Rumizen, 1998). Perhaps the most widely known practical tacit knowledge transferral examples in Japan have been the collaborations between and within research and academic scientists (Zucker, Darby, & Armstrong, 1998, 2001).

Apart from the use of teamwork in the west, "expert networks" have been created, whereby queries from employees are redirected to specialists within or external to the organisation (Bloodgood & Salisbury, 2001). Nevertheless it has been noted employees are often reluctant to use this approach for fear of being perceived as incompetent. Alternatively, "knowledge maps" representing personnel with their areas of expertise have also been adopted in some organisations (Bennett & Gabriel, 1999). The latter approaches do not necessarily aid in team-based tacit knowledge transfer. Given the IT oriented workplace today, what impact has technology had on soft knowledge transfer? As regards to the benefits of IT being extolled, are there disadvantages from a knowledge management point of view?

The Role of Information Technology in Tacit Knowledge Transfer

Companies have a tendency to invest in information technology rather than in developing social relationships, and not many have attempted the cultural and organisational transformation needed to promote knowledge transmission and circulation ... Information technology is part of the essential infrastructure of the knowledge revolution, but it is a necessary, not sufficient, condition (Clarke & Rollo, 2001).

On the one hand there is no denying the positive role IT has had in the working life of companies (Hustad, 2004; Syed-Ikhsan & Rowland, 2004).[c, d, e] On the other hand, what often takes place within the western firm is an orientation towards the management of tacit knowledge from an IS/IT perspective,[f] such as the encouragement given to the explication of tacit knowledge in the expert systems domain (Stenmark, 2000/2001). There is no denying the role of expert systems; it is an honourable attempt to make expert knowledge more widely available to the organisation. On the down side, apart from the loss of the true tacit component of the knowledge (i.e., the in-articulable component), the cost factor of making knowledge explicit often outweighs the benefits (Bloodgood & Salisbury, 2001), and the (expert) systems developed were often an attempt at "thinking machines" rather than supplements to "human thinking" (Goh, 2005).[g] Another example is that roughly seventy percent of knowledge management publications in the year 1998 were focused on IT/IS issues (Swan, Newell, Scarbrough, & Hislop, 1999). From a knowledge management perspective however it is acknowledged that informal employee networks are more effective (Jorgensen, 2004).[h] In short, the technologically based approaches provide the infrastructure, but not the social networking processes necessary for sense making (Swan et al., 1999).

Some current IT based knowledge diffusion approaches include the use of intranets, video-conferencing, company encyclopaedias, *LotusNotes*™ databases and the use of email sifting tools such as *Tacitmail*™ (Bennett & Gabriel, 1999). With regard to this last point, email whilst a popular means for communication is nevertheless really only a *communication tool*. In fact executive management have often stated that although they may have sent email to someone, they did not necessarily feel they had communicated. Indeed executive management in at least one study noted that there is an "implicit understanding that efficient communication and transfer of knowledge requires some type of face to face interaction" (Jacob & Ebrahimpur, 2001 p. 79). The limitations of email are outlined by Lee (1994), who stated that "in the view of information richness theory, electronic mail filters out important cues such as body language and tone of voice and, unlike face-to-face meetings, is not conducive to immediate feedback" (p. 143). The alternative proposed by Nonaka et al. (1996) and Johannessen, Olaisen, and Olsen (2001) is for external meeting places where interaction, visual cues and information media provide greater enrichment in the tacit knowledge transferral process, that is to say an approach that avoids the de-contextualisation of knowledge in general from tacit knowledge specifically (Clarke & Rollo, 2001). At this point it is worth noting that Organisations X, Y, and Z in the study all make extensive use of e-mail, faxes, and phones as accepted communication tools. The *extent* to which they do so will become clearer later on.

What is needed are better means of permitting tacit knowledge to flow amongst personnel, to which end information technologies suffer limitations. Whilst knowledge workers cannot be prevented from taking their tacit knowledge home with them (Kreiner, 2002), it is at least possible to improve IT communication systems, which in turn improve communication with knowledgeable people (Stenmark, 2000/2001). How well do Organisations X, Y and Z provide an atmosphere for knowledge sharing? If IT does not necessarily aid directly in the soft knowledge transferral process, then what does? To try to answer these questions, an examination of the role of human networks is necessary.

Knowledge and Human Networks as a Means of Knowledge Diffusion

Software may be appropriate for information transfer, but individuals are generally considered appropriate for "knowledge" transfer (Jacob & Ebrahimpur, 2001).

Granted that tacit knowledge is difficult to diffuse technologically (Haldin-Herrgard, 2000), some evidence (Asheim & Dunford, 1997) would suggest that for knowledge to be transferred, it needs to be codified. If tacit knowledge is both socially embedded (Keane & Allison, 1999; Lado & Zhang, 1998), and contextually based (Busch, Richards & Dampney, 2003), tacit knowledge is not likely to be effectively transferred. In essence, the marginal cost of transmitting tacit knowledge rises with distance (Audretsch, 1998), which explains at a macro level at least, the conglomeration of industry based on access to tacit knowledge (Dahlstrand, 1999; Keane & Allison, 1999) of which Silicon Valley provides us with an excellent example (Shariq, 1999). One of the reasons for "conglomeration" is that Tacit Knowledge is best transmitted through face-to-face interaction and repeated contact (Audretsch, 1998; Hustad, 2004; von Hipple, 1994). Furthermore the non-rival[i] nature of tacit knowledge (Arrow 1962), means that its' benefits are able to spread to other knowledge domains, which would tend to suggest why tacit knowledge possesses attributes corresponding to low environmental support for its distribution (Sternberg, 1995), insofar as the value of the knowledge to one individual is also likely to benefit another. In other words, as there is low environmental support we keep it to ourselves. This last point however, is not what organisations necessarily desire (Syed-Ikhsan & Rowland, 2004),[j] at least at an *intra*-organisational level, whilst we acknowledge diffusion is even more difficult at an *inter*-organisational level (Rycroft & Kash, 1999). Another salient point is that knowledge exists as part of a **holistic** system, for "knowledge is not a thing in, and of, itself, but is rather a bundle or network of various elements: bodies, machines, communications technologies and materials of all sorts … No one has ever observed a fact, a theory or a machine that could survive outside of the networks that gave birth to them. Still more fragile than termites, facts and machines can travel along extended galleries, but they cannot survive one minute in this famous and mythical 'out-thereness' so vaunted by philosophers of science (Latour, 1987, p. 248).

Networks thus form the vital infrastructure needed for knowledge and particularly tacit knowledge transfer. A number of definitions for networks exist. The *Macquarie Diction-*

ary (1997) defines a network as "**1.** any netlike combination of filaments, lines, passages, or the like ... [and more relevantly] **9.** to establish social contact with particular people because it is thought that they may prove to be useful" (p. 1446). It is this latter point that emphasises the role that humans play in the transfer of knowledge. In other words people seek council with individuals who are likely to help us them in their goals. More relevantly in the Social Network sense of the term (covered in the following chapter), they represent a distinct set of nodes or actors linked together by a set of edges or relations (Wasserman & Faust, 1994). Networks form social conduits (Ansell, 1997) with a person's position in the network determining how effective knowledge transfer is likely to be. Traditionally one means of diffusing tacit knowledge in the workplace, reliant also upon one's role in the network, has been through "**war stories**", where employees discussed ways they achieved technical success. Indeed management at *Xerox*™ had tried to prevent this, and then decided it was for the best (Brown, 2000). An alternative to "war stories" is "**storking**" or popping one's head up from cubicle dividers (Leonard & Sensiper, 1998; Wild, Bishop, & Sullivan, 1996). Other examples involve the use of modern technology such as wireless Palm VII computers to relay encoded or articulated Tacit Knowledge gathered from the field to help technical service workers (Walczak, 2005).[k]

While some employees are perhaps unaware of their own tacit knowledge (Nahapiet & Ghoshal, 1998; Spender, 1994), colleagues will nevertheless seek out employees whom they feel will provide the expertise they require, in technical or academic terms this is referred to as *Social Capital Theory*.

The fundamental proposition of social capital theory is that network ties provide access to resources. One of the central themes in the literature is that social capital constitutes a valuable source of information benefits (i.e., "who you know" affects "what you know"). Coleman (1988) notes that information is important in providing a basis for action but is costly to gather. However, social relations, often established for other purposes, constitute information channels that reduce the amount of time and investment required to gather information (Nahapiet & Ghoshal, 1998).

Other than counting the movements of highly skilled persons from one section of the organisation to the next (Stevens, 1996), the researcher is forced to examine the networks of relationships between individuals in an organisation to determine knowledge and particularly tacit knowledge flows. Indeed evidence suggests this must necessarily be so, for "Krackhardt and Hansen (1997) have argued that intra-organizational networks are the sites at which the real action in companies takes place" (Jacob and&, 2001 p. 77). The questions then remain, what role do the *attributes* of these intra-organisational networks themselves play? Are larger networks more effective than smaller ones? And what is the role of Information Technology in transferring the knowledge? In answer to the former question, some would argue that weak ties in networks increase knowledge diffusion through minimising redundant relationships (Burt, 1992; Nahapiet & Ghoshal, 1998). Others in relation to the latter question (Leonard & Sensiper, 1998) stress the importance of factors such as body language and physical demonstrations of skill requiring personal intimacy which can only be distributed in person. What of the type of relationships between individuals? Is the frequency with which one colleague meets another likely to influence tacit knowledge flows? What role does the status of the individual play?

Relationship Formality in the Knowledge Transfer Process

Having established that the means of tacit knowledge diffusion are through networks, what roles do the attributes of the networks play in the diffusion process? These attributes may be classified into firstly the importance and frequency of contact with other individuals in the network, which in turn encompasses the strength of the relationship. It is possible that the *frequency* of communication between individuals is likely to be far less important than the *type* (meaning importance) of the person involved in the relationship (Bennett & Gabriel, 1999; Lee, 1994). Knowledge networks may be considered hard and soft as well as long and short. Generally speaking softer networks or contacts between people tend to be shorter, generate softer facts, require fewer resources and leave room for negotiation (French, 2000; Latour, 1987). In other words within a community of practice where people know one another and the work practices and contexts are familiar, hard networks become less common, there is greater discretion between individuals in terms of the interpretation of knowledge, and in turn greater likelihood for the transferral of tacit knowledge. In certain professional communities of practice, such as the accounting discipline, a high degree of discretion has been noted; nevertheless professional bodies do act in self regulating manner (Clegg, 1989; French, 2000). The transferral of harder "facts" is noted to be implicit in "harder" networks which utilise specific means of articulation to transfer information, for example the use of forms, metrics and so on (French, 2000; Latour, 1987).

The second major attribute relates to the type of meeting that takes place. If tacit knowledge is only able to be passed in personal settings, what type of meeting is more appropriate? McAdam and McCreedy (1998) had conducted a survey of 97 UK firms showing that in actual fact a majority (81%) of tacit knowledge was elicited through *informal* meetings, whereas a substantially lesser amount had been acquired through *formal* discussion (44%). Similarly the study had indicated that lessons learned on the job were largely passed onto colleagues through discussion groups (54%) rather than through presentations (7%). What of the type of interaction at the micro-organisational level? For example, Daft and Lengel (1984) note that there exists a five step knowledge transfer richness continuum being comprised of: 1. face-to-face interaction, 2. the telephone, 3. written personal communication, 4. written formal communication and lastly 5. numeric formal communication. The face-to-face medium is considered the richest means for transferring knowledge, with the telephone being less rich due to the absence of visual cues.

Written forms of communication are less rich, nevertheless personal forms of communication such as e-mails are considered to exhibit more richness than formal communication which may be addressed to more than one individual (Koskinen & Vanharanta, 2002). As an aside, it is interesting to note the knowledge continuum outlined here exhibits a strong positive correlation with a knowledge hierarchy first proposed by Dampney and Busch in earlier work.[1]

What are the micro-level communication patterns within organisations X, Y, and Z? To what extent do people in these organisations make use of phones to transfer their information? [m] Do informal or formal meetings take place? Are the communities of practice in these organisations based around hard networks (for example with formal meetings), or softer and shorter networks involving casual discussions on an ad-hoc face-to-face basis? The point being that the type of interaction will directly affect the likelihood of tacit knowledge flows.

The Impact of Strong and Weak Ties

... social network research could provide a more complete account of the role of instrumental network ties in organizations by considering search and transfer as well as various forms of knowledge that flow through network relations ... A strong tie will constrain search, whereas a weak tie will hamper the transfer of complex knowledge (Hansen, 1999).

Apart from ascertaining the importance of informal networks in regard to soft knowledge transfer, attention may also be given to the strength of ties that make up the networks themselves. Ties between individuals constitute a fundamental principle in Social Network Analysis. Pivotal in Social Network Analysis (SNA) has been the work of Granovetter (1973 in Fernie, Green, Weller, & Newcombe, 2003). In addition to links (relationships) between nodes (individuals) forming a means by which soft knowledge can be transferred, Granovetter had long noticed that the strength of ties between people influenced the likelihood of knowledge transfer. "Strong ties, identified by high-trust, lengthy timeframes and close relationships, are ideal for the sharing of tacit, complex knowledge. Weak ties, on the other hand, limit the exchange of knowledge and even information" (Fernie et al., 2003; Granovetter, 1973).

Other recent research has revealed that the picture is not necessarily so black and white. Hansen (1999) had found that weak *interunit* ties will impede the flow of tacit knowledge, but do aid in forcing units themselves to seek information from other units. Strong ties within a group often means the group satisfies their demands for knowledge within that group (Hansen, 1999), and provides the infrastructure for repeated contact necessary for soft knowledge transfer (Polanyi, 1967). At the same time strong ties do increase the likelihood of the receiver of tacit knowledge possessing what Daft and Lengel (1984) label **absorbtive capacity** (Augier & Vendelø, 1999; Daft & Lengel, 1984) coinciding with our understanding of the importance of the receiver in the knowledge flow process (Busch et al., 2003). In other words "two actors that are strongly tied tend to have developed a relationship-specific heuristic for processing noncodified knowledge between them" (Hansen, 1999). Whereas codified knowledge is transferred easily through either strong or weak ties, evidence would seem to suggest tacit knowledge can truly only be passed through strong ties. The disadvantage in the latter case being that redundant knowledge is likely to be transferred as well (Hansen, 1999).

Summary

It is known that tacit knowledge is gained through experience or working with people who possess "know-how" (Roberts, 2001). Furthermore the dissemination of tacit knowledge can be a problem where organisations rely too heavily on information technology (Koski, 2001; Walsham, 2001). For an organisation to benefit from its tacit knowledge resources it must undertake to examine the richness of the different forms of communication mediums it makes use of (Koskinen, 2000; Schulz & Jobe, 2001). Aside from studying the role of semiotics in interpreting meanings flowing between individuals (McHaffie, 2002), at a more practical level, research indicates the only way for soft knowledge to be effectively transferred is through the socialisation process (Roberts, 2001).

It has been established that current knowledge management practices have almost exclusively focused on explicit knowledge. In keeping with the explicit knowledge theme, knowledge management has often been synonymous with IT or IS management. What is understood is that although information technologies have empowered many organisations, they are precisely that, *information* technologies. *Knowledge* technologies tend to be embedded within the human context. Attention needs to be paid to understanding the tacit flows that take place within an intra-organisational context. Social networks of one form or the other provide the fundamental means by which this process is able to take place. The characteristics of social networks vary based on the attributes of the networks themselves. Information richness, which in turn will affect knowledge richness, is dependent upon the type of media utilised. In combination with the effect of the media used, the strength of networks between individuals is expected to heavily influence the degree to which tacit knowledge is transferred. In order to study flows one must begin with a source and destination for tacit knowledge. Organisational staff members provide the source and destination of such knowledge. These employees will likely be affected by biographical factors, such as speaking a language other than English. The tools and methodologies for observations of knowledge measurement and diffusion, that is to say Social Network Analysis will be examined next, but before this step, this chapter concludes with the research goals,[n] questions[o] and assumptions[p] related to this study.

Research Goals

1. To formalise definitions for tacit knowledge along qualitative lines (Chapter III).

2. To test for tacit knowledge in IS/IT individuals (Chapter IV).

3. To determine if organisational size and type affect tacit knowledge flows (Chapter V).

4. To ascertain if there exists a set of "quasi-experts" to be referred to as expert non-experts. This group of people should potentially be identified by their tacit knowledge inventory results. These expert non-experts thus become another group high in tacit knowledge that would be able to help lesser tacit knowledge rich colleagues (Chapter VI).

5.   To model the probable intra-organisational diffusion patterns of tacit knowledge among information systems personnel (Chapter VII).

Research Questions

1.   Are there observable tacit knowledge differences between how (yet to be defined) "experts" handle the tacit knowledge issues in the organisation from those of (yet to be defined) novices? In other words how do experts differ in their approaches to those of novices?

2.   Can one identify other tacit knowledge rich personnel based on the similarity of their answers with that of the expert group?

3.   Are there certain biographical parameters (i.e. age, gender, ethnicity, years of IT experience, ACS level, highest formal qualification) that differentiate IS individuals who have accumulated more tacit knowledge from those with significantly less tacit knowledge?

4.   Do people clique[q] with one another based on biographical factors such as ethnicity? If so, does it affect tacit knowledge transfer?

5.   Is there evidence of tacit knowledge "bottlenecking"[r] taking place?

6.   Are there observable differences in knowledge diffusion patterns between IS personnel depending upon the character of the organisation?

Research Assumptions

1.   That contract staff will take tacit knowledge assets with them, that is to say will not leave behind "soft knowledge", when they leave the organisation, which will have a detrimental affect on the performance of the organisation (Walczak, 2005; Syed-Ikhsan and Rowland, 2004).[s, t]

2.   That organisations are at least implicitly if not explicitly decreasing their proportions of contract staff in acknowledgement of the understanding that soft knowledge is being taken away when contractual or short term staff leave.

3.   That organisations will try as much as possible to capture the expertise of their experienced staff by implementing knowledge capture systems such as *Tacitmail*™ or *LotusNotes*™, or by involving staff in a mentoring program, whereby staff who are recognised as being proficient at what they do will make good mentors for lesser experienced staff.

4.   That in practice not all tacit knowledge can be articulated.

5.   That the tacit knowledge that can be articulated is in fact really implicit knowledge, rather than truly tacit knowledge.

6. That the tacit knowledge being empirically tested in this empirical study is in actual fact implicit knowledge that can be articulated, which we can refer to as *implicit articulable IT managerial knowledge.*

7. That employees will form certain cliques or workplace groups.

8. That the formation of cliques will have a detrimental affect on the transference of tacit knowledge.

9. That those within a certain clique with a higher proportion of tacit knowledge savvy individuals will benefit from being within that clique; that is to say that access to tacit knowledge is considered to be beneficial.

References

Anand, V., Manz, C., & Glick, W. (1998). An organizational memory approach to information management. *The Academy of Management Review, 23*(4), 769-809.

Ansell, C. (1997). Symbolic networks: The realignment of the French working class 1887 – 1894. *The American Journal of Sociology, 103*(2), 359(32) (electronic).

Arrow, K. (1962). Economic welfare and the allocation of resources for invention. In R. Nelson (Ed.), *The rate and direction of inventive activity.* Princeton, NJ: Princeton University Press.

Asheim, B., & Dunford, M. (1997). Regional futures. *Regional Studies, 31*(5), 445(11).

Audretsch, D. (1998).Agglomeration and the location of innovative activity. *Oxford Review of Economic Activity, 14*(2), 18.

Augier, M., & Vendelø, M. (1999). Networks, cognition and management of tacit knowledge. *Journal of Knowledge Management, 3*(4), 252-261.

Bassie, L. (1997). Harnessing the power of intellectual capital. *Training and Development, 51*(12), 25-30.

Bennett, R., & Gabriel, H. (1999). Organisational factors and knowledge management within large marketing departments: An empirical study. *Journal of Knowledge Management, 3*(3), 212-225.

Bloodgood, J., & Salisbury, D. (2001). Understanding the influence of organisational change strategies on information technology and knowledge management strategies. *Decision Support System,* 31, 55-69.

Bonner, D. (2000). Knowledge: From theory to practice to golden opportunity. *American Society for Training & Development,* September-October, 12-13.

Broadbent, M. (1998). The phenomenon of knowledge management: What does it mean to the information profession? *Information Outlook, 2*(5), 23.

Brown, J. (2000). Growing up digital: The future impact of the World Wide Web. *Change, 32*(2), 11 (electronic).

Burt, R. (1992). *Structural holes: The social structure of competition.* Cambridge, MA: Harvard University Press.

Busch, P., Richards, D., & Dampney, C. (2003). The graphical interpretation of plausible tacit knowledge flows. *Australian Symposium on Information Visualisation* (InVis. au). Adelaide, South Australia, February 3 - 4.

Clark, P., Carter, C., & Szmigin, I. (2000). The spectrum of (Explicit) knowledge in firms and nations. *Prometheus, 18*(4). [Review article of *Tacit knowledge in Organisations* by Philippe Baumard (1999)], pp. 453-460.

Clarke, T., & Rollo, C. (2001). Corporate initiatives in knowledge management. *Education + Training, 43*(4/5), 206-214.

Clegg, S. (1989). *Frameworks of power.* London: Sage Publications.

Coleman J. (1988). Social capital in the creation of human capital. *American Journal of Sociology, 94,* 95-120.

Daft, R., & Lengel, R. (1984). Information richness: a new approach to managerial behavior and organizational design. In B. Staw & L. Cummings (Eds.), *Research in Organizational Behavior*, Vol. 6. Greenwich, CT: JAI Press, 191-223.

Dahlstrand, A. (1999). Technology based SME's in the Goteborg region: Their origin and interaction with universities and large firms. *Regional Studies, 33*(4), 379.

Durrance, B. (1998). Some explicit thoughts on tacit learning (Cover Story). *Training & Development, 52*(12), 24(6).

Ellis, L. (1981). Evaluating multicultural library service: An urban case study. In D. Whitehead, R. Rasmussen, & A. Holmes (Eds.), *Multiculturalism and libraries: Proceedings of the National Conference on Multiculturalism and Libraries,* Monash University 1980, Published by the Conference committee in 1981.

Fernie, S., Green, S., Weller, S., & Newcombe, R. (2003). Knowledge sharing: Context, confusion, and controversy. *International Journal of Project Management, 21*(3), 177-187.

French, S. (2000). Re-scaling the economic geography of knowledge and information: Constructing life assurance markets. *Geoforum, 31,* 101-119.

Giunipero, L., Dawley, D., & Anthony, W. (1999). The impact of tacit knowledge on purchasing decisions. *Journal of Supply Chain Management, 35*(1), 42-49.

Goh, A.L.S. (2005). Harnessing knowledge for innovation: An integrated management framework. *Journal of Knowledge Management, 9*(4), 6-18.

Granovetter, M. (1973). The strength of weak ties. *American Journal of Sociology, 78*(6), 1360-1380.

Hackett, B. (2000). *Beyond knowledge management, New ways to work and learn.* Retrieved October 1, 2002 from: www.conferenceboard.org

Haldin-Herrgard, T. (2000). Difficulties in diffusion of tacit knowledge in organisations. *Journal of Intellectual Capital, 1*(4), 357-365.

Hansen, M. (1999). The search-transfer problem: The role of weak ties in sharing knowledge across organizational subunits. *Administrative Science Quarterly, 44*(1), 82-111.

Hustad, E. (2004). Knowledge networking in global organizations: The transfer of knowledge. *SIGMIS'04*, April 22–24, Tucson, Arizona, 55-64.

Jacob, M., & Ebrahimpur, G. (2001). Experience vs. expertise: The role of implicit understandings of knowledge in determining the nature of knowledge transfer in two companies. *Journal of Intellectual Capital, 2*(1), 74-78.

Johannessen, J., Olsen, B., & Olaisen, J. (1997). Organising for innovation. *Long Range Planning, 30*(1), 96-109.

Jorgensen, B. (2004). Individual and organisational learning: A model for reform for public organisations. *Foresight, 6*(2), 91-103.

Kankanhalli, A., Tanudidjaja, F., Sutanto, J., & Tan, B. (2003). The role of IT in successful knowledge management initiatives. *Communications of the ACM, 46*(9), 69-73.

Keane, J., & Allison, J. (1999). The intersection of the learning region and local and regional economic development: Analysing the role of higher education. *Regional Studies, 33*(9), 896.

Koski, J. (2001). Reflections on information glut and other issues in knowledge productivity. *Futures, (London, England), 33*(6), 483-495.

Koskinen, K. (2000). Tacit knowledge as a promoter of project success. *European Journal of Purchasing & Supply Management, 6*, 41-47.

Koskinen, K, & Vanharanta, H. (2002). The role of tacit knowledge in innovation processes of small technology companies. *International Journal of Production Economics, 80*(1), 57-64.

Krackhardt, D., & Hanson, J. (1997). Informal networks: The company. In L. Prusak (Ed.), *Knowledge in Organizations.* Boston: Butterworth-Heinemann, 37-49.

Kreiner, K. (2002). Tacit knowledge management: The role of artefacts. *Journal of Knowledge Management, 6*(2), 112-123.

Lado, A., & Zhang, M. (1998). Expert systems, knowledge management and utilisation, and sustained competitive advantage: A resource based model. *Journal of Management, 24*(4), 489(2).

Latour, B. (1987). *Science in action: How to follow scientists and engineers through society.* Milton Keynes, UK: Open University Press.

Lawson, C., & Lorenz, E. (1999). Collective learning, tacit knowledge and regional innovative capacity. *Regional Studies,* June, Cambridge.

Lee, A. (1994). Electronic mail as a medium for rich communication: an empirical investigation using hermeneutic interpretation. *MIS Quarterly,* 143-157.

Lee, J. (2000). Knowledge management: The intellectual revolution. *IIE Solutions,* October, 34-37.

Leonard, D., & Sensiper, S. (1998). The role of tacit knowledge in group innovation, *California Management Review Berkeley, 40*(3).

Macquarie Dictionary (1997). Published by the Macquarie Library, 3rd. ed. Macquarie University, Australia: Macquarie Library.

Martinez, M. (1998). The collective power of employee knowledge. *HR Magazine, 43*(2), 88-94.

McAdam, R., & McCready, S. (1998). The emerging trend of knowledge management within organisations: A critical assessment of both theory and practice. *1998 Annual Conference of the British Academy of Management,* University of Nottingham (electronic).

McHaffie, P. (2000). Surfaces: Tacit knowledge, formal language, and metaphor at the Harvard lab for computer graphics and spatial analysis. *International Journal of Geographical Information Science, 14*(8), 775-773.

Nahapiet, J., & Ghoshal, S. (1998). Social capital, intellectual capital, and the organisational advantage. *Academy of Management Review, 23*(2), 242-266.

Nonaka, I., Takeuchi, H., & Umemoto, K. (1996). A theory of organisational knowledge creation. *International Journal of Technology Management, 11*(7/8), 833-845.

Platts, M., & Yeung, M. (2000). Managing learning and tacit knowledge. *Strategic Change, 9*, 347-355.

Polanyi, M. (1967). *The tacit dimension.* London: Routledge & Kegan Paul.

Roberts, J. (2001). The drive to codify: Implications for the knowledge-based economy. *Prometheus, 19*(2), 99-116.

Rosendo, J. (n.d.). *Sweating it out in Finland.* Retrieved on March 28, 2003 from: http://more.abcnews.go.com/sections/business/biztrav0129/

Rubenstein-Montano, B., Liebowitz, J., Buchwalter, J., McCaw, D., Newman, B., & Rebeck, K. (2001). A systems thinking framework for knowledge management. *Decision Support Systems, 31,* 5-16.

Rumizen, M. (1998). Report on the second comparative study of knowledge creation conference. *Journal of Knowledge Management, 2*(1), 77-81.

Rycroft, R., & Kash, D. (1999). Innovation policy for complex technologies. *Issues in Science and Technology, 16*(1), 73.

Schulz, M., & Jobe, L. (2001). Codification and tacitness as knowledge management strategies: An empirical exploration. *Journal of High Technology Management Research, 12,* 139-165.

Shariq, S. (1999). How does knowledge transform as it is transferred? Speculations on the possibility of a cognitive theory of knowledgescapes. *Journal of Knowledge Management, 3*(4), 243-251.

Smith, E. (2000). Applying knowledge – Enabling methods in the classroom and in the workplace. *Journal of Workplace Learning: Employee Counselling Today, 12*(6), 236-244.

Smith, E. (2001). The role of tacit and explicit knowledge in the workplace. *Journal of Knowledge Management, 5*(4), 311-321.

Spender, J. (1994). Knowing, managing and learning: A dynamic managerial epistemology. *Management Learning, 25,* 387-412.

Stenmark, D. (2000/2001). Leveraging tacit organizational knowledge. *Journal of Management Information Systems, 17*(3), 9-24.

Sternberg, R. (1995). Theory and management of tacit knowledge as a part of practical intelligence. *Zeitschrift für Psychologie, 203*(4), 319-334.

Stevens, C. (1996). The knowledge-driven economy. *OECD Observer,* June-July, n200, 6(5) (electronic).

Stewart, T. (1997). *Intellectual capital.* New York: Currency/Doubleday.

Swan, J., Newell, S., Scarbrough, H., & Hislop, D. (1999). Knowledge management and innovation: Networks and networking. *Journal of Knowledge Management, 3*(4), 262-275.

Syed-Ikhsan, S., & Rowland, F. (2004). Knowledge management in a public organization: A study on the relationship between organizational elements and the performance of knowledge transfer. *Journal of Knowledge Management, 8*(2), 95-111.

von Hippel, E. (1994). Sticky information and the locus of problem solving. *Management Science, 40,* 429-439.

von Krogh, G., Ichijo, K., Nonaka, I., (2000) *Enabling Knowledge Creation: How to Unlock the Mystery of Tacit Knowledge and Release the Power of Innovation* Oxford University Press New York U.S.A.

Wah, L. (1999). Making knowledge stick. *Management Review,* May, 24-29.

Walczak, S. (2005). Organizational knowledge management structure. *The Learning Organization, 12*(4), 330-339.

Walsham, G. (2001). Knowledge management: The benefits and limitations of computer systems. *European Management Journal, 19*(6), 599-608.

Wasserman, S., & Faust, K. (1994). *Social network analysis: Methods and applications.* Cambridge, UK: Cambridge University Press.

Wild, H., Bishop, L., & Sullivan, C. (1996). Building environments for learning and innovation. *Institute for Research on Learning Report to the Hewlett Packard IRL Project,* Menlo Park, CA.

Zucker, L., Darby, M., & Armstrong, J. (1998). Geographically localised knowledge: Spillovers or markets? *Economic Inquiry, 36*(1), 65(22).

Zucker, L., Darby, M., & Armstrong, J. (2001). *Commercializing knowledge: University science, knowledge capture, and firm performance in Biotechnology.* National Bureau of Economic Research (NBER), Working Paper 8499, October. URL: http://www.nber.org/papers/w8499

Endnotes

[a]   An ethnic group is one "other than those of Anglo-Celtic origin, [the latter group] who form the majority in Australia" (Ellis, 1981, p. vi).

[b]   "… of or relating to members of the community who are migrants or the descendants of migrants and whose native language is not English" (*Macquarie Dictionary,* 1997, p. 727). N.b.

this definition is not necessarily intended in the Australian context to refer to Scots, Welsh, or Irish Gaelics.

[c]   "Technological development is a crucial part of modernization, and the development of ICT is a crucial part of globalization. Specifically, the role of IT can be explained by the way it supports and enables time-space distances. IT enables integrated production processes that are distributed more or less globally. Control of global logistics processes such as global just-in-time (JIT) is a typical example. IT enables organizations to be distributed globally while at the same time being tied together into one organization and business processes are coordinated globally by IT" (Hustad, 2004, p. 57).

[d]   "These [results - Syed-Ikhsan & Rowland, 2004] show that technology plays key roles in managing knowledge in an organisation are considered as an effective means in of capturing, storing, transforming and dissemination information. Although ICT is not the answer to the success of implementing knowledge management, ICT infrastructure seems to allow individual sin the organisation to create and share knowledge efficiently and contribute to the performance of knowledge transfer ... With regard to ICT tools, the test shows that there is a positive significant relationship between ICT tools and knowledge assets, but not a significant one with the performance of knowledge transfer. Although descriptive analysis shows that most respondents agreed that the use of various tools helps them in sharing knowledge, the test shows no significant relationship with the performance of knowledge transfer. Pertaining to ICT know-how, the test shows that there is a positive relationship between ICT know-how and both the performance of knowledge transfer and knowledge assets. The results individuate that giving adequate training internally on using computers and software will allow employees to contribute to the performance of knowledge transfer and the creation of knowledge assets" (Syed-Ikhsan & Rowland, 2004, p. 108).

[e]   "The driving force behind the transformation to greater inter-connectivity, accelerated data transmission and reduced costs of communications is no other than information and communication technologies (ICTs). In most developed nations, ICT has been the key driver of the knowledge economy-providing faster ways of delivering and accessing information and real-time communication. Undoubtedly, the greatest benefit of ICT is its reach and one of its most important roles in KM is its knowledge-sharing benefits" (Goh, 2005, p. 13).

[f]   "Information management has largely been defined from an information systems perspective and equated with the management of information technology" (Anand, Manz, & Glick, p. 796).

[g]   "As early as in the 1980s, there were great expectations that knowledge-based systems (e.g. expert systems or decision support systems) should exploit the use of IT as a tool for knowledge creation. For almost two decades, the search for these tools was centred on stand-alone information systems (IS) such as expert system shells. But now, the internet offers a means for enterprise-wide knowledge-based initiatives to be better accomplished through groupware conferencing systems like Lotus Notes or intranets. In retrospect, part of the problem was that developers have focused too much, perhaps overly so, on developing "thinking machines" using, for instance, artificial intelligence (AI) techniques, rather than designing these "machines" to augment "human thinking" (Goh, 2005 p. 8).

[h]   "Informal employee networks and modified workplace practices have been shown to more effective at knowledge management than IT centric approaches (Hackett, 2000). As von Krogh *et al.,* (2000) argue, much of what people know is held tacitly and cannot be codified" (Jorgensen, 2004 p. 92).

[i]   "Goods are called non-rival when they can be consumed by many agents simultaneously" URL: www.econlinks.com/glossary/non_rival_goods.php (accessed 11/3/04).

j   "Rubenstein-Montano *et al.* argue that people and the culture of the workplace are the driving forces that ultimately determine the success or galore of knowledge management initiatives" (Rubenstein-Montano *et al.,* 2001 p. 5 in Syed-Ikhsan and Rowland, 2004 p. 108).

k   "Field service knowledge workers use Palm VII palm PCs and wireless connectivity to access explicitly encoded performance support knowledge. The source of the performance support knowledge is encoded tacit knowledge from other field service knowledge workers and teams as well as product development engineers, thus creating virtual knowledge teams to best satisfy the core competency of customer service. These virtual teams conform to the knowledge management goal of mutual support through technology for high-volatility service firms as specified by Kankanhalli *et al.,* (2003)" (Walczak, 2005 p. 337).

l   The author had as early as 2000 proposed a knowledge hierarchy from the most basic knowledge at the bottom to the most formalized knowledge being represented at the top of the "knowledge hierarchy". The levels were from tacit knowledge, to articulable tacit knowledge (subset of former that can be codified), codified knowledge (all print and electronic information), categorized knowledge (knowledge classified, such as classification systems etc.) and finally formalized knowledge (mathematics, models and so on).

m   At the time the survey component of the research was undertaken (2001-2002), respondents were not asked if they made use of virtual reality in their electronic communication (just phone, fax and email).

n   Goals represent the macro-level achievements sought in the book.

o   The research questions are those for which an answer is being directly sought.

p   Assumptions form the underlying basis upon which the research will progress from here. They are not necessarily intended to be proven or rather disproven in a Popperian logical positivist sense.

q   These are sub-groups within a network. For most practical Social Network Analysis purposes, a clique is defined as at least 3 people

r   In other words because of cliques in the organisation, has a bottleneck formed which fails to deliver tacit knowledge to a "disadvantaged" group, where disadvantaged refers to a "tacit knowledge poor" or "expert-poor" group?

s   "The results [from their empirical study] also indicate that there is a positive relationship between procedures for staff turnover and knowledge transfer performance and knowledge assets. Although the results do not show a strong relationship between the variables having adequate procedures to retain the knowledge and know-how of officers who leave the organisation is very important" (Syed-Ikhsan and Rowland, 2004 p. 109).

t   "Whenever a knowledge worker leaves one knowledge team and joins another, the knowledge worker takes all of the acquired tacit knowledge from the previous team, such as best practices or lessons learned" (Walczak, 2005 p. 335).

Chapter VII

Social Network Analysis

The basic idea of SNA is that individual people are nested within networks of face-to-face relations with other persons. Families, neighborhoods, school districts, communities, and even societies are, to varying degrees, social entities in and of themselves (Hanneman, 2002). The social network analyst is interested in how the individual is embedded within a structure and how the structure emerges from the micro-relations between individual parts (Hanneman, 2002). This could then be applied at an organizational level to see how the "actors" (e.g., employees, departments, etc.) relate to each other via their interactions. Through SNA, a knowledge map could be generated to aid in the knowledge audit process (Liebowitz, 2005 p. 79).

Introduction

If one seeks to measure (knowledge) flows amongst individuals, then the means of doing so are limited. Observation is one technique but is hindered by certain constraints. The first constraint is that the researcher cannot always place him or herself in the organisation for political or managerial reasons, especially if management is concerned that the work being conducted is confidential or "cutting edge" in nature. Secondly, people are known to modify their behaviour if being observed. Finally even if permission were to be given to observe workers and staff supposedly did not modify their behaviour, the nature of ICT work is largely desk or meeting-bound such that observation is not likely to reveal what it might in say occupations that were more "physical" or active in character. To that end, Social Network Analysis becomes a serious contender in seeking to examine knowledge flows between staff based on the relationships they have with one another.

Social Network Analysis

In the traditional workplace, organisational members can interact with each other frequently, thereby converting existing tacit knowledge to new tacit knowledge. Very often, these meetings with colleagues follow an impromptu mode where people "bump" into each other, be it near the elevator, the coffee percolator or the photocopying machine. Meetings might also take the less impromptu form of going out for lunch or for an after hours' drink. Invariably, these informal meetings follow a pattern where people share news about their work related problems and how they went about solving these problems (Raghuram, 1996, p. 862).

Not only is tacit knowledge typically transferred in the above manner within an organisation, but in order for the knowledge to be passed, the groups are on average required to be very small, because "larger communities of knowledge can share certain practices, routines, and languages, but for new tacit knowledge to emerge through socialization the group must be small" (von Krogh, Ichijo, & Nonaka, 2000 in Allred, 2001, p. 162). This teamwork then permits knowledge to be transmitted back into the organisation, through various but usually social means. Observation or more specifically participant observation (Scott, 1990, 1992) also has been utilised for observing tacit knowledge flows. In short "participant observation is characterised by the observer (researcher) becoming a part of the situation being observed. Participant observation typically exists along a continuum with the role of 'complete observer' on one end and the role of 'complete participant' on the other" (Leedy, 1997, p. 159). The limitations of participant observation are however that one is required to be physically present in the field of study. Furthermore subjects being studied are likely to alter their behaviour given that they are being observed (Yin, 1994). Nonetheless participant observation has been shown to be useful for collecting data on proceedings that specifically take place *within* the organisation (Williams, May, & Wiggins, 1996). Participant observation also tends to be useful if the subjects are undertaking physical tasks, which lend themselves to observation.

Social Network Analysis,[a] on the other hand, is far less intrusive in the workplace domain, as individuals filling out the questionnaire can anonymously[b] elect whom they network with. This latter technique essentially maps the relationships between individuals and has numerous practical applications having had its origins in fields as diverse as anthropology, graph theory and sociology (Knoke & Kuklinski, 1982; Scott, 1991; Wasserman & Faust, 1994). The advantage of using SNA is multitudinous. Participant observation of tacit knowledge is difficult because IT practitioners on the whole do not undertake physically active tasks to the extent of say nurses (Scott, 1990, 1992), police officers or fire-fighters, therefore attempting to view the actions and knowledge transferral of IT practitioners is difficult. What is clear is that SNA is effective in determining the communication patterns between individuals by way of their relationship networks as discussed by Krackhardt and Hanson (1993):

Using network analysis ... managers can translate a myriad of relationship ties into maps that show how the information organization gets work done. Managers can get a good overall picture by diagramming three types of relationship networks: The advice network shows the prominent players in an organisation on whom others depend to solve problems and provide technical information. The trust network tells which employees share delicate political information and back one another in a crisis. The communication network reveals the employees who talk about work – related maters on a regular basis (p. 105 italics added).

This research is concerned largely with the first and last networks. Along the lines of other Social Network Analysis research (Brass, Butterfield, & Skaggs, 1998; Cross, Borgatti, & Parker, 2001; Cross & Parker, 2004; Dekker, 2001; Freeman, Webster, & Kirke, 1998; Koehly & Shivy, 1998; Labianca, Brass, & Gray, 1998; Liebowitz, 2005; Paxton, Schutz, Wertheim, & Muir, 1999; Sawer & Groves, 1994; Scott, 1991; Snowden, 2005; Wasserman & Faust, 1994; Wetherell, 1998; Wilward & Provan, 1998), a social network analysis component gives added strength to the research insofar as it replaces participant observation (Scott, 1990, 1992) as a means of determining how effectively soft knowledge was likely to be transferred within the IT workplace. Furthermore both sides of a relationship may be mapped, reducing the likelihood of one-sided bias (Cavusgil, Calantone, & Zhao, 2003). The addition of social network analysis nevertheless significantly complicates the research effort, as it does not allow the questionnaire to be anonymous, for individuals have to log in to be identified so that they in turn may categorize their working relationships. Apart from the increased difficulty of passing such a questionnaire by the University Ethics Committee,[c] it also naturally meant that respondents would likely be less inclined to want to participate in the research in case they felt they could be identified.

Social Network Underpinnings

Social network analysis has as its basis four major underpinnings. Firstly, **actor**s or participants in the system are viewed as interdependent upon one another, rather than independent. Such an assumption highlights the holistic nature of SNA research. Social Network Analysis does not in other words adopt a methodological-individualist stance. The second underpinning is that relations among actors are considered as channels or thoroughfares of resources. Third, the interaction among actors is directly constrained or aided by the structure of the relationships themselves. Finally, the relations that take place between the actors determine all economic, political and social structures (Koehly & Shivy, 1998; Wasserman and Faust, 1994; Wetherell, 1998). The second and third points are particularly relevant for the tacit knowledge research undertaken here, insofar as an assumption is made that articulable tacit knowledge will be transferred from actor A to actor B and vice versa, depending on the directions of the relationships.

Criticisms of SNA

Admittedly SNA is not without censure, for "critics argue that SNA's excessive focus on structural relationships tend to minimise the role of individual agency, and that this represents a major weakness of the approach" (Brint, 1992; Emirbayer & Goodwin, 1994; Haines, 1988; Wetherell, 1998). Wetherell (1998) notes SNA has strong support among community network analysts who consider human behaviour as instrumental and that humans tend to interact with one another quite consciously. Snowden (2005) notes that a disadvantage with SNA is that the *role* of the individual can often be confused with the individual him or herself. With the departure of that given individual in the firm one ordinarily gets the impression that a (knowledge) vacuum will be created. However if respondents are asked to choose *identities*[d] they network with, rather than individuals, the problem can be overcome to some degree. Nevertheless in practice it is hard to separate the individual from their role, and when results were canvassed in this research individuals were asked to identify individuals they collaborated with.

Whole Network vs. Egocentric Network Approach

When undertaking SNA research, one is faced with the choice of undertaking such research at what may be termed the **Whole Network** (WN) or **Egocentric Network** (EC) approach (Wetherell, 1998).[e] The former approach attempts to model all ties between all **actor**s in the system, the boundary for which will have been determined at the commencement of the research. The latter technique concentrates on particular individuals and seeks to focus on selected individuals and how they interact with one another. To a large extent this research takes the former approach. All actors were modelled in the system design, although not all were chosen to participate in the research. The focus on the research is to study the macro information flows between the actors in the system to determine whether tacit knowledge bottlenecking is taking place. However before information flows can be studied, participants in the study need to be determined.

Membership Rules

Membership defines the **actor**s who will participate in the study for the purposes of SNA. Given the closed membership nature of the research, little difficulty was inherent in choosing personnel who would participate. All IT staff members' names were hardcoded into the questionnaire. To that end the research takes the whole network approach. The personnel chosen to participate in filling out the questionnaire were up to Chief Information Officer (CIO) or appointed nominee level. In the case of Organisation X, the CIO was a manager in charge of 200-300 IT staff members, out of a total of 1,400 IT staff nationwide. In the case of Organisation Y, the CIO was in charge of some 14 staff. Similarly the CIO for Organisation Z was in charge of 15-20 IT staff members.

Information Elicitation

Unlike small actor networks within which observation, face to face or telephone interviews may suffice, in the information elicitation process "when the actors are people and respondents can directly report the relation(s) of interest, questionnaires are the most commonly used technique" (Koehly & Shivy, 1998). The questionnaire approach also has as its strengths the possibility of attaining closed sets of data insofar as the respondent is given limited opportunity to provide the researcher with irrelevant or unnecessary information. Additionally from a workplace information elicitation point of view, far greater levels of resources and permission are required in order to conduct interviews or even open-ended questionnaires, given the time constraints that management understandably impose on their staff.

Sociomatrices

In creating social network analysis datasets, the first approach tends to be conversion of the questionnaire data into **sociomatrix** format. Sociomatrices are as their name suggests square, although they need not be symmetric. Data represented in the ijth cell of a sociomatrix refer to relationship information from **actor** i to actor j. Actors i tend to be represented in rows, whilst actors j are represented in columns. Data represented in each of the cells may be either binary if the data in its simplest format is to represent whether a relationship takes place between actor i or j, in which case a 1 is present, and 0 otherwise (Hanneman, 2002; Liebowitz, 2005).[f] Valued relations tend to make use of positive or negative integer values that express the intensities (supportive or antagonistic) of relationships between the actors. An example of such a sociomatrix in provided in Figure 1. The row data in this instance presents titles in full, of respondents who have participated (e.g., 3014 … 3020E). Column titles on the other hand have been shortened to include only the initial integer value of the same value represented in the rows. To clarify, it is obvious that the matrix is square. There are seven rows and columns. Each of the rows and columns is numbered 1 through to 7. Row and column titles for respondents who will eventually be seen as nodes in a graph drawing package are also provided in Figure 1.

Furthermore, valued data instead of binary data is evidenced through the fact that the integer values in the sociomatrix vary from 0 (no relation) through to 7 (maximum or highest strength of relation). Note the incidence of 0 values diagonally to indicate the relations people have with themselves, that is to say relationships of technically no value.

Naturally valued data provides more information than simple binary data; however certain dedicated SNA packages such as UCINET™ occasionally need to convert data to binary in order to perform statistical functions such as the QAP[g] procedure. Having established a sociomatrix, it is often important to manipulate the numerical data. One example of manipulation is symmetrising.

Figure 1. Providing an example of a sociomatrix

```
              1  2  3  4  5  6  7
              3  3  3  3  3  3  3
             -- -- -- -- -- -- --
1  3013E      0  7  7  6  6  6  5
2   3014      6  0  0  6  6  6  6
3  3016E      6  6  0  6  6  6  6
4   3017      6  6  5  0  5  6  4
5  3018E      7  6  6  0  0  0  0
6  3019E      6  6  6  6  6  0  6
7  3020E      0  5  5  4  4  5  0
```

Symmetrising

Symmetrising takes place when what should logically be a symmetrical relation appears in the dataset to be otherwise. For example, if asking two actors with regard to the number of times they communicate with one another, and the answers from the two appear quite different, one has the option in SNA software to recalculate the communication values. Formally this is expressed as, for all of matrix X, force X(i,j) to equal X(j,i), for all *i* and *j*. Recalculation tends to find the average between the two values given, although a number of options are possible:

Replace xij and xji by their maximum, minimum, average, sum, absolute difference, product or xij/xji (provided xji is non zero) i < j. Alternatively, make the lower triangle equal the upper triangle or the upper triangle equal the lower triangle (Analytic Technologies 2002) ... Among the more unusual choices is the possibility of setting both X(i,j) and X(j,i) equal to 1 if X(i,j) = (Xj,i) and 0 otherwise. In effect, this creates a new matrix that indicates whether each dyad is in agreement or not (Borgatti, Everett, & Freeman, 2001 p. 4.7).

Figure 1 above provided an example where actor 3013E (in this case an "expert") finds his or her strength of relationship (whatever it is being measured) with 3014 (the second person along in the columns), a weight of 7. Person 3014, on the other hand, has chosen a strength of relationship with 3013E as being that of 6. At this juncture the researcher may choose to either take the maximum, minimum or average value of these two. If then satisfied with the sociomatrix, various statistical computations may be performed on the dataset, for example calculating the degree (in and out), measures of centrality, and determining the cliques that individuals belong to. The graphical interpretation of data thus represents another aspect to Social Network Analysis altogether. The researcher is also able to perform statistical functions on the data before even attempting a visual interpretation. One such quantitative function relates to degree.

Degree

Degree is an important SNA concept insofar as it can relate to higher order SNA concepts dealing with **actor** power, centrality and prestige. Degree relates to the ties an actor has with another. Formally, this may be expressed as $d(n_i) = \sum_j X_{ij} = \sum_j X_{ji}$. The concept of degree can be broken down into indegree and outdegree. "The indegree of a point is the total number of other points which have lines directed towards it; and its outdegree is the total number of other points to which it directs its lines. The indegree of a point, therefore, is shown by is column sum in the matrix of the directed graph [formally, $d_i(n_i) = \sum_j X_{ji}$], while its outdegree is shown by its row sum [formally $d_o(n_i) = \sum_j X_{ij}$]" (Scott, 1991, p. 72; [relevant formalisms from Wasserman & Faust, 1994]). From a graphical perspective, Figure 2 provides an example of in and out-degree. For instance one can see that node X has a degree of 3, an in-degree of 3, and an out-degree of 2. Node A has a degree of 2, an in-degree of two and out-degree of one.

Figure 2. Illustrating in and out-degree

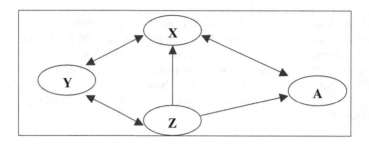

Another way of viewing in-degree and out-degree relations is the popularity of an individual in the case of the former, and the extroverted-ness of an individual in the case of the latter measure. In other words one can expect an individual with a higher in-degree factor to be popular with their colleagues. Although the experts in this tacit knowledge related research might be knowledgeable, they may have a low in-degree factor, which would suggest they are not effectively contacted. Alternatively an expert, or perhaps a non-expert who nevertheless scores similarly on the tacit knowledge scale with an expert, may not have a high measure of out-degree. Should a low out-degree measure prove to be the case then one could expect expert personnel to be ineffectively transmitting their knowledge.

Centrality and Prominence

Connected with in and out degree, **centrality** relates to an **actor**s level of social prestige. Should relations between actors prove non-directional, the centrality of people is determined by the number of ties relating to each of the actors (Koehly & Shivy, 1998). Where ties are directional however, "a central actor is one who sends many ties, either directly or indirectly, to other network members, and a prestigious actor is one who receives many ties from others" (Koehly & Shivy, 1998, p.9). Centrality may be further distinguished as local or global. Local centrality refers to an actor who has a high degree of connectedness with actors directly around them, ignoring the indirect links this actor may have with other actors further away. Local centrality is not concerned with any central point existing in the network of actors. Global centrality on the other hand is based upon what Freeman (Borgatti et al., 2001; Freeman et al., 1998) proposes as a "closeness of points".

A point is globally central if it lies at short distances from many other points ... If the matrix of distances between points in an undirected graph is calculated, the sum distance of a point is its column or row sum in this matrix (the two values are the same). A point with a low sum distance is "close" to a large number of other points, and so closeness can be seen as the reciprocal of the sum distance. In a directed graph ... paths must be measured through lines which run in the same direction, and for this reason, calculations based on row and column sums will differ (Scott, 1991, p. 89).

The reader can see with regard to Figure 2 above that none of the actors are *particularly* central, save that individuals X and Z may be considered more so than actors Y and A. Extending such a concept is what has been termed betweenness (Freeman, 1978/1979; Scott, 1991). In other words actors may have more than one path available to them to transfer information from actor A to actor B. The logic behind betweenness is that actors are likely to use the shortest path for information transfer. One would hope that the tacit knowledge experts possess a high betweenness centrality enabling their soft knowledge to be easily transferred.

Density and Inclusiveness

Density may be taken as a sign of how many interactions are taking place between **actor**s. We define the density of a non-directed graph as the number of links between actors as a proportion of the maximum possible number of links. Formally, Scott (1991) illustrates this concept as follows:

$$\frac{l}{n(n\text{-}1)/2}$$

where l are the number of lines present. If, for example, four actors are connected by a maximum possible number of ties which would be six links, then the inclusiveness of the graph would be 1.0, that is to say complete, there being no isolated nodes or actors. The sum of the degrees in the case of four actors and six links would be 12, there being an in-degree and out-degree for each of the links. The density of this complete graph would also be 1.0, in other words complete. There can be no other connections between the actors, for all means of connectivity or knowledge communication flows will have been achieved. If, however, four actors are all joined by only four links, then the inclusiveness will still be 1.0. In other words, the actors are all still connected with one another, however not all directly; it will be necessarily for communication flows for some actors to have to pass through another, rather like an IBM Token Ring network. Given four links, the sum of in and out-degrees becomes eight, instead of 12, with the network density being 0.7, instead of 1.0 (Scott, 1991).

Cliques and Discrete Networks

The **clique** is one of the fundamental components of social network analysis and may be thought of as a "sub-grouping of a network. This sub-grouping is built up, or developed out of the combining of dyads and triads into larger, but still closely connected structures. Studying the role of cliques can be insightful in understanding how the network as a whole behaves or why it behaves in such a way" (Higgins, 2000, p. 5.2.4). Cliques form an important social construct due to the fact that they are formed by all subgroup members choosing one another. More formally, we may state a clique is a "'maximal complete sub-graph' (Harary, 1969;

Luce & Perry, 1949). That is to say, a clique is a sub-set of points in which every possible pair of points is directly connected by a line and the clique is not contained in any other clique" (Scott, 1991, p. 117). If one were to have three **actor**s participating in a clique, this would mean that the number of links connecting them would be three. Once again, for four actors, as with measures relating to density, the number of links would be six, encompassing all possible links directly from one actor to the next. In reality, however, these maxims have proved too strict for practical social network analysis, and so researchers tend to make use of *n*-clique arrangements whereby *n* represents the maximum path length through which a neighbour is connected with another. For example with a 2 *n* clique network, each actor in the system would be reached either directly by the neighbour next to them, or through at most one other person. Once again, a Token Ring, analogy would be a machine passing a token to the machine next to it, or alternatively passing the token to the neighbouring machine, which would in turn pass it to the next machine where the token would remain.

A practical example of clique or discrete networks is given in the following description. "… For example, if Joe has a link to Mary and Barbara and Barbara also has a link to Mike, these nodes would all be in one group. If Joe has a link to Mary and Barbara and Mike has a link to Sara, there would be two separate networks and therefore separate groups. If there were also nodes with no links, they would all appear in one group" (From Netmap solutions, 1998. *User guide for the Netmap data visualiser* [Netmap/DV] System Release 4.14 1998). Depending on the software utilised, it is possible to identify these "emergent groups" potentially as "discriminant analysis could be performed to evaluate statistically whether actor attributes such as gender actually differentiate such group memberships" (Arabie, 1984 in Koehly & Shivy, 1998, p. 12). As Wasserman and Faust (1994) point out, what makes data far more meaningful however are the composition variables, which provide the attribute related data, in this case for respondents who have taken part in the tacit knowledge questionnaire. One may note from Figure 3 for example, that a clique (far left grouping) has formed based on Cantonese being used by the clique members as a second language. In other words, these group members have chosen each other to associate with based on their first language other than English.

Figure 3. Illustrating clique (or emergent group) (left hand side) of Cantonese speakers (source Organisation X)

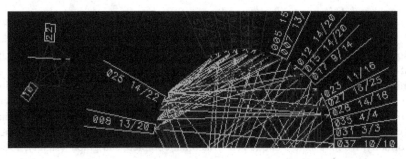

Sociograms

Having established a sociomatrix for SNA data, and having performed numerical process-ing on the data in question, leads typically to the establishment of a **sociogram** or network diagram. Sociograms represent sociomatrix data by way of graph theoretical constructs, insofar as objects such as respondents are implemented as nodes, whilst relations between respondents are illustrated as edges or lines connecting the nodes. A difficulty arises however when the graph includes more than a limited number of nodes, in that the edges of the graph soon begin to cross over. "One common technique has been to construct the sociogram around the circumference of a circle, so that the pattern of lines becomes more visible" (Scott, 1991, p. 149). The Netmap datasets adopt such an approach, which can be considered diagram-matically powerful through the appropriate use of colour to highlight attribute-based data, such as age groups and gender. The reader will see an example of a sociogram in Figure 4. Colour can also be used to indicate attributes such as gender. In the original colour figures, blue represents males, and green females. Red indicates that respondents have not indicated their gender as part of the questionnaire.

A disadvantage with circular diagrams, however, is their loss of mathematical information, for "the points are arranged [typically] in arbitrary positions, and the drawn lengths of the various lines reflect this arbitrary arrangement. It is not possible to infer anything about the actual position of points relative to one another or about the distances between them" (Scott, 1991, p. 150). To that end social network analysis has moved towards producing more mathematically true graphs utilising Multi-Dimensional Scaling (MDS).

Figure 4. Illustrating a sociogram

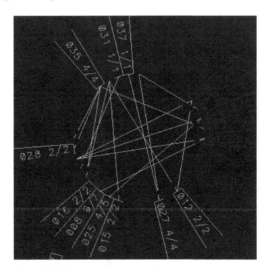

Multi-Dimensional Scaling

The introduction of MDS permits space and distance to be incorporated into graphical displays. Utilising graph theory, MDS calculates the number of lines connecting two nodes, and based on this measure is able to determine the distances apart the nodes should be spaced. "**Multi-dimensional scaling** at its simplest, is an attempt to convert graph measures such as path distance into metric measures analogous to physical distance ... MDS can take graph theoretical measures of the "closeness" of points and can express these relations of closeness and distance in metric terms. This involves, more formally, the use of "proximity data" to construct a metric configuration of points" (Scott, 1991, p. 152). An example of multi-dimensional scaling can be seen in Figure 5. It is the strength of multidimensional scaling which greatly permits researchers to determine the likelihood of knowledge transferral.

Some further SNA measures are discussed in detail in Chapters XI, XII, and XIII where the SNA results are presented. It is felt that the reader will gain a better understanding of these metrics if they can be offered along with actual results. Examples of such techniques include measures of information centrality and global centrality (based upon closeness and betweenness).

Figure 5. Illustrating an example of multi-dimensional scaling

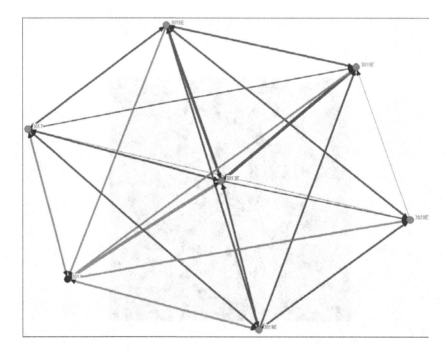

Summary

In summarising the methodological underpinnings covered in this chapter, one needs to bear in mind the suitability of means for assessing tacit knowledge diffusion. The Sternberg means of testing for tacit knowledge is considered to be the most practical approach for undertaking research in the organisational domain. If one wishes to measure knowledge flows amongst personnel in organisations there are limitations in the approaches that can be adopted. After some consideration had been given to Participant Observation along the lines of Scott (1990, 1992), it was felt a more appropriate alternative would be Social Network Analysis. This approach by its very nature is not only less intrusive than participant observation, but is able to be incorporated into the same questionnaire, meaning that employees would be disturbed for an overall lesser period of time. Indeed the last point is of particular relevance when conducting research with active professionals who do not necessarily represent a captive audience. Social Network Analysis is based on graph theory and is well established in many disciplines. There are critics of SNA but in general the benefits outweigh the disadvantages. The technique is based upon a number of underpinnings, chief among which is that if a relationship exists between individuals then communication will flow between personnel. The attention now turns toward examining the micro-methodology used in the study with a view toward helping other researchers and practitioners replicate this study should they wish to.

References

Allred, B. (2001). Enabling knowledge creation: How to unlock the mystery of tacit knowledge and release the power of innovation. *The Academy of Management Executive, 15*(1), 161-162.

Arabie, P. (1984). Validation of sociometric structure by data on individuals' attributes. *Social Networks, 6,* 373-403.

Borgatti, S., Everett, M., & Freeman, L. (2001). *UCINET 5.8 Version 1.00* Natick: Massachusetts: Analytic Technologies.

Brass, D., Butterfield, K., & Skaggs, B. (1998). Relationships and unethical behavior: A social network perspective. *The Academy of Management Review, 23*(1), 14-31.

Brint, S. (1992). Hidden meanings: Cultural content and context in Harrison White's structural sociology. *Sociological Theory, 10,* 194-208.

Cavusgil, S.T., Calantone, R.J., & Zhao, Y. (2003). Tacit knowledge transfer and firm innovation capacity. *Journal of Business and Industrial Marketing, 18*(1), 6-21.

Cross, R., Borgatti, S., & Parker, A. (2001). Beyond answers: Dimensions of the advice network. *Social Networks Journal, 23*(3), 215-35.

Cross, R., & Parker, A. (2004). *The hidden power of social networks.* Boston: Harvard Business School Press.

Dekker, A. (2001). Visualisation of social networks using CAVALIER. *Information Visualisation 2001: Proceedings of the Australian Symposium on Information Visualisation,* Vol. 9, December, Sydney, Australia, 49-55.

Emirbayer, M., & Goodwin, J. (1994). Network analysis, culture and the problem of agency. *American Journal of Sociology, 99,* 1411-1454.

Freeman, L., Webster, C., & Kirke, D. (1998). Exploring social structure using dynamic three – dimensional color images. *Social Networks, 20,* 109-118.

Freeman, L. (1978/1979). Centrality in social networks: Conceptual clarification. *Social Networks, 1,* 215-239.

Haines, V. (1988). Social network analysis, structuration theory and the holism-individualism debate. *Social Networks, 10,* 157-182.

Hanneman, R. (2002). *Introduction to social network methods.* Retrieved June 15, 2006 from http://faculty.ucr.edu/~hanneman/nettext/.

Harary, F. (1969). *Graph theory.* Reading, MA: Addison-Wesley.

Higgins, P. (2000). *An exploratory case-study into the existence of technological convergence in Australia.* Unpublished honours thesis, Department of Computing, Macquarie University, Australia.

Knoke, D., & Kuklinski, J. (1982). *Network analysis.* Beverly Hills, CA: Sage Publications.

Koehly, L., & Shivy, V. (1998). Social network analysis: A new methodology for counseling research. *Journal of Counseling Psychology, 45*(1), 3-17.

Krackhardt, D., & Hanson, J. (1993). Informal networks: The company behind the chart. *Harvard Business Review,* July-August, 104-111.

Labianca, G., Brass, D., & Gray, B. (1998). Social networks and perceptions of intergroup conflict: The role of negative relationships and third parties. *Academy of Management Journal, 41*(1), 55-68.

Leedy, P. (1997). *Practical research: Planning and design, 6th. Ed.* New York: Merrill.

Liebowitz, J. (2005). Linking social network analysis with the analytic hierarchy process for knowledge mapping in organizations. *Journal of Knowledge Management, 9*(1), 76-86.

Luce, R., & Perry, A. (1949). A method of matrix analysis of group structure. *Pyschometrika, 14,* 95-116.

Netmap solutions (1998). *User guide for the Netmap data visualiser,* (Netmap/DV), System Release 4.14.

Paxton, S., Schutz, H., Wertheim, E., & Muir, S. (1999). Friendship clique and peer influences on body image concerns, dietary restraint, extreme weight – loss behaviours, and binge eating in adolescent girls. *Journal of Abnormal Psychology, 108*(2), 255-266.

Raghuram, S. (1996). Knowledge creation in the telework context. *International Journal of Technology Management, 11*(7/8), 859-870.

Sawer, M., & Groves, A. (1994). The women's lobby: Networks, coalition building and the women of middle Australia. *Australian Journal of Political Science, 29,* 435-459.

Scott, D. (1990). Practice wisdom: The neglected source of practice research. *Social Work, 35*(6), 564-568.

Scott, D. (1992). Reaching vulnerable populations: A framework for primary service expansion. *American Journal of Orthopsychiatry, 62*(3), 333-341.

Scott, J. (1991). *Social network analysis: A handbook.* London: Sage Publications.

Snowden, D. (2005). From atomism to networks in social systems. *The Learning Organization, 12*(6), 552-562.

von Krogh, G., Ichijo, K., & Nonaka, I. (2000). *Enabling knowledge creation: How to unlock the mystery of tacit knowledge and release the power of innovation.* New York: Oxford University Press, Inc.

Wasserman, S., & Faust, K. (1994). *Social network analysis: Methods and applications.* Cambridge, UK: Cambridge University Press.

Wetherell, C. (1998). Historical social network analysis. *International Review of Social History, 43*(Supplement 6), 125-144.

Williams, M., May, T., & Wiggins, R. (1996). *Introduction to the philosophy of social research.* University College, London: UCL Press Limited.

Wilward, H., & Provan, K. (1998). Measuring network structure. *Public Administration, 76,* 387-407.

Yin, R. (1994). *Case study research: Design and methods.* Applied Social Science Research Methods series, Vol. 5. Beverly Hills, CA: Sage.

Endnotes

[a]   "Social network analysis is a general set of procedures that use indices of relatedness among individuals to produce representations of the social structures and social positions that are inherent in dyads or groups by attending to the reciprocal interactions among two or more network members. A social network is simply a set of actors—individuals or other social entities—and their relationships with each other" (Koehly & Shivy, 1998, p. 3).

[b]   Meaning their peers need not know whether they have chosen them as part of their communication/friendship network.

[c]   Ethics Committees exist at all Australian universities. As their name suggests, such Committees provide a check on research conducted and prohibit research not falling within what the Committee sees as being "ethical." The committee is typically made up of perhaps twenty to thirty people from both academic and lay backgrounds, including legal and medical personnel, indigenous representatives and members of the clergy. Such committees do from time to time however come in for criticism, for example, http://www.abc.net.au/rn/healthreport/stories/2006/1680645.htm#transcript (accessed 14th July 2006).

[d]   Identity of people filling a particular *role*, rather than the name of the individual themself

[e]   "One method is called 'full network methods' whereby information about each actor's ties with all other actors is collected. One major limitation of this technique is that it may be costly and difficult to collect full network data. A second group of methods is called the 'snowball methods' whereby the analyst begins with a focal actor or set of actors. Then, each of these

actors is asked to name some or all of their ties to other actors. Then, these 'other actors' are asked for some or all of their ties, and the snowball effect continues until no new actors are identified (or until some stopping rule is determined). The limitations with this method are that those who are 'isolated' may not be identified and it may be unclear as to where to start the snowball rolling. The third major strategy used in SNA is the use of egocentric networks. With this approach, one would begin with a selection of focal nodes (egos) and identify the nodes to which they are connected. Then, one would determine which of the nodes identified in the first stage are connected to one another. Egocentric methods focus on the individual, rather than on the network, as a whole" (Hanneman, 2002 in Liebowitz, 2005, p. 79).

[f]   "The zero-one binary scale is an example of a nominal scale and would show if ties are absent (zero) or present (one). The multiple-category nominal measures of relations is similar to multiple choice versus the true-false binary representation. The ordinal measures of relations are similar to a Likert scale and can determine the 'strength' of ties. However, the third class of measures of relations, namely the interval/ratio method, is the most advanced level of measurement that allows the actors to discriminate among relations (e.g., this tie is three times as strong as that tie)" (Hanneman, 2002 in Liebowitz, 2005, p. 79).

[g]   Quadratic Assignment Procedure. An example of a statistical test available in UCINET™ to check for significance of association between a couple of networks.

Section III

This third section of the book, covering Chapter VIII, introduces the reader to the methodology used in the book. As this is a research monograph, a methodology is necessary so that other researchers may follow in the footsteps of this one should they choose to do so. In essence, the methodology was comprised of a sequence of stages along the following lines. Initial qualitative analysis was conducted on the tacit knowledge literature, which revealed the organisationally based nature of tacit knowledge along with its highly individualistic character. If one wishes to undertake empirical organisationally based research, the choice of practical research instrument is limited. It is felt one of the better approaches is that along the lines of Sternberg. If one wishes to analyse likely knowledge flows within a company, the incorporation of Social Network Analysis provides a means of increasing rigour. The IT nature of the research domain validates the use of an Internet means of data collection. A Web-based questionnaire permits respondents to participate at a time and place that suits them. An individual login (due to the SNA component as we need to record who is networking with whom), requires that individuals must be de-identified for ethical reasons. A pilot testing process is considered advisable which in the case of this research involved 28 people in Organisation X. A comparison is drawn between the results of experts and non-experts as defined by personnel within the organisations under study. As this research is a multiple case study, the emphasis of the investigation was to chiefly examine specific organisational cases with a view to expounding exploratory theories, rather than conducting statistical generalisations on specific populations. To that end graphical tools were used in addition to basic descriptive statistics. One such example of a graphical tool is that of Formal Concept Analysis, which is in turn based on lattice theory. It is expected that the methodological outline provided in this chapter is replicable to the extent that others may engage in similar study should they wish to.

Chapter VIII

Methodology[a, b]

Sometimes existing theories may prove useful in accounting for the observed results, while on other occasions the findings cannot be adequately explained by existing theory and the researcher must discover the theory hidden in the empirical findings (Stenmark, 2000/2001, p. 16).

Introduction

There is more than reasonable support for the idea that the conduct of tacit knowledge related research is best *commenced* from a qualitative perspective (Stenmark, 2000/2001; 2000). The atypical nature of tacit knowledge does not lend itself easily to controlled experiments, whilst the knowledge itself is very much grounded within the organisation and the interactions personnel have with one another. To begin with a set of hypotheses and then seek to disprove these would arguably limit the researcher from the outset. Although both interpretivistic and positivistic research approaches have their advantages, it was felt that a positivistic approach would be more desirable because this would enable the author to broadly follow in the footsteps, though not necessarily *precisely* replicate, the work conducted by Sternberg's group at Yale University. As psychologists utilising questionnaires with a statistical interpretation to their results, Sternberg's group is firmly grounded in a positivistic epistemology. Nevertheless, as Chapter 4 has revealed and as other authors (Cutcliffe, 2000; Partington, 2000) have noted, there is strength in combining both epistemological approaches to a greater or lesser degree. Finally, the methodology adopted did not in any way intend at the start to adopt a critical social science perspective. That is to say, the initial intent of the researcher was not necessarily to force change in the organisation (Neuman, 1997), although recommendations in the concluding chapters of the book may lead to action being taken.

The (Empirical) Conduct of Tacit Knowledge Research

The researcher must take into account that whereas tacit knowledge may be a much talked about phenomenon, when it comes to actually experimenting or observing how tacit knowledge could be collected, measured or transferred, the options are limited.

General Methodological Overview

The research process must necessarily commence with an extensive literature review, for it is important to firstly establish what could be said to comprise tacit knowledge, indeed this process is lengthy in itself as Appendix A reveals (see also Chapter 3). Granted researchers may not agree on what constitutes an appropriate definition, the exercise in formulating a definition nevertheless allows the researcher to determine essentially two things. Firstly, the knowledge area of the study, that is to say whether the research may be conducted purely theoretically, or should take place within a "real world" domain. And secondly, in relation to the selection of research instrument or tools that will permit data collection and analysis. As an example of this process, although tacit knowledge has been codified along set-theoretic lines (Dampney, Busch, & Richards 2002b), the combination of the formalisms with the qualitative interpretation of the data permitted a new definition to be established. For the purposes of empirical testing within the study, the definition for tacit knowledge thus became *articulable implicit IT managerial knowledge*.

The literature review revealed that although much mention is made of tacit knowledge, little is actually extrapolated for the conduct of measurement or testing for tacit knowledge, other than predominantly the works of Sternberg (1999; Sternberg, Grigorenko, & Stella, 2001), Reed, Hock, and Lockhead (1993) and others in psychology. Alternatively we have the works of Magnus and Morgan (1997, 1999) in econometrics, which does not take a workplace testing approach, rather more of a traditional **methodological-individualistic** econometric modelling technique in relation to the role of tacit knowledge in the wider society. Certainly much mention is made of tacit knowledge in the knowledge management domain; for it is here that the empirical study takes place, investigating the likely flows of **intra-organisational** tacit, or rather implicit "soft knowledge" flows from one individual to another. To this end the most feasible approach to testing intra-organisational knowledge flows among IT practitioners was felt to be Sternberg's work which tests along psychological lines for differences in "tacit" knowledge from one individual to the next. Sternberg's approach does have its critics (Jensen, 1993, 1998; Ree & Earles, 1993; Schmidt & Hunter, 1993) who feel the tests are simply tests of workplace knowledge. Nevertheless even "Schmidt and Hunter acknowledge that alternative measures such as work sample test and job knowledge tests have comparable and perhaps even higher validities than do general ability tests, and provide incremental prediction above such tests" (Sternberg et al, 2001 in Lachman, 2001, p. 234). In spite of this, it has been acknowledged that in broadly adhering to Sternberg's approach, a greater sense of research credibility would be maintained.[c]

Although the techniques of Sternberg's (1999; Sternberg, Wagner, Williams, & Horvath 1995; Wagner & Sternberg, 1991a; 1991b), research into Tacit Knowledge at Yale University is broadly followed, the research is specifically focused in the Information Systems domain. Tacit knowledge is contextual. As such, this research along with others (Colonia-Willner, 1999; Sternberg, 1999) begins by using expert vs. novice comparisons within the *same* organisation. Again this last point relates to the intra-organisational nature of the research.

At a macro-level, the approach adopted within this study was to firstly define tacit knowledge. The following step was to adopt a **research instrument** for testing of IT tacit knowledge in individuals. The third component of the study required analysing tacit knowledge data. The next stage was to examine communication patterns between individuals by way of their relationships. The final step is to present findings and recommendations. At the micro-level, the conduct of the study was composed of broadly four phases with a total of seventeen steps. The first phase included background research with an emphasis on a literature review and establishment of research questions. The second phase involved the construction of the research instrument, in this case a **tacit knowledge inventory** and **pilot testing**. The third phase involved the live questionnaire in three selected organisations, with the fourth phase comprising interpretation of research results. Let's examine each of the phases in more detail, beginning with the literature review.

Phase 1: Background to the Research

Stage 1: Literature Review

Any tacit knowledge research must necessarily undertake a substantial literature review that attempts to define what the parameters are for the subject under study. Particular emphasis needs to be placed on literature that deals with methodology, rather than mere discussion of tacit knowledge and the usefulness of its role within the organisation. Furthermore the adoption of an initial qualitative perspective means that rather than starting with specific research questions in mind, the researcher is forced to read widely on topics relating to tacit knowledge. These topic areas include but are not limited to psychology, artificial intelligence, economics, sociology, philosophy, and of course information systems.

Stage 2: Qualitative Analysis of the Tacit Knowledge Literature

An initial or indeed complete qualitative approach to studying the phenomenon of tacit knowledge is not unique to the work presented here. Other researchers have also undertaken tacit knowledge research with a qualitative approach (Herrington & Oliver, 2000; Jacob & Ebrahimpur, 2001; Scott, 1990, 1992; Stenmark, 2000/2001). Given the textual nature of tacit knowledge definitions and the fact that authors do not precisely agree on these (Appendix 1), a useful method is to *initially* undertake a grounded theory approach. A further advantage of such a technique is that like qualitative research in general, it does not commit to any particular theoretical model from the outset (van Maanen, Dabbs, & Faulkner, 1982). First proposed by Glaser and Strauss in the 1960s, grounded theory has proven to be popular in a number of disciplines. In short "it is a set of procedures for "analysing data that will lead to the development of theory useful to that discipline" (Strauss & Corbin, 1990, p. 27).

The grounded theory component of the research utilised *Atlas.ti*™. Such software enables the mark-up of text so that network maps amongst other outputs may be used to examine themes arising from (subjectively) created codes. Needless to say other qualitative analysis software may be adopted, or the analysis process may be undertaken manually. The initial stage in the qualitative analysis involved creating a "hermeneutic unit" labelled Tacit Knowledge involving the coding up of 64 primary text documents (Busch & Dampney, 2000; Dampney et al., 2002a, 2002b). These documents contained separately the refined definitions of other author's attempts at defining this knowledge type (Appendix 1). Coding is initially open, that is to say a code is allocated to a particular sentence or paragraph as the text is being marked up. Axial coding is then utilised where the codes created are further re-allocated to text that encompasses similar themes to text already coded (Leedy, 1997). For example, there were eventually a total 1,310 code instances in the qualitative database, which were derived from marking up the documents.

Coding up of the documents permits us from a content analysis point of view to determine which of the definitions (Appendix 1) appear most frequently in the literature. An examination of Table 1 illustrates only codes with an occurrence in the qualitative database of greater than eight instances or "groundedness" in the literature. For example Knowledge was the most common keyword theme seen in the literature, with 80 instances within the 64 coded up textual documents. Note however the prominence of Individuals/Individuality: (50 instances) and role of the Organisational Domain: (46 instances). The occurrence of other representative codes such as Context Specific: (24 instances), Action: (12 instances), Practical: (9) instances is also not trivial.

The second major stage in the qualitative analysis had been to create network maps (Appendix B), which permitted a visual definition of tacit knowledge. In order to create network maps, one must first create a "code family" that encapsulates codes that are similar. This process may be labelled selective coding. The code family is created on the subjective understanding of the researcher. Several code families were established, principal among these were: code occurrence > 8; competition; culture; social environment; group interaction; individuals; and learning. The next stage is then to create network maps that permit a graphical

Table 1. Illustrating occurrence of codes >8 within the network maps (note the incidence of "knowledge," "skill," and "individuals" (Busch & Richards, 2000)

Knowledge	80		Action	12
Individuals	50		Expertise	11
Organisational domain	46		Culture	10
Skill	35		Contingency based	9
Non-Codification	28		Environment	9
Non-verbal	27		Externalisation	9
Experience	26		Knowing	9
Context specific	24		Not easily communicated	9
Intuition	20		Practical	9
Learned	16		Sub-consciousness	9
Know how	15		Understanding	9
Not formal	13		**Totals**	**1310**

view of themes comprising tacit knowledge. Map creation involves simply using the codes established as part of the initial marking up process, as nodes in a network map. The task the researcher then faces is to construct the edges, links or relationships between the nodes. Whilst one relation is able to be expressed between any two nodes, and this relation is fixed throughout the hermeneutic unit, any number of relations may be created, representing all sorts of relationships between the other nodes.

For the sake of research logistics, limitations in relationship diversity are necessary as the application of a similar relation to another set of codes enables easier comparison, both visually (by way of colour) and in terms of hierarchy that may exist between one relation and another. For example whilst certain relations are subsumed by others, some are at the same level of hierarchy, but simply represent different relationships between nodes. Typical relations are those of: is-associated-with; is-part-of; is-cause-of; is-composed-of; contradicts; is-an-example-of; is-a; leads-to; and is-property-of. Examination of the network maps reveals two numerical values on each code. The former relates to the **groundedness** or occurrence of this "theme" in the literature. The second numerical value on each code relates to the **density** of this code in the network, that is to say with how many other codes this code is related to. Both of these values permit the researcher to gain some understanding of the importance of one code over another. Figure 1 illustrates just such a network map of a code family relating to tacit knowledge and organisations.

The centrality of organisational domain (groundedness of 46, density of 21) is obvious from the network map. Note however other pivotal codes such as competitive advantage (3:8), competitive (2:1), sub-consciousness (9:13), job knowledge (4:5), tasks (6:2) and particularly the centrality of codes such as task management (1:8). The role of apprenticeship (7:8) is noticeable in the diagram as indeed it is in the literature, reflecting the teacher-student relationship in tacit knowledge transfer. What network mapping has enabled is the unearthing of

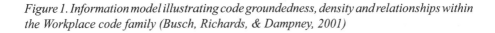

Figure 1. Information model illustrating code groundedness, density and relationships within the Workplace code family (Busch, Richards, & Dampney, 2001)

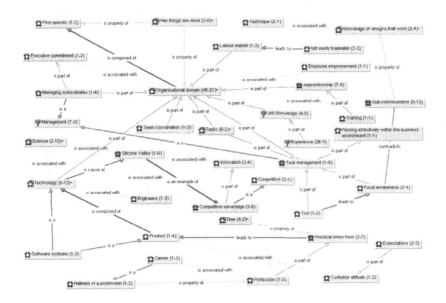

dominant themes within tacit knowledge so that a better understanding of the phenomenon can be gained.

Notice also the importance of colour (apparent in the original network diagrams). Although network maps may be represented in black and white, the consequence is that a large amount of information is lost. Not only is the user more easily able to identify the relationships between each code by way of the text represented on each relationship line, the use of colours which is so necessary in such a network map immediately permits the viewer to identify the levels of complexity of the relationships themselves. For example, a red colour has been used to identify contradiction between one node and another. In other words where a code conflicts with another one is able to visually identify this trend. Colour coding thus permits instances of "aggressiveness/passiveness," "superclass/subclass," or "similarity/dissimilarity" in the codes to emerge from the literature. Simply put, colour provides the reader with a more intuitive interpretation of the maps. Further such examples may be evidenced in Appendix B.

The purpose of such an exercise is to establish theory, which is considered to be "conceptually dense" (Leedy, 1997). As evidence of the subjective nature of this qualitative approach, one investigator will specify the name and groundedness allocated for each code, where another individual may allocate slightly different code names and use a certain code more often than another. Qualitative research does not necessarily aim to be wholly objective or necessarily replicable for that matter either.

What the qualitative stage of the research has done is acknowledge both the organisational as well as individualistic nature of tacit knowledge. Given that the phenomenon was discovered to be: (1) heavily grounded in the workplace; (2) individualistic in nature; (3) greatly contextual; and (4) experience based, it was felt that interpretational case studies were the best approach to be taken (Gall, Borg, & Gall, 1996; Leedy, 1997). As further testimony to the appropriateness of using a case study approach, Yin (1984) notes that "… case studies, like experiments, are generalisable to theoretical propositions and not to populations, or universes. In this sense, the case study, like the experiment, does not represent a 'sample,' and the investigator's goal is to expand and generalise theories (analytic generalisation) and not to enumerate frequencies (statistical generalisation)" (p. 21). As will become clear, the data analysis approach used in this study adopts a largely visual approach to data presentation and interpretation rather than a purely statistical technique.

Phase 2: Initial Construction of the Tacit Knowledge Inventory

Stage 3: Interviewing of Domain Experts

Once a case study approach had been settled upon, the next task was to determine the most appropriate instrument for tacit knowledge data collection. Pre-eminent in the field of tacit knowledge testing has been that of Professor Robert Sternberg. Sternberg's approach is generally to use situational job inventories as a means of determining the differences in "street smarts" amongst organisational personnel. An organisational-based approach is considered most appropriate for testing of articulable implicit IT managerial knowledge. A further strength in using the Sternberg approach is that there is a general acceptance in the research community of situational job inventories (McDaniel, Morgeson, Finnegan, Campion, & Braverman, 2000). To that end, the methodology follows Sternberg's approach, beginning with interviewing of personnel within the knowledge domain under study.

When interviewing IT staff, it is considered appropriate to ascertain workplace situations where interviewees encountered successful and unsuccessful situations. Sternberg's group was permitted to determine *who* was *un*successful in the workplace as well as a means of determining what might constitute unsuccessful applications of practical knowledge. Permission to determine who was unsuccessful was not granted at Macquarie University, as it was felt this was **covert research** and therefore unethical.[d] Nevertheless permission was given for ascertaining who might be successful persons and what it was that personnel had done correctly and incorrectly in the IT workplace.

Interviews comprising both open and closed questions ranging from 26 to 52 minutes in duration were conducted with 14 IT practitioners. The purpose of this exercise was to elicit enough information that would enable the creation of a tacit knowledge inventory along the lines of Sternberg's technique. Personnel were selected on the basis of seniority/non-seniority, as the literature seemed to indicate that age and experience affected use of tacit knowledge. Moreover it was felt desirable to include a mix of both practitioners and theoreticians to provide balance to the tacit knowledge inventory. Some IT practitioners were reluctant to mention unsuccessful workplace experiences, stating that what they did was always successful and of a high standard.

Stage 4: Creation of Tacit Knowledge Inventory

Interviews were transcribed and the transcripts enabled the creation of 24 IT workplace scenarios with answer options for dealing with each scenario. The answer options varied from six to 13 means of dealing with each selected scenario. Each answer option was specific to that particular scenario, although broadly similar themes began to emerge from interviewing practitioners and theoreticians along the lines of "management" related information, which was retrospectively discovered in Wagner and Sternberg's (1991a, 1991b) views on tacit knowledge being management related information concerning management of self, others, and tasks. In short tacit knowledge may be considered "management" knowledge. What Sternberg's group means by this is management of one's life, management of tasks necessary to achieve day-to-day success, and management of people who people interact with:

Tacit knowledge about managing self refers to practical know-how about self motivation and self-organisational aspects of performance. An example of tacit knowledge about managing oneself is about knowing how to overcome the problem of procrastination. Tacit knowledge about managing tasks refers to practical know-how about how to do specific work related tasks well. An example of tacit knowledge about managing tasks is knowing how to make an effective oral presentation. Tacit knowledge about managing others refers to practical know-how about managing relations among subordinates, peers, and superiors. An example of tacit knowledge about managing others is knowing how to reward individuals so as to maximise both their job satisfaction and their productivity (Wagner & Sternberg, 1991b, p. 2)

In short, the approach adopted is one of workplace scenarios with options for dealing with a situation, which are "tested" by respondents. Admittedly some alternative means for undertaking tacit knowledge testing do exist (Herbig, Büssing, & Ewert, 2001; Larkin, 1980; Noh, Lee, Kim, Lee, & Kim, 2000; Reber, 1993; Reber & Lewis, 1977; Reed et al., 1993), the various merits of these approaches having been discussed (Chapter 4). The initial 24 scenarios were later reduced to 16, when it was realised there was a crossover between some of the scenarios. Sternberg's group at Yale has used in the order of 12 scenarios with four to 12 answer options per scenario.

Stage 5: Testing of the Tacit Knowledge Scenarios (Pre-Pilot Study)

With the scenarios finalised they were duplicated and handed out randomly to 30 IT practitioners both on and off Macquarie University campus as a form of pre-pilot study. The purpose of this exercise was to establish **face validity** of the workplace inventories, a similar approach having also been adopted by Subramaniami and Venkatraman (2001). The personnel were selected at random, and were specifically chosen to be practitioners, rather than theoreticians. In other words, they were chosen for their experience and on the basis of their ability to conduct **member checking**[e] as objectively as possible. Undergraduate or postgraduate computing students were not asked to critique scenarios, as the study was not concerned with student experience. It was decided to use mostly university-based IT staff as the difficulties in obtaining external IT staff who would be prepared to provide feedback on the scenarios without remuneration proved difficult indeed. Evidence of this negative attitude was reflected in comments by IT superiors who intimated that although they would try and persuade their staff to provide some feedback, as the staff members were not compulsorily required to provide feedback, there was little likelihood that anything like a 100 percent success rate could be achieved. This was an attitude to resurface later when tacit knowledge testing in selected organisations went live.

What was in fact called for was a "reality check" of the scenarios and answer options. Each practitioner randomly received no more than four scenarios with applicable answer options, as it was felt that concentration spans would lapse if they were asked to critique any more. As it turned out, even critiquing four scenarios proved taxing. In short what was desired was that they provide feedback on only a few scenarios, but that they take the scenarios seriously, rather than simply declare there was little wrong with them. In randomly assigning scenarios it was hoped that as diverse a range of opinions as possible would be provided, so that by the time the critiqued scenarios would be retrieved, all 16 scenarios would have had the attention of at least a few people. Typical feedback comments included, "questions seem okay, but the responses don't seem to me to be industrial strength in reflecting realities in business" (i.e., relating to the scenario/answer wording), to "pretty realistic scenario, including register of language and tone" and "wow! realistic scenario, this actually happened to me!" Feedback in terms of the language and terminology used was also called for.

Though the tacit knowledge inventory was specifically aimed at IT practitioners (typically graduate level), some responded that "not everybody would know what an expert system was," or "not everyone would know what UML (Unified Modelling Language) is." To that end it was also expected that critiquers were required to stipulate which parts or wording of the inventory components they did not understand. Having retrieved the scenarios from the critiquers, a refinement process took place whereby all comments were utilised to update the tacit knowledge inventory before it could be integrated into the complete questionnaire.

Stage 6: Incorporation of the Tacit Knowledge Inventory within a Broader Questionnaire

Having established that tacit knowledge testing takes place at the individual level, is context specific, and aids in the knowledge management domain, it was felt desirable to *also* test for *likely* tacit knowledge "loss" from the organisation. To this end, the research not only sought to test along psychological lines for who may be said to have more tacit knowledge than others, but also how well tacit knowledge is being transferred between individuals. Scott's (1990, 1992) work into tacit knowledge and the nursing domain, utilised participant observation as a means of observing the transfer of tacit knowledge from one individual to another; for example, the observation of how nurses and new mothers interacted in relation to the handling of a new-born infant in the hospital environment. It was felt that participant observation would not be effective within the Information Systems domain given the usually deskbound working style of IT practitioners. In other words work practices that typically involve a human and a monitor. Other difficulties involved the limited likelihood of being granted permission to observe IT professionals in organisational meetings, whether official or unofficial (at the coffee machine or photocopier for example), given the University's Human Research Ethics Committee (HREC) gave a negative impression of any form of covert research. There was a possibility that IT personnel could be asked for permission to be videotaped, however given the reluctance of busy private sector IT practitioners to even completing an online questionnaire, it is doubtful video taping personnel in workplace settings would have been successful.

As a result of the above factors, it was considered that rather than utilise participant observation, a more appropriate means of determining information flows, and more specifically tacit knowledge flows amongst individuals, would be to incorporate Social Network Analysis into the research. To this end, the questionnaire incorporated three major components. Firstly a biographical section, secondly a social network analysis section, and finally the tacit knowledge inventory itself.

Section A: Biographical

The first component of the questionnaire included questions relating to:

* *gender*, as this was felt to make a difference in tacit knowledge utilisation (Somech and Bogler, 1999; Horgan and Simeon, 1990).
* *age*, as executives for example were known to use tacit knowledge differently depending on age (Colonia-Willner, 1999), and
* *language other than English*, as culture was felt to have a bearing on tacit knowledge utilisation.[f]

It also was felt desirable to determine whether personnel making greater or lesser use of tacit knowledge could be said to be front office (i.e., client facing) or back office employees (i.e., more technically focused staff). The expectation being that the job types would have differing knowledge transferral demands. It was felt[g] there was likely to be a difference between the two staff types. To that end, questions were asked as to

* *occupation* of employees today,
* 3 years ago and
* 6 years ago.

The latter question largely related to how long the person had been in the IT occupation.

Initial interviews with IS management revealed an interest in determining whether the hiring of contract staff was desirable because of the ever-present conception that tacit knowledge would "walk out the door." To that end, one of the questions asked was whether staff were contract or permanent. Other questions related to **Australian Computer Society** (ACS) levels. It was felt there would be a connection between higher ACS levels (therefore levels of expertise) and increased use of tacit knowledge (this is a recurring theme in chapter 2). ACS levels were derived from the results of an ACS remuneration survey from 2000 (ACS 2000). Also of interest were numbers of years of IT experience as well as the number of years with the current organisation. Also as far as management experience was concerned, it was felt important to ask how many subordinates were junior to the respondent. Sternberg et al.'s research seems to indicate that "... tacit knowledge tends to increase with experience on the job. In other words, people who have been in a job longer tend to have more tacit knowledge than those who have not been in the job as long, [although admittedly], ... The important variable appears to be not amount of time in the job per se, but what the person has learned from being in the job" (1995 p. 329).

Questions were also asked about highest formal qualifications obtained and technically specific computing qualifications. Given the responses from the pilot study, which indicated that there were far too many types of computing "on-the-job" qualifications for most people to remember, it was felt prudent to simply list vendors under the computing specific qualification section of the questionnaire. Advice was given that it was inappropriate to *insist* upon respondents providing age and gender related data, although the option existed for them do so.

Figure 2. Illustrating the initial social network analysis component of the questionnaire used in the pilot study

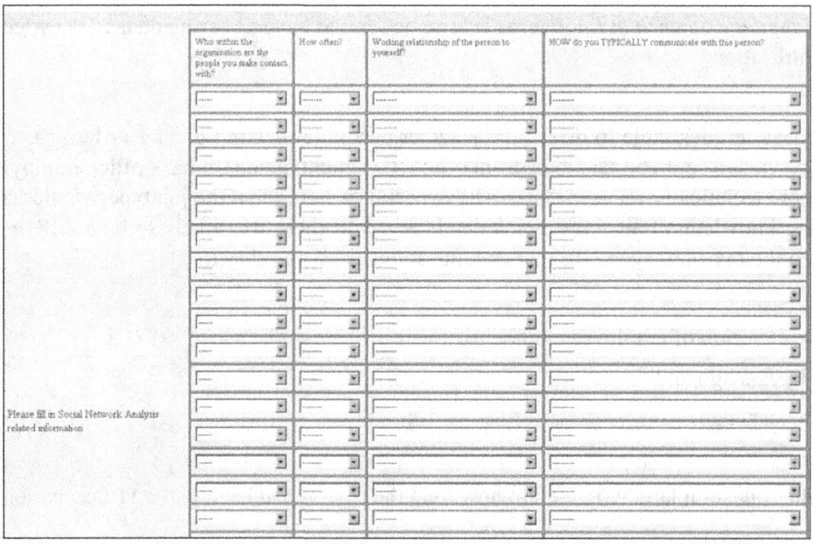

Section B: Social Network Analysis

It was considered that diffusion of articulable tacit knowledge could be measured through the adoption of social network analysis. Traditionally such a process has taken place via a pen and paper format enabling respondents to select from a matrix-like structure. Problems with a pen and paper approach included amongst other things a very "busy" look to the sheet, which made filling out and maintaining order for that particular question difficult.[h] For that reason encouragement was given early on that providing an electronic means for gathering Social Network Analysis information would be preferable. To that end, a prototype questionnaire component was programmed, and feedback obtained on the suitability of the questions being asked. As the pilot study was only to involve 28 people, a simple matrix (with 28 rows) was constructed as illustrated in Figure 2. Respondents were to select (a) the person with whom they networked, (b) how often, (c) the type of working relationship with the person, in other words whether the colleague was superior or subordinate to the respondent, and lastly (d) the type of meeting/communication pattern that takes place. The latter point is particularly important, as evidence would suggest that much information is transmitted in face-to-face, in other words tacit knowledge is *not* communicated in electronic form.

Section C: Tacit Knowledge Inventory

Because the questionnaire was to be electronic, it was possible to randomise the allocation of scenarios from the test bank of 16, so that respondents would be presented with a given number of scenarios in a random order. This was preferable because a respondent who had finished earlier could not necessarily inform a colleague of the sorts of questions to expect. Admittedly there was some likelihood that a colleague would be presented with at least one scenario the same as their co-worker.

For each one of the answer options presented, there were Likert scales from 1 to 7 (Extremely Bad, Very Bad, Bad, Neither Good nor Bad, Good, Very Good and Extremely Good respectively). Participants did not see a numerical value; only the wording from *Very Bad* through to *Extremely Good* was visible, the reason being that it was felt inadvisable to bias respondents unduly with numerical weightings to questions. Furthermore, no advantage was noted to be gained by increasing the Likert scale to 9 points or more (Bass, Cascio, & O'Connor, 1974).

Two Likert Scales per scenario were presented, requesting both an Ethical and a Realistic value as a means of working out how much a variation there would likely be between what a person "should" be doing, as opposed to what they would actually sensibly do.[i] Indeed Wagner and Sternberg (1991a; 1991b) as it turned out, utilised a similar approach. One such example of a tacit knowledge scenario with a Likert scale answer arrangement used in this research may be seen in Figure 3.

Having completed each scenario with relevant answer options, respondents were to click the <*submit*> button at the bottom of the page and be presented with the next scenario until all scenarios had been completed. Upon completion of scenarios, a concluding page was presented which advised the user to log out of the browser. This was done to prevent work colleagues from back-paging to refill out a questionnaire under someone else's login. The

Figure 3. Illustrating scenario 3, answer 2 of the IS articulable tacit knowledge inventory

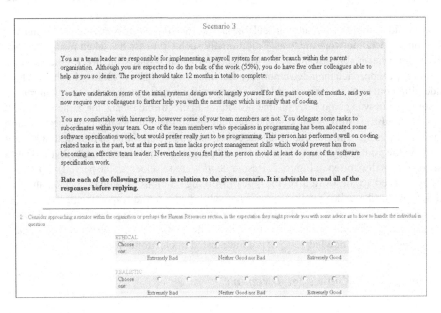

examination of submitted electronic result pages did not appear to indicate that personnel had acted mischievously.

Stage 7: Ethics Committee Approval

After an initial literature review, a preliminary research design was submitted to the Ethics Committee in September of 1999. The HREC wished to see the completed questionnaire before permission could be given for live testing. The main objection the committee had with the approach adopted by Yale University (Sternberg), was asking within an organisational setting who is "not proficient" at what they do. Asking as part of the research who *was* actually proficient was acceptable. Provided this condition was met, the committee was satisfied the research could continue. Finally the questionnaire was at a stage where it could be shown to the HREC for their final approval by late March of 2001. One final requirement from the committee was that research results be kept secure for at least five years and that the means of identification of subjects be available only to the principal researchers.

Stage 8: Selection of IT Organisations

The information systems background of the researcher predestined that the research take place within IS/IT organisations. Additionally evidence suggested that tacit knowledge research with an emphasis on the knowledge management area was needed (Anand, Manz, & Glick, 1998; Cavusgil, Calantone, & Zhao, 2003; Smith 2000; Subramaniami & Venka-traman, 2001). Moreover, along the lines of Xu and Quaddus (2005) and McDaniel et al. (2001), it is acknowledged "studies of students [are best] excluded to avoid concerns over generalisability to work-related settings" (p. 734). Furthermore the work of Lam (2000) us-ing Mintzberg's typology (1983, 1991a, b, c, d, e) had indicated that organisations are likely to differ in their tacit knowledge characteristics. For all of these reasons, ICT organisations were chosen to provide a degree of organisational breadth.

The selection process took place in December of 2000. One of the academics of the depart-ment was a member of DAMA (DAta Management Association), Sydney, Australia, which aided in finding appropriate organisations. Organisations were approached on the basis of being sent formal letters to their CIOs (Chief Information Officers), asking them if they were interested in having their IT section participate. Given the poor response, follow up phone calls were necessary.

Of the 28 organisations sent letters with follow up phone calls, eight felt interested enough to ask for further details about the research. Of these eight, it was decided to proceed with one of these for the pilot testing, within which one CIO was particularly interested in what was being researched. For the purposes of confidentiality, this organisation shall be referred to as Organisation X, it is however a large privately listed, nationally based company with a software engineering staff profile of some 400 personnel, and a total IT profile of 1,400 personnel nationwide.

As a final point it is worth noting that nonprobability sampling was adopted; more specifi-cally convenience sampling was the approach implemented. That is to say the researcher "takes the units as they arrive on the scene or as they are presented to the researcher by mere happenstance" (Leedy, 1997, p. 204). In fact, the researcher had little choice with regard to the sample population. The personnel chosen to participate in the study were entirely up to the CIO's discretion in each of Organisations X, Y, and Z. All were however IT staff. As it turned out, the sample group consisted of 100 percent of the IT staff in the case of both organisations Y and Z.

Stage 9: Programming of the Questionnaire

Given that IT related tacit knowledge was under investigation and that only IT practitioners were to be participants in our research, an electronic Internet based questionnaire was felt justified. To that end January to March of 2001 saw programming of the questionnaire take place, incorporating the three sections. The coding utilised Javascript with a CGI and Perl backend, which was extensively custom-tailored from sample templates that existed on the Internet. Each component of the questionnaire consisted of a separate "Web page." The biographical section was one page, the SNA section another, and then each subsequent tacit knowledge inventory component yet another. In filling out a page, a "form" with answers would be sent back to the host machine at Macquarie University. Error checking routines built into the program ensured that all questions save those dealing with gender and age, had to be answered. Advice was provided[j] that one could not insist upon personnel providing age or gender related information. The entire questionnaire may be seen in Appendix G.

As the questionnaire was going to incorporate an SNA component, anonymity would only be possible through individual de-identification. Incorporating an SNA module meant that respondents would have to identify themselves as well as identifying other respondents they interacted with. At the same time, it was not felt advisable by the researcher to *force* people to indicate with whom they interacted, or for that matter stipulating in the questionnaire a minimum number of people with whom they had to provide details of their workplace interaction. Both of these requirements are subjective to the degree that some personnel may network with many and others with very few. Removing error checking routines from the social network component of the questionnaire thus enabled participants to either not choose any networks with other staff, or alternatively to choose as many contacts with other staff as they may have had.

It was felt that given the time constraints on the average IT practitioner, requiring respondents to spend up to two hours filling out a questionnaire (the time noted in some of Sternberg's studies) would have been unreasonable. It is also likely to have led to a very low response rate, with a high error rate due to the questionnaire not being taken seriously. To that end, the questionnaire for the pilot study incorporated only 6 scenarios with answer options. As two answer values would have to be provided for each answer option (an ethical and realistic value), multiplied in turn by between five to 13 answer options per scenario, multiplied by six scenarios; a social network analysis section; and some 13 biographical questions meant that a respondent had in excess of 120 answers to provide. At this stage, pilot testing could take place.

Stage 10: Pilot Testing

The group of participants to be chosen for the complete pilot study was the decision of the senior Software Development Engineer in Organisation X. Two pilot groups were involved. Each of the groups was sent a personal letter from the researcher, also signed by the boss of the two groups. The letter contained clarification that the research had been sanctioned by the University Ethics Committee and contained the respondent's personal username and password. One group consisting of 26 people were to be the "control" group, the other group consisting of seven personnel were to be the "expert" group. They were deemed to be experts by their peers, in other words they were highly proficient in achieving their workplace tasks and were generally admired by their peers. Respondents had simply been telephoned afterwards and asked to identify colleagues whom they thought of as proficient. These "experts" were then contacted individually by phone and asked to fill in the online questionnaire. Response rates for the control group were 20 out of 26 (77 percent). The response rate for the expert group was 100 percent, which may have had something to do with the fact that the "expert" respondents were told they were as such, and that their results would provide comparisons with the "control" group.

Specifically for the pilot testing, the incorporation of an open-ended (free text) question for each tacit knowledge scenario permitted extra feedback (Figure 4). Once again no error checking routines were placed on *this* particular question, even though such routines were on all Likert scale questions for the scenarios. It was not felt feasible (or fair) to force respondents to have to answer the open-ended question. The idea behind incorporating this

Figure 4. Illustrating the question used to elicit feedback from respondents in relation to tacit knowledge questions

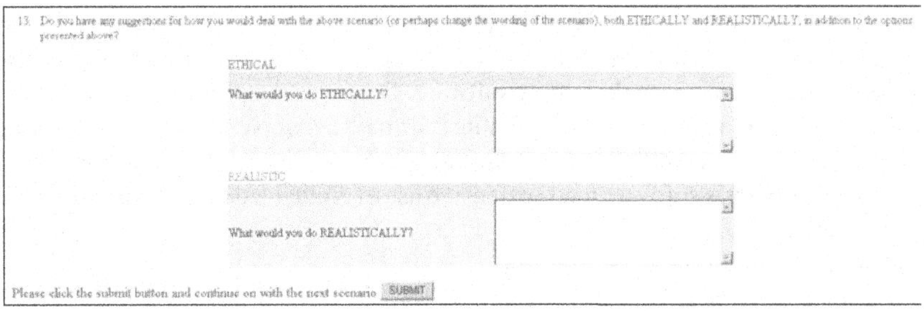

last question in each scenario was to obtain feedback from IT practitioners in relation to the tacit knowledge scenarios; this last approach thus incorporated extra "member checking".

Remarkably, the questionnaire seemed to take respondents only 20 to 30 minutes to fill out. It is felt the reason for this was its electronic nature.

Stage 11: Processing of Data

The completion of each electronic page of the questionnaire meant numbers of pages submitted were in the order of eight pages or forms per person (biographical, social network analysis, and six tacit knowledge scenario pages). The contents of these forms were entered into a spreadsheet so that the data could be further sorted. Information was transposed correctly into the proper format from where it could be used for statistical analysis. The text wizard in MSExcel™ permitted data to be read in either tab delimited or comma delimited format. Data was aligned so that rows represented objects and attributes were represented in columns. In other words for both the Formal Concept Analysis and Social Network Analysis formats, the respondents were listed in rows, and their attributes (biographical information, social network analysis contacts and tacit knowledge answers), were represented in columns, one cell after the other in a row. It is from this stage onwards that data preparation began to assume alternative formats.

Stage 11a: Data Preparation for Formal Concept Analysis

Apart from descriptive statistical analysis, the data had to be prepared in a spreadsheet so that it could be fed into MSAccess™ from whence it could be utilised by Anaconda™ and then in turn Toscana™. Anaconda™ is data preparation software that formats the data in such a way that it is acceptable to Toscana™. Toscana™ is the actual lattice modelling software.

Stage 11b: Data Preparation for Social Network Analysis

For the SNA component of the research NetMap™ software from the NetMap Analytics™ company was chosen due to its ability to enable one to visualise complex personal relationships. Once again data had to be sorted into a spreadsheet format so that NetMap™ was able to interpret the data correctly into its software. Data was then saved from MSExcel™ spreadsheet format into ASCII comma delimited format so that NetMap™ in turn was able to read the data into its own format. Interestingly both the Formal Concept Analysis and Social Network Analysis software made extensive use of embedded SQL (Structured Query Language) statements.

Stage 12: Modelling of the Data

Two major means of modelling the questionnaire results were those of SNA itself, and Formal Concept Analysis. The data models appear as part of the results in the following chapters.

Stage 13: Preparation of a De-Identified Report for Organisations who had Participated

Because the respondents were not captive, an incentive had to be provided to management of the organisations in order for adequate data samples to be obtained. The incentive was a de-identified report that illustrated likely soft knowledge flows within their particular organisation. In effect, this was handled as a "donation in kind" knowledge management consultancy.

Phase 3: Major Surveys

Stage 14: Modifications to the Questionnaire

Having conducted a pilot study on 28 personnel, the major component of the questionnaire that would need to be changed involved the social network analysis section. What was needed was an approach that allowed respondents to select a far greater number of colleagues. Whilst the pilot study prototype incorporated only the names of 28 people involved in the study, the complete questionnaire would literally have 1,400 personnel hardcoded. The SNA component of the questionnaire now appeared along the following lines (Figure 5).

The inclusion of a separate window on the right hand side of the screen also enabled the respondent to view the relationship combinations they had chosen. This enabled people completing the questionnaire to delete and redo a relationship upon further reflection. It was also felt prudent to incorporate a *<section>* selection button (top left hand corner),

Figure 5. Illustrating the updated Social Network Analysis component of the questionnaire, allowing selection of personnel

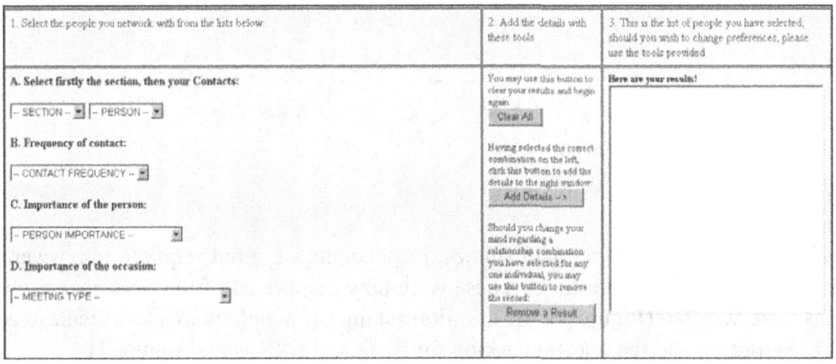

which would in turn permit the presentation of a subset of individuals for that given section. An alternative approach to incorporating a *<section>* button would have been to list staff members of any given organisation alphabetically. A disadvantage noted by this approach would be that respondents may not necessarily know the surnames of the people they are working with, although they would likely know the sections the people are located in.[k] A more sophisticated approach was the recommendation given to incorporating photographs of staff next to names in the questionnaire; so that one would be able to select colleagues by face should respondents wish to do so. This was felt to be overly complicated and not practical for the purposes of the research, for enough difficulties were experienced in obtaining staff names, let alone staff photographs. To this end, the final version of the questionnaire incorporated only sections and names.

The Social Network Analysis section also incorporated extra questions asking for people who were difficult to contact (Figure 6). In incorporating such a question, it was hoped to identify soft knowledge bottlenecks that could possibly occur within the IT domain.

Following Sternberg's approach to tacit knowledge testing, which compares the results of "experts" with others, it was felt best to identify "experts" or proficient people at the time that participants undertook the questionnaire (Figure 7). Although the term "good" had at first been utilised rather than "proficient," it was felt that "good" was too morally loaded a term for use in research.[l]

Figure 6. Illustrating question asking respondents to identify individuals they typically had difficulties contacting in the workplace

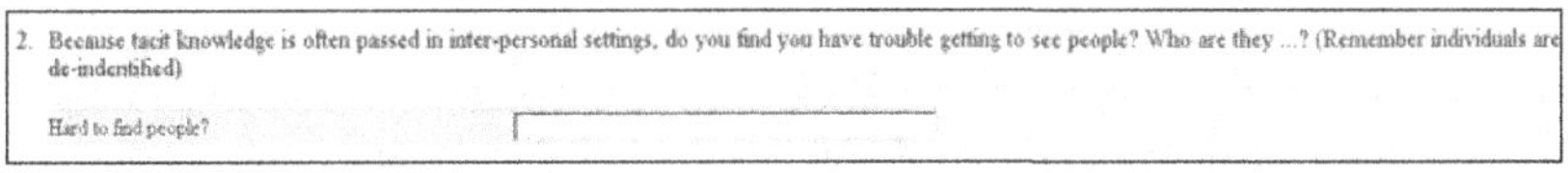

Figure 7. Illustrating questionnaire asking respondents to identify personnel they felt were particularly proficient at what they did

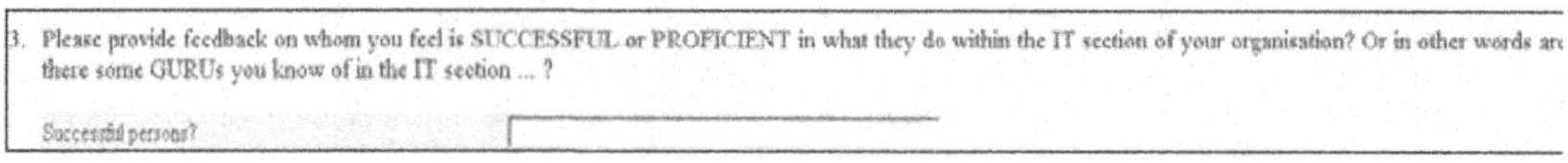

It should be noted that for the main studies, respondents were not required to answer the Social Network Analysis questions. These were now comprised of the SNA menu where contacts were selected (Figure 5), the question asking for people who are difficult to contact/see (Figure 6), and the question asking for proficient colleagues (Figure 7).

It was not felt appropriate to include error-checking routines (in other words an error message that did not permit forward page movement unless questions had been answered), into the SNA component of the questionnaire, as one could not necessarily force people to identify their workplace relationships. For that reason no error checking routines existed for the second (hard to find) and third (proficient) questions on this Web page either. A number of respondents did nevertheless answer the second and third questions as well however, some exclaiming that "all their colleagues were professionals," others stating the proficient ones "had all left."

Stage 15: Live Questionnaire

It was expected that up to 1,400 IT personnel in Organisation X would potentially participate in the study. The pilot study with six scenarios took respondents in the order of 20 to 30 minutes to fill out. Advice was given that it would be acceptable to have fewer scenarios with a larger sample size.[m] Furthermore discussions with Sternberg's group at Yale indicated in the order of 50 items of information per respondent they considered acceptable.[n] To that end it was decided to administer only 4 tacit knowledge scenarios to each Organisation X participant. The hope was that in having respondents in Organisation X answer fewer scenarios, they would be less tired, more likely to concentrate and generally take the questionnaire more seriously. Results indicate that this was in fact the case. Very few of the respondents who eventually *did* participate simply "copped out" by routinely choosing the central non-committal Likert scale value of "Neither Good nor Bad." One or two respondents did however. With the structure of the questionnaire as it now stood with a biographical section, SNA section and the tacit knowledge inventory with roughly four scenarios presented, it was feasible for an IT practitioner to complete the questionnaire in the order of 20 minutes.

In all, 1,400 individually addressed letters (on appropriate Macquarie University letterhead paper with Ethics Committee approval), were to be internally mailed to IT personnel in Organisation X. The letters contained personal usernames and passwords for the participants. Unfortunately due to an unexplained combination of political and managerial factors within

Organisation X, only 164 of the 1,400 letters were internally distributed. The complete questionnaire went live in November of 2001. In January of 2002 follow up letters and phone calls convinced more staff to participate. By late February of 2002 some 108 staff had completed the questionnaire.

As organisations Y and Z were significantly smaller than Organisation X it was felt advisable to require respondents to answer a larger number of scenarios, remembering that scenarios are electronically randomly assigned from the test bank of 16 possible scenarios. This would mitigate the likelihood of no one scenario within any test organisation going unanswered. Once again participants were sent individually addressed letters. Respondents within organisation Y (seven participants out of eight in total) answered seven scenarios each. Participants in Organisation Z (13 participants out of 15 in total) answered six scenarios each. The change in scenarios to be attempted was easy to administer. Merely changing the "number-of-scenarios-to-be-attempted" parameter in the configuration file accomplished this. Fortunately, the goodwill of the respondents in all the organisations ensured that almost none of the scenarios contained blank Likert scale values, or that respondents simply logged out part way through. Expecting respondents to answer more than about seven scenarios as part of the questionnaire process was considered highly inadvisable, as it was felt people would not take the questionnaire seriously and likely log out after about 40 minutes. Once again, one must realise the respondents were private sector IT practitioners, not captive undergraduates, for whom in the case of the former, no *direct* incentive (or commandment) existed for participating in the research.

Stage 16: Modifications to Social Network Analysis Processing

For analysing the main questionnaire results in addition to using NetMap™, utilisation was also made of UcinetV™ SNA software and its associated graph drawing package NetDraw™. The primary reason for this decision being that NetDraw added the benefit of using Multi-Dimensional Scaling in addition to sociomatrices and sociographs.

Phase 4: Analysis of Data

Stage 17: Interpretation of Data

Analysis of the data took place with the Formal Concept Analysis software, Anaconda™ and Toscana™. Although statistical testing was included in the research (Wilcoxon test), the use of Formal Concept Analysis permitted a finer granularity of data interpretation with its lattice-based approach to data visualisation. The incorporation of Social Network Analysis aided in determining communication flows between individuals at an intra-organisational level.

Summary

In summary, the methodology was comprised of a sequence of stages along the following lines.

- Initial qualitative analysis revealed the organisationally based nature of tacit knowledge along with its highly individualistic character.

- If one wishes to undertake empirical organisationally based research, the choice of practical research instrument is limited. It is felt that the best approach is that along the lines established by Sternberg at Yale University.

- Member checking when using the Yale based approach is considered to greatly increase the face validity of the research instrument.

- Given the knowledge diffusion nature of the research, the incorporation of social network analysis is considered desirable.

- The IT nature of the research domain validates the use of an Internet means of data collection. A Web-based questionnaire permits respondents to participate at a time and place that suits them.

- Individual login due to the social network analysis component means in turn that individuals must be de-identified.

- A pilot testing process is considered advisable which in the case of this research involved 28 people in Organisation X.

- A comparison is drawn between the results of experts and non-experts as defined by personnel within the organisations under study.

- For all forms of organisationally based research, permission from the University Ethics Committee was required.

- As this research is a multiple case study, the emphasis of the investigation was to examine specific organisational cases with a view to expounding exploratory theories, rather than conducting statistical generalisations on specific populations. To that end graphical tools were used in addition to basic descriptive statistics. One such example of a graphical tool is that of Formal Concept Analysis, which is in turn based on lattice theory.

- It is expected that the methodological outline provided in this chapter is replicable to the extent that others may engage in similar study should they wish to.

Next the focus turns to the results of the research, beginning with the organisational backgrounds, respondent biographies and tacit knowledge inventory outcomes.

References

A.C.S. (2000). *A.C.S. Remuneration Survey.* APESA: Australian Computer Society.

Anand, V., Manz, C., & Glick, W. (1998). An organizational memory approach to information management. *The Academy of Management Review, 23*(4), 769-809.

Bass, B., Cascio, W., & O'Connor, E. (1974). Magnitude estimations of expressions of frequency and amount. *Journal of Applied Psychology, 59*(3), 313-320

Busch, P., & Dampney, C. (2000). Tacit knowledge acquisition and processing within the computing domain: An exploratory study. *2000 Information Resources Management Association International Conference,* Anchorage, AK, 1014-1015.

Busch, P., & Richards, D. (2000). Graphically defining articulable tacit knowledge. In *Proceedings of PAN-Sydney Area Workshop on Visual Information Processing* (VIP'2000). December 1, University of Sydney, http://www.cs.usyd.edu.au/~vip2000/presentation. html

Busch, P., Richards, D., & Dampney, C. (2001). Visual mapping of articulable tacit knowledge. In P. Eades & T. Pattison (Eds.), *Australian Symposium on Information Visualisation* (InVIS'2001), December 10-11, Melbourne, pp. 37-47.

Cavusgil, S.T., Calantone, R.J., & Zhao, Y. (2003). Tacit knowledge transfer and firm innovation capacity. *Journal of Business and Industrial Marketing, 18*(1), 6-21.

Colonia-Willner, R.(1999). Investing in practical intelligence: Ageing and efficiency among executives. *International Journal of Behavioral Development, 23*(3), 591-614.

Cutcliffe, J. (2000). Methodological issues in grounded theory. *Journal of Advanced Nursing, 31*(6), 1476-1484.

Dampney, C., Busch, P., & Richards, D. (2002a). A definition of tacit knowledge. *Information Systems Foundations Workshop,* October 1–2. Canberra, Australia: Australian National University.

Dampney, C., Busch, P., & Richards, D. (2002). The meaning of tacit knowledge. *Australian Journal of Information Systems,* December, 3-13.

Dowall, D. (1987). Back offices and San Francisco's office development growth gap. *Cities, 4*(2), 119-127.

Gall, M., Borg, W., & Gall, J. (1996). *Educational research:An introduction,* 6th Ed. New York: Longman.

Herbig, B., Büssing, A., & Ewert, T. (2001). The role of tacit knowledge in the work context of nursing. *Journal of Advanced Nursing, 34*(5), 687-695.

Herrington, J., & Oliver, R. (2000). An instructional design framework for authentic learning environments. *Education Technology Tesearch and Development, 48*(3), 23-48.

Horgan, D., & Simeon, R. (1990). Gender, mentoring, and tacit knowledge. *Journal of Social Behaviour and Personality, 5*(1, Special Issue), 153 171.

Jacob, M., & Ebrahimpur, G. (2001). Experience vs. expertise: The role of implicit understandings of knowledge in determining the nature of knowledge transfer in two companies. *Journal of Intellectual Capital, 2*(1), 74-78.

Jensen, A. (1993). Test validity: G versus "Tacit Knowledge." *Current directions in psychological science: A Journal of the American Psychological Society, 2*(1), 9-10.

Jensen, A. (1998). The *g* factor and the design of education.In R. Sternberg & W. Williams (Eds.), *Intelligence, instruction and assessment: Theory into practice.* Mahwah, NJ: Lawrence Erlbaum Associates, 111-131.

Lachman, M. (2001). *Handbook of midlife development.* New Jersey: Wiley and Sons.

Lam, A. (2000). Tacit knowledge, organizational learning, and societal institutions: An integrated framework. *Organization Studies, 21*(3), 487-513.

Larkin, J. (1980). Skilled problem solving in physics: A hierarchical planning model. *Journal of Structural Learning, 6*(4), 271-297.

Leedy, P. (1997). *Practical research: Planning and design, 6th. Ed.* New York: Merrill.

Magnus, J., & Morgan, M. (1997). Design of the experiment. *Journal of Applied Econometrics, 12,* 459-465.

Magnus, J., & Morgan, M. (1999). *Methodology and tacit knowledge: Two experiments in econometrics.* Chichester, West Sussex, England: John Wiley and Sons.

Mathe, H., & Dagi, T. (1996). Managing technology for the globalisation of service operations. *International Journal of Technology Management, 12*(5/6), 577-607.

McDaniel, M., Morgeson, F., Finnegan, E., Campion, M., & Braverman, E. (2001). Use of situational judgment tests to predict job performance: A clarification of the literature. *Journal of Applied Psychology, 86*(4), 730-740.

Mintzberg, H. (1991a). The professional organisation. In *The Strategy Process: Concepts, Contexts, Cases,* 2nd Ed. Englewood Cliffs, NJ: Prentice Hall, pp. 704-717.

Mintzberg, H. (1991b). The entrepreneurial organisation. In *The Strategy Process: Concepts, Contexts, Cases,* 2nd Ed. Englewood Cliffs, NJ: Prentice Hall, 604-613.

Mintzberg, H. (1991c). The machine organisation. In *The Strategy Process: Concepts, Contexts, Cases,* 2nd Ed. Englewood Cliffs, NJ: Prentice Hall, pp. 630-646.

Mintzberg, H. (1991d). The diversified organisation. In *The Strategy Process: Concepts, Contexts, Cases,* 2nd Ed. Englewood Cliffs, NJ: Prentice Hall, pp. 666-677.

Mintzberg, H. (1991e). The innovative organisation. In *The Strategy Process: Concepts, Contexts, Cases,* 2nd Ed. Englewood Cliffs, NJ: Prentice Hall, pp. 731-746.

Mintzberg, H. (1983). *Structures in fives: Designing effective organisations.* Englewood Cliffs, NJ: Prentice Hall Inc.

Neuman, W. (1997). *Social research methods : Qualitative and quantitative approaches,* 3rd ed. Boston: Allyn and Bacon.

Noh, J., Lee, K., Kim, J., Lee, J., & Kim, S. (2000). A case-based reasoning approach to cognitive map-driven tacit knowledge management. *Expert Systems with Applications, 19,* 249-259.

Partington, D. (2000). Building grounded theories of management action. *British Journal of Management, 11*(2), 91-102.

Reber, A. (1989). Implicit learning and tacit knowledge. *Journal of Experimental Psychology: General, 118*(3), 219-235.

Reber, A., & Lewis, S. (1977). Implicit learning: An analysis of the form and structure of a body of tacit knowledge. *Cognition, 5*(4), 333-361.

Ree, M., & Earles, J. (1993). G is to psychology what carbon is to chemistry: A reply to Sternberg and Wagner, McClelland, and Calfree. *Current Directions in Psychological Science: A journal of the American Psychological Society, 2*(1), 11-12.

Reed, S., Hock, H., & Lockhead, G. (1983). Tacit knowledge and the effect of pattern recognition on mental scanning. *Memory & Cognition, 11*(2), 137-143.

Schmidt, F., & Hunter, J. (1993). Tacit knowledge, practical intelligence, general mental ability, and job knowledge. *Current Directions in Psychological Science: A Journal of the American Psychological Society, 2*(1), 8-9.

Scott, D. (1990). Practice wisdom: The neglected source of practice research. *Social Work, 35*(6), 564-568.

Scott, D. (1992). Reaching vulnerable populations: A framework for primary service expansion. *American Journal of Orthopsychiatry, 62*(3), 333-341.

Smith, E. (2000). Applying knowledge – Enabling methods in the classroom and in the workplace. *Journal of Workplace Learning: Employee Counselling Today, 12*(6), 236-244.

Somech, A., & Bogler, R. (1999). Tacit knowledge in academia: Its effect on student learning and achievement. *The Journal of Psychology, 133*(6), 605-616.

Stenmark, D. (2000). Turning tacit knowledge tangible. *Proceedings of the 33rd International Conference on System Sciences*, 1-9.

Stenmark, D. (2000/2001). Leveraging tacit organizational knowledge. *Journal of Management Information Systems, 17*(3), 9-24.

Sternberg, R. (1999). Epilogue – What do we know about tacit knowledge?: Making the tacit become explicit. In R. Sternberg & J. Horvath (Eds.) *Tacit knowledge in professional practice: Researcher and practitioner perspectives*. Mahwah, NJ: Lawrence Erlbaum and Associates, 231-236.

Sternberg, R., Grigorenko, E., & Stella, O. (2001). The development of intelligence at midlife. Chapter 7, In M. Lachman (ed.), *Handbook of Midlife Development*. New Jersey: John Wiley and Sons.

Sternberg, R., Wagner, R., Williams, W., & Horvath, J. (1995). Testing common sense. *American Psychologist, 50*(11), 912-927.

Strauss, A., & Corbin, J. (1990). *Basics of qualitative research: Grounded theory procedures and techniques*. Newbury Park, CA: Sage Publications.

Subramaniam, M., & Venkatraman, N. (2001). Determinants of transnational new product development capability: Testing the influence of transferring and deploying tacit overseas knowledge. *Strategic Management Journal, 22*, 359-378.

van Maanen, J., Dabbs, J., & Faulkner, R. (1982). *Varieties of qualitative research*. California: Sage Publications.

Wagner, R., & Sternberg, R. (1991a). *TKIM: The common sense manager: Tacit knowledge inventory for managers: Test booklet*. San Antonio: The Psychological Corporation Harcourt Brace Jovanovich.

Wagner, R., & Sternberg, R. (1991b). *TKIM: The common sense manager: Tacit knowledge inventory for managers: User manual.* San Antonio: The Psychological Corporation Harcourt Brace Jovanovich.

Xu, J., & Quaddus, M. (2005). Adoption and diffusion of knowledge management systems: An Australian survey. *Journal of Management Development, 24*(4), 335-361.

Yin, R. (1994). *Case study research: Design and methods.* Applied Social Science Research Methods series, Vol. 5. Beverly Hills, CA: Sage.

Endnotes

[a]   The following chapter has been written along the lines of a "conduct of study." Oftentimes people attending talks relating to this research topic at conferences would ask questions with regard to specifically how the research was undertaken, with a view to conducting similar research themselves.

[b]   This chapter assumes a social science conduct to research.

[c]   Personal communication with Assoc. Prof. Brett Myors, Organisational Psychologist (Semester 1, 2000), formerly Macquarie University, now at the Department of Psychology, Griffith University, Queensland.

[d]   Ethics Committees exist at all Australian universities. As their name suggests, such Committees provide a check on research conducted and prohibit research not falling within what the Committee sees as being "ethical." The committee is typically made up of perhaps 20 to 30 people from both academic and lay backgrounds, including legal and medical personnel, indigenous representatives and members of the clergy. Such Committees do from time to time however come in for criticism, for example, http://www.abc.net.au/rn/healthreport/stories/2006/1680645.htm#transcript (accessed 14th July 2006).

[e]   Member checking is the process whereby those intimately involved with the subject domain ("members"), for example organisational staff or subject specialists etc., check the validity of the methodology and/or results under study.

[f]   Personal communication with Ms. Sibba Gudlaugsdottir, Associate Lecturer, Department of Statistics, Macquarie University; February 2001.

[g]   Personal communication with Mr. Alan Hansell, Program Director, IT Executive Program, Gartner Group, March 2000; (also Dowall, 1987; Mathe & Dagi, 1996).

[h]   Personal communication with Dr. John Galloway, Director, Netmap Analytics; Adjunct Professor U.T.S., Sydney 2000

[i]   Experience from the pre-pilot showed that respondents felt they should be given opportunity to state how they *would* answer questions in addition to how they *should* answer them.

[j]   Personal communication with Ms. Sibba Gudlaugsdottir, Associate Lecturer, Department of Statistics, Macquarie University; April 2001.

[k]   Personal communication with Dr. John Galloway, Director, NetMap Analytics; Adjunct Professor U.T.S., Sydney 2000.

[l]   Personal communication with Mr. Alan Hansell, Program Director, IT Executive Program, Gartner Group, March 2000.

[m]   Personal communication with Dr. Einat Amitay, Department of Computing, Macquarie University, June 2001.

[n]   Personal communication with Dr. John Antonakis, PACE centre, Yale University, October 2001.

Section IV

This fourth section of the book, covering Chapters IX, X, XI, XII, and XIII, introduces the reader to the results of the study. There were in essence two datasets, which were interrelated, but nevertheless somewhat independent. With the tacit knowledge dataset the goal of the research was to establish if colleagues considered some of their peers to be experts. Secondly, did these experts answer tacit knowledge related questions differently from others? Thirdly, were there other individuals who answered the inventory similarly to experts? Fourthly, what did these experts and expert novices resemble with regard to their biographical parameters? These results are presented in Chapters 9 and 10. Chapter 9 specifically presents the results from the statistical testing. Chapter 10 presents the results through the use of Formal Concept Analysis. The reader may recall that the use of FCA permitted a finer level of granularity of data interpretation. Statistical testing was applied to the results but did not reveal significant differences between experts and others. The use of Formal Concept analysis did however allow the identification of individuals whose answers were consistently like those of experts. Through taking the results of these expert novices and placing them in with experts and re-conducting the statistical test, some significance from the results was derived.

The second set of data focused on the interrelationships of employees. Chapters XI, XII, and XIII thus focus on the Social Network implications of the research, with Chapter XI concentrating on the results of Organisation X, Chapter XII on the results of Organisation Y and Chapter XIII on the results of Organisation Z. It was found with regard to Organisation X that there were some parameters that could influence tacit or soft knowledge flows. There were certainly quite a number of cliques in this firm, where some of the cliques were likely to be highly tacit knowledge intensive with high levels of contact between experts. At the same time less powerful cliques of employees seemed to have reduced contact to expert personnel, and could thus be conceivably tacit knowledge poorer as a result. Organisation

Y was totally different. It was a much smaller firm, highly knowledge intensive and consisted of effectively just one clique. The biographical makeup of its staff was also quite different. Organisation Z was similar although on a smaller scale to Organisation X, although the CIO seemed to play a more prominent role as knowledge transferor.

Chapter IX

Initial Results

Statistics do not enable us to predict a specific phenomenon, but merely to express a total result relative to a sufficiently large quantity of analogous phenomena [a] (Borel, [b] n.d.).

Introduction

Chapter V revealed how the three IT organisations varied in their structure. Remember that Organisation X is an insurance company; however what is referred to as Organisation X herein is the IT support group for the wider organisation. Organisation Y differed insofar as it is a management consultancy with a specialisation in IT; to that end, the staff under study represent the *core* of the organisation, rather than the IT support staff, as is the case in Organisation X. Organisation Z is a home and office furniture supply company, however what is referred to as Organisation Z here is the IT group providing support to the logistics of storing and selling furniture items. Thus, Organisation X and Z under study are similar insofar as they provide a service role to the wider organisation. Organisation Y differs, as its mission is to deliver IT/IS managerial expertise. The population of the organisations not surprisingly reflects this. For example Organisation Y is made up of predominantly senior mono-cultural "first language is English" personnel. The other two organisations have a much broader staff profile with a far higher level of multiculturalism.

There are a couple of other issues need to be clarified at this stage because they are continually referred to from now on. They are the Australian Computer Society (ACS, 2000; ACS SA, 1999) levels because of the nature of their role in relation to employee experience in each of the firms. It is also considered worthwhile to provide a short discussion on the selection of our "expert" sample population at this stage.

Table 1. Illustrating ACS levels

ACS Level 0:	Clerical level computing work
ACS Level 1:	Little practical experience in I.T. work, may be supervising ancillary staff
ACS Level 2:	Experienced and capable of performing wide range of general I.T. work
ACS Level 3:	Experienced in specialised I.T. areas, well developed liaison skills
ACS Level 4:	Managing a number of teams and the allocation of resources
ACS Level 5:	Typically report to CEO, manage major function, extensive I.T. coordination

Australian Computer Society Levels

Although brief mention of the Australian Computer Society was made in Chapter V, the ACS levels are discussed in further detail here. Since evidence (Sternberg, 1999) would tend to suggest that tacit knowledge increases with experience on the job, ACS levels thus become a useful indicator of know-how. There actually are five levels, ranging from 1 to 5 (most senior) (Table 1).

The stage graduates are at upon graduation is that of level 1. Because of the interest by some clerical staff in participating in the research, an ACS level 0 also was also introduced. Level 1 clearly stipulates that a graduate could possibly be supervising ancillary staff but would in fact likely have little practical experience in IT work. As will become clearer later, quite a number of the sample population, particularly in Organisation X is at level 3; in other words experienced in more specialised IT areas, and perhaps more importantly having well developed liaison skills which would permit greater communication across the workplace. The fifth level is not commonly encountered in the population samples, as one would expect, given this is Chief Information Officer (CIO) level. As a final point of note, it should be remembered that respondents were not asked *if* they were a member of the ACS,[c] rather they were simply asked to choose what they considered their relevant ACS level to be, based on their own subjective understanding of their range of experience.

The Expert Sample

When filling out the social network analysis component of the questionnaire, respondents were asked to choose colleagues they felt were particularly proficient at what they did. This list of people within each organisation was identified as comprising the **expert** group. If two or more peers identified individuals as being of above average workplace proficiency, the identified persons were classified as experts. As the researcher was not responsible for choosing experts, this meant that people who worked closely with proficient colleagues were best able to determine in a "street smart" sense who was most savvy within their IT group. The choice of expert sample was not established by any pre-determined set of parameters such as how people answered a set of questions, or whether staff had obtained a certain level of formal or workplace qualification.

With these points in mind, the focus turns to the backgrounds of the organisations themselves, followed by the outcomes of the tacit knowledge inventory component of the research. In each case a brief history and role of each organisation will be provided followed by more detailed discussion of tacit knowledge inventory results.

The Tacit Knowledge Inventory

The **tacit knowledge inventory** was composed of 16 IT workplace scenarios with relevant answer options for each given scenario. In total there were 126 answer items for all 16 scenarios together. The number of answer items varied from as few as six answers (Scenarios 5, 9, 13) up to 12 answers (Scenario 3). Again respondents had to select Likert scale options twice (ethical and realistic) for each answer option relating to any randomly assigned scenario. In other words, if a respondent was fortunate to randomly receive Scenario 5, then for that scenario they would have to click 12 Likert scale buttons on the electronic questionnaire. If they were randomly assigned Scenario 3, then they would have to click 24 Likert scale radio buttons. Once again error-checking routines built into the questionnaire, prevented respondents from only partially filling out a questionnaire page before moving onto the next scenario. The reader also is reminded that the random nature of scenario assignment meant that copying of answers from one respondent to the next was likely to be minimised.

The purpose of the tacit knowledge inventory for the research was essentially two-fold: first of all to ascertain whether identified experts were answering the inventory differently from **novice**s and secondly to identify personnel, who were not actually identified by their peers as being experts, but according to inventory results, gained scores close to that of the expert sample. The point of such an exercise was to determine whether some form of soft knowledge bottlenecking could be said to be taking place, that is to say, if a group of personnel can be identified as having results on a soft knowledge test close to that of the expert sample, but this group of personnel are not necessarily identified as expert by their co-workers, one could reasonably conclude the former group are "hiding their light under a bushel." Remember if one wishes to establish a means of testing for "soft knowledge" within an organisational domain, there are few practicable approaches available. The generally accepted approach is the one along Sternberg's lines. Their test for this soft or tacit knowledge, which is in reality a form of managerial knowledge, seeks to establish whether (a) experts or "proficient" personnel answer soft knowledge situations in a manner different from that of "normal" people. Traditionally the testing also seeks (b) to identify staff that may or may not be identified as experts but may make suitable management "material" within any given organisation. In other words the inventory has traditionally been very management general, rather than IT management specific. Secondly the purpose of the original Sternberg (Wagner & Sternberg, 1991a, b) inventory was to establish suitable management candidates. In fact, it is worth noting that such selection techniques had their origins in German and then British military systems as a means of selecting suitable officer candidates[d] (Thornton & Byham, 1982).

The purpose of this research was not to identify staff that would be suitable for a formal managerial role per se, rather to establish which personnel might also have high concentrations of soft managerial knowledge; and more importantly, to determine how well these identified staff members (both expert and **expert-non-expert** [ENE]) were transferring or withholding their tacit knowledge.

A careful examination of the results enabled personnel to be identified who whilst not being identified as experts, did have scores that were close to those of experts. The identification process proceeded along the following lines. Firstly all, descriptive statistics were produced for all questionnaire results, which included: Mean, Median, Standard Deviation, Minimum and Maximum values (1 to 7 in the case of the Likert scale), Count (of the number of respondents who had answered the scenario/answer combination) and Confidence Level (95 percent). This process was repeated for each organisation's data. Each set of answers for each scenario thus had the aforementioned statistics produced for them. As Likert scale data is ordinal, descriptive statistics were able to provide an indication of:

1.   Whether experts in general were answering the tacit knowledge inventories differently from novices.

2.   Which particular scenarios and answer options experts were answering differently?

3.   Which scenarios and answer options showed the greatest degree of variation between how experts differed in terms of their ethical and realistic answers as compared to novices.

4.   Which individuals who were not actually identified by their peers as being experts, ended up having answers (ethically and realistically) close to that of experts. This identified group thus becoming "expert non-experts" (ENE).

Identification Process of Expert Non-Experts

Dealing with the final point first of all, the tacit knowledge data retrieved from the questionnaire was numerical, being integer in format from 1 (Extremely Bad), to 4 (Neither Good nor Bad), through to 7 (Extremely Good). The respondent did not see a numerical value attached to any particular value on the Likert scale. Nevertheless, converting the integer values into descriptive statistics meant that an indication could be obtained in relation to how respondents had answered the questions. In addition, the creation of a **formal concept lattice** for each scenario answer showing how both experts and novices provided both an ethical and realistic value meant that a profile could be created of personnel who had answered close to that of experts. Let us examine this process in closer detail, beginning with a sample scenario and answer option. In this case, Scenario 3 (Figure 1) is illustrated, with an answer option (no. 12) and associated descriptive statistics (Table 2). This particular piece of data is taken from Organisation X.

For the given sample scenario with answer 12, the descriptive statistics as shown in Table 2, illustrate several things. Firstly, the control group (or novice group's) statistics are provided on the left hand side, with the expert's statistics on the right. Starting with the count given

Figure 1. Illustrating sample scenario 3 and answer 12 from the tacit knowledge inventory

Scenario 3

You as a team leader are responsible for implementing a payroll system for another branch within the parent organisation. Although you are expected to do the bulk of the work (55%), you do have five other colleagues able to help as you so desire. The project should take 12 months in total to complete.

You have undertaken some of the initial systems design work largely yourself for the past couple of months, and you now require your colleagues to further help you with the next stage which is mainly that of coding.

You are comfortable with hierarchy, however some of your team members are not. You delegate some tasks to subordinates within your team. One of the team members who specialises in programming has been allocated some software specification work, but would prefer really just to be programming. This person has performed well on coding related tasks in the past, but at this point in time lacks project management skills which would prevent him from becoming an effective team leader. Nevertheless you feel that the person should at least do some of the software specification work.

Rate each of the following responses in relation to the given scenario. It is advisable to read all of the responses before replying.

Answer 12

Give him fewer but more specific tasks to do, because it is simply not worth the effort to argue with him. Besides his skills in coding mean that he will be able to effectively contribute here, and then you can be rid of him, to concentrate on testing with other team members of your choice.

Table 2. A sample of descriptive statistics from Scenario 3, answer 12

Answer 12 **(Novice)**	Ethical	Realistic
Mean	**3.2**	**3.8**
Median	**3.0**	**4.0**
Standard Deviation	**1.6**	**1.6**
Range	5.0	6.0
Minimum	**1.0**	**1.0**
Maximum	**6.0**	**7.0**
Count	**23.0**	**23.0**
Largest(1)	6.0	7.0
Smallest(1)	1.0	1.0
Confidence Level(95.0%)	0.7	0.7

Answer 12 **(Expert)**	Ethical	Realistic
Mean	**2.5**	**3.6**
Median	**2.0**	**4.0**
Standard Deviation	**1.4**	**1.6**
Range	5.0	6.0
Minimum	**1.0**	**1.0**
Maximum	**6.0**	**7.0**
Count	**17.0**	**17.0**
Largest(1)	6.0	7.0
Smallest(1)	1.0	1.0
Confidence Level(95.0%)	0.7	0.8

towards the bottom of each table, we see that 23 novices answered this question dealing with this scenario, whereas 17 experts did so.

Once again these figures represent those in Organisation X who answered this section of the inventory. The Means were 3.2 (ethical) and 3.8 (realistic) for novices, but 2.5 (ethical) and 3.6 (realistic) for the experts. The experts were inclined to be a little more negative or pessimistic (ethically) when dealing with this answer, than the novices on the whole. Likewise, the experts were also marginally more negative realistically (3.6), than the novices (3.8). Examining the median values however, note that experts were even more negative ethically (2.0, or Very Bad) than the novices (3.0 or Bad). Realistically both groups were actually fairly non-committal (4.0 or Neither Good nor Bad). More substantial statistical testing took place in the form of a Wilcoxon test.

The Wilcoxon Test Results

Recall that Chapter IV mentioned the Wilcoxon test for matched pairs to determine if there was some statistical significance in the differences of responses between experts and novices in the tacit knowledge inventory results. With regard to undertaking a test between experts and novices, the following results were achieved (using the medians). A number of tests were conducted, first for all the organisational data combined[e] And secondly a test just for the largest of our organisations (Organisation X), which of any of the organisations, would have had the largest statistically significant data set. Thirdly (and the main purpose of the test), was to see if there was any difference between the scores of experts and novices.

- All three Organisations combined:

  Null hypothesis: declares there is no difference in the scores (Likert scale 1-7) between *experts* and *novices*.

  Statistical significance: $z = -1.1$

  Answer: One cannot reject the null hypothesis (as the statistical outcome (-1.1) is not considered meaningful enough according to tables provided in Siegel (1956)).

- Just Organisation X (the largest of our organisations):

  Null hypothesis: declares there is no difference in the scores (Likert scale 1-7) between experts and others.

  Statistical significance: $z = 1.4$.

  Answer: One cannot reject the null hypothesis (Siegel, 1956).

Admission of Failure or Change of Tack?

Statistically, results could not be derived that stated categorically there were no differences between how the expert sample population and others (novices) answered the tacit knowledge inventory. It is however possible had the instrument been refined further, differences may have been apparent in the results.

Remember that formal concept analysis was adopted because the author was looking for a means of examining questionnaire results that would allow both finer granularity interpretations than is possible with numerical processing, and secondly that would permit result validity with smaller sample sizes. Through an examination of all of the tacit knowledge inventory results with formal concept analysis, the authors was able to determine a subset of respondents who were achieving results or dealing with the scenarios in the same way as the peer-recognised expert cohort. Through a laborious process of examining a concept lattice for each scenario-answer permutation[f] user-ids could be identified where certain non-expert personnel were routinely choosing the same sorts of answers in the tacit knowledge inventory as recognised experts. This last point is important, for part of the research was to establish whether (a) such individuals existed and (b) who they were.[g]

Returning to the issue of minimal validity of the statistical results, one may hypothesize a reason for this is that our expert novices or Expert Non-Experts (ENEs as they shall henceforth be referred to), were included with the novice control population. Although such personnel have not actually been identified by their peers as being experts, their tacit knowledge results indicated they *should* be. A procedural approach taken therefore was to place "expert non-expert" results in with the "expert" sample. One could then expect to see differences between how the new "expert" group performed compared to the control population. The author acknowledges that further experimentation is needed to test the validity of this approach, vis-a-vis the purely operational approach of choosing the experts.

Wilcoxon Test with Expert Non-Expert Sample Included in the Expert Sample Results

Having included ENE results in with the expert sample some statistical validity appears. Beginning with *ethical* values only: differences between experts and novices (true novices and expert non-experts/expert novices/ENEs) in terms of how they answer the scenarios.

- **Null hypothesis**: That there is no difference between experts (experts + expert non-experts) and novices in terms of how they ethically answer IT scenario tacit knowledge questions.

  Statistical significance: $z = -1.8$ (with a 3% significance).

  Answer: The null hypothesis *can be* rejected at the 3% level (Siegel, 1956).

- Followed by *realistic* values only: difference between experts and novices in terms of how they answer the scenarios realistically:

  Null Hypothesis: That there is no difference between experts (experts + expert non-experts) and novices with regard to *realistically* answering scenario related questions.

  Statistical significance: $z = -1.4$

  Answer: One cannot reject the null hypothesis (Siegel, 1956).

- *Experts* only: Examining the responses of experts only.

  Null hypothesis: That there will be no difference between ethical and realistic values for the experts (experts and expert non-experts).

  Statistical significance: $z = -1.0$

  Answer: One cannot reject the null hypothesis (Siegel, 1956).

- *Novices* only: Once again with regard to novices, stating a null hypothesis.

  Null hypothesis: That there will be no difference between ethical and realistic values for the novices.

  Statistical significance: $z = -0.9$

  Answer: One cannot reject the null hypothesis (Siegel, 1956).

- Differences within each of the groups (novices and experts) and then determining the difference between experts and novices.

  Null hypothesis: That there will be no significant difference between experts and novices in terms of how they answer internally within their scenario/answer combinations.

  Statistical significance: $z = -0.473$

  Answer: One cannot reject the null hypothesis (Siegel, 1956).

What has thus been discovered? That the *non*-inclusion of ENEs into the expert sample population, provides us with only minimal *statistically significant* differences between experts and novices. On contemplation this makes some sense, for there are likely to be personnel who are as capable as experts but "hide their light under a bushel."[h] In doing so the expert non-expert sample population could be said to be "polluting" the novice results with expert data. Upon taking the ENE results and placing them in with experts, the picture now changes with a *statistical* significance for ethical results at least. Realistic results show no difference between the two sample populations. Remember again the reason for using Formal Concept Analysis was to use visualisation in data interpretation. Also in using FCA a more qualitative approach could be adopted, as the researcher knew the sample size would likely not be large enough to permit *substantial* statistical interpretation to take place. To summarise, FCA permitted finer granularity of data interpretation, and in doing so the ENE sample population could be revealed.

Summary

After being introduced to the Australian Computer Society and the concept of what comprises an expert, statistical testing was applied to the results leading to the conclusion that the findings as they stood could not reveal significant differences between experts and others. The use of formal concept analysis did however allow the identification of individuals whose answers were consistently like those of experts. By taking the results of the expert novices and placing them in with experts and re-conducting the statistical test, some statistical significance was evident.

Remembering some key points, the aim of the research was to establish if colleagues considered some of their peers to be experts. Secondly, did these experts answer tacit knowledge related questions differently from others? Thirdly, were there other individuals who answered the inventory similarly to experts? Fourthly, what did these experts and expert novices look like? And finally, how well did these individuals network with their colleagues who were not necessarily similarly blessed with higher levels of tacit knowledge aptitude? Point one could be answered with part b of the questionnaire. Points two and three required the use of formal concept analysis to adequately answer these questions. Point four could be answered with either statistics or formal concept analysis, and point five required the use of social network analysis. Next the tacit knowledge inventory results are examined through the use of formal concept analysis.

References

A.C.S. (2000). *A.C.S. Remuneration Survey.* APESA: Australian Computer Society.

A.C.S. (S.A.) (1999). *Careers in Information Technology.* Australian Computer Society, http://www.iss.net.au/ACSSA/careers/sacit99.pdf

Nelson, D. (Ed.) (1998). *Dictionary of Mathematics,* 2nd Ed. London: Penguin Books.

Siegel, S. (1956). *Nonparametric statistics: For the behavioural sciences.* New York: McGraw-Hill.

Sternberg, R. (1999). Epilogue – What do we know about tacit knowledge?: Making the tacit become explicit. In R. Sternberg & J. Horvath (Eds.) *Tacit knowledge in professional practice: Researcher and practitioner perspectives.* Mahwah, NJ: Lawrence Erlbaum and Associates, 231-236.

Thornton, G., & Byham, W. (1982). *Assessment centers and managerial performance.* New York: Academic Press.

Wagner, R., & Sternberg, R. (1991a). *TKIM: The common sense manager: Tacit knowledge inventory for managers: Test booklet.* San Antonio: The Psychological Corporation Harcourt Brace Jovanovich.

Wagner, R., & Sternberg, R. (1991b). *TKIM: The common sense manager: Tacit knowledge inventory for managers: User manual.* San Antonio: The Psychological Corporation Harcourt Brace Jovanovich.

Endnotes

[a]   Source: http://koti.mbnet.fi/neptunia/science/statist1.htm (accessed on 21 July 2006).

[b]   Borel, Félix Edouard Émile (1971-1956) French mathematician noted for his work on set theory and measure theory. Borel also introduced a definition for the sum of divergent series (Nelson, 1998, p. 36).

[c]   It is customary in Australia today to ask potential employees if they are "eligible" for membership in professional organisations, rather than if they are "members" of such organisations per se. Such a practice presumably eliminates any perceived discrimination as to whether one is a member of the "club" or not.

[d]   It is interesting but not wholly unsurprising to discover that the military had long been in favour of testing informal knowledge. The application of street smarts is of course vital in the many tasks a military officer must undertake. Before the 20th century officer candidates (or their families) purchased commissions, however the horrors and ineptitudes of the First World War caused a change in mindset towards far more rigorous testing of officer candidates. From the 1920s we see an early form of testing taking place in the German military system, and then followed by the British (and thus Canadian and Australian) military systems after this point in time.

[e]   It was recommended (personal communication with Ms. Sibba Gudlaugsdottir, Department of Statistics, Macquarie University), to combine the data from all three organisations so as to increase the size of the sample data set.

[f]   Some 126 scenario-answer permutations in all, remembering there were 16 scenarios with anywhere from six to 13 answers per scenario.

[g]   With a view toward ascertaining if they were perhaps suitable to play a mentoring role to lesser tacit knowledge rich colleagues.

[h]   To have talent, but not really allow the talent to show. Performed at the correct time and place, this may actually represent a judicious usage of tacit knowledge.

Chapter X

Results with Formal Concept Analysis

Objects, attributes, and concepts are basic notions of conceptual knowledge; they are linked by the following four basic relations: an object has an attribute, an object belongs to a concept, an attribute abstracts from a concept, and a concept is a subconcept of another concept. These structural elements are well mathematized in formal concept analysis (Luksch & Wille, 1991, p. 157).

Introduction

Chapter V provided some introduction to formal concept analysis through the visualisation of biographical results from the tacit knowledge questionnaire. The attention now turns to the strength of using FCA by examining the tacit knowledge inventory results which are one of the two major underpinnings of this work. To remind the reader, FCA had its beginnings at the Technical University of Darmstadt in Germany, and was the work of Professor Rudolf Wille. Formal Concept Analysis is a means of illustrating via a lattice like structure all sorts of information in virtually any discipline. The lattice-like structure illustrates relationships between objects (typically any type of noun), and their corresponding attributes (typically any kind of adjective). Through connecting these "concepts" together, sense is gained for the body of knowledge dealt with. The application of FCA to questionnaire results is rare but not unheard of, but its application to better understanding tacit knowledge is.

Usage of Formal Concept Analysis

Even if statistics was not the major tool used for processing questionnaire results, some use was nevertheless made of descriptive statistics to provide an indication which Likert scale values had been chosen by the respondents. With the addition of a formal concept analysis lattice further meaning could be derived from the data. Figure 1 provides an illustration of the lattice structure for a Likert scale result, in this case scenario 3, answer 12. A reminder that the lattice is read starting from the outer ellipses (ethical values) through to the inner lattice structures (realistic values). The reader will see that the answers are inclined toward the negative end of the spectrum. Note also that some personnel (1528, 17, 15E, 14E, 7, 33E, 35E, 5, 34E) whilst ethically feeling negative about this particular answer for dealing with scenario 3, nevertheless feel positive about the answer from a realistic standpoint. Alternatively note that individuals 20 and 13E feel positive ethically about this answer, but negative about it realistically. Generally speaking however the ethical feeling tends to be more negative than the realistic one.

The point of this exercise is that in examining each formal concept lattice for each answer option for each scenario, the researcher is slowly able to build up a picture for how novices have answered relative to that of experts. For example, in Figure 1, one can see that 1525, 1025, 1583, 2375, 1524, 1528, 17, 1507, 9, 7, 5, 1 and 20 have answered the same way as experts. By noting this similarity for all 125 answers (examining all concept lattices) novices can be listed in descending order of similarity with expert answer responses. Those novices with the greatest incidence of similarity with experts, head the list. For Organisation X, an extra 25 personnel were able to be identified who scored close to that of experts using the aforementioned technique, without necessarily being identified by their peers as being experts. Examining the closeness of the scores in descending order, it was decided the top 32 percent of ENEs warranted inclusion as a group as this group appeared to present a

Figure 1. Illustrating formal concept lattice for Scenario 3, answer 12

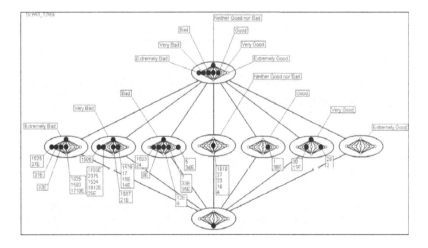

natural cut-off point from those who scored below them. These were individuals {1, 2, 4, 5, 7, 9, 16, 17, 20, 23, 24, 27, 28, 1023, 1507, 1521, 1524, 1527, 1534, 1536, 1538, 1543, 1778, 1792 and 1796}.

When dealing with Organisation Z, there were four other individuals who obtained scores close to that recorded by experts. At least two of the individuals were of non-English speaking origin. Participant 3334 decided not to provide any biographical details, 3339 declined to provide gender. Note once again bachelor's degrees and high school certificate as being the highest formal qualifications. As there were only two individuals (out of seven participants) who were not actually identified as experts in Organisation Y, the same technique was not adopted.

The ramifications for identifying ENEs are that this sample group are likely to constitute employees who also have high levels of tacit or "soft" managerial knowledge. One needs to bear this mind when examining the interactions of staff when looking at the social network analysis results. The point of such an exercise being, that if one can (a) identify another group who are similar to experts, and (b) see how well they interact/communicate in the workplace, one can also determine the likelihood of their soft knowledge expertise being transferred to lesser experienced staff.

Tacit Knowledge Scenarios: Differences and Similarities

Further to the identification of expert non-experts, was there a variation between answer options and scenarios between how experts answered (ethically and realistically) as opposed to novices? In other words,

1.   *which* scenarios + answers were answered *fundamentally* differently by experts when asked to provide an ethical answer and a realistic answer to a given response for a scenario, as opposed to novices? At the same time,

2.   *which* scenarios + answers for *both* experts and non experts indicated no difference between how *each* group answered ethically and realistically?

Variations Between Experts and Novices in Questionnaire Scenario-Answer Combinations

Dealing with the first point, all respondents from the three companies answered the same questionnaire. Respondents were grouped into expert and novice categories; and as each individual had an identification number, all such personnel could be identified in each organisation. It was therefore feasible to pool the data together to form a larger dataset.[a] As a next step it is possible to examine the difference for each group (expert/novice) independently to determine if there has been a variation in tacit knowledge scenario answers. Examining

Table 1, column A, reveals the actual scenarios and answer options that show *significant* (>1.0 on the Likert Scale) variation in answers. Column B indicates differences between ethical and realistic Likert values provided by novices, that is to say how much novices varied in their ethical answers to a question as opposed to the realistic value they gave. So for Scenario 10, 2nd question, novices varied as much as a whole point on the Likert scale for how they answered this question ethically and realistically. Column C illustrates the same concept for experts. Column D highlights the differences between the two groups (experts and novices). As an aside, a number (59) of other scenario + answer combinations showed variations between experts and novices but were equal to or below 1.0 variance and will not be discussed here.

Beginning with Scenario 10, 2nd question as shown in Figure 2, like much in the way of tacit knowledge tests, the situational inventories tend to be subjective. There need not necessarily be any one correct answer; rather answers are a shade of grey. In the case of this IT workplace scenario the respondent is asked about system success. The answer for dealing with this scenario relates to what is more important, for example should the IT practitioner keep the client happy, and at what cost? If one looks at Table 1 it will be apparent that the value for novices is –1.0, whilst for experts it is 2.0, the difference being that of whole 3 points on the Likert scale.

The numerical figures provided in Table 1 illustrate differences between ethical and realistic answers. For each of the columns B and C, the ethical value (1.0 through to 7.0) on the Likert scale has been subtracted from the realistic value. Thus –1.0 for novices indicates that realistic Likert value was actually lower than that of the ethical value. In other words,

Table 1. Illustrating scenarios (with answers) which showed substantial variation (>1.0) (diff. = difference) between ethical and realistic values provided by novices as opposed to expert samples for all organisations collectively

Column A	Col. B	Col. C	Col. D
Medians	*Novice*	*Exp*	*Diff.*
Scenario 10 - 2nd Question	-1.0	2.0	3.0
Scenario 2 - 2nd Question	0.0	2.0	2.0
Scenario 2 - 6th Question	0.0	2.0	2.0
Scenario 6 - 1st Question	-2.0	0.0	2.0
Scenario 5 - 2nd Question	-0.5	1.0	1.5
Scenario 6 - 2nd Question	0.0	1.5	1.5
Scenario 12 - 5th Question	-1.0	0.5	1.5
Scenario 13 - 5th Question	-1.0	0.5	1.5
Scenario 14 - 1st Question	-2.0	-0.5	1.5
Scenario 3 - 6th Question	0.0	-1.5	-1.5
Scenario 6 - 6th Question	2.0	0.5	-1.5
Scenario 4 - 2nd Question	1.0	-1.0	-2.0
Scenario 8 - 8th Question	1.0	-1.0	-2.0
Scenario 10 - 4th Question	1.0	-1.0	-2.0

Figure 2. Illustrating scenario 10, answer 2 as an example of a scenario and answer option with large variation between experts and novices in terms of ethical and realistic answers

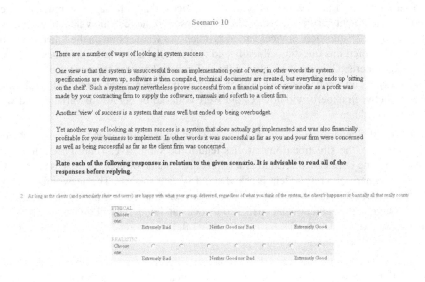

Figure 3. Illustrating answer 4 for scenario 10 (shown in Figure 2)

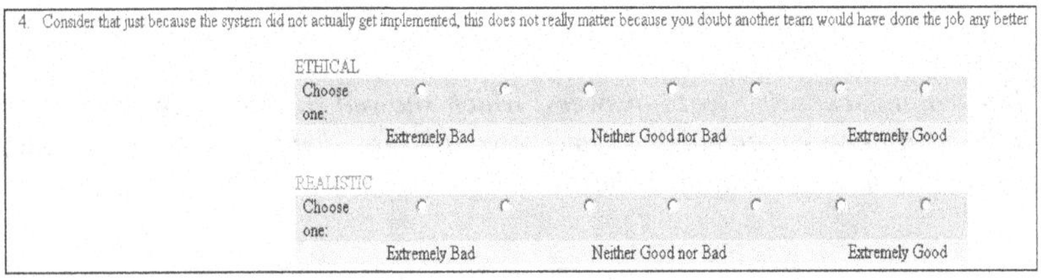

the novices as a group felt more inclined to provide a negative realistic value than an ethical one in relation to answer 2 for dealing with scenario 10. Another way of looking at this is that novices felt *ethically* keeping the client happy is important, but in *reality* this is less important. The experts as a group felt substantially the opposite way. Examining column C (Table 1) and remembering that the ethical value was subtracted from the realistic one, indicates in the case of the expert sample that their realistic value was higher (more toward the positive end of the Likert scale) than their ethical one. So in relation to answer 2 with regard to Scenario 10 (Figure2), the experts as a group felt that realistically keeping the client happy is far more important than what it is perceived to be ethically. Examining table 10.1 again for the same scenario, but for answer 4 (Figure 3) produces the opposite response.

In this case the novices as a group felt more positive realistically about answering this question than they did ethically. The experts felt the opposite way; their ethical answer was higher

Figure 4. Illustrating tacit knowledge inventory scenario 6, with answer 1

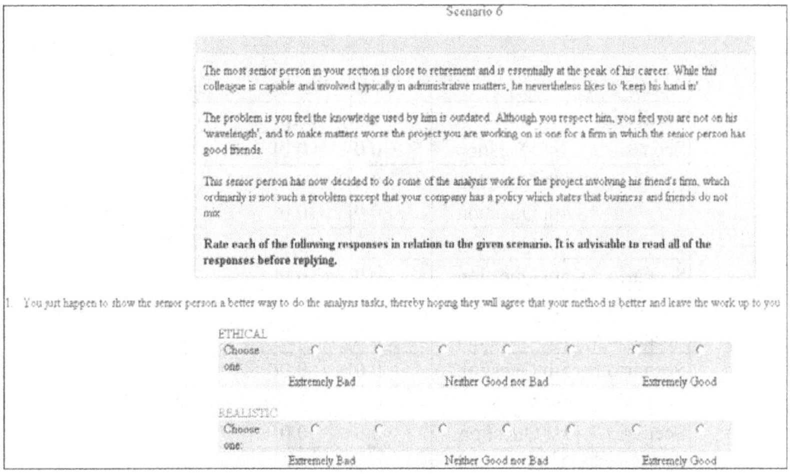

on the Likert scale (more positive) than their realistic answer. In short, one could conclude that novices were generally happier realistically in not having their system implemented, but ideally speaking it was rather a shame it wasn't. The experts in comparison were in reality disappointed the system wasn't implemented, but ideally or ethically speaking the non-implementation of the system generally meant less to the experts. Examining another scenario and answer option, this time scenario 6, answer 1 one can see (Table 1) that the experts are fairly consistent in terms of differences between ethically and realistically dealing with this answer, for this scenario (Figure 4). The novice group on the other hand realistically feel more negatively disposed towards this answer than they do ethically. To rephrase, the results would indicate that the novice group feel ethically showing the senior hand a better way of doing things is a generally more positive thing than they feel about showing the senior person in reality. The experts on the other hand feel the same way either *ethically* or *realistically*. In fact the actual results for this answer are novices (*ethical* 5.5; *realistic* 3.5), experts (*ethical* 3.5, *realistic* 3.5). *Realistically* at least, both groups tend to verge on neutrality (Likert scale value 4: Neither Good nor Bad). The novices perhaps a little more naïvely, consider getting the senior person to follow the way of the junior is a better idea (5.5, Good to Very Good), *ideally* speaking.

Ethical and Realistic Options with No Variation Between Experts and Novices

At the opposite extreme in terms of differences between ethical and realistic responses by novices vs. experts, viewing Table 2 there remain a number of scenario + answer combina-

Table 2. Illustrating scenarios and answers for which both novices (Col. B) and experts (Col. C) each show no variation (using median) between how the groups feel ethically and realistically

Column A Medians	Col. B Novice	Col. C Exp	Col. D Difference
Scenario 1 - 3rd Question	0.0	0.0	0.0
Scenario 1 - 6th Question	0.0	0.0	0.0
Scenario 2 - 4th Question	0.0	0.0	0.0
Scenario 3 - 4th Question	0.0	0.0	0.0
Scenario 3 - 5th Question	0.0	0.0	0.0
Scenario 4 - 6th Question	0.0	0.0	0.0
Scenario 4 - 7th Question	0.0	0.0	0.0
Scenario 5 - 5th Question	0.0	0.0	0.0
Scenario 5 - 6th Question	0.0	0.0	0.0
Scenario 7 - 1st Question	0.0	0.0	0.0
Scenario 7 - 2nd Question	0.0	0.0	0.0
Scenario 7 - 6th Question	0.0	0.0	0.0
Scenario 7 - 7th Question	0.0	0.0	0.0
Scenario 8 - 1st Question	0.0	0.0	0.0
Scenario 8 - 2nd Question	0.0	0.0	0.0
Scenario 9 - 3rd Question	0.0	0.0	0.0
Scenario 11 - 2nd Question	0.0	0.0	0.0
Scenario 11 - 5th Question	0.0	0.0	0.0
Scenario 11 - 6th Question	0.0	0.0	0.0
Scenario 12 - 3rd Question	0.0	0.0	0.0
Scenario 12 - 8th Question	0.0	0.0	0.0
Scenario 14 - 2nd Question	0.0	0.0	0.0
Scenario 14 - 5th Question	0.0	0.0	0.0
Scenario 14 - 8th Question	0.0	0.0	0.0
Scenario 15 - 2nd Question	0.0	0.0	0.0
Scenario 15 - 7th Question	0.0	0.0	0.0

tions with no variation. With this in mind, examine a couple of these cases to contrast the differences with prior examples, beginning with scenario 1, answer 3 (Figure 5). Scenario 1 deals with a technique to be used for modelling a new database. Although the novice and expert groups both show no variation ethically and realistically for how they would deal with answer 3 (deciding to make an issue of the modelling exercise with the Data Administrator, because of other workload commitments), the answers they provide do actually differ. Novice values (medians) are (ethical 2.0, realistic 2.0) in other words *Very Bad*. Expert values are (ethical 4.0, realistic 4.0) in other words *Neither Good nor Bad*. The novice group therefore feels protesting is both from an idealistic and in fact realistic point of view, really quite a

Figure 5. Illustrating tacit knowledge inventory Scenario 1 with answer 3

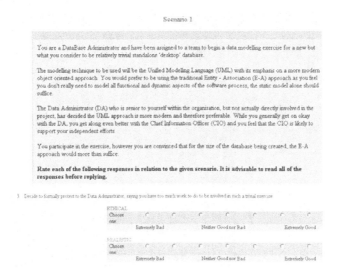

bad idea. The expert group on the other hand appears far less fazed with the suggestion of protest to a senior member of staff.

As an aside, it is interesting to note the differences between how the genders dealt with the issue, at least from a realistic point of view (Figure 6). One can see that whilst females fairly

Figure 6. Illustrating tacit knowledge inventory scenario 1, with answer 3, realistic values * gender

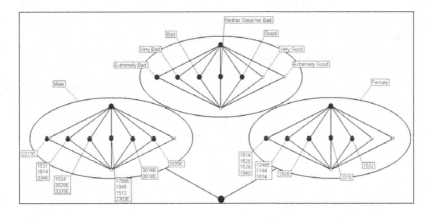

Figure 7. Illustrating tacit knowledge inventory scenario 15, with answer 7

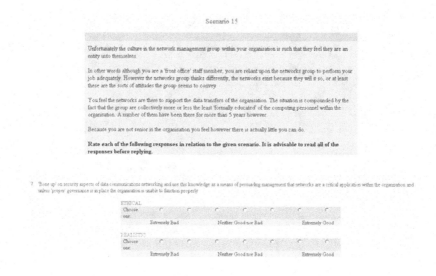

consistently believed the third answer option for scenario 1 was really quite a bad idea; the males did not necessarily feel quite the same way.

Scenario 15, with answer 7 (Figure 7) deals with a difficult data communications network management group who implicitly feel they possess more power than others in the organisation consider they should. This specific example was one particularly noteworthy case in point observed by IT personnel as part of the initial interviewing, information elicitation process. The answer approach to dealing with this situation suggests "boning up" (gaining a good understanding) in the area of the organisation causing difficulties, as a means of gaining some leverage with management. Both expert and novice groups for this situation felt the same way ethically and realistically. Not only this, but the results for novices (4.0) and experts (4.0) indicated a generally non-committal attitude by both groups. The idea of "boning up" is greeted neutrally by both parties. It is neither a good nor bad idea.

Thus, to answer our original questions relating to this section dealing with difference between ethical and realistic responses by expert and novice categories, one sees that 14 (out of 128 total) scenario + answer responses had significant (>1.0) variation between experts and novices. Whereas 26 (out of 128) had no variation in terms of differences ethically and realistically for how both groups had answered these situations. The remaining 88 scenario + answer combinations showed *some* or *minor* variation between expert and novice groups, in terms of differences between ethical and non-ethical responses.

Overall Differences Between Expert and Novice Groups

It is time to investigate the second initial question for this chapter, namely which particular scenarios and answer options were being answered differently by experts? Were there particular scenarios with answer options that were answered substantially differently between the groups? That is to say, rather than comparing the differences *between* ethical and realistic values for each particular group, which scenarios and answers did the two groups overall differ on firstly from an ethical standpoint, secondly from a realistic point of view. Table 3 highlights the major areas of disagreement between experts and novices, from a purely *ethical* point of view. In other words statistics have been compared that assesses the differences between the expert and non-expert groups purely on the basis of their ethical points of view. The previous set of data had instead examined differences within each group in terms of how they had varied for each given answered ethically and realistically, and then contrasted those differences between novice and expert groups.

Table 3. Indicating significant (>1.0) difference between experts and non-experts in terms of ethical values (medians) for given scenarios and answers

Scenarios + answers	Exp-Novice (differences)
Scenario 1 - 3rd Question	2.0
Scenario 1 - 8th Question	2.0
Scenario 12 - 1st Question	1.5
Scenario 13 - 3rd Question	1.5
Scenario 16 - 1st Question	1.5
Scenario 5 - 2nd Question	-1.5
Scenario 7 - 8th Question	-1.5
Scenario 12 - 4th Question	-1.5
Scenario 12 - 6th Question	-1.5
Scenario 12 - 7th Question	-1.5
Scenario 13 - 4th Question	-1.5
Scenario 16 - 6th Question	-1.5
Scenario 2 - 6th Question	-2.0
Scenario 2 - 7th Question	-2.0
Scenario 4 - 6th Question	-2.0
Scenario 6 - 1st Question	-2.0
Scenario 10 - 6th Question	-2.0
Scenario 11 - 7th Question	-2.0
Scenario 6 - 7th Question	-2.5
Scenario 16 - 5th Question	-2.5
Scenario 10 - 2nd Question	-3.0

Here the situation is less complex as the desire is to see examples of situations where experts differed on certain points from an ethical point of view. Again, the novice results have been subtracted from the expert Likert scale vales as a means of highlighting the differences. Scenario/answer combinations highlighted have been so chosen because they are also reflected in the realistic differences (Table 4), which follow. It is prudent to examine the same situations concurrently.

Returning to scenario 1, (Figure 5), one can see question/answer 3 is contentious, but this point has already been covered. Nevertheless, it is clear from looking at the table that experts are inclined to feel a whole 2 points on the Likert scale more positively about this issue than the novices were. Remember this issue dealt with protesting to the data administrator about having too much work to do, where the experts were unfazed about this idea (4.0, Neither Good nor Bad), but our novices thought it was a far worse idea (2.0, Very Bad).

Examining the same scenario, but answer option 8 this time (Figure 8), note a similar ethical variation between how experts feel in relation to novices. The scenario was in relation to modelling for a database, but this time the answer takes the opposite tack to answer 3. Whereas before there was whinging about overwork, now enthusiasm is shown in the hope the attention is noticed and "better" projects are allocated in future. Seeing as these highlighted scenario/answer combinations appear in the realistic table as well (Table 4), note that experts are even *more* positive *realistically* about this situation than the novices, a whole 3 points (median) on the Likert scale in fact. Indeed the results for novices are (*ethical* 2.0 Very Bad, *realistic* 4.0 Neither Good nor Bad). Alternatively the experts feel (*ethical* 4.0 Neither Good nor Bad, *realistic* 5.0 Good). It would appear that ethically being enthusiastic

Figure 8. Illustrating a particular situation (scenario 1, answer 8) where there significant difference (>1.0) between how experts and novices feel ethically *and* realistically *about a certain situation*

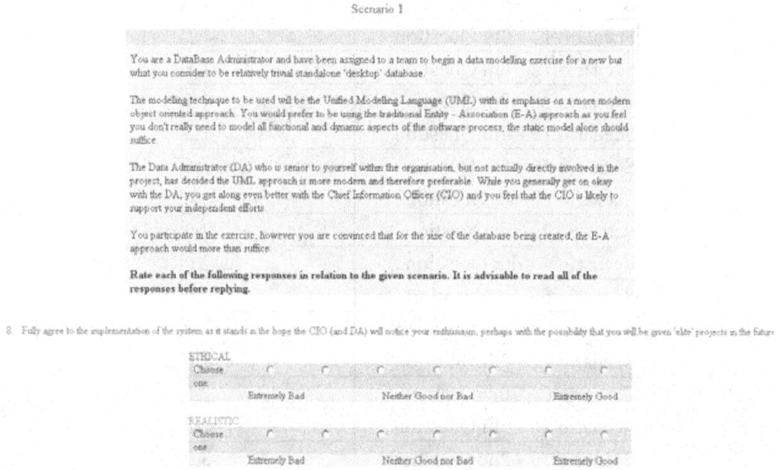

Scenario 1

You are a DataBase Administrator and have been assigned to a team to begin a data modelling exercise for a new but what you consider to be relatively trivial standalone 'desktop' database.

The modeling technique to be used will be the Unified Modeling Language (UML) with its emphasis on a more modern object oriented approach. You would prefer to be using the traditional Entity - Association (E-A) approach as you feel you don't really need to model all functional and dynamic aspects of the software process, the static model alone should suffice.

The Data Administrator (DA) who is senior to yourself within the organisation, but not actually directly involved in the project, has decided the UML approach is more modern and therefore preferable. While you generally get on okay with the DA, you get along even better with the Chief Information Officer (CIO) and you feel that the CIO is likely to support your independent efforts.

You participate in the exercise, however you are convinced that for the size of the database being created, the E-A approach would more than suffice.

Rate each of the following responses in relation to the given scenario. It is advisable to read all of the responses before replying.

8. Fully agree to the implementation of the system as it stands in the hope the CIO (and DA) will notice your enthusiasm, perhaps with the possibility that you will be given 'elite' projects in the future

ETHICAL
Choose one
Extremely Bad — Neither Good nor Bad — Extremely Good

REALISTIC
Choose one
Extremely Bad — Neither Good nor Bad — Extremely Good

Table 4. Indicating significant (>1.0) difference between experts and novices in terms of realistic values (medians) for given scenarios and answers

Scenarios + answers	Exp-Novice (differences)
Scenario 1 - 8th Question	3.0
Scenario 1 - 3rd Question	2.0
Scenario 2 - 1st Question	2.0
Scenario 3 - 1st Question	1.5
Scenario 6 - 2nd Question	1.5
Scenario 14 - 1st Question	1.5
Scenario 6 - 6th Question	-1.5
Scenario 6 - 7th Question	-1.5
Scenario 12 - 2nd Question	-1.5
Scenario 13 - 4th Question	-1.5
Scenario 16 - 3rd Question	-1.5
Scenario 16 - 5th Question	-1.5
Scenario 1 - 4th Question	-2.0
Scenario 2 - 7th Question	-2.0
Scenario 4 - 2nd Question	-2.0
Scenario 4 - 6th Question	-2.0
Scenario 7 - 5th Question	-2.0
Scenario 7 - 8th Question	-2.0
Scenario 9 - 6th Question	-2.0
Scenario 12 - 7th Question	-2.0
Scenario 16 - 6th Question	-2.0

about a project is no big deal, whereas for novices it seems to have negative connotations. In reality however the expert group seems to think that being enthusiastic is actually a good idea, something the novices are lukewarm about.

Looking at another area of disagreement between experts and novices, in this case scenario 4, answer 6 (Figure 9), notice from both Tables 9 and 10, that experts are more negatively disposed ethically *and* realistically than the novices. Scenario 4 in this instance deals with a situation where clients from the company you are producing a system for, are involved with the system design. Unfortunately the visitors/clients seem to be holding up the works. The answer option in this case relates to being diplomatic in the short term, but non-accountable in the long term.

Note from the results given in both ethical and realistic tables, that experts feel a whole two points on the Likert scale more negatively about the way of dealing with this situation than the novices. In fact, the actual results are, novices (*ethical/realistic* 3.0 Bad), experts (*ethical/realistic* 1.0 Extremely Bad). Actually even the standard deviations bear out the

Figure 9. Illustrating scenario 4, answer 6 as an example of where experts and novices appear to substantially (>1.0) disagree both ethically and realistically

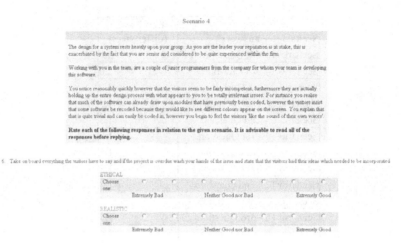

differences between the two groups: novices (S.D. ethical 1.3, realistic 1.5), experts (S.D. ethical 0.7, realistic 0.5). Fundamentally, the experts feel strongly disinclined to "wash their hands" of important affairs.

Turning the attention to scenario 12 with answer 7 (Figure 10) as another example of how experts and novices differ markedly in relation to dealing with a situation, one are faced with a range of implicit issues. Firstly, the speed at which a subordinate is undertaking tasks is considered inappropriate. Secondly, there is the issue of what senior within the organisation on this occasion means? Does senior relate to number of years with the organisation, status in terms of job title, or level of formal qualification?

In practice, seniority is often a varying combination of all three. The answer suggestion in this case relates to asking the slow individual whether and which extra resources would aid them. The differences between experts and novices were 1.5 *ethically* and 2.0 *realistically*. Interestingly whilst the novices felt very positive about the suggestion (*ethical/realistic* 6.0 Very Good, S.D. 1.1, 1.3), experts were lukewarm about the offer (*ethical* 4.5, *realistically* 4.0 Neither Good nor Bad, S.D. 1.2, 1.2).

Examining one final example of differences between the two groups is that of scenario 13, answer 4 (Figure 11). The situation the respondent faces here is one where an outside influence comes to bear on the organisation; furthermore the implication is that the external factor is not considered to be value for money. This scenario was developed after consultation with IT staff, who when interviewed indicated such examples had directly taken place in their organisation, for which they were understandably less than impressed.

The question asks whether sending an email to someone senior in the organisation as a means of getting management to change its mind, might not be a good idea. The novices

Figure 10. Illustrating scenario 12, answer 7 as an example of a situation where experts and novices appear to differ substantially (>1.0) both ethically and realistically

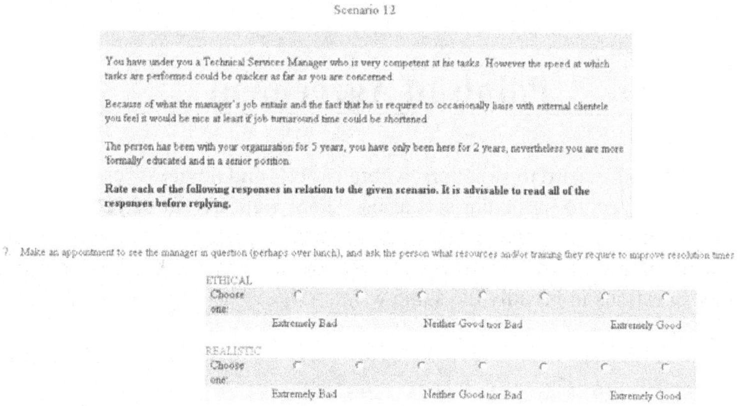

Figure 11. Illustrating scenario 13, answer 4 for which experts and novices appear to substantially (>1.0) disagree both ethically and realistically

generally felt non-committal about the issue (*ethical/realistic* 4.0/3.5 Neither Good nor Bad, S.D. 1.6/1.5). The experts on the other hand were far more negative about the suggestion (*ethical/realistic* 2.5/2.0 Very Bad, S.D. 2.0/1.5). Although both groups felt more negatively about the issue in reality than idealistically speaking, it is somewhat interesting to note the slight tightening up in terms of the standard deviation amongst the experts when examining their responses to how they would deal with the issue in reality. In other words, whilst the experts might be somewhat more divided on this issue *ethically* (nevertheless still feeling negative about the suggestion), *realistically* in terms of what they would do, the experts would appear to have closed ranks somewhat. Obviously the experts are of the opinion that approaching senior management is not a good idea.

Points of Agreement

Examine Table 5 with regard to situations where experts and novices were totally in agreement for given answers to particular scenarios. There were 21 out of 125 situations were both parties produced effectively the same set of results. That is to say, on 17 percent of occasions, when the results from all three organisations are pooled, the two groups answered the inventory questions in broadly the same way.

Table 5. Showing scenarios and answers where both experts and novices are in agreement (medians)

Scenario + answers	Exp-Novices (diff.) (Eth. and Real.)
Scenario 1 - 2nd Question	0.0
Scenario 1 - 6th Question	0.0
Scenario 2 - 4th Question	0.0
Scenario 5 - 5th Question	0.0
Scenario 7 - 1st Question	0.0
Scenario 7 - 2nd Question	0.0
Scenario 7 - 4th Question	0.0
Scenario 8 - 2nd Question	0.0
Scenario 9 - 1st Question	0.0
Scenario 9 - 3rd Question	0.0
Scenario 9 - 4th Question	0.0
Scenario 10 - 5th Question	0.0
Scenario 11 - 5th Question	0.0
Scenario 12 - 8th Question	0.0
Scenario 13 - 2nd Question	0.0
Scenario 14 - 5th Question	0.0
Scenario 14 - 7th Question	0.0
Scenario 15 - 1st Question	0.0
Scenario 15 - 7th Question	0.0
Scenario 15 - 10th Question	0.0
Scenario 16 - 4th Question	0.0

Figure 12. Illustrating scenario 5, answer 5 as an example of an answer scenario, which showed very no variation (medians) from a ethical point of view between experts and novices

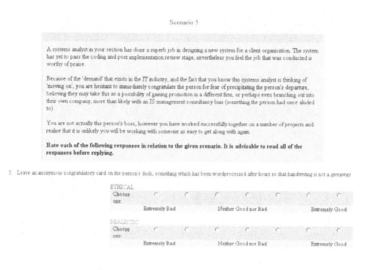

With this in mind, briefly examine a couple of the situations where both groups were in agreement with one another. First of all, scenario 5 (Figure 12) deals with interpersonal relations, whereby an analyst had performed well on a project, but implicitly there is some concern that if the analyst is too aware of their skills, they may leave the organisation taking their tacit knowledge with them. Answer 5 (Figure 12), which suggests leaving an anonymous note, is agreed by both parties (experts and non experts) to be an extremely bad idea (1.0 ethical and realistically).

To take one other similarity between the two groups, scenario 16 (Figure 13) places the respondent in the shoes of a systems manager, whereby large-scale systems integration is required to take place in the near future. The answer (4) for which experts and novices are in agreement (Figure 13), relates to constructing a questionnaire to gather further feedback in relation to the organisation's application portfolio. Both groups from an *ethical* point of view agreed this was a very good idea (6.0). *Realistically* they were both inclined to be a little more pessimistic (5.0). Both groups ethically felt creating a questionnaire was a good idea. In practice however, both considered it only a good, rather than a very good, means of eliciting information.

Perhaps the groups felt this way, because of prior experience in completing questionnaires themselves, with all the associated problems of low response rates. Alternatively the groups may simply have understood in practice, the extra workload the establishment of a questionnaire would bring.

Figure 13. Illustrating scenario 16, answer 4 as an example of a situation where no variation (medians) from an ethical point of view existed between experts and novices

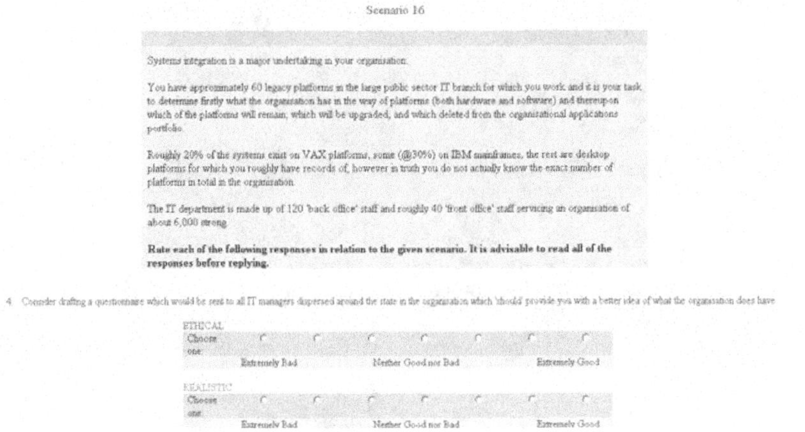

Scenario 16

Systems integration is a major undertaking in your organisation.

You have approximately 60 legacy platforms in the large public sector IT branch for which you work and it is your task to determine firstly what the organisation has in the way of platforms (both hardware and software) and thereupon which of the platforms will remain, which will be upgraded, and which deleted from the organisational applications portfolio.

Roughly 20% of the systems exist on VAX platforms, some (@30%) on IBM mainframes, the rest are desktop platforms for which you roughly have records of, however in truth you do not actually know the exact number of platforms in total in the organisation.

The IT department is made up of 120 'back office' staff and roughly 40 'front office' staff servicing an organisation of about 6,000 strong.

Rate each of the following responses in relation to the given scenario. It is advisable to read all of the responses before replying.

4. Consider drafting a questionnaire which would be sent to all IT managers dispersed around the state in the organisation which 'should' provide you with a better idea of what the organisation does have

ETHICAL
Choose one:
Extremely Bad | Neither Good nor Bad | Extremely Good

REALISTIC
Choose one:
Extremely Bad | Neither Good nor Bad | Extremely Good

Summarisation of Contentious Scenario/Answer Combinations

There were after examination of scenario and answer combinations as indicated in tables in this section, a number of issues where experts and novices appeared to differ. (1) Firstly, differences between ethical and realistic values amongst novices, compared against the same differences amongst experts. (2) Secondly, differences between what experts consider to be *ideally/ethically* appropriate compared to novices. (3) Thirdly, differences between the same two groups but this time how the groups differ fundamentally from a *practical/realistic* point of view. First examine the differences between how novices and experts answered ethically and realistically within each scenario/answer combination. Results are summarised in Table 6. Shaded areas indicate overlap in scenario/answer combinations between the three summary tables. A somewhat colloquial style has been adopted in certain places in the scenarios and the summarisation at the end of the chapter to give the reader a "street-smart" feel to what is taking place. Endnotes are provided should the reader require them.

Significant Ethical Differences Between the Two Groups

Now examine the scenarios and answer situations where experts and novices differed between the two groups in terms of ***ethical*** responses only, in other words how experts and novices felt about an issue ideally, disregarding what they would do in practice. A summation of these scenario/answer combinations is provided in Table 7.

Table 6. Highlighting areas where experts and novices disagreed significantly (>=2.0 on Likert value median scores) in terms of ethical and realistic values within each group

Scenario	Controversial answer (way of dealing with the scenario)	Attitudinal differences between the groups
Scenario 2: A network manager wishes to install a network (IBM Token Ring). You are that persons junior, but realise there is a better way. You have IT experience yourself. You are a CNE (Certified Novell Engineer). The manager has more work experience. The manager has been able to get the equipment cheaply. You think Ethernet is cheaper and simpler.	**Answer 2**: It's best not to "get above your station." You are junior, leave it there.	Experts differentiate ethically and realistically. In reality experts are more favourable. Novices don't differentiate.
	Answer 6: Ignore the situation. There is little you can do. If something goes wrong, it's not your fault.	Experts differentiate ethically and realistically. Ethically, experts are more negative. Novices don't differentiate.
Scenario 4: You are conducting system design for another organisation. You are a team leader, senior and experienced. There are junior programmers in your team from a *client* firm. The junior *client* programmers make irrelevant suggestions for inclusion in the project. You begin to feel they like the sound of their own voices.	**Answer 2**: Talk to someone senior in the *client* organisation. Express your concerns. Hope *their* senior management can sort out issues.	Both groups differentiate realistically. In reality, experts are more negative, novices are more positive.
Scenario 6: The senior person in your section is close to retirement. He is mostly an administrator at this stage of life, but likes to "keep his hand in."[b] You feel his knowledge is outdated. You respect him, but you are not on the same the "wavelength."[c] The senior person wants to help with systems analysis on a project for a client firm. He has a friend in the client firm. Your company policy is business and friends don't mix.	**Answer 1:** Show the senior person a better way to do analysis tasks. Hope he will "see the light."[d] In other words, see your better way of doing things.	Both groups agree realistically. Ethically novices are more positive.
Scenario 8: You have been with your current IS job for two years. You are working on a software project. You are possessive of the project. If you insist upon completing it yourself, it will not be done on time. Some colleagues have volunteered to help you. You feel their backgrounds are not appropriate. However you really would rather not have the boss make extra staffing help decisions for you.	**Answer 8:** Send out an e-mail asking for expressions of interest to help you. You are "casting a wider net" in effect. Decide upon replies whom to have help you. If there are no replies, then accept the boss's decision as to who will be allocated to you.	Both groups vary ethically and realistically. Experts are ethically slightly more positive, realistically slightly more negative than the novice group.

Table 6. continued

Scenario	Controversial answer (way of dealing with the scenario)	Attitudinal differences between the groups
Scenario 10: There exist a number of ways of looking at system success. A system that meets the specifications within cost but "sits on the shelf"[e] may be successful. A system that works perfectly but over budget may also be considered successful. Another view of success is a system that is utilised and is on or under budget.	**Answer 2:** As long as the clients are happy, regardless of your opinions, this is all that counts.	Both groups agree realistically. Ethically experts are more negative about this. Novices are more positive than their realistic values.
	Answer 4: Just because the system wasn't implemented, it doesn't matter because another team couldn't have done the job better anyway.	Both groups vary ethically and realistically Experts are ethically slightly more positive, realistically slightly more negative than the novice group.

Table 7. Highlighting significant (>=2.0 median) areas of contention between expert and novice groups purely on ethical value judgements

Scenario	Controversial answer (way of dealing with the scenario)	Expert opinion
Scenario 1: You are a DBA. You are in a team working on a database modelling exercise, which you think is trivial. UML with object orientation is being used. You feel a simple relational E-A model would suffice. Your senior, the DA has decided the UML object approach will be used. You get on okay with the DA, but even better with the CIO.	**Answer 3:** You protest to the DA, saying you have too much work to do to be involved in this trivial exercise.	+2.0 (agree more ethically)
	Answer 8: Fully go along with it and hope the DA and CIO will notice your enthusiasm. The point being you hope you will be given better projects in the future in lieu of cooperation.	+2.0 (agree more ethically)
Scenario 2: A network manager wishes to install a network (IBM Token Ring). You are that persons junior, but realise there is a better way. You have IT experience yourself. You are a CNE (Certified Novell Engineer). The manager has more work experience. The manager has been able to get the equipment cheaply. You think Ethernet is cheaper and simpler.	**Answer 6:** Ignore the situation. There is little you can do. If something goes wrong, it's not your fault.	-2.0 (disagree more ethically)
	Answer 7: Agree "in principle" with the network manager, hoping the network manager will support you for one of your projects in the future	-2.0 (disagree more ethically)

Table 7. continued

Scenario	Controversial answer (way of dealing with the scenario)	Expert opinion
Scenario 4: You are conducting system design for another organisation. You are a team leader, senior and experienced. There are junior programmers in your team from a *client* firm. The junior *client* programmers make irrelevant suggestions for inclusion in the project. You begin to feel they like the sound of their own voices.	**Answer 6:** Listen to the junior visitors, but if the project is overdue "wash your hands" of the matter, saying the visitors wanted these irrelevant features included.	-2.0 (disagree more ethically)
Scenario 6: The senior person in your section is close to retirement. He is mostly an administrator at this stage of life, but likes to "keep his hand in." You feel his knowledge is outdated. You respect him, but you are not on the same the "wavelength." The senior person wants to help with systems analysis on a project for a client firm. He has a friend in the client firm. Your company policy is business and friends don't mix.	**Answer 1:** Show senior person better way to do the analysis tasks. Hope he will "see the light." See your better way of doing things.	-2.0 (disagree more ethically)
	Answer 7: Place the "no business/friends" company directive on the workplace noticeboard after hours.	-2.5 (disagree more ethically)
Scenario 10: There exist a number of ways of looking at system success. A system that meets the specifications within cost but "sits on the shelf" may be successful. A system that works perfectly but over budget may also be considered successful. Another view of success is a system that is utilised and is on or under budget.	**Answer 2:** As long as the clients are happy, regardless of your opinions, this is all that counts.	-3.0 (disagree more ethically)
	Answer 6: System success is just a matter of resource allocation. In this case the combination of time and/or skills wasn't correct.	-2.0 (disagree more ethically)
Scenario 11: A new team member seems to lack basic software engineering competency. The person is more of a technical writer. You feel nevertheless he should be more technically competent. You are not the team leader, but you feel you should point out software deficiencies. The current project has critical deadlines; you are facing a fine time deadline.	**Answer 7:** Consider asking the boss for an extra team member, implying new team member is not most suited to the project, but his skills will improve.	-2.0 (disagree more ethically)

Table 7. continued

Scenario	Controversial answer (way of dealing with the scenario)	Expert opinion
Scenario 16: You are working in a large public sector organisation. There are 120 "back office" IT staff and 40 "front office" IT staff supporting 6,000 people. Systems integration is a major task. You are responsible for updating the organisational application portfolio. Some platforms: hardware/software have to go. You don't actually know all the platforms the organisation has.	**Answer 5:** Establish a pilot team to evaluate organisational systems. Once management has made up its mind which systems it wants to keep, keep those, and decommission the remainder. You are stalling/ "passing the buck" basically.	**-2.5** (disagree more ethically)

Table 8. Highlighting significant (>=2.0 median) areas of contention between expert and novice groups purely on realistic value judgements

Scenario	Controversial answer (way of dealing with the scenario)	Expert opinion
Scenario 1: You are a DBA. You are in a team working on a database modelling exercise, which you think is trivial. UML with object orientation is being used. You feel a simple relational E-A model would suffice. Your senior, the DA has decided the UML object approach will be used. You get on okay with the DA, but even better with the CIO.	**Answer 3:** You protest to the DA, saying you have too much work to do to be involved in this trivial exercise.	**+2.0** (agree more in reality)
	Answer 4: Consider asking the DA to clarify why the use of UML, so the other team members can see the benefits of using this technique. You hope in doing so the DA rethinks his decision. Either that or the other team members see things your way.	**-2.0** (disagree more in reality)
	Answer 8: Fully go along with the plan and hope the DA and CIO will notice your enthusiasm. The point being you hope you will be given better projects in future because of your cooperation.	**+3.0** (agree more in reality)

Table 8. continued

Scenario	Controversial answer (way of dealing with the scenario)	Expert opinion
Scenario 2: A network manager wishes to install a network (IBM Token Ring). You are that persons junior, but realise there is a better way. You have IT experience yourself. You are a CNE (Certified Novell Engineer). The manager has more work experience. The manager has been able to get the equipment cheaply. You think Ethernet is cheaper and simpler.	**Answer 1**: Approach network manager with contacts of your own, who could offer an even better deal.	+2.0 (agree more in reality)
	Answer 7: Agree "in principle" with the network manager, hoping the network manager will support you for one of your projects in future.	-2.0 (disagree more in reality)
Scenario 4: You are conducting system design for another organisation. You are a team leader, senior and experienced. There are junior programmers in your team from a *client* firm. The junior *client* programmers make irrelevant suggestions for inclusion in the project. You begin to feel they like the sound of their own voices.	**Answer 2:** Talk to someone senior in the *client* organisation. Express your concerns. Hope *their* senior management can sort out the issues.	-2.0 (disagree more in reality)
	Answer 6: Listen to the junior visitors, but if the project is overdue "wash your hands" of the matter, saying the visitors wanted these irrelevant features included.	-2.0 (disagree more in reality)
Scenario 7: You are a senior "back office" programmer, working in a team. The "Front office" team has been busy liaising with clients. Front office team has not communicated well with your team on this project. Documentation occurred but front office simply handed over to your team. Front office team had also made some extra "promises" to the client in terms of deliverables. Not only is your team a little in the dark about total deliverables, but also your group may have to redo some front office tasks, conducting some interviews with clients yourselves. Basically the project is not working to plan.	**Answer 5:** Ignore the whole issue. If anything goes wrong, chances are the front office will take the blame anyway.	-2.0 (disagree more in reality)
	Answer 8: Perhaps the front office is correct after all. Decide at the end of the day to follow their lead.	-2.0 (disagree more in reality)

Table 8. continued

Scenario	Controversial answer (way of dealing with the scenario)	Expert opinion
Scenario 9: Your team is from an outsourced firm working on a large QA system for a public sector organisation. Many teams are involved, even from other outsourced firms. The probity (checking) team will work on the project after you. You are generally satisfied with the way things have gone. A certain component is niggling you. Your team has done as the specifications required, but you realise the system won't properly work as is.	**Answer 6:** Fix the problem yourself even if this means unpaid overtime.	**-2.0** (disagree more in reality)
Scenario 12: There is a technical services manager under you. He is very competent, but a little slow in completing tasks as far as you are concerned. Because of his job requirements and his having to liaise with external clients you feel it would be better if job turnaround time were reduced. The technical manager has been in the organisation for five years, you have only been here for two. You are admittedly more "formally" educated and in a more senior position.	**Answer 7:** Make an appointment to see the manager in question (perhaps do lunch). Ask him what extra resources/training he might require to improve through time.	**-2.0** (disagree more in reality)
Scenario 16: You are working in a large public sector organisation. There are 120 "back office" IT staff and 40 "front office" IT staff supporting 6,000 people. Systems integration is a major task. You are responsible for updating the organisational application portfolio. Some platforms: hardware/software have to go. You don't actually know all the platforms the organisation has.	**Answer 6:** Decide to travel to all branches of the organisation to get a better feeling for the most important platforms. Those not mentioned, need not be maintained. Backup tapes exist of the data anyway. Should any hardware/software ultimately be re-required, your organisation has a mirroring arrangement with another organisation in the public sector.	**-2.0** (disagree more in reality)

Significant Realistic Differences Between the Two Groups

At the same time, there was another set of answers for some of the same scenarios for which experts and novices disagreed on a *realistic* level. How experts and novices actually handled the situation in *practice* differed, and are summarised in Table 8.

Summary

What can be gathered from the summarisation of each of the significant scenario/answer combinations? Even though *significant* differences in the inventory results were limited, the following themes emerge:

1.   One gains some understanding of experts having a greater awareness of status related issues ("best not to get above one's station"[f]).

2.   Perhaps the major difference that seems to arise from the tables is that experts also seem to be a little more attuned to the problems related to avoiding responsibility for issues. Novices seem to be a little happier to "pass the buck."[g]

3.   Experts also seem to feel that "going over a superior's head"[h] is less of a good idea.

4.   At the same time, the expert sample group also views taking issues outside of the organisation slightly less favourably.

5.   Experts seem to see less wrong ideally with showing a senior person a better way to do things. Admittedly this probably reflects their higher levels of expertise and the fact they are likely to be more often called upon for advice.

6.   One can also surmise that experts seem to have a slightly better grasp of differentiating when it comes to getting help, between what might be a good idea in theory, and the logistical implications of involving extra people on a task.

7.   Experts seem to feel a little guiltier if a system is implemented that makes the clients happy but is perhaps not quite what was intended or what they feel to have been a better idea. This may reflect a higher ego involved in system design and implementation.

From a purely *ethical* point of view:

1.   The experts seem more comfortable with telling superiors that their plate is full enough.

2.   Yet at the same time, if they are to be given extra work, then it is best not to grumble but tackle the task at hand.

3.   This last point in turn helps explain why experts seem less enthusiastic ideally speaking about passing responsibility for tasks onto others.

4.   Whilst it seems experts would prefer to be noticed for working harder, they do seem less comfortable with being a "yes"[i] person.

5.   From an ethical point of view, experts seem to feel less at ease with covert means of gaining advantage. Perhaps this reflects the likelihood they are less likely to need to be secretive about getting their points across. Their opinions are more likely to be respected in any case.

6.   Experts seem ethically speaking, to be more responsible for a project's success. Perhaps this reflects a possible greater loss of status if a project does not succeed, than it would for someone who may not have quite the same reputation.

From a *realistic* point of view, subtle differences that seem to characterise experts are the following.

1.   Experts seem far happier in practice to say they are already overcommitted. Again this would reflect their recognition of being in demand. People who are less employable are less likely to complain about being given extra work.

2.   Experts seem far less comfortable in practice questioning the decisions of a superior. Perhaps this relates to this group having a greater awareness of status issues. Inadvertently gaining negative attention appears to be somewhat more implicitly recognised as a problem by the expert group.

3.   Conversely agreeing with superiors if the task at hand needs to be done seems to rate more highly with experts in practice. This may signal either greater levels of responsibility amongst expert personnel, or alternatively an understanding of the reward structure that is likely to be forthcoming.

4.   Experts seem more content in practice with offering management alternatives if they know of them. This probably reflects their greater levels of overall expertise.

5.   Experts appear less inclined practically to want to achieve goals with ulterior motives. Perhaps this reflects a diminished need on their part to have to. They may be able to acquire resources or permission for their interests more easily than novices in any case.

6.   It would also appear from a practical point of view that experts are less inclined to "pay lip service."[j]

7.   This last point seems to tie in with their reduced interest in "passing the buck." Perhaps they feel not accepting responsibility at an early stage (paying lip service), will lead to negative consequences in later stages (passing the buck).

8.   There would also appear to be some indication of experts being leaders from a practical point of view, rather than followers.

9.   Yet they seem at the same time to be less interested in practice to have to put in unpaid overtime. Perhaps this reflects an attitude that "it shouldn't have gone wrong to begin with."

10. Experts also seem less interested in practice in asking subordinates what extra help they may require. This may reflect a self-focus on the part of experts. Alternatively experts may feel asking a somewhat lesser competent person (than themselves) could conceivably "open a can of worms."[k]

11. Similarly it would appear the expert group also seems a little more reluctant to commit itself to exercises where outcomes are likely to be less clear.

One can see there exist a number of areas ethically and realistically where the expert sample differs from the novice group. Returning to the points relating to whether experts were answering the inventory differently from non-experts, the answers are as follows: *Yes*, experts do tend to answer the IT tacit knowledge inventory items differently from that of novices. Only 17 percent of the 125-scenario/answer combinations reveal close similarities between the ways the two groups would deal with these "tacit managerial knowledge" situations. In turn, that means that 83 percent of the time, the two groups feel and handle them differently. At the same time we were able to identify a whole group of expert novices who were not officially identified by their peers as being experts but whose results did place them in an expert category. With these points in mind, organisational social network patterns are examined next to determine the likelihood of tacit knowledge being transferred in different organisational domains based on the communication patterns between expert "elites" (experts and ENEs) and novices.

References

Luksch, P., & Wille, R. (1991). A mathematical model for conceptual knowledge systems. In H Bock & P. Ihm (Eds.), *Classification, data analysis, and knowledge organization.* Heidelberg, Germany: Springer Publishers.

Endnotes

[a] On the recommendation of a staff member from the Department of Statistics, Macquarie University.

[b] Keep up practically speaking with what is going on.

[c] Not on the same level of understanding.

[d] See the way things actually are. See the truth, whatever that may be.

[e] Created for a purpose, but not actually utilised.

[f] Implicitly understanding one's status or place is society (even in Australia) is often advantageous and less likely to lead to conflict. In other words it is best to avoid negative attention. This is an example of tacit knowledge.

[g] Passing responsibility onto someone else if a negative event occurs.

h   Approaching a higher level of authority in the anticipation they will see your point of view. Whilst at the same time you hope you come to the higher authority's attention in a positive light.

i   Consistently agreeing with the boss regardless of what you actually feel, in order to gain future favour.

j   Listening to someone in relation to a particular matter. Acting as if you agree, and then going ahead and doing your own thing in any case.

k   Open up a whole range of issues, which are typically best left uncovered.

Chapter XI

Large Company (X)

One's access to social knowledge depends on one's position in the network of communication and social interaction. People who are well placed in the communication network also tend to be the central players in terms of power and influence. Those who have valuable social connections within the organizations are also fortunate ... we can say that power is a function of one's position in the network of communications and social relations, where this position is assessed not only simply in terms of structural centrality, but also in terms of power of the people with whom one is connected (Pfeffer, 1992, p. 111).

Introduction

In many ways the quote from Pfeffer (1992) illustrates the importance of tacit knowledge communication; or rather what takes place if the communication breaks down. This chapter deals with communication flows between personnel in the first of three organisations. An understanding of tacit knowledge patterns was gained in the previous chapter. It was noted that experts do in fact produce different responses generally speaking from that of the novices and that there existed a group of staff whose results made them effectively "expert" non-experts (ENEs). There existed in effect a certain street-smarted-ness to varying degrees amongst the IT staff studied in the three organisations. Through modelling the relationship patterns of individuals one is able to determine the consequences of knowledge flowing from one individual to the next. Implicit within this assumption is that those within a clique of higher tacit knowledge savvy individuals are more likely to benefit by gaining access to soft knowledge. Conversely those not within expert-rich cliques are likely to be disadvantaged by their lack of access to scarce knowledge related resources.

Large Organisation (X)

The major organisation sample of respondents was that of Organisation X. Although Organisation X offers the largest dataset of the three organisations, the increase in data introduces visualisation complications, to that end some of the data is simplified insofar as only those participants, who filled out the questionnaire, are illustrated in the graphs. The reader will recall that some 1,400 names were hard-coded into the IS tacit knowledge inventory. Not all of these 1,400 personnel ultimately participated for political, logistical or managerial reasons known only to the CIO. Furthermore because biographical (part A) and tacit knowledge inventory scores (part C) were not available from people who may nevertheless have been identified in part B of the questionnaire, it was felt prudent to omit these people. To provide the reader with an understanding of these issues, Table 1 illustrates the different workgroups of people identified in the questionnaire of 1,400 hard-coded names. Table 2 illustrates people who *actually* participated and the workgroups to which they belong. Clearly a smaller number of organisational workgroups emerges.

Table 1. Workgroups and physical locations of personnel identified in Organisation X

Department Name	Physical location
Account Management	
Account Services	
Business Intelligence Systems	Level 27, 580 Flossy Street
Bus Req Engin Team	Level 27, 580 Flossy Street
Business Solutions	Level 27, 580 Flossy Street
Business Solutions Centre 1	Level 16, 580 Flossy Street
Business Solutions Centre 2	Level 16, 580 Flossy Street
Business Solutions Centre 3	Level 16, 580 Flossy Street
Business Solutions Centre 4	Level 16, 580 Flossy Street
Business Solutions Centre 5	Level 16, 580 Flossy Street
Business Sol Manag	Level 16, 580 Flossy Street
CFO Information Services	Level 16, 580 Flossy Street
Claims Systems	Level 16, 580 Flossy Street
CTP/ Workers Comp Team	Level 16, 580 Flossy Street
Customer Data Management	Level 16, 580 Flossy Street
Customer Support Services	Level 16, 580 Flossy Street
Dev Env & Tools	Level 16, 580 Flossy Street
Doc Design & Dev	Level 16, 580 Flossy Street
Financial Services	Level 16, 580 Flossy Street

Table 1. continued

Department Name	Physical location
Huon Dev	Level 28, 580 Flossy Street
Huon Services	Level 28, 580 Flossy Street
Infrastructure Projects	Level 28, 580 Flossy Street
IS IT Victoria	Aristo Park 550 Fairy Hwy Vic
IS Management Services	Aristo Park 550 Fairy Hwy Vic
IS Operations	Aristo Park 550 Fairy Hwy Vic
IS Program Office	Aristo Park 550 Fairy Hwy Vic
IS SAP Basis	Level 29, 580 Flossy Street
IS SAP Development	Level 29, 580 Flossy Street
Manager Admin Supp	Level 29, 580 Flossy Street
Member Services IT&T	Level 16, 580 Flossy Street
Middleware	Level 16, 580 Flossy Street
National Prod Plat User Grp	Level 16, 580 Flossy Street
National Test Centre	Level 30, 580 Flossy Street
Online Receipting	Level 30, 580 Flossy Street
Operations	Aristo Park 550 Fairy Hwy Vic
Print Logistics Team	Aristo Park 550 Fairy Hwy Vic
Print Logistics	Aristo Park 550 Fairy Hwy Vic
Printing & BMT	Aristo Park 550 Fairy Hwy Vic
Product Analysis	Aristo Park 550 Fairy Hwy Vic
Production Enablement	Level 16, 580 Flossy Street
Production Support	Level 29, 580 Flossy Street
SAP Systems	Level 29, 580 Flossy Street
SE Insurance Systems	Level 29, 580 Flossy Street
SE Professional Development	Level 29, 580 Flossy Street
SGIC IT Group Facilities	Level 29, 580 Flossy Street
SGIO IT Technical Services	Level 29, 580 Flossy Street
Software Development Esprit IT	Level 28, 580 Flossy Street

Table 1. continued

Department Name	Physical location
Software Engineering Victoria	Aristo Park 550 Fairy Hwy Vic
Sol Dev IBM/GSA Cont	Level 14, 580 Flossy Street
South Australia Business Sol	Level 7, Story Square Adel SA
Strategy Planning & Architec	Level 14, 580 Flossy Street
Western Australia Business Sol	Level 14, 580 Flossy Street
Windows & Unix Sol	Level 27, 580 Flossy Street

Organisational X Structure, Experts, and Expert Non-Experts

Examining some of the numerical Social Network Analysis results relating to Organisation X personnel, experts were colour coded green in the original tables and ENEs blue. This allowed a simple check on the positioning of these two types of important people with respect to others who have not been identified so.

Organisation X Metrics

Organisation X Cliques[a]

... power relationships within groups communities and organisations can operate to skew benefit towards compliant individuals (Bush & Baum, 2001) while isolating others. Practices such as these are likely to contribute to the erosion of trust with adverse implications for the sustainment of organisational growth and creative effort (Jorgensen, 2004, p. 97).

Cliques represent a way of ascertaining how well people are connecting to one another in a group. In reality there are two ways of viewing cliques in Organisation X. The first approach simply includes all cliques where *at least one* member of the clique has participated in the research, in which case 265 cliques were identified in Organisation X. The second approach views cliques as composed of *only* actors who participated, that is to say a clique is true if *all* actors represented in the clique took part in this research. Taking the latter meaning to be more relevant, there existed 54 cliques in Organisation X (Table 3). These cliques

Table 2. Workgroups and physical location of personnel identified in Organisation X who actually participated

Department name	Physical location
Business Intel Sys	Level 27, 580 Flossy Street
Business Solutions Centre 1	Level 16, 580 Flossy Street
Customer Data Management	Level 16, 580 Flossy Street
HXXX Development	Level 28, 580 Flossy Street
IS IT Victoria	Aristo Park 550 Fairy Hwy Vic
IS SAP Basis	Level 29, 580 Flossy Street
IS SAP Development	Level 29, 580 Flossy Street
Manager Admin Sup	Level 29, 580 Flossy Street
Member Services IT&T	Level 16, 580 Flossy Street
National Test Centre	Level 30, 580 Flossy Street
Operations	Aristo Park 550 Fairy Hwy Vic
Production Enablement	Level 16, 580 Flossy Street
Production Support	Level 29, 580 Flossy Street
SAP Systems	Level 29, 580 Flossy Street
Software Dev Esprit IT	Level 28, 580 Flossy Street
Software Engineering Victoria	Aristo Park 550 Fairy Hwy Vic
Sol Dev IBM/GSA Contractors	Level 14, 580 Flossy Street
South Australia Business Sol	Level 7, Story Square Adel SA
Strategy Planning & Architec	Level 14, 580 Flossy Street
Windows & Unix Solutions	Level 27, 580 Flossy Street

have been calculated by UCINET™ (Analytic Technologies 2002). Examining the cliques one begins to see some (4, 5, 7, 10, 11) are composed almost exclusively of either experts (green) or expert non-experts (light blue). From a tacit knowledge transferral point of view in terms of seniors and "apprentices" working together, this would be considered less than ideal insofar as the knowledge is potentially bottlenecked amongst the actors in this clique. Whilst one may term number 4 a "power clique" given its exclusive large membership of experts and ENEs, the likelihood of these members transferring tacit knowledge amongst them is likely to be high. The organisation would hope they are transferring tacit knowledge outside of this power clique.

Table 3. Showing 54 cliques within Organisation X where the condition is every member of each clique has participated in the research

	Clique participants – All Organisation X actors who actually participated in the research										
1	1039	1046	1246E	1710E	1719E						
2	1039	1528	1534	1537							
3	1039	1534	1537	1543							
4	1	5	7	24	27	28	13E	14E	15E	21E	25E	8E
5	5	1023	14E	8E							
6	20	1531	1543	1732E							
7	20	27	28	15E	21E						
8	20	1507	1514								
9	20	1514	1543								
10	20	1543	2286E								
11	20	1507	2286E								
12	27	1931	25E	8E							
13	1337	1790	1805E								
14	1337	1791	1805E								
15	1337	1801	1805E								
16	1337	1802	1805E								
17	1337	1811	1805E								
18	1337	2383	1805E								
19	1337	1789E	1805E								
20	1337	1638	1642								
21	1337	1796	2386	1812E							
22	1337	1796	1789E	1812E							
23	1337	1790	1796	1812E							
24	1337	1796	1810								
25	1337	1796	1811	2386							
26	1337	1798	1789E	1795E							
27	1337	1799	1789E								
28	1337	1811	1795E								
29	1337	1790	1795E								
30	1507	1514	1534								
31	1514	1534	1543								
32	1525	1531	1532	1534	1543						
33	1525	1528	1531	1534							
34	1526	1527	1538								
35	1531	1532	1534	1537	1543						
36	1528	1531	1534	1537							
37	1531	1593	1607								
38	1528	1531	1593								
39	1046	1531	1246E								
40	1638	1642	1835E								

Table 3. continued

41	1790	1719E	1805E	
42	1790	1796	1806	
43	1790	1806	1805E	
44	1791	1806	1805E	
45	1792	1794	1809	
46	1796	1806	1811	
47	1796	1806	1789E	
48	1798	1795E	2385E	
49	1799	1810	1814	
50	1801	1806	1805E	
51	1806	1811	1805E	
52	1806	2383	1805E	
53	1806	1789E	1805E	
54	2257	15E	25E	8E

At the other end of the scale, cliques such as 20, 37, 38, and 49 have no expert or ENE in them at all. One could reasonably conclude they are missing out on tacit knowledge being transferred from their "seniors." Of course one must balance these points of view with an acknowledgement that the overwhelming majority of the cliques do in fact include a proportion of both experts and/or ENEs. Furthermore people who are involved in a "tacit knowledge deficient" clique[b] do at the very least participate in other cliques. At the same time it is worth noting that some novice members of certain cliques seem to have exposure only to one particular expert or ENE, for example personnel such as 1801, 1836, and 2383 only seem to have exposure to the knowledge of expert 1805E. One gains understanding of the likelihood of tacit knowledge transferral through an examination of clique patterns, however other measures of flows from individuals such as the densities of networks and the degrees of individuals are also informative. Having glanced briefly at the clique patterns making up the Organisation X sample, the density of the actual networks as they relate more specifically to experts, ENEs and the remainder of staff more generally, are now examined.

Degrees (Local Centrality)

The local centrality value of **degree**[c] also provides us with an understanding of how approachable or contactable an individual is. Once again only information has been provided that illustrates information for individuals who participated in the research, rather than all individuals who were actually identified. Table 4 presents the symmetrised degrees, that is to say degrees for participants where the data has been symmetrised to account for discrepancies in questionnaire responses. While the mean for symmetrised degrees is only 23.4 (taking into account all 378 *identified* actors as opposed to 108 actual *participants*), it is evident that experts and expert non-experts are clearly grouped above 41 degrees to use a specific cut-point. In other words, there seems to be a strong positive correlation with these two "elite" groups of staff being concentrated in the higher degree end of the table.

Table 4. Showing the degrees for individuals who participated in relation to contact frequency (experts = green; expert non-experts = blue)

Degree			Degree			Degree	
ID#	Degree		ID#	Degree		ID#	Degree
1039	338		1	71		2386	28
1337	325		28	69		1525	27
1710E	276		12E	66		1614	27
20	241		17	59		1792	26
1531	228		1582	57		1798	22
1534	169		1795E	57		1791	21
1543	165		1684E	54		2383	21
1555E	152		1790	52		1246E	21
23	137		4	51		1533	19
2286E	134		1796	50		1023	18
1507	128		1536	47		1801	18
2303E	123		1789E	47		1642	17
1732E	110		1812E	46		1802	16
5	107		1538	44		1793	14
2257	106		1835E	44		1581	12
14E	102		16	43		1607	12
1806	98		1811	41		2385E	12
1719E	98		1528	40		2375	11
8E	97		1799	40		1527	10
1593	89		1794	38		1591	10
25E	88		1526	37		1586	7
15E	87		1778	37		1530	6
1805E	85		1514	34		1540	6
21E	84		1810	34		1535	5
27	83		1931	34		1524	3
9	82		2277E	33			Degree
1046	80		1638	31		Mean	23.4
7	79		1809	31		StdDev	41.2
2	78		1537	30		Min.	0
1532	78		1513	28		Max.	338
13E	75		1539	28			
24	73		1814	28			

If we examine the degrees from an asymmetrical point of view using the person importance data, then a slightly different pattern emerges (Table 5). The means are both 7.5 (where out

Table 5. Showing the degrees for individuals who participated in relation to person importance, in descending order of in-degree (prestige)

Degrees	Out	In
8E	18	51
1543	65	47
20	170	34
21E	15	30
1789E	3	29
9	42	27
1732E	43	27
1046	31	26
28	8	25
2	25	24
23	67	24
1719E	44	24
1538	22	23
12E	22	22
2286E	62	22
25E	25	21
1811	4	20
1	27	19
1534	91	18
4	29	17
1513	2	17
17	11	16
7	28	15
27	13	15
1507	78	15
1514	4	15
1536	26	15
1790	6	15
14E	30	15
16	13	14
1246E	4	14
15E	22	14
1525	4	12

Degrees	Out	In
1533	0	12
1812E	16	12
5	38	11
1526	28	11
1539	21	11
13E	29	11
1537	9	10
1794	8	10
2303E	72	10
24	24	9
1528	26	9
1791	2	9
1792	3	9
1796	19	9
1607	0	8
1642	0	8
1801	0	8
1810	10	8
1814	9	8
2383	2	8
2386	12	8
1591	0	7
1798	11	7
1809	8	7
1795E	27	7
2385E	0	7
1531	165	6
1638	6	6
1802	0	6
1684E	60	6
1710E	157	6
1337	0	5
1527	3	5

Degrees	Out	In
1793	2	5
1805E	48	5
1532	56	4
1586	0	4
2277E	20	4
1540	0	3
1799	13	3
2257	85	3
1555E	79	3
1023	8	2
1039	268	2
1530	3	2
1535	2	2
1593	54	2
1144	0	0
1521	4	0
1524	4	0
1529	0	0
1581	8	0
1582	28	0
1614	13	0
1778	40	0
1806	58	0
1931	16	0
2375	10	0
1835E	25	0
	Out	In
Mean	7.5	7.5
Std Dev	25.6	7.8
Min	0	0
Max	268	75

of 378 actors, only actual participants are shown) for in and out degrees, where the results are in descending order of in-degree. There is by far and away a larger standard deviation in the out than in-degrees (25.6 out-degree, 7.5 in-degree). In other words the difference in values by staff that approach others (out-degree) seems to be greater, than for staff that are approached (in-degree). Clearly the experts and expert non-experts do seem to occupy higher in-degree values than many of the "normal" personnel. In fact, if results are presented in descending order of out-degree (Appendix E; Table 1), then the experts and expert non-experts tend to overwhelmingly occupy the higher places in the table. An interesting observation concerns that of 1039 with an out-degree of 268, but an in-degree of only 2. This actor clearly has high centrality, but low prestige.

Conversely certain expert actors (8E, 21E, 1789E, 1732E), and expert non-expert actors (1543, 20, 9, 28, 2, 23, 1538) to name but the top few, have the highest orders of prestige. Actor 20, who acts as a bridge between different cliques, also seems to have a very high centrality rating (170).

Global Centrality

Perhaps more important is the issue of global **centrality**[d] when considering the impact experts and expert non-experts are likely to make on knowledge diffusion within the firm. Rather than simply examining which personnel have the highest in-degree as a means of determining how popular the individual is, looking at global centrality permits the greater picture to emerge. Global centrality, as its name suggests is an algorithm that tests for how related or close an actor is to all others in the network, not simply the in- or out-degree they have from one actor to another directly connected one.

Freeman's measure of global centrality is expressed in terms of the distances among the various points. It will be recalled that two points are connected by a path if there is a sequence of distinct lines connecting them, and the length of a path is measured by the number of lines which make it up. In graph theory, the length of the shortest path between two points is a measure of the distance between them. The shortest distance between two points on the surface of the earth lies along the geodesic, which connects them, and, by analogy, the shortest path between any particular pair of points in a graph is termed a "geodesic." A point is globally central if it lies at short distances from many other points. Such a point is "close" to many of the other points in the graph (Scott, 1991, p. 89).

Another way of phrasing this is that "**closeness** indexes which members of a group of people can reach all the others in the fewest number of steps, and Freeman has suggested that it serves as an indicator of independences, because if one is close to all the others in the communication network, one cannot as readily have his or her access to those others controlled by someone else" (Freeman, 1979 in Pfeffer, 1992 italics added). Less pessimistically "… actors occupying central locations with respect to *closeness* can be very productive in communicating information to other actors. If the actors in the set of actors are engaged in problem solving, and the focus is on communication links, efficient solutions occur when one actor has very short communication paths to the others" (Wasserman & Faust, 1994, pp. 183-184). The algorithm for calculating closeness is as follows:

For a given network with vertices v1 ... vn and maximum closeness centrality cmax, the network closeness centralization measure is Σ(cmax - c(vi)) divided by the maximum value possible, where c(vi) is the closeness centrality of vertex vi (Analytic Technologies - Ucinet manual).

Betweenness values on the other hand, are, as the term suggests, a means for determining which actors are important for sitting between nonadjacent actors and are thus able to act as a means of knowledge transfer. In other words "an actor is central if it lies between other actors on their geodesics, implying that to have a large betweenness centrality, that actor must be between many of the actors via their geodesics" (Wasserman & Faust, 1994, p. 189). The algorithm for calculating betweenness is as follows:

For a given network with vertices v1 ... vn and maximum betweenness centrality cmax, the network betweenness centralization measure is Σ(cmax - c(vi)) divided by the maximum value possible, where c(vi) is the betweenness centrality of vertex vi (Analytic Technologies - Ucinet manual).

Examining our measures relating to global centrality (Table 6), it is clear that the elite groups of experts and ENEs are distributed throughout the table. Although there does appear to be a weak positive correlation between closeness and betweenness percentages. Clearly experts 1710E, 1732E, 13E and 14E are the closest with regards to reachability to others.

Expert non-expert 20 (who appears from graphical information to be revealed shortly, to play a central role) does have a closeness percentage of 9.3. Her betweenness percentage of 4.7, is thus above the average of 1.6 but nowhere near the maximum of 21. This would tend to indicate that she is not important insofar as she is close to many people but does play a role in being between numbers of adjacent actors and is thus able to pass on knowledge. Who then are personnel 1337 and 1806 who have the highest closeness ratings? Respondent 1337 is a male 25 to 29 year old Greek-Australian technical analyst who happens to be a permanent member of staff and has five to nine years of IT experience. Whilst he claims to be ACS level 4, he has actually only been with the organisation between seven and 12 months. The fact that he is ACS level 4 is interesting insofar as he has not been identified as being either an expert nor have his tacit knowledge inventory results shown him to be an expert non-expert. Person 1806 is a female 35 to 39 year old Mauritian Australian Software Engineer, also with five to nine years of IT experience who has been with the organisation for one to two years. Unlike person 1337 she claims to be of ACS level 3. While her closeness percentage is the same as that for person 1337, her betweenness percentage is considerably lower (9.7 percent as opposed to 21 percent). This tends to indicate that person 1337 is not officially or unofficially recognised as being elite, yet he seems to socially interact with many others and forms an important conduit between others.

Table 6. Illustrating values relating to global centrality for personnel in Organisation X

	Close.	Bet.
1337	9.9	21.0
1806	9.9	9.7
1710E	9.8	6.2
1732E	9.8	10.1
2257	9.7	6.1
13E	9.7	3.7
1593	9.7	7.6
14E	9.7	4.6
1506	9.7	5.3
1026E	9.7	3.9
27	9.6	4.1
1538	9.6	8.6
1504	9.6	1.6
1246E	9.6	3.3
1684E	9.6	3.3
5	9.6	1.1
1796	9.5	1.7
1	9.5	0.5
7	9.5	0.5
1046	9.5	3.2
1039	9.5	2.5
1514	9.5	3.2
1810	9.5	4.5
1555E	9.5	3.0
1531	9.5	4.8
1507	9.5	1.6
1798	9.4	2.3
2386	9.4	0.9
1591	9.4	0.8
24	9.4	0.5
1526	9.4	2.3
1534	9.4	2.9
1581	9.4	0.9
12E	9.4	5.5
1805E	9.4	1.1
1031	9.4	1.1
1513	9.4	0.2
1638	9.4	0.9
1029E	9.4	0.7
28	9.3	1.1
20	9.3	4.7

	Close.	Bet.
1607	9.3	1.6
1642	9.3	0.2
1778	9.3	0.2
1811	9.3	0.4
1719E	9.3	0.8
1791	9.3	0.1
1801	9.3	0.1
1794	9.3	1.4
1614	9.3	0.0
1501	9.3	0.1
1795E	9.3	0.2
1512	9.3	0.1
1539	9.3	1.2
1931	9.3	0.6
1508	9.2	0.0
1543	9.2	2.8
25E	9.2	0.2
2286E	9.2	0.0
15E	9.2	0.1
1789E	9.2	0.2
21E	9.2	0.1
1586	9.2	0.9
2383	9.2	0.3
1793	9.1	0.0
1802	9.1	0.0
1792	9.1	0.0
1582	9.1	1.2
1530	9.1	0.5
1790	9.1	0.0
2375	9.1	0.0
1532	9.1	0.6
1812E	9.0	0.1
1809	9.0	0.4
1025E	9.0	0.0
1540	9.0	0.3
1799	9.0	1.8
2	9.0	0.1
17	9.0	0.1
23	9.0	0.1
1814	9.0	1.5
4	9.0	0.1

	Close.	Bet.
16	9.0	0.1
1537	9.0	0.0
8E	9.0	0.0
1023	8.9	0.1
1536	8.9	0.1
1525	8.9	0.0
1524	8.9	0.0
1521	8.8	0.1
1535	8.8	0.5
1529	8.8	0.0
2303E	8.8	0.0
1528	8.7	0.0
9	8.7	0.0
1527	8.6	0.0
1835E	8.5	0.0
2277E	8.3	0.0
2385E	0.9	0.0
31E	0.9	0.0
32E	0.9	0.0
33E	0.9	0.0
34E	0.9	0.0
35E	0.9	0.0
36E	0.9	0.0
37E	0.9	0.0

	Close.	Bet.
Mean	8.6	1.6
Std Dev	2.2	2.9
Min	0.9	0.0
Max	9.9	21.0
Cent= 2.62%	Cent. Index = 19.56%	

With regard to the overall network centralisation figure at 2.62 percent (Table 6) one can see there is an overall low level of centrality, that is to say there is little in the way of a central clique of actors when all of the actors are taken into consideration. In other words there are few actors who are clearly identifiable as being central when all of the actors are taken into consideration. There is another measure of centrality, but this one relates to information flow likelihood.

Information Centrality

Information centrality values can also be important as they provide us with some means of determining the likelihood of "information" transferal between two actors (Greve & Benassi, 2003; Marsden, 2002; Stephenson & Zelen, 1989). The information algorithm first developed by Stephenson and Zelen (1989) who were of the opinion that "information is inversely proportion[ate] to the distance of a path and the information in a combined path is equal to the sum of the information of the individual paths … [and that] … the higher the weight the more important the communication between the incident points on the line" (pp. 8, 14). Greve and Benassi (2003) rephrase this concept of information centrality through stating that paths between actors represent flows of communication or rather information specifically. When information passes through several actors in a network, the information centrality algorithm takes into account likely information loss, such that longer paths carry less information than shorter ones. The end point of this algorithm is to "assess the knowledge that can accumulate to any actor due to their position in the network, given all nodes have equal knowledge. Information centrality thereby provides a measure of the distribution of social capital within the network" (Greve & Benassi, 2003, p. 22). Phrased another way, "one considers the combined path from one actor to another, by taking all paths, including the geodesics, and assigning them weights. A weighted function of this combined path is then calculated, using as weights the inverses of the lengths of the paths being combined. The weights assigned to the paths making up the combined path are determined so that the "information" in the combined path is maximized" (Wasserman & Faust, 1994, p. 193).

Examining Table 7, observe that the experts and ENEs seem to be scattered throughout the table. Numbers are low because an average statistical value has been obtained amongst the 378 actors who were identified in the questionnaire. Only those actors who actually *participated* in the questionnaire have been included here. What is also readily apparent is that there are experts with the lowest information centrality scores (at the end of the table). These experts who are also greater than 1 point below the mean value for the power value, represent personnel who provided tacit knowledge results (hence their being identified as experts), but did not answer the social network analysis component of the questionnaire (remembering the SNA component of the questionnaire was not compulsory). Note also that information centrality results for the sample population demonstrate that experts (green) and ENEs (blue) are evenly distributed amongst the staff that participated in the questionnaire. There is no strong positive correlation with assemblage of either of these two "elite" groups at the upper end of the table, which in turn would ordinarily indicate higher information flow likelihood. There is however a weak positive correlation of these groups having slightly higher than mean values for information centrality. Observe that some expert non-experts (namely 20, 1534, 1507, and 23 in particular) are perceived by the information centrality algorithm to be better transferors of information flows than many of the experts. This is perhaps not so surprising given that an expert may perceive their time to be more valuable and so are less likely to be effective transferors of their intellectual property in practice. Interestingly certain personnel of neither of the two elite groups (namely 1039, 1531, 1337, 2257, 1046, 1532 9, 1593, and 1806) appear to have higher information centrality values.

Table 7. Illustrating "information" centrality values for personnel who participated in Organisation X

Info. values		Info. values		Info. values	
1039	2.28	1795E	2.15	1802	1.98
1710E	2.27	27	2.15	1023	1.96
20	2.27	1789E	2.15	1614	1.96
1531	2.26	7	2.15	1642	1.94
1534	2.26	13E	2.14	2277E	1.93
1543	2.26	28	2.14	1607	1.90
1507	2.25	1514	2.14	2385E	1.82
23	2.25	24	2.14	2375	1.79
2286E	2.25	1	2.14	1591	1.77
1732E	2.24	1024	2.14	1527	1.76
1337	2.24	1812E	2.14	1581	1.76
2257	2.24	1811	2.13	1586	1.68
2303E	2.24	1537	2.13	1530	1.64
1719E	2.23	1835E	2.12	1540	1.64
1046	2.22	1513	2.11	1535	1.57
1555E	2.22	1799	2.11	1524	1.29
1532	2.21	1525	2.11	1144	0.10
2	2.21	1536	2.11	1521	0.10
9	2.21	1538	2.10	1529	0.10
1593	2.20	1810	2.09	31E	0.10
1805E	2.20	1684E	2.08	32E	0.10
1806	2.19	1526	2.06	33E	0.10
12E	2.19	2386	2.06	34E	0.10
17	2.18	1809	2.05	35E	0.10
4	2.18	1931	2.05	36E	0.10
8E	2.18	1582	2.04	37E	0.10
15E	2.17	2383	2.04		
5	2.17	1533	2.04	Mean	1.7
14E	2.17	1814	2.04	Std Dev	0.4
25E	2.16	1539	2.04	Minimum	0.1
16	2.16	1638	2.03	Maximum	2.3
1528	2.16	1778	2.03		
21E	2.16	1801	2.00		

Density Values

Whereas reach-ability refers to any particular geodesic path existing, density relates specifically to the type of network relationships individuals have with one another. Density allows one to determine whether individuals have a number of different associates and perhaps for that reason only loose contact with them. Alternatively, some individuals may have fewer contacts but they maintain very close ties with them. For each of the following tables the parameters represented are the following:

1. **Size**: Size of ego network
2. **Ties**: Number of directed ties
3. **Pairs**: Number of ordered pairs
4. **Density**: Ties divided by Pairs
5. **AvgDis**: Average geodesic distance
6. **Diameter**: Longest distance in egonet
7. **EgoBetween**: Betweenness within the egonet
8. **UnReach**: # of ordered pairs with infinite distance

Examining Table 8, note that ENEs 1023, 1527, "normal" people 1535, 1539, and 1607 also display network densities of 100 as well as expert 2385E. An examination of the table does reveal that generally speaking the personnel with less dense networks do seem to have greater sized networks. There also appears to be a weak positive correlation between slightly greater numbers of experts concentrated at the bottom of the table, that is to say greater numbers of experts have more ties with others, but the densities of their networks tend to be consequently smaller. For example expert 1710E has a network size of 67 other people, which is reflected in his network density being only 3.8 instead of 100, where 100 refers to perfect one on one contact with each member of the network.

Table 8. Showing densities in Organisation X (remainder were 0's or did not participate in the research)

	1	2	3	4	5	6	7	8
	Size	Ties	Pairs	Density	AvgDis	Dia.	EgoBet	UnReac
1023	3	6	6	100	1	1	0	0
1527	2	2	2	100	1	1	0	0
1535	2	2	2	100	1	1	0	0
1539	5	20	20	100	1	1	0	0
1607	2	2	2	100	1	1	0	0

246 Busch

Table 8. continued

	1	2	3	4	5	6	7	8
	Size	Ties	Pairs	Density	AvgDis	Dia.	EgoBet	UnReac
2385E	2	2	2	100	1	1	0	0
7	13	146	156	93.6	1.1	2	5	0
16	7	38	42	90.5	1.1	2	2	0
1	14	160	182	87.9	1.1	2	11	0
24	14	160	182	87.9	1.1	2	11	0
13E	14	160	182	87.9	1.1	2	11	0
28	13	132	156	84.6	1.2	2	12	0
17	9	60	72	83.3	1.2	2	6	0
2386	4	10	12	83.3	1.2	2	1	0
21E	15	170	210	81	1.2	2	20	0
1513	6	24	30	80	1.2	2	3	0
1525	5	16	20	80	1.2	2	2	0
27	15	158	210	75.2	1.3	3	26	0
1537	6	22	30	73.3	1.3	2	4	0
25E	16	168	240	70	1.3	3	36	0
1642	3	4	6	66.7	1.3	2	1	0
1798	4	8	12	66.7	1.3	2	2	0
1801	3	4	6	66.7	1.3	2	1	0
1802	3	4	6	66.7	1.3	2	1	0
15E	16	160	240	66.7	1.4	4	40	0
4	9	46	72	63.9	1.4	2	13	0
12E	11	68	110	61.8			21	0
2	13	94	156	60.3	1.4	2	31	0
1809	5	12	20	60	1.4	2	4	0
9	13	90	156	57.7	1.5	3	33	0
1538	8	32	56	57.1	1.5	3	12	0
14E	18	172	306	56.2	1.4	2	67	0
1536	8	30	56	53.6	1.5	3	13	0
1794	6	16	30	53.3	1.5	3	7	0
5	19	172	342	50.3			85	0
1526	8	28	56	50	1.6	3	14	0
1638	5	10	20	50	1.6	3	5	0
1791	4	6	12	50	1.5	2	3	0
2383	4	6	12	50	1.5	2	3	0
8E	17	128	272	47.1			72	0
1796	8	26	56	46.4	1.6	3	15	0
1811	7	18	42	42.9	1.7	3	12	0
1799	6	12	30	40	1.7	3	9	0
1810	6	12	30	40	1.7	3	9	0

Table 8. continued

	1 Size	2 Ties	3 Pairs	4 Density	5 AvgDis	6 Dia.	7 EgoBet	8 UnReac
1528	10	32	90	35.6	1.7	3	29	0
1789E	9	24	72	33.3	1.8	3	24	0
1812E	8	18	56	32.1			19	0
1792	5	6	20	30			7	0
1046	15	62	210	29.5	1.9	4	74	0
1795E	10	22	90	24.4			34	0
1514	7	10	42	23.8			16	0
1732E	23	114	506	22.5			196	0
1790	10	20	90	22.2			35	0
1805E	16	52	240	21.7			94	0
23	26	138	650	21.2			256	0
1532	15	42	210	20			84	0
1931	6	6	30	20			12	0
2286E	25	114	600	19			243	0
1543	35	146	1190	12.3			522	0
1507	31	102	930	11			414	0
1814	5	2	20	10			9	0
1719E	23	50	506	9.9			228	0
1835E	7	4	42	9.5			19	0
1806	19	32	342	9.4			155	0
1534	38	116	1406	8.3			645	0
20	53	184	2756	6.7			1286	0
2303E	29	54	812	6.7			379	0
2257	29	38	812	4.7			387	0
1593	23	22	506	4.4			242	0
1710E	67	166	4422	3.8			2128	0
1778	8	2	56	3.6			27	0
1531	68	156	4556	3.4			2200	0
1337	58	88	3306	2.7			1609	0
1039	85	178	7140	2.5			3481	0
1555E	34	6	1122	0.5			558	0

Physical Organisational Location of Experts

Another important factor that may influence likelihood of knowledge transfer relates to the layout of the organisation structure. Where are experts and expert non-experts located?

Table 9. Showing physical locations of experts

1022E	Business Intelligence Systems	Level 27, 580 Flossy Street
1024E	Business Intelligence Systems	Level 27, 580 Flossy Street
1025E	Business Intelligence Systems	Level 27, 580 Flossy Street
1026E	Business Intelligence Systems	Level 27, 580 Flossy Street
1027E	Business Intelligence Systems	Level 27, 580 Flossy Street
1029E	Business Intelligence Systems	Level 27, 580 Flossy Street
1246E		Level 27, 580 Flossy Street
1555E		Level 27, 580 Flossy Street
1710E		Level 16, 580 Flossy Street
1719E		Level 29, 580 Flossy Street
1732E	SAP Systems	Level 29, 580 Flossy Street
1789E	Software Engineering Victoria	2/500 Fairy Highway Aristo Park, Victoria, 3174
1795E	Software Engineering Victoria	2/500 Fairy Highway Aristo Park, Victoria, 3174
1805E	Software Engineering Victoria	2/500 Fairy Highway Aristo Park, Victoria, 3174
1812E	Software Engineering Victoria	2/500 Fairy Highway Aristo Park, Victoria, 3174
1835E	Sol Development IBM/GSA Contractors	Victorian Admin Centre
2277E	South Australia Business Solutions	Level 7, Story Square Adelaide SA
2286E	Strategy Planning & Architecture	Level 14, 580 Flossy Street
2303E	Strategy Planning & Architecture	Level 14, 580 Flossy Street
2385E	Software Engineering Victoria	2/500 Fairy Highway, Aristo Park, Victoria, 3174

Table 9 illustrates that the experts are physically located in the Flossy St. building, and indeed even on the same floor. Values missing in the table represent data that was simply unknown. Similarly the expert non-experts (Table 10) are also located within similar buildings, although they seem to be a little more dispersed than the experts.

Expertise and Placement within the Organisational Structure

Examination of Figures C.0 (a, b, c, d, e, f, g, h, and i in appendix c) reveals a weak positive correlation with senior placement in the organisational sections (from organisational structure charts that were actually available). Again experts are represented in green, ENEs in blue. XXXX indicators represent personnel who did not participate in the research and hence for whom no biographical, social network or tacit knowledge inventory data exists.

Table 10. Showing physical locations of expert non-experts

1021ENE	Business Intelligence Systems	Level 27, 580 Flossy Street
1023ENE	Business Intelligence Systems	Level 27, 580 Flossy Street
1031ENE	Business Intelligence Systems	Level 27, 580 Flossy Street
1500ENE	IS SAP Basis	Level 29, 580 Flossy Street
1501ENE	IS SAP Basis	Level 29, 580 Flossy Street
1502ENE	IS SAP Basis	Level 29, 580 Flossy Street
1504ENE	IS SAP Development	Level 29, 580 Flossy Street
1506ENE	IS SAP Development	Level 29, 580 Flossy Street
1507ENE	IS SAP Development	Level 14, 580 Flossy Street
1508ENE	IS SAP Development	Level 29, 580 Flossy Street
1512ENE	IS SAP Development	Level 29, 580 Flossy Street
1521ENE	Member Services IT&T	Level 30, 580 Flossy Street
1524ENE	Member Services IT&T	Level 29, 580 Flossy Street
1527ENE	Member Services IT&T	Villawood
1534ENE	Member Services IT&T	Level 16, 580 Flossy Street
1536ENE	Member Services IT&T	Villawood
1538ENE	Member Services IT&T	Villawood
1543ENE	Member Services IT&T	Level 16, 580 Flossy Street
1598ENE	National Test Centre	Level 30, 580 Flossy Street
1610ENE	National Test Centre	Level 30, 580 Flossy Street
1778ENE	Software Development Esprit IT	Level 28, 580 Flossy Street
1792ENE	Software Engineering Victoria	2/500 Fairy Highway, Aristo Park, Victoria, 31##
1796ENE	Software Engineering Victoria	2/500 Fairy Highway, Aristo Park, Victoria, 31##
2295ENE	Strategy Planning & Architecture	Level 14, 580 Flossy Street

Noticeable also from an examination of the figures, is that expert non-experts (again shown in blue) are not necessarily always subordinate to experts (e.g., Figure C.0d).

Difficult to Locate Individuals

Finally it was observed via the questionnaire (appendix f) that a select number of individuals were "**difficult to locate.**" They were experts 1024E and 2303E, and expert non-experts 1023ENE, 1031ENE, and 1527ENE. Novices 1046, 1793, 1811, and 2257 were also noted by their peers as being difficult to contact. This is of slight tacit knowledge transference concern as it means that a majority of the individuals described as difficult to locate are "elites." One may surmise that difficulty in locating novices is less consequential from a soft knowledge diffusion point of view.

Graphical Interpretation of Data

Having discussed some of the numerical parameters associated with social networking in Organisation X, what is able to be discerned visually? The reader should note that the graphical data is presented from three different perspectives to provide us with a more complete picture of the interactions. The figures have simply been printed in black and white from colour, rather than first converted to black and white and then printed in black and white. The latter approach resulted in poorer quality illustrations. The first graphs with a (originally) red theme explore the frequency of contact between individuals. The second series of graphs adopts a (originally) blue theme with an emphasis on the perceived importance of individuals. The third set of graphs adopting a (originally) green theme explores the types of meetings personnel have with one another, for example "bumping into people" around the workplace, or perhaps meeting colleagues in a formal meeting environment. An extension to the green theme is also to focus on meeting occasions that involve only face-to-face contact, as these meeting types are most likely to transfer tacit knowledge. Finally, the author acknowledges the graphs can appear quite full of activity or "busy". The reader will note that the nodes representing individuals or actors are in the same position from diagram to diagram. It was intended the reader would visualise actors dropping in and out of relationships. Two actors may appear in the same places in a diagram; however the edges or lines connecting them in diagrams will appear and disappear. It was possible to delete actors not actually participating in a relationship; however each diagram would then appear totally different, with no continuity.

Contact Frequency and Organisation X Personnel

The degree of tacit knowledge transfer depends on the closeness of the two partners. Frequent interactions afford the two parties the ability to understand each other's needs and satisfy the needs accordingly. For example, the transfer of tacit knowledge is not likely to be complete first time ... (Cavusgil, Calantone, & Zhao 2003, p. 15).

Given the number of nodes illustrated in Organisation X figures, a simplistic means of identifying expert non-experts has been to append ENE to their identification numbers. Males are represented as squares, females as circles.[e] Staff who have decided not to provide their gender or for whom other biographical information has not been included are shown as grey upright triangles. Permanent staff members are illustrated in black, contract staff in red. A key is provided (Figure 1) which illustrates the colour significance for links between the nodes for contact frequency related information.

Figure 1. Illustrating legend for contact frequency links between nodes

1= Quarterly (light yellow)
2= Bi-Monthly (Bright Yellow)
3= Monthly (Salmon Pink)
4= Fortnightly (Mid Orange)
5= Weekly (Dark Orange)
6= Daily (Bright Red)
7= Hourly (Dark Red)

One of the major points of interest to CIOs or the organisations under study was to what extent contract staff contributed to the knowledge flows of their organisation. If contractors were to leave the firm, what sort of impact would this have on their soft knowledge flows within the firm? Beginning with the first figure (2) for Organisation X, we are able

Figure 2. Here we have all the people who have participated in the research, for whom biographical information was provided.

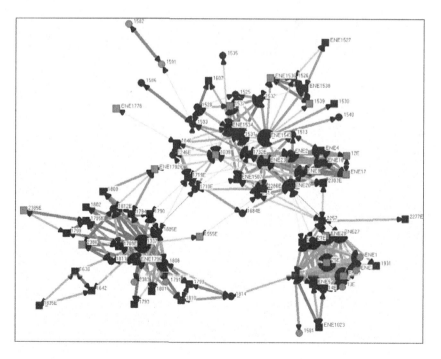

Figure 3. Illustrating our communication picture with the removal of contractors

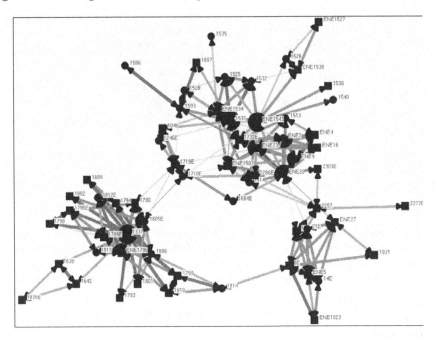

Figure 4. Illustrating people who contact each other quarterly

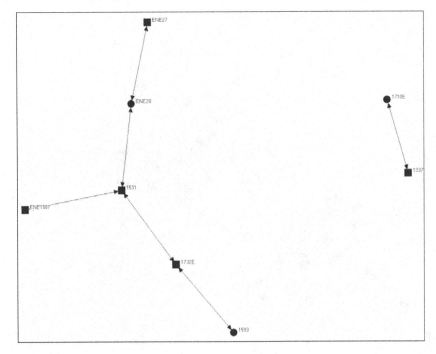

to see there are 3 macro-cliques. Some points are already obvious; actor ENE1543 in the top clique seems to be highly central, as is actor 25E in the bottom right hand clique. Actor 2257 in the latter clique appears to form a communication bridge to the major clique, as do actors 1555E, 1814, ENE1792, and ENE20. Observe the bottom right hand clique is very dense and closely spaced, indicating a high degree of interrelationship amongst the actors. Some idea is gained of the impact the removal that contractors would have on the firm in the following figure (3).

Note that two of our bridges have already disappeared (ENE1792, 1555E), both of whom may be regarded as experts, either officially (E) or unofficially (ENE). Furthermore we lose other seemingly important individuals, such as actor 1039 (top clique) and actor 25E (bottom right hand clique). With this in mind, some of the relationships between Organisation X actors are explored in closer detail. With regard to quarterly (Figure 4) and bi-monthly meetings (Figure 5) between staff, it is obvious that only a small proportion of them actually engage in either of these types of meetings. Actor 1531, who is neither an expert nor ENE, does appear to act as a bridge between other expert/ENE actors. This actor is an Indonesian speaking 45 to 49 year old male business analyst who has between zero and four subordinates and has been with the organisation for only one to two years. Examining bi-monthly meetings (Figure 5); actor 1531 seems to be prominent again, but not as much as ENE actor 20, who is a female software engineer aged 35-39. In fact, actor 20 plays a prominent role in a number of other relationships. Indeed she also participated in quarterly communications with actor 1531.

Almost all bi-monthly contact seems to take place between either experts or ENE permanent staff, the one exception being the communication that our female software engineer has with an expert 35-39 year old male contract system administrator (ENE28, bottom right hand corner). Like the quarterly communication patterns, the bi-monthly communication seems to be disjoint and of little relevance in the scheme of things. These could simply be social contacts rather than work related ones. If they are work related, they may be in relation to an occasional project meeting.

As expected, when asked whether monthly communication is taking place (Figure 6), many more respondents answered in the affirmative. Again our female software engineer (ENE20) takes part, as does Indonesian 1531. Flows still seem to be disjoint, although some actors such as 1719E, a permanent 35 to 39 year old male project manager seems to be central to

Figure 5. Illustrating bi-monthly contact between certain staff members

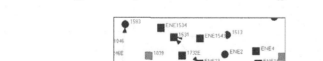

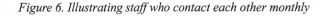

Figure 6. Illustrating staff who contact each other monthly

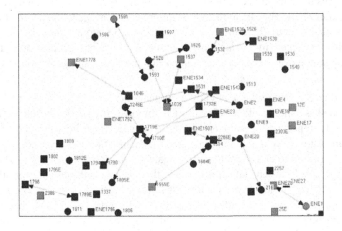

some information flows. Note that much of the monthly communication takes place between the largest clique, and rather less in the other two. Actor ENE20 does however provide a means for two of the cliques to interact, as does actor 1719E.

The picture changes slightly with regard to fortnightly communication patterns (Figure 7). To begin with far more contractors (red colour) are involved in the communication pattern,

Figure 7. Illustrating staff who meet each other fortnightly

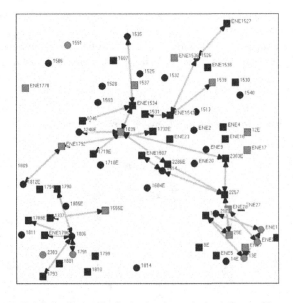

than had been the case up until now. This would seem to indicate that infrequent conversations explored in figures already covered, might be those of longer term "friendships" that persist over time, rather than short term "business conversations" on work related matters. Actor ENE20 does not participate, 1531 does, but only in a minor capacity with ENE1543. The latter is a male 40 to 44 year old project manager who seems to have some centrality. This is not surprising given his job title. Similarly, ENE1534 is also a male 40 to 44 years old, but a business systems analyst.

Actors with either highest centrality or prestige would appear to be contractor 1039 (45 – 49 year old project director, middle of figure), 1806 (bottom left centre, female 35 to 39 year old Mauritian Creole software engineer), actor 2257 (centre right, 55 to 59 year old project director). Indeed the smaller bottom right clique is only communicating through the main clique by way of this last actor. Naturally more staff communicate with one another on a weekly basis (Figure 8).

What is interesting is that none of the cliques actually communicate with each other. Activity intensifies *within* each clique, but not *between* them. Some understanding is gained when it is realised that the cliques are to some extent physically separate. The bottom left hand clique is actually located in Victoria, whilst the two right hand cliques more or less occupy separate floors of the same building in Sydney. Communication appears to be particularly dense with the group located on level 27 of the downtown Sydney office at Flossy St. As a point of interest, ENE1 actually resides on level 30; this individual is a female contractor who declined to provide age related information.

Figure 8. Illustrating staff who meet each other weekly

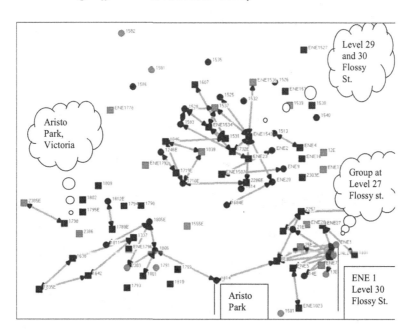

256   Busch

Figure 9. Illustrating people who meet each other daily

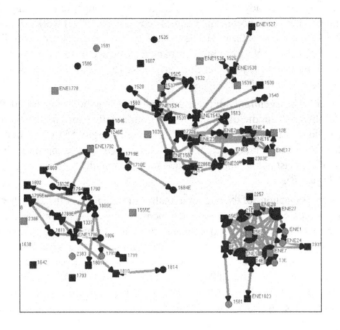

Figure 10. Illustrating people who meet each other hourly

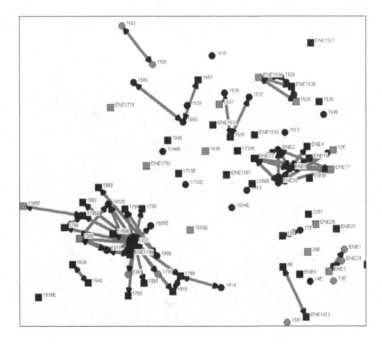

When considering interaction between participants on a daily basis (Figure 9), one can see communication patterns become far denser. The entire group on level 27 Flossy Street are in communication with each other daily, with the exception of 2257 (a 55 to 59 year old male project manager) and 2277E (a male 45 to 49 year old contract application programmer, formerly systems programmer). One would be inclined to think that the former is not taking part in daily communication because of his seniority, and that the latter is isolated from a daily communication point of view because of his specialisation as an application or systems programmer. The Victorian clique (bottom left) and the largest Sydney clique (top), tend to have quite a few isolates. At the same time the core of these cliques is far less dense.

In Figure 10 it is apparent there is no contact between the groups, and very little hourly contact between what was formerly a very dense clique on level 27, Flossy St. (bottom right hand corner). In fact this hourly communication takes place between only two sets of expert types, namely 8E and 1023ENE, and ENE7 and ENE1. Now see that the density of the Victorian clique (bottom left) is greater than that of the other groups. Clearly actor 1337 seems to have greatest centrality and prestige, remembering again the data has been symmetrised. Actor 1337 is neither an expert nor ENE. This actor is a male 25 to 29 year old Greek-Australian Technical Analyst.

Ethnicity and Social Networks

There were some people in Organisation X who were meeting one another and had an ethnic language in common. One could reasonably conclude they met partially because of their ethnicity. Whilst it will be observed that there is some ethnic "collaboration", in fact

Figure 11. Illustrating a meeting clique of Cantonese speakers

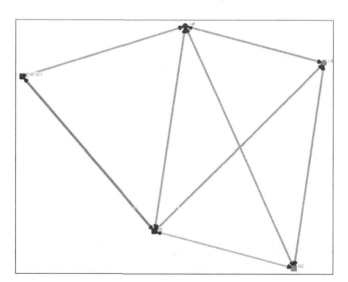

Figure 12. Illustrating specific area where Cantonese clique is based

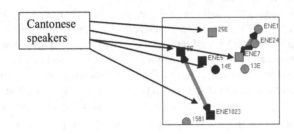

this is not significant for two reasons. Either the organisations (X, Z) tend to be so diverse ethnically, that little collaboration is possible on an ethnic basis because the ethnicities tend to be disparate. Or the organisation is largely mono-cultural (Y) in which case cliquing behaviour on the basis of ethnicity is not taking place, simply because it cannot. One instance where some cliquing on the basis of ethnicity is taking place is that of Cantonese speakers (Figure 11).

In terms of where these Cantonese-speaking individuals belong in the organisation (Figure 12), it is evident that they belong to the group housed on level 27 of Flossy St. (Figure 12 represents a section of Figure 8), not only are these people on the same floor, but the small figure provides an example of their physical proximity in terms of multidimensional scaling. Remember that the social network analysis software also factors in a person's distance from someone else in terms of how they chose the relationships they hold with other individuals. In other words, the closeness of dots actually has some indication of the relationship distance the person holds with the other person in real life.

Figure 13a. A couple of Greek speakers meet hourly   *Figure 13b. A couple of Japanese speakers meet daily*

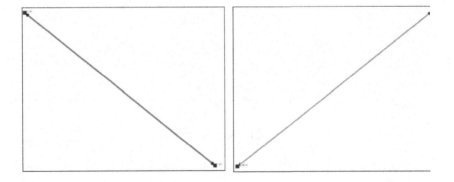

Figure 14. Illustrating our Serbian speakers in Organisation X

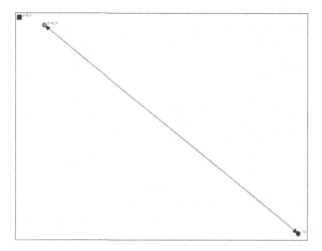

There was a trivial amount of association, rather than cliquing (remembering that a clique is at least three persons), taking place based on other ethnicities. For example, two Greek speakers (Figure 13a) met on an hourly basis (both located in Victoria), whilst two Japanese speakers (Figure 13b) met on a daily basis (both located in Sydney).

Also a couple of Serbian speakers were noted to meet up fortnightly (Figure 14). Note the third Serbian speaker (upper left hand corner) who whilst sharing the same language (and one concludes ethnicity), does not in fact communicate with the other two Serbian speakers.

No other relations between ethnic groups were distinctly identified. Again this is due to the highly multicultural nature of the organisation, meaning that cliquing on the basis of ethnicity was actually limited.

Networking According to "Front Office" or "Back Office" Roles

It had been suggested,[f] that there would likely be a difference in soft knowledge communication patterns based on "front" or "back" office IT roles. However no significant differences were observed by way of formal concept analysis when interpreting the questionnaire results. [g] Front office roles tend to be client facing and include such job titles as business systems analyst, data administrator, project manager or director. Back office roles are classically technical, such as applications programmer, technical analyst, network support and so on. One sees the roles identified by the respondents in table 11. As a point of note, the researcher has placed roles into these two categories. The respondents themselves did not decide upon the categories. Although no significant differences in terms of how back office or front office

Table 11. Showing roles identified by respondents in the questionnaire grouped by front office or back office occupations

Front Office	Back Office
Analyst	Account Manager
Analyst: Business	Analyst: Technical
Business Development Manager	Application Programmer
Business Systems Analyst	Computer Engineer
Clerical Support	Computer Systems Engineer
Data Architect	Contractor
Help Desk Support	Data Administrator
Information Management Consultant	Database Administrator: Junior
Information Modeller	Network Manager
IT Salesperson/Consultant	Programmer
Project Director	Software Engineer
Project Manager	System Administrator

Figure 15. Our front office occupations and how they network

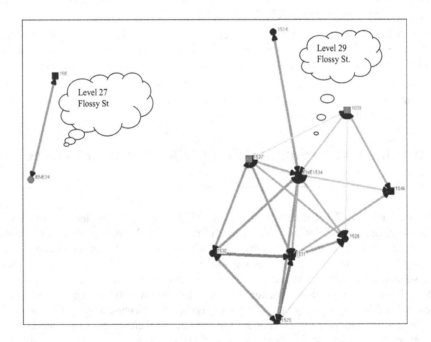

respondents answered the tacit knowledge inventory could be found, the question remains, do the two groups network differently?

Beginning with Figure 15, observe that front office roles tend to be fewer (than the following back office figure provides), and what is evident is that the front office roles amongst themselves, tend not to communicate so much on an hourly basis, rather either daily, weekly or fortnightly. Note that front office personnel tend to only be located in Sydney, and on separate floors of the same building.

Figure 16 illustrates the far denser networks that exist between back office personnel. As opposed to the front office staff, it is apparent that the back office is more widely physically distributed, but more cohesive within their groups. Observe how many hourly relationships (dark red) are also taking place, centred on certain people such as ENE 23 and ENE20 (top middle clique) and person 1337 (middle of the bottom clique located in Victoria), a male permanent staff member who is neither an expert nor expert non-expert. What is taking place is that the back office personnel obviously enjoy a closer working relationship than would appear to be the case with front office personnel. This in turn is a fairly safe indication that in actual fact it is more than likely the *back office* rather than the front office is making greater use of tacit knowledge, even if one assumes the underlying knowledge base is apt to be more technically oriented.

Figure 16. Clearly most of our Organisation X staff fit more within the back office mould

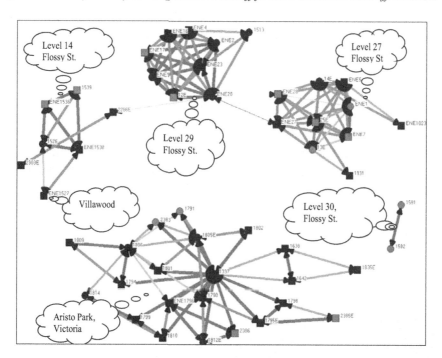

Hierarchy and Clique Behaviour

With regard to hierarchy in the organisation and communication patterns, Figure 17 illustrates how the most senior personnel interact at most on a daily rather than an hourly basis. Two distinct groups are visible, with a fortnightly communication link between them. What are presented are: personnel who supervise either 50+ staff (1046, interestingly considered neither an expert by peers/colleagues, nor an ENE by way of questionnaire results); people who supervise 40-44 people (1246E); those who supervise 25-29 subordinates (1719E); or those supervising 10-14 subordinates (1534 and 12E). It is worthwhile noting that 12E, even though of a senior level, appears to have no direct communication with other senior personnel. Figure 17 illustrates that the organisational IT structure for Organisation X is actually quite flat. Note that all of these staff are permanent and largely male (with the exception of 1246E, left hand side, is a 40 to 44 year old female, Cantonese and Mandarin speaking software engineer).

Including personnel who supervise only five to nine subordinates there are now up to 18 staff included in the figure (18). Clearly the added middle management layer tends to be quite small. Only ENE 20 interacts on an hourly basis with expert 12E, the remaining communication flows are daily, weekly fortnightly, monthly or bi-monthly. The remaining members of staff (90 in all) therefore supervise one to four people or simply none at all. One should expect this, given that the organisation is composed of professionals who would be expected to largely work independently.

Figure 17. Showing our highest ranking people, 1046 has 50+ subordinates, 1246E has 40-44 subordinates, 1719E has 25 to 29 subordinates, 1534 and 12E have 10-14 subordinates

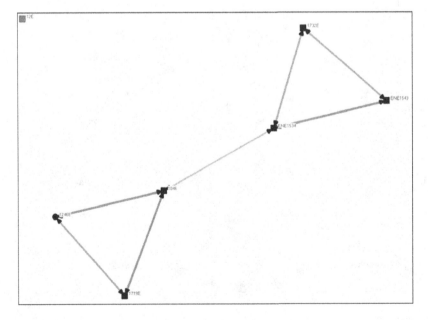

Figure 18. Now including people with five to nine subordinates

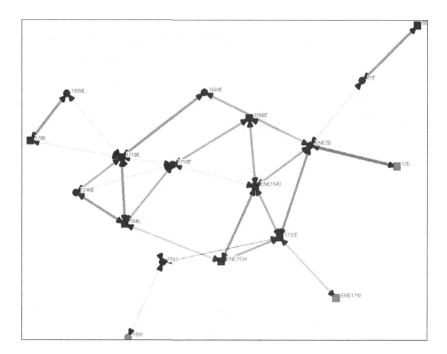

Person Importance and Organisation X

Just as important as examining the meeting types of our personnel, is that of understanding the level of **importance** they attach to one another. Remember at this stage these relationship patterns have not been symmetrised, unlike those for contact frequency (previous) and meeting type (following). With regard to person importance a better picture is gained of who the most important people are considered to be. Figure 19 illustrates the colour scheme used for person importance. Figure 20, on the other hand, illustrates least important individuals (light colour) in terms of their needing to be seen, through to most important (darkest colour).

Again, three macro level cliques are obvious in this organisation. Note also the red lines in the clique mainly on the right hand side of the figure. Exploring this clique in further detail (Figure 21), we see people who are avoided, insofar as the question asked "whom do you try not to see".

The negative attention seems to be wholly focused on this group who are located on level 27 of the Flossy St. building. One may interpret this in one of two ways. Either the staff members are generally feeling negative about one another, and there is a social misfit between the group members. Or alternatively the staff have a close working relationship and

Figure 19. Key for person importance

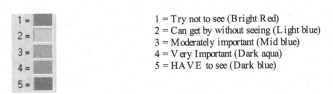

1 = Try not to see (Bright Red)
2 = Can get by without seeing (Light blue)
3 = Moderately important (Mid blue)
4 = Very Important (Dark aqua)
5 = HAVE to see (Dark blue)

Figure 20. Everyone and the importance of the individual

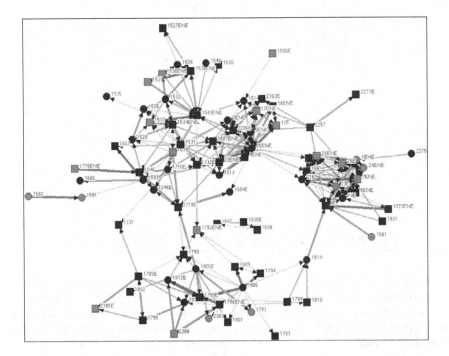

understand each other's time commitments, preferring to avoid disturbing one another as much as possible. It is nevertheless interesting to note that the staff/nodes in the figure are located so physically close to one another, indicating a high degree of interoperability.

With regard to staff they can get by without seeing (Figure 22), the picture immediately changes to a far more complete set of links between the nodes, that indicate from a practical point of view, one can get by without seeing quite a number of the staff. Remember that it

Figure 21. People who try to avoid one another

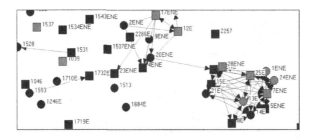

Figure 22. Can get by without seeing

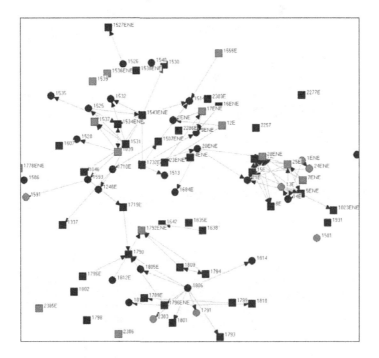

was possible for staff to choose more than one relationship type with colleagues, so whilst they can get by for certain things, this may not always prove to be the case. Evidence for this exists in the tightly knit clique on the right hand side, where these same staff members had previously mentioned they "tried not to see" the same individuals.

Figure 23. Moderately important to see the individual

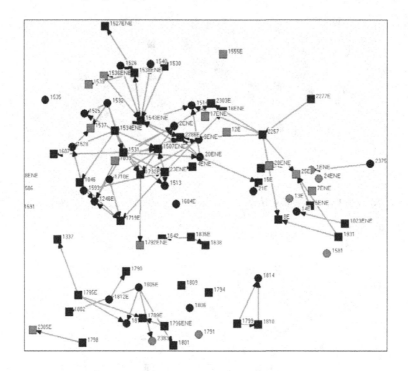

Figure 24. Very important to see these individuals

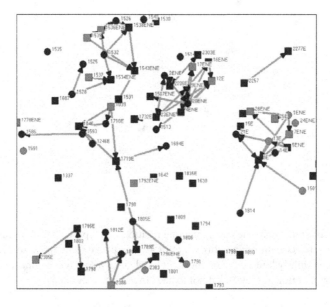

Asking the staff whom they considered moderately important tended to include almost all staff (Figure 23), with an equal balance of permanent and contract staff not considered to be moderately important. A somewhat similar pattern emerges for very important people (Figure 24).

With reference to people that simply have to be seen (Figure 25), the main contenders seem to be expert non-experts 1538ENE, 1543ENE, 17ENE, 4ENE, 9ENE, 20ENE, 1023ENE, 24ENE, 1ENE, and experts 21E, 8E, 1796E. One would expect these types of people to be the most important ones given their classification. What is a little surprising is that there are also some extremely important novice personnel, namely 1591, 2386, 1809, 1794, and 1513. Person 1591 is a 25 to 29 year old female contract business systems analyst, whereas 2386 is a 35 to 39 year old male application programmer. Person 1809 is a male 40 to 44 year old software engineer, whilst 1794 is a 35 to 39 year old male, Greek-speaking software engineer. Lastly, actor 1513 is a 50 to 54 year old female Cantonese, Malay and Hokkien speaking technical analyst. Whereas communication paths with regard to less important person rankings ("can get by without seeing," "moderately important," and "very important") tend to cross (to some degree) from one clique to the next, with respect to "having to see" the given individual, relationships tend to only occur within the given cliques.

Notice also the circled individuals. These were people identified as difficult to find (Figure 7 in Chapter VIII). It would appear there is a conflict only with regard to novices 1046 (middle left) and 1811 (bottom left), insofar as they have to be seen, but are difficult to find. One may surmise that this may represent a slight tacit knowledge bottleneck, nevertheless

Figure 25. These individuals have to be seen, circled actors were noted to be difficult to find

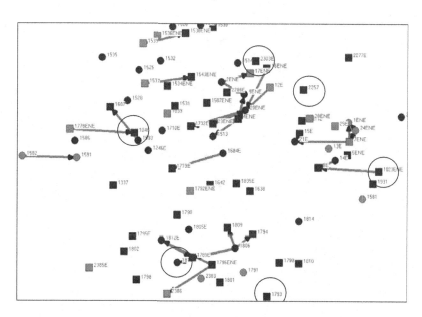

the experts and ENEs identified as difficult to find are not represented here. These actors are however identified in lesser important capacities in previous figures (22-24). Other individuals identified as difficult to find did not necessarily participate with regard to the social network analysis component of the questionnaire.

Meeting Types Using Electronic Mediums

There have been some (albeit limited) studies on the impact on ICT on knowledge management practices. Hendrick's (2001) study[h] like many tends to be descriptive without necessarily being empirical. Clearly what is needed is research that can provide further insight into the impact of ICT on the knowledge transferral process. With regard to Organisation X what is most of concern with regard to the transferral likelihood of tacit knowledge is the use of **electronic communication** (Figure 26 phone; and Figure 27 e-mail) as mentioned in Chapter 6. Remember that at the time of the survey (early 2002), questions were not asked of teleconferencing, Web-casting, or other internet/telephony based means of contacting one another on a "face-to-face" basis.

Remember there is strong evidence that people who contact one another by phone, e-mail or fax are simply unable to transfer tacit knowledge (Jacob & Ebrahimpur, 2001; Johannessen,

Figure 26. People who contact one another by phone

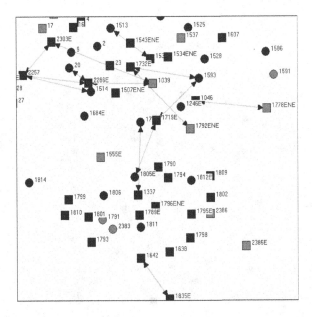

Olaisen, & Olsen, 2001; Lee, 1994; Smith, 2000). They may transfer codified information, but certainly not tacit knowledge. To what extent are these electronic mediums made use of in Organisation X? Fortunately it appears the use of these mediums appears to be limited. There does appear to be slightly higher use being made of e-mails in the clique located on level 27 of Flossy St. in Sydney. This is the Business Intelligence Systems group and does appear to be well populated with "experts." From a tacit knowledge transferral point of view this would not make for good tacit knowledge management practice.

The Software Engineering Victoria group does not appear to make much use of e-mails, and one may note that only person 1790 contacts expert 1719E in this manner. Again little use is made of e-mails by other levels of Flossy St. in Sydney. One final point worth mentioning is that it appears almost no contractors seem to be involved in the phone communication process (Figure 26). Phoning one another seems to be an activity undertaken by permanent staff. E-mail contact, on the other hand, does seem to involve more contract staff. One may interpret this to mean that the latter form of communication seems to be more relied upon for staff that come in at odd times and are less likely to be available by way of random phone call. Perhaps less likely is that the location of contractors is such that permanent (and other contract staff) don't know how to contact contractors other than by e-mail.

Figure 27. People who contact each other by e-mail

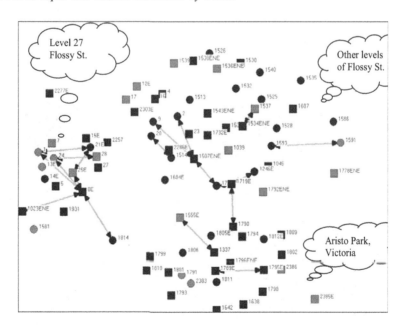

Meeting Type of Only Face-to-Face Contact

... tacit knowledge cannot be easily specified, close partners may have opportunities to de-tect the knowledge needed. Besides, partnering relationships include a monitoring[i] process. Monitoring is especially valuable where tacit knowledge is concerned, since such knowledge is not readily codified, and hence cannot be transmitted in the form of reports and balance statements ... (Cavusgil et al., 2003, p. 10).

Figure 28. Legend for only those people who have face-to-face meetings (i.e., are more likely to pass on tacit knowledge)

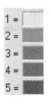

1 = Formal organisational meetings
2 = Informal but pre-arranged meetings
3 = See one another outside of work
4 = Meet each other at morning/afternoon tea or lunch
5 = Bump into each other in the workplace

Figure 29. Showing only those people who conduct face to face meetings with one an-other

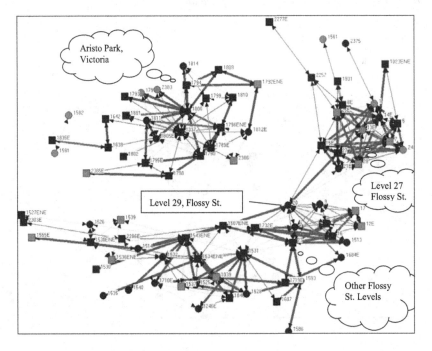

Fortunately examining only the staff interactions of those who meet in **face-to-face** scenarios, one observes many more of the Organisation X personnel did engage in forms of communication that were considered conducive to tacit knowledge diffusion. For Organisation X specifically, a purple theme had (originally) been adopted in relation to colour coding tacit-rich knowledge flows (Figure 28).

For example note from Figure 29 that different colour shades have been used relative to the increasing likelihood of tacit knowledge being transferred, again only showing relationships indicative of the likelihood of tacit knowledge transferral.

Three broad cliques are visible, which represent the different areas of the organisation. Note how individual ENE 20 again acts as a "go-between" level 29 and other floors of Organisation X. Examining Figure 30 observe the extent to which staff participate in formal organisational meetings; notice there are personnel who bump into each other around the workplace. With regard to formal meetings (which would provide a means for tacit knowledge transfer, but perhaps a less obvious one than "bumping into one another"), a light pink theme has been adopted (Figure 30).

Meetings seem to be focused around certain personalities, such as actor 1805E (top left), actor 25E (top right), and particularly actor 1543E (bottom centre). This last actor is not surprisingly a project manager who is a male permanent member of staff between 40 and 44 years of age. Indeed he appears to have been a project manager for at least the last six years and has more then 20 years of experience in the IT industry. It is interesting to note

Figure 30. Formal organisational meetings

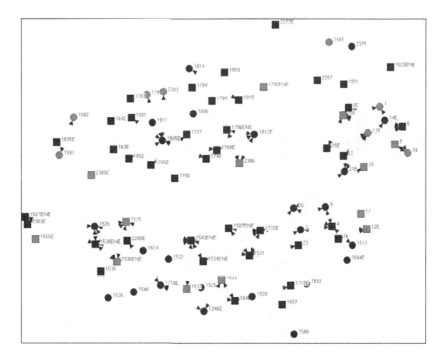

Figure 31. Informal organisational meetings

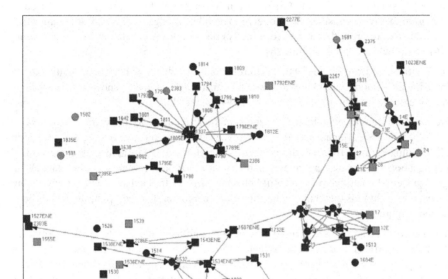

that not all staff participate in formal organisational meetings, in fact only two thirds appear to. Contrast this last point with informal organisational meetings (Figure 31), and the picture changes considerably; almost all staff participate in such meetings. Again meetings seem to be centred on certain actors such as 1337 (a male permanent 25 to 29 year old Greek speaking technical analyst). Again, individual 20 features prominently.

With regard to contact outside of work (Figure 32), only person 20 and expert 1684E seem to engage in a knowledge exchange. Both of these people are female and between 35 and 44 years of age. The former is a software engineer, the latter a project manager. They both appear to be of the same ethnic background, that is to say Anglo-Celtic Australian. One

Figure 32. Outside of work

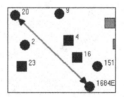

could reasonably conclude they share common interests outside the work environment and are simply friends. Clearly then extra-occupational knowledge flows seem to be limited in the case of organisation X.

Concerning staff that meet on other "social" occasions, such as lunch or morning/afternoon tea (Figure 33), again the communication pattern is limited. Clearly some of the Victorians do (top clique), and such contact takes place only between permanent staff members. For those on level 29 of Flossy St. this form of communication seems a little more popular amongst the contract staff. No one else on other floors or sections of the organisation in Sydney seems to communicate this way.

An examination of Figure 34 does reveal good opportunities for tacit knowledge interaction. Note how some of the cliques (level 29) appear particularly dense with regard to "bumping into one another," and that in the case of the level 29 clique, a number of the participants are

Figure 33. Lunch/morning/afternoon tea

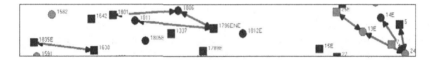

Figure 34. Bump into each other in the workplace

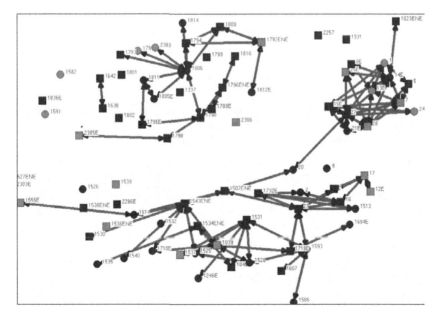

actually contractors. The other areas of the organisation do seem to have fewer contractors participating in this way.

Summary

What has been gleaned from Organisation X in terms of the likelihood of tacit knowledge flows? These are numerous and include the following; first, there is a potential that some of the tacit knowledge of contractors is not being transferred to the extent that it could be. Second, certain key members, such as ENE 20 seem to be pivotal in transferral of knowledge from one section of the organisation to another. Third, little other inter-macro-clique knowledge transfer appears to be taking place outside these selected individuals. Fourth, intra-clique communication patterns tend to be quite dense. Fifth, there exist many (54) "micro" level cliques (Table 3). Sixth, some micro cliques do not involve the presence of experts or ENEs and that for some "normal" people their access to these actors is indeed limited. Seventh, novices have access to at least one expert, or expert non-expert. Eighth, there exist "power" cliques made up almost exclusively of staff who are considered experts by their peers, or those who have gained IT tacit knowledge inventory scores which place them in a similar league to the experts (thus they become expert non-experts). Finally, that measures of degree; centrality, information centrality and betweenness indicate there is not necessarily a perfect or even strong positive correlation between expertness or expert non-expertness and higher scores on these parameters, which in turn indicates that tacit knowledge diffusion could be improved. It is time to examine an organisation where almost the opposite situation takes place; for Organisation Y is almost totally different.

References

Analytic Technologies (2002). *Microsoft Windows Help for UCINET SNA software,* Version 5.8.

Bush, R., & Baum, F. (2001). Health, inequities, community, and social capital. In R. Eckersley, J. Dixon, & B. Douglas (Eds.), *The social origins of health and well-being.* Cambridge: Cambridge University Press, 189-204.

Cavusgil, S.T., Calantone, R.J., & Zhao, Y. (2003). Tacit knowledge transfer and firm innovation capacity. *Journal of Business and Industrial Marketing, 18*(1), 6-21.

Greve, A., & Benassi, M. (2003). Exploring the contributions of human and social capital to productivity. Paper prepared for *Hawaii International Conference On System Sciences*, HICSS-37, January. Retrieved July 19, 2006 from: http://www.chass.utoronto.ca/~agreve/Greve-Benassi_soc&hum.pdf

Hendriks, P. (2001). Many rivers to cross: From ICT to knowledge management systems. *Journal of Information Technology, 16*(2), 57-72.

Horgan, D., & Simeon, R. (1990). Gender, mentoring, and tacit knowledge. *Journal of Social Behaviour and Personality, 5*(4, Special Issue), 453-471.

Jacob, M., & Ebrahimpur, G. (2001). Experience vs. expertise: The role of implicit understandings of knowledge in determining the nature of knowledge transfer in two companies. *Journal of Intellectual Capital, 2*(1), 74-78.

Johannessen, J., Olaisen, J., & Olsen, B. (2001). Mismanagement of tacit knowledge: The importance of tacit knowledge, the danger of information technology and what to do about it. *International Journal of Information Management, 21,* 3-20.

Jorgensen, B. (2004). Individual and organisational learning: A model for reform for public organisations. *Foresight, 6*(2), 91-103.

Lee, A. (1994). Electronic mail as a medium for rich communication: an empirical investigation using hermeneutic interpretation. *MIS Quarterly,* 143-157.

Marsden, P. (2002). *Social Network Analysis: Seminar.* Department of Sociology, Harvard University. Retrieved August 18, 2003 from: http://www.courses.fas.harvard.edu/~soc275//; http://icg.harvard.edu/~soc275/assignments/Workshop_2_2002.PDF

Ng, J.M., & Li, K.X. (2003). Implications of ICT for knowledge management in globalization. *Information Management & Computer Security, 11*(4), 167-174.

Pfeffer, J. (1992). *Managing with power: Politics and influence in organizations.* Boston: Harvard Business School Press

Scott, J. (1991). *Social network analysis: A handbook.* London: Sage Publications.

Smith, E. (2000). Applying knowledge – Enabling methods in the classroom and in the workplace. *Journal of Workplace Learning: Employee Counselling Today, 12*(6), 236-244.

Somech, A., & Bogler, R. (1999). Tacit knowledge in academia: Its effect on student learning and achievement. *The Journal of Psychology, 133*(6), 605-616.

Stephenson, K., & Zelen, M. (1989). Rethinking centrality: Methods and applications. *Social Networks, 11*(1), 1-37.

Wasserman, S., & Faust, K. (1994). *Social network analysis: Methods and applications.* Cambridge, UK: Cambridge University Press.

Endnotes

[a] These were sub-groups within a network (Chapter 6). For most practical SNA purposes a clique is defined as at least three people.

[b] One that has little tacit knowledge likely to be transferred because of the absence of a high, say >50 percent proportion of experts or novices.

[c] Degree related to how many interactions were taking place between one actor and another.

[d] Personal communication with Prof. Mike McGrath, Victoria University, Melbourne, July 2003.

e   There is some indication gender is considered to make a difference to tacit knowledge utilisation (Horgan & Simeon 1990; Somech & Bogler 1999), although no significant evidence has been found for this parameter here. Admittedly the 1999 and 1990 studies did not focus on the IT industry where males are traditionally more strongly represented.

f   Communication with Mr. Alan Hansell (Program Director, IT Executive Program, Gartner Group consulting).

g   FCA analysis was undertaken also with a view toward establishing whether there were differences between how front and back office personnel answered the questionnaire. No significant differences could be found, other than the fact that most senior people tended to be within the front office category. However, there was not necessarily a strong positive correlation between Experts and ENEs being senior personnel.

h   As the Hendriks (2001) model lacks empirical data and the discussion of the five dimensions shows that linking ICT to knowledge management is a difficult task, study should be carried out to obtain further findings by means of empirical data (Ng & Li, 2003, p. 172).

i   Where monitoring means a to and fro communication process from the sender to the receiver.

Chapter XII

Small Company (Y)

Preparing the organization is the first step in developing a "knowledge culture" and often involves changing the culture of the organization, changing the way employees work and interact. Organizational culture shifts are difficult to accomplish (Roth, 2004). Smaller organizations, 200 or fewer employees, and newer entrepreneurial organizations will have an advantage in making the prescribed culture shift over larger and older organizations that have a long history of corporate culture and a more rigid managerial structure (Becerra-Fernandez, Gonzalez, & Sabherwal, 2004 in Walczak, 2005, p. 331).

Introduction

In many ways, the dynamics of this smaller company is diametrically opposed to that of the previous one. Its mission one may recall was different, it was an IS management consultancy with a staff base that was senior (40s/50s) in age with relatively long years of IT experience. Although the sample population was very small (7), it was essentially a small firm with basically a mono-cultural (Anglo-Celtic) staff mix. Coupling these basic parameters with a physical layout that represents only one floor of a building, punctuated perhaps by a couple offices there is clearly a very different organisational structure. Organisation Y provides an opportunity to examine likely knowledge flows in a small entrepreneurial or professional firm.

Small Organisation (Y)

The dynamics of organisation Y are in many ways *very* different, given the substantially smaller size of the organisation. What is most noticeable from social network analysis results is the extensive interconnectivity between the actors. Observe from the dendogram[a] (Figure 1) and all graphs illustrating interaction patterns at Organisation Y, that the personnel are highly interconnected; there is only one clique in which all staff participate.

Organisational Y Structure, Experts, and Expert Non-Experts

Figure 11 (from Chapter V), reveals the experts are by and large **located** in senior positions. Given the type of organisation this is perhaps just as well, where consultants are able to pass through the organisation and gleam important knowledge from senior personnel.

Figure 1. Dendogram for Organisation Y

Figure 11 (from Chapter V). Structure chart of Organisation Y

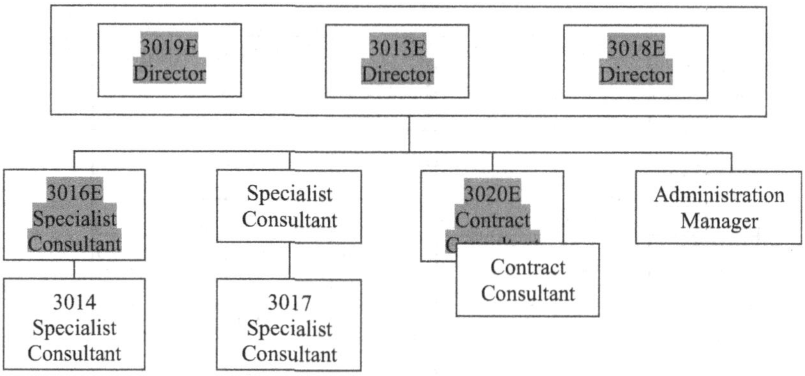

Organisation Y Metrics

Examining Table 1 with regard to values of personnel in Organisation Y, some points are quite obvious. Starting on the far right of the table viewing the **closeness** and **betweenness** values, which relate to global centrality, the measures are 100 for the former and 0 for the latter (again expressed as percentages), this indicates that all people are equally close to one another and none stand between one another. All actors are equally interconnected, which is also borne out by the fact that the network centralisation value was 0 percent. The table has been sorted in descending order of prestige (in-degree) where expert 3020E has the highest reading of 25 (in other words 25 mentions by his colleagues of being contacted). However, the most central actor (highest out-degree) is that of 3013E (26 instances recorded), this is perhaps not surprising as 3013E is the CIO. From a symmetrised degree point of view (contact degree), actor 3014, the 35-39 year old Cantonese and Malay speaking female business analyst with a master's degree is interesting. While she is not of the same **ethnic** background as the remaining monolingual respondents, and not as experienced in terms of years of IT background, she does nevertheless tend to have high contact degree in general (37), she is overtaken in this regard only by the CIO himself (3013E).

Degrees (Local Centrality)

Once again degrees for contact frequency and meeting type (Table 1) utilise symmetrised data, which means only one degree is visible. In relation to person importance, note an in and out-degree, as it was not appropriate to symmetrise this data. From a contact frequency point of view, 3013E, one of the senior partners at 50-54 years of age, was clearly the most contacted individual. The Cantonese and Malay speaking 35-39 year old business analyst was next most popular once again. Also note that novice 3017, a 30-34 year old male mono-

Table 1. Illustrating summarised values for SNA measures relating to Organisation Y; Sorted in descending order of in-degree

	Contact Degree	Person Out Degree	Person In Degree	Closeness %	Betweenness %
3020E	31	12	25	100	0
3016E	37	20	24	100	0
3013E	38	26	20	100	0
3014	37	24	18	100	0
3018E	34	14	18	100	0
3019E	36	18	16	100	0
3017	33	22	15	100	0
Mean	35.1	19.4	19.4		
Std Dev	2.4	4.7	3.5		
Minimum	31	12.0	15		
Maximum	38	26.0	25		

lingual business analyst, with four to five years less IT experience than 3014 is by almost all accounts lower on degree and power values than the latter. Perhaps this is borne out by the fact he has only been with the organisation one to two years, whereas 3014 has been with the organisation three to four years.

With regard to person importance, remember the in degree represents the number of flows in to see that individual, which represents a measure of prestige. The data presented has been sorted in descending order of in-degree on the basis of whether a person is likely to be contacted for advice rather than making contact themselves. To that end it is possible to see (Table 1), that 3020E and 3016E are the most popular from an in degree point of view. The former is a male 50 to 54 year old monolingual information management consultant with no subordinates and the lowest out-degree reading. The latter is a 55 to 59 year old monolingual male information management consultant with five to nine subordinates, and a senior partner of the firm. The most contact passing out of any actor is through 3013E (out degree 26) specifically. In themselves the in and out-degrees tend to vary quite markedly.

In the case of out degrees the minimum for any actor is 15 up until 25 and in the case of in degrees the variation is from 12 to 26. Clearly some actors are far more active than others with regard to their communication patterns for the maximum out degree in this case is by 3013E again. This senior actor is higher in person importance centrality but slightly less high in person importance prestige. While some actors such as 3013E are important in terms of giving directions to staff within the firm, others such as 3020E would appear to be approached for their expertise, but play a far lesser role in approaching others and telling them what to do. Individual 3020E with the highest prestige has between 10 to 14 years

IT experience, whilst 3013E who has the highest centrality, claims to have 30 to 34 years of IT experience.

Turning to the last two columns relating to the global centrality measures for Organisation Y (Table 1), closeness and between-ness values indicate total equality, that is to say everybody is connected to everybody else, all are equal players. No one actor is more globally central than another.

Information Centrality

The **information centrality**-based values (Table 2), suggest that participants in Organisation Y are similar from information flow likelihood. The best distributor of information would appear to be expert 3013E, closely followed by the only female 3014. The youngest male novice 3017 appears to be the second least effective from an information transferral point of view. Again all actors are not markedly dissimilar from one another in information values, however.

Table 2. Illustrating information values for personnel in Organisation Y

Information values	
3013E	24.7
3014	24.4
3016E	24.4
3019E	24.1
3018E	23.4

3017	23.0
3020E	22.3
Mean	23.8
Std Dev	0.8
Minimum	22.303
Maximum	24.737

Table 3. Showing density values for Organisation Y in descending order of actor density

	1	2	3	4	5	6	7	8
	Size	Ties	Pairs	Density	Avg Dist	Diameter	Ego Betw	UnReach
3018E	6	28	30	93.3	1.1	2	1	0
3020E	6	27	30	90.0	1.1	2	1.5	0
3013E	6	26	30	86.7	1.1	2	2	0
3014	6	26	30	86.7	1.1	2	2	0
3016E	6	26	30	86.7	1.1	2	2	0
3017	6	26	30	86.7	1.1	2	2	0
3019E	6	26	30	86.7	1.1	2	2	0

Density

From a density point of view (Table 3), the picture changes slightly as 3018E is the most popular individual (93). Given the interconnectedness of the actors the lowest density based on contact frequency is not less than 86.7, though. The average distances of communication paths between individuals are limited to 1.0 to 1.1, that is to say very interconnected, with a short if non-existent flow-betweenness ratio, that is to say the path of communication between individuals is typically one path long. It takes only one person to see another directly, without having to go through anyone else. Illustrated evidence for this will become apparent when examining the sociographs.

Difficult to Locate Individuals

There were noted to be no individuals in Organisation Y who were difficult to track down. Having viewed numerical values associated with Organisation Y actors; let's examine the results using the medium of sociographs.

Contact Frequency and Organisation X Personnel

With regard to the issues of communication patterns amongst members of organisation Y, one point is clear, namely all personnel are highly interconnected in their knowledge flows. Evidence for this interaction is illustrated in Figure 2. Note the evenness of the distance between the actors. Note their interconnectedness; there are no communication bridges as such. There are no isolates. There are no pendants.[b] All of the Organisation Y graphs appear very similar.

With regard to attribute determinacy and interaction patterns amongst the staff, no particular patterns can be seen to exist, save that with the removal of the contractor (3020E; Figure 12.3), six (out of 20) fewer channels of information amongst the staff members. The one contractor occupies 30 percent of the communication "bandwidth" in this organisation; furthermore this staff member is actually acknowledged as being an expert.

Figure 4 reveals that whilst only two of the staff members conduct fortnightly meetings, four participate in weekly (Figure 5) and seven participate in daily (Figure 6) meetings, even if only four of the seven staff members contribute to hourly meetings (Figure 7). Two of these four staff (3013E, 3016E) members are in fact senior partners of the firm. The role of one of the senior two partners (3013E) starts to become a little more obvious in relation to this person's role in hourly meetings. Clearly this individual is a major actor. One interpretation is that the meeting of all staff is likely to be formal in nature, whilst the hourly meetings are probably likely to be personnel working on specific projects. The point remains that all staff are highly interconnected. From a purely meeting frequency based point of view, one may surmise that tacit knowledge transferral is likely to be less between staff members (3020E

Figure 2. Illustrating all relationships by gender and employment type for Organisation Y

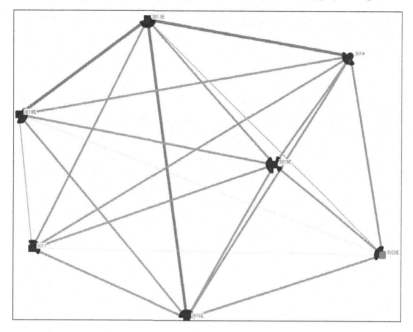

Figure 3. Illustrating our contractor removed

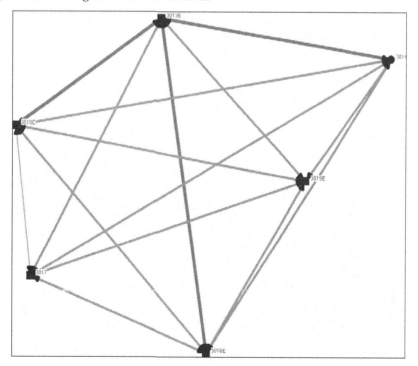

and 3017) and (3020E and 3018E), as these three personnel conducted fortnightly meetings. However, the interaction the staff members in general have with one another would tend to cancel out any likelihood of soft knowledge transfer blockage.

Figure 4. Illustrating fortnightly meetings amongst Organisation Y members

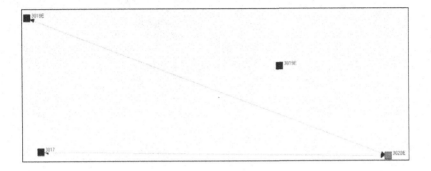

Figure 5. Illustrating weekly meetings amongst Organisation Y staff members

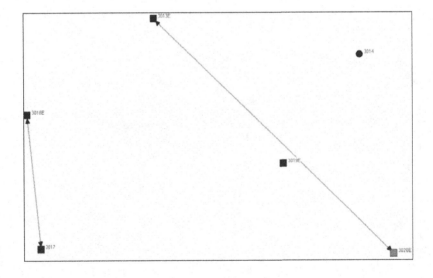

Figure 6. Illustrating daily staff meetings amongst Organisation Y staff members

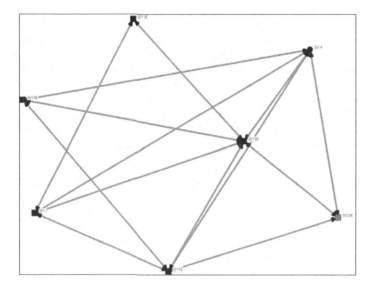

Figure 7. Illustrating hourly meetings in Organisation Y

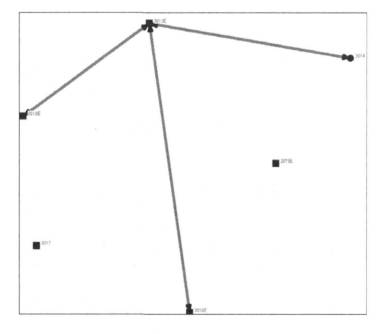

Person Importance and Organisation Y

Although none of the Organisation Y staff seemed to avoid any other staff members ("try not to see"), when asked to indicate staff they could get by without seeing (Figure 8), expert contractor 3020E the highest person-**importance** prestige individual, chose three others. One of these was the Cantonese and Malay speaking younger female (3014), another was the young male (3017), and also another expert (3018E). This final expert individual is a 50 to 54 year old monolingual information management consultant who claims to have an ACS level of 5, he is not however responsible for any subordinates, meaning his results are contradictory. Assuming his ACS level is still 3 or 4, he nevertheless has 10 to 14 years of IT experience and he has nonetheless only been with the organisation for one to two years.

One may surmise that the expert contractor with a high prestige rating may not need to see the former two because they are younger and perceived to be less useful to him in terms of workplace experience. Nevertheless, as a service provider one would hope the contractor *should* be seeing the other staff, at the very least to pass on some of this tacit knowledge. One may assume expert contractor 3020E may feel he does not need to see expert 3018E because of the latter's shorter tenure with the organisation at present. Recall that expert contractor 3020E was still having fortnightly meetings with both 3014 and 3018E. All seven staff members were considered both moderately important (Figure 9) and very important to be seen (Figure 10).

Figure 8. Can get by without seeing

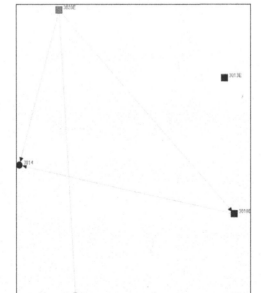

Figure 9. Illustrating moderately important people

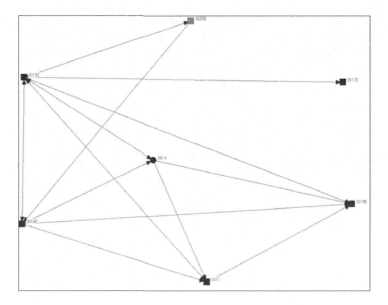

Figure 10. Illustrating very important people

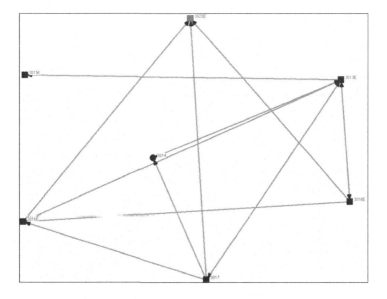

With regard to moderate importance, the expert contractor is only identified as such by expert 3019E. When however higher levels of importance are examined, the expert contractor begins to play a more important role. Figure 10 illustrates that expert contractor 3020E now has a person importance in-degree of 3. With the exception of the CIO (one of the senior partners, 3013E) the contractor has a very high prestige rating, his centrality however is low. At the same time 3019E is quite isolated, and is in fact a pendant at this stage. Without the CIO taking an interest in him, his importance would be greatly curtailed, and indeed

Figure 11. Illustrating people who just have to be seen

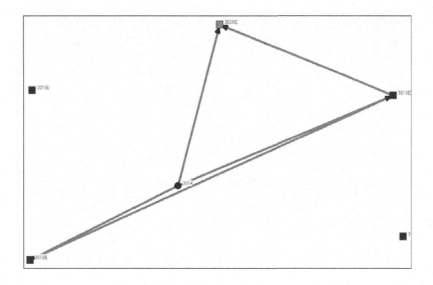

Figure 12. Illustrating key to communication patterns

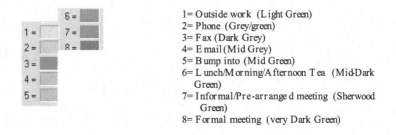

1= Outside work (Light Green)
2= Phone (Grey/green)
3= Fax (Dark Grey)
4= Email (Mid Grey)
5= Bump into (Mid Green)
6= Lunch/Morning/Afternoon Tea (Mid-Dark Green)
7= Informal/Pre-arranged meeting (Sherwood Green)
8= Formal meeting (very Dark Green)

when examining individual 3019E in relation to people who simply have to be seen (Figure 11), 3019E becomes an isolate. This is somewhat unusual because he is a 50 to 54 year old monolingual business systems analyst with 30 to 34 years of IT experience, who has been with the organisation for five to six years. On the other hand he has no subordinates. Perhaps this reflects a certain degree of independence, whereas as an experienced IT practitioner he really does not have to see anyone, nor does it seem others feel a need to have to see him.

Individuals considered *particularly* important were those of 3020E and 3016E (in-degree 2 each). Actor 3013E was also acknowledged as very important (in-degree 1). The Cantonese and Malay speaking junior in this case has a high centrality (out degree 4), but appears to have no prestige at this level (in-degree 0). It would appear that whilst she may be highly educated formally (she is one of only two with a Masters degree), she appears to seek advice from some of the senior males, the CIO being one of them.

Communication Patterns: Meeting Type and Organisation Y

Because **electronic** forms of communication are minimal in both organisations Y and Z a (originally) common green theme was used to illustrate *all* communication forms, rather than the two different colour themes that were used for Organisation X. Figure 12 illustrates a similar greyish theme has again been utilised for less likely tacit knowledge flows, but all other forms of communication are shown in green. In short a simplified scheme is presented for communication flows in organisations Y and Z.

As was previously discussed, the type of interaction is likely to greatly influence the means by which tacit knowledge can be transferred. In Organisation Y, none of the staff members had indicated they used electronic forms of communication (phones, faxes, e-mails). Whilst this may at first strike the reader as odd, it is worth noting that all actors occupy one floor within the same building. It has been acknowledged (Audretsch, 1998; von Hipple, 1994) that **face-to-face** transferral is important for soft knowledge transfer, even if not for codified knowledge transferral, to that end some idea is gained from Figure 13 that at least two out of the seven staff members do "bump into each other" around the workplace. This is somewhat surprising given that the staff share office accommodation. The younger female and an older male expert are the ones who bump into one another. One may speculate that others had not chosen "bump into each other" as this took place all too commonly, however the option was present in the questionnaire and only two staff members chose this answer.

Examining informal, but nevertheless pre-arranged meetings (Figure 14), note all the staff are involved, although the CIO (3013E), 3016E, and 3018E (another senior consultant) do not touch base this way. Perhaps the fact that the staff seem not to be bumping into one another, but rather conducting informal type meetings, means staff are engaged on specific projects, and only come together at specific meeting times?

What is unusual is that the female, who whilst not necessarily identified as an expert, but who does enjoy high power ratings, is left out of the formal organisational meeting process altogether (Figure 15). At this level, she becomes an isolate. One may at first conclude it is

Figure 13. Organisation Y staff members who tend to just bump into each other

Figure 14. Our staff who participate in informal yet pre-arranged meetings

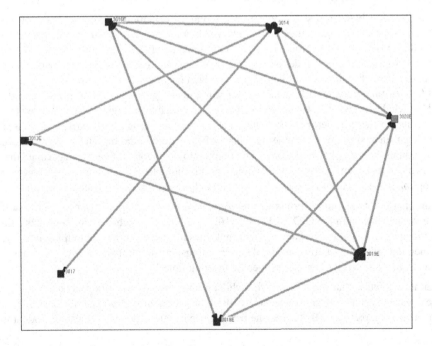

Figure 15. Illustrating formal meetings that take place between Organisation Y

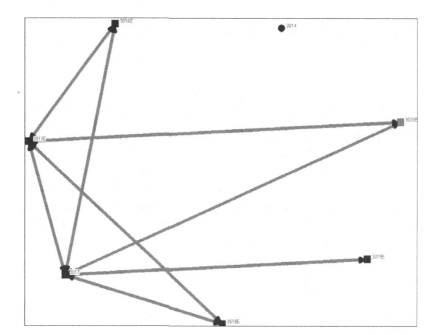

due to her junior level (both in terms of age, and IT experience, or perhaps fewer years of experience with the firm). However the *even more* junior male 3107, *is* included in formal meetings, and even acts as a communication bridge with senior expert actor 3019E, who would otherwise be isolated in such a meeting situation.

Summary

What do these results reveal regarding communication patterns in Organisation Y? First, the small "cottage industry" size of the organisation would indicate higher densities of communication patterns with fewer actors acting as communication bridges. Second, the lack of electronic means of information communication would already greatly benefit the probability of tacit knowledge transfer. Third, the fact that all staff meet face to face regularly (at least daily, if not hourly), would indicate a high confidence in the tacit knowledge transfer process. Fourth, the evidence that staff appear to have no major areas of conflict in terms of not wishing to see colleagues would tend to indicate a fairly harmonious working relationship. Fifth, the numerical values of information and other measures of centrality, along with values given for degrees, indicate that "normal" actor 3104 is as important or "central" as *most* of the experts, with the exception of perhaps one of the managing directors, 3013E. Finally, the presence of only one clique indicates all actors are interconnected without any go-between. What then of the final Organisation?

References

Audretsch, D. (1998). Agglomeration and the location of innovative activity. *Oxford Review of Economic Activity, 14*(2), 18.

Becerra-Fernandez, I., Gonzalez, A., & Sabherwal, R. (2004). *Knowledge management challenges, solutions, and technologies.* Upper Saddle River, NJ: Pearson Prentice Hall.

Roth, G. (2004). Lessons from the desert: Integrating managerial expertise and learning for organizational transformation. *The Learning Organization, 11*(3), 194-208.

von Hippel, E. (1994). Sticky information and the locus of problem solving. *Management Science, 40,* 429-439.

Walczak, S. (2005). Organizational knowledge management structure. *The Learning Organization, 12*(4), 330-339.

Endnotes

[a]   A branching tree like diagram.

[b]   A node with degree 1.

Chapter XIII

Medium Company (Z)

To enhance the knowledge flows between people to stimulate innovative thinking, organizations should first conduct a knowledge audit and develop a knowledge map of the sources, sinks, and flows of knowledge in the organization. In other words, whom do people go to in the organization for answers to questions or how are departments in the organization interacting within and between each other? (Liebowitz, 2005, p. 77).

Introduction

Company Z represents a microcosm of Company X. Whereas the previous firm was a small consultancy organisation, Z on the other hand is essentially a smaller version of X, for Z exists to support the mission of the organisation (selling furniture), rather than ICT being an end in itself as with Company Y. Organisation Z has a strong CIO who participates in most cliques and is considered by his peers to be an "expert." Almost all staff members meet one another on a daily basis, if not weekly, at the same time there seem to be few staff avoiding one another. There are few contract staff members that present the risk of taking tacit knowledge with them. Electronic forms of communication exist but are minimal, which is not surprising given the small IT staff complement.

Medium Organisation (Z)

Organisation Z comprises a small-scale version of Organisation X in terms of its staffing profile and mission. Similar to Organisation X, there were staff members who had participated in the tacit knowledge inventory component of the questionnaire but had not participated in the social network analysis component. To that end contact-frequency and meeting-type relationships were required to be symmetrised. Staff members of Organisation Z tended to be heavily concentrated around a singular CIO. Staff were physically **located** in the same building and in the same workspace. As a reminder, remember there were five experts (3333E, 3335E, 3336E, 3340E, 3343E) and four expert non-experts (3334ENE, 3339ENE, 3342ENE and 3344ENE) identified through the tacit knowledge inventory section of the questionnaire.

Organisational Z Structure, Experts, and Expert Non-Experts

A cursory examination of Figure 16 (again from Chapter V), reveals a strong positive correlation between seniority and expertness. Those positions for which no identification numbers are available, relate to personnel who did not participate in the study. Whilst it has been noted that a help desk person was an ENE, this individual is actually part of the

Figure 16 (from Chapter V). Structure chart for Organisation Z

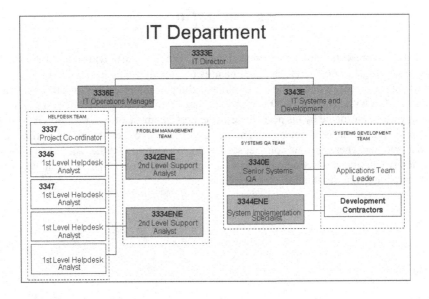

problem management team in the organisational structure chart. Either way it is clear that non-elite personnel do appear to have access to both experts and ENEs and that the latter group appear evenly dispersed.

Organisation Z Metrics

Organisation Z Cliques

Examining Table 1, what is most obvious is the participation of 3333E and 3340E in almost all the cliques. The former happens to be the CIO. What also is apparent is the participation of at least one expert (again identified by E's) and expert non-experts (3334, 3339, 3342 and 3344), in each of the cliques, thus there is no single micro level clique that does not contain one of these "elite" actors.

The same sets of cliques are represented in Figure 1 below. Reading the identification numbers vertically, the dominance of 3333E and 3340E participating in all cliques is obvious. What is also noticeable is that everyone (15 in all who fully participated when relationships are symmetrised) participated in at least one clique (3338 for example participated in at least one clique).

Table 2 provides a summarised set of values of other measures relating to the network patterns of employees. Again the table has been sorted on the basis of descending order of a person's in-degree, or the extent to which individuals are being approached by others (i.e., their prestige). What is immediately obvious is the strong positive correlation in the case of

Table 1. Indicating cliques and clique members

Clique No:	Participants of the clique as numbered on the left							
1:	3333E	3337	3339	3340E	3341	3342	3343E	3346
2:	3333E	3339	3340E	3341	3342	3344	3346	
3:	3333E	3337	3339	3340E	3342	3345	3346	
4:	3333E	3339	3340E	3342	3346	3347		
5:	3333E	3338	3339	3340E	3341	3342		
6:	3333E	3336E	3337	3340E	3341	3342	3343E	
7:	3333E	3335E	3336E	3340E	3341	3342	3343E	
8:	3333E	3336E	3340E	3341	3342	3344		
9:	3333E	3336E	3337	3340E	3342	3345		
10:	3333E	3336E	3340E	3342	3347			
11:	3333E	3335E	3340E	3341	3342	3343E	3346	
12:	3334	3336E	3337	3340E	3341	3342	3343E	
13:	3334	3337	3340E	3341	3342	3343E	3346	

Figure 1. Illustrating single link hierarchical clustering of cliques in Organisation Z

```
          3           3         3 3       3
      3 3 3 3 3 3 3 3 3 3 3 3 3 3 3 3
      3 3 3 3 3 3 3 3 3 3 4 3 4 3 3 3
      3 3 5 4 4 3 6 3 4 3 0 4 3 4 4
      8 4 E 4 5 9 E 7 1 E E 2 E 6 7

          1 1                 1 1 1 1
Level 6 2 3 2 3 7 4 5 9 1 8 0 1 4 5
----- - - - - - - - - - - - - - - -
  13  . . . . . . . . . . XXX . . .
  11  . . . . . . . . . . XXXXX . .
   9  . . . . . . . . . XXXXXXX . .
   6  . . . . . . . XXXXXXXXXXXXXXX .
   5  . . . . . XXXXXXXXXXXXXXXXX .
   2  . XXXXXXXXXXXXXXXXXXXXXXXXXXX
   1  XXXXXXXXXXXXXXXXXXXXXXXXXXXXXX
```

Table 2. Illustrating values for Organisation Z

	Contact Degree	Person Out Degree (Centrality)	Person In Degree (Prestige)	Global Closeness	Global Betweenness
3333E	75	30	32	93.3	4.9
3343E	63	15	32	77.8	1.1
3336E	71	32	31	82.4	3.6
3340E	87	36	30	100	6.5
3337	58	8	24	77.8	1.1
3344	43	5	20	66.7	0.2
3334	39	0	18	66.7	0.1
3347	37	0	18	63.6	0.2
3335E	40	10	18	66.7	0.1
3342	87	43	17	100	6.5
3345	44	9	17	66.7	0.2
3338	29	0	14	60.9	0
3341	68	35	11	87.5	3.6
3346	66	25	11	87.5	3.9
3339	77	55	10	82.4	3.2
Mean	58.9	20.2	20.2	78.7	2.3
Std Dev	18.4	17	7.5	12.7	2.3
Minimum	29	0	10	60.9	0
Maximum	87	55	32	100	6.5

Organisation Z between expertness and high levels of in-degree, the one exception being expert 3335E. The latter is a 30 to 34 year old male Hindi speaking business systems analyst. He is one of the few contract staff in this IT branch of the firm (the others being novice actor 3346 and ENE 3339 who we would otherwise label 3339ENE). Although actor 3335E has been with the firm for seven to eight years, he has no subordinates. What is apparent is the high prestige of expert actors 3333E (CIO) and 3343E, both senior personnel.

Degrees (Local Centrality)

Degrees represent at a more simple level the contact people have with one another purely from an inward or outward flow of communication. Beginning with degrees in relation to contact frequency, Table 2 illustrates 3340E and 3342 possess the highest degree purely on the basis of being contacted (87), down to 3338 with the lowest degree (29). Whereas there is a strong positive correlation between prestige (in degree) and expert stature, the ENEs (blue) do not score so well with regard to prestige (3344: 20; 3334: 18; 3342: 17, and 3339: 10). With regard to centrality (out degree) the picture for at least two of the ENEs (3342, 3339) begins to change quite radically (3342: 43; 3339: 55). One could surmise that experts are approached for advice on matters, although certain novices (3341; 3346) seem to be just as proactive as experts generally speaking when it comes to contacting other people in the organisation. The latter point would make sense and indicate that certain novices probably need to attain advice from more expert personnel.

Global Centrality

Scrutinizing measures relating to global centrality (Table 2), the most globally central person using **closeness** as a measure, is that of 3340E who is a 55 to 59 year old Cantonese and Mandarin speaking business development manager with 20 to 24 years of IT experience. Clearly his peers identify this individual as being an expert (hence his being selected as an expert), at the same time his global centrality also bears this out. Interestingly his position in the organisational structure chart (Figure 5.16, at the beginning of this section) reveals he is not necessarily close to the top of the organisation. The CIO (3333E) does not quite have the same global centrality rating as 3340E (93.3 as opposed to 100). At the same time, his **betweenness** value is also less than 3340E (4.9 as opposed to 6.5). One other individual of the same global centrality is expert non-expert 3342ENE, a male 20 to 24 year old help desk support officer with less than four years of IT experience. This is very interesting as it reveals that one at the opposite end of the spectrum in the organisation to the "powerful" expert can be just as important to the running of the firm. In many ways ENE 3342 could not differ more in comparison to expert 3340E, in terms of age, experience, job type and ethnicity. One is officially recognised as knowledgeable by his peers, the other seems to be equally so but is not so recognised. Broadly speaking there is a weak positive correlation between higher ranges of prestige and global centrality for the elite groups. This, in combination with evidence that elites are involved in all cliques indicates a high likelihood for successful tacit knowledge transferral, at least in the case of this organisation.

Yet again there appears to be a strong positive correlation between betweenness values and extent of expertness. On the other hand, there only is a weak positive correlation between global closeness and expertness. Novice actors 3341 and 3346 for example appear to have high global centrality scores. The former is a male 35 to 39 year old Chinese speaking software engineer. The latter is 30 to 34 year old male Anglo Celtic Australian programmer.

Pertaining to how centralised Organisation Y is as a whole, a network centralization figure of 47.5 percent is realised. In other words there appears to be a high percentage of centralisation taking place, certainly very high as opposed to the 2.6 percent realised in Organisation X, and definitely extremely high when contrasted with the 0 percent (or non-existant centralisation) observed in Organisation Y. Let's now examine the density values for each of our Organisation Z personnel. Remember density provides some indication of connectedness actors have with one another.

Information and Organisation Z

The **information centrality** values (Table 3), reveal expert 3340E's prominence in facilitating information flows. He happens to be a male 55 to 59 year old Cantonese and Mandarin

Table 3. Illustrating information values for personnel in Organisation Z

Information values	
3340E	36.8
3342	36.8
3339	34.7
3333E	34.6
3336E	33.6
3341	33.0
3346	32.7
3343E	31.7
3337	30.5
3345	26.3
3344	26.1
3335E	25.0
3334	24.6
3347	23.9
3338	20.5
Mean	**30.0**
Std Dev	**5.0**
Minimum	**20.5**
Maximum	**36.8**

speaking business development manager. Note that ENE 3342 (a male 20 to 24 year old help desk support worker) has effectively the same information centrality as the former. At the other end of the scale certain experts (3335E, the 30 to 34 year old Hindi business systems analyst) and expert non-experts 3344 (a female 20 to 24 year old Indonesian and Cantonese speaking help desk support officer) and 3334 (no biographical details supplied) scored low for information centrality values. The difference in terms of information centrality for one help-desk support officer (3342) compared to another (3344) is noteworthy.

Density

The density values for contact frequency varied from 100 (3338) to 3342 (Table 4). From a person importance point of view, the density varied from 95 (3338), down to 40.7 (3340E). Finally from a meeting importance point of view, 3338 again has the highest density (100), down to 3342 (with a density of 64.8). It should be noted the reason the density tends to be higher for an actor such as 3338, in that the size of their ego networks is much smaller (typically 5-6) as opposed to personnel such as 3340E (14). That is to say, one would expect the density of relations to be higher for a staff member who is involved in fewer relations with people, and indeed this has proved to be the case in Organisation Z.

The relevance of this last point relates to strong ties being more conducive to tacit knowledge flows, but less for innovative flows (Fernie, Green, Weller, & Newcombe, 2003; Hansen,

Table 4. Showing densities in Organisation Z

	1	2	3	4	5	6	7	8
	Size	Ties	Pairs	Density	Avgas Dist	Diameter	Ego Betw	UnReach
3338	5	20	20	100.0	1.0	1	0	0
3334	7	40	42	95.2	1.0	2	1	0
3335E	7	40	42	95.2	1.0	2	1	0
3344	7	38	42	90.5	1.1	2	2	0
3345	7	38	42	90.5	1.1	2	2	0
3347	6	26	30	86.7	1.1	2	2	0
3337	10	76	90	84.4	1.2	2	7	0
3343E	10	76	90	84.4	1.2	2	7	0
3341	12	96	132	72.7	1.3	2	18	0
3339	11	78	110	70.9	1.3	2	16	0
3346	12	90	132	68.2	1.3	2	21	0
3333E	13	106	156	67.9	1.3	2	25	0
3336E	11	72	110	65.5	1.3	2	19	0
3340E	14	118	182	64.8	1.4	2	32	0
3342	14	118	182	64.8	1.4	2	32	0

1999). Another way of phrasing this is that the experts and the more popular expert non-experts are involved with a greater number of people, but their network density is somewhat retarded, meaning their knowledge may have to flow through another individual to reach its final destination (the diameters in the density ego nets varying from 1 to 3).

What do the numerical values explain? That the relatively small numbers of personnel in this organisation are quite different in their interaction patterns from the single clique seen in Organisation Y. Although the IT staff in Organisation Z comprised basically double the number of IT staff of Y, there are 13 cliques in the former, as opposed to 1 in the latter. One also can see that experts and expert non-experts do at least display a weak positive correlation with higher degree results, both in and out degree for that matter. It would also appear that experts and expert non-experts generally seem to interact with larger numbers of staff, but that their densities consequently tend to be lower, meaning in turn that while they come into contact with more personnel, some of this contact may be indirect (in other words through another individual).

Difficult to Locate Individuals

More controversially for Organisation Z, is that five individuals out of the 15 who participated were noted to be difficult to find. They were experts 3333E (CIO), 3343E and 3335E, expert non-expert 3334 and novice 3338. The fact that four "elites" out of 15 staff are difficult to get to would indicate that soft knowledge flows could be improved.

Contact Frequency and Organisation Z

Figure 2 reveals once again there were several (four) staff members who chose not to provide biographical details in the questionnaire. While error checking prompts were in place, a small minority of IT staff members similarly to that of Organisation X, choose to circumvent biographical questions and proceeded onto the social network and tacit knowledge sections of the questionnaire. To that end these information non-providers are shown in some of the figures as grey triangles. The ENEs have been identified with cross-hatching. Note for example the communication flows taking place through ENE contractor 3339. Although only two staff members were engaged in fortnightly meetings (3337, 3341), all staff who did complete the questionnaire were engaged at least in weekly meetings (Figure 3), if not daily meetings (Figure 4). What is clear from weekly meetings, which are likely to be some form of staff meeting, is that 3333E and 3346 have a high *weekly* degree (six each). In fact, 3333E is the CIO. One is able to see from Figure 3 that these two personnel also occupy a central role in knowledge diffusion, insofar as their removal from this picture would create a considerably lower communication flow. Examining the daily meeting interaction (Figure 4), and it is apparent that much of the communication flow takes place through expert 3340E, who is not the CIO, but rather a Cantonese and Mandarin speaking 55-59 year old (daily in and out degree 8).

Figure 2. Contact frequency of everyone in Organisation Z

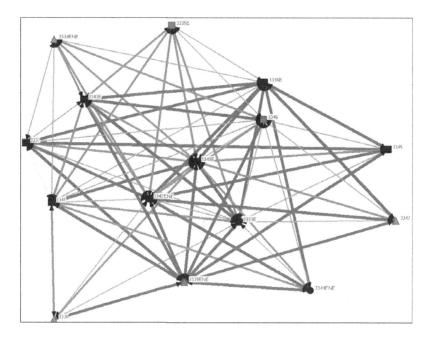

Figure 3. Illustrating weekly meetings taking place in Organisation Z

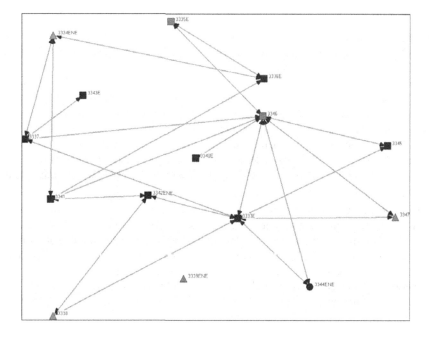

Figure 4. Illustrating daily meetings taking place between Organisation Z people

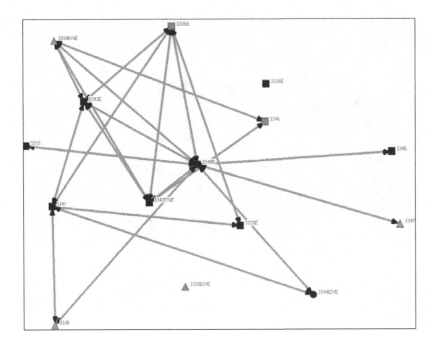

Removing this individual creates isolates (3347, 3337 and 3345) (Figure 5). Whilst the CIO (3333E) is still involved in communication, this is only between two other individuals (3341, 3335E). From an hourly meeting point of view (Figure 6), the emphasis now shifts to expert non-expert 3339ENE, who while not actually providing gender based information, is a Persian and Assyrian speaking 35-39 year old contractor with the organisation one to two years (hourly in-degree 8). Also notable is the importance of 3336E (hourly in-degree 7) in the communication process, even though he is not quite as centrally placed as 3339. If actor 3339 is removed (Figure 7), then some communication problems may conceivably take place. Note how 3339 forms an hourly communication backbone to other members of staff. Actor 3339 has not been identified as an expert but clearly plays a central communication role.

Age does not seem to play a critical role in Organisation Z in determining communication patterns. However, there is some cliquing taking place on the basis of a shared language, of which in Organisation Z, there are only the Chinese languages in common amongst three staff members (3340E, 3344, 3341 in Figure 8). One is able to see (Figure 8) that these staff members are all permanent as indicated by the black coloured nodes. Daily meetings take place between 3340E and 3344, and also between 3344 and 3341. Hourly meetings take place between 3340E and 3341.

Figure 5. Illustrating the effects of 3340E being removed from the communication picture

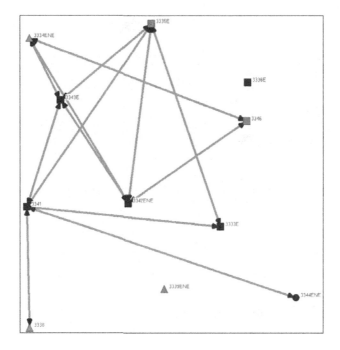

Figure 6. Illustrating hourly meetings taking place between our personnel in Organisation Z

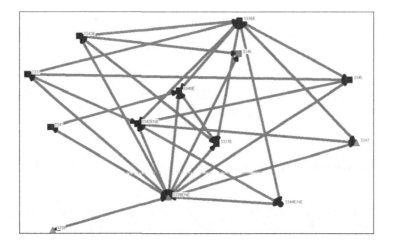

Figure 7. Illustrating the removal of 3339

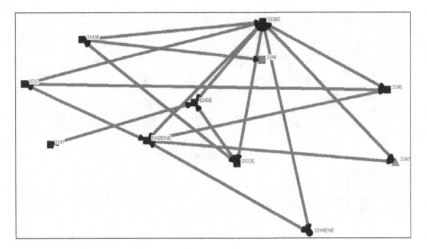

Figure 8. Illustrating staff members who share a common language, in this case a Chinese language

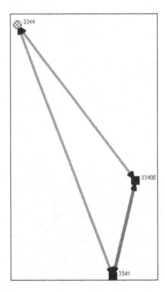

Person Importance and Organisation Z

There exist a number of interesting communication patterns, for example there are a few personnel who are avoided by 3342ENE (Figure 9), being those of contractor novice 3346,

Figure 9. Illustrating situations where 3342 tries to avoid other staff members

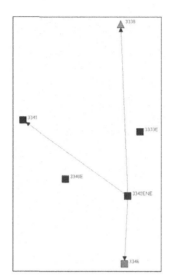

permanent novice 3341 and no biography novice 3338). Interestingly these feelings are not reciprocated. Somewhat disturbingly 3342 is an ENE who is avoiding staff who are neither experts, nor ENEs. In other words staff that can less afford to not acquire knowledge.

With regard to getting by without seeing the individual (Figure 10), a totally different pattern emerges. It is clear that almost all staff can get by without seeing another should they need to, at the same time if asked who they consider are moderately important (Figure 11), practically all staff are chosen again. Whereas staff such as 3342 may have a high centrality, prestige with regard to tacit knowledge is the more important determinant as it is important to know who is approached for ways of doing things. One can see that contractor 3335E is moderately important (in degree 4).

With regard to who are considered the very important people (Figure 12), one can see that the centrality of ENE 3342 is obvious as is the actor prestige of experts 3336E, 3340E and 3343E (in-degree 5 each).

Perhaps most telling are those individuals that simply have to be seen, no matter what. Clearly from Figure 13, 3339 has a high degree of centrality (out degree 11), but low prestige (in degree 0). Actors with highest prestige are those of 3333E (the CIO), 3343E, 3340E and 3337. The last actor mentioned is interesting as this person is not senior, rather a 20-24 year old Greek LOE[a] speaker, who is currently in the help desk support role, and prior to this was not even in the IT industry. This last point would tend to emphasise the importance of the help desk role for the diffusion of tacit knowledge, but what of the roles of the other two? Individual 3343E is a 30-34 year old monolingual project manager, but considers himself to

306 Busch

Figure 10. Can get by without seeing the individual

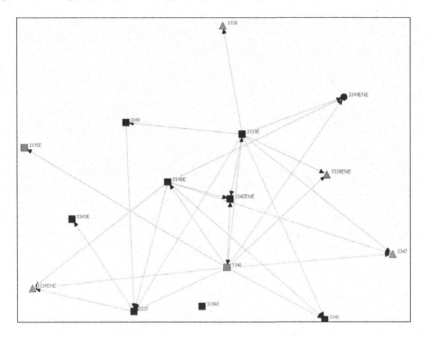

Figure 11. Moderately important

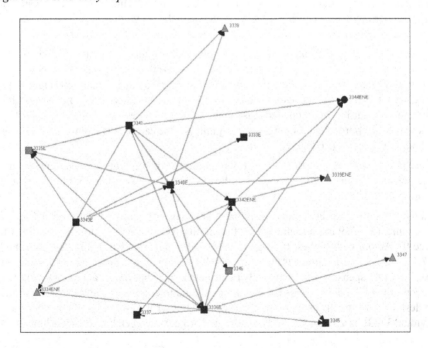

Figure 12. Very important

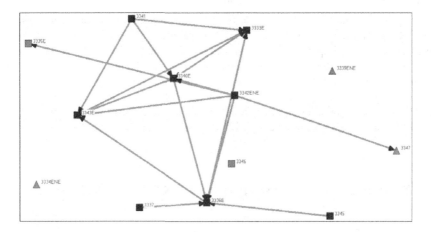

Figure 13. Illustrating individuals that simply have to seen in Organisation Z

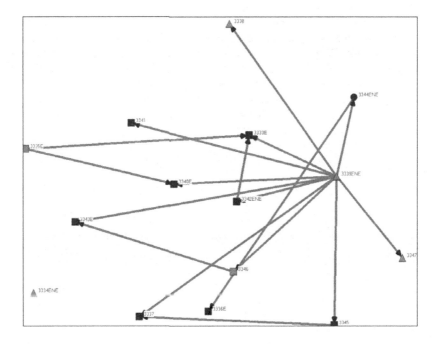

be ACS level 5 (remembering that in fact there can only be one CIO, who is actually 3333E). Person 3340E is a Chinese 55-59 year old business development manager.

There may be some bottlenecking of soft knowledge taking place if ENEs are avoiding some personnel who may have greater necessity of their expertise. While generally all staff were viewed as moderately important, it is clear only the identified experts were generally considered to be *very* important. However in terms of personnel who just had to be seen, while the experts were prominent again, a help desk officer was just as important with the same in degree rating as the experts identified. In other words, while experts are more obvious targets for staff attention, they still need to rely on the humble role of the help desk officer. With this in mind, what type of meetings did Organisation Z people engage in?

Meeting Types Using and Electronic Medium

What is evident from Figure 14 is that telephone communication is limited in Organisation Z. Only two staff contacted each other this way, one is an ENE (3334). In fact both of these people are 20-24 year old help desk officers, one of Greek and the other of Chinese extraction. From a tacit knowledge point diffusion point of view, telephone conversations would likely impede flow, but at least voice intonation is possible to decipher and at least the nature of the communication medium is limited in this organisation.

With regard to e-mail contact amongst staff (Figure 15) the situation drastically changes. Remembering that e-mail is an information rather than knowledge transfer tool, the proportion of staff making use of such a medium could conceivably create tacit knowledge bottlenecking *if* this were the primary means of communication. Note also the high e-mail prestige of actor 3346 (degree 8), a monolingual 30-34 year old contract programmer with 10 to 14 years of IT experience. What is interesting is that someone with such a high prestige ranking, who has been in the industry for so long, is not actually acknowledged by his peers as being an expert, or even appears by way of the IS tacit knowledge inventory to be an expert non-expert. Perhaps this reflects a high quotient on the part of the individual of codified knowledge, but less in the way of "street smart" knowledge.

Figure 14. Illustrating the respondents communicating by way of telephone

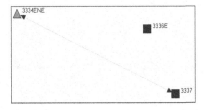

Figure 15. Illustrating e-mail contact amongst Organisation Z respondents

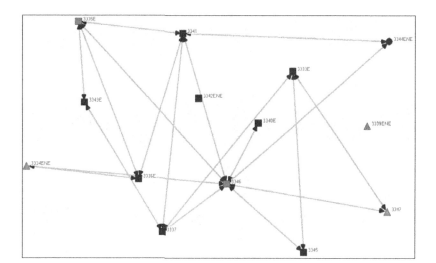

Meetings Involving Face-to-Face Contact

Figure 16 illustrates the meeting types where face-to-face contact takes place for Organisation Z. What is apparent is that there are no isolates or even pendants. The darkest flows represent "bumping into one another in the workplace", and it is here that the contractors seem to miss out. This could be of some concern for the organisation wishing to best enable contactors to pass on their knowledge while it is on "the tip of their tongues" (Jüttner, 1980). Examining formal organisational meetings specifically (Figure 17), only one contractor appears to be involved (3335E our Hindi speaking business systems analyst) who has actually been with the organisation for seven to eight years. The other two contractors (novice 3346 and expert non-expert 3339ENE) have been with the organisation from seven to 12 months in the case of the former and one to two years in the case of the latter. Interestingly, the Hindi speaker supervises no one, but expert non-expert 3339ENE supervises between five and nine people. No job title has been given by 3339ENE other than "contractor." What is clear from this figure is that quite a number of staff do not necessarily participate in formal organisation meetings, whilst everybody (Figure 18) participates in at least informal organisation meetings. Although there are no isolates from an informal meeting point of view, expert contractor 3335E, expert permanent staff member 3336E and expert non-expert 3334ENE are pendants. At least two contractors don't appear to "bump into" other staff members (Figure 19). Unfortunately, they are either expert non-experts (3339ENE) or experts (3335E).

Figure 16. Illustrating all Organisation Z people who participate in face to face meetings

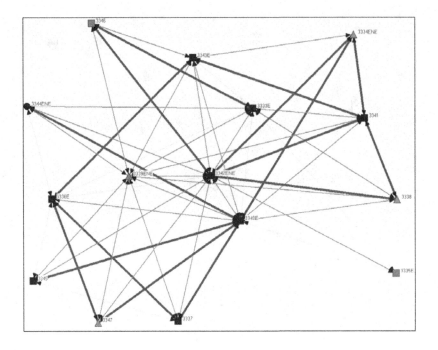

Figure 17. Those who meet in formal organisational meetings

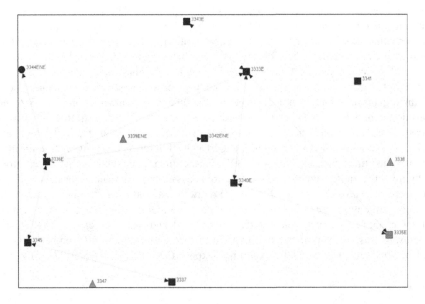

Figure 18. Those who meet in informal but pre-arranged meetings

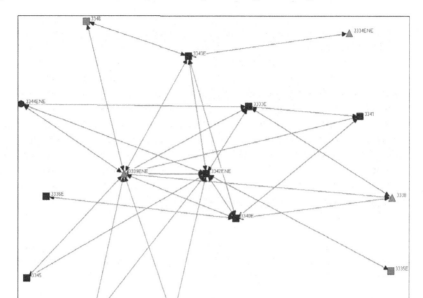

Figure 19. Those who bump into one another (note none of the organisation Z people an-swered that they met at lunch/morning/afternoon tea or outside of work)

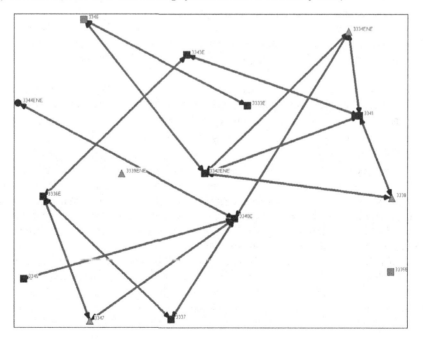

Organisation Z Summary

What can be gleaned from the communication paths of Organisation Z? First, there are a large number of cliques (13), remembering the minimum number for a clique was three people, given the number of staff who participated were 15 out of a total of 16. This is interesting, as small Organisation Y had only one clique. Nonetheless, experts and particularly the CIO (3333E) participate in almost all the cliques. With regard to power, 3339ENE and 3342ENE as expert novices outrank some of the experts. Remember the former was a 35 to 39 contractor; while the latter was a 20 to 24 year old help desk support officer. It would also appear that network densities reflected a weak negative correlation with regard to the tacit-ness quotient of the individuals, that is to say those people who one would expect to have higher readings of tacit knowledge (our experts and ENEs) have lower network densities. Concurrently, these people tend to be connected with higher numbers of individuals. With regard to degrees, a pattern emerges that indicates whilst experts may not be the most oft contacted, or making contact, they do generally appear to have the highest prestige rating in relation to values of person importance. Therefore, while a help desk officer or perhaps a contractor may be important to contact, they are not necessarily considered quite as *important* in general as an expert, unless the contractor also happens to be an expert, in which case the expertness would tend to take precedence over the contract nature of employment.

Second, the size of the organisation tends to indicate quarterly or monthly meetings are not appropriate and so the least people see each other is weekly, with daily meetings involving an overwhelming proportion of the staff as well. The key players here tend to be the CIO, as well as personnel such as 3346 who is neither an expert nor ENE, but is a help desk contractor. Some important people such as 3339ENE, don't tend to be involved in weekly or daily meetings, but are heavily involved in hourly meetings. Given the contract nature of 3339's employment and his qualifications in Microsoft and Sun Systems, one could reliably conclude he is a technical specialist engaged on specific projects. Because of the relatively diverse **ethnic** nature of Organisation Z, there does not appear to be any significant cliquing on the basis of language other than English, although hourly meetings do take place between a couple of the Chinese speakers, one of whom is a 35 to 39 year old software engineer. The other is an expert 55-59 year old Business Development Manager. The former has a masters degree, the latter a bachelors degree. On the surface, there does not appear to be any specific reason why they would conduct hourly meetings, but this may likely relate to a project they may be working on. No other specific ethnic cliques can be identified in this organisation.

Third, there appears to be some superficial antagonism between a few of the people (four in all) in terms of one of the expert non-experts attempting to avoid seeing three others, however this is the only such example. Generally all staff members are considered moderately important by at least one other individual. Noticeably, but understandably the CIO is considered moderately important by just one other, an expert. The CIO is considered very important and a "must see" by 3 or more people. One may gather from this that unlike Organisation Y, Organisation Z tends to be more hierarchical, such that only some really need to see the CIO, while those at a lower level would likely have little direct reason for doing so. In fact, only six out of 15 staff members are considered very important, and these are all experts, with the exception of one expert non-expert. Furthermore, considering that people who simply *have* to be seen number 13 out of 15, this seems unusual, however as the person importance data remains unsymmetrised, it is essentially ENE 3339 who has chosen many of these people, as such the data is somewhat biased. To that end, selecting individuals who have been chosen by more than just 3339, number just four (3337, 3343E, 3340E and the CIO 3333E), again these comprise either experts, or a help desk person. Clearly in regard to people who have to be seen, 3339 has high centrality, but not prestige. In other words, expert non-expert 3339 may be a good spreader of tacit knowledge, but does not appear to be a person who is approached in relation to tacit knowledge.

Fourth, while phone conversations are limited, e-mail is used extensively. Whatever is transferred by e-mail is certainly not tacit knowledge. The people contacted via e-mail tend to be experts (3333E, 3336E), contractors (3346) or both (3335E). At the same time 3337 and 3341 also seem to have high e-mail centrality and prestige; the former is a help desk support person; the latter is a software engineer. Certainly in an organisation of this size, it would appear most people are "bumped into", but particularly experts and expert non-experts. With regard to at least informal meetings, all staff are involved to varying degrees, but clearly the actors with higher prestige and centrality tend to be the experts and expert non-experts. While the CIO may participate in formal organisational meetings, it seems far fewer IT people in this organisation generally do. At least 15 people (if not 16) participate in informal meetings, as one individual did not participate in the research; only nine took part in formal meetings.

Summary

With respect to the actors themselves, the expertness of individuals is not necessarily a direct indicator of high prestige or centrality. However, there is at least a weak positive correlation between the latter parameters and elitism of actors in all three organisations. Whereas firms X and Z are similar in mission and composition, Y provides a balance that also coincides with differences in tacit knowledge diffusion likelihood. That Organisation Y has but one clique is certainly a useful indicator that all staff network and share their tacit knowledge effectively. Although many more cliques exist in Organisation Z and either experts or ENEs are spread throughout both of them, some cliques certainly could be considered more disadvantaged with regard to novices attaining access to tacit knowledge savvy individuals. In many ways Organisation Z may not have quite the staff diversity of Organisation X; however it would appear the CIO in the case of the former acts as the focus for tacit knowledge diffusion. The CIO in comparison is nowhere near as central in Organisation X. Firm Y on the other hand operates in a far less hierarchical way with knowledge pooled readily amongst the staff. The centralization indices of each of the organisations bear this out as well. Clearly Y has no centre and this is evident not only in examining the firm's structure chart, but also the single clique arrangement. The centralisation index of 0 percent is not surprising. Organisation Z on the other hand, with a centralization figure of 47.5 percent represents a structure that revolves around some key players, the CIO being one of them. However other actors such as expert 3340E are almost equally, if not equally prominent. The largest firm, X, has a low centralization figure of 2.62 percent, but this is not surprising when one examines its broad 3 macro-level cliques. Typically within these macro-cliques are to be found 54 micro-cliques in which no particularly prominent actors take a particularly pivotal role. The size of the firm and its dispersed physical layout would understandably inhibit this. While tacit knowledge is not likely to be severely bottlenecked in Organisation Z, the author is of the opinion that transfer is likely to be far less easy than for example in Organisation Y. Organisation X on the other hand will almost certainly not achieve the same level of tacit knowledge diffusion as Y.

References

Fernie, S., Green, S., Weller, S., & Newcombe, R. (2003). Knowledge sharing: Context, confusion, and controversy. *International Journal of Project Management, 21*(3), 177-187.

Hansen, M. (1999). The search-transfer problem: The role of weak ties in sharing knowledge across organizational subunits. *Administrative Science Quarterly, 44*(1), 82-111.

Jüttner, C. (1980). Nichtbewußtes Wissen, Mustererkennung und der Entwurf eines Gedächtnismodells. *Psychologische Beiträge, 22*(1), 70-87.

Liebowitz, J. (2005). Linking social network analysis with the analytic hierarchy process for knowledge mapping in organizations. *Journal of Knowledge Management, 9*(1), 76-86.

Endnote

[a] Language Other than English

Section V

This fifth section of the book, covering Chapters XIV and XV, provides the reader with the conclusions and recommendations to arise from the study. Chapter XIV revealed there were a number of parameters that would influence organisational knowledge flows varying from organisational type along Mintzberg lines, through to the composition of the workforce, to the extent to which electronic forms of communication were being made use of and so on. Finally, Chapter XV presents some recommendations for organisations including among which are use of appropriate mentoring arrangements, the adoption of the tacit knowledge inventory as shown in appendix F to identify potential ICT management candidates and the use of Social Network Analysis to identify potential tacit knowledge voids.

Chapter XIV

Discussion

... Transfer of tacit knowledge needs complicated administrative, organizational, and monitoring support that tends to be only available to large firms. Second, in comparison with large firms, small firms usually do not have the resources or expertise to exploit tacit knowledge in its most sophisticated forms; rather, these small firms have a distinctive marketing style characterized by little or no adherence to formal structures and frameworks, and by heavy reliance on intuitive ideas, decisions, and common sense (Cavusgil, Calantone, & Zhao, 2003, pp. 11-12).

Larger communities of knowledge can share certain practices, routines, and languages, but for new tacit knowledge to emerge through socialization the group must be small (von Krogh, Ichijo, and Nonaka, 2000 in Allred, 2001, p. 162).

Introduction

One must, after reading the above two quotes, make up one's own mind as to the composition of tacit knowledge, for it seems Cavusgil et al., (2003) are certainly not discussing the *same* tacit knowledge as von Krogh et al. (2000). The tacit knowledge studied herein is more akin to that discussed by the latter set of authors, that is to say a form of knowledge that is passed through what Nonaka and colleagues have labelled socialisation in intimate person to person settings. In time the organisation builds up a stock of such soft knowledge, which is lost when staff leave and not replaced again either until further skilled staff arrive, or the ones remaining acquire it through experience over time. Whilst earlier work in this empirical study examined the phenomenon of tacit knowledge in depth (including a multitude of definitions as revealed in Appendix A), what was ultimately settled upon for the empirical research in this study was that of *articulable implicit managerial IT knowledge*.

Tacit Knowledge within the Context of this Research

Why is it the above two sets of authors differed so greatly with regard to their discussion of organisational tacit knowledge? In many ways, the former definition examines tacit knowledge from an accounting point of view with regard to articulation and capture of the knowledge into an expert system. The organisational emphasis of the first quote is focused on *articulation* and best practice with regard to "capturing" soft knowledge to aid in organisational learning processes. The conduct of the research in this book has *not* been along those lines, or with those aims in mind. Rather, the focus here has been more along the lines of the second quote, namely an examination of issues relating to tacit knowledge *diffusion* in an IT domain, using a variety of organisations to add rigour to the research. That is to say focusing on that portion of the tacit knowledge conception cycle Nonaka and colleagues refer to as *socialisation*. Although an inter-organisational comparison was not one of the original goals of the study, the idea for using three separate organisations arose out of a need to examine whether the organisational type (along Mintzberg lines) was likely to affect tacit knowledge diffusion in the firm. Evidence would seem to suggest there was a difference in the transfer likelihood based on organisational characteristics, chief among which was size.

The reader may recall the initial qualitative research using grounded theory had established that tacit knowledge was (1) largely individualistic, (2) organisationally based, and (3) contextual. All of these parameters meant that a laboratory conduct of study within academe would have been unsuitable. In conducting the research a number of controls needed to be implemented. First it was considered desirable to undertake empirical research within an outside world context, that is to say non-purely theoretical work. Many studies of a truly empirical nature are often conducted on undergraduate students which whilst permitting larger sample sizes nevertheless limit the study to typically inexperienced students in any given subject area. Conversely, conducting research in an organisational domain is compounded by the difficulties inherent in gaining management permission for staff to be distracted from their tasks for the sake of pleasing the visiting researcher. Then there is the issue of the staff itself. Typically students tend to be compliant. They respect the role of the teacher/researcher and are generally happy to comply if faculty wish them to participate in a study. Those who do not actually participate tend be small in number. Organisationally based staff members, who in our domain tend to be university graduates, are naturally far more independently minded. They do not *have* to participate, especially if the research is to be conducted non-anonymously. They are often very busy, and at their stage of lives are likely to have commitments outside of their workplaces. Furthermore, as they are graduates, they have expectations about the value of their time, to that end there is less impetus for them to devote half an hour, let alone two hours to investigations, particularly when they are not likely to see or experience the results of the study.

Second, the firms themselves were chosen for their differences. Even allowing for the fact that organisations do not typically leap at the opportunity to participate in research, it was determined they should at least be diverse in makeup. Whilst two of them were typical IT service providers to the wider organisation (X and Z), this was balanced with a small information systems management consultancy that had a cottage industry feel to it. The intention of the research was to establish likely tacit knowledge flows (or indeed bottlenecks) specifically in the IT sector, not in any other discipline. Remember these firms were chosen, because they represented examples of what may be called small (Y), medium (Z) and large (X) organisations. They were Mintzberg professional bureaucracies, although in the case of the first and last organisation might have been considered (Mintzberg) machine in nature. Finally, they all happened to be within the private sector.

Third, the participants in the study were required to be IT professionals. The reason for this stipulation was that the inventory itself was to be based on IT managerial situations, for which it was felt individuals who were neither professional or in the IT domain would be able to answer competently. Nevertheless allowance was made for the inclusion of ACS level 0's as some clerical IT staff had expressed an interest in participating in the research, nonetheless the overwhelming majority of the participants were university graduates (or their workplace equivalent in terms of work experience). The results demonstrated a fairly clear bell curve with a large proportion of respondents at level 3, that is to say personnel experienced in specialised IT areas. Naturally there were few level 5s (CIOs). As a point of interest, there were also very few level 1s (recent graduates).

Parameters in Knowledge Diffusion

According to Cavusgil et al., (2003) both organisational and workgroup size (Hansen, 1999) *should* have an impact on knowledge transfer, including of course tacit knowledge transfer. The studies reported in this book seem to confirm this. Smaller firms and workgroups do appear more likely to be successful at transferring tacit knowledge. This is also shown to be the case in the work of Nonaka (von Krogh et al., 2000 in Allred, 2001), who had conceded for tacit knowledge to be transferred in an intra-organisational setting, the group size must necessarily be small. Indeed Hansen (1999) had alluded to the same principles but added that networks of ties needed to be strong and continual for tacit knowledge to be effectively transferred. Previous studies have provided very little in the way of empirical evidence for these claims however.[a]

Another important variable concerned the extent to which electronic communication was made use of in the three firms. The situation in Organisation Y was very straightforward, as no specific such means of communication were identified. Organisation Z had made extensive use of e-mail, but face-to-face meetings took place on at least a daily if not hourly basis for all concerned. Organisation X saw somewhat more use of phone and e-mail but really only between macro level cliques. Remember the survey instrument did not ask for Web/Internet enabled forms of communication such as podcasting, Web conferencing and so on.

As a reminder to the reader, the next section steps through the organisations and examines the tacit knowledge diffusion implications for each. Before summarising such outcomes, let us examine what has been covered in the book so far. The book has been divided into a number of sections. The first section explored the knowledge management domain and the sub-domain of tacit knowledge specifically. The first chapter outlined the aims for wishing to examine the management of the tacit knowledge resource within the firm. The second chapter explored the discipline of knowledge management as a way of setting the stage for the discussion on tacit knowledge that would follow. Chapter 3 then provided a review of the literature concerning tacit knowledge and provided a general discussion of its character. Through the adoption of grounded theory a definition of tacit knowledge became *articulable implicit IT managerial knowledge*.

The second section of the book introduced the reader to the logistics of testing for tacit knowledge in organisations and how flows of knowledge can be measured, culminating with explaining the widely accepted technique of Social Network Analysis. It was the role of Chapter 4 to introduce ways researchers could undertake empirical testing of tacit knowledge. The reader will have noted there are limitations in ways of doing so for logistical and political reasons. Although a few practical approaches exist, a commonly accepted way is to use Sternberg's workplace scenarios as a means of measuring differences between personnel in organisations. At the same time, Formal Concept Analysis was introduced as a means to interpreting questionnaire date where statistical analysis was not considered satisfactory. Chapter 5 introduced the concept of organisations, and then the three firms under study here. A Mintzberg framework was utilised and the participating organisations placed within this. Chapter 6 introduced the concept of knowledge flows and the sorts of parameters that will affect them. These included culture, either at the organisational or individual/ethnic level. More recent research (Busch 2007-2008, yet to be published) examines the role of ethnicity, generations (Baby Boomer, Generation X, and Generation Y) and gender with regard to the knowledge management of tacit or soft knowledge in the IT domain; however this monograph discussed the role of culture at the organisational level. Another parameter affecting diffusion was the role of IT. Yet another parameter was human networks and particularly the relationship formality between individuals, which relates to the strength of ties between individuals. Chapter 7 introduced the first of the techniques and tools that were used in producing the results for this monograph, namely that of Social Network Analysis. Given that Chapter 6 had illustrated human networks were important for the flow of soft knowledge, it was SNA that arguably provided the best means of measuring or viewing this flow between personnel.

Section three comprised only of Chapter 8, provided the methodology or conduct of study used to gain results.

The fourth section presented the results from the empirical research of all three of the firms. More specifically, Chapter 9 illustrated initial results, including the results of a statistical test (Wilcoxon test). Chapter 10 demonstrated there was an alternative to statistical testing, yet still maintaining rigour, this form of result processing was through Formal Concept Analysis, a graph based approach, which was used to examine questionnaire results with a finer level of granularity than would be possible using statistics only. The use of FCA also allowed the identification of another group of individuals who were just as soft knowledge savvy as their peers but not recognised by their peers as such. Chapter 11 explored the results of Organisation X with a focus on SNA. Chapter 12 presented results for Company Y, and Chapter thirteen for Organisation Z.

There is one final matter before turning the attention to summarising the results from the organisations. Although the work conducted in this book was based at an underlying level on interpretivism, the research conducted has been largely positivistic. Whereas interpretevism recognises that generalisations cannot necessarily be drawn[b] from one or even perhaps several case studies, it nevertheless is felt desirable to summarise the findings in general so that some benefit for similar sized organisations be obtained. The overarching methodology and instruments adopted in the book do take a positivist approach, which is to say two things. First that the conduct of experimentation should be replicable should others wish to follow suit, and second that the results should be generalisable. With these points in mind, Organisation X is summarised first.

Organisation X (Large)

Organisation X was certainly the most challenging of the firms to come to terms with. The size of the company under study; the diversity of its population; the physical layout of the offices spread throughout several buildings and the levels of hierarchy within the firm, all represent challenges to any phenomenologist.[c] It would appear from this research that whilst relations between colleagues in the organisation were generally more than cordial, some bottlenecking could be seen to be occurring with certain work groups tending to avoid one another. Admittedly the avoidance of colleagues was a minor issue. There only seemed to be one particular group displaying indication of this behaviour. The majority of personnel made at least monthly, if not daily contact with one another.

The physical layout of the organisation presents a problem if one desires face-to-face contact. Certainly knowledge management practitioners argue face-to-face means of contact are possible if using **teleconferencing**, for one does not necessarily need to meet in the same room.

Respondents were not asked this question at the time of the data collection. With staff spread over a number of states (of which only two were sampled), meant that there was a strong likelihood that cliques would form at the local level, while management as in any bureaucratic organisation would take an overall leadership role and spread knowledge around at their level, but not necessarily at levels lower down. "Filtering down" of knowledge will require personnel at each location; clearly this is an area where teleconferencing can "cut corners." From a physical location perspective, one saw how ICT staff members were spread over a number of floors in the same building. The SNA diagrams illustrated a number of cliques formed along the lines of floor, upon which staff were located. Not surprisingly the back office personnel also maintained tighter groups than the front office staff, which in some ways is a positive. One would expect teams of programmers and analysts working in carrels to maintain close links with one another. Front office staff such as salespersons or managers one would contrarily expect to be more dispersed as their mission involves establishing contact with clientele external to the company, or perhaps internal, but external to one's particular work section.

Where electronic mediums of communication were drawn upon, there was some usage of phones, faxes and e-mail as expected in most modern firms. Interestingly the extent of this electronic communication was not significant insofar as it affected clique formation. It is surprising given how pervasive phones, faxes, and e-mails are in the modern organisation, that use of them in Organisation X is actually quite minimal (Figures 11.26 and 11.27). Even had more modern forms of electronic communication been allowed for in the questionnaire, it is doubtful many more personnel would have answered in the affirmative. It is the author's opinion based on a number of years of experience, that teleconferencing is not undertaken by all levels of staff within a company. Rather it presents a means of communication through which various levels of management and to a lesser degree professional level staff within the organisation, can establish some means of face-to-face contact, where flying to a meeting is either too expensive or time consuming. The impact of more modern forms of teleconferencing using ones own terminal with a camera mounted on top, remains to be seen and would make an interesting study. Even given the absence of high levels of electronic communication, viewing the SNA graphs one can see personnel still maintained contacts with one another regardless of their phone/faxing/e-mail communication patterns. Considering as some of the literature suggests that electronic communication acts as a tacit knowledge transferral limiter, then there is little to worry about in Organisation X and next to nothing to worry about in the other two companies.

With regard to interactions of employees in the company, some of the interaction and mentoring patterns within the firm could be improved. For example certain **"power" clique**s could be seen to comprise dense networks of colleagues in certain work areas, whereas other "novice" colleagues could be seen to be missing out on access to groups high in tacit knowledge density. Remembering that social network analysis measures of degree, betweenness, global, and information centrality did not show a perfect or even strong positive correlation between higher measures on these performance indicators and elite-ness (where elite was defined as expert or expert non-expert), one perceives an organisation that could improve its mentoring of novices.

The issue of access to expert knowledge is paramount to almost every organisation, and it is for this reason that KM comes into play. Whether the technique adopted is that of codifying use knowledge bases such as Lotus Notes, adopting storytelling or establishing communities of practice, organisations need to draw increasingly heavily upon their knowledge capital. The access and adoption of this knowledge capital is more important than ever due the need in the case of western firms to compete on a knowledge footing, considering secondary industry is now effectively being accomplished offshore. For western or westernised countries not overly prolific in primary industry (Britain and Japan representing but a couple of possible examples, due to both their small relative sizes, but highly developed economies), the need to thus focus heavily on maximising knowledge capital in their tertiary, quaternary and quinary sectors is critical.[d]

Australia is no exception to this rule, and various governments both progressive and conservative, have talked up the notion for Australia to embrace the concept of being or at least becoming a "knowledge nation". Becoming such a nation requires embracing the concept of knowledge capital at a far lower level, including of course the workplace.

Organisation Y (Small)

In many ways the dynamics of Organisation Y have proved ideal with regard to the intra-organisational transfer of tacit knowledge. The "boutique" size of the firm and the dense social interaction patterns have combined to form a harmonious working environment where all members are well interconnected and transfer their knowledge on a solidly face-to-face basis. The advantages of soft knowledge transfer in this firm are compounded by the general lack of electronic means of interaction indicating that wherever possible the employees see passing knowledge in a personal setting as preferable. The frequency with which meetings are conducted in this organisation indicates that any misunderstandings, which might occur because of a possible loss of tacit knowledge transfer, can easily be remedied given the almost hourly contact that takes place between the staff. A further advantage for the firm is the physical layout of the offices and buildings, which illustrates a firm that is able to make maximum use of its intra-organisational communication.

The staff makeup of this organisation was also very different. They were largely **mono-cultural** and typically experienced in IT. What is interesting are the few staff (two) members who tend to "bump into one another." This is interesting, because again the physical layout of the building is such that it comprises only four to five rooms and is located on the one floor. One gets the impression that staff members have simply overlooked this option in the questionnaire, either that, or they bump into one another so often that they don't give it much consideration. From the researcher's experience with the firm, this is a company where daily face-to-face contact represents the norm as consultants come together to discuss the projects they are working on for outside clientele. There is no doubt when considering all of the parameters for this firm, that tacit knowledge transferral is likely to be very high indeed, indeed for a firm of this type it is a necessity for survival.

Organisation Z (Medium)

In many ways this sized firm is perhaps the most interesting. It would appear that the potential for soft knowledge to flow is high in this firm given the fairly intimate size of its work-group and their location within the same building. There are examples of tacit knowledge bottlenecking occurring here. Factors that affect the knowledge flow for this firm include for example the number of cliques. Unlike the small organisation with only one clique, this medium sized firm displays thirteen. Fortunately elites are found in all of the cliques, unlike the situation that exists in the large firm (X). The number of cliques in turn also indicates a certain hierarchy with few appearing to need to contact the CIO, even though he does participate in almost all cliques. Whilst numerous cliques by themselves do not necessarily present a problem, what could be improved in an organisation of this size is greater tacit knowledge diffusion with regard to improving the staffing composition of the cliques.

There is an argument on the other hand that this number of cliques for such a small IT staff complement means that opinions are likely to flow readily enough among clique members. If there are "street smarts" that are known by members in one clique, then the overlap of these members in other cliques is likely to transfer this knowledge successfully. For example, it would appear that the network densities reflect a weak positive correlation with the tacitness quotient of the individuals. In other words, those people who one would expect to have higher readings of tacit knowledge (our experts and ENEs) have lower network densities. Concurrently, these people tend to be connected with higher numbers of individuals. Furthermore, there appears to be a situation in this firm (and arguably in ones of similar size), where a pattern emerges that indicates whilst experts may not be the most oft contacted or making contact, they do appear to have the highest prestige rating in relation to values of person importance. Therefore, while a help desk officer or perhaps a contractor may be important to contact, they are not necessarily considered quite as *important* in general as an expert, unless the contractor also happens to be an expert.[e] Finally, there is some utilization of electronic means of communication. The use of e-mail is extensive, and where it not for the fact that the staff complement is small enough and that staff are seeing one another in other forms of meetings, there would be some cause for concern. This sized organisation clearly seems to feel it requires electronic mediums of data transfer, but not quite to the extent of the large firm.

Optimal Firm

Tacit knowledge can be gained through personal experience. Nevertheless, should it need to be transferred from one individual to the next, this must ordinarily take place through verbal and visual interaction. Generally speaking, it would appear the larger the organisation, the more the firm is inclined towards electronic forms of data administration and transfer. There would appear, from the results presented here, to be a strong positive correlation between organisational size and diminishing ease with which tacit knowledge *is* being transferred. Furthermore, the research seems to indicate that there is not a strong positive correlation between technically qualified or formally qualified personnel and their tacit knowledge richness. Nor for that matter is there a strong positive correlation between increasing age and tacit knowledge richness.

Based on these observations, from a tacit knowledge transfer effectiveness point of view the **optimal firm** would be that of Y. That is to say a small firm along the lines of an operating adhocracy (Lam, 2000) or perhaps professional bureaucracy (Mintzberg, 1991a). What more specifically were the factors that were helpful here? These factors included first of all a single clique arrangement. There is no doubt a single grouping of staff where all are interacting and there are no isolates is going to be ideal from a knowledge transferral point of view. Even if one of the members decides never to talk, their body language would provide plenty of information, which would naturally be interpreted through contextual knowledge. Second, if a closeness ratio of 100 percent exists, this also means all staff members are connected. Third, a betweenness ratio of 0 percent means there is a lack of (communication) steps from one individual to the next; in other words, each individual is *directly* connected. The importance of direct communication cannot be underestimated. There are countless examples where the use of communication intermediaries has entirely changed the message that is being transferred. Probably one of the more famous examples dates from the trenches in the First World War (1914-1918), where the instruction being given was "send reinforcements, we are going to advance" which became "send three and four pence, we are going to a dance!"[f] Another benefit Organisation Y has is a lack of widespread use of electronic forms of communication; even though it is true face-to-face forms of electronic communication would (although to a somewhat limited degree) enable the tacit knowledge transferral process.

Another benefit that makes Organisation Y a good forum for tacit knowledge transferral relates to the dense communication patterns, insofar as daily meetings involved all the staff. Furthermore, no staff members were strongly avoided, many meetings in this firm were largely informal and the staff all occupied the same floor of the building. The character of the staff themselves will also have a positive effect on knowledge transferral. Given that the organisation revolves around a management consultancy, which is naturally communication intensive, it is a benefit to the company that the staff are senior management types, a role that is by definition strongly communication based. These management employees are also mainly Anglo-Celtic Australians meaning cultural distance is reduced. Finally, the staff members hold each other in high esteem, given that the overwhelming majority were selected as experts, although the cynic might interpret this behaviour as egotistical. In view of these factors, it is highly unlikely that tacit knowledge bottlenecking could be said to be taking place, certainly not on any noticeable scale. It is highly probable that similar sized firms with similar communication patterns would also be effective in transferring their tacit knowledge.

In terms, therefore, of tacit knowledge diffusion likelihood, the firm best placed for its transfer is clearly the small one (Y), but the next best would have to be the medium one (Z) followed by X.

One could with *some* degree of certainty make claims to the effect, that the larger the firm the less likely tacit knowledge is to be successfully transferred from one individual to the next. To this end the model proposed by Busch and Dampney (2000) maintains its validity with regard to tacit knowledge and organisational size.[g] Somewhat similar research by Cavusgil et al. (2003) indicated the same pattern. Having examined the tacit knowledge flow and bottleneck issues in the three companies, let us return to answering the research questions, goals and assumptions. For ease of reading they are reproduced below, but now include a series of short answers to each question.

Observations

There are a number of parameters that are definitely going to affect soft knowledge flows. The size of the organisation is one parameter. The smaller the company, the more of a cottage industry feel it has about it, the higher the likelihood the company will make great use of tacit knowledge in its day to day activities. As the size increases, the organisation tends to become more bureaucratic, knowledge has to be codified and there are increasing numbers of employees such that they cannot all see one another on a regular basis. The physical layout of the firm will also play a part, for where staff members naturally are in a position to visually see each other they are far more likely to engage in some sort of conversation, also involving body language which will transfer tacit knowledge.

The age groups of employees are another factor that can be expected to have an impact of tacit knowledge creation and flow within the organisational context. Current research (Busch, Venkitachalam, & Richards, 2007-2008 yet to be published), indicates that between generations employees may actually be processing ICT tacit knowledge in different ways. **Generation**s are defined in this case as Baby Boomers (1945 to 1964), Generation X (1965 to 1979), and Generation Y as 1980 to present. The dates given for these generations also are in line with Yu and Miller (2005). There is certainly evidence to suggest that younger employees are more IT savvy, especially with regard to Generation Y (Jorgensen, 2003; Stein & Craig, 2000; Todd, Mardis, & Wyatt, 2005). This is so firstly because they are a generation that have grown up with computers as the norm in their day-to-day lives and second because the Internet as a viable resource, really only began with the appearance of Mosiac as the first sophisticated search engine in the early 1990s. As we all know, Mosiac forever changed the face of the World Wide Web such that we now take Netscape Navigator, Internet Explorer and Mozilla Firefox for granted.

The differences in the generations are exemplified in a number of ways, including their uptake of technology, their ambition in the workforce, their commitment to the workplace and their expectations with regard to job security (Amar, 2004; Jorgensen, 2003). This last parameter in particular has changed the power status in many organisations as younger employees are less likely to recognize or care about issues of status where their parents may have done.

Generational difference is an issue for engaging in KM. For example, it has been noted by Amar (2004) that Generation Y is not motivated in the same way as X or the Baby Boomers before them. Whereas Boomers and X expected to graduate from formal education and work their way up the company ladder one step at a time, Generation Y expects to change jobs every couple of years, are far less interested in the corporate ladder, and require motivation to stay in the same position and/or company (Martin, 2005), a trend known as "job-hopping" (Bova & Kroth, 2001).

There is a renewed necessity to capitalise on knowledge that is in the heads of employees, who (a) may either not be as present on a day to day basis as workers in the past, and (b) may have trouble communicating as effectively or perhaps may communicate in another way as compared with workers of the past. There are knowledge management ramifications of having several generations in a workforce. For example in an earlier study, Bova and Kroth (1999, p.12) had identified some relevant parameters: "(1) work and the work environment must support continuing learning; (2) mentors and organizational leaders must lead by example and (3) Generation X employees place major importance upon living multidimensional lives." There are also knowledge transfer implications for a workplace that is not tuned to its generations (Syed-Ikhsan & Rowland, 2004).

Generational differences in IT soft knowledge handling has also been examined (Busch et al., 2007-2008, yet to be published). It was found that there were four parameters that depicted differences across the three generations. These were issues with regard to the handling of status; principles of commitment to the workplace; the need by younger generations in particular for recognition of their achievements; and the idealistic attitudes displayed by Generation X and even more so by Generation Y. It was also found that these parameters influenced desired soft knowledge outcomes, such as maturity in work practices displayed by the Baby Boomers; open and frank knowledge exchange and reduced employee turnover and so on.

Another parameter examined relates to the differences between **genders** in their processing of tacit knowledge (Richards, Busch, & Venkitachalam, 2007-2008 yet to be published). It was noticed that certain of the tacit knowledge scenarios were approached differently depending on gender. While there is no right or wrong way to respond to a particular scenario answer option, some strategies will work better than others depending on the situation and the people involved. For example, some of the scenarios relate to seeking help or cooperation from others. It seems that males try to solve problems by themselves where the incorporation of input from other team members would actually produce better results. At the same time, it seems the female cohort was more likely to try to seek input from others. These generalizations are not a great surprise and align with many of Broverman, Vogel, Broverman, Clarkson, and Rozenkrantz's (1972) characterisations and common gender stereotypes. We are finding that an important message for organisations is that a mix of genders will probably achieve the best result when it comes to soft knowledge utilisation and transfer. Understanding these differences will lead to better soft knowledge management and innovation.

Finally, there is some indication (Busch 2006) that organisation type along Mintzberg (1991a, b, c, d, e) lines will also have an impact on tacit knowledge transferral. It is likely that the entrepreneurial firm and the operating adhocracy are the most likely to use and exchange their tacit knowledge assets. With these points in mind, which factors determine an optimal firm for soft knowledge diffusion? All of these parameters will naturally have an affect on how KM takes place within the organisation, from the successfulness or otherwise of the establishment of knowledge networks, the usefulness of "storytelling" or the degree to which the implementation of knowledge bases using Lotus Notes or similar tools will be beneficial in the long run.

Research Questions

At this stage, let us revisit the research questions that were posited in chapter five. First of all, we wished to know if "there were observable tacit knowledge differences between how 'experts' handled the tacit knowledge issues in the organisation from those of novices? In other words, how did experts differ in their approaches to those of novices?" The answer here was in the affirmative, depending on the tacit knowledge situations posed. There were certain identifiable areas where experts differed from "others" with regard to how they would deal with IT managerial workplace situations from both an ethical and realistic point of view. While statistical tests indicated only minor differences between the two groups, the use of Formal Concept Analysis did permit a finer level of granularity of data interpretation, which revealed more significant differences.

The second research question was "could we identify other tacit knowledge rich personnel based on the similarity of their answers with that of the expert group?" The answer here was another group of tacit knowledge rich personnel *were* identified in the course of the research, largely through the use again of Formal Concept Analysis. This group of actors were not identified by their peers as experts but scored test results close to that of experts. As such they were considered to also be a valuable source of tacit knowledge. This group were referred to as expert non-experts (ENE). The value of using FCA to answer this question cannot be underestimated. The finer level of granularity that the technique afforded permitted us to examine results down at the level of the individual and compare these results across the board. Using a statistical approach would have meant collapsing the data into numerical cohorts where the results of an individual across all questions would have been harder to identify.

The third research question was "were there certain biographical parameters (i.e., age, gender, ethnicity, years of IT experience, ACS level, highest formal qualification) that differentiated IS individuals who have accumulated more tacit knowledge from those with significantly less tacit knowledge? To which end, we can answer that biographical parameters did not play a *significant* role with regard to tacit knowledge utilisation and IS personnel. Furthermore, there was *some* evidence for experts being on the whole either younger or older than the average age of personnel included in the study. That is to say, experts seemed to be well represented on the left and right ends of a bell curve. It has also been discovered, in all three companies, that experts are *not* particularly well qualified formally with regard to technical computing credentials. Experts were also *not* noted to be of a particularly high ACS level (4 or 5), or necessarily even the most formally qualified personnel, that is to say having any qualification higher than a pass/ordinary bachelors degree. No significant differences could be found with regard to gender and how tacit knowledge usage differed. There was *some* indication for a higher than average distribution in Organisation X of experts being of Chinese extraction (proportionately speaking with regard to all the ethnic groups represented). All of these outcomes certainly were true at the time of data processing; however more recent research (Busch et al., 2007-2008 yet to be published) is revealing there are some differences amongst cultures at the ethnic level in terms of how they are handling these ICT soft knowledge situations. There also appear to be differences among the genders in terms of how they deal with tacit knowledge, and also at the generational level (Baby Boomer, Generation X, and Generation Y).

The fourth research question was "do people clique with one another based on biographical factors such as ethnicity? If so, does it affect tacit knowledge transfer?" To which we can say there was little evidence for cliquing on the basis of ethnicity. There was however some evidence for cliquing amongst Chinese speakers, a number of whom were considered experts. However, the overwhelmingly multicultural nature of Organisations X and Z meant that cliquing on the basis of ethnicity was not possible to any but a very minor degree. There was found to be negligible evidence of cliquing on the basis of any of the other biographical factors. Had the organisations been less ethnically diverse, but with larger numbers of certain groups, then it is felt there would be a stronger likelihood that cliquing along ethnic lines would probably take place.

The fifth research question asked "is there evidence of tacit knowledge "bottlenecking"[h] taking place?" To which we can answer, there exists evidence for small-scale tacit knowledge bottlenecking in Organisation Z. Somewhat more bottlenecking appears to take place in Organisation X. No major bottlenecking appears to occur in Organisation Y. Although this is perhaps the most important research question for the KM practitioner, it also is the hardest one to answer. Again it is very difficult if not impossible to gauge the degree to which soft knowledge transfer is taking place between individuals. Social Network Analysis provides the researcher with one tool to gauge if knowledge transfer is happening, however this is based on the presumption that an interaction will lead to knowledge transfer. There is no absolute way of knowing, other than reading people's minds.

The final research question asked "are there observable differences in knowledge diffusion patterns between IS personnel depending upon the character of the organisation?" To which we can answer the size of the organisation would appear to be the greatest determinant *indirectly* with regard to whether tacit knowledge is likely to be effectively transferred from tacit knowledge rich personnel to lesser knowledge rich personnel. It would appear the smaller the firm the more likely its members will communicate on a face-to-face basis and therefore make use of and pass around tacit forms of knowledge. Other factors include the extent to which companies make use of electronic forms of communication, which by their nature generally *do not* transmit tacit knowledge. Another factor affecting diffusion was the density of cliques; Organisation Y involved the most connected actors who formed one clique, while Organisation X had a number of cliques involving actors who had no direct access in their clique to a tacit knowledge rich actor (either expert or expert non-expert). Organisation Z whilst quite centralised nevertheless had 13 cliques where tacit knowledge rich actors were present in each of these cliques.

Summary

Perhaps some of the more obvious findings uncovered here are that there are a number of parameters affecting tacit knowledge utilisation and transfer. Commencing from the outside, the classification type of the organisation will have some affect. Certain organisations are by their very mission going to be tacit knowledge rich and others far more heavily reliant on a codified knowledge base. Within the organisation itself, the number of employees, departments and work teams is going to affect how reliant the company is on codifying their knowledge and trying where possible to codify their tacit knowledge. At the level of the employees themselves, there are also a number of parameters that will affect how well the tacit knowledge is likely to flow. Ethnic differences, how proficiently and extensively a common language such as English is utilised by the employees, their gender and also their age group along generational lines, will all have a bearing on how well tacit knowledge is made use of and then transferred. At this stage, let us turn our attention to the final component of this book, namely the directions for future research.

References

Allred, B. (2001). Enabling knowledge creation: How to unlock the mystery of tacit knowledge and release the power of innovation. *The Academy of Management Executive, 15*(1), 161-162.

Amar, A.D. (2004). Motivating knowledge workers to innovate: A model integrating motivation dynamics and antecedents. *European Journal of Innovation Management, 7*(2), 89-101.

Bova, B., & Kroth, M. (2001). Workplace learning and Generation X. *Journal of Workplace Learning, 13*(2), 57-65.

Broverman, I., Vogel, S., Broverman, D., Clarkson, F., & Rozenkrantz, P. (1972). Sex-role stereotypes: A current appraisal. *Journal of Social Issues, 28*(2), 59-79.

Busch, P. (2006). Organisation design and tacit knowledge transferal: An examination of three IT firms. *Journal of Knowledge Management Practice, 7*(2). Retrieved October 19, 2006 from http://www.tlainc.com/articl111.htm

Busch, P., & Dampney, C. (2000). Tacit knowledge acquisition and processing within the computing domain: An exploratory study. *2000 Information Resources Management Association International Conference,* Anchorage, AK, 1014-1015.

Cavusgil, S.T., Calantone, R.J., & Zhao, Y. (2003). Tacit knowledge transfer and firm innovation capacity. *Journal of Business and Industrial Marketing, 18*(1), 6-21.

Hansen, M. (1999). The search-transfer problem: The role of weak ties in sharing knowledge across organizational subunits. *Administrative Science Quarterly, 44*(1), 82-111.

Jorgensen, B. (2003). Baby Boomers, Generation X and Generation Y: Policy implications for defence forces in the modern era. *Foresight, 5*(4), 41-49.

Lam, A. (2000). Tacit knowledge, organizational learning, and societal institutions: An integrated framework. *Organization Studies, 21*(3), 487-513.

Martin, C. (2005). From high maintenance to high productivity: What managers need to know about Generation Y. *Industrial and Commercial Training, 37*(1), 39-44.

Mintzberg, H. (1991a). The professional organisation. In *The Strategy Process: Concepts, Contexts, Cases,* 2nd Ed. Englewood Cliffs, NJ: Prentice Hall, pp. 704-717.

Mintzberg, H. (1991b). The entrepreneurial organisation. In *The Strategy Process: Concepts, Contexts, Cases,* 2nd Ed. Englewood Cliffs, NJ: Prentice Hall, 604-613.

Mintzberg, H. (1991c). The machine organisation. In *The Strategy Process: Concepts, Contexts, Cases,* 2nd Ed. Englewood Cliffs, NJ: Prentice Hall, pp. 630-646.

Mintzberg, H. (1991d). The diversified organisation. In *The Strategy Process: Concepts, Contexts, Cases,* 2nd Ed. Englewood Cliffs, NJ: Prentice Hall, pp. 666-677.

Mintzberg, H. (1991e). The innovative organisation. In *The Strategy Process: Concepts, Contexts, Cases,* 2nd Ed. Englewood Cliffs, NJ: Prentice Hall, pp. 731-746.

Neuman, W. (1997). *Social research methods : Qualitative and quantitative approaches,* 3rd ed. Boston: Allyn and Bacon.

Nonaka, I. (1991). The knowledge creating company. *Harvard Business Review, 69*(6), 96-104.

Nonaka, I., Ray, T., & Umemoto, K. (1998). Japanese organizational knowledge creation in Anglo – American Environments. *Prometheus, 16*(4), 421-439.

Nonaka, I., Takeuchi, H., & Umemoto, K. (1996). A theory of organisational knowledge creation. *International Journal of Technology Management, 11*(7/8), 833-845.

Smith, E. (2001). The role of tacit and explicit knowledge in the workplace. *Journal of Knowledge Management, 5*(4), 311-321.

Stein, A., & Craig, A. (2000). The dot.com generation: IT practices & skills of transition students. *ACM International Conference Proceeding Series; Vol. 8 Proceedings of the Australasian Conference on Computing Education*, Melbourne, Australia, 220-227.

Syed-Ikhsan, S., & Rowland, F. (2004). Knowledge management in a public organization: A study on the relationship between organizational elements and the performance of knowledge transfer. *Journal of Knowledge Management, 8*(2), 95-111.

Todd, K., Mardis, L., & Wyatt, P. (2005). We've come a long way, baby! But where women and technology are concerned, have we really? *User Services Conference archive: Proceedings of the 33rd annual ACM SIGUCCS conference on User services,* Monterey, CA, 380-387.

von Krogh, G., Ichijo, K., & Nonaka, I. (2000). *Enabling knowledge creation: How to unlock the mystery of tacit knowledge and release the power of innovation.* New York: Oxford University Press, Inc.

Yu, H., & Miller, P. (2005). Leadership style: The X Generation and Baby Boomers compared in different cultural contexts. *Leadership & Organization Development Journal, 26*(1), 35-50.

Zackarias, P., Samiotis, K., & Poulymenakou, A. (2001). Learning in knowledge-incentive organisations: Methods and tools for enabling organisational learning processes. *7th International Conference on Concurrent Enterprising,* Bremen, Germany. Retrieved February 18, 2003 from: http://www.knowledgeboard.com/library/organisational_learning.pdf

Endnotes

[a]   "Zackarias et al. (2001, p. 7) and Smith (2001 p. 421) claim that adequate training may enable employees to translate their knowledge into the organisations tacit and explicit knowledge, whereas those who lack training will have to struggle to keep up. However, the Spearman test shows that there is no significant relationship between training and knowledge transfer performance but shows a positive significant relationship with knowledge assets" (Syed-Ikhsan & Rowland, 2004 pp. 108-109).

[b]   Neuman (1997) points out that whereas positivism attempts to generalise at the conclusion of research, interpretivistic scholarship treats each case on an individual basis, recognising the dangers in overgeneralisation. The treatment of the latter epistemology with regard to generalisation is indicative of its strongly human oriented focus where unlike the physical world one finding cannot necessarily be said to hold true for all findings.

[c]   Whilst the study was not intended to be specifically phenomenological, it is acknowledged by the writer that tacit knowledge is a phenomenon.

[d]   "The **tertiary sector** of industry (also known as the service sector or the service industry) is one of the three main industrial categories of a developed Economic economy, the others being the secondary industry (manufacturing), and primary industry (extraction such as mining, agriculture and fishing). Services are defined in conventional economic literature as 'intangible

goods.' The tertiary sector of industry involves the provision of services to businesses as well as final consumers. Services may involve the transport, distribution (business) and sale of goods from producer to a consumer as may happen in wholesaler wholesaling and retailer retailing, or may involve the provision of a service, such as in pest control or entertainment. Goods may be transformed in the process of providing a service, as happens in the restaurant industry. However, the focus is on people interacting with people and serving the customer rather than transforming physical goods. Since the 1960s, there has been a substantial shift from the other two industry sectors to the Tertiary Sector in industrialised countries. The service sector consists of the 'soft' parts of the economy such as insurance, tourism, banking, retail and education. In soft sector employment, people use time to deploy knowledge assets, collaboration assets, and process-engagement to create productivity (effectiveness), performance improvement potential (potential) and sustainability. Typically the output of this time is content (information), service, attention, advice, experiences, and/or discussion (aka, 'intangible goods'). Other examples of service sector employment include: Franchising, Restaurants, Retailer|Retailing, Entertainment, including the Record industry, Music industry, Radio, Television and Film Movies, News media, Leisure industry, Consulting, Transport, Healthcare" (Anon. *Tertiary Sector of Industry* URL: http://en.wikipedia.org/wiki/Tertiary_sector_of_industry accessed on 17th. October 2006).

"The **Quaternary sector** of industry is the sector of industry that involves the intellectual services. That is research, development, and information. It is considered the fourth basic industry out of all of them: primary, secondary, tertiary and quaternary. It was once, and by some still is, considered just a subset of the general service-oriented tertiary sector of industry This includes the high technology industry, with information and communication technology and some forms of scientific research, as well as education and consulting, and information industry. The quaternary sector can be seen as the sector in which companies invest in order to ensure further expansion. Research will be directed into cutting costs, tapping into markets, producing innovative ideas, new production methods and methods of manufacture, amongst others. To many industries, such as pharmaceutical giants such as Pfizer, the sector is the most valuable because it creates future branded products, which the company will profit from. According to some definitions, the quaternary sector also includes all other pure services, such as the entertainment industry. There is also the notion of a **'quinary sector'** which would encompass health, education, culture and research" (Care & Heard, 2006 *Quaternary Sector of Industry* URL: http://en.wikipedia.org/wiki/Quaternary_sector accessed on 17th October 2006).

[e]   In which case the expertness would tend to take precedence over the contract nature of employment.

[f]   "A common (likely apocryphal) story in the UK is of a general who sent the message "Send reinforcements, we are going to advance" back to HQ. After passing through many intermediaries it finally arrived as "Send three and fourpence, we are going to a dance" (*Chinese Whispers* URL: http://en.wikipedia.org/wiki/Telephone_(game) accessed 18th October 2006).

[g]   The schematic model proposed by Busch and Dampney (2000) (figure 2.5) was not necessarily intended to be tested within the research presented here. Rather the model represented a generalisation of trends that seemed to be present within the tacit knowledge literature.

[h]   In other words because of cliques in the organisation, has a bottleneck formed which fails to deliver tacit knowledge to a "disadvantaged" group? Where disadvantaged refers to a "tacit knowledge poor" or "expert-poor" group.

Chapter XV

Conclusion and Recommendations

A much quoted historical pronouncement by the late British Prime Minister Winston Churchill is that "The empires of the future are empires of the mind." Perhaps this comment has never been more visionary than now when OECD economies and organizations are restructuring around new managerial concepts such as: knowledge management; knowledge, groupware and the Internet; the learning and teaching organization; and collaborative intelligence. In the future the strength of organizations and their economic value-adding to the economy will depend more than ever on knowledge where issues such as "What do we know?," "How do we use what we know?," and "How quickly can we learn something new?" will become the central questions for high performing organizations (Wood, 2003, p. 144).

Introduction

From examining the discipline of KM and tacit knowledge more specifically through to elaborating research questions that have allowed us to test for soft knowledge diffusion in three ICT organisations and then presenting the results through a number of different instruments, we are at the stage where there is little more that can be achieved other than making recommendations for firms to consider should they wish to explore their ICT soft knowledge assets in closer detail. It is of course up to reader to decide the value of this book; nevertheless the author suggests at least a few options management may consider to be of some value.

Recommendations for Organisations

The phenomenon of tacit knowledge was examined in three ICT organisations with regard to how the former is likely to flow and what the likely bottlenecks will be. Parameters that are going to affect soft knowledge flows will vary from composition of staff complement, through to degree of non-face-to-face meeting types, to physical layout of the organisation to name but a few. We are at the stage where we can at last make some recommendations for organisations.

First and foremost, a tacit knowledge measurement instrument capable of being used within the ICT domain has been presented. Organisations could choose to introduce a tacit knowledge inventory for employees upon entering the organisation. To a degree, certain organisations are already doing so in the form of asking employees to fill in questionnaires or take tests to determine if they fit the "culture" of the firm (Coates, 2001). Tests for fit are essentially assessments for ascertaining if potential employees possess the soft knowledge required to belong and contribute to their company. The strength of the inventory in this book relates more toward determining potential management candidates. A company employing the inventory as provided in Appendix F would gain some idea of which of their ICT employees have the street smarts to perform well in a management role where soft knowledge is vital. The inventory also asks personnel to determine which of their peers they consider to be particularly proficient at their tasks. To that end management can gain an informal view of their company's expertise where the formal organisational charts *will* not typically provide this. Certainly organisational structure charts will illustrate hierarchy or seniority within the firm and to some degree expertise as it relates to work group area. Structure charts will not necessarily identify tacit knowledge richness within work group areas and this is where the inventory may prove useful.

The identification of tacit knowledge savvy staff can also help the company adopt effective mentoring arrangements. Once **soft knowledge savvy** individuals have been identified, they may be able to pass their skills onto those less fortunate. All of this assumes a degree of cooperation on the part of the employees themselves. There are noted to be few organisations and Buckman Laboratories would be one (Chua, 2003; Kankanalli, Tanudidjaja, Sutanto, & Tan, 2003; Robbins, Bergman, Stagg, & Coulter, 2003), where true knowledge sharing is aggressively championed. The temptation on the part of the individual to horde their precious information resource is naturally understandable. It is our tacit knowledge, our tricks of the trade, our street credibility, that gives us the edge over our fellow employee and makes us that much more marketable, both in our own workplace as well as the workplace we may be heading to next.

The tacit knowledge inventory is also useful in so far as it is subjective. That is to say, fellow employees are the ones who choose successful peers. There is no attempt with regard to *this* inventory to state that if employees answer a certain way, then they may be regarded as an expert. Rather, it is only with *post* processing that one can examine the results of individuals who have been identified by their peers as proficient in their occupations, and only then begin to assess the results of "others." Should others hold similar results, one can then ascertain if they too could be considered experts. The alternative approach might take an organisational structure chart for example and in doing so get the most senior people in each section to provide their tacit knowledge results. Comparisons could then be made against them. The latter method is likely to be less successful for reasons provided above.

The incorporation of the social network analysis component allows an organisation to see where their employees lie. Through an examination of groupings, management are better enabled to bring in other employees who may gain from the knowledge that soft knowledge rich cliques may share. Again this assumes that groups will be willing to allow an outsider to gain access to their knowledge, and for that matter that an outsider will be a keen and grateful recipient of the knowledge. The strength of viewing the social networks of their employees at the same time allows management to determine if there are knowledge poor cliques who would benefit from the "injection" of an adviser who can perform storytelling on how particular tasks or problems were solved. Given the importance of teamwork to companies today, the need for organisations to understand their group dynamics has become more important than ever before.

Another benefit of the social network analysis component is that it provides management with a view of the *negative* or even non-existent social interactions of their employees. The graphs showing lack of interaction between work groups could also help management identify tacit knowledge sinks where knowledge may be being passed in, but not out of a particular group. The lack of communication amongst staff is the most debilitating parameter affecting the knowledge organisation. There was some evidence in Organisation X of employees avoiding one another, and fortunately no examples in the other firms. Evaluating non-communication patterns will allow companies to rearrange its staff to better allow for soft knowledge communication. Perhaps encouragement could even be given for companies to permit staff to socialise in a carefree environment. Support might be given for socialisation after hours or perhaps for recreational facilities to be made available for knowledge workers whereby they are able to exchange their ideas in relaxed and non-judgemental surroundings.

Finally management may wish to use the instruments illustrated in this book and extend the approach to the *inter*-**organisational domain**. The coalface with other firms is where much interaction between consultants and clients takes place. What are the soft knowledge flow patterns between partner firms? What are the issues of **multi-national organisation**al knowledge transfer? Certainly there are some references that allude to knowledge flows within multinational organisations (Butler, 2001; Cantwell & Santangelo, 2000; Malik, 2004), but with regard to tacit knowledge flows, truly empirical studies tend to be few and far between.

Finis

We, in Western societies in particular, have tended to emphasise the value of what Sternberg (1999) refers to as "book smarts." The consumption of codified knowledge has been commensurate with the increasing size and complexity of organisations, which in turn has led to lesser emphasis being placed on "street smarts." Certain cultures such as the Japanese have managed to better maintain their respect for tacit knowledge all the while modernising into the workforce they have today. They have managed to do this because they try to provide maximum opportunity for face-to-face discussion both within and external to the workplace itself. It is little coincidence that the small firm (Organisation Y) presented the best prospects for tacit knowledge transfer. One saw how the parameters conducive to tacit knowledge transfer, such as intimate meetings, lack of electronic communication and repeated contact were ideal for tacit knowledge flows. Certainly it is more difficult for large organisations such as X to achieve this model. But for the sake of effective soft knowledge management, one must at least try.

The Industrial Revolution[a] in the West spelt the demise of cottage industries where dexterous workers laboured at home. The move from domestic environments also brought with it a certain amount of deskilling, as workers were collected into workgroups in the urban industrialised factories. Gone oftentimes too were many skills transferred through traditional guilds and passed on from the master to the apprentice (i.e., tacit knowledge transfer). True, the rise of machinery demanded new expertise, but in many ways human skill had taken second place to the machine. What will be important to us in the 21st century will be to ensure we do not have an Information Age[b] that sees the deskilling of the tacit knowledge component at the expense of the codified bottom line.

With the disappearance of pre-structured and progressive career paths, employees experience themselves and their professional development very differently. While 20 years ago employees could relatively easily plot their future career paths in a hierarchical, bureaucratic organisation, employees today are encouraged to see themselves effectively as "self-employed," with employers being their customers. This new approach shifts the perspective of life-time employment to the pressure for life-time employability. This means that workers are impelled to develop a set of transferable skills and adaptive strategies in order to maintain their employability (Savickas, 2000 in Loogma, Ümarik, & Vilu, 2004, p. 329).

References

Butler, R. (2001). How can we conquer the tyranny of scale? *The Age, 21,* 21.

Cantwell, J., & Santangelo, G. (2000). Capitalism, profits, and innovation in the new techno-economic paradigm. *Journal of Evolutionary Economics, 10*(1-2), 131-157.

Chua, A. (2003). Knowledge sharing: A game people play. *Aslib Proceedings, 55*(3), 117-129.

Coates, P. (2001). Headhunters and collectors. *The Weekend Australian,* Saturday, July, 7, 1st edition.

Kankanhalli, A., Tanudidjaja, F., Sutanto, J., & Tan, B. (2003). The role of IT in successful knowledge management initiatives. *Communications of the ACM, 46*(9), 69-73.

Loogma, K., Ümarik, M., & Vilu, R. (2004). Identification-flexibility dilemma of IT specialists. *Career Development International, 9*(3), 323-348.

Macquarie Dictionary (1997). Published by the Macquarie Library, 3rd. ed. Macquarie University, Australia: Macquarie Library.

Malik, K. (2004). Coordination of technological flows in firms. *Journal of Knowledge Management, 8*(2), 64-72.

Robbins, S., Bergman, R., Stagg, I., & Coulter, M. (2003). *Management,* 3rd. ed. French's Forest, NSW Australia: Prentice Hall/Pearson Education.

Savickas, M. (2000). Renovating the psychology of careers for the 21st century. In A. Collin & R. Young (Eds), *The future of career.* Cambridge: Cambridge University Press, 53-68.

Sternberg, R. (1999). Epilogue – What do we know about tacit knowledge?: Making the tacit become explicit. In R. Sternberg & J. Horvath (Eds.) *Tacit knowledge in professional practice: Researcher and practitioner perspectives.* Mahwah, NJ: Lawrence Erlbaum and Associates, 231-236.

Wood, J. (2003). Australia: An under performing knowledge nation? *Journal of Intellectual Capital, 4*(2), 144-164.

Endnotes

[a]   "1. The radical social, economic and physical transformation of a country by the general introduction of mechanical means of manufacture. 2. The period in history when such a development took place in many Western countries; beginning in Britain in the late 18th century and continuing in the 19th century in other Western European countries and the U.S" (*Macquarie dictionary,* 1997, p. 1090).

[b]   "That period in the history of the world in which possession or provision of information is seen as a key element in society" (*Macquarie Dictionary,* 1997, p. 1095).

Appendices

Appendix A

Prior Definitions of Tacit Knowledge

Allred (2001)

- generally the source of a firm's competitive advantage
- knowledge that is understood and applied by those possessing it
- not easily communicated to others
- knowledge that is difficult to replicate or imitate
- often even those possessing it cannot fully describe it

Armbrecht et al. (2001)

- contained in an expert's head
- sources like corporate knowledge, core competencies, customers' perspectives, and external information, are combinations of tacit and explicit

Arora (1996)

- components of technology that are not codified into blueprints, manual patents and the like
- intangible knowledge
- rules of thumb
- heuristics
- tricks of the trade

Athanassiou and Nigh (2000)

- inherently non-transferable

Baldwin and Baldwin (1978)

- personal, subjective knowledge based on direct experience with social or nonsocial environment (Bridgman 1952, 1959; Polanyi 1959, 1960, 1966 and Skinner 1969 in above)
- understanding of action/attached meanings
- *Verstehen* (Weber)
- contingency shaped behaviour (learned behaviour from direct experience, without rules of verbal guidance)
- personal discovery/real life experience
- need not rely on verbal elements to be vivid and subjectively real
- subjective quality to contingency shaped knowledge
- explicit verbal accounts are not necessarily involved, although may be invented on an ad hoc basis after learning experience
- maxims
- rule of thumb
- customs
- proverbs
- shop lore
- aphorisms
- information [often] second hand/crude
- culturally accumulated rules

Bassellier, Reich and Benbasat (2001)

- experience and cognition

Bhatt, Gupta and Kitchens (2002)

- difficult to capture, codify and share
- requires a people-centred strategy of knowledge management (Polanyi 1966)
- distribute tacit knowledge in forms of rituals, histories, and organizational stories
- research has shown that the use of rituals, stories, and organizational histories can provide a basis of "collective memories" (Weick 1995)

Breschi and Lissoni (2001)

- highly contextual and difficult to codify, and therefore is more easily transmitted through face-to-face contacts and personal relationships, which require spatial proximity, in other words it is a public good, but a local one
- "tacitness" as an intrinsic property of some scientific or technical fields' knowledge base (stock)
- synonym for non-codifiability
- this goes against the most recent developments in the economics of knowledge codification, which suggest that tacitness ought to be referred to knowledge flows rather than stocks, and codification to be both a means for diffusion, and a powerful tool for exchanging messages which appear tacit to outsiders (Cowan et.al. 2000, Steinmuller 2000)
- fundamentals of tacit knowledge, which requires mutual understanding of working practices
- knowledge exchanges may tacit, even when they are trusted to very formal means of communications (such as mails, scientific articles, or even public conferences). This is because technical knowledge (and even more so scientific knowledge) is highly specific, and the jargon by means of which it can be transmitted is not the same jargon of the broader social community, which hosts the firm and its workers. Rather, it is the jargon of a much closer and restricted community (an "epistemic community")

Brockmann and Anthony (1998)

- work related practical knowledge (Wagner and Sternberg, 1986 in above)
- that which is neither expressed nor declared openly but rather implied or simply understood and is often associated with intuition
- intuition and tacit knowledge closely related

Bruynseels and Vos (2000)

- is unstructured knowledge that is implicitly present in a community, but is not readily organised or available for its members.

Burton (2001)

- is assumed to be that business-related knowledge that has not been articulated (either in verbal or written form)

Casonato and Harris (1999)

- personal knowledge resident within the mind/behavior/perceptions of individuals
- skills/experiences/insight/intuition/judgment
- typically shared through discussion/stories/analogies/person-to-person interaction; therefore, it is difficult to capture or represent in explicit form

- because individuals continually add personal knowledge which changes behavior and perceptions, tacit knowledge is by definition uncapped

Chambers (1998)

- resisting capture in symbolic form (Polanyi in above)
- know-how
- can be learned/transmitted however normally slow process, requires direct contact eg. apprenticeship
- difficult to evaluate
- can normally only be seen by looking at results and context to make inferences about the knowledge that must have been involved

Chaseling (1994)

- knowledge that is existing, but it is not articulated

Clarke and Wilcockson (2001)

- the expert knowledge that professionals use but find difficult to articulate is known as tacit knowledge (Meerabeau 1992, Meyer and Batehup 1997 in above)

Coff (1997)

- management is a tacit skill (Castanias & Helfat 1991 in above)
- management requires that we identify tacit constructs, including asset specificity, social complexity, causal ambiguity, and asymmetric information

Collins (2001)

- concealed knowledge
- mismatched salience
- ostensive knowledge
- unrecognised knowledge
- unrecognised/unrecognisable knowledge

Colonia-Willner (1999)

- instantiation of practical knowledge acquired in situations where the information is not openly expressed
- hard to articulate
- usually not explicitly verbalised or taught

Cowan, David and Dominique (2000)

- Unarticulated: knowledge that is not invoked explicitly in the typical course of knowledge activities

Dahl (2000)

- internalised through formal training and practice. Such knowledge can be verbalised and made part of conscious reasoning again.
- inarticulable knowledge', alluding to the potential for verbalisation.

Dahlbom and Mathiassen (1999)

- no idea how we do a lot of the things that we know how to do
- very fast feats of perception
- recognition
- attention
- information retrieval
- motor control
- know how to see and smell
- how to recognise a friend's face
- how to concentrate on a mark on the wall

Davenport, De Long and Beers (1998)

- knowledge that resides in the minds of the people in an organization but has not been put in structured, document-based form

David (1992)

- the concept of tacit knowledge refers to the common perception that we all are often generally aware of certain objects without being focused on them (based on Polanyi)

Desrochers (2001)

- "dependent on the particular circumstances of time and place"
- therefore cannot be acquired by traditional market research procedures or transmitted by advertising or long-distance learning
- little truth in the belief information is expensive to produce but can be replicated at little cost for using information from others is always more difficult than using your own information

Devinney (1997)

- *Systemic* ..... existing knowledge base of the individuals: firm must be able to convert its implicit understanding into codified *conceptual knowledge*: by this stage: information
- *Operational knowledge* how firm able to do something
- *Socialisation*: finally, the individual must be able to meld the know how into their internal schemas

Durrance (1998)

- result of involuntary learning that guides how people behave and act
- deeper than explicit knowledge because it is internalised when individuals are least conscious that learning is taking place
- actions that become second nature to workers
- lines that become spontaneous to speakers
- abilities, such as biking and driving, that are performed without any effort and cannot be explained to another person
- lives in our hunches, intuition, emotions, values, and beliefs
- non-intellectual qualities/mental models—form the basis of how we behave and act
- filter through which we see the world

Eraut (2000)

- that which we know but cannot tell (Polanyi, 1967)
- that which cannot be abstracted from practice (Spender, 1995)

Falkenberg, Russell and Ricker (2000)

- abstract knowledge
- deeply rooted in action
- involvement in a specific context

Fleck (1997)

- wholly embodied in individuals
- rooted in practice/experience
- expressed through skilful execution
- transmitted by apprenticeship/training, through 'watching and doing' forms of learning
- differs from informal and contingent knowledge in not being readily articulable and therefore not easily communicable or tradeable in Winter's terminology

- skill formation is very pertinent here: mentally mediated rather than bodily mediated skills ('informating' rather than 'automating') across many different sectors (Zuboff 1988 in above)

- carriers almost entirely restricted to individuals in direct contact with one another, owing to the intimate interpersonal form of learning necessary

- component of expertise consequently the most crucial in restricting the social distribution of knowledge, and has been widely identified as a major constraint on the diffusion of both science (Fleck 1935; 1979 in above) and technology (Winter 1987 in above)

- because of wholly personal embodied nature: not tradeable as any form of artefact, but necessarily has to be traded through labour markets

- in extreme cases, individuals possessing highly valued tacit knowledge become very influential if not powerful, and rather than simple status, personal charisma results

- during the growth heyday of `Silicon Valley', personnel with the latest know-how (or `black art') of chip design and fabrication commanded massive transfer fees and remuneration packages on being head-hunted from one company to another

  a.   distributed

  b.   apparently trivial

  c.   highly specific to the particular application domain

  d.   accidental to the general process of technology development

- effective acquisition and exploitation of contingent knowledge can be seen to be a key factor in the success of Japanese manufacturing practices

  - Ishikawa diagrams: accumulating information about causes of problems or defects, statistical process control charts for monitoring quality trends etc.

  - habit of displaying these charts on the walls of the workplace, where they are visible and can therefore be accessed by many, can be seen as an explicit coding or embodiment of contingent knowledge directly into the immediate context

  - use of labels providing immediate maintenance procedures directly on the machines affected (as is now usual with photocopying machines, for instance) can be interpreted as a way of making more explicit and concentrated the contingent knowledge arising from everyday operations and remedial tasks

- contingent knowledge differs from formal knowledge in that it lacks systematic codification and is concrete rather than theoretical

  - it is a form of informal knowledge, perhaps, but tends to remain tied to the context, rather than being informally passed on as more or less generalisable `rules of thumb' or `tricks of the trade'

  - it is very specific to the particular arrangements or physical kit and often 'written' (sometimes literally) in that context

- informal knowledge exists more in the interactions between people than it is embodied in any one place or individual

- contingent knowledge may appear to be a form of tacit knowledge when mediated through one individual
- differs from other sorts of tacit knowledge in being more related to particularities of the context rather than cognitive or motor skills
  - *contingent knowledge*: known through an individual or individuals
  - *contingent information*: 'written' directly into the context and available for interpretation by knowledgeable individuals
- contingent knowledge is embodied in specific context in some form, even when mediated through people

Fodor (1968)

- *inter aila*, a theoretical term in psychology
- computational operations of some optimal simulation of an organism
- relation the term designates presumably holds between the organism itself and proposition, rule, maxim, or technique
- in attributing tacit knowledge to an organism, we infer from a fact about a simulation of the organism to a fact about the mental life of the organism
  - one might reasonably want to know what sort of inference this could possibly be

Giunipero, Dawley and Anthony (1999)

- common sense or intuition
- common sense may elude the outsider or novice
- common sense = type of tacit knowledge
- "we can know more that we can tell" (Polanyi 1966 in above)
- personal quality about it that is rooted in action, commitment, involvement in a specific context
- body of hidden knowledge people have deep within themselves developed over the years
- people use this knowledge to make decisions and often do not realize that they are doing so
- conceptualised as an idiosyncratic, subjective, highly individualized store of knowledge
- practical know-how gathered through years of experience and direct interaction within a domain or profession (Wagner and Sternberg 1985 in above)
- experience becomes integrated, actions become second nature, collected impressions guide actions that are often below the consciousness of individuals and groups (Wagner and Sternberg 1985 in above)
- generally thought of as practical intelligence or know-how about the real world

- personal competence or a thinking in practice (Nonaka 1994 in above)
- automatic, subconscious process that draws upon experientially established cognitive structures
- cognitive structures are schemata (mental maps) or knowledge formed from abstractions of experience that simplify, but may bias, the decision making (Hitt and Tyler 1991 in above)
- learned independently of direct instruction
- individuals often unable to articulate tacit knowledge
- managers do not often enjoy the luxury of making their decisions on the basis of orderly rational analysis, but depend largely on intuitive or judgmental responses to decision-demanding situations (Barnard 1966 in above)
- contains two dimensions (Nonaka and Takeuchi 1995 in above)

  1. *know how*: developed from years of doing a particular job eg. experienced trade craftsman: wealth of skills in his or her mind, difficult to easily discuss or transfer this knowledge in terms of underlying principles and theories

  2. *cognitive*: consisting of all the mental models, perceptions, and beliefs that are ingrained in all individuals

     - cognitive dimension reflects our perspective of the world around us as it exists and what it ought to be

- most precious knowledge can neither be taught nor passed on, but comes from direct experience (Levitt 1991 in above)
- innovator Craig McCaw: "I try to be an idiot savant. Look at the obvious and ignore everything else. To me, it's all intuition, it's all obvious and hits you. Market research is there to confirm what you feel, not tell you what you should think (Hill and Hardy 1997 in above)"
- intuition not magic and is much more than a glorified guess
- intuition is a subspecies of logical thinking, one in which the steps in the process are hidden in the subconscious portion of the brain (Agor 1986 in above)
- *bounded rationality*: disparity between traditional Western management training on rational decision making and the use of tacit knowledge in decision making (March and Simon 1958 in above)
- difficult to measure and observe, purchasers must realize that it will play a major role in their buying decision

Goldman (1990)

- possessed/utilised on an implicit/subsidiary level without conscious awareness
- "knowing how"
- involved in acquisition/use of physical skills/mental abilities/processes which combine both
- beyond conscious awareness of the user

- contained/expressed in actions rather than conscious thoughts
- recognis[ing] one special human face in a crowd
- recognising mood and attitude communicated via that human face
- distinguish[ing] face of toxic infant from irritated/tired child.
- precise amount to tension to exert upon the suture
- felt/shown during the practice of skill
- how to use/feel through a tool
- how to know the spatial position of the tip of the instrument as if it were one's own
- expert pianist who can perform brilliantly, but freezes in mid – concert if begins to concentrate on the movement of his fingers instead of the music
- implicit
- unspecifiable in proposition
- required to interpret and decide the relevant from explicit information
- used to recognise and apply the appropriate explicit rules to a given problem
- knowledge beyond physical findings/lab data/clinical rules when intensivist fine tunes controls of mechanical ventilator
- knowledge which integrates/permits choice/use of appropriate explicit rules/methods
- knowledge excluded from decision trees/software systems
- expert radiologist (Polanyi 1962 in above), can sort through range of vague shadows/shapes, find concealed panorama of significant details
- which rules to employ when
- which case requires use of which information
- achieving diagnostic closure, deciding upon management course without knowing every routine used in that mental process
- may introspectively reconsider process in more explicit detail
- will not necessarily reflect tacit knowledge inherent in the decision - making process
- may not be aware of that knowledge
- may be fully unaware of ever coming to possess certain knowledge in his skills
- may simply find himself using knowledge by practicing the skill
- knowing-in-action (Schon 1983; Schon 1987)
- clinician does not always reach conclusions one would predict by assuming adherence to rational decision theory
- formal decision theory fails because lacks certain essential knowledge possessed by the clinician in actual practice

Greeno (1987)

- needed for performing a task
- presence unsuspected by the performer
- "such as we have of something we are in the act of doing" (Polanyi 1959 in above).
- not "set out in written words or maps, or mathematical formulae"
- we do not know how to display it directly.
- only communicated implicitly, as unseen and unanalysed component of performance
- exists "between the lines" (Bundy, 1975, in above)

Halter (2001)

- is gained by experience and interaction and also by acquiring and combining skills (Polanyi, 1958, p. 82)
- connects the knower with the world, discerns patterns from experience, and scribes meaning to the patterns

Hannigan (2001)

- by reflecting-in-action, practitioners use a form of tacit knowledge, in which the "science" or "theory" informing activity is embedded in the activity itself

Hedlund (1994)

- cross cultural negotiation skills
- team coordination in complex work
- corporate culture
- customer's attitudes to products and expectations (adapted from Hedlund and Nonaka, 1993, in above)
- nonverbalised/nonverbalisable
- intuitive
- unarticulated (Polanyi, 1962, in above)

Henderson (1995)

- knowledge which is not verbalised: either because it cannot be or because it may simply be taken for granted or regarded as too trivial to warrant verbalisation
- all types of knowledge, however pure consists in part of tacit rules which may be impossible to formulate in principle (Laser example Collins, 1972, p. 46 in above)
- residual category which encompasses many dimensions of non-verbal knowledge

Hicks (1995)

- tacit/unpublishable knowledge = foundation of scientific/technical credibility
- gestalt shift: personal judgement, embodied (Gelwick, 1977, in above)

Horak (2001)

- has been estimated that between 50 and 90 percent of the knowledge in an organisation is tacit
- information that is in people's heads in the form of insights, ideas, perceptions, and values.

Howells (1995a)

- is non-codified, disembodied know how that is acquired the informal take-up of learned behaviour and procedures
- does not involve the generation and acquisition of tangible products and processes, or the more formal element of intangible knowledge flows association with specific research, technical or training programmes
- skills
- cannot be directly or easily transmitted (knowledge and task performance, individual specific)
- "learning by doing" (Arrow, 1962, in above)
- "learning by using" (Rosenberg, 1982, in above)
- "learning to learn" (Ellis, 1965; Estes, 1970; Argyris and Schon, 1978; Stigilitz, 1987, in above) = critical elements within tacit knowledge acquisition
- something that cannot be easily codified or learnt
- high *speed and simultaneity* of information processing: may force a learner of a new skill to work out the details of the coordination for himself/herself. In this case, the actual performance cannot be slowed down and practicing cannot be done slowly
- sometimes difficult to *articulate* all that is necessary to master a skill since the action is embedded in the context: if one of the many context variables changes too much there will be no performance and all the 'ifs' cannot be meaningfully expressed
- involves learning and skill … in a way that cannot be communicated in any direct, codified way
- "learning by doing"
- "learning by using"
- "learning to learn" are therefore crucial elements in tacit knowledge acquisition associated with *direct*, on the job contact with new equipment/workpractice/operation
- hard to conceive of situations where tacit knowledge can be acquired indirectly as this would involve some kind of codification and lack of direct experience
- direct experience

- person-embodied
- not directly codifiable via artefacts
- firm/organisation can possess tacit knowledge through workforce or via operational milieu that exists and is created and sustained within the organisational structure
- personnel within firm gain tacit knowledge via direct work experience
- not a static stock of knowledge
- continually being built upon/learnt
- involving intuition and trial and error (although equally it can be forgotten; see Douglas, 1987; Johnson, 1992, in above)

Howells (1995b)
- non-verbal knowledge

Johannessen, Olsen and Olaisen (1997)
- emerges and develops through closeness to the work processes
- if work processes change .... may be made superfluous

Joly and Mangematin (1996)
- learning processes are localised/cumulative
- circulates very badly

Johnston (1989)
- can be possessed by itself

Lamberton (1996)
- not written
- cannot be articulated
- acquired/stored/used in course of experience
- inextricably interwoven with human and organisational contexts

Langlois (2001)
- it is always possible in principle to create a codebook, but that codebook will never capture all the knowledge held by the individuals whose code it is
- need not be idiosyncratic

Larkin (1980)

- *Explicating tacit knowledge*: structure and context are often *not* obvious either to the person using it, or to a casual observer

Lawson and Lorenz (1999)

- co-ordinate actions and act capably without needing, or being able, to articulate in words or diagrams exactly how they accomplish this
- must draw upon knowledge that they have come to hold tacitly by acting within, and reproducing, the organizations routines (Cyert and March, 1963, in above)
- not necessarily/typically result of clearly thought out or explicit intentions
- often have no idea of the history leading to/benefits of following, certain routines
- tacit/articulated knowledge are complements
- underlies manual dexterity: knowing how to swim/ride a bike
- underlies scientific capability
- observation/imitation/experience = only method for acquiring skills to formulate scientific problems/develop strategies aimed at their solution (Senker, 1995a, in above)
- process of articulating/codifying knowledge does not simply amount to transforming something which remains unaltered in its meaning or content into a more easily communicated form

Lei (1997)

- unwritten know-how/'know-why"
- understood only by the person, team, unit, or firm that has long worked with it on a deeply personal or embedded level
- becomes part of the personality/guiding process/organisational routines of the person, team of group/firm that possess it, respectively
- much less transparent then explicit knowledge
- often has "sticky" quality to it (Ghemawat, 1991; Polanyi, 1967; Dosi, 1988; Hoskisson and Hitt, 1994; von Hippel, 1994; Wright, 1994, in above)
- very context specific
- deeply embedded within organisation's routines/practices
- generally unseen by those who have not worked with it on a personal level
- requires "learning by doing" that often first begins with imitation/direct observation/practice
- more "art" than "science"
- embedded in organisation's dynamic routines
- becomes part of firm's social fabric of interrelationships/interactions among people (Teece, 1986; Teece, Pisano and Shuen, 1994; Badaracco, 1991; Nonaka, 1991, in above)

Lei, Hitt, and Bettis (1996)

- "learning by doing", "learning by using" (Badaracco, 1991; Dierickx and Cool, 1989; Dosi, 1988; Polanyi, 1967; Reed and deFillippi, 1990; Sahal, 1981; Teece, Rumelt, Dosi and Winter, 1992, in above)

- neither easily imitated nor clearly understood outside the firm

- firm specific

- often cannot be written or encoded (Dougherty, 1992; Nelson and Winter, 1982; Nonaka, 1991; Polanyi, 1967)

- immutable, hard-to-decipher quality that cannot be easily transmitted to others

- often represents a shared experience among organisation members

- richer than universal knowledge (Dougherty, 1992)

- skills required to implement a new production process successfully are often specific to the organisation or its team members in ways that outsiders cannot easily duplicate

- high barriers erected to imitability through causal ambiguity (Barney, 1991; Reed and deFillippi, 1990).

  1. *Scientific*: social, abstract, highly mobile
  2. *Conscious*: individual focused, taken for granted
  3. *Communal*: interrelated/occurs with organisational culture
  4. *Automatic*: individual focused, taken for granted (Spender in above)

- appropriability is an important issue (of less concern with automatic or conscious)

- learned by "apprenticeship"

- learned by doing through collaborative arrangements

Leonard and Sensiper (1998)

- tacit knowledge: not yet explicated (Spender, 1996, in above)

- some knowledge unlikely ever to be wholly explicated, whether embedded in cognition or in physical abilities

- semiconscious/unconscious tacit knowledge produces insight/intuition/decisions based on "gut feel"

- largely tacit: coordination/motor/physical (muscle)/negotiation skills, artistic vision

- common element = inability of the knower to totally articulate all they know

- tacit knowing embodied in physical skills in muscles/nerves/reflexes, learned through practice, i.e., through trial and error

- tacit knowing in cognitive skills, learned through experience, resides in unconscious/semiconscious

- individual level (Polanyi in above)

Love (2001)

- unverbalisable and skill-oriented learning that contributes to the education of a professional and classified him or her as an expert
- practice-oriented knowledge that is acquired without explicit instruction

McDaniel, Morgeson, Finnegan, Campion and Braverman (2001)

- "practical know-how that usually is not openly expressed or stated and which must be acquired in the absence of direct instruction" (Wegener, 1987, p. 1236)

MacKenzie (1996)

- motor skills
- intuition
- common sense
- judgment that cannot be transmitted in words or equations alone
- *Los Alamos*: nuclear weaponry: repeated discovery that explicit knowledge alone is not enough
- *expert systems* in artificial intelligence: attempts to render tacit knowledge fully explicit have repeatedly disappointed

MacKenzie and Spinardi (1995)

- tacit knowledge, on the other hand, is knowledge that has not been (and perhaps cannot be) formulated explicitly, and therefore, cannot be effectively stored or transferred entirely by interpersonal means

McAulay, Russell and Sims (1997)

- proximal knowledge (Polanyi, 1962; Athanassiou and Nigh, 1996, in above)
- *proximal knowledge*: more widely referred to as "tacit" knowledge, is everything which distal knowledge is not
  - cannot be
  - documented
  - formalised
  - easily talked about with newcomers
  - turned into procedures
  - reproduced through statements
  - techniques or models
  - replicated easily by competitors, hence it is a source of competitive advantage.

- precisely the knowledge taken for granted, built up through close working relationships over long period of time
- underlying knowledge taken for granted as managers carry out everyday actions in response to events, or instructions of superiors, or create kinds of organisation they would like to work for
- need not be made explicit as long as it appears to be leading the organisation in the direction it wants to go
- need not be made explicit as long as colleagues share sufficient experience/understanding of underlying meaning of what it is to be a financial director/treasurer/financial controller
- given such sharing of experience and meaning, to spell out and explicitly define these roles is simply a waste of time
- exceptionally difficult
- taken-for-granted knowledge simply used as part of organisational norms and routines, explaining tacit knowledge is unnecessary.

(The) *Macquarie Dictionary* (1997)

- silent; saying nothing
- not openly expressed, but implied, understood or inferred
- unspoken

Meerabeau (1992)

- helicopter pilots: expert practitioners view situations holistically, draw on past concrete experience, whereas the merely competent or proficient must use conscious problem solving (Benner, 1984, on Dreyfus & Dreyfus in above).
    - *Tacit Knowledge*: Experts do not use same pattern of skills as learners; view situations holistically, much of their knowledge embedded in their practice (Polanyi, 1958, 1967)
    - *Proximal/Distal knowledge*: when we know something only by relying on our awareness of it for attending to a second activity
- psychomotor skills: co-ordination of respiration necessary to swim/action of hammering a nail
- attention to the parts makes us unable to perform the whole
- success depends on personal contact between scientists (Laser construction Collins 1974 in above)
- learning from a careful examination of artistry (Schön, 1987, in above).
- "reflection in action", reflection upon that reflection (Schön, 1987, in above)
- expressed only in practice, learned through experience (Oakeshott, 1962; Polanyi; Eraut, 1985, in above)
    1. *Replication*: "regurgitation"

2. *Application*: knowledge in new situations, although still following rules
3. *Interpretation*: professional education, involving judgement, "ways of seeing" a situation, although these ways may be unquestioned, effort to break free and see situations in new ways may be considerable
4. *Association*: intuition, metaphors, images (Broudy *et al.*, 1964 in above)

- medical practice: practitioner cannot suspend action in absence of convincing evidence, or afford to be sceptical, often has to think on his or her feet (Freidson, 1971, in above)
- medical sociology: tacit knowledge may be a positive asset
- the hallmark of a profession (Jamous and Peloille, 1970; Atkinson *et al.*, 1977)
- technicality: procedures that can be mastered and communicated in the form of rules
- indeterminacy: variety of tacit/private knowledge which cannot be made wholly explicit (Jamous and Peloille, 1970; Atkinson *et al.*, 1977)

Murphy (2001)
- useful stuff you know about that no one bothers to ask

Murray and Teal (2002)
- deeply embedded in individual's actions and experiences

Nelson and Winter (in Lamberton, 1997)
- "we know more than we can tell"
- "knowledge that cannot be articulated"

Nightingale (1998)
- assuming that "meaning" of information is somehow contained in it
- obviously false, as most technical scientific papers only understood by scientists who are well versed in the subject
- tacit knowledge that enables them to understand science is dependent on the intrinsic biology of the brain
- knowledge dependent on embodied ability to recognise similarity, this implies a brain (and tacit knowledge), information approaches have to invoke "tacit knowledge" in order to explain it
- once we invoke tacit knowledge, "information processing" drops out of the equation as irrelevant, because the tacit recognition of patterns explains our ability to understand information
- information cannot be disembodied, because sense of what it "means" depends somehow on "us"

- from tacit knowledge perspective, science cannot be described without scientists
- innovation dependent on this conception of similarity
- problem is made worse as knowledge is not only embodied, also embedded in social networks
- tacit knowledge vital to our understanding of even simple words like "cut" in sentences "cut the grass" and "cut the cake" (Searle, 1995)
- we know the appropriate meaning because we have tacit background knowledge to compare the words to
- "see as", rather than "see" (Gregory, 1980, 1981 in above)
- capacity to interpret information and comprehend things that cannot be codified, like how to ride a bicycle
- backgrounds of interwoven experience
- automatic capacity we have to relate experience to it.
- hard (if not impossible) to codify/transmit because it is the background to which codified transmitted information is compared

Noh et al. (2000)
- is intangible because it represents intuition, subjective insights, beliefs and expertise (Dutta, 1997; Wagner and Sternberg, 1985)
- will disappear along with turnover or retirement of employees since it is highly personal, and context dependent
- hard to formalise, communicate, and share with others (Wagner & Sternberg, 1985)
- often elicited by means of figurative languages and symbolism to express thee inexpressible (Numata, Hane, Lei & Iwashita, 1997)

Nonaka (1991)
- highly personal
- hard to formalise
- difficult to communicate to others
- deeply rooted in action/individual's commitment to a specific context
- consists partly of technical skills
- know-how
- mental models
- beliefs

Nonaka, Ray, and Umemoto (1998)
- concerns an individuals feelings
- often difficult to express in a manner that others can understand

- covers hidden areas
- quite probably partially hidden from knowledge-holding individuals

Nonaka, Takeuchi, and Umemoto (1996)

- personal
- context specific
- hard to formalise and communicate

Olsson and Gullberg (1988)

- formed under long tradition/experience
- mostly mediated by interchange—ritual and maintenance—routine

Osterloh and Frey (2000)

- acquired by and stored within individuals and cannot be transferred or traded as a separate entity
- crucial source of sustainable competitive advantage because it is difficult for competitors to imitate it (e.g., Teece, 1998)

(The) *Oxford English Dictionary* (1989)

- unspoken; unvoiced, silent, emitting no sound; noiseless, wordless
- not openly expressed or stated, but implied; understood, inferred

Persaud, Kumar, and Kumar (2001)

- cannot be easily coded/transferred
- not easily accessible
- knowledge people carry in their heads
- intuitive and experience based
- represents a disproportionately large part of the knowledge needed to conduct cutting-edge R&D
- cultural or situational specificity is a major component of tacit knowledge
- assigns meaning to data and facts
- often inseparably linked to processes and people

Platts and Yeung (2000)

- can be summarized as knowledge that has not been articulated
- may be a "skill" or "know-how"

- might usefully consider explicit knowledge to mean know-what and tacit knowledge to mean "know-how"

Polanyi (1968)

- triad controlled by knower
  1. subsidiary particulars
  2. focal target
  3. knower who links first to the second

Powell (1995)

- open culture
- employee empowerment
- executive commitment

Pylyshyn (1981)

- cannot be freely accessed/updated by every cognitive processes within the organism
- nor can it enter freely into any logically valid inference
- much of it is not introspectable or verbally articulable, e.g., grammatical/logical rules/social conventions
- no doubt what makes it possible for people to hold contradictory beliefs or to have beliefs that are only effective within certain relatively narrow classes of tasks
- might well be that many people only have access to their tacit knowledge of physics when they are acting upon the world (e.g. playing baseball, or perhaps when they are engaged in something we call *visualising* some physical process, but not when they have to reason verbally or answer certain kinds of questions in the abstract

Raghuram (1996)

- personal quality
- hard to formalise and communicate
- traditions
- values
- organisational cultures

Richards (1998)

- is difficult to communicate and share with others
- it is built on our experiences, feelings, values and learning styles
- represents the understanding of the external world

Roberts (1998)
- embedded in people
- in their heads
- not at all easy to copy of transfer from one individual to another

Roberts (2000)
- collective rather than individual

Ruppel and Harrington (2001)
- tacit knowledge, such as insights, intuitions and hunches is not as easily codified and is more difficult to articulate and transfer
- tacit knowledge most strongly facilitates learning, builds intellectual capital and provides value and competitive advantage to organizations. This is because it is more difficult for competitors to replicate.
- Tacit knowledge includes technical knowledge, such as personal skills and "know-how", and cognitive models that we take for granted.
- Inkpen and Dimur suggest that an organization's goal is to convert tacit to explicit knowledge so it can be shared more easily.

Sako (1999)
- "we know more than we can tell" (Polanyi, 1966, in above)
- hands-on teaching
- the way things are done in the firm (Nelson and Winter, 1982, in above)

Sanderson, Nixon and Aron (2000)
- The very nature of tacit knowledge is that an expert may possess the experiences, and skills from which the explicit knowledge is created, but may not even realise that he/she could provide an answer.

Schmidt and Hunter (1993)
- practical intelligence simply more general and broadly applicable form of tacit knowledge
- knowledge does not attain special construct status merely because it is "tacit"
- "often...not openly expressed or stated" or typically acquired informally
- most human knowledge is acquired informally
- just knowledge
- in the job context, it is simply job knowledge
- job knowledge explains wider range of phenomena

- has well studied relationships with intelligence, job experience, job performance
- relates nicely to known principles of learning theory

Schulz and Jobe (2001)

- difficult to express and to communicate to other people by means of symbols (Hill & Ende, 1994; Nelson & Winter, 1982; Spender, 1993)
- more difficult to transmit than codified knowledge
- travels particularly poorly between organisations (Kogut & Zander, 1993)
- efficient transmission of tacit knowledge requires its codification into explicit forms
- depends on sense making of participants
- stimulates creativity, "creative chaos", innovative forms of response and coordination

Scott (1990)

- practice wisdom
- practitioner "has a feeling" about a particular case and its likely causes or outcome

Senker (1995a)

- ability to recognise facts
- knowledge that can be possessed by itself
- all knowledge is *either tacit* or *rooted in tacit knowledge* (Polanyi, 1969, p. 144 in above)
  1. Knowledge implies understanding: acquisition of knowledge is a purely perceptual, cognitive process
  2. Skill: knowing how to make something happen; cognition; manual dexterity; sensory ability, may be based entirely on tacit knowledge
- important to distinguish between tacit knowledge: which is embodied in skills and can therefore be copied, and tacit knowledge which cannot be demonstrated and so is very difficult to transfer (e.g., The recognition of a musical note)
- this differentiation between tacit knowledge/skills marks a fundamental disagreement with Nonaka (forthcoming), who suggest that tacit knowledge involves cognitive dimensions (schemata, paradigms, mental models, etc.), as well as a technical dimensions (concrete knowledge, crafts and skill which apply to specific contexts)
- skills based on appropriate combinations of tacit and formal knowledge in specific contexts might be better defined as "expertise" [It should of course be recognised that the term expertise rightly extends beyond the narrowly cognitive or technical domains to encompass the social context which gives meaning and status to one set of knowledge and skills over another]
- must be acquired by example or experience; in "person-embodied" form

- personal interaction or movement only channel (for the most part) by which tacit knowledge can be transferred
- hypothesise that tacit knowledge is a very important element of the knowledge transferred through personal networks.
- accumulated "on the job"
- learning-by-doing
- most of the associated knowledge had not yet been published or documented anywhere
- firms recruit scientists and engineers who personally embody the required skills and tacit knowledge; by conducting in-house R & D; and by promoting networking
- primarily transferred by example/practical experience
- channels primarily person-embodied rather than literature based

Senker (1995b)
- we know more than we can tell
- ability to recognise faces
- ride a bicycle
- knowledge of techniques, methods, designs that work in certain ways, with certain consequences, even when one cannot explain exactly why (Rosenberg, 1982, in above)
- can be possessed by itself
- explicit knowledge must rely on being tacitly understood and applied (Polanyi, 1969, in above)
- all knowledge either tacit or rooted in tacit knowledge
  - *knowledge*: implies understanding
  - *acquisition of knowledge*: perceptual and cognitive process
  - *skill*: knowing how to make something happen

Shipman and Marshall (1999)
- poses a particularly challenging problem for adding formal structure and content to any system
- by its very nature people do not explicitly acknowledge tacit knowledge

Sidani and Gonzalez (2000)
- implicit knowledge
- describes a form of "compiled" knowledge that an expert utilizes when dealing with a situation
- knowledge that is hidden, implied, intuitive or judgemental

Skeris (1999)

- no one can capture and codify tacit knowledge in software, hardware, and processes
- hatched of experience
- often nonverbal
- even subconscious in nature
- users can transfer it without direct contact with the owner
- tacit knowledge on the other hand, resides in the acting persons
- the coordination and motor skills to run a large crane are largely tacit
- the negotiation skills required in a corporate meeting or the artistic vision embodied in the design of a new computer program interface
- tacit knowledge entails a body of perspectives
  - our view of customers is framed by ours firm's experience
- perceptions
  - customers seem disinclined to try our new product
- beliefs
  - investment in new technology will lead to breakthrough new products that will create new customer needs
- values
  - do what is right for the customer
- people usually acquire tacit knowledge in face-to-face interactions
- large part of interaction is nonverbal
- social interaction is especially critical for teams of individuals responsible for delivering new products, services, and organizational processes.

Somech and Bogler (1999)

- informal and implicit knowledge used to achieve one's goals

Sparrow (2001)

- recognition that *subconscious* knowledge (in the form of skills and tacit feel) figures in human performance

Stenmark (2000)

- we are not necessarily aware of our tacit knowledge
- on a personal level, we do not need to make it explicit in order to use it,
- we may not want to give up a valuable competitive advantage
- is knowledge that cannot be easily articulated and thus only exists in people's hands and minds, and manifests itself through their actions

- in contract Polanyi does not make such a distinction. Instead, he envisions tacit knowledge as the backdrop against which all understanding is distinguished.
- is thus a cultural, emotional, and cognitive background, of which we are only marginally aware This tacitness is a precondition for focal knowledge (Polanyi, 1998; Prosch, 1986)
- Polanyi's view has sometimes been criticised for being overly concerned with the tacit aspects and this becoming almost monistic
- Polanyi's opinion that the tacit and the explicit are mutually constituted and should thus not be treated as two separate types of knowledge supported by, for example Tsoukas (1996), who argues that trying to split these two inseparably related entities is to miss the point.

Stenmark (2000/2001)

- inherently elusive
- not necessarily aware of our tacit knowledge
- on a personal level, we do not need to make it explicit in order to use it
- may not want to give up a valuable competitive advantage
- cannot be easily articulated and thus only exits in people' hands and minds, and manifests itself through their actions

Sternberg (1995)

- knowledge you need to succeed in an endeavour
- not formally taught
- often is not even verbalised
- typically acquired on the job or in the situation where it actually used
- typically informal
- not actually a part of any discipline formally taught anywhere
- in theory, can be verbalised/taught (in which case we still refer to it as "tacit knowledge" even though strictly speaking it is no longer tacit)
- differs from more formal knowledge in that there is often resistance to its revelation
  - e.g., company whose stated promotion policies encourage innovation but whose true promotion policies reward conformity or perhaps membership in certain groups, is not likely to want these facts to be known
- often not readily available for the asking
- must be inferred simply by spending time in an environment
- carefully observing what is happening in that environment
- tacit knowledge is contextually relative
  - formal knowledge is not

- tacit knowledge almost always acquired as people interact with real environment in which they have to adapt
- rarely acquired in artificial situations, whether in the classroom of otherwise
- others may have various agendas, lead them purposely to obscure/hide tacit knowledge
- far more important to shaping/adaptation to the environment than is formal knowledge
- organisational cultures = vast repositories of tacit knowledge, when culture changes, so much tacit knowledge
- metacognitive understanding of own tacit knowledge generally weaker than such understanding of formal knowledge
- procedural as opposed to declarative
- practical: knowledge for use in actual organisation/everyday situation
- to be exploited effectively, need to know both procedures (actions) and their link to environment (when and where to use them)
- not enough to know what to do: have to know when/where to do it, when/where not to
- much is scripted (Schank & Abelson, 1977, in above): it is part of script/schema people follow in certain situations
- can be taught

Sternberg (1998)
- action oriented
- typically acquired without direct help from others
- allows individuals to achieve goals they personally value (Sternberg, Wagner, Williams & Horvath, 1995, in above)
  - a.   it is procedural
  - b.   it is relevant to the attainment of goals people value
  - c.   it typically is acquired with little help from others
- important part of practical intelligence: particular notion of tacit knowledge used here derived from triarchic theory of intelligence (Sternberg, 1985a, 1997a, in above)
- form of "knowing how" rather than of "knowing that" (Ryle, 1949, in above)
- we view condition - action sequences (production systems) as a useful formalism of understanding the mental representation of tacit knowledge (Sternberg *et al.,* 1995; see also Horvath *et al.*, 1996)
- always wedded to particular uses in particular situations or classes or situations.
- practically useful
- instrumental to attainment of goals that people value

- people use this knowledge in order to achieve success in life, however they may define success
  - abstract academic knowledge about procedures for solving problems with no relevance to life should not be viewed, in this perspective as constituting tacit knowledge
- typically is acquired without direct help from others
- others can guide one to acquire this knowledge
- environmental support for the acquisition of this knowledge is minimal
- sometimes organisation actually suppress the acquisition of tacit knowledge
- wedded to contexts: tacit knowledge that would apply in one context would not necessarily apply in another context
- to help someone develop tacit knowledge, one would provide mediated learning experiences rather than direct instruction as to what to do, when
- *wisdom*: application of tacit knowledge as mediated by values toward the goal of achieving a common good
  a.   through a balance among multiple intrapersonal, interpersonal, and extrapersonal interests
  b.   in order to achieve balance among responses to environmental contexts
- adaptation to existing environmental contexts
- shaping of existing environmental context
- section new environmental context

Sternberg and Wagner (1989)
- rules of thumb that are useful to know to perform well in a given field

Sternberg (2000)
- comprises the lessons of life that are not explicitly taught and that often are not even verbalised (Sternberg, Wagner, Williams & Horvath, 1995).
- thus, tacit knowledge has three main features:
  a.   it is procedural
  b.   it is relevant to the attainment of goals people value
  c.   it typically is acquired through experience or mentoring, rather than through direct classroom or textbook instruction
- an example of tacit knowledge is knowing how to write and present an article for ensure publication
- forms an essential component of practical intelligence

Sternberg, Wagner and Okagaki (1993)

- practical know how usually not directly taught or even openly expressed or stated
- kind of knowledge that one picks up on a job or in everyday kinds of situations, rather than through formal instruction
- used in adaptation to environments
    - also in deciding when an environment is unsatisfactory and a new one needs to be sought out (environmental selection)
- when present environment can be shaped in a more nearly optimal one (shaping of the environment)
- most relevant to contextual or practical subtheory of the triarchic account of intelligence
- knowledge base that enables us to face the everyday world

Sternberg, Wagner, Williams and Horvath (1995)

- action oriented knowledge
- acquired without direct help from others
- procedural in nature
- relevant to the attainment of goals people value
- acquired with little (direct) help from others
- must be inferred from actions or statements
- always wedded to particular uses in particular situations or in classes of situations
- practically useful
- rules of thumb may permit explicit training of at least some aspect of tacit knowledge
- typically implied rather than stated explicitly
- complex, multiconditional rules for how to pursue particular goals in particular situations
- articulating general rules in roughly declarative form
- abstract/summary representation for family of complex specified procedural rules
- unspoken/underemphasized/poorly conveyed relative to its importance for practical success
- how to seek out, create, and enjoy challenges
- maintaining appropriate levels of
- self-motivation, self-direction, self-awareness, and personal
- completing tasks and working effectively within the business environment

Subramaniam and Venkatraman (2001)

- largely "indwells" in the minds of people as perspectives on, or images of, reality (Polanyi, 1966)
- define tacit overseas knowledge as "the knowledge of the differences among overseas markets that is difficult to codify and transfer in a systematic way".
- an unspoken and often subtle understanding of differences in cultures, tastes, habits, or customs (Jain, 1989; Subramaniam et al., 1998).

Sveiby (1997)

- used as a tool to handle what is being focused on
- functions as background knowledge that assists in accomplishing the task in focus
- varies from one situation to another
- often operates as a constraint
- articulated through models or concepts
- externalisation: combining thoughts into actual designs
- most person to person communication
- out of the corner of the eye
- unconscious
- teaches codes of behaviour and skills

Swaak and de Jong (2001)

- intuitive knowledge is hard to verbalise
- in explicit tasks sometimes labelled "inert"

Swap, Leonard, Shields and Abrams (2001)

- intangible assets exist in the tacit dimensions of knowledge
- built up over time in peoples' heads, hands and relationships

Takeuchi (1998)

- something not easily visible and expressible
- highly personal
- hard to formalise
- difficult to communicate or share with others
- subjective insights
- intuitions
- hunches

- inspirations
- deeply rooted in an individual's action/experience/ideals/values/emotions
- two dimensions
- technical: informal/hard to pin down skills/crafts often captured in the term "know-how"
- cognitive: beliefs/perceptions/ideals/values/emotions/mental (*Weltanschauung?*)

Takii (2000)

- even an instructor can not clearly describe what she wants to say
- What she can do is show several examples
- trainee must attempt to infer what the instructor wants to say from these examples
- the transfer of tacit knowledge requires long term face-to-face contact

Talisayon (2001)

- Many people know what works well in particular situations at work, at home and at play.
- embodied unconsciously in talented people or embedded in unrecognised excellent work routines
- unseen, not because they are hidden from view, but because we do not look for them or we do not know how to look for them

Tibau (2000)

- class participants realised that these concepts are influenced by their distinct culture, i.e., by deep tacit assumptions about how the world is, and ought to be, that they share as a group
- assumptions determine perceptions, thoughts, feelings, and, to some degree overt behaviour (Schein, 1996).
- implied, without being openly expressed
- highly personal
- deeply ingrained in action
- individual commitment to their specific economic context (Janssens and Tibau, 1995)

Torff and Sternberg (1998)

- practical know-how
- usually not directly taught or even openly expressed or stated
- kind of knowledge one acquires on the job or in everyday kinds of situations, rather than through formal instruction

- knowing how to convince others of the worth of your idea or product is not kind of knowledge likely to be taught, rather the kind of knowledge one picks up through experience
- procedural in nature, taking the form of "knowing how" (procedural knowledge) rather than "knowing that" (declarative knowledge)
- practically useful; it is directed toward attainment of goals that people value
- acquired under conditions of low environmental support; one often gains tacit knowledge on one's own, without much direct instruction
- generally unspoken, underemphasized, conveyed in indirect manner (Sternberg *et al.,* 1995, in above)
- knowledge about managing: (a) one's self, (b) others, and (c) tasks
- crossed with two orientations of tacit knowledge: local (oriented toward the attainment of short term goals, e.g., how to organise daily tasks)
- global (oriented toward the long term, e.g. how to get a promotion) (Wagner and Sternberg, 1985, in above)

Turner (1989)

- tacitness will refer strictly to the reproducible expectations
- assumptions
- presuppositions
- cognitive skills

van Daal, de Haas and Weggeman (1998)

- implicit knowledge: tacit knowledge, experience, skills and attitude, shared through demonstration, attainable through imitation in socialisation processes, can be used as power
- ESA: Experience, Skills and Attitude

Wachter (1999)

- personal and context specific, which is often developed over a long period of time through direct experience.
- due to the extent of embedded learning that supports it, such knowledge is frequently difficult to formalise and communicate.
- such knowledge is internalised and might not be readily transferable to a written report of step-by-step manual
- tacit knowledge also includes cognitive and technical elements
- technical element of includes concrete know-how, craft, and skill

Wagner and Sternberg (1985)

- knowledge usually not openly expressed/taught
- probably disorganised/informal/relatively inaccessible
- ill-suited for direct instruction
- not necessarily inaccessible to conscious awareness/unspeakable/unteachable
- not directly taught to most of us
  - *knowledge of managing self*: relative importance of tasks one faces, knowledge about more/less efficient ways of approaching tasks, knowledge about how to motivate oneself to maximise accomplishment
  - *knowledge of managing others*: managing subordinates/social relationships, assign/tailor tasks to take advantage of individual's strengths, minimise effects weaknesses, reward to maximise job performance/job satisfaction, how to get along with others
  - *knowledge about managing career*: career reputation established/enhanced, convince superiors of ideas/products, extent one's priorities reflect what is valued by organisation/field, how to gain respect/confidence of those who judge your work/determine promotions, how to convince others that your work as good as it is
- not automatically acquired with years of experience
- all purpose algorithms (Scriber, 1983, in above)
- abstract, high-level goals, plans developed as result of experience (Soloway, Erlich, Bonar, and Greenspan, 1982, in above)

Wagner and Sternberg (1987)

- knowledge usually not openly expressed/stated (*Oxford English Dictionary,* 1933, in above)
  - a. *content*: whether knowledge concerns management of oneself, management of others, management of one's tasks
  - b. *context*: whether knowledge concerned with short/long term accomplishments
  - c. *orientation*: whether knowledge concerns ideal quality or practically of judgements/decisions

Wagner and Sternberg (1990)

- work related practical know how that is learned informally on the job (Wagner and Sternberg, 1986, in above)
- "learning the ropes"
- "getting one's feet wet"
- "what goes on without saying around here"

West and Meyer (1997)

- organizational capabilities which are embedded in routines
- unobservable
- difficult to change

Woherem (1991)

- difficult to express
- gained through social/cultural interactions in society and area of work." (Gill, 1988a, in above)
- knowledge gained through apprenticeship

Wong and Radcliffe (2000)

- something that is gained through experience
- can only be observed through action
- inarticulable and uncodifiable
- extremely difficult, if not impossible, to articulate, put in writing or codify

Wyatt (2001)

- tacit knowledge (or intuition) defies recording. This kind of knowledge underlies personal skill, and its transfer requires face-to-face contact or even apprenticeship

Zack (1999)

- subconsciously understood/applied
- difficult to articulate
- developed from direct experience/action
- usually shared through highly interactive conversation/storytelling/shared experience

Zeira and Rosen (2000)

- Often referred to as intuition, common sense, or practice wisdom, is the implicit store of knowledge used in practice
- Is a meaningful and important source of information that influences practitioner's decisions and actions (Schon, 1983; Scott, 1990)
- Easily accessed on demand
- Remains elusive to critical examination and verification by scientific procedures (Reber, 1993)

Appendix B

Tacit Knowledge Maps Created Through a Qualitative Analysis of Tacit Knowledge Definitions

Figure B.1. Code family—Code groundedness of >9 instances

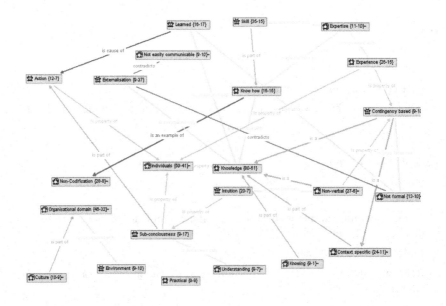

Figure B.2. Code family—Competition

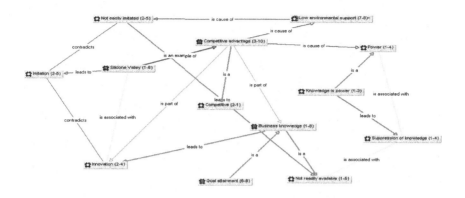

Figure B.3. Code family—Culture

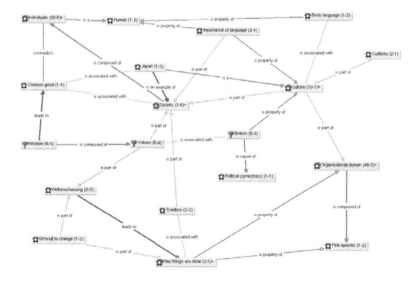

Figure B.4. Code family—Social environment

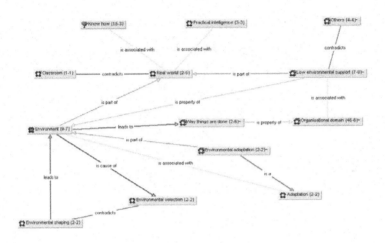

Figure B.5. Code family—Group interaction

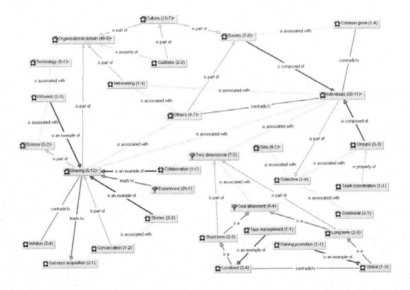

Figure B.6. Code family-Individuals

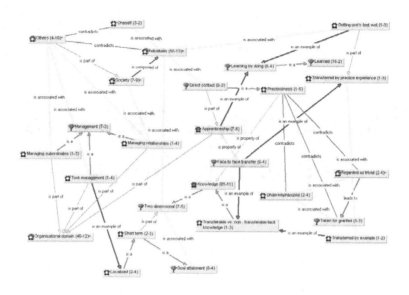

Figure B.7. Code family-Learning

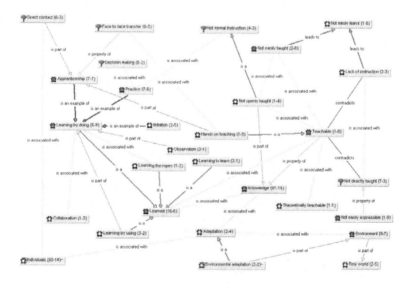

Appendix C

The Structure Charts for Organisation X

Figure C.1. Organisation X—Technology services—Development support (XXXX represent persons who did not participate in the research).

Figure C.2. Organisation X—Development support—Production enablement

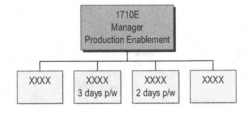

Figure C.3. Organisation X—Technology services—Development 1 (experts = green)

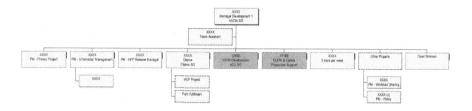

Figure C4. Organisation X—Technology services—Development 3 (experts = green; experts non-experts = blue)

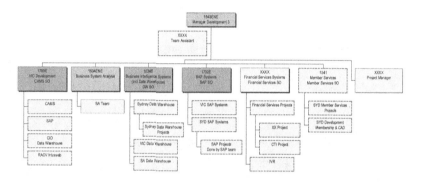

Figure C.5. Organisation X—Development 3—Business intelligence systems (experts = green; expert non-experts = blue)

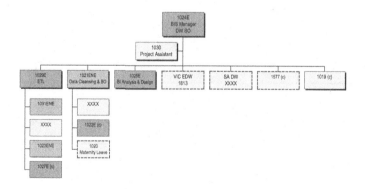

Figure C.6. Organisation X—Technology services—Development 3—Financial services (expert non-expert = blue)

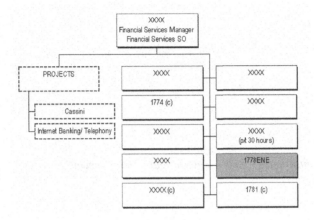

Figure C.7. Organisation X—Development 3—Member services (expert non-experts = blue)

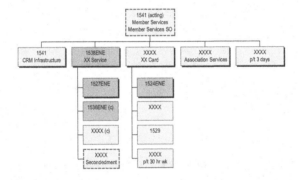

Figure C.8. Organisation X—Technology services—Development 3—SAP systems

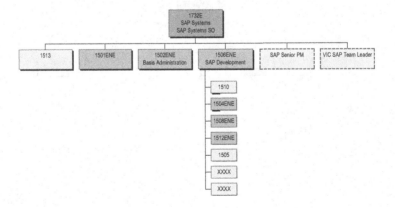

Figure C.9. Organisation X—Technology services—Development 3—VIC Development

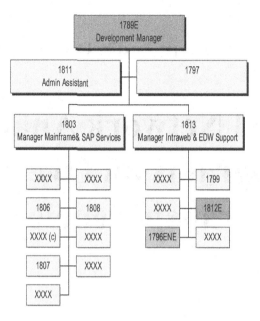

Appendix D

Social Network Analysis Sociograms on Overhead Transparencies

D.1 Organisation X

D.1.1 Organisation X and Contact Frequencies

Figure D.1. Illustrating legend for contact frequency links between nodes

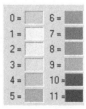

1= Quarterly (light yellow)
2= Bi-Monthly (Bright Yellow)
3= Monthly (Salmon Pink)
4=Fortnightly (Mid Orange)
5=Weekly (Dark Orange)
6=Daily (Bright Red)
7=Hourly (Dark Red)

Figure D.2. Here we have all the people who have participated in the research, for whom biographical information was provided

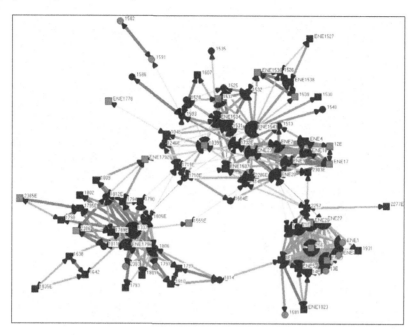

Figure D.3. Illustrating our communication picture with the removal of contractors

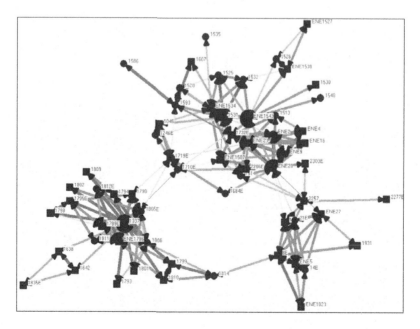

Figure D.4. Illustrating bi-monthly contact between certain staff members

Figure D.5. Illustrating staff who contact each other monthly

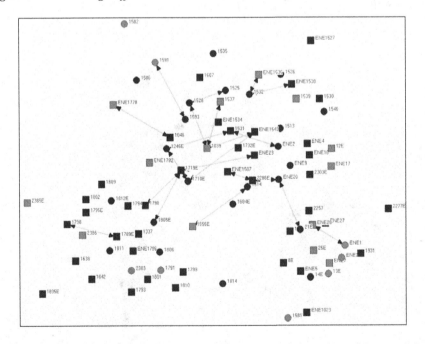

Figure D.6. Illustrating staff who meet each other fortnightly

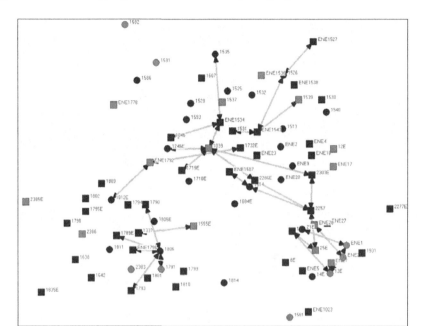

Figure D.7. Illustrating staff who meet each other weekly

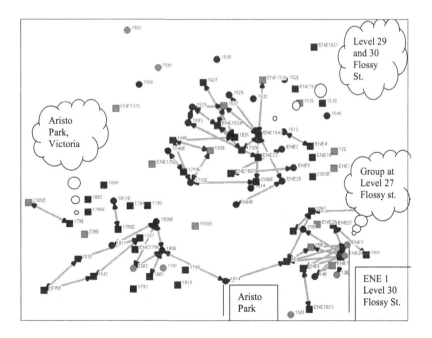

Figure D.8. Illustrating people who meet each other daily

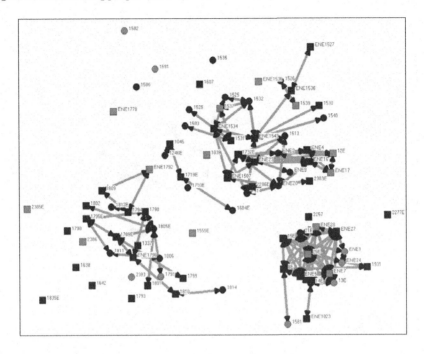

Figure D.9. Illustrating people who meet each other hourly

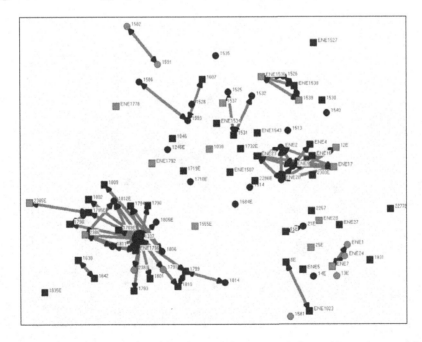

D.1.2 Organisation X and Hierarchy/Clique Behaviour

Figure D.10. Showing our highest ranking people, 1046 has 50+ subordinates, 1246E has 40-44 subordinates, 1719E has 25 to 29 subordinates, 1534 and 12E have 10-14 subordinates

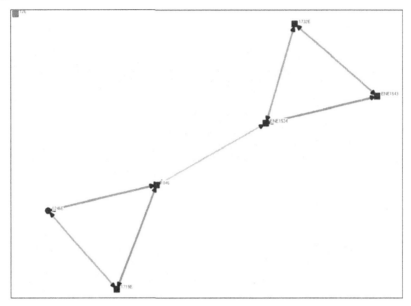

Figure D.11. Now including people with 5 to 9 subordinates

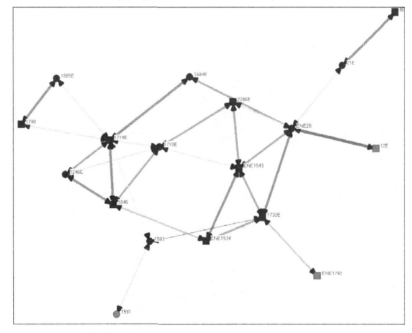

D.1.3 Organisation X and Person Importance

Figure D.12. Key for person importance

1 = Try not to see (Bright Red)
2 = Can get by without seeing (Light blue)
3 = Moderately important (Mid blue)
4 = Very Important (Dark aqua)
5 = HAVE to see (Dark blue)

Figure D.13. Everyone and the importance of the individual

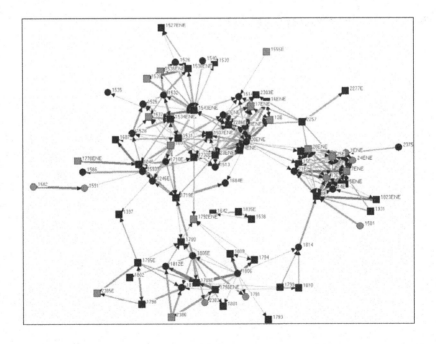

Figure D.14. People who try to avoid one another

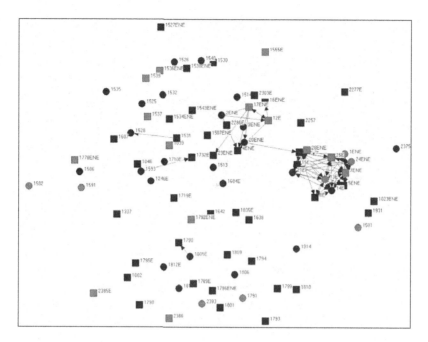

Figure D.15. Can get by without seeing

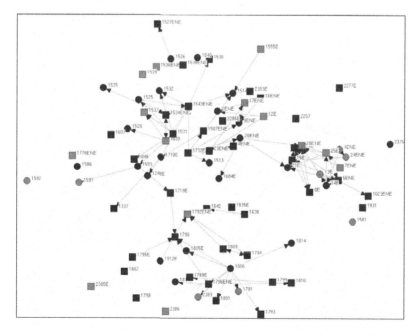

Figure D.16. Moderately important to see the individual

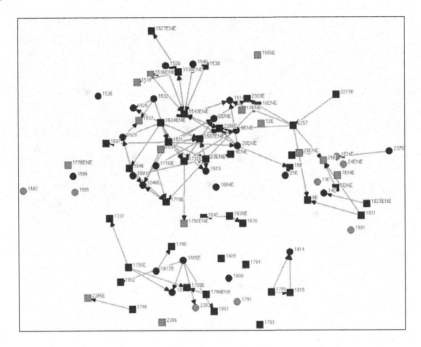

Figure D.17. Very important to see these individuals

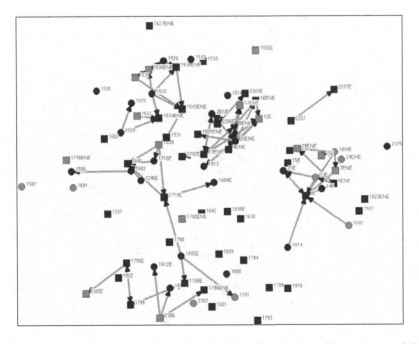

Figure D.18. These individuals have to be seen

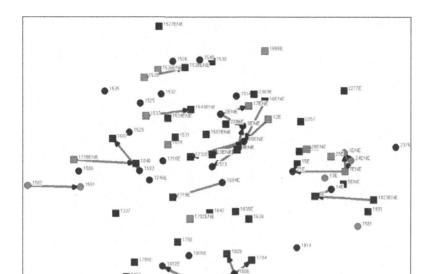

D.1.4 Organisation X and Meeting Types with an Emphasis on Electronic Mediums

Figure D.19. Illustrating key to communication patterns

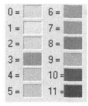

1= **Outside work** (Light Green)
2= **Phone** (Grey/green)
3= **Fax** (Dark Grey)
4= **Email** (Mid Grey)
5= **Bump into** (Mid Green)
6= **Lunch/Morning/Afternoon Tea** (Mid-Dark Green)
7= **Informal/Pre-arranged meeting** (Sherwood Green)
8= **Formal meeting** (very Dark Green)

Figure D.20. People who contact one another by phone

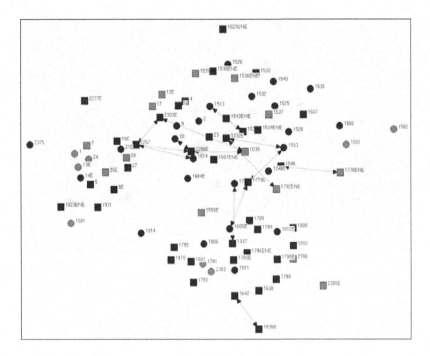

Figure D.21. People who contact each other by e-mail

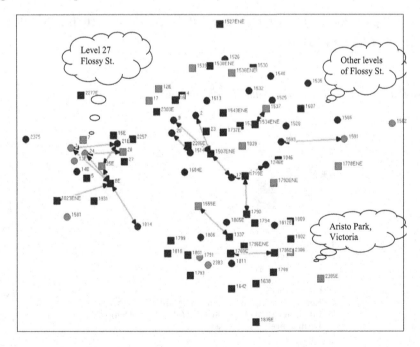

D.1.5 Organisation X with an Emphasis on Face-to-Face Meetings

Figure D.22. Legend for only those people who have face to face meetings (i.e. are likely to pass on tacit knowledge)

1 = Formal organisational meetings
2 = Informal but pre-arranged meetings
3 = See one another outside of work
4 = Meet each other at morning/afternoon tea or lunch
5 = Bump into each other in the workplace

Figure D.23. Showing only those people who conduct face to face meetings with one another

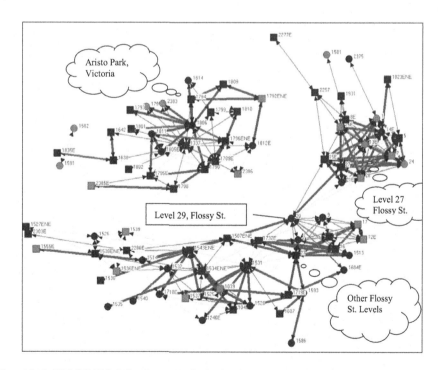

Figure D.24. Formal organisational meetings

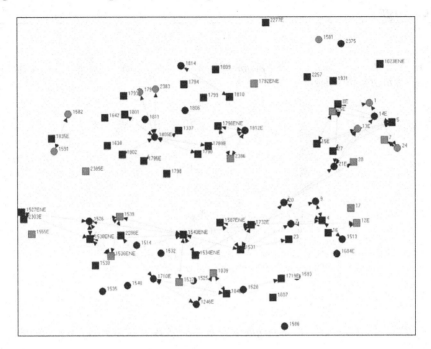

Figure D.25. Informal organisational meetings

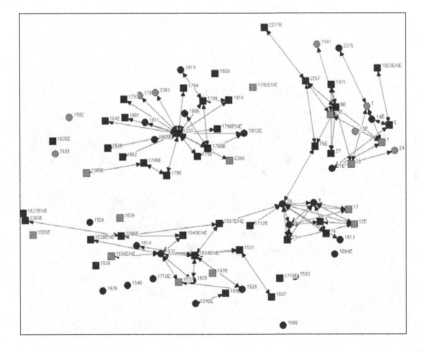

Figure D.26. Outside of work

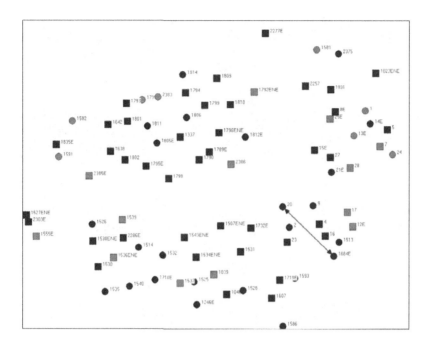

Figure D.27. Lunch/morning/afternoon tea

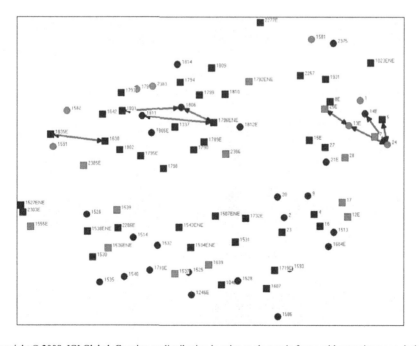

Figure D.28. Bump into each other in the workplace

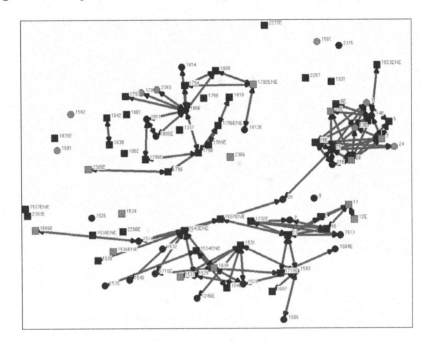

D.2 Organisation Y

D.2.1 Organisation Y and Contact Frequencies

Figure D.29. Illustrating legend for contact frequency links between nodes

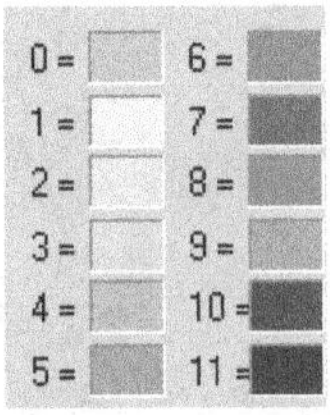

0 =	6 =
1 =	7 =
2 =	8 =
3 =	9 =
4 =	10 =
5 =	11 =

1= Quarterly (light yellow)
2= Bi-Monthly (Bright Yellow)
3= Monthly (Salmon Pink)
4=Fortnightly (Mid Orange)
5=Weekly (Dark Orange)
6=Daily (Bright Red)
7=Hourly (Dark Red)

Figure D.30. Illustrating all relationships by gender and employment type for Organisation Y

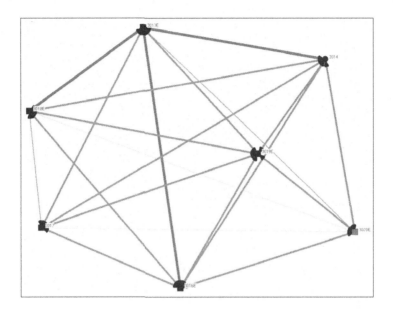

Figure D.31. Illustrating our contractor removed

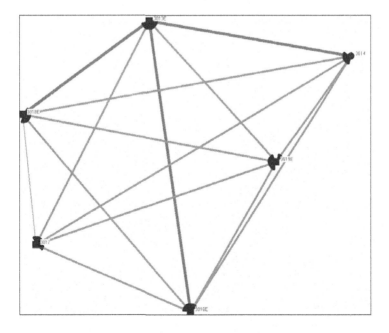

Figure D.32. Illustrating fortnightly meetings amongst Organisation Y members

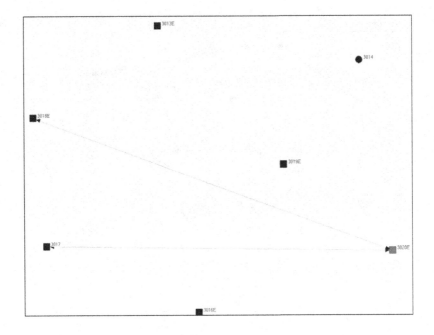

Figure D.33. Illustrating weekly meetings amongst Organisation Y staff members

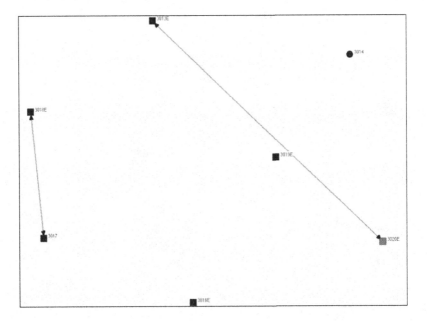

Figure D.34. Illustrating daily staff meetings amongst Organisation Y staff members

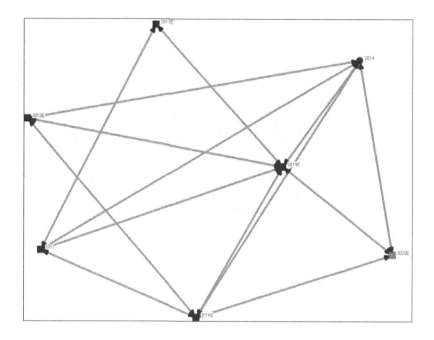

Figure D.35. Illustrating hourly meetings in Organisation Y

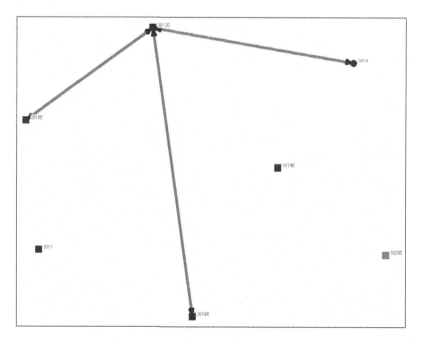

D.2.2 Organisation Y and Person Importance

Figure D.36. Key for person importance

1 = Try not to see (Bright Red)
2 = Can get by without seeing (Light blue)
3 = Moderately important (Mid blue)
4 = Very Important (Dark aqua)
5 = HAVE to see (Dark blue)

Figure D.37. Can get by without seeing

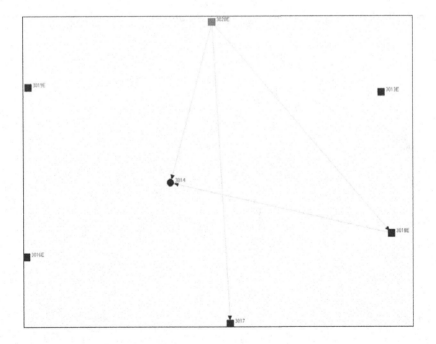

Figure D.38. Illustrating moderately important people

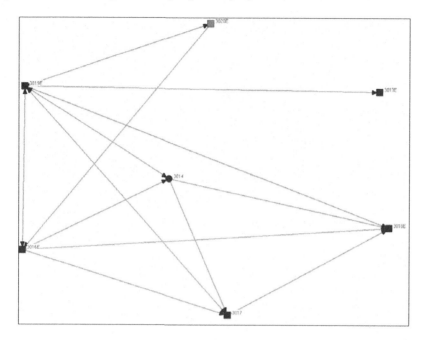

Figure D.39. Illustrating very important people

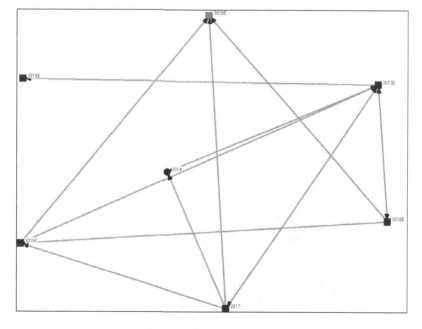

Figure D.40. Illustrating people who just have to be seen

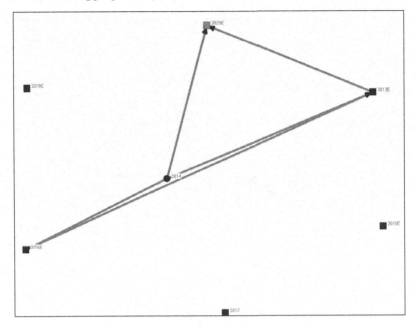

D.2.3 Organisation Y and Meeting Types[a]

Figure D.41. Illustrating key to communication patterns

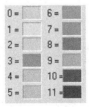

1= Outside work (Light Green)
2= Phone (Grey/green)
3= Fax (Dark Grey)
4= Email (Mid Grey)
5= Bump into (Mid Green)
6= Lunch/Morning/Afternoon Tea (Mid-Dark Green)
7= Informal/Pre-arranged meeting (Sherwood Green)
8= Formal meeting (very Dark Green)

Figure D.42. Organisation Y staff members who tend to just bump into each other

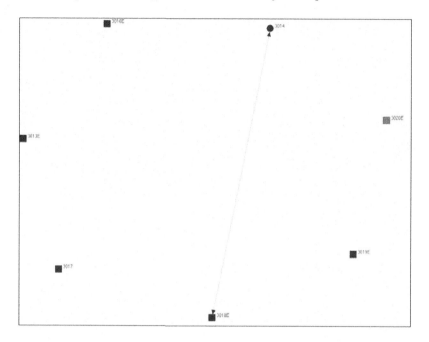

Figure D.43. Our staff who participate in informal yet pre-arranged meetings

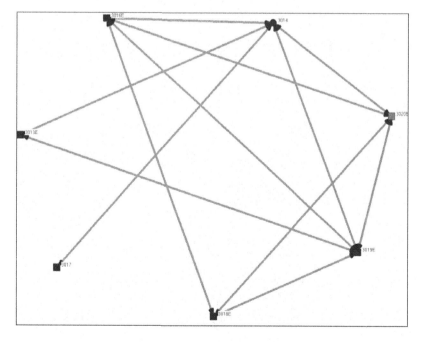

Figure D.44. Illustrating formal meetings that take place between Organisation Y

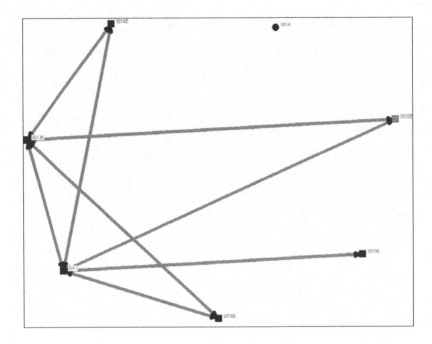

D.3 Organisation Z

D.3.1 Organisation Z and Contact Frequencies

Figure D.45. Illustrating legend for contact frequency links between nodes

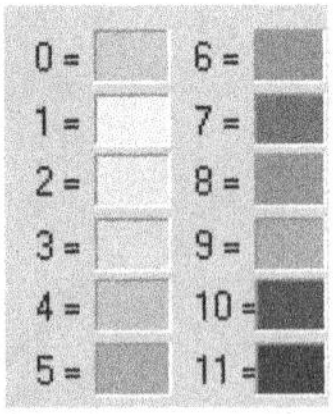

1= Quarterly (light yellow)
2= Bi-Monthly (Bright Yellow)
3= Monthly (Salmon Pink)
4=Fortnightly (Mid Orange)
5=Weekly (Dark Orange)
6=Daily (Bright Red)
7=Hourly (Dark Red)

Figure D.46. Contact frequency of everyone in Organisation Z

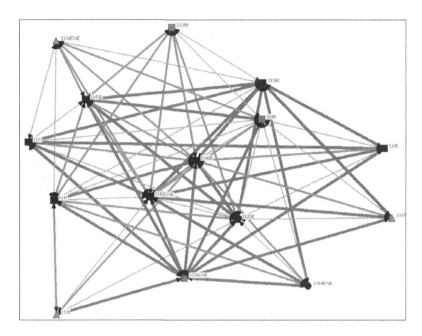

Figure D.47. Illustrating weekly meetings taking place in Organisation Z

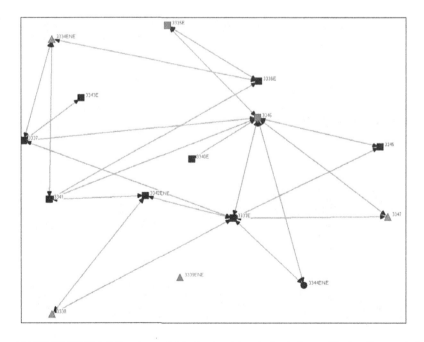

Figure D.48. Illustrating daily meetings taking place between Organisation Z people

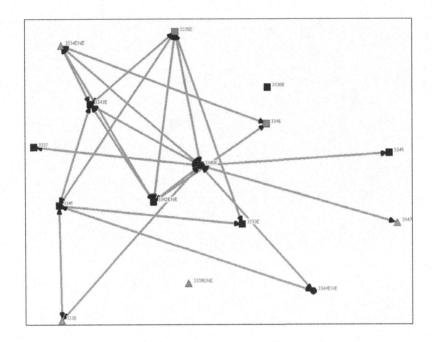

Figure D.49. Illustrating the effects of 3340E being removed from the communication picture

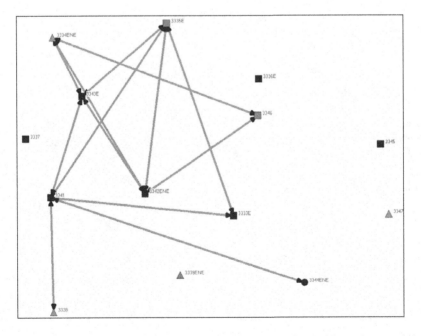

Figure D.50. Illustrating hourly meetings taking place between our personnel in Organisation Z

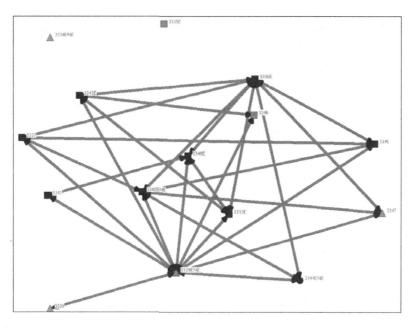

Figure D.51. Illustrating the removal of 3339

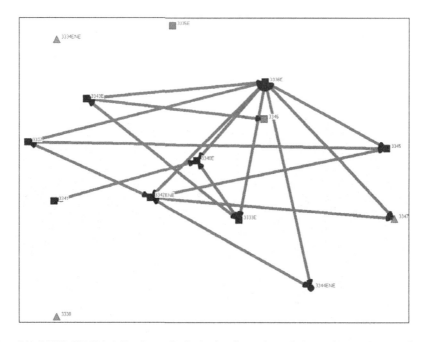

D.3.2 Organisation Z and Person Importance

Figure D.52. Key for person importance

1 = Try not to see (Bright Red)
2 = Can get by without seeing (Light blue)
3 = Moderately important (Mid blue)
4 = Very Important (Dark aqua)
5 = HAVE to see (Dark blue)

Figure D.53. Illustrating situations where 3342 tries to avoid other staff members

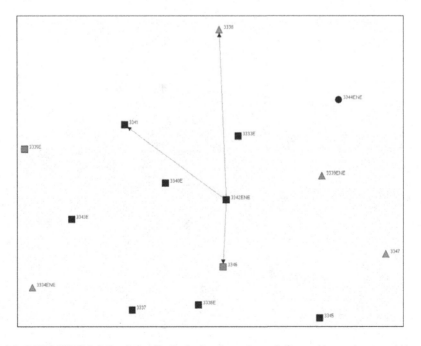

Figure D.54. Can get by without seeing the individual

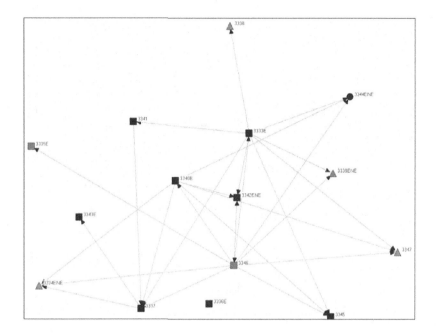

Figure D.55. Moderately important

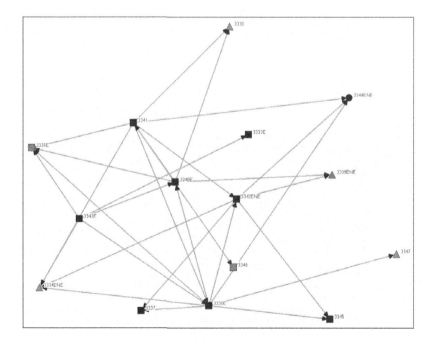

Figure D.56. Very important

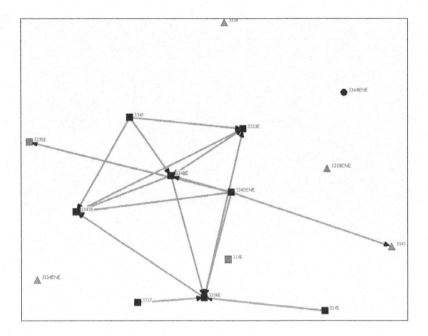

Figure D.57. Illustrating individuals that simply have to seen in Organisation Z

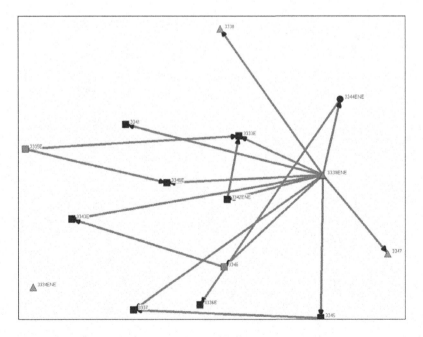

D.3.3 Organisation Z and Meeting Types

Figure D.58. Illustrating key to communication patterns

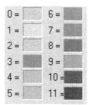

1= Outside work (Light Green)
2= Phone (Grey/green)
3= Fax (Dark Grey)
4= Email (Mid Grey)
5= Bump into (Mid Green)
6= Lunch/Morning/Afternoon Tea (Mid-Dark Green)
7= Informal/Pre-arranged meeting (Sherwood Green)
8= Formal meeting (very Dark Green)

Figure D.59. Illustrating the respondents communicating by way of telephone

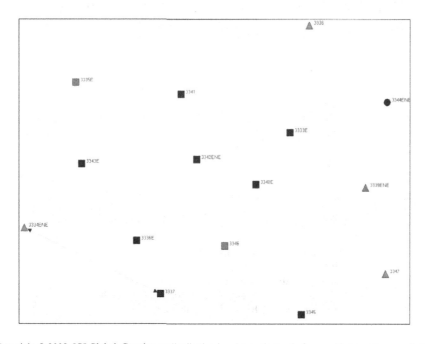

Figure D.60. Illustrating email contact amongst Organisation Z respondents

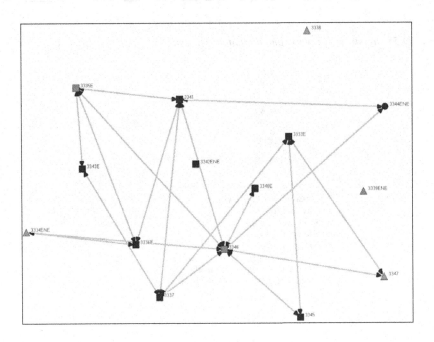

D.3.4 Organisation Z and Meetings of a Face-to-Face Nature

Figure D.61. Legend for only those people who have face to face meetings (i.e. are likely to pass on tacit knowledge)

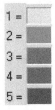

1 = Formal organisational meetings
2 = Informal but pre-arranged meetings
3 = See one another outside of work
4 = Meet each other at morning/afternoon tea or lunch
5 = Bump into each other in the workplace

Figure D.62. Illustrating all Organisation Z people who participate in face to face meetings

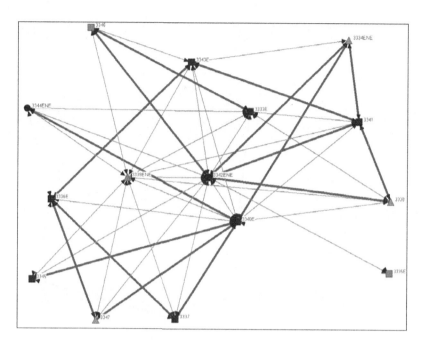

Figure D.63. Those who meet in formal organisational meetings

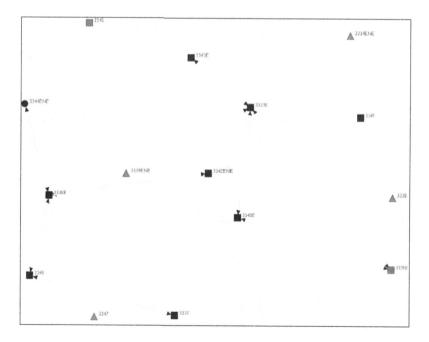

Figure D.64. Those who meet in informal but pre-arranged meetings

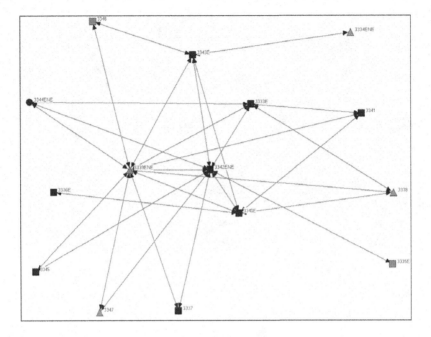

Figure D.65. Those who bump into one another (note none of the organisation Z people answered that they met at lunch/morning/afternoon tea or outside of work).

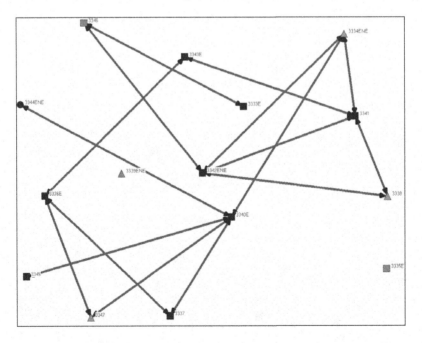

Endnote

[a]   Remember only the one colour scheme was used here for both face to face and electronic communication because of the small nature of the organisation.

Appendix E

Extra Social Network Analysis Supporting Data

E.1 Section A

E.1.1 Organisation X (Extra Supporting Data)

Table E.1. Illustrating in and out degrees for respondents from Organisation X, in descending order of out-degree

Degrees	Out	In
1039	268	2
20	170	34
1531	165	6
1710E	157	6
1534	91	18
2257	85	3
1555E	79	3
1507	78	15
2303E	72	10
23	67	24
1543	65	47
2286E	62	22
1684E	60	6
1806	58	0

1532	56	4
1593	54	2
1805E	48	5
1719E	44	24
1732E	43	27
9	42	27
1778	40	0
5	38	11
1046	31	26
14E	30	15
4	29	17
13E	29	11
7	28	15
1526	28	11
1582	28	0
1	27	19

1795E	27	7
1528	26	9
1536	26	15
2	25	24
1835E	25	0
25E	25	21
24	24	9
1538	22	23
12E	22	22
15E	22	14
1539	21	11
2277E	20	4
1796	19	9
8E	18	51
1931	16	0
1812E	16	12

Table E.1. continued

21E	15	30
16	13	14
27	13	15
1614	13	0
1799	13	3
2386	12	8
17	11	16
1798	11	7
1810	10	8
2375	10	0
1537	9	10
1814	9	8
28	8	25
1023	8	2
1581	8	0
1794	8	10
1809	8	7

1638	6	6
1790	6	15
1514	4	15
1521	4	0
1524	4	0
1525	4	12
1811	4	20
1246E	4	14
1527	3	5
1530	3	2
1792	3	9
1789E	3	29
1513	2	17
1535	2	2
1791	2	9
1793	2	5
2383	2	8

1144	0	0
1337	0	5
1529	0	0
1533	0	12
1540	0	3
1586	0	4
1591	0	7
1607	0	8
1642	0	8
1801	0	8
1802	0	6
2385E	0	7
	Out	In
Mean	7.5	7.5
Std Dev	25.6	7.8
Min	0	0
Max	268	75

E.2 Section B

The following set of diagrams represent social network analysis graphs for Organisation X where only those participants who chose a particular meeting type, contact frequency or person importance in relation to themselves is revealed.

For example the reader may note that in chapter 7 nodes (actors) are identified who do not have links with one another. This was done to maintain a consistency between viewing one actor network with the next to visualise where edges (lines of communication between actors) *dropped out*.

The following figures show only actors who have chosen a particular relationship type; hence all nodes have edges between them. The disadvantage of this approach is that one is unable to 'overlay' one map to the next. The SNA software instead recalculates the positions (actors) to best fit them on the screen, so no one actor is ever in the same place for the next diagram and so on.

E.2.1 A Closer View: Contact Frequency Patterns

Figure E.1. A closer view of staff who contact each other bi-monthly

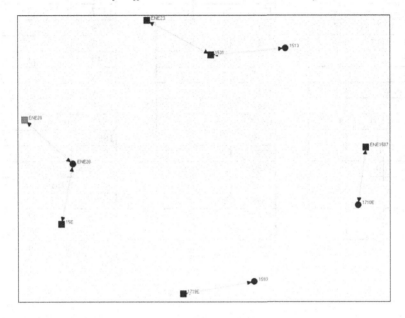

Figure E.2. Illustrating a closer view of staff who see each other monthly

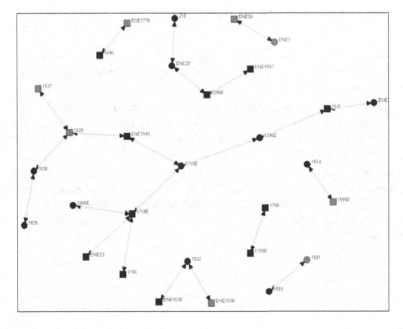

Figure E.3. Organisation X staff members who contact each other fortnightly

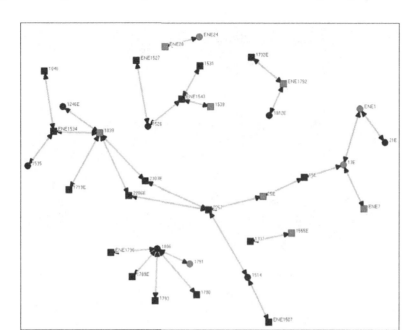

Figure E.4. Illustrating in closer detail, staff at Organisation X who contact each other weekly

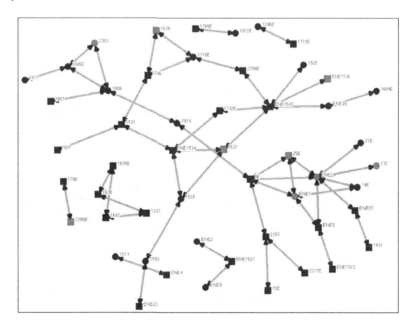

Figure E.5. Showing more clearly staff who contact one another daily

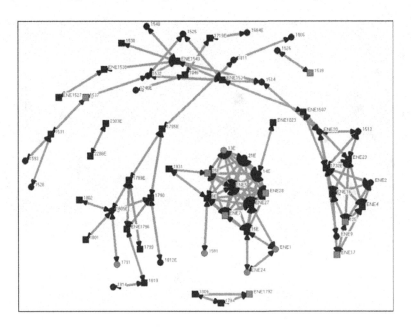

Figure E.6. A closer look: Hourly meetings

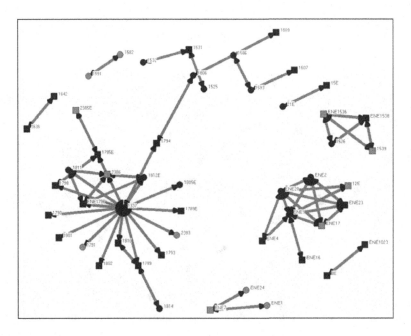

E.2.2 A Closer Look: Person Importance

Figure E.7. Try not to see

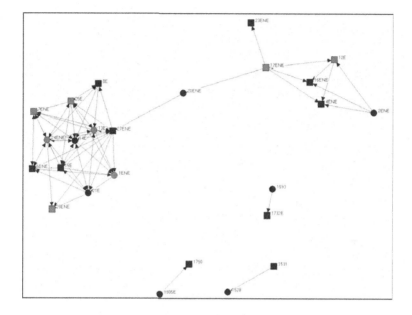

Figure E.8. Can get by without seeing

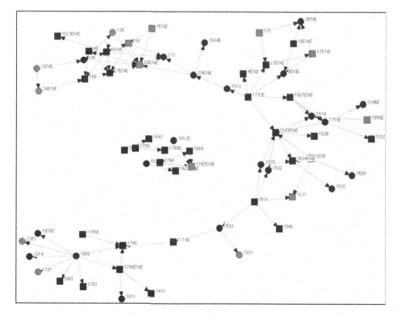

Figure E.9. Illustrating people who are moderately important to be seen

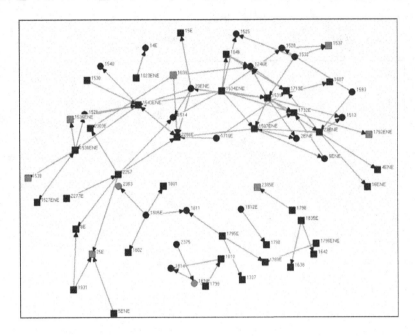

Figure E.10. Very important to see

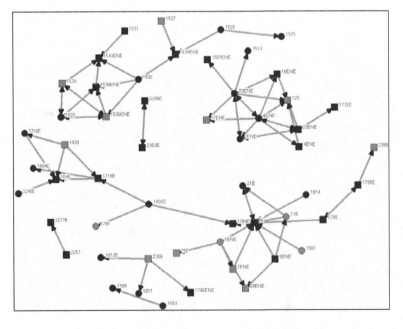

Figure E.11. Just have to be seen

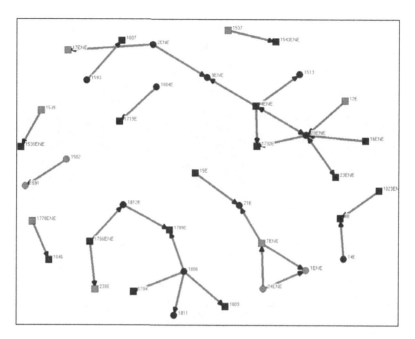

E.2.3 Meeting Types and Organisation X

Figure E.12. Only formal organisational meetings

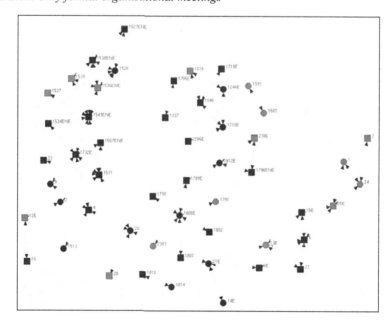

Figure E.13. Informal organisational meetings

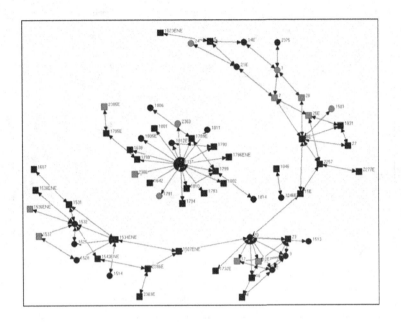

Figure E.14. Lunch/morning/afternoon tea

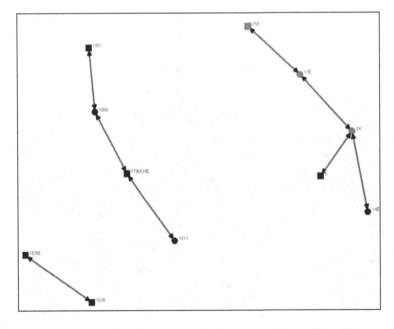

Figure E.15. bump into each other in the workplace

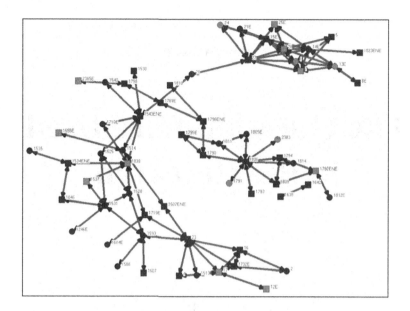

Appendix F

The Questionnaire Used in the Research

F.1 Part A: Biographical Details

An examination of articulable Tacit Knowledge within the Information Systems domain

Introduction

The following forms a component of a methodology aimed at extracting levels of *articulable Tacit Knowledge* within the computing domain. Tacit knowledge relates to 'management' ability, not necessarily just management of other people, but of resources, time, even one's own career, as research in Psychology at Yale University in the United States has indicated. What we present here is a questionnaire along the lines used in other tacit knowledge tests, except that in this instance the questionnaire has been made more Information Systems relevant. Furthermore the processing of our results will also take a unique approach insofar as we seek to examine the diffusion of tacit knowledge throughout the IS organisational domain.

Although I used to be a Netscape fan, I find myself confessing that the questionnaire 'looks better' on Internet Explorer. Ultimately of course, which platform you choose to use is up to you :-)

Please remember results are anonymous, all individuals will be de-identified, furthermore the experimentation has passed the rigours of a University Ethics Committee. In any case we do not consider the scenarios and answer options to be particularly contentious.

Directions

It would be much appreciated if participants simply perform the following sequence of instructions

1. Please close down as many other applications 'as possible' so that the questionnaire software is able to properly load. If this is inconvenient at present, then choose a more appropriate time to complete the questionnaire

2. Fill in the Biographical Details (Part A)

3. Continue (after pressing the submit button) through to the Social Network Analysis (Part B) relationship related information

4. Complete the Tacit Knowledge Inventory (Part C) by selecting the most appropriate measure on the Likert Scale (7 point scale) for each answer option in relation to each of the 6 chosen scenarios

Naturally results from this questionnaire are confidential.

Part A: Biographical Details

1. Gender:

○ Male	○ Female

2. Please provide information pertaining to your age

Please select your age group	Age range [<PLEASE SELECT> ▼]

3. IF a language OTHER than English is spoken in your home environment, please select these from the lists below:

Please fill in the language related information, where applicable	Please begin by answering the MAIN language other than English spoken in the home [-- ▼] If applicable, select the next major language in order of usage in the home [-- ▼] And the next language after that? [-- ▼] And yet another? [-- ▼]

4. Please provide details relating to occupational status, simply select the occupation CLOSEST to your role

Current occupational status	What IS the CLOSEST MAIN job you are CURRENTLY in? [<PLEASE SELECT> ▼] What was your MAIN position three (3) years ago? [<PLEASE SELECT> ▼] Finally what was the MAIN position you were in six (6) years ago? [<PLEASE SELECT> ▼]

5. Please type the occupation you were engaged in before joining the IT industry

Occupation prior to your IT occupation?	[_____]

6. How many years of I.T. experience would you say you had?

Choose an experience range	Years of experience? [<PLEASE SELECT> ▼]

7. Are you a contract or permanent employee of this organisation?

○ Contract staff member	○ Permanent staff member

8. How long have you been with the current organisation?

Choose a value	Years with the present organisation? [<PLEASE SELECT> ▼]

9. Please provide information concerning the number of subordinates under you

How many subordinates do you have?	How many? [<PLEASE SELECT> ▼]

10. What Australian Computer Society (ACS) level would you consider yourself to be?

What Australian Computer Society level would you be?	Australian Computer Society level [<PLEASE SELECT> ▼]

11. Are you a member of a professional computing organisation?

Which organisation would this be?	Organisation [-- ▼]
Other Societies/Associations?	[_____]

12. Please select the HIGHEST formal qualification (or equivalent) you have obtained

Highest qualification?	Qualification? [<PLEASE SELECT> ▼]

13. Do you have any TECHNICAL (COMPUTING SPECIFIC) qualifications?

Please click the submit button thereby continuing on to the next page SUBMIT

F.2 Part B: Social Network Analysis Details

Part B: Social Network Analysis

1. Please select individuals of relevance to yourself, select the levels of importance and frequency and type of contact. In question 2 below, you may say if you have trouble getting hold of them.

Please note that you may have more than one (1) type of intra-organisational relationship with someone, if so please select another set of relationship information for the same individual

2. Because tacit knowledge is often passed in inter-personal settings, do you find you have trouble getting to see people? Who are they ...? (Remember individuals are de-indentified)

Hard to find people?

3. Please provide feedback on whom you feel is SUCCESSFUL or PROFICIENT in what they do within the IT section of your organisation? Or in other words are there some GURUs you know of in the IT section ... ?

Successful persons?

When satisfied with your Social Network Analysis Relations, click the submit button below which will take you to the Tacit Knowledge Section.

SUBMIT

F.3 Part C: Tacit Knowledge Inventory

F.3.1 Scenario 1

Part C: (articulable) Tacit Knowledge Inventory for Information Systems

We realise that any of the following questionnaire scenarios may be tackled from an IDEAL (ethical) and a REALISTIC (perhaps unethical) point of view. We would like you to select BOTH an IDEAL AND REALISTIC value for each answer option.

Read each scenario and select what you consider to be the most appropriate scale for each answer option. Remember we would like you to select BOTH an IDEAL AND REALISTIC value for each answer option.

Scenario 1

You are a DataBase Administrator and have been assigned to a team to begin a data modelling exercise for a new but what you consider to be relatively trivial standalone 'desktop' database.

The modelling technique to be used will be the Unified Modelling Language (UML) with its emphasis on a more modern object oriented approach. You would prefer to be using the traditional Entity - Association (E-A) approach as you feel you don't really need to model all functional and dynamic aspects of the software process, the static model alone should suffice.

The Data Administrator (DA) who is senior to yourself within the organisation, but not actually directly involved in the project, has decided that the UML approach is more modern and therefore preferable. While you generally get on okay with the DA, you get along even better with the Chief Information Officer (CIO) and you feel that the CIO is likely to support your independent efforts.

You participate in the exercise, however you are convinced that for the size of the database being created, the E-A approach would more than suffice.

Rate each of the following responses in relation to the given scenario. It is advisable to read all of the responses before replying.

1 Help the others in the team but take very much a 'back seat' role yourself, so that if the design should have problems or go overtime because of excessive modelling effort, at least you have not wasted too much of your time.

2 Simply decide that resistance for such a 'trivial' exercise is futile and decide to go along with the others in the team, even though you still feel the E-A technique would have sufficed

ETHICAL Choose one: Extremely Bad   Neither Good nor Bad   Extremely Good
REALISTIC Choose one: Extremely Bad   Neither Good nor Bad   Extremely Good

3 Decide to formally protest to the Data Administrator, saying you have too much work to do to be involved in such a trivial exercise

ETHICAL Choose one: Extremely Bad   Neither Good nor Bad   Extremely Good
REALISTIC Choose one: Extremely Bad   Neither Good nor Bad   Extremely Good

4 Consider asking the Data Administrator to clarify the basis for using UML, so that other team members might better see the benefits making use of this modelling technique, in the hope that either the DA is forced to rethink his decision or the other team members start to see your way of doing things

5 Try to assign someone else to the team in your place and hope that the problem will eventually go away

ETHICAL
Choose one:
Extremely Bad   Neither Good nor Bad   Extremely Good

REALISTIC
Choose one:
Extremely Bad   Neither Good nor Bad   Extremely Good

6 Participate in the exercise, however decide to take it upon yourself to produce your own version in E-A format to be used later in a 'hold you to' deliverance

ETHICAL
Choose one:
Extremely Bad   Neither Good nor Bad   Extremely Good

REALISTIC
Choose one:
Extremely Bad   Neither Good nor Bad   Extremely Good

7 Find that all of a sudden your diary is very full, therefore you are unable to participate in the project because of a paper you realise you need to be delivering at the conference in Singapore next month

ETHICAL
Choose one:
Extremely Bad   Neither Good nor Bad   Extremely Good

REALISTIC
Choose one:
Extremely Bad   Neither Good nor Bad   Extremely Good

8 Fully agree to the implementation of the system as it stands in the hope the CIO (and DA) will notice your enthusiasm, perhaps with the possibility that you will be given 'ride' projects in the future

ETHICAL
Choose one:
Extremely Bad   Neither Good nor Bad   Extremely Good

REALISTIC
Choose one:
Extremely Bad   Neither Good nor Bad   Extremely Good

9 Do you have any suggestions for how you would deal with the above scenario (or perhaps change the wording of the scenario), both ETHICALLY and REALISTICALLY, in addition to the options presented above?

ETHICAL
What would you do ETHICALLY?

REALISTIC
What would you do REALISTICALLY?

Please click the submit button and continue on with the next scenario SUBMIT

F.3.2 Scenario 2

Part C: (articulable) Tacit Knowledge Inventory for Information Systems

We realise that any of the following questionnaire scenarios may be tackled from an IDEAL (ethical) and a REALISTIC (perhaps unethical) point of view. We would like you to select BOTH an IDEAL AND REALISTIC value for each answer option.

Read each scenario and select what you consider to be the most appropriate scale for each answer option. Remember we would like you to select BOTH an IDEAL AND REALISTIC value for each answer option.

Scenario 2

The network manager wishes to install a token ring network. This person has been with the organisation for 6 years, you however are a junior technical analyst, but realise that a Ethernet backbone would better suit the layout of the building

You have been with the organisation for three years, but before that you were a network administrator for a couple of years in another small organisation.

To complicate matters further you are a Certified Novell Engineer (CNE), the manager does not actually have this qualification but has 'work experience' instead. Admittedly you realise the network manager has been able to acquire the necessary hardware and software at 'reasonable' rates (because the administrator is good friends with the suppliers of equipment), however you know that an Ethernet network would be simple to install and also relatively 'affordable'.

Rate each of the following responses in relation to the given scenario. It is advisable to read all of the responses before replying.

1 Approach the network manager with contacts of your own (made during your time in the previous organisation), whom you feel could offer an even better deal

ETHICAL
Choose one:
Extremely Bad   Neither Good nor Bad   Extremely Good

REALISTIC
Choose one:
Extremely Bad   Neither Good nor Bad   Extremely Good

2. As you have only been in the organisation for three years you feel you would be 'getting above your station' to in any way disagree with the network manager

ETHICAL
Choose one:

Extremely Bad			Neither Good nor Bad			Extremely Good

REALISTIC
Choose one:

Extremely Bad			Neither Good nor Bad			Extremely Good

3. Diplomatically 'inform' the network manager that an advantage to a CNE or indeed similar qualification, is that many case studies are examined where networking scenarios are explored in depth and 'best possible' solutions theoretically decided upon. You hope by using such an approach to get the network manager to see things your way

ETHICAL
Choose one:

Extremely Bad			Neither Good nor Bad			Extremely Good

REALISTIC
Choose one:

Extremely Bad			Neither Good nor Bad			Extremely Good

4. You quietly go about drawing up your own set of specifications that will ultimately show that you are correct, hoping to eventually show this to the chief information officer

ETHICAL
Choose one:

Extremely Bad			Neither Good nor Bad			Extremely Good

REALISTIC
Choose one:

Extremely Bad			Neither Good nor Bad			Extremely Good

5. Politely approach the network manager and let the person know of your thoughts, hoping this will change the situation

ETHICAL
Choose one:

Extremely Bad			Neither Good nor Bad			Extremely Good

REALISTIC
Choose one:

Extremely Bad			Neither Good nor Bad			Extremely Good

6. Ignore the situation, although you are not comfortable with it, you realise that realistically there is little you can do and in case if something should go wrong it's not going to be your fault

ETHICAL
Choose one:

Extremely Bad			Neither Good nor Bad			Extremely Good

REALISTIC
Choose one:

Extremely Bad			Neither Good nor Bad			Extremely Good

7. You agree 'in principle' to agree with the network manager, hoping that this person will support you when you want to implement a system of your own you have planned that may not be the most cost effective for the organisation, but nevertheless will help the organisation in the long run

ETHICAL
Choose one:

Extremely Bad			Neither Good nor Bad			Extremely Good

REALISTIC
Choose one:

Extremely Bad			Neither Good nor Bad			Extremely Good

8. Do you have any suggestions for how you would deal with the above scenario (or perhaps change the wording of the scenario), both ETHICALLY and REALISTICALLY, in addition to the options presented above?

ETHICAL

What would you do ETHICALLY?

REALISTIC

What would you do REALISTICALLY?

Please click the submit button and continue on with the next scenario [SUBMIT]

F.3.3 Scenario 3

Part C: (articulable) Tacit Knowledge Inventory for Information Systems

We realise that any of the following questionnaire scenarios may be tackled from an IDEAL (ethical) and a REALISTIC (perhaps unethical) point of view. We would like you to select BOTH an IDEAL AND REALISTIC value for each answer option.

Read each scenario and select what you consider to be the most appropriate scale for each answer option. Remember we would like you to select BOTH an IDEAL AND REALISTIC value for each answer option.

Scenario 3

You as a team leader are responsible for implementing a payroll system for another branch within the parent organization. Although you are expected to do the bulk of the work (55%), you do have five other colleagues able to help as you so desire. The project should take 12 months in total to complete.

You have undertaken some of the initial systems design work largely yourself for the past couple of months, and you now require your colleagues to further help you with the next stage which is mainly that of coding.

You are comfortable with hierarchy, however some of your team members are not. You delegate some tasks to subordinates within your team. One of the team members who specialises in programming has been allocated some software specification work, but would prefer really just to be programming. This person has performed well on coding related tasks in the past, but at this point in time lacks project management skills which would prevent him from becoming an effective team leader. Nevertheless you feel that the person should at least do some of the software specification work.

Rate each of the following responses in relation to the given scenario. It is advisable to read all of the responses before replying.

1. Call him into your office at the end of the working day and question him about his recalcitrance, hoping to overcome the obstacle very early on in the project

2. Consider approaching a mentor within the organisation or perhaps the Human Resources section, in the expectation they might provide you with some advice as to how to handle the individual in question

3. Replace him in the team, suspecting that he will probably be 'too much of a handful' anyway, and choose to simply wear the consequences; the chances are that he will be found other work to do anyway

4. Having called him into your office, discuss the overall project with him, telling him he is being assigned specific tasks because of his unique skills. Phrase things in such a way that it at least appears that what he being assigned is as important as any aspect of the project

5. Leave the person within the team, but in a subtle way perhaps verbally and physically (by way of body language), make it clear to the person that if they intend to be difficult, so will you

ETHICAL
Choose one: Extremely Bad — Neither Good nor Bad — Extremely Good

REALISTIC
Choose one: Extremely Bad — Neither Good nor Bad — Extremely Good

6. Let him have his say, encourage him to express his ideas, find out his goals to see if you can meet him at least part way

ETHICAL
Choose one: Extremely Bad — Neither Good nor Bad — Extremely Good

REALISTIC
Choose one: Extremely Bad — Neither Good nor Bad — Extremely Good

7. Be confrontational with him, tell him that he does what he is asked or he leaves the group, something that may not look good on his CV

ETHICAL
Choose one: Extremely Bad — Neither Good nor Bad — Extremely Good

REALISTIC
Choose one: Extremely Bad — Neither Good nor Bad — Extremely Good

8. Make up your mind not to have this person as part of the team, but talk to senior management in an effort to try and find other employment for the person within the firm

ETHICAL
Choose one: Extremely Bad — Neither Good nor Bad — Extremely Good

REALISTIC
Choose one: Extremely Bad — Neither Good nor Bad — Extremely Good

9. Call a 'staff meeting' of your team and without mentioning names, say that the project is a very important one and for it to be completed on time and within budget, everyone is going to have to 'pull together', hoping thereby that the message will be received where it needs to be

ETHICAL
Choose one: Extremely Bad — Neither Good nor Bad — Extremely Good

REALISTIC
Choose one: Extremely Bad — Neither Good nor Bad — Extremely Good

10. Conduct regular team meetings to allocate tasks and discuss progress. Take input from everyone on allocation issues and problems – encouraging this member in particular. However, don't forget who is in charge and responsible.

ETHICAL
Choose one: Extremely Bad — Neither Good nor Bad — Extremely Good

REALISTIC
Choose one: Extremely Bad — Neither Good nor Bad — Extremely Good

11. Discretely approach senior management about the issue and say that you are doing what you can as team leader but if the project is not completed on time, you know the reason why. Because you get on fairly well with management you do not feel they will think any less of you for having come to see them

ETHICAL
Choose one: Extremely Bad — Neither Good nor Bad — Extremely Good

REALISTIC
Choose one: Extremely Bad — Neither Good nor Bad — Extremely Good

12. Give him fewer but more specific tasks to do, because it is simply not worth the effort to argue with him. Besides his skills in coding mean that he will be able to effectively contribute here, and then you can be rid of him, to concentrate on teeing with other team members of your choice

ETHICAL
Choose one: Extremely Bad — Neither Good nor Bad — Extremely Good

REALISTIC
Choose one: Extremely Bad — Neither Good nor Bad — Extremely Good

Please click the submit button and continue on with the next scenario [SUBMIT]

F.3.4 Scenario 4

Part C: (articulable) Tacit Knowledge Inventory for Information Systems

We realise that any of the following questionnaire scenarios may be tackled from an IDEAL (ethical) and a REALISTIC (perhaps unethical) point of view. We would like you to select BOTH an IDEAL AND REALISTIC value for each answer option.

Read each scenario and select what you consider to be the most appropriate scale for each answer option. Remember we would like you to select BOTH an IDEAL AND REALISTIC value for each answer option.

Scenario 4

The design for a system rests heavily upon your group. As you are the leader your reputation is at stake, this is exacerbated by the fact that you are senior and considered to be quite experienced within the firm.

Working with you in the team, are a couple of junior programmers from the company for whom your team is developing this software.

You notice reasonably quickly however that the visitors seem to be fairly incompetent, furthermore they are actually holding up the entire design process with what appears to you to be totally irrelevant issues. For instance you realise that much of the software can already draw upon modules that have previously been coded, however the visitors insist that some software be recoded because they would like to see different colours appear on the screen. You explain that that is quite trivial and can easily be coded in, however you begin to feel the visitors 'like the sound of their own voices'.

Rate each of the following responses in relation to the given scenario. It is advisable to read all of the responses before replying.

1   Politely but firmly let the visitors know that their issues are irrelevant, and that if they wish to include their ideas the whole project will be delayed, perhaps indicating that their boss trusts your team with the project it is conducting

ETHICAL
Choose
one:
      Extremely Bad   Neither Good nor Bad   Extremely Good

REALISTIC
Choose
one:
      Extremely Bad   Neither Good nor Bad   Extremely Good

2   Discretely talk to someone senior in the client organisation expressing your concerns at the potential system delay, in the hope their management sort out the situation

ETHICAL
Choose
one:
      Extremely Bad   Neither Good nor Bad   Extremely Good

REALISTIC
Choose
one:
      Extremely Bad   Neither Good nor Bad   Extremely Good

3   In the forthcoming team meeting you acknowledge the contributions of all the team members and particularly that of the visitors with the hope of getting them on your side so that you can then take control of the project

ETHICAL
Choose
one:
      Extremely Bad   Neither Good nor Bad   Extremely Good

REALISTIC
Choose
one:
      Extremely Bad   Neither Good nor Bad   Extremely Good

4   All of sudden find a reason to be appointed to a different project, so that you may 'wash your hands' of the whole issue

ETHICAL
Choose
one:
      Extremely Bad   Neither Good nor Bad   Extremely Good

REALISTIC
Choose
one:
      Extremely Bad   Neither Good nor Bad   Extremely Good

5 Talk to your boss expressing your concerns, in an attempt to 'cover yourself' should the project be delayed unnecessarily

ETHICAL
Choose one:
Extremely Bad   Neither Good nor Bad   Extremely Good

REALISTIC
Choose one:
Extremely Bad   Neither Good nor Bad   Extremely Good

6 Take on board everything the visitors have to say and if the project is overdue wash your hands of the issue and state that the visitors had their ideas which needed to be incorporated

ETHICAL
Choose one:
Extremely Bad   Neither Good nor Bad   Extremely Good

REALISTIC
Choose one:
Extremely Bad   Neither Good nor Bad   Extremely Good

7 'Humour' the visitors in relation to their requests, diplomatically 'biting your tongue' if in disagreement with what they are saying, and decide that arguing with them is not worth the effort. If the project looks like being delayed you will simply have to put in some unpaid overtime as team leader to ensure that it is eventually successful

ETHICAL
Choose one:
Extremely Bad   Neither Good nor Bad   Extremely Good

REALISTIC
Choose one:
Extremely Bad   Neither Good nor Bad   Extremely Good

Please click the submit button and continue on with the next scenario SUBMIT

F.3.5 Scenario 5

Part C: (articulable) Tacit Knowledge Inventory for Information Systems

We realise that any of the following questionnaire scenarios may be tackled from an IDEAL (ethical) and a REALISTIC (perhaps unethical) point of view. We would like you to select BOTH an IDEAL AND REALISTIC value for each answer option.

Read each scenario and select what you consider to be the most appropriate scale for each answer option. Remember we would like you to select BOTH an IDEAL AND REALISTIC value for each answer option.

Scenario 5

A systems analyst in your section has done a superb job in designing a new system for a client organization. The system has yet to pass the coding and post implementation review stage, nevertheless you feel the job that was conducted is worthy of praise.

Because of the 'demand' that exists in the IT industry, and the fact that you know this systems analyst is thinking of 'moving on', you are hesitant to immediately congratulate the person for fear of precipitating the person's departure, believing they may take this as a possibility of gaining promotion in a different firm, or perhaps even branching out into their own company, more than likely with an IS management consultancy bias (something the person had once alluded to).

You are not actually this person's boss, however you have worked successfully together on a number of projects and realise that it is unlikely you will be working with someone as easy to get along with again.

Rate each of the following responses in relation to the given scenario. It is advisable to read all of the responses before replying.

1 Talk as soon as possible with the analyst and 'come straight out with it', telling the person that they did a good job, making no mention of employment possibilities in the industry, simply 'assuming' they will stay on

ETHICAL
Choose one:
Extremely Bad   Neither Good nor Bad   Extremely Good

REALISTIC
Choose one:
Extremely Bad   Neither Good nor Bad   Extremely Good

2. Admit to yourself that the workplace is a professional environment and as the IT industry is competitive, the analyst deserves every chance they can get. With that in mind you don't hesitate approaching the person to congratulate them even if it looks as if you are trying to 'sidle up' to them

ETHICAL
Choose one:

Extremely Bad			Neither Good nor Bad			Extremely Good

REALISTIC
Choose one:

Extremely Bad			Neither Good nor Bad			Extremely Good

3. Consider talking to the team leader and mentioning the hard work put into the exercise by the systems analyst. What the leader decides to do from there is out of your control

ETHICAL
Choose one:

Extremely Bad			Neither Good nor Bad			Extremely Good

REALISTIC
Choose one:

Extremely Bad			Neither Good nor Bad			Extremely Good

4. Do nothing positive or negative, simply 'act normal', if and when the analyst arrives comes seeking advice of any kind you can simply let it slip that you thought they did an okay job

ETHICAL
Choose one:

Extremely Bad			Neither Good nor Bad			Extremely Good

REALISTIC
Choose one:

Extremely Bad			Neither Good nor Bad			Extremely Good

5. Leave an anonymous congratulatory card on the person's desk, something which has been wordprocessed after hours so that handwriting is not a giveaway

ETHICAL
Choose one:

Extremely Bad			Neither Good nor Bad			Extremely Good

REALISTIC
Choose one:

Extremely Bad			Neither Good nor Bad			Extremely Good

6. Next time a social occasion arises, just happen to mention 'off the cuff' to the analyst's colleagues that you thought the person did a great job

ETHICAL
Choose one:

Extremely Bad			Neither Good nor Bad			Extremely Good

REALISTIC
Choose one:

Extremely Bad			Neither Good nor Bad			Extremely Good

Please click the submit button and continue on with the next scenario   SUBMIT

F.3.6 Scenario 6

Part C: (articulable) Tacit Knowledge Inventory for Information Systems

We realise that any of the following questionnaire scenarios may be tackled from an IDEAL (ethical) and a REALISTIC (perhaps unethical) point of view. We would like you to select BOTH an IDEAL AND REALISTIC value for each answer option.

Read each scenario and select what you consider to be the most appropriate scale for each answer option. Remember we would like you to select BOTH an IDEAL AND REALISTIC value for each answer option.

Scenario 6

The most senior person in your section is close to retirement and is essentially at the peak of his career. While this colleague is capable and involved typically in administrative matters, he nevertheless likes to 'keep his hand in'.

The problem is you feel the knowledge used by him is outdated. Although you respect him, you feel you are not on his 'wavelength', and to make matters worse the project you are working on is one for a firm in which the senior person has good friends.

This senior person has now decided to do some of the analysis work for the project involving his friend's firm, which ordinarily is not such a problem except that your company has a policy which states that bosses and friends do not mix.

Rate each of the following responses in relation to the given scenario. It is advisable to read all of the responses before replying.

1. You just happen to show the senior person a better way to do the analysis tasks, thereby hoping they will agree that your method is better and leave the work up to you

ETHICAL
Choose one:

Extremely Bad			Neither Good nor Bad			Extremely Good

REALISTIC
Choose one:

Extremely Bad			Neither Good nor Bad			Extremely Good

2   Simply admit to yourself that you are junior in the organisation and leave it there, it's not your problem

ETHICAL
Choose
one:
　　　　　　Extremely Bad　　　　　　Neither Good nor Bad　　　　　　Extremely Good

REALISTIC
Choose
one:
　　　　　　Extremely Bad　　　　　　Neither Good nor Bad　　　　　　Extremely Good

3   Pacify yourself by saying that this is likely to be the senior person's last significant project anyway, and besides what does having friends in the client organisation really do to affect things?

ETHICAL
Choose
one:
　　　　　　Extremely Bad　　　　　　Neither Good nor Bad　　　　　　Extremely Good

REALISTIC
Choose
one:
　　　　　　Extremely Bad　　　　　　Neither Good nor Bad　　　　　　Extremely Good

4   Have a meeting with the senior person and 'clear the air', expressing your respect and high regard for him, but that a more current approach may be beneficial for this project

ETHICAL
Choose
one:
　　　　　　Extremely Bad　　　　　　Neither Good nor Bad　　　　　　Extremely Good

REALISTIC
Choose
one:
　　　　　　Extremely Bad　　　　　　Neither Good nor Bad　　　　　　Extremely Good

5   Approach the big boss and let her know that you are concerned about the possible ramifications of the senior person working on the project

ETHICAL
Choose
one:
　　　　　　Extremely Bad　　　　　　Neither Good nor Bad　　　　　　Extremely Good

REALISTIC
Choose
one:
　　　　　　Extremely Bad　　　　　　Neither Good nor Bad　　　　　　Extremely Good

6   Avoid this person by finding a reason to be reallocated to another team hopefully avoiding any questions that might be raised

ETHICAL
Choose
one:
　　　　　　Extremely Bad　　　　　　Neither Good nor Bad　　　　　　Extremely Good

REALISTIC
Choose
one:
　　　　　　Extremely Bad　　　　　　Neither Good nor Bad　　　　　　Extremely Good

7   Place a photocopy of the company directive that states business and friends don't mix, up on the workplace noticeboard after hours

ETHICAL
Choose
one:
　　　　　　Extremely Bad　　　　　　Neither Good nor Bad　　　　　　Extremely Good

REALISTIC
Choose
one:
　　　　　　Extremely Bad　　　　　　Neither Good nor Bad　　　　　　Extremely Good

8   Talk with the other members of the team on separate occasions casually mentioning the company's policy, basically leaving it for them to do anything about it

ETHICAL
Choose
one:
　　　　　　Extremely Bad　　　　　　Neither Good nor Bad　　　　　　Extremely Good

REALISTIC
Choose
one:
　　　　　　Extremely Bad　　　　　　Neither Good nor Bad　　　　　　Extremely Good

Please click the submit button and continue on with the next scenario   SUBMIT

F.3.7 Scenario 7

Part C: (articulable) Tacit Knowledge Inventory for Information Systems

We realise that any of the following questionnaire scenarios may be tackled from an IDEAL (ethical) and a REALISTIC (perhaps unethical) point of view. We would like you to select BOTH an IDEAL AND REALISTIC value for each answer option.

Read each scenario and select what you consider to be the most appropriate scale for each answer option. Remember we would like you to select BOTH an IDEAL AND REALISTIC value for each answer option.

Scenario 7

You are a senior programmer, working as part of a 'back office' team.

The 'front office' team has been busily at work engaging the clients, trying to understand what it is they require from the project. Unfortunately on this particular project the front office team has not consulted your team.

What has in effect taken place is that requirements were identified for what the project should do, documented, and then the front office team simply handed over the tasks to the back office.

No agreement was entered into up front between the front office staff and your team as to what would be delivered. The front office had also provided some 'promises' (not necessarily contractual) to the client.

It now appears the back office not only doesn't have a clear understanding of what the front office has promised, but your team may actually have to redo some of the front office tasks, with a possibility of conducting some interviews with the clients yourself. In short, you realise the project is not working according to plan.

Rate each of the following responses in relation to the given scenario. It is advisable to read all of the responses before replying.

1   Approach the senior member of the front office team with your concerns and try to set ground rules for communication between teams

ETHICAL
Choose one:

Extremely Bad   Neither Good nor Bad   Extremely Good

REALISTIC
Choose one:

Extremely Bad   Neither Good nor Bad   Extremely Good

2   Call a meeting to discuss the situation so that everyone is aware of all the issues and what the best way forward may be

ETHICAL
Choose one:

Extremely Bad   Neither Good nor Bad   Extremely Good

REALISTIC
Choose one:

Extremely Bad   Neither Good nor Bad   Extremely Good

3   Have a quiet word with the client and tell them the project is really not what they want, and they should perhaps raise some issues with the 'front office' staff at this still fairly early stage

ETHICAL
Choose one:

Extremely Bad   Neither Good nor Bad   Extremely Good

REALISTIC
Choose one:

Extremely Bad   Neither Good nor Bad   Extremely Good

4   Approach management and raise the issues with them, in other words 'wash your hands of the matter' and expect management to sort it out

ETHICAL
Choose one:

Extremely Bad   Neither Good nor Bad   Extremely Good

REALISTIC
Choose one:

Extremely Bad   Neither Good nor Bad   Extremely Good

5. Ignore the whole issue because you know deep down the front office are going to take blame if anything goes wrong anyway

ETHICAL
Choose one:

Extremely Bad		Neither Good nor Bad		Extremely Good

REALISTIC
Choose one:

Extremely Bad		Neither Good nor Bad		Extremely Good

6. As you are the senior member of the back office team, change the specifications to what you feel they should be and let your team go ahead with the job

ETHICAL
Choose one:

Extremely Bad		Neither Good nor Bad		Extremely Good

REALISTIC
Choose one:

Extremely Bad		Neither Good nor Bad		Extremely Good

7. Don't concern yourself any further with the issue because you have it in writing that your team's job is to develop the software from a clear set of specifications and that is precisely what you will end up doing

ETHICAL
Choose one:

Extremely Bad		Neither Good nor Bad		Extremely Good

REALISTIC
Choose one:

Extremely Bad		Neither Good nor Bad		Extremely Good

8. Consider that the front office may actually be correct after all, perhaps they do know better than the client what is really required, in other words, simply decide to follow their lead

ETHICAL
Choose one:

Extremely Bad		Neither Good nor Bad		Extremely Good

REALISTIC
Choose one:

Extremely Bad		Neither Good nor Bad		Extremely Good

9. Draw up a revised set of specifications and get the front office team and clients to sign off on them, meaning there will be some loss of face in front of the client but at least any misunderstandings are cleared up

ETHICAL
Choose one:

Extremely Bad		Neither Good nor Bad		Extremely Good

REALISTIC
Choose one:

Extremely Bad		Neither Good nor Bad		Extremely Good

Please click the submit button and continue on with the next scenario SUBMIT

F.3.8 Scenario 8

Part C: (articulable) Tacit Knowledge Inventory for Information Systems

We realise that any of the following questionnaire scenarios may be tackled from an IDEAL (ethical) and a REALISTIC (perhaps unethical) point of view. We would like you to select BOTH an IDEAL AND REALISTIC value for each answer option.

Read each scenario and select what you consider to be the most appropriate scale for each answer option. Remember we would like you to select BOTH an IDEAL AND REALISTIC value for each answer option.

Scenario 8

You have been in the IS Department for about 2 years now and are coding some software that will be used to process photographs from speed cameras

The problem is if you insist upon completing the project yourself, it will not be due on time, consequently you need to consider having other people helping you

Several people have volunteered, but you consider that their skills are not appropriate. You are also somewhat possessive of this project and rather than have the boss come in and delegate people, you would prefer to deal with the issue of help yourself

The fact that your last project which you mostly (70%) completed by yourself, happened to work fairly well, means that you feel confident you will be successful as an individual once again.

Rate each of the following responses in relation to the given scenario. It is advisable to read all of the responses before replying.

1. Approach your friend in the organisation and ask her to put aside what she is doing and help you

ETHICAL
Choose one:

Extremely Bad		Neither Good nor Bad		Extremely Good

REALISTIC
Choose one:

Extremely Bad		Neither Good nor Bad		Extremely Good

2 Talk to the boss and say that the people who have volunteered are not what you would consider to be ideal, but you could consider 'outsourcing' part of the project

ETHICAL
Choose one:
Extremely Bad   Neither Good nor Bad   Extremely Good

REALISTIC
Choose one:
Extremely Bad   Neither Good nor Bad   Extremely Good

3 Decide to work excessive amounts of overtime so that the project will be completed on time. You will remain the sole person doing the coding, but likely will need a holiday upon completion of it. The project should be completed in two weeks, at which time you have three weeks leave coming to you anyway

ETHICAL
Choose one:
Extremely Bad   Neither Good nor Bad   Extremely Good

REALISTIC
Choose one:
Extremely Bad   Neither Good nor Bad   Extremely Good

4 Decide that as the boss is simply going to allocate some 'volunteers' to the project, whom you have already decided are not suitable, simply hand the project over to these 'volunteers' and go and do something else

ETHICAL
Choose one:
Extremely Bad   Neither Good nor Bad   Extremely Good

REALISTIC
Choose one:
Extremely Bad   Neither Good nor Bad   Extremely Good

5 Talk to a friend or your partner about what you should do, perhaps over a drink or dinner. Agree to yourself that whatever they advise, that is what you will do

ETHICAL
Choose one:
6
Extremely Bad   Neither Good nor Bad   Extremely Good

REALISTIC
Choose one:
Extremely Bad   Neither Good nor Bad   Extremely Good

7 Arrange a meeting with your boss and key members of your Department to air your concerns and discuss further options. At this meeting you decide to ascertain the priorities and implications of the project

ETHICAL
Choose one:
Extremely Bad   Neither Good nor Bad   Extremely Good

REALISTIC
Choose one:
Extremely Bad   Neither Good nor Bad   Extremely Good

8 Send out your own department wide email asking for expressions of interest in helping you on the project. Decide from the short list of replies what to do from there. If there are no replies (or very few) then admit to yourself that the boss can simply allocate extra help, otherwise you will narrow down the list to those who can help you

ETHICAL
Choose one:
Extremely Bad   Neither Good nor Bad   Extremely Good

REALISTIC
Choose one:
Extremely Bad   Neither Good nor Bad   Extremely Good

9 Isolate yourself by perhaps working from home where you are less likely to be interrupted in the hope that you will make the deadline

ETHICAL
Choose one:
Extremely Bad   Neither Good nor Bad   Extremely Good

REALISTIC
Choose one:
Extremely Bad   Neither Good nor Bad   Extremely Good

Please click the submit button and continue on with the next scenario   SUBMIT

F.3.9 Scenario 9

Part C: (articulable) Tacit Knowledge Inventory for Information Systems

We realise that any of the following questionnaire scenarios may be tackled from an IDEAL (ethical) and a REALISTIC (perhaps unethical) point of view. We would like you to select BOTH an IDEAL AND REALISTIC value for each answer option.

Read each scenario and select what you consider to be the most appropriate scale for each answer option. Remember we would like you to select BOTH an IDEAL AND REALISTIC value for each answer option.

Scenario 9

Your team is working on a large QA system for a large public sector organisation. Your team however is from an outsourced organisation.

The project is an ongoing one, and because of its size other outsourced firms are also involved. In this instance the team immediately following yours will be the probity (integrity) team, whose task it will be to check the 'correctness' of work completed on the system.

You are actually quite satisfied with the work that has been done, however a component (not necessarily mission critical) of the system is niggling you. You realise that it won't properly work, however you have done as the specifications have asked.

Rate each of the following responses in relation to the given scenario. It is advisable to read all of the responses before replying.

1   Inform the leader of the probity team up front and express your team's concerns lest your team potentially be made responsible for the shortcomings of the system

ETHICAL
Choose one:
Extremely Bad   Neither Good nor Bad   Extremely Good

REALISTIC
Choose one:
Extremely Bad   Neither Good nor Bad   Extremely Good

2   Ignore the problem because the specifications are quite unambiguous and you know your team cannot be held legally accountable for anything that may fail at system run time

ETHICAL
Choose one:
Extremely Bad   Neither Good nor Bad   Extremely Good

REALISTIC
Choose one:
Extremely Bad   Neither Good nor Bad   Extremely Good

3   Take the matter up with the coordinating project management group before the probity team actually arrives. Regardless of the project management group's response, at a minimum insist upon documenting your concerns and making such concerns known to the probity team

ETHICAL
Choose one:
Extremely Bad   Neither Good nor Bad   Extremely Good

REALISTIC
Choose one:
Extremely Bad   Neither Good nor Bad   Extremely Good

4   Fix the problem, regardless of what the specifications actually ask for. This may mean up to one weeks overtime, but you feel you would be able to persuade management that the effort is worth it in any case

ETHICAL
Choose one:
Extremely Bad   Neither Good nor Bad   Extremely Good

REALISTIC
Choose one:
Extremely Bad   Neither Good nor Bad   Extremely Good

5   Recommend the probity team make an example of this 'mistake' in the hope that specifications may be tightened up in future

ETHICAL
Choose one:
Extremely Bad   Neither Good nor Bad   Extremely Good

REALISTIC
Choose one:
Extremely Bad   Neither Good nor Bad   Extremely Good

6   Fix the problem yourself even if it means unpaid overtime on your behalf

ETHICAL
Choose one:
Extremely Bad   Neither Good nor Bad   Extremely Good

REALISTIC
Choose one:
Extremely Bad   Neither Good nor Bad   Extremely Good

Please click the submit button and continue on with the next scenario   SUBMIT

F.3.10 Scenario 10

Part C: (articulable) Tacit Knowledge Inventory for Information Systems

We realise that any of the following questionnaire scenarios may be tackled from an IDEAL (ethical) and a REALISTIC (perhaps unethical) point of view. We would like you to select BOTH an IDEAL AND REALISTIC value for each answer option.

Read each scenario and select what you consider to be the most appropriate scale for each answer option. Remember we would like you to select BOTH an IDEAL AND REALISTIC value for each answer option.

Scenario 10

There are a number of ways of looking at system success.

One view is that the system is unsuccessful from an implementation point of view, in other words the system specifications are drawn up, software is then compiled, technical documents are created, but everything ends up 'sitting on the shelf'. Such a system may nevertheless prove successful from a financial point of view insofar as a profit was made by your contracting firm to supply the software, manuals and soforth to a client firm.

Another 'view' of success is a system that runs well but ended up being overbudget.

Yet another way of looking at system success is a system that *does* actually get implemented and was also financially profitable for your business to implement. In other words it was successful as far as you and your firm were concerned as well as being successful as far as the client firm was concerned.

Rate each of the following responses in relation to the given scenario. It is advisable to read all of the responses before replying.

1. There is really only one view of system success, in other words a system that delivers what the specifications asked of it, within budget

    ETHICAL
    Choose one:

Extremely Bad		Neither Good nor Bad		Extremely Good

    REALISTIC
    Choose one:

Extremely Bad		Neither Good nor Bad		Extremely Good

2. As long as the clients (and particularly their end users) are happy with what your group delivered, regardless of what you think of the system, the client's happiness is basically all that really counts

    ETHICAL
    Choose one:

Extremely Bad		Neither Good nor Bad		Extremely Good

    REALISTIC
    Choose one:

Extremely Bad		Neither Good nor Bad		Extremely Good

3. Consider that success or failure are essentially subjective judgements and that there are really no true measures in this regard. For example users may often underestimate what they require and as such any shortcomings may not be due to the developer or the technical capabilities of the system itself

    ETHICAL
    Choose one:

Extremely Bad		Neither Good nor Bad		Extremely Good

    REALISTIC
    Choose one:

Extremely Bad		Neither Good nor Bad		Extremely Good

4. Consider that just because the system did not actually get implemented, this does not really matter because you doubt another team would have done the job any better

    ETHICAL
    Choose one:

Extremely Bad		Neither Good nor Bad		Extremely Good

    REALISTIC
    Choose one:

Extremely Bad		Neither Good nor Bad		Extremely Good

5 If a system didn't get implemented, consider going back to the client organisation in your own time afterwards to more deeply ascertain why it was not implemented

ETHICAL
Choose one:

Extremely Bad		Neither Good nor Bad			Extremely Good

REALISTIC
Choose one:

Extremely Bad		Neither Good nor Bad			Extremely Good

6 Consider that system success is merely dependent on correct allocation of resources. In this instance a system wasn't successful because the right combination, in other words of time and/or skills were employed on the task

ETHICAL
Choose one:

Extremely Bad		Neither Good nor Bad			Extremely Good

REALISTIC
Choose one:

Extremely Bad		Neither Good nor Bad			Extremely Good

7 Success and failure are terms of relevance to project managers, you are a junior programmer

ETHICAL
Choose one:

Extremely Bad		Neither Good nor Bad			Extremely Good

REALISTIC
Choose one:

Extremely Bad		Neither Good nor Bad			Extremely Good

Please click the submit button and continue on with the next scenario   SUBMIT

F.3.11 Scenario 11

Part C: (articulable) Tacit Knowledge Inventory for Information Systems

We realise that any of the following questionnaire scenarios may be tackled from an IDEAL (ethical) and a REALISTIC (perhaps unethical) point of view. We would like you to select BOTH an IDEAL AND REALISTIC value for each answer option.

Read each scenario and select what you consider to be the most appropriate scale for each answer option. Remember we would like you to select BOTH an IDEAL AND REALISTIC value for each answer option.

Scenario 11

A newly appointed team member appears to lack competency in certain software engineering aspects that your group is working on

Admittedly this person's background is more in the technical writing area, however you feel he should be a little more competent in understanding algorithms, parameter passing, functional and object oriented structures of software

Although you are not the team leader, you feel it is your duty to point out the deficiencies in your colleague's software oriented knowledge

The critical nature of this project means that failures will not be well tolerated and you are facing a fast time deadline

Rate each of the following responses in relation to the given scenario. It is advisable to read all of the responses before replying.

1 Quietly pull the team member aside and suggest they may be better off engaging themselves on a different project

ETHICAL
Choose one:

Extremely Bad		Neither Good nor Bad			Extremely Good

REALISTIC
Choose one:

Extremely Bad		Neither Good nor Bad			Extremely Good

2. Consider the issues and that you *likely* don't know all the team needs, thereupon you decide to keep your concerns to yourself. Besides this person's skills may be redeployed elsewhere on your team

ETHICAL
Choose one

Extremely Bad · Neither Good nor Bad · Extremely Good

REALISTIC
Choose one

Extremely Bad · Neither Good nor Bad · Extremely Good

3. Chat with the team leader to raise your concerns, and suggest that the person be sent on training courses to catch up on their software engineering knowledge

ETHICAL
Choose one

Extremely Bad · Neither Good nor Bad · Extremely Good

REALISTIC
Choose one

Extremely Bad · Neither Good nor Bad · Extremely Good

4. Contemplate mentoring the person, after all much knowledge is actually passed in person to person interactions, rather than by way of written words, perhaps this person just needs the 'human touch'

ETHICAL
Choose one

Extremely Bad · Neither Good nor Bad · Extremely Good

REALISTIC
Choose one

Extremely Bad · Neither Good nor Bad · Extremely Good

5. 'Have it out' with the person and tell them of your criticisms in front of the group in the hope they will see your side of things

ETHICAL
Choose one

Extremely Bad · Neither Good nor Bad · Extremely Good

REALISTIC
Choose one

Extremely Bad · Neither Good nor Bad · Extremely Good

6. At the next team meeting (or however tasks are allocated), suggest that the new person take on tasks of lesser technical ability (not necessarily worded this way), but which are still essential - like documentation, development of user manuals and so on

ETHICAL
Choose one

Extremely Bad · Neither Good nor Bad · Extremely Good

REALISTIC
Choose one

Extremely Bad · Neither Good nor Bad · Extremely Good

7. Consider seeing the boss and asking for an extra team member, explaining that the balance of the team would be better served with an extra member, implicitly stating therefore that the newest addition to the team (the technical writer) is not the most suited for the project, but his skills will prove useful nonetheless

ETHICAL
Choose one

Extremely Bad · Neither Good nor Bad · Extremely Good

REALISTIC
Choose one

Extremely Bad · Neither Good nor Bad · Extremely Good

8. Take it upon yourself to use this experience to create a 'competency hurdle' (minimum qualification level) for your section that can be used as a benchmark for technical knowledge capabilities in the future

ETHICAL
Choose one

Extremely Bad · Neither Good nor Bad · Extremely Good

REALISTIC
Choose one

Extremely Bad · Neither Good nor Bad · Extremely Good

Please click the submit button and continue on with the next scenario SUBMIT

F.3.12 Scenario 12

Part C: (articulable) Tacit Knowledge Inventory for Information Systems

We realise that any of the following questionnaire scenarios may be tackled from an IDEAL (ethical) and a REALISTIC (perhaps unethical) point of view. We would like you to select BOTH an IDEAL AND REALISTIC value for each answer option.

Read each scenario and select what you consider to be the most appropriate scale for each answer option. Remember we would like you to select BOTH an IDEAL AND REALISTIC value for each answer option.

Scenario 12

You have under you a Technical Services Manager who is very competent at his tasks. However the speed at which tasks are performed could be quicker as far as you are concerned.

Because of what the manager's job entails and the fact that he is required to occasionally liaise with external clientele you feel it would be nice at least if job turnaround time could be shortened.

The person has been with your organisation for 5 years, you have only been here for 2 years, nevertheless you are more 'formally' educated and in a senior position.

Rate each of the following responses in relation to the given scenario. It is advisable to read all of the responses before replying.

1   Approach the Technical Services Manager personally and diplomatically ask him to 'pull his socks up' in a manner of speaking, making him aware of his strengths and weaknesses

ETHICAL
Choose one.
Extremely Bad   Neither Good nor Bad   Extremely Good

REALISTIC
Choose one.
Extremely Bad   Neither Good nor Bad   Extremely Good

2   Decide simply speaking to the Technical Services Manager is a non issue and doing so would probably not improve service delivery anyway, it may actually worsen it

ETHICAL
Choose one.
Extremely Bad   Neither Good nor Bad   Extremely Good

REALISTIC
Choose one.
Extremely Bad   Neither Good nor Bad   Extremely Good

3   Send the Technical Services Manager an email, perhaps hinting that the IT industry is generally fast moving   and leave it there

ETHICAL
Choose one.
Extremely Bad   Neither Good nor Bad   Extremely Good

REALISTIC
Choose one.
Extremely Bad   Neither Good nor Bad   Extremely Good

4   Select a project. Tell the manager that it is a very important one with a critical time frame. Offer to work with the manager to assist in overcoming obstacles. Use this as an opportunity to gauge the situation and offer training and/or guidance as necessary

ETHICAL
Choose one.
Extremely Bad   Neither Good nor Bad   Extremely Good

REALISTIC
Choose one.
Extremely Bad   Neither Good nor Bad   Extremely Good

5   Pacify yourself by considering that how fast a person actually performs a task is not particularly important in any case, all that really matters is whether the job is done so properly

ETHICAL
Choose one.
Extremely Bad   Neither Good nor Bad   Extremely Good

REALISTIC
Choose one.
Extremely Bad   Neither Good nor Bad   Extremely Good

6   Consider getting a colleague to speak to the Manager, preferably one who is on good terms with the person

ETHICAL
Choose one.
Extremely Bad   Neither Good nor Bad   Extremely Good

REALISTIC?
Choose one.
Extremely Bad   Neither Good nor Bad   Extremely Good

7   Make an appointment to see the manager in question (perhaps over lunch), and ask the person what resources and/or training they require to improve resolution times

ETHICAL
Choose one.
Extremely Bad   Neither Good nor Bad   Extremely Good

REALISTIC
Choose one.
Extremely Bad   Neither Good nor Bad   Extremely Good

8. Leave a humourous card on the manager's desk that makes a slight joke about slow service

Please click the submit button and continue on with the next scenario [SUBMIT]

F.3.13 Scenario 13

Part C: (articulable) Tacit Knowledge Inventory for Information Systems

We realise that any of the following questionnaire scenarios may be tackled from an IDEAL (ethical) and a REALISTIC (perhaps unethical) point of view. We would like you to select BOTH an IDEAL AND REALISTIC value for each answer option.

Read each scenario and select what you consider to be the most appropriate scale for each answer option. Remember we would like you to select BOTH an IDEAL AND REALISTIC value for each answer option.

Scenario 13

A large consultancy corporation has been called in to do an IT security audit of your company.

As you are a computing professional, you are more than usually interested in what they have to do and say.

You find that when you get to read the report it appears to be rote written with your company's name substituted on top (at least as far as you are concerned). In other words, although the report looks professionally written and bound, it does not really address the IT security peculiarities of your organisation.

Rate each of the following responses in relation to the given scenario. It is advisable to read all of the responses before replying.

1. Decide that this is simply another management exercise and as you are not management there is little point in questioning the whole activity

2. Feel that as you are not actually a security IT person (your area is desktop database platforms), perhaps upon reflection, it would be wiser to keep quiet about the report but make sure you are not responsible for it's perceived inaccuracies in any case

3. Decide to take it upon yourself to write a report, identifying issues that management would agree are critical or important. Assess the outcomes of the security report against the management criteria you have identified, highlighting implications of any shortcomings. You realise care should be taken to present a balanced report coming from yourself

4. Send an email to the CIO asking diplomatically whether it may not be better to either get the internal networks group to deal with an audit next time, or if an external audit is actually warranted, perhaps a cheaper consultancy company

5   Try to obtain a copy of a similar report written for another organisation and present that (anonymously) to management as a means of highlighting the rote-like nature of it, what management does from there is up to them

ETHICAL
Choose one:
Extremely Bad   Neither Good nor Bad   Extremely Good

REALISTIC
Choose one:
Extremely Bad   Neither Good nor Bad   Extremely Good

6   Merely accept the opinions of the data communications (networking) group within the organisation, there is little you can do about the situation anyway

ETHICAL
Choose one:
Extremely Bad   Neither Good nor Bad   Extremely Good

REALISTIC
Choose one:
Extremely Bad   Neither Good nor Bad   Extremely Good

Please click the submit button and continue on with the next scenario   SUBMIT

F.3.14 Scenario 14

Part C: (articulable) Tacit Knowledge Inventory for Information Systems

We realise that any of the following questionnaire scenarios may be tackled from an IDEAL (ethical) and a REALISTIC (perhaps unethical) point of view. We would like you to select BOTH an IDEAL AND REALISTIC value for each answer option.

Read each scenario and select what you consider to be the most appropriate scale for each answer option. Remember we would like you to select BOTH an IDEAL AND REALISTIC value for each answer option.

Scenario 14

You have been with the present organisation for the last three months. You have just updated your qualifications with a coursework Masters in Computing

For the last 3 years prior to this, you were working in the IS Department of a bank. As a new appointee you find that the last four weeks have been hectic to say the least and you have experienced an enormous learning curve in your new role as technical analyst for the IS branch of a large public sector organisation in which you are employed

You are generally affable and reasonably talented, but you don't mind admitting to yourself that your technical knowledge in the Unified Modelling Domain is not what it could be. Ordinarily you would not worry, however a project is due to be completed later this month and your supervisor has allocated you to the task of ensuring the UML component is correct and up to date.

Your predecessor on the project however had some 'unusual' notational techniques you are having added problems coming to terms with.

Rate each of the following responses in relation to the given scenario. It is advisable to read all of the responses before replying.

1   Quietly inform your boss that in actual fact you would be better off assigned to another task as your knowledge would not be sufficient for what is expected of you

ETHICAL
Choose one:
Extremely Bad   Neither Good nor Bad   Extremely Good

REALISTIC
Choose one:
Extremely Bad   Neither Good nor Bad   Extremely Good

2   You decide to furiously learn up on UML in the hope you will pass the organisational 'acceptance' and thereby 'social' acceptance hurdle

ETHICAL
Choose one:
Extremely Bad   Neither Good nor Bad   Extremely Good

REALISTIC
Choose one:
Extremely Bad   Neither Good nor Bad   Extremely Good

3   Approach someone else in your section to help you 'come up to speed' with your requirements in the project

ETHICAL
Choose one:
Extremely Bad   Neither Good nor Bad   Extremely Good

REALISTIC
Choose one:
Extremely Bad   Neither Good nor Bad   Extremely Good

4   As the project is not high security, you decide to enlist the services of your colleague in another organisation to help you with what you need to achieve with regard to this particular project

ETHICAL
Choose one:
Extremely Bad   Neither Good nor Bad   Extremely Good

REALISTIC
Choose one:
Extremely Bad   Neither Good nor Bad   Extremely Good

446 Busch

5. Decide to stage an 'accident' whereby you will be put out of work for at least a week, meaning that the assignment will have to be delegated to someone else

6. Approach someone elsewhere in the organisation (but definitely not on your team) to help you 'come up to speed' with your requirements in the project

7. Simply admit to all and sundry from the outset that you are only human, you do not know everything and you are certainly not an expert in UML, and whilst you don't mind working on the task as part of a team, you would not be able to complete your part of the bargain as an individual by the due date if left to your own devices

8. Put your best foot forward and try to bluff your way through the development process, should any questions be raised about some of the notation or techniques for how your analyst component was handled, simply pretend this is the 'very latest' in style (alluding to the fact this was what you had learnt as part of the Masters)

Please click the submit button and continue on with the next scenario SUBMIT

F.3.15 Scenario 15

Part C: (articulable) Tacit Knowledge Inventory for Information Systems

We realise that any of the following questionnaire scenarios may be tackled from an IDEAL (ethical) and a REALISTIC (perhaps unethical) point of view. We would like you to select BOTH an IDEAL AND REALISTIC value for each answer option.

Read each scenario and select what you consider to be the most appropriate scale for each answer option. Remember we would like you to select BOTH an IDEAL AND REALISTIC value for each answer option.

Scenario 15

1. Provide the best service you are able to, but make sure problems due to poor network service are apportioned to the networks group both in client and external meetings

2   Approach the boss first about the issue and ask her to take on the issue without necessarily having your name mentioned, in the meantime however you decide to let the CIO know what is taking place

ETHICAL
Choose one:

Extremely Bad			Neither Good nor Bad			Extremely Good

REALISTIC
Choose one:

Extremely Bad			Neither Good nor Bad			Extremely Good

3   Decide to minimise service you are able to deliver to clientele (whether internal or external), and when complaints begin to arise from poor service, you simply blame the networks group as a means of highlighting your plight

ETHICAL
Choose one:

Extremely Bad			Neither Good nor Bad			Extremely Good

REALISTIC
Choose one:

Extremely Bad			Neither Good nor Bad			Extremely Good

4   Approach the networks group in a surreptitiously complimentary manner, acting as if you fully appreciate their importance in the organisation and their degree of overwork with the intention of getting on their better side, the hope being they provide you and your group with better service

ETHICAL
Choose one:

Extremely Bad			Neither Good nor Bad			Extremely Good

REALISTIC
Choose one:

Extremely Bad			Neither Good nor Bad			Extremely Good

5   Consider being transferred to a different sector of the organisation where you are less likely to affected by the networks group

ETHICAL
Choose one:

Extremely Bad			Neither Good nor Bad			Extremely Good

REALISTIC
Choose one:

Extremely Bad			Neither Good nor Bad			Extremely Good

6   Bring the inefficiencies of the networks group to the attention of as many people in the organisation as you dare as a means of highlighting your group's plight

ETHICAL
Choose one:

Extremely Bad			Neither Good nor Bad			Extremely Good

REALISTIC
Choose one:

Extremely Bad			Neither Good nor Bad			Extremely Good

7   'Bone up' on security aspects of data communications networking and use that knowledge as a means of persuading management that networks are a critical application within the organisation and unless 'proper' governance is in place the organisation is unable to function properly

ETHICAL
Choose one:

Extremely Bad			Neither Good nor Bad			Extremely Good

REALISTIC
Choose one:

Extremely Bad			Neither Good nor Bad			Extremely Good

8   The next time a 'soft crash' of the network takes place, you bring the issue to the attention of the CIO, using this as a means of illustrating how reliant the organisation as a whole is upon reliable networks

ETHICAL
Choose one:

Extremely Bad			Neither Good nor Bad			Extremely Good

REALISTIC
Choose one:

Extremely Bad			Neither Good nor Bad			Extremely Good

9   You decide to attend all problem coordination meetings (or however else the problems are managed), both to make sure problems are recorded against the networks group rather than your own group and to raise issues with the networks group in a forum with other staff

ETHICAL
Choose one:

Extremely Bad			Neither Good nor Bad			Extremely Good

REALISTIC
Choose one:

Extremely Bad			Neither Good nor Bad			Extremely Good

10   You decide to 'test' a new application that 'unfortunately' has the habit of crashing the network. You use this to create a certain degree of 'overtime' amongst the network staff, to 'keep them on their toes' and thereby highlight problems

ETHICAL
Choose one:

Extremely Bad			Neither Good nor Bad			Extremely Good

REALISTIC
Choose one:

Extremely Bad			Neither Good nor Bad			Extremely Good

Please click the submit button and continue on with the next scenario   [SUBMIT]

F.3.16 Scenario 16

Part C: (articulable) Tacit Knowledge Inventory for Information Systems

We realise that any of the following questionnaire scenarios may be tackled from an IDEAL (ethical) and a REALISTIC (perhaps unethical) point of view. We would like you to select BOTH an IDEAL AND REALISTIC value for each answer option.

Read each scenario and select what you consider to be the most appropriate scale for each answer option. Remember we would like you to select BOTH an IDEAL AND REALISTIC value for each answer option.

Scenario 16

Systems integration is a major undertaking in your organisation.

You have approximately 60 legacy platforms in the large public sector IT branch for which you work, and it is your task to determine firstly what the organisation has in the way of platforms (both hardware and software) and thereupon which of the platforms will remain, which will be upgraded, and which deleted from the organisational applications portfolio.

Roughly 20% of the systems exist on VAX platforms, some (@30%) on IBM mainframes, the rest are desktop platforms for which you roughly have records of, however in truth you do not actually know the exact number of platforms in total in the organisation.

The IT department is made up of 120 'back office' staff and roughly 40 'front office' staff servicing an organisation of about 6,000 strong.

Rate each of the following responses in relation to the given scenario. It is advisable to read all of the responses before replying.

1   Take stock of the organisation at this point in time, compare it to similar sized organisations with similar levels of activity both here and abroad (in similar countries). Prepare a report for senior management that states what the applications portfolio *should* consist of, admitting to yourself that you are likely never to fully find out what the organisation does have in the way of applications software.

2   You realise you would have difficulty completing a task like this by yourself so you decide to establish a 'working party' that can report back to management on the applications portfolio status

3   As management has confidence in your abilities, take it upon yourself to insist that all platforms need to be of standard desktop configuration, those that are not should within the next 6 months be decommissioned

4   Consider drafting a questionnaire which would be sent to all IT managers dispersed around the state in the organisation which 'should' provide you with a better idea of what the organisation does have

5   Establish a pilot team, with up to 20 diverse users to evaluate the entire organizational systems. Once management decides on the hardware and software to be used, you keep these systems and simply decommission the remainder. In other words you 'pass the buck' to some extent to senior management

ETHICAL
Choose one:

Extremely Bad   Neither Good nor Bad   Extremely Good

REALISTIC
Choose one:

Extremely Bad   Neither Good nor Bad   Extremely Good

6   Undertake to travel to all branches of the organization and interview relevant personnel to gain a better feeling of which are the most important platforms. Those that do not get mentioned need not be maintained. Backup tapes exist for all data used in the organization in any case. Should any particular hardware or software be required, another public sector organization with mirror applications would be able to help.

ETHICAL
Choose one:

Extremely Bad   Neither Good nor Bad   Extremely Good

REALISTIC
Choose one:

Extremely Bad   Neither Good nor Bad   Extremely Good

7   Determine the true mission statement for the organization as a whole and let this guide you as to which applications to update or delete insofar as the applications portfolio should only support the 'true' needs of the organization

ETHICAL
Choose one:

Extremely Bad   Neither Good nor Bad   Extremely Good

REALISTIC
Choose one:

Extremely Bad   Neither Good nor Bad   Extremely Good

Please click the submit button and continue on with the next scenario SUBMIT

F.4 Final Thank-You Screen

Articulable Tacit Knowledge Survey

You have completed the survey. Thankyou for your participation.

Results will be made available in the form of a de-identified report

Please exit from the Browser

Appendix G

Glossary of Common Terms Used in this Book

Actor: The common Social Network Analysis term for participant or respondent or person who is being modeled with regard to their communication pattern with other people.

Articulable implicit managerial IT knowledge: That subset of articulable tacit knowledge that is under study in this thesis. For the purposes of this research we are focusing on a soft set of skills, which is managerial in its nature. It is expected more competent IT people will have a higher store of articulable implicit managerial IT knowledge.

Articulable tacit knowledge: That subset (whether major or minor) of tacit knowledge that can eventually be articulated. Strictly speaking the knowledge elicited is then no longer tacit knowledge. Examples of this sort of tacit knowledge include "tricks of the trade," "trade secrets," "street smarts," and so on.

CNE: Certified Novell Engineer. An individual qualified in making sure Novell networks run correctly.

DA: Data Administrator/Architect. A person who undertakes senior level data/information/knowledge planning for the organisation. This is an individual who is typically managerial rather than technical.

DBA: DataBase Administrator. The technical person in charge of the organisation's information systems.

Delphi method: An approach that brings experts together with a view toward getting them to brainstorm ideas.

Dendogram: A branching tree like diagram used in a number of disciplines to illustrate a relationship between a number of attributes or parameters.

E-A: Entity-Association/Entity-Relationship. A data modelling convention typically used for relational database design

Ethernet: A LAN protocol.

Expert non-expert: Individuals who by way of the Formal Concept Analysis interpretation of their tacit knowledge inventory results, were identified as having scores close to that of experts. The expert non-experts were not necessarily identified by their peers as being an expert.

Expert: One who has been identified by his peers as being of above average ability with regard to their workplace performance

FCA: Formal Concept Analysis. A lattice based technique for data interpretation

Inarticulable tacit knowledge: That subset (whether major or minor) of tacit knowledge that cannot be truly articulated. Typically this knowledge is based upon sense, feeling and experience the individual must come to feel for themselves. It cannot be transferred verbally and only to a limited degree by example.

LAN: Local Area Network. A communication network typically at building or multi-building/organisation level.

Meaning: Another important ingredient in inarticulable tacit knowledge. Together with sense the individual gains a feeling for this type of knowledge which simply cannot be verbalised or even passed on fully by way of example.

Novell: A LAN protocol.

Novice: One who has not been identified by their peers as being of above ordinary or exception IT workplace performance.

Sense: The important ingredient necessary for the individual to experience inarticulable tacit knowledge. This together with meaning allows the person to gain a feel for this type of tacit knowledge, which enriches their knowledge base.

SNA: Social Network Analysis. A technique for examining how people interact which is likely to affect how knowledge and other resources are transferred between individuals.

Tacit knowledge: Typically knowledge that is unspoken, hard to articulate. It is knowledge that is interpreted between the lines. Many previous definitions have been offered in Appendix B.

Token Ring: A LAN protocol (and typology) whereby data packets pass around a ring like network in one direction only

UML: Unified Modelling Language. A current modelling technique giving greater emphasis to object-orientation.

About the Author

Peter Busch is a lecturer in the Department of Computing at Macquarie University, but his background is somewhat more diverse than this discipline. With an interest in human settlement patterns and faraway places, he studied both geography and German as an undergraduate at the University of Adelaide. Having always been keen on books, and libraries more specifically, he obtained a position in the library at Adelaide University. His library experience led him to want to undertake a Masters degree in Librarianship at Monash University in Melbourne. Realising the future lay very much in IT whilst having an interest in experiencing Tasmania, encouraged him to complete further studies in Computing at the University of Tasmania. A few years were then spent as an associate lecturer in the Department of Computer Science and thereafter the School of Information Systems at that university. With an interest in an academic career he completed his Ph.D. under the supervision of the late C.N.G. "Kit" Dampney at Macquarie University in Sydney, examining the knowledge management implications of tacit knowledge diffusion. His current research focuses on knowledge management, organisational learning, and human capital. As with almost all academics he teaches as well, having a strong interest in databases, information modelling, management of IT, and enterprise integration.

Index

E

"expert" non-experts (ENEs) 231
economics 19
egocentric network (EC) approach 153
electronic communication 268
electronic mediums 268, 308
embodied knowledge 77
embrained knowledge 103
entrepreneurial firm 102
epistemology 77
Erklären 43
ethnicity 257
expert group 213
expert non-experts, identification process 197
expert sample 195
expert systems 20, 24
explicit knowledge 141
exploratory research 76
externalisation 48, 51

F

face-to-face contact 270, 309
face-to-face relations 150
face validity 173
formal concept analysis (FCA) 78, 85, 86
formal concept analysis, results 204
formal concept analysis, usage of 205
formalisms 58
front office roles 259

G

global centrality 240, 297
globalisation 21
groundedness 170
group decision support systems (GDSSs) 25
groupware conferencing systems 25

H

hierarchy 262
holistic system 137
human-based knowledge management 4
human capital 18

I

ICT in knowledge management 24
implicit. *See* tacit
inarticulable tacit knowledge 58
inclusiveness 157
individual questionnaire 78
informal knowledge 75

information, definition 1
information and communication technologies
    (ICTs) 4, 148
information centrality 243, 281, 298
information elicitation 153
information management 2
information processing approach 80
information science 19
information systems (IS) 2, 19, 148
information technology 3
information technology, role of 136
innovative firm 104
intellectual capital 1, 5
inter-organisational domain 334
internalisation 48, 51
intra-organisational communication 322
intra-organisational tacit knowledge 167
intra-organisational testing 77
IS domain 49

J

J-Form organisation 104

K

knowledge, codified 1
knowledge, definition 1, 18
knowledge, tacit 1
knowledge diffusion 137
knowledge diffusion, parameters in 318
knowledge engineering 19
knowledge flows 133
knowledge hierarchy 18, 36
knowledge management (KM) 2, 4, 17, 42,
    134
knowledge management, definition 19
knowledge management evolution/classifica-
    tion 20
knowledge management in the workplace 4
knowledge map 150
knowledge repositories 26, 27
knowledge society 19, 21
knowledge technologies 141
knowledge transfer 2, 5
knowledge transfer process 139

L

large company (X) 231
large organisation (X) 232
learning by doing 53
learning by using 53
learning organisation (LO) 22